The Holy Land and the Early Modern Reinvention of Catholicism

A shared biblical past has long imbued the Holy Land with special authority as well as a mythic character that has made the region not only a revered spiritual home for Muslims, Christians, and Jews, but also a source of a living sacred history that informs contemporary realities and religious identities. This book explores the Holy Land (1517–1700) as a critical *place* in which many early modern Catholics sought spiritual and political legitimacy during a period of profound and disruptive change. The Ottoman conquest of the region, the division of the Western Church, Catholic reform, the integration of the Mediterranean into global trading networks, and the emergence of new imperial rivalries transformed the Custody of the Holy Land, the venerable Catholic institution that had overseen Western pilgrimage since 1342, into a site of intense intra-Christian conflict by 1517. This contestation underscored the Holy Land's importance both as a frontier and sacred center of an embattled Catholic tradition, and in consequence, as a critical site of Catholic renewal and reinvention.

Megan C. Armstrong is Associate Professor of History at McMaster University. A scholar of Early Modern European history in a global context, she is the author of *The Politics of Piety: Franciscan Preachers during the Wars of Religion, 1560–1600* (2004).

The Holy Land and the Early Modern Reinvention of Catholicism

MEGAN C. ARMSTRONG
McMaster University

CAMBRIDGE
UNIVERSITY PRESS

University Printing House, Cambridge CB2 8BS, United Kingdom

One Liberty Plaza, 20th Floor, New York, NY 10006, USA

477 Williamstown Road, Port Melbourne, VIC 3207, Australia

314–321, 3rd Floor, Plot 3, Splendor Forum, Jasola District Centre, New Delhi – 110025, India

79 Anson Road, #06-04/06, Singapore 079906

Cambridge University Press is part of the University of Cambridge.

It furthers the University's mission by disseminating knowledge in the pursuit of education, learning, and research at the highest international levels of excellence.

www.cambridge.org
Information on this title: www.cambridge.org/9781108832472
DOI: 10.1017/9781108957946

© Cambridge University Press 2021

This publication is in copyright. Subject to statutory exception and to the provisions of relevant collective licensing agreements, no reproduction of any part may take place without the written permission of Cambridge University Press.

First published 2021

A catalogue record for this publication is available from the British Library.

ISBN 978-1-108-83247-2 Hardback

Cambridge University Press has no responsibility for the persistence or accuracy of URLs for external or third-party internet websites referred to in this publication and does not guarantee that any content on such websites is, or will remain, accurate or appropriate.

to Michael, Lori, Jack, and Patrick

Contents

List of Figures	*page* ix
Acknowledgements	x
Introduction	1
1 A Catholic Gateway to the Holy Land: The Custodia Terrae Sanctae	26
1.1 A Venerable Pilgrimage Institution	28
1.2 Ottoman Rule	39
1.3 A Shared Sacred Landscape	42
1.4 Conclusion	66
2 Altars and Christian Precedence in the Holy Places	68
2.1 The Disputes over Altars	71
2.2 Islamic Law and Christian Privileges	84
2.3 Christian Precedence, Sacred History, and Religious and Political Change	100
2.4 Conclusion	119
3 The Order of the Holy Sepulcher	121
3.1 The Order of the Holy Sepulcher	123
3.2 A Spiritual Brotherhood	127
3.3 Reformation Polemic and Knightly Treatises	147
3.4 The Knight As Spiritual Expert	162
3.5 Conclusion	180

4	**France, the Protector of the Holy Places**	182
	4.1 The Dispute of 1661	185
	4.2 Turning the Custody "French"	197
	4.3 The Pursuit of Christian Hegemony	223
	4.4 Conclusion	257
5	**The Congregation of the Propaganda Fide**	258
	5.1 The Expansion of Papal Influence	260
	5.2 A Catholic *Frontier*	280
	5.3 A Spiritual *Center*	295
	5.4 Conclusion	300
6	**A Franciscan Holy Land**	302
	6.1 Fraternal Conflicts, 1517–1700	305
	6.2 An Observant Sacred History	321
	6.3 A Franciscan Holy Land: Francis of Assisi	325
	6.4 Apostolic Succession	336

Conclusion. The Holy Land: Renewal, Revelation, and Reinvention	361
Bibliography	368
Index	391

Figures

1.1	Map, Custody of the Holy Land, 1670	*page* 39
1.2	Map, pilgrimage routes	50
1.3	Map, Jerusalem	61
4.1	Painting, Marquis de Nointel at Jerusalem (1674)	256

Acknowledgements

This book was a long time in the making. What began initially as a comparative study of three early modern Franciscan missions in diverse global contexts increasingly, inexorably became a study of the Custody of the Holy Land. I do sometimes regret having to leave aside Guatemala; all the evidence points to a fascinating world there that would have been wonderful to explore. However, the early modern Holy Land had its own ineffable character that drew me in, and it still exerts a powerful hold. Because this project has involved so many archives, side journeys, surprise discoveries, and welcome collaborations along the way, it is difficult to adequately pay tribute to every institution, scholar, and friend who has helped it come to fruition. To begin with, I want to give my sincere gratitude to Beatrice Rehl, my editor at Cambridge University Press. In addition to skilfully shepherding this manuscript through the many stages to completion at the press, she expressed interest and encouragement for this project at a very early and crucial stage of the writing process and has remained a vital source of encouragement and advice from that point to the present. I also cannot thank enough the readers of the manuscript for Cambridge University Press. They clearly spent a great deal of time poring over the text and provided excellent comments that have greatly improved its quality. I take full responsibility for any problems that remain.

I have also been very fortunate to receive financial support from a number of institutions, beginning with the University of Utah, which generously gave me a travel grant during my time there as a member of the history department. McMaster University, my academic home since 2005, has also generously provided research and conference grants to further develop the project in addition to a SSHRC grant that funded three years at archives in Italy, Spain, Israel, and France. Because this project took me to many archives, I worked with many archivists. In each place, they were unfailingly kind and patient: at the majestic archives in Simancas (it has a moat!), the National Archives in Madrid, the Archives Nationales in Paris, the Propaganda Fide in Rome, and the state archives in Venice. I had a special experience working in Jerusalem at the archives of the Custody of the Holy Land, which is still housed at the convent of the Holy Saviour that dates back to the sixteenth century. Every morning for several weeks, I walked through the Old City from the Jewish quarter to the via dolorosa and followed it to the convent to meet friar Cristoforo, the assistant archivist. It is hard to convey the profundity of the experience of being in the same places and walking in the footsteps of the early modern friars and to have a chance to talk each day to a member of the modern community. Father Narcyz Klimas, the archivist, was also unfailingly generous with his knowledge of the collection and its history. I am also grateful to Patrick DeLuca (GISP), GIS Specialist and Lecturer, School of Earth, Environment and Society, at McMaster University for producing my maps. This collective support has been enormously important to the success of this project and I cannot thank these institutions and specialists enough.

I feel equally indebted if not more so to the many colleagues who have shared their expertise and research and read and commented on chapters. To begin with, I thank my former colleagues (and dear friends) at the University of Utah, including Isabel Moreira, Janet Theiss, Becky Horn, Bradley Parker, Nadja Durbach, Raul Ramos, David Igler, and Susie Porter, for encouraging me to stretch my wings and move outside of France to think a bit bigger about the Catholic tradition, especially in global terms. Their dinner parties, I will add, remain unparalleled social events and my husband and I miss Utah deeply for that reason among many others. At McMaster in Canada, I have found wonderfully supportive colleagues as well. I thank Tracy McDonald, Juanita DeBarros, Virginia Aksan, Bonny Ibahwoh, Nancy Christie, Michael Gauvreau, and Stephen Heathorn, all of whom have read grant applications and chapters or just listened sympathetically when my chapters were not going well. It is hard to overstate the value of having colleagues in different fields who ask the big questions. For example, why does this matter? And what does *this* mean? I owe a special debt to Virginia Aksan, who, much to my chagrin, retired recently though is thankfully still in Hamilton and available for virtual cocktails. Ginny has been unfailingly generous with her knowledge of the Ottoman Empire and her contacts with other Ottoman and Mediterranean scholars. It was through Ginny and her colleagues that I met Leslie Peirce, Molly Greene, Nathalie Rothman, Tijana Krstić, Eric Dursteler, Jacob Norris, Rob Clines, Gillian Weiss, Junko Takeda, Carina Johnson, Felicita Tramontana, and Ana Sekulic. Natalie Rothman put me on the trail of the Venetian dispacci, a wonderful piece of advice that led me not only to an amazing documentary base but also to other Venetianists, in particular Eric Dursteler, Saundra Weddle, and Roisin Cossar. I am deeply indebted to scholars who work on the Holy Land, including Adam Beaver, Zur Shalev, and Yamit Rachman-Schrire, who have generously shared their own research and ideas on Catholic engagement. In general, it has been a humbling but also exciting experience to be "schooled" on the history of an unfamiliar regime in an unfamiliar landscape, and I am grateful for the many conversations with these and other scholars over the last years at the RSA and the SCSC as well as in the archives. My hope is that this study does justice to the fascinating Ottoman context of the Custody, in particular, and at the very least doesn't misrepresent it. If I failed to do so, then fault lies entirely with me because these scholars have been unfailingly generous and rigorous.

In addition to these colleagues, I owe thanks to so many others including Allyson Poska and Gerhild Scholz Williams who, in the course of many conversations over the years, usually over a glass of wine, have pushed me to think more deeply about what I am doing and why, both in terms of research and as a historian more generally. The same is true for Craig Harline and Brian Catlos, whose rich conversations helped me think through my project from very early on and for Alison Forrestal, whose own work on the Lazarists and conversations on the nature of mission have been immensely formative upon my thinking about the Franciscans for many years. It was through participation in a multiyear project organized by Alison, Sean Smith, and other colleagues at NUI Galway that my thinking about the Holy Land as a Catholic frontier took concrete form, and it led to an article included in a subsequent collection of essays edited by Alison and Sean, *The Frontiers of Mission: Perspectives on Early Modern Missionary Catholicism* (2016). More recently, Karen Melvin and Ana Sekulic have become delightful fellow explorers of the Franciscan tradition. It has been illuminating to bring the early modern friars of New Spain, Bosnia, and Jerusalem into conversation with one another. Doing so has only reinforced my conviction that it is helpful to think about this religious group as an international community and network inasmuch as we think of Franciscan convents as local institutions.

One of the most satisfying parts of the present project has been to retain a scholarly connection with early modern France even though it has moved geographically to a very different place. My journey to the Holy Land began in Paris, when I discovered a cluster of contracts involving a pilgrimage confraternity, the Order of the Holy Sepulcher, affiliated with the Franciscan Grand Couvent. These men went to Jerusalem as did some of my French friars and so I followed them. From the very beginning, as well, I have relied upon the continuing expertise and rigor as well as friendship of colleagues who work on early modern France. My generation grew up with a plethora of mentors including Mack Holt, Jim Collins, and Barbara Diefendorf, who were rigorous and supportive in equal measure. As a young scholar, the sight of their raised hands was both encouraging and nerve-wracking because the questions were never easy. Now they are friends who are no less demanding and rigorous, and I am grateful for that. I feel just as grateful for the continuing support and friendship of a cohort that has been developing since the dissertation days. With regard to this project, I am indebted in particular to Eric Nelson, who has read everything I have published and who has more generally been a wonderful partner in crime exploring the many dimensions of early modern Catholicism. Sara Chapman Williams, who I have known from the very beginning, has also read chapters and significantly shaped my thinking about La France "outremer." Brian Sandberg, Marco Penzi, Stuart Carroll Kay Edwards, Tom Worcester, Andrew Spicer, Jotham Parsons, and Michael Breen, all dear friends, have been a ready and opinionated group of commentators. Finally, forming a "virtual convent" with Sara Beam, Penny Roberts, Virginia Reinburg, and Hilary Bernstein was a stroke of brilliance. While we have been consistently poor at adhering to the vows (which involve among other things limiting administrative work), this reading group has helped massage a hodgepodge of writings into a coherent book. It has become an invaluable support system in the process.

It has not been easy completing this book in the middle of a pandemic. A persistent sense of anxiety, of the unknown, however, is something we can share with people living in the sixteenth and seventeenth Mediterranean since they too were experiencing profound and disruptive change firsthand. One can only hope that our modern experience of global disease will lead us to find pathways to transformative change that will deal with the pressing concerns of climate change, poverty, authoritarianism, racism, and religious intolerance among others. As this pandemic makes clear, thinking and planning as a global community is more important than ever for promoting peace, equality, economic security, and a healthy planet. Finding consolation in the power of positive, transformative change has helped me manage a much more personal tragedy, the loss of my dearly beloved brother Michael. He passed suddenly and unexpectedly in the summer of 2019 and our family hasn't been the same since. He left behind two young sons and a wife, his soul mate Lori. He was a very good person (with a wicked sense of humour) who believed in the innate goodness and worthiness of all people, and so it is a source of some solace to know that he is now with our mother who was much the same way. Michael's passing has made me immeasurably grateful for my family and friends, pets (two dogs and three cats), my career as a historian, and the privilege of living in a stable and beautiful place like Canada. I feel so fortunate to have been handed such wonderful parents, Jack and Noreen, siblings Michael, Gillian, and Tom, and equally wonderful in-laws in the Opekar family. My husband Alex makes every day a lively adventure, culinary and otherwise, a gift in itself. This book, however, is dedicated to my brother Michael and his family, Lori, Jack, and Patrick, because they embody the spirit that is needed more than ever: love, respect, compassion, humour, and optimism.

Introduction

In his *Trattato di Terra Santa e dell' Oriente*, published in 1524, the Venetian friar Francesco Suriano wrote the following about the Holy Land. God, he said, "decreed this land to be the habitation of the Holy Spirit, that is of His Son ... in which He should work the salvation of the world by his birth, life and death." He had "ennobled, decorated and adorned with every prerogative of sanctity and grace above all other parts of the world as the principle which contains every perfection of the world." From this land "has diffused all graces in all parts of the world, just as from the heart of the animal the vital spirits are diffused to all the members of the animal, as from the fountain runs down the water in rivulets, and as the lines are drawn from the center of this land ..."[1] In this passage, Suriano evokes a Holy Land that would have been familiar to his devout early modern Catholic readers. It was a sacred landscape, beloved of God, because it was the divinely appointed home of Christ. It was in consequence a powerful and transformative place of encounter with a living Christ because the region continued to resonate with his divinity. Of special relevance to our investigation here, however, is Suriano's depiction of the Holy Land as the *source* of Christian perfection. The region described in this passage is a powerful, active force of divinity and a central actor in a global story of redemption – "a beating

---

[1] The seminal modern edition of Francesco Suriano's treatise is the *Trattato di Terra Santa e dell'Oriente* (Assisi: Artigianelli, 1900). The translation used here comes from the excellent English edition, *Treatise of the Holy Land*, trans. Theophilus Bellorini and Eugene Hoade (Jerusalem: Franciscan Printing Press, 1949): 22–23.

heart," an ever-flowing "fountain of sacrality," that "diffused all graces in all parts of the world."

Suriano's conception of a powerful, unbounded source of sacrality sets the frame for the following exploration of Catholic engagement in the Holy Land between 1517 and 1700. In doing so, it contributes to broader discussions on a region that remains a focus of intense interest to this today. Bookstore shelves heave with publications penned by modern day travelers, popular historians, and journalists as well as academics. The vigorous production of scholarship on medieval and early modern pilgrimage is especially striking, all the more because it shows little sign of slowing down.[2] That the Holy Land continues to generate such intense interest makes sense for many reasons that also shape the present study, not the least of which is its possession of a shared biblical past. This shared past has imbued the Holy Land with a special authority and mythic character that have made the region not only a revered spiritual home for Muslims, Christians, and Jews and a site of extraordinary religious diversity but also a source of a living sacred history that continues to inform present-day realities and religious identities. As Moshe Sharon argues so eloquently in a recent study of medieval pilgrimage, "the Holy Land is more than a geographical name; it is a concept, it is a focus

---

[2] A small sampling of the diverse and rich nature of recent scholarship on shrines and pilgrimage in the Holy Land includes Marianne Ritsema van Eck, "Encounters with the Levant: The Late Medieval Illustrated Jerusalem Travelogue by Paul Walter Von Guglingen," *Mediterranean Review* 32(2018): 153–188; Adam G. Beaver, "From Jerusalem to Toledo: Replica, Landscape and the Nation in Renaissance Iberia," *Past and Present* 218 (2013): 55–90; James Grehan, *Twilight of the Saints: Everyday Religion in Ottoman Syria and Palestine* (Oxford: Oxford University Press, 2014); Katharine Blair Moore, "The Disappearance of an Author, the Appearance of a Genre: Niccolò da Poggibonsi and Pilgrimage Guidebooks between Manuscript and Print," *Renaissance Quarterly* 66 (2013): 357–411; Arad Pnina, "Mapping Divinity: Holy Landscape in Maps of the Holy Land," in *Jerusalem As Narrative* Space, ed. Annette Hoffmann and Gerhard Wolf (Leiden: Brill, 2012), 263–276; Paris O'Donnell, "Pilgrimage or Anti-Pilgrimage? Uses of Mementoes and Relics in English and Scottish Narratives of Travel to Jerusalem, 1596–1632," *Studies in Travel Writing* 13 (2009): 125–139; Alexandra Cuffel, "From Practice to Polemic: Shared Saints and Festivals As 'Women's Religion' in the Medieval Mediterranean," *Bulletin of the School of Oriental and African Studies, University of London* 68 (2005): 401–419; Josef W. Meri, *The Cult of the Saints among Muslims and Jews in Medieval Syria* (Oxford University Press, 2002; reprint, 2004); Daniel Vitkus, "Trafficking with the Turk: English Travelers in the Ottoman Empire during the Early Seventeenth Century," in *Travel Knowledge: European "Discoveries" in the Early Modern Period*, ed. Ivo Jamps and Jyotsna G. Singh (Basingstoke: Palgrave, 2001), 35–52; Lucia Rostagno, "Pellegrini italiani a Gerusalemme in Età Ottomana: Percorsi, Esperienze, Momenti d'incontro," *Oriente Moderno* 17 (1998): 63–157; Amikam Elad, *Medieval Jerusalem and Islamic Worship* (Leiden: Brill, 1995).

of identity, it is a source of inspiration, it is legend and reality intermingled and interchanged."[3]

The present monograph explores one particularly important dimension of the Holy Land for early modern Catholics, namely, its function as a powerful source of spiritual and political legitimacy. By 1517, the forces of religious reform were shaking the foundations of the Catholic tradition, threatening many of its traditional structures of authority including the papacy. The westward expansion of the powerful Muslim Ottoman Empire, the emergence of new Catholic empires and encounters with cultures previously unknown to Europeans were other forces that tested the fabric of the Church, reshaping it as it ventured into the modern era. A central argument of this book is that the Holy Land became a critical *place* in which many early modern Catholics sought legitimacy for their changing tradition. They did so through an imaginative engagement with its storied Christian past, an engagement that was no less material and political as it was ideological in nature because, for Catholics, the material was another critical conduit of its authority. Being *there*, performing the liturgical rites, possessing convents, churches, and shrines as well as practicing central Christian tenets demarcated a place for the Catholic tradition *in* the sanctifying power of the region, and in doing so facilitated its reinvention.

This inventive function of the Holy Land is well on display in the passage penned by Francesco Suriano, one of the reasons why his treatise serves as our starting point for our analysis of Catholic engagement in the early modern Holy Land. Another reason is that Suriano was a known expert on the sacred landscape because of his many years of service to the Custodia Terrae Sanctae (the Custody of the Holy Land), the venerable pilgrimage institution that is the focus of our investigation here. The Custody was first established in 1342 to oversee Western pilgrimage to the Holy Places, the sacred sites associated with the life and death of Christ. Political boundaries have shifted since the sixteenth century, leaving modern-day Christian pilgrims to wander through the modern states of Egypt, Syria, Israel, and Lebanon in pursuit of this Christian past. As in earlier centuries, however, the Custody continues to fulfill its central pilgrimage mandate from the convent of the Holy Saviour in Jerusalem, its administrative base since 1558. It also remains in the hands of the

---

[3] Moshe Sharon, ed., "Introduction," in *The Holy Land in History and Thought*. Papers Submitted to the International Conference on the Relations between the Holy Land and the World Outside it (Johannesburg 1986) (Leiden: Brill, 1988).

Franciscan order, marking a continuous history of Franciscan governance of almost seven hundred years. Dressed in their distinctive brown robes, the brothers are a familiar site in the streets of the Old City, as they lead groups of Catholic pilgrims in well-choreographed visitations of the sacred Christian sites.

Suriano would have been well familiar with these sacred itineraries because he spent years in the ministry of the Custody involved in a wide array of tasks – tending to the material and spiritual needs of pilgrims, maintaining Latin altars in the Holy Places, and providing pastoral care to local Catholic merchants. Typical of the mobile nature of the Franciscan ministry, the Venetian friar moved around while in the Custody, assigned to communities in Beirut and Jerusalem. Suriano thus gleaned a great deal of experience while there, but his official status as *custos* also invested his *Trattato* with added authority. Suriano held the post twice, between 1481 and 1484, and 1512 and 1514. As *custos*, Suriano served simultaneously as the head (guardian) of the Franciscan community and as the most powerful representative of the Western Church within the boundaries of the Custody. Thus, from the main convent in Jerusalem, Suriano oversaw the operations of an institution that was an important local political as well as spiritual manifestation of the Catholic tradition in a region of immense significance to Christians, a region that at the time lay under the authority of a great Muslim power, the Mamluk Sultanate of Egypt.

Whether Suriano was aware of the changes to come is unclear from his treatise. Most of it was written during the 1480s, following his first tenure as *custos* with some revisions made later during the first two decades of the sixteenth century. By the time he was living in Jerusalem during his second term, however, the Venetian friar must have noticed the steady westward expansion of Ottoman influence along the southern shores of the Mediterranean. In 1516/1517, only two years after Suriano left Jerusalem for good, the forces of Selim I (d. 1520) swept the regions of the Holy Land into the embrace of the Ottoman Empire. As a prominent Catholic official, the Venetian friar may also have heard the rumblings of reform that were growing increasingly louder in the Catholic Church by this time and which would soon rupture the once united Catholic body, creating a much more diverse Christian landscape in Europe after 1517. Certainly, as a Franciscan, Suriano would have been aware as well of the deep ideological divisions then besetting his own Order by this time, divisions that – in a curious case of historical synchronicity – took formal form in 1517 when the Order recognized the creation of two separate branches: Conventual, and Observant.

As the following investigation will show, these profound changes, along with the increasing integration of the Mediterranean into global trading networks and the emergence of new imperial rivalries, would have important consequences for the operations of the Custody after 1517 because of its intimate association with the Holy Land. One of the most important consequences, and the focus of the present investigation, was the transformation of the Custody into a site of intense intra-Christian conflict. This monograph asserts that these conflicts, when studied in the context of the profound changes shaping the early modern Church, illuminate the Holy Land's valued function as a powerful source of spiritual and political legitimacy for members of an embattled Catholic tradition and, in consequence, an influential role for the Custody as its gatekeeper.

To make this case, the following study probes five of the more persistent challenges to the jurisdiction of the Franciscan brothers from other Christians between 1517 and 1700. These conflicts assumed different forms and involved a diverse array of Christian institutions and communities including not only other Christians (Greek Orthodox, Protestant reformers) but also fellow Catholics. Close investigation of these conflicts thrusts into relief a decidedly traditional conception of the Holy Land as a powerful material vessel of Christ's authority, one that many Catholics found as useful for legitimizing claims to spiritual leadership *within* the Catholic Church as it was for affirming the authenticity of the Catholic faith vis-à-vis other Christian traditions. Indeed, the authority vested in the Holy Land helps to explain not only the intensity and nature of Catholic engagement in the region after 1517 but also why it was meaningful for European powers such as those of France, Spain, and the papacy, to exercise jurisdiction over the administration of the Custody.

With this argument in mind, this monograph makes three assertions that will be developed over the course of six chapters. Firstly, that the early modern Catholics studied here privileged the authority of the Holy Land because they considered it the *place* of Christ. To be there, in contact with the region, was to lay claim to its transformative power and thus to spiritual expertise and authority. Buoyed by this belief, the Catholics of this study emphasized their first-hand experience of the region in their writings, marked its landscape with material evidence of their presence in the form of buildings, art, and Catholic bodies, and, in some cases, exercised jurisdiction *there*. Secondly, along with manifesting a presence *there*, Catholics turned to sacred pasts in the Holy Land to articulate their claims to spiritual authority and leadership. Thirdly, accessing the sacralizing power of the Holy Land required working both through, and with, Islamic structures of authority since the sacred landscape resided within the boundaries of a powerful Muslim regime. The Holy Land had spent most of its history under the rule of a succession of Muslim rulers, the most recent at this point being the Ottoman rulers based in Constantinople (modern day Istanbul). Indeed, the Custody was a construct of both Islamic and canon law, and its operations were also significantly informed by the broader Ottoman context in which it operated.[4] This Ottoman context we should note included a rich diversity of Muslim, Jewish, and Christian communities, a reality that recognized the Holy Land's traditional importance for all three Religions of the Book inasmuch as it does the historically diverse religious and ethnic character of the Ottoman Empire. In other words, a particular concern of this study is to assert the influence of local relations (political, religious, legal) in shaping not only the nature of Catholic engagement in the Holy Land but also the meaning of this sacred landscape for early modern Catholics.

The organization of chapters requires some explanation, especially since it ends with the Franciscan brothers of the Holy land who serve as our central lens into the conflicts involving the Custody. It is precisely because they operate at the center of this investigation, however, that this monograph gives the friars the last word on the Holy Land. Indeed, in Chapter 6 they provide us with not only the last but also the most poignant of the sacred histories considered here. We begin instead from the outside, with conflicts that take us to the frontiers of Catholic engagement with other Christians, in this case the Greek Orthodox and Protestant reformers. From there we move steadily inwards to examine relations between the friars and other Catholics including Catholic institutions (the French state, the papacy, other Franciscans). These final three chapters probe particular cases of jurisdictional conflict to shine a light on a Catholic body riven by reforming currents and the forces of political change – a body that was also slowly transforming in response to these changes.

Chapter 1 introduces the Custody by situating the venerable institution in three contexts critical for understanding its historic role as a gateway to

---

[4] On Ottoman governance vis-à vis non-Muslim subjects (*dhimmi*), see among others, Oded Peri, *Christianity under Islam in Jerusalem: The Question of the Holy Sites in Early Ottoman Times* (Leiden: Brill, 2001); and Ronald C. Jennings, *Christians and Muslims in Ottoman Cyprus and the Mediterranean World, 1571–1640* (New York: New York University Press, 1993).

the Holy Land for early modern Catholics: Western pilgrimage, a shared sacred landscape, and Ottoman governance. By the sixteenth century, the Custody had operated within a multi-faith site of pilgrimage for several centuries, an experience that informed its character and influence as much as its roots in Catholic spirituality. The Ottoman conquest severed the Holy Land from its former Mamluk rulers in 1517, bringing the region into a new political and religious context that had formative consequences for the Franciscan brothers of the Holy Land and their management of Western pilgrimage. This discussion, along with an exploration of the Holy Land as a shared sacred landscape and the Holy Places as shared shrines provides an important context for interpreting the disputes between the friars and other Christians, beginning with the conflicts with the Greek Orthodox in Chapter 2.

The remaining chapters each explore a specific jurisdictional challenge faced by the Franciscan brothers of the early modern Custody, to highlight the Custody's role as a valued gatekeeper to the legitimizing authority of the Holy Land during an era of profound religious and political change. Central to the discussion in each one is recognition of the Custody's role in manifesting a material, spiritual, and legal place for the Catholic tradition *in* the Holy Land and most importantly *in* the Holy Places. Chapter 2 examines the rekindling of a rivalry between the Latin (Catholic) and the Greek Orthodox communities in Jerusalem over the possession of altars in the Holy Places. These disputes, which were legal, political, and liturgical in form, also engaged a broad international Catholic community in defense of Latin altars. It is the argument of this chapter that these disputes functioned as rites of Christian legitimacy involving two ancient Christian traditions with universalist ambitions, both of which could trace a long material and spiritual presence in the Holy Land. In addition to highlighting the influence of these sacred histories in shaping relations between the two Christian communities during the Early Modern Period, a central objective of this chapter is to feature the hybrid character of the Custody. As both an Islamic and Catholic institution, one that straddled Ottoman and Western structures of authority, the Custody played a critical role in mediating Western access to the Holy Places through its legal possession of altars.[5]

---

[5] Some scholars prefer the term "Islamicate" to explain evidence of cultural mixing, syncretism, in shaping the character of institutions such as the Custody. It does apply to the Custody, but for the purposes of this monograph, I find it especially helpful to think of this institution as a product of, and imbedded in, multiple structures of authority both

Chapter 3 shifts our attention to the European Reformation as another Christian context shaping the meaning of the Holy Land for early modern Catholics, in this case focusing upon the religious engagement of a brotherhood of devout Catholics known as the Order of the Holy Sepulcher. The Reformation sparked intense discussion over the efficacy of the rite of pilgrimage by 1520, a debate that made the Holy Land pilgrimage a particular locus of confessional debate almost immediately. Several members of the Order used their pilgrimage treatises to engage in this debate, revealing in the process a distinctive and devout Catholic brotherhood that privileged a role for members as spiritual leaders through their personal experience of the Holy Land. In particular, these men celebrated their participation in the pilgrimage, the crusading past of the Order, and a spiritual partnership with the Franciscan brothers of the Holy Land as critical foundations of their claims to spiritual expertise on the contested rite. Their writings, moreover, which played upon the visceral experience of the Holy Land pilgrimage, suggest that one important legacy of the Reformation controversies was the intensification of the material cast of the Catholic tradition and the reification of the Holy Land as a material manifestation of the Word.

Chapter 4 uses an intriguing dispute that erupted in 1661 during the Easter pilgrimage to explore growing conflict between the French state and the brothers of the Holy Land over jurisdiction in the Custody. Beginning in the 1620s, we find the Bourbon regime using its Ottoman status as Protector of the Holy Places to transform the Custody into a visibly French Catholic institution. The French state was granted this status in the Capitulations of 1604, and it used it to press for the assignment of French religious (French missionaries as well as French Franciscans) to work in the Custody. The legal cases that followed reveal a Bourbon regime turning to its mythic past as defender of the Holy Land to strengthen a French state badly weakened by decades of religious and political civil conflict in France and which was also facing a powerful imperial rival in the form of the Spanish Habsburg rulers. In this context, an alliance with the Ottoman regime and France's storied crusading past invested the status of Protector of the Holy Places with significance both as a marker of Catholic orthodoxy and Christian leadership.

---

within the Ottoman Empire and in Europe. On the usage of the term, see, for example, the discussion in Brian A. Catlos, *Muslims of the Medieval Latin Christendom, c. 1050–1614* (Cambridge: Cambridge University Press, 2014).

Chapter 5 examines the Custody's place in the construction of the global ambitions of a post-Tridentine papacy by looking at relations between the Franciscan brothers and the newly established Congregation of the Propaganda Fide (1622). The correspondence found in the archives of the Propaganda Fide reveals a persistent effort on the part of the Congregation to erode the autonomy of the friars and mold them to a new model of ministry that better reflected the globalizing ambitions of the post-Tridentine Church. Of critical importance in this regard was the Custody's jurisdiction in the Holy Places. These sacred spaces offered crucial sites of contact with other Christian communities while mediating the flow of the sanctifying authority of the region to Rome. Thus, this chapter ponders the Holy Land's function both as a Catholic *frontier* and a spiritual *center* of a globalizing Catholic Church, functions that help to explain, in particular, the papacy's concern with the conversion of local Eastern Christians.

In Chapter 6, we turn our attention to the meaning of the Holy Land for the Franciscan brothers, an international Franciscan community that found itself divided internally by the seventeenth century over competing conceptions of the Franciscan ideal. This conflict emerges into view in a series of disputes during the seventeenth century following the arrival of members of the Capuchin, Recollect, and *Riformati* reforming traditions in the Custody. For the brothers of the Holy Land, most of whom were drawn from mainstream or "regular" communities of the Order of Friars Minor (OFM), these reformed brethren posed a direct threat to their administration of the Custody. Why they did so is clear when we consider these disputes in conjunction with contemporary Franciscan writings on the Holy Land. These illuminate a decidedly Franciscan understanding of the Holy Land that privileged it as a Franciscan sacred landscape through its association with the life and spirituality of Francis of Assisi. In these sacred histories, the Custody was a legacy of Christ to Francis, one that recognized his role, and that of his most faithful followers, as latter-day apostles.

***

This monograph marks a continuation of over two decades of research on, and fascination with, the Franciscan tradition. What began as a dissertation and then a book on the political and spiritual influence of Franciscan preachers during the French Wars of Religion (1560–1600)[6]

---

[6] Megan C. Armstrong, *The Politics of Piety: Franciscan Preachers during the French Wars of Religion, 1560–1600* (Rochester: University of Rochester Press, 2004).

has since developed into a more broadly construed study of a revered pilgrimage administration, one that had global reach because it was managed by an international community of friars at a site of global pilgrimage. This study of the Custody of the Holy Land is also by necessity an international project because most of its internal records were destroyed in the nineteenth century,[7] a reality that requires the researcher to look outward to other archives to fill in key gaps in the historical record. Thankfully, the friars were actively in communication with a diverse array of Catholic institutions and powers throughout their history, leaving important repositories of documents in archives across Europe. In addition to the archives of the Custody in Jerusalem, which has an extensive collection of firmans (Ottoman decrees) and a registry of the Order of the Holy Sepulcher among other documents, this research has culled documents from a multitude of archives in Spain, France, and Italy, three regions that enjoyed particularly close ties with the Custody throughout the Early Modern Period. With regard to particular archives, the extraordinary richness of those belonging to the Congregation of the Propaganda Fide (Rome) and the Venetian ambassador to the Ottoman Porte, the latter found at the national archives in Venice, have been especially important. The royal archives at Simancas in Spain, the National Historical Archives in Madrid, and the Archives Nationales in France also contain valuable collections of diplomatic and Franciscan correspondence. In addition to these archival sources, this study has relied extensively upon travel accounts to the Holy Land. Pilgrimage treatises, in particular, have been a rich resource, treated here simultaneously as historical records, literary narratives and, perhaps most importantly, as sacred histories. In addition to pilgrimage treatises, of which they produced quite a few, the friars associated with the Custody also wrote a broad array of other texts including chronicles. Together, these diverse writings provide another important filter through which this project has examined the meaning of the Holy Land for early modern Catholics.

As should be abundantly clear from this discussion, the present project has cast a wide net with the objective of studying a diverse array of Catholic actors and diverse modes of religious and political engagement in the early modern Holy Land. It does not claim to be an exhaustive let alone definitive study but rather an interjection into recent scholarly

---

[7] On the destruction of the archives, see, in particular, Narcyz Klimas, "I danni subiti nei secoli dall'Archivio gerosolimatano: Principale causè e fattori," *Antonianum* 3 (2009): 531–564.

discussions on a number of concerns that touch upon the significance of the Holy Land for a Catholic tradition embattled by the forces of change. The long time frame of this study (1517–1700) should be considered suggestive rather than restrictive in terms of defining the nature and impact of these changes, chosen to evoke the convergence of some of the more transformative ones and to trace evidence of their long-term impact upon the Custody as well as the Catholic tradition more generally. Many of these changes were already underway before the period studied here and their ripple effects in most cases were still being felt well into the eighteenth century. Accepting as well that the disputes involving the Custody were likely shaped by other factors that are not considered here, this investigation ventures a number of observations on four areas of vigorous discussion among historians of the Mediterranean and the Catholic tradition: the distinctive character of early modern Catholicism, sacred space, religion and empire-building, and the role of Catholic institutions as critical sites of religious and political engagement in the eastern Mediterranean.

First, with regard to early modern Catholicism, John O'Malley coined the term, seeking an explanatory framework that better encompassed some of the more striking elements of a religious tradition that was changing by the sixteenth century.[8] For O'Malley and many other scholars, this change resulted from the confluence of multiple forces that included those of internal reform, confessional conflict, and the growing global spiritual engagement of the Church. With this broadly construed framework in mind, the view from the Holy Land suggests that one particular consequence of Reformation debates over the nature and locus of the sacred was the intensification of the material cast of the Catholic tradition. In making this argument, this monograph is very much in line with Alexandra Walsham and other scholars who have been pushing back hard at an older paradigm of the Reformation as the beginnings of "de-sacralization" of the world, instead embracing a more nuanced conception of religious change. For Walsham and these scholars, the older paradigm put forth so persuasively by Weber and later by Keith Thomas linking modernity to Protestant rejection of a sacralised world is no longer tenable. That the Reformation fundamentally altered how the sacred was understood by Protestants as well as Catholics is difficult to deny. Even as it was rethought and reformulated in important ways, the

---

[8] John O'Malley, *Trent and All That: Renaming Catholicism in the Early Modern Era* (Cambridge, MA: Harvard University Press, 2000).

sacred remained integral to the construction of Protestant as well as Catholic piety long after Luther posted his theses on the doors of Wittenberg Cathedral.[9] Walsham suggests, in fact, that it might be much more useful to abandon the paradigm of disenchantment entirely and replace it with a cyclical one in which periods of desacralization and resacralization followed one another, and at times even overlapped. In this new paradigm, the material could retain and even renew its importance as a tangible source of sacrality for diverse Christians, something that I will suggest was happening for many Catholics in the century after the Reformation.

With particular relevance to this project, the robust scholarship examining the resurgence of local and long-distance pilgrimages in Europe provides a particularly strong case for the persistence of Catholic belief in a tangible holiness.[10] Rome emerged as an especially popular and revered pilgrimage destination under the active patronage of the papacy, attracting many thousands during its Jubilee years.[11] This resurgence was manifestly material in form, visible in the flow of pilgrims on the roads, the vigorous trade in relics and pilgrim's mementoes, and the restoration of local shrines as well as the construction of new ones.[12] That the resurgence of pilgrimage represented a layered response to the profound

---

[9] Alexandra Walsham, "The Reformation and 'The Disenchantment of the World' Reassessed," *The Historical Journal* 51 (2008): 497–528. Walsham rightly attributes Robert Scribner with making an early, influential argument against the Weberian thesis of desacralization. See, in particular, "The Reformation, Popular Magic, and the "Disenchantment of the World," *The Journal of Interdisciplinary* History 23 (1993): 475–494. For a more recent engagement with this paradigm, see William Whyte, "Buildings, Landscapes and Regimes of Materiality," *Transactions of the Royal Historical Society* 28 (2018): 135–148.

[10] Some of the excellent recent scholarship in a vast literature includes Elizabeth Tingle, "Long-Distance Pilgrimage and the Counter Reformation in France: Sacred journeys to the Mont Saint-Michel 1520–1750," *The Journal of Religious History* 41 (2016): 158–180; Craig Harline, *Miracles at the Jesus Oak: Histories of the Supernatural in Reformation Europe* (New Haven: Yale University Press, 2003).

[11] On the pilgrimage in Rome, see, in particular, Simon Ditchfield, "Reading Rome as a Sacred Landscape, c. 1585–1635," in *Sacred Space in Early Modern Europe*, ed. Will Coster and Andrew Spicer (Cambridge: Cambridge University Press, 2005), 167–192. It is also discussed in Rostagno, "Pellegrini italiani a Gerusalemme."

[12] Work that has shaped my thinking about the material nature of post-Reformation pilgrimage and shrines includes Virginia Reinburg, *Storied Places: Pilgrims Shrines, Nature, and History in Early Modern France* (Cambridge: Cambridge University Press, 2019); Eric Nelson, *The Legacy of Iconoclasm: Religious War and the Relic Landscape of Tours, Blois and Vendôme, 1550–1750* (St. Andrews: St. Andrews Studies, 2013); and the seminal collection of articles in Will Coster and Andrew Spicer, eds., *Sacred Space in Early Modern Europe* (Cambridge: Cambridge University Press, 2005).

challenges posed by the division of the Western Church after 1517 is widely accepted, interpreted (dependent upon context), for example, as rites of purification and restoration, as well as expressions of an emergent Catholic confessional identity.[13] These more confessionally charged responses coexisted alongside the more traditional devotional, penitential, and thaumaturgical ones. For many believers, the Holy Land pilgrimage also served these myriad functions, but it is the specific observation here that the importance given to possessing, protecting, and promoting a material presence in the Holy Land in the form of Catholic structures, bodies, and jurisdiction in the Holy Places sets into relief the special role of these sacred sites as stable, tangible sources of Christ's authority.

In making this argument, I agree with the rich scholarship emerging that argues for the importance of *place* in shaping the meaning and function assigned to sites of holiness.[14] I argue, more precisely, that the *locus* of the sacred mattered to early modern Catholics, especially in a time in which traditional institutional bastions of Catholic authority were under siege. Moreover, it was important *to be there* to experience its sacrality. Emphasizing this point may seem to argue against research that points to the many signs of Catholic renewal generated within the main institutional structures of the Church, including the papacy and the new religious orders. Rather, this study intentionally broadens the framework to argue for a much more diffuse understanding of spiritual authority, one in which the divine could express itself through diverse agents including ecclesiastical institutions, scriptures, monarchies, mystics, and also sacred places. A diffuse understanding of Catholic authority helps to explain, in particular, the alacrity with which many Catholics living in regions hard hit by interfaith violence turned to rebuilding local shrines and other

---

[13] On the myriad functions of pilgrimage in the specific context of the Reformation, see, for example, Alexander Walsham, *The Reformation of the Landscape: Religion, Identity, and Memory in Early Modern Britain and Ireland* (Oxford: Oxford University Press, 2011) and the diverse articles in Coster and Spicer, eds., *Sacred Space in Early Modern Europe*.

[14] Some of the more important works from across disciplines that have shaped my thinking about *place* include Virginia Reinburg's, *Storied Places: Pilgrims Shrines, Nature, and History in Early Modern France* (Cambridge: Cambridge University Press, 2019); Robert Ousterhout, "Architecture As Relic and the Construction of Sanctity: The Stones of the Holy Sepulcher," *Journal of the Society of Architectural Historians* 62 (2003): 4–23; Jonathan Z. Smith, *To Take Place: Toward a Theory of Ritual* (Chicago: Chicago University Press, 1987); and Shampa Mazumdar and Sanjoy Mazumdar, "Religion and Place Attachment: A Study of Sacred Places," *Journal of Environmental Psychology* 24 (2004): 385–397.

valued sites of holiness by the late sixteenth century. More to our immediate purpose here, such acts of restoration offer a striking point of comparison with the attentiveness of the Franciscan brothers to the renovation and ornamentation of Catholic chapels in the Holy Places. By the sixteenth century, Catholics in Europe as well as those in the Holy Land were living in regions marked by significant religious diversity that expressed itself, in particular, through the distinctive design and ornamentation of its own religious spaces and, far too often, through the destruction of those belonging to other religious communities. In comparing these two distinctive religious contexts – post-Reformation Europe and the Holy Land – it does seem as though that, at least for Catholics, conflicts over religious spaces intensified their significance not only as identifiers of the Catholic faith but also as local sources of divinity and thus authority. Such a view makes sense when we consider Catholic acceptance of the material world as a legitimate host of divinity.[15] The destruction of shrines did little to harm their inherent sacrality because the sacred was *de natura* eternal and thus always present in that place. It remained present even as the authority of texts, the local clergy, the papacy, and other traditional institutional structures of the Church came under serious criticism.

In an era of deep unease about the direction of the Western Church and growing religious conflicts such as we find in the Early Modern Period, sacred places thus offered even the ordinary believer a stable and accessible source of Christian authority. It must have been comforting for many Catholics to know that a holy well lay only a few hours down the road, or that Mary had marked a tree in the nearby forest with her presence. It must have also been reassuring to the armchair pilgrim who read about the journey to the Holy Land, the European diplomat who passed through Jerusalem on the way to Constantinople, as well as the friars who tended to Catholic altars in the Holy Places to know that Christ was truly living *there*, infusing the region with his presence and serving as an ever-flowing source of sacrality. That the sacred was both nearby, accessible to one's touch, and powerful also helps to explain the flourishing of pilgrimage treatises and other genres of sacred history associated with

---

[15] See, for example, Carolyn Bynum Walker, *Christian Materiality: An Essay on Religion in Late Medieval Europe* (Cambridge, MA: MIT press, 2011); and Sara Ritchey, *Holy Matter: Changing Perceptions of the Material World in Late Medieval Christianity* (Ithaca: Cornell University Press, 2014).

shrines during the Early Modern Period.[16] These writings suggest that mapping the presence of the sacred in the world of early modern Catholics became all the more important in the century after the Reformation, redrawing the traditional sacred geography in many regions to include newly sacralized places as well as charting new miracles at existing sites. Pilgrimage texts and traveling pilgrim bodies worked together to legitimize these sites as holy, and in doing so participated in the reconstruction of Catholic authority in the century after the Reformation. This point is raised in a number of recent works studying the reconstruction of shrines in the wake of the Wars of Religion in France. One is struck, for example, by the visible resurgence of the Catholic faith in the regions of Tours, Blois, and Vendôme studied by Eric Nelson, manifested in new sacred structures in landscapes that still bore the material scars of earlier bouts of iconoclasm. For Virginia Reinburg, the Marian shrines appearing in many communities in southern France played a crucial role in rebuilding, indeed reinventing, local Catholic identity. In these communities, *place* certainly mattered, their shrines drawn from the sinews of the local landscape, reemerging from the ruins as important sites of local meaning and authority that had been profoundly shaped by recent religious and political change.[17]

As a final related point in this broader discussion about the manifestly material nature of early modern Catholicism, it seems important to ponder the continuing influence of Franciscan spirituality. Medievalists have paid tribute to its formative influence upon late medieval piety, in particular its fostering of a more visceral and Christocentric devotional life.[18] This monograph suggests that we keep the Franciscans at the center

---

[16] Regarding the nature and function of sacred history, this project owes an intellectual debt in particular to Mack Holt and the rich sacred history constructed by his *vignerons* in early modern Burgundy. Mack P. Holt, *The Politics of Wine in Early Modern France* (Cambridge: Cambridge University Press, 2018). The excellent collection of articles on sacred history edited by Katherine Van Liere, Simon Ditchfield, and Howard Louthan has also been extremely important: *Sacred History: Uses of the Christian Past and the Renaissance World* (Oxford: Oxford University Press, 2012).

[17] Eric. P. Nelson, *The Legacy of Iconoclasm*; and Reinburg, *Storied Places*.

[18] Franciscan promotion of a more "human" conception of Christ (the infant Christ, *ecce uomo*, suffering on the Cross) influenced Renaissance art, modes of preaching, scholastic theology (i.e., Bonaventure of Nursia). See, for example, Rona Goffen, *Piety and Patronage in Renaissance Venice: Bellini, Titian, and the Franciscans* (New Haven: Yale University Press, 1986). On preaching, see, for example, Megan C. Armstrong, *The Politics of Piety*; and Corrie Norman, "The Franciscan Preaching Tradition and Its Sixteenth-Century Legacy: The Case of Cornelio Musso," *The Catholic Historical Review* 85 (1999): 208–232.

of our thinking about early modern Catholicism as well, especially when we consider the global reach of this tradition, its missionary mandate, and direct management of Western pilgrimage in the most sacred of Christian sacred landscapes. The administration of the Holy Land offered the friars an especially useful global platform for disseminating their distinctive message of reform because it placed the brothers in the Holy Land at the center of Christendom and in contact with Christ. Friars wrote pilgrimage treatises, developed and exported liturgical practices, and circulated pilgrim mementoes produced in the Holy Land that collectively forged a material and ideological connection between the outer Catholic world and the ministry of the brothers based in Jerusalem. These Franciscan "products" were inflected with Franciscan spirituality, an argument that receives support from many scholars working on New Spain, including Louise Burkhart, Karen Melvin, and William Taylor.[19] For Taylor, the mystical and material dimensions of Franciscan piety were especially influential, contributing to the popularity of not only *via crucis* processions but also image shrines, because it privileged the material realm as an active and continuing site of divine engagement and revelation.[20]

The second observation builds upon the first. It asserts the special authority of the Holy Land, through its containment of Christ, to legitimize a Catholic tradition that was embattled but also changing. That the Holy Land operated at the apex of a hierarchy of sacred spaces in the Catholic tradition was well established by the time considered in this study. Quite simply, it was regarded as the most powerful and most authentic reservoir of Christian authority available in the material world. The rich and growing body of scholarship on Holy Land pilgrimage treatises, architectural replicas, and pilgrim's mementoes suggests convincingly, moreover, that its popular status as a material vessel of Christ only intensified as the Church ventured into the sixteenth century. For scholars such as Robert Outsterhout, Kathryn Rudy, Marie-Christine Gomez-Géraud, and many others, these literary and material recreations brought the Holy Land into the local realities of devout European Christians,

---

[19] Louise M. Burkhart, *Holy Wednesday: A Nahua Drama from Early Colonial Mexico* (Philadelphia: University of Pennsylvania Press, 1996); William J. Taylor, *Theatre of a Thousand Wonders* (Cambridge: Cambridge University Press, 2016); and Karen Melvin, "The Travels of *El Devoto Peregrino*: A Franciscan Holy Land Comes to New Spain," in *Five Hundred Years of Franciscans in New Spain*, ed. Thomas Cohen, Jay Harrison and David Rex Galindo (forthcoming).

[20] Taylor, *Theatre of a Thousand Wonders*, 55–56.

rendering its authority accessible. That these "copies" reflected an increasingly Christocentric Western piety by the fifteenth century seems a reasonable assumption as does their function as "mental" pilgrimages and as local proxies or conduits of the reformative power of the real Holy Places.[21]

Where this study diverges from some of the scholarship is with the suggestion that these mobile Holy Lands reflected the Holy Land's relegation to the role of symbol in the Catholic tradition by the Early Modern Period rather than as a vital reservoir of Christian authority and thus an important *place* of Catholic engagement. While it is certainly true that the number of pilgrims boarding ships for Jerusalem sharply dropped during the early sixteenth century and that the journey was even at the best of times far too expensive and arduous for most Catholics to make, it is clear from this research that the Holy Land not only remained a meaningful site of spiritual engagement for most Catholics but also that its importance as a powerful localized source of authority intensified. This was because Christ both lived and died *there*. In the Catholic tradition, the Holy Sepulcher was a uniquely powerful sacred place through its association with the final days of Christ (*passio*). The grand Basilica, which was first erected by the Roman emperor Constantine in the fourth century to promote the Holy Land pilgrimage, covers the most important soteriological moments of Christ's life: his crucifixion and resurrection. In traditional Catholic teachings on this Holy Place, the presence of Christ rendered the space immaterial, making it one of the most visible symbols

---

[21] On pilgrimage treatises, see, for example, Marie Christine Gomez-Geraud, *Le Crépuscule du Grand Voyage. Les récits de pèlerins à Jérusalem (1458–1612)* (Paris: Honoré Champion, 1999); Wes Williams, *Pilgrimage and Narrative in the French Renaissance: The Undiscovered Country* (Oxford: Oxford University Press, 1999); Kathryn Rudy, *Virtual Pilgrimages in the Convent: Imagining Jerusalem in the Late Middle Ages* (Turnhout: Brepols, 2011); and Kathryn Rudy, "A Guide to Mental Pilgrimage: Paris, Bibliothèque de l'Arsenal Ms. 212)," *Zeitschrift fur Kunstgeschichte* 63 (2000): 494–515. Fascinating studies of early modern architectural replicas include Kathryn Blair Moore, *The Architecture of the Christian Holy Land: Reception from Late Antiquity through the Renaissance* (Cambridge: Cambridge University Press, 2017); Bram de Klerck, "Jerusalem in Renaissance Italy: The Holy Sepulcher on the Sacro Monte de Varallo," in *The Imagined and the Real Jerusalem in Art and Architecture*, ed. Jeroen Goudeau, Mariette Verhoeven, and Wouter Weijers (Leiden: Brill, 2014), 215–236; and Adam G. Beaver, "From Jerusalem to Toledo: Replica, Landscape and the Nation in Renaissance Iberia," *Past and Present* 218 (2013): 55–90. On medieval examples, see Robert G. Ousterhout, "The Church of Santo Stefano: A 'Jerusalem in Bologna'," *Gesta* 20 (1981): 311–321.

of the sacrifice of Christ but even more importantly, an eternal place of encounter with Him.[22]

As the most sacred of the Christian Holy Places, the Holy Sepulcher was also the most powerful and transformative of all. But many other sites in the Holy Land also felt the footsteps of Christ, Mary, and the apostles. Understanding this conception of the Holy Land as the most authentic source of Christ's authority helps to explain the significant investment (financial, political) made by the great Catholic powers of early modern Europe, for example, in the preservation and acquisition of Latin altars and convents, as well as the importance given by pilgrims such as the knights of the Holy Sepulcher to the transformative experience of visiting the region. While the European replicas of the Holy Places were certainly important to the devotions of Catholics in Europe, they drew their authority *from* their association with the real Holy Places and, in particular, their material association. Hence the importance given to measuring the Holy Places. Pilgrims like Don Fadrique de Enriquez carried ribbons or pieces of rope to gather the measurements of the distances between the Holy Places as well as their interior dimensions and listed these sacred measurements in their treatises. They also used them to construct copies of the Holy Places and design local processional routes for the *via crucis*. These measurements were also conduits of sacrality, linking the authentic Holy Place with its copies wherever they appeared. The perceived material connection between the authentic Holy Place and its copy is what made the latter powerful.[23]

The Holy Land was thus no ordinary sacred landscape but *the* ultimate source of Christian perfection. It was, and is in consequence, regarded as a material manifestation of the *biblia sacra*[24] since it contained the wisdom of Christ but also that of the biblical patriarchs because they had also lived *there*. Maintaining a Catholic presence in the region in the form of Catholic churches, convents and hospices, liturgical rites, legal

---

[22] On discussions of the unique spiritual significance of the Holy Sepulcher in the Catholic tradition, see, for example, Colin Morris, *The Sepulcher of Christ and the Medieval West: From the Beginning to 1600* (Oxford: Oxford University Press, 2005); Jonathan Z. Smith, *To Take Place*; and Ousterhout, "Architecture As Relic."

[23] See, for example, Zur Shalev, *Christian Pilgrimage and Ritual Measurement in Jerusalem*. Preprint 384 (Berlin: Max Planck Institute for the History of Science, 2009); and Felipe Pereda, "Measuring Jerusalem: The Marquis of Tarifa's Pilgrimage in 1520 and Its Urban Consequences," *Città et Storia* VII (2012): 77–102.

[24] Of particular influence upon my thinking of the Holy Land is Alphonse Dupront, *Du sacré: Croisades et pèlerinages-images et langages* (Paris: Editions Gallimard, 2013).

jurisdiction, and the bodies of Catholic priests and pilgrims was thus important to many early modern Catholics because it anchored their tradition in the most authentic source of Christian wisdom, thus authenticating Catholic claims to Christian perfection. For the Catholics of this study, maintaining a Catholic presence was fundamental to asserting Catholic precedence locally among the other Christian traditions in the Levant, but it was no less useful for legitimizing an embattled Catholic tradition as the "true" faith in the context of growing religious diversity in Europe. In fact, one could argue that the material cast of Catholic engagement in the Holy Places directly challenged Protestant reification of the Scriptures as the sole source of Christian wisdom. It did so by representing the Holy Land as the Word rendered material. As our early modern Catholics insisted, the Holy Land was another vessel of the *biblia sacra*, one that was just as authoritative as that of the written text and readily accessible to the devout believer because its wisdom flowed continually outwards into Catholic Europe through its many material conduits.

As a powerful source of Christian legitimacy, the Holy Land also served as an important mechanism of spiritual reinvention. Scott Hendrix makes a similar argument about the Scriptures to explain the growing diversity of the Protestant tradition during the sixteenth century. For Hendrix, this diversity belied an important shared ideological conception of the Scriptures as the sole source of Christian wisdom.[25] That Protestant reformers developed divergent opinions by going *ad fontem* was secondary to their shared reverence for the textual source. The Catholics of our study went to their source – the Holy Land – to legitimize their claims to Christian authenticity and to claim its authority for their own tradition. In reality, as discussed already, they were seeking legitimacy for a Catholic tradition that was changing. This view of the Holy Land as a source of Catholic reinvention adds support for Alexandra Walsham's powerful call to rethinking sacred spaces as important actors shaping the religious world of the early modern devout and not simply viewing them as sites "acted upon."[26] Certainly, the Holy Land in this study emerges as a powerful, energizing force, one that increasingly enjoyed a global reach. Indeed, it may not be going too far to give it a central role in shaping an emergent global Catholicism because of its function as a spiritual "center," a role that was predicated upon a broadly

---

[25] Scott Hendrix, "Re-Rooting the Faith: The Reformation as Re-Christianization," *Church History* 69 (2000): 558–577.
[26] Walsham, *The Reformation of the Landscape*, 14.

shared conception of the Holy Land as *the* place of Christ. Such a view does not significantly challenge recent works that emphasize the adaptation and indigenization of Mary and the Holy Places as local responses to the expansion of the faith outside of Europe.[27] This book argues, rather, that for many early modern Catholics, it was also important to locate Christ *in* the Holy land, concretizing his presence at the historical place where his ministry began. The innumerable distinctive ways in which the Holy Land was evoked locally reflected the influence of indigenous cultures across the global footprint of the Catholic Church and further underscores the inventive function of the Holy Land. Its authority was useful for legitimizing new Catholic traditions that differed, at times substantially, from that found in contemporary parishes in Europe.

A third broad observation that emerges from this study concerns the role of religion in the construction of early modern empires. That the Custody became a site of intense political, religious, and economic competition between Spain and France by the sixteenth century is one striking indication that the Holy Land remained important to shaping imperial ambitions. Again, this function was by no means something new to the Early Modern Period let alone Western European in origin. For centuries, a succession of powers fought (and indeed continue to do so today) for possession of the region, each victor marking the landscape with the visible signs of its authority. Mamluk and the Ottoman rulers each in turn actively promoted Jerusalem as a site of pilgrimage, filling the city with structures that simultaneously facilitated the movement of Muslims, Jews, and Christians through the innumerable shrines important to their faiths and marked their jurisdiction. Shut out of direct jurisdiction, European powers filled Catholic altars with beautiful ornaments, clothed priests in fine vestments, and renovated Catholic convents and other spaces to articulate their own claims to Catholic leadership.

That the Holy Land emerged by the end of the sixteenth century as an important venue in a global rivalry between France and Spain reflected the imperial ambitions of these two powers but also the increasing confessionalization of Europe in the wake of the Reformation.[28]

---

[27] Two recent examples include Karin Vélez, *The Miraculous Flying House of Loreto: Spreading Catholicism in the Early Modern World* (Princeton, Princeton University Press, 2019); and Olivier Christin, Fabrice Flückiger, and Naïma Ghermani, eds., *Marie mondialisée: L'Atlas Marianus de Wilhelm Gumppenberg et les topographies sacrées de l'époque* (Neuchâtel: Presses universitaires suisses, 2014).

[28] On Confessionalization theory and its influence, see, for example, Bodo Nischan, John M. Headley, Hans Joachim Hillerbrand, and Anthony J. Papalas, eds.,

"Confessionalization" is an intensely debated term. However, it is useful for thinking about the role of religion in shaping the political identities of European states in the wake of the Reformation. Indeed, Chapter 4 argues that the intensification of the Catholic character and identity of the French and Spanish monarchies helps to explain their interest in exercising influence over the Custody of the Holy Land. Taken in conjunction with the growing body of work touting the importance of religious institutions as global agents of Spanish and French influence,[29] this study provides further support for considering the Catholic faith as formative in shaping early modern conceptions of empire. Certainly in the case of France and Spain, these powers forged a visible presence in the Holy Land to manifest claims to Catholic orthodoxy and thus Catholic leadership.[30] But more than that, an intimate material and ideological association with the Holy Land, one also mediated through possession of jurisdiction over the Custody, had potentially far-reaching political and economic as well as religious implications for these powers, especially when we consider the Holy Land's significance as a site of global pilgrimage. Firstly, the Holy Places were shared religious spaces and important sites for marking Catholic identity in a diverse Christendom. Secondly, pilgrimage was also a business, one that could both be enormously profitable as well as ideologically useful for a growing Christian empire. Spanish monarchs realized this early on and worked closely with the friars of the Custody to establish an increasingly global trading network in alms and pilgrimage mementoes during the sixteenth and seventeenth centuries. This trade brought goods created in workshops in Bethlehem on Spanish ships to

---

Confessionalization in Europe, 1550–1700: Essays in Honor and Memory of Bodo Nishan (Aldershot: Ashgate, 2004).

[29] Recent scholarship illuminates a complex engagement between indigenous cultures, European states, and the religious orders. A few representative examples include Keith Luria, "Catholic Marriage and the Customs of the Country: Building a New Religious Community in Seventeenth Century Vietnam," *French Historical Studies* 40 (2017): 457–473; Ryan Dominic Crewe, "Pacific Purgatory: Spanish Dominicans, Chinese Sangleys, and the Entanglement of Mission and Commerce, 1580–1620," *The Journal of Early Modern History* 19 (2015): 337–365; Osvaldo Pardo, *The Origins of Mexican Catholicism: Nahua Rituals and Christian Sacraments in Sixteenth-Century Mexico* (Ann Arbor: University of Michigan Press, 2006); Dominique Deslandres, *Croire et faire Croire: Les missions françaises au XVIIe siècle* (Paris: Fayard, 2003).

[30] Adam G. Beaver makes precisely this point in his work on Spanish patronage of the Custody of the Holy Land. Beaver, "A Holy Land for the Catholic Monarchy: Palestine in the Making of Modern Spain, 1469–1598," PhD diss., Harvard University, 2008; and "From Jerusalem to Toledo: Replica, Landscape and the Nation in Renaissance Iberia," *Past and Present* 218 (2013): 55–90.

European ports and from there to Spanish colonies in the Atlantic under the supervision of Spanish friars.[31] But whether discussing Spain, France, Venice, or the papacy, central to the construction of their hegemonic ambitions was the visible manifestation of their imperial identities in the Holy Places in the form of expensive ornaments in Latin chapels and public demonstration of jurisdiction over the Custody.

As a fourth and final observation, this study argues for Catholic institutions as crucial sites of Western religious and political engagement in the Muslim-governed regions of the Levant. This may seem to be an obvious point given that Catholic convents and friaries offered Western powers rare points of institutional contact once Islamic powers consolidated their control of the eastern and southern regions of the Mediterranean.[32] While Mamluk and Ottoman scholars recognize these institutions as political institutions,[33] Europeanists until recently have tended to privilege traditional diplomatic representatives such as consuls, envoys, and ambassadors, as well as merchants, as cultural and political mediators. The Custody, however, suggests that Catholic institutions frequently offered Western travelers and political authorities a deeper geographic penetration into these regions. Catholic institutions also typically operated in close contact with local authorities and engaged more broadly with the local populace. To be sure, Catholic institutions also relied significantly upon the linguistic and administrative expertise of the *dragoman*, a highly trained official who was central to European relations

---

[31] Felicita Tramontana, "Per ornamento e servizio di questi luoghi: L'arrivée des objets de devotion dans les santuaires de Terre Sainte," *Archives sciences sociales des religions. Façonner l'objet de dévotion chrétien. Fabrication, commerce et circulations* 183 (2018): 227–240; Jacob Norris, "Exporting the Holy Land: Artisans and Merchant Migrants in Ottoman-Era Bethlehem," *Journal of Middle East Migration Studies* 2 (2013): 14–40, and Melvin, "The Travels of *Il devoto peregrino*."

[32] See, in particular, Bernard Heyberger, *Les Chrétiens du Proche-Orient au temps de la Réforme Catholique* (Rome: Ecole Française de Rome, 1994); and Peri, *Christianity under Islam in Jerusalem*.

[33] Ottoman and Mamluk scholars are at the forefront of studying religious institutions as political institutions. See, for example, Anton Molnar, *Le Saint-Siège, Raguse et les missions Catholiques de la Ongrie ottoman (1572–1647)* (Budapest: METEM, 2007); Ana Sekulic, "Conversion of the Landscape: Environment and Religious Politics in an Early Modern Ottoman Town," PhD diss., Princeton University, 2020; Hasan Çolak, "Between the Ottoman Central Administration and the Patriarchates of Antioch, Jerusalem and Alexandria," PhD thesis, University of Birmingham, 2008; Febe Armanios, *Coptic Christianity in Ottoman Egypt* (Oxford: Oxford University Press 2011); and Halil Inalcik, "The Status of the Greek Orthodox Patriarch under the Ottomans," *Turcica* 23 (1991): 407–436.

with Ottoman authorities.[34] During the Early Modern Period, however, the Franciscan family of the Holy Land also included members trained in Arabic and other local languages who could also engage directly with local authorities and the populace more generally. This broader arena of engagement offered by Catholic convents also owed something to the mendicant nature of their ministries. The Franciscan brothers of the Custody, for example, had a mobile ministry that linked their convents with the Catholic mercantile colonies in the major urban centers and the Holy Places. But even more importantly, the Custody was a critical site of political and religious engagement for Catholics because it was a construct of Islamic as well as canon law. To adapt the terminology of Natalie Rothman, the Custody was a *trans-imperial* institution,[35] one that offered Catholics a legitimate place *in* the Holy Land because it was a legally and politically constructed locus of Catholic engagement. Grounded as it was upon Islamic and canon law, and subject to local as well as imperial structures of authority in the Holy Land, the Custody could offer shelter to Western travelers, protect them before local judges in cases of dispute, provide them with expert advice on local political relations and contact with important officials. The longevity of the Custody as an institution added to its utility for Western authorities as well, giving it a respected and well-connected community of men to act as envoys on a variety of matters with local religious and political leaders.

As should be clear, this investigation privileges the local influence of the older, well-established religious communities (mostly mendicant) over the Jesuits, Capuchins, and the other religious orders that began establishing communities in the Ottoman Empire at this time. That historians of the Jesuit tradition have been quite successful in making this Order, in particular, the recognized face of early modern missions is difficult to ignore.[36] It is also not an entirely accurate representation, though the Jesuits were certainly innovative and influential and rightly deserve

---

[34] On the importance of these officials as cultural and political mediators, see the extensive publications of Natalie Rothman including *The Dragoman Renaissance: Diplomatic Interpreters and the Routes of Orientalism* (Ithaca: Cornell University Press, 2021).

[35] I am taking liberties with Rothman's usage, applying it not to subjects but also to institutions. I find the term extremely useful for thinking about institutions that have a place *within*, as well as *between*, multiple cultures, legally, politically, and in this case, spiritually. Natalie Rothman, *Brokering Empire: Trans-Imperial Subjects between Venice and Istanbul* (Ithaca: Cornell University Press, 2012).

[36] *Pace* to my many friends and colleagues who work on the Jesuit tradition. One of the great pleasures of my professional career has been our lively, vigorous debates over "our Orders," inevitably followed by cocktails at the bar and continuing debate.

significant attention. Moreover, the rich scholarship on the Jesuits and Capuchins has been central to rethinking the nature and influence of early modern missions. My point here is simply to suggest that the mendicant traditions remained central to the operations of European religious and political authority in the Mediterranean throughout the Early Modern Period and were not replaced by the early modern religious Orders. Indeed, mendicant communities could trace a long presence in the eastern Mediterranean dating back to the thirteenth century.

Many of these communities remained vigorous institutions throughout the Early Modern Period and locally influential because they were a part of the material and political fabric of their local communities. It is because the friars possessed extensive local ties and expert knowledge that the Jesuits, Capuchins, and other newly arrived missionaries could not easily dislodge them from their jurisdiction in the Custody. For the same reasons, the papacy and the French, Venetian, and Spanish states were eager to bring the venerable institution and its Observant administrators within their respective spheres of political influence. As a final but important point, we need to remember that the older mendicant orders also expanded globally during the Early Modern Period and were culturally influential, a point that scholars working on New Spain, in particular, would agree with.

The Custody, with its many convents, hospices, and traveling friars thus offered Western powers as well as merchants and other travelers a well-recognized, indeed crucial site of political as well as religious engagement in the Levant. Though much more work needs to be done on this front, the sources suggest that the Custody was simultaneously a critical transmitter of cultural influence back to Europe throughout the Medieval and Early Modern Periods. This was because it was a trans-regional and trans-imperial institution but also because it was administered by a religious Order that embraced a mobile spiritual ideal and that had its own extensive, indeed global, network of Franciscan institutions. More attention needs to be given in particular to the role of the Custody in mediating the influence of Muslim, Jewish, and the Eastern Christian traditions upon Catholic devotional rites in Europe. It is worth considering, to begin with, that Christian worship in the Holy Places was regulated by Islamic law, which determined not only where and when worship took place but also even its liturgical form. Secondly, the Holy Land was an extraordinarily diverse religious landscape and the Holy Places were shared sites of worship. Thirdly, the Franciscan brothers of the Custody actively promoted the dissemination of the Holy Land rites to Europe and elsewhere through their local proxies – Franciscan friaries. Indeed, the Franciscan Order embraced an extensive and expanding institutional network of Franciscan communities during the Early Modern Period. Beyond its dissemination of a Franciscan brand of Catholic spirituality through these popular devotions, it does seem time to think about these devotions as creations of a diverse religious landscape. It raises, in particular, a provocative question: To what extent was medieval and early modern Catholic devotion informed by Islam?

I

A Catholic Gateway to the Holy Land

The Custodia Terrae Sanctae

In 1605, François Savary de Breves arrived at the gates of Jerusalem to begin the traditional pilgrimage. The Holy Land was one of a number of places visited by the French ambassador and his party during the course of several months touring the eastern Mediterranean. Savary de Breves was a devout Catholic, however, and his account shows that the sacred landscape was an especially meaningful destination, Jerusalem in particular. Indeed, the following description of his visit could have been lifted directly from a pilgrimage treatise rather than a diplomatic relation because it recreates the traditional itinerary followed by early modern pilgrims, describing each sacred place, its biblical past, and the performance of the liturgical rites. More to our immediate purpose here, Savary de Breves' description of the visitation of the Holy Places introduces us to the Custodia Terrae Sanctae, illuminating important dimensions of a unique Catholic institution that had served the needs of Western pilgrims for centuries in a sacred landscape shared among many faiths and presided over by Ottoman rulers.

We begin with the moment that the French ambassador caught sight of Jerusalem glimmering in the distance, suddenly aware that the holy city was within reach. He and his party immediately dismounted, kissed the ground, and prayed. Savary de Breves was grateful for their safe arrival, but his prayers also paid special tribute to the holy city itself, giving thanks to God "for giving us the grace of his city," a city "beloved and ennobled by his son our Saviour." The French party was eager to experience its sacred mysteries, he says, because it offered a path to redemption. Having made their prayers, the men walked on foot to the city gates, passing "an infinity ... of churches and monasteries" along the way.

At the gates, the French party waited, first for permission from the *sangiac* (local ottoman official) to enter and then for the arrival of the Franciscan vicar to take them to the hospice attached to the convent of the Holy Saviour.

Turkish scrutiny did not end there because another official arrived at the convent to make sure they were not hiding arms and searched their bags. Refreshments in the refectory of the convent followed and then a solemn mass in the church, which formally welcomed the men through the traditional ritual washing of the feet. The pilgrimage had officially begun for the French party, but though the men must have been exhausted after the busyness of their first day in the sacred city, they followed a number of the brothers up to a terrace overlooking Jerusalem. Savary de Breves' description of this moment conveys a distinct sense of place and time. We learn that it was already the evening and that to reach the terrace the men had to climb up several steps. There they found two dogs (*bons chiens*) sleeping, their role apparently to protect the convent from potential pillaging. From the terrace of the Catholic convent, safely ensconced inside the walls of the ancient city, the pilgrims had their first intimate view of a place that loomed large in the Catholic imaginary and which most Catholics would never experience in person. Savary de Breves describes an excited Catholic party "full of desire to contemplate this holy city" and pestering the brothers with questions, and the brothers doing their best to respond to "our impatient curiosity," gesturing with their hands to "the most remarkable places."[1]

The French ambassador's account conveys some of the emotional intensity of the pilgrimage experience for early modern Catholics as well as the special reverence with which they held the Holy Land. At the same time, it illuminates the central role played by the Franciscan brothers in mediating Catholic experience of the region. The friars greeted the pilgrims at the gates, hosted them at their convents, and shared their expertise on the many wonders to be found in Jerusalem and the other sacred places. The brothers also worked closely with local authorities to protect Western access to the Holy Places, a necessity when working in a region that lay well outside the jurisdiction of the Catholic Church, especially

---

[1] "... là les Religieux nous monstroient au doigt, les plus remarquables lieux, selon que confusément nostre impatiente curiosité les en solicitoit." *Relation des voyages de Monsieur de Brèves, tant en Grèce Terre Saincte et egypte qu'aux royaumes de Tunis et Arger* (Paris: Nicolas Gasse, 1628), 112–113. The relation is based upon his memoirs and written by one of his secretaries named Jacques du Castel.

one governed by Muslim rulers. As shall soon be clear, this was a task that became harder in the immediate wake of the Ottoman conquest of the region in 1516/1517, though it was by no means the only challenge faced by the friars to their administration during the Early Modern Period including from other Christians. In preparation for a close analysis of the intra-Christian disputes that are the focus of the remaining chapters, this chapter grapples with the unique character of the Custody as a religious institution, arguing that its emergence as a site of intra-Christian contestation after 1517 rested to a significant degree upon its intimate material, historic, and spiritual association with the most sacred of Christian landscapes. By the time Savary de Breves and his French party made their way to Jerusalem, the Custody was a revered pilgrimage institution that had devoted centuries to forging a liturgical and material place for the Catholic tradition in the Holy Land.

The Custody was a unique institution, one that straddled Western and Ottoman structures of authority and that was profoundly shaped by its long history of engagement with the many local Christian, Muslim, and Jewish communities. The Custody was, in other words, a product of the Holy Land in as much as it was a product of Catholic spirituality. To make this argument, the following discussion will situate the Custody in three contexts that were especially formative, contexts that are visible as well in the relation of Savary de Breves: Western pilgrimage, Ottoman governance, and the Custody's location in a shared sacred landscape.

1.1 A VENERABLE PILGRIMAGE INSTITUTION

The Custody of the Holy Land looks back on a long and storied history, one that had its roots in the Crusades – or more accurately – their failure to secure a Western foothold in a region sacred to Muslims, Christians, and Jews. Today, the sacred landscape known as the Holy Land traverses the modern states of Israel, Egypt, Lebanon, Jordan, and Syria, though early modern European travelers knew the regions somewhat differently, as Egypt, Syria, and Palestine. The Custody was formally established in 1342 to manage Western (Catholic) pilgrimages to the Holy Places, a role that it continues to play to this day. The term "custody" (*custodia*) marks this medieval institution as simultaneously Franciscan and extraterritorial in character. The Franciscan order, which played a central role in the formation of the Custody of the Holy Land, organized its convents in regional administrative clusters known as custodies. In the context of the

Western Church, more generally, custodies usually designated Catholic administrations in regions outside its direct influence. The Holy Land was just such a place because it lay under the governance of Muslim rulers – first the Mamluk Turks of Egypt (1250–1517) and later the Ottomans. Mamluk authority expanded throughout Egypt, Syria, and Palestine during the thirteenth century, assuming definitive control following the collapse of Crusader influence in the region by 1291. Accounts vary on the origins of the Custody, though it seems fair to say that the rulers of the kingdoms of Aragon and Naples were negotiating independently to reestablish a formal Latin (Western Catholic) clerical presence in Jerusalem to facilitate pilgrimage.[2] Western pilgrimage had flourished during the era of the Crusades but largely collapsed by 1291. Negotiations between Robert and Sancia (Sancha) of Naples and Sultan al-Malik al-Nasir Muhammad (1310–1341) of Egypt for a permanent Latin ministry in the region seem to have begun in earnest during the 1320s and bore fruit in 1333, when the Sultan granted altars to the Latin Church in the Cenacle and the Basilica of the Holy Sepulcher, two of the most significant of the Christian shrines, or Holy Places. The Holy Sepulcher was first constructed by Emperor Constantine and his mother Helen to venerate the sites of the Crucifixion and Resurrection, while Christians venerated the Cenacle as the site of the Last Supper. It was here, attached to the Cenacle, that the Franciscan brothers received permission to build the convent of Mount Sion, which became the celebrated center of custodial administration until its loss in 1551.[3]

Obtaining these altars and establishing an administrative base in Jerusalem were consequential achievements for the Catholic tradition because they symbolically, materially, and legally restored its access to the most sacred of Christian landscapes. Papal recognition of the negotiations came swiftly in the form of a series of papal bulls in 1342.[4] From this time forward, devout Catholics could worship in the hallowed

---

[2] The most detailed study of the origins is Felix del Buey and Cristoforo Alvis, "Origenes de la custodia de Tierra Santa," *Archivo ibero-americano* 65 (2005): 7–96. On the negotiations between Aragon and Robert of Anjou, the King of Naples, see also Sabino de Sandoli, *The Peaceful Liberation of the Holy Place in the Fourteenth Century* (Jerusalem: Franciscan Center, 1991), 36. In terms of the history of the Custody more generally, see Girolamo Golobovich, ed., *Biblioteca bio-bibliografica della Terra Santa e dell'Oriente Francescano*, 5 vols. (Florence: Quaracchi, 1906–1927).

[3] Del Buey and Alvis, "Origenes," 26–28.

[4] The papal bulls *Gratias agimus* and *Nuper carissimae* (November 12, 1342) officially recognized the establishment of the Custody of the Holy Land.

Christian shrines of the Holy Land. Just as importantly, they had a liturgical presence in some of the most significant of them in the form of the Franciscan brothers. Indeed, the selection of the Franciscans as their first administrators inaugurated a formative relationship between this religious order and the Custody that continues to the present day. For the rulers of Naples, the choice of the friars to manage the fledgling institution may have reflected a personal taste for this spiritual tradition since they were already favoured recipients of royal patronage at home. It was just as likely a pragmatic decision, however, because the friars were a well-established Western presence in the eastern Levant by this time.

The Franciscan Order was active in establishing missions in Syria, Palestine, and Egypt during the thirteenth century, so much so that by the time the Order assumed oversight of the Custody it numbered twelve convents: five in Syria (Acre, Antioch, Sidon [Saida], Tripoli, and Tyre), two in Palestine (Jerusalem and Jaffa), one in Egypt (Damietta), and four on Cyprus (Nicosia, Limassol, Famagusta, and Paphos).[5] With regard to Jerusalem, in particular, the friars claim to have possessed a small house near the House of Simon of Cyrene (Station V) on the via dolorosa by 1229, the same year that Frederick II Hohenstaufen, the Holy Roman Emperor, restored the cities of Jerusalem, Nazareth, and Bethlehem to the Kingdom of Jerusalem. This base proved to be impermanent, however, once Ayyubid forces swept through the city in 1244. Mamluk forces moved in shortly after and consolidated their authority over Syria and Palestine by 1250. The friars were forced to retreat to Cyprus during this time. While surviving accounts of these early decades are rather sparse in terms of detail, they do reveal small bands of friars traveling back and forth to Jerusalem during the holy season of Easter when permitted by the political conditions (and sometimes when not). Moreover, it seems clear that they did so with the permission of Mamluk authorities, who allowed limited Western access to the religious sites for the purposes of worship. By the 1270s, the friars seemed to have established a more regular presence of sorts on Mount Sion, presaging the later establishment of their first convent known as Mount Sion.[6]

---

[5] Buey and Alvis, "Origines," 12–14. See also Golubovich, ed., *Biblioteca Bio-Bibliografica*, vol. 1 (1906), 158, 356, 413.

[6] Jason Welle, "The Status of Monks in Egypt under Early Mamluk Rule: The Case of Ibn Taymiyya," *LOGOS: Journal of Eastern Christian Studies* (2014): 57. Welles mentions that Queen Sancia of Naples sent four friars to this city to establish a convent or hospice in the *funduq* of Marseilles' merchants. See pp. 57, ft. 39.

Whether it was because of their tenacious ministry in the region, hard-won experience working with local authorities, or favoured status with the Neapolitan rulers, the Franciscan Order assumed control of the administration from the start. Indeed, some friars may have played a role in the early negotiations for the Custody. Franciscan chronicles credit Friar Roger Guerin, in particular, with securing sole jurisdiction for the Latin (Western) Church over the main altar of the Cenacle as well as permission to establish the convent of Mount Sion and for a small Franciscan community to live inside the Basilica of the Holy Sepulcher.[7] In recognition of his hard work, Guerin became the first friar appointed as *custos*, a papal office that from this time forward was held simultaneously with that of *guardian* of the main convent of Mount Sion in Jerusalem. In Franciscan communities, the guardian was the administrative head of the community, responsible for overseeing the spiritual and other duties of the friars. The office of *custos* invested Guerin with much broader jurisdiction. Over time, the authority of the *custos* expanded. By the start of this investigation in 1517, the *custos* was invested with episcopal authority and the role of apostolic delegate, making its holder the single most powerful Latin official within the boundaries of the Custody and one of the most powerful in the Levant.

As one finds with any long-lasting institution, the administration of the Custody changed over time. Particularly impactful was the shift of its jurisdiction from the Conventual to the Observant branches of the Franciscan Order in 1430/1431, a move that reflected the growing influence of the new reformed tradition in the spiritual brotherhood and stirred more than a little controversy at the time.[8] Indeed, the issue of reform bedeviled the administration of the Custody periodically throughout its history, including during the period of this investigation. Divisions within the Observant branch (Order of Friars Minor) sparked renewed conflict over office-holding during the seventeenth century, reshaping

---

[7] On the role played by Roger Guerin, see among others, Del Buey and Alvis, "Origines," 29–30, and Andrew Jotischky, "The Franciscan Return to the Holy Land (1333) and Mt Sion: Pilgrimage and the Apostolic Mission," in *The Crusader World*, ed. Adrian Boas (London: Routledge, 2016), 241–258.

[8] According to the *Registro de' fatti memorabili*, Martin V gave Niccolò d'Osimo permission to reform the conventual brothers of the Holy Land in 1426. The Observants were given the guardianship officially in 1430/1431, and the conventuals were subsequently forced out of the Custody. Leonhard Lemmens, ed., "Registro de' fatti memorabilia di Terra santa in Collectanae Terrae Sanctae," in *Biblioteca bio-bibliografica della Terra Santa e dell'Oriente Francescano*, vol XIV nuova serie, ed. Girolamo Golobovich (Florence: Quaracchi, 1933), 7–8, and n. 1.

internal administration in important ways that will receive specific attention in Chapter 6. Looking broadly over the long span of custodial administration, however, one still notes its fundamentally Franciscan character. In particular, it was a mobile community. As per the mandate of Franciscan regulations, most brothers spent only three years on assignment in the Custody, circulating among the convents as required by the *custos*. It is true that Mamluk and later Ottoman decrees also stipulated a three-year limit, but more than likely Islamic regulations recognized and institutionalized existing Franciscan administrative practices. Three-year terms were in fact normative in convents throughout the Order long before the sixteenth century, especially for the highest offices in a community such as guardian and vicar. There was an ideological reason for this mandate, rooted in Franciscan skepticism of office-holding as worldly oriented and thus a potential source of corruption. In a famous passage from chapter VI in the Rule of 1223, which became the guiding constitution of the order, Francis urged his followers to remain "pilgrims and exiles" in the world, which meant among other things rejecting the many ties (material, sexual, political) that could distract them from leading a truly spiritual life and spreading God's message of reform.[9] Making the most important offices elective and also ensuring a regular circulation of friars through offices and on diverse assignments were among the mechanisms intended to preserve the "otherworldly" character of the spiritual brotherhood. These same mechanisms – short-term office-holding, mobility – also came to distinguish the Franciscan tradition from the earlier medieval monastic traditions such as the Benedictine and Cistercian.

A broad survey of the administration highlights the regular rotation of brothers in and out of the Custody throughout the Early Modern Period, though some friars clearly stayed much longer than the mandated three-year term. The Venetian friar Francesco Suriano spent an unusually long time in the Holy Land overall, though it was interrupted by periods during which he was recalled to his home province in the Venetian state. From his *Trattato*, we know that between 1481 and 1512 he fulfilled two three-year terms as *custos* based in Jerusalem, but this was in addition to a number of years based in Egypt as well as other parts of the Custody. The seventeenth-century friar Jacques Goujon spent five years in the Holy Land holding diverse offices. One finds friars who stayed for even longer

---

[9] For a discussion of the spiritual meaning attached to Franciscan mobility, see, for example, Megan C. Armstrong, *The Politics of Piety: Franciscan Preachers and the French Wars of Religion, 1560–1600* (Rochester: University of Rochester Press, 2004).

periods, including the seventeenth-century French Recollect friar Hilaire Tounon who spent over thirty years there.[10] All of this suggests that both the Franciscan administration in Rome and the Congregation of the Propaganda Fide, two authorities that claimed oversight of the Custody during the Early Modern Period, were willing to be flexible in certain cases to meet the practical demands of manning such a unique institution, one that relied upon a trained, multilingual ministry to tend to the needs of an international pilgrimage. European pilgrims encountered friars in the Holy Places who were drawn from across Europe as well as from the eastern Mediterranean. While Italian was the common language of the administration, French, Spanish, Flemish, Polish, and Arabic were among the many other languages spoken by members.

While the demands placed upon the Custody to field a diverse ministry help to explain why some friars stayed several years in the region, the archives of the Propaganda Fide suggest even so that three-year terms still remained normative throughout the Early Modern Period. One important consequence of this practice was that the Holy Land family – the name that the brothers themselves often used to refer to their unique Franciscan community in the Holy Land – was perpetually changing as new men arrived every three years at the ports of the Levant from Europe and others made their way back home after completing their terms. Just as importantly, the constant circulation in and out of Europe ensured a continuous and routinized mode of communication between the brothers of the Holy Land and Catholic authorities in Europe, ties that would be called upon time and time again during their disputes over altars. But inasmuch as friars circulated to and from the Holy Land, they also circulated *through* it in ways that are important for understanding the operations of the Custody, in particular its responsibilities as both a Western pilgrimage institution and as a local representative of the Catholic faith. Indeed, the mobility of the friars increased during the course of the fourteenth and fifteenth centuries in response to the steady expansion of the spiritual geography of the Custody. During the fourteenth century alone, the sacred topography of the Latin tradition expanded to include other important altars: one in the Church of the Nativity in the nearby city of Bethlehem (1347) and the Tomb of the Virgin Mary (1363), which lies in the Valley of Jehosophat just outside the walls of Jerusalem. In 1392, the friars also received permission to

---

[10] On Tounon, see Chapter 6.

officiate in the Grotto of the Garden of Gethsemane. At the time of the Ottoman conquest in 1516/1517, the Custody included two convents in Jerusalem (Mount Sion, Holy Sepulcher) and one each in the cities of Bethlehem, Aleppo, and Beirut. These were in addition to two other convents on Cyprus (Famagusta, Nicosia) and two hospices (Ramleh and Jaffa).[11]

As the above discussion should suggest, the Custody was a well-established pilgrimage institution by 1517. It was, moreover, a decidedly Franciscan one in terms of not only its structure and operations but also its membership. Early modern sources can be frustratingly opaque when it comes to tracking individual friars. This is especially true of the lay brothers who were charged with the more domestic tasks of the Custody and not its central administration. We do catch periodic glimpses of some of them – doing errands, singing in the choir, traveling to and from Europe with their companion brothers, or, at times, reprimanded for disobedience. Even such brief glimpses into the daily lives of the friars, however, reveal a strong sense of community. As with any family, however, relations were not always harmonious. In the case of the brothers of the Holy Land, the bonds of fraternal affection were tested periodically by difficult personalities, regional rivalries, and even different conceptions of the Franciscan ideal. Still, the friars of this study also belonged to a spiritual tradition that bound them as a spiritual family that shaped their experience of life in the Holy Land. Chapters 4 and 6 will allow us to delve more deeply into internal relations, but we can learn a great deal as well about the nature of this community from the material form of its ministry.

Franciscan chronicles and administrative records as well as pilgrimage accounts provide us with the richest window into the material character of the Custody at this time, describing a Latin presence that must have seemed quite modest when compared to many of the monastic institutions found in European cities. With the exception of the two main communities in Jerusalem and Bethlehem, the convents housed only a few friars each. A fascinating document, which seems to have been generated as part of a broad, internal survey of Franciscan provinces in 1627, gives us some understanding of the general distribution of the Franciscan population among its many institutions in the Custody as well as its material

---

[11] Lucas Wadding, *Annales Minorum in quibus res omnes trium ordinum a S. Francisco institutum*, vol. XV (Rome: Typis Rochi Bernabò, 1836), 405. The date of the list is 1506.

character. The *Registrum omnium conventuum, provinciarum tam Familiae quam Reformationis, necnon Monialium cismontanae Familiae* begins by stating that Custody of the Holy Land included six convents, seven chaplaincies, and a number of hospices and churches where they officiated ("alcuni hospitii e chiese officiate"). Proceeding systematically, it mentions that twenty-eight friars lived at the convent of the Holy Saviour and another eight (seven priests, one laic) at the monastery in the Holy Sepulcher. The convent that had been recently reestablished in Nazareth had six brothers, while the convent of Santa Maria dell'Arnica in Cyprus had three priests and one laic. Three priests and a laic were also assigned to the Church of the Holy Conception in Aleppo for the pastoral service of the Venetian nation, and another friar was attached to the "casa" of the French consul in the city.[12] For some reason, the *Registrum* does not give the size of the Franciscan family in Bethlehem, which was the second largest community in the Custody. We know from other sources, however, that it hovered in the range of twelve to fifteen members around this time. The *Registrum* does nevertheless include information on other sites of Franciscan engagement, noting that eleven friars were appointed to six different chaplaincies (consulate chapels) as well as in service to the local merchant colonies: two each were assigned to Alexandretta (Iskanderon), Damascus and Saida (Sidon), four to Cairo (three Venetian, one French), one in Rosetta, and two in Alexandria (French and Venetian).

Whether these numbers are accurate is difficult to say with certainty, though it does seem to support other sources that place the typical annual number of friars in the range of 80–100 by the early seventeenth century. Of these, more than half of the friars were assigned to convents in Jerusalem and Bethlehem. The larger size of the communities in Jerusalem and Bethlehem, both in terms of the structures themselves as well as membership, makes sense when we consider that they were located close to the most important Holy Places and had to bear the brunt of the administrative and liturgical burden of the ministry in the Custody. The description of the Bethlehem convent in the *Registrum* illuminates its unique economic as well as liturgical role within the institutional context of the Custody, serving both as busy site of pilgrimage and a manufacturing hub for an increasingly global commerce in Holy

---

[12] Leonhard Lemmens, ed., "Conspectus Missionum Familiae Cismontanae Ordinis Fratr. Minorum an. 1627–1628 conscriptus." *AFH* 22 (1929): 379–390.

Land pilgrimage mementoes.[13] The community had a beautiful convent "filled with cells and workshops," and "a beautiful walled garden surrounded with high walls, a vine yard described as "assai bella" which the friars harvested for grapes, wine and fruit.[14] The *Registrum* also counted three churches belonging to the Bethlehem community – a large church "with three naves and the most beautiful stone columns on both sides," the church of Saint Catherine, where the friars said the divine office, and a chapel in the Grotto of the Nativity. Similar to the Basilica of the Holy Sepulcher, the Grotto was a layered sacred place, containing numerous altars that were associated not only with the life of Christ but also later holy figures, notably the early Christian patriarchs and martyrs. The *Registrum* lists nine: the site of Christ's birth, the adoration of the magi, the Holy Manger (Presepio), Saint Joseph, the holy innocents, Saint Eusebius, Saint Paula, the Sepulcher of Saint Jerome, and the oratorio of Saint Geronimo.

Though concise, the *Registrum* provides us with a useful picture of a Bethlehem community burdened with heavy liturgical and economic responsibilities, which were manifested in its cells, workshops, multiple altars, and shrines. Because of its importance as an administrative center, the convent of the Holy Saviour in Jerusalem receives even more attention. As it does to this day, the convent is located just to the east of the New Gate inside the walls of the Old City at a short distance from the via dolorosa and the Holy Sepulcher. The structure one finds today likely bears little resemblance to its early modern counterpart since it has been extensively renovated over the subsequent centuries. Contemporary sources nevertheless suggest it had been a substantial institution. Pilgrimage accounts frequently mention the spacious dormitories awaiting pilgrims in the main hospice, the refectory where they shared meals with the friars, and the Church where they were welcomed on the night of their arrival with the traditional ritual washing of the feet by the *custos*. From the *Registrum* one learns about other important parts of the complex, including a spicery (*speciaria*), infirmary, and a library.

Surviving inventories of the main library in Jerusalem (Mount Sion and later the Holy Saviour) show that it contained books useful both to the Franciscan community and to visiting pilgrims, including numerous

---

[13] Jacob Norris, "Exporting the Holy Land: Artisans and Merchant Migrants in Ottoman-Era Bethlehem," *Mashriq & Mahjar* 2 (2013): 14–40
[14] Lemmens, ed., "Conspectus," 388.

pilgrimage guides, breviaries, lives of saints, and dictionaries.[15] The convent of the Holy Saviour also included two gardens, an oven for making bread, and eight cisterns, both small and large. In an obvious nod to the dangers of working in a region well outside the boundaries of Western Christendom – Franciscan convents were raided periodically – the *Registrum* also notes that the convent had "many hidden rooms for concealing brothers and property when required."[16]

As the above suggests, the two main communities of the Custody were sizeable institutions because of their pilgrimage responsibilities. Franciscan convents that were not located near a Holy Place tended to be much smaller, including those established for the merchant colonies based in the port cities and other major economic centers. Perhaps because these were relatively modest operations, they tend to receive much less attention from pilgrim authors, though we find some exceptions. The Italian pilgrim and author, Aquilante Rocchetta, for one, provides a rare description of the church of the Holy Conception in Aleppo. Rocchetta traveled from his home in Calabria to the Holy Land in late 1598 and published an account of it in 1630. At the Church of the Holy Conception, he describes a room of moderate size that included wooden pews (*banchi*), and an altar with many levels above it that held twelve candlesticks, and "many gold vases with flowers." Rocchetta also mentions that a chair sat to the right of the altar, which was reserved for the Venetian consul of the city, another indication of the local importance of this official within the colony. The consul represented the Venetian state and local merchants in their commercial and political dealings with

---

[15] On the library of the Custody, see, for example, Michele Campopiano, "Islam, Jews and Eastern Christianity in Late Medieval Pilgrims' Guidebooks: Some Examples from the Franciscan Convent of Mount Sion," *Al-Masaq* 24 (2012): 75–89. Books feature prominently in the internal records of the Custody, in particular in correspondence discussing the sending of books from Europe but also inventories and alms-registers. A letter dated April 6, 1630, for example, sent by friar Agostino Maria, the procurator of the Holy Land to the Propaganda Fide, requested a number of texts including a breviary entitled *Breviarum Cronologium*, a latin dictionary, and the "*Esercitio de perfettione del Rodriges*," referring to the important work by the Jesuit Alonso Rodrigez the *Ejercicio de perfección y virtudes cristianas* (1609). It had received a number of editions by 1630 including in Italian. APF SC Terra Santa I, f. 1.

[16] Lemmens, "Conspecto," 386. "In questo convento vi è una bella speciara et infermaria et anco libraria; vi sono due giardinetti; vi é il forno da fare il pane; vi sono 8 cisterne tra grandi e piccolo, e vi sono anco molte stanze secrete per nasconder frati e robbe nell'occurrenze."

Ottoman officials among other matters.[17] The Italian pilgrim's description more than hints at the wealth of the Venetian colony, noting that the Church had "so many friezes and silver ornaments" that it could not be outdone by an archbishopric in Naples, and that it owned a profusion of silk vestments "made of diverse colours and with gold and silver brocade" for use of the friars in the performance of the liturgical rites.

Useful as it is as a window into its material character, Rocchetta's discussion of the Venetian church also hints at the thinly spread nature of the Franciscan administration and its mobile character. As the map of the Custody shows (see Figure 1.1), Aleppo lay several hundred kilometers to the north of Jerusalem. Despite the distance, Rochetta notes that the Franciscan *custos* made it a point of preaching in this church on the most important feast days including in the Spring. The geographic spread of the Custody and the relatively small size of the brotherhood challenged the Franciscan ministry even at the best of times, while local conflict and outbreaks of disease could seriously disrupt it. The plague that hit Jerusalem and the surrounding regions in 1619–1620, for example, brought the ministry to a virtual halt when it felled a reported twenty-four brothers. The remaining friars were forced to move to Bethlehem until the contagion died down. In a fascinating letter to the commissioner general of the Holy land based in Madrid, then guardian Tommaso Obicino da Novara described the event as devastating, noting the loss of some of the most prominent officeholders including the vicar and procurator. In addition to the twenty-four killed, as many as eight or ten other brothers were so weakened by the illness that, "though they healed, they were almost useless in the service of the Holy Places." Novara ended by saying that he felt pained "to see myself with so few friars, and with the responsibility of carrying out so many furious obligations as I do."[18]

---

[17] Aquilante Rocchetta, *Peregrinatione di Terra Santa ed' altre Provincie di Don Aquilante Rocchetta, Cavaliere del Santissimo Sepolcro* (Palermo: Aflonso dell'Isola, 1630), 58–59. "... sopra l'altare sono molti scalini, ne'quali stanno d'ordinario dodici candilieri, e molti vasi dorati con fiori, e nelle due corna ò lati dell'Altare sono due candilieri grande, ove si pongono due grosse intorcie." On Rocchetta himself, see José Sarzi Amade, "Peregrinazione di Terra Santa di Don Aquilante Rocchetta sul finire del secolo XVI."

[18] AHNOP legajo 1/27/a&b, 3. "Y por acabar con este trabajo de la peste; *Digo que han muerto delli veynte y quatro frayles, y otros ocho o diez que han sido heridos deste mal*; y aunque han sanado que d[.] casi innutiles para el servicio de estos santos lugares. Y yo me hallo affligido por verme con tan pocos frayles, y con cargo de acudir a tantas y tan furiosas obligaciones como ay."

A Catholic Gateway to the Holy Land

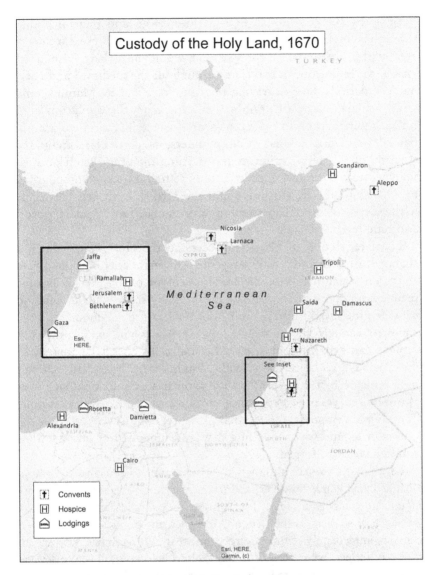

Figure 1.1 Map, Custody of the Holy Land, 1670

1.2 OTTOMAN RULE

While the Custody was challenging to manage at times, it was a vigorous and well-established pilgrimage institution, one that by the time of the Ottoman conquest had a physical presence near most of the most important Holy Places and which was supported and given purpose by the continuous flow of Franciscan and pilgrim bodies through its myriad spaces. This material and liturgical presence operated within an imperial context that would have been also quite visible to the European travelers throughout the medieval and early modern periods. Ships carrying pilgrims were met by Mamluk (and later Ottoman) officials upon arrival, and from there pilgrims continued their journey to the Franciscan hospice in Jerusalem accompanied by armed soldiers. One wonders, in particular, about the reaction of the devout pilgrim approaching the grand front door of the Basilica of the Holy Sepulcher only to find it locked and guarded by a Muslim official. Muslims could enter freely, but Christian access to the sacred center of Christendom was regulated by a Muslim porter and required a fee.

Local regulation of Christian access to the Holy Places did not change fundamentally following the Ottoman conquest in 1516/1517, an event that saw the replacement of one powerful Islamic regime with another. Unfortunately, surviving records for this period provide little insight into the minds of the friars at the moment of the conquest, though one can imagine that the friars who lived in the path of Ottoman expansion must have been anxious about the security of the Custody. While relations with Mamluk authorities had at times been difficult, by the sixteenth century, the friars could look back over two hundred years of experience working with this Muslim regime. The Mamluk empire was a familiar presence, in other words, while the Ottoman regime was something new and unfamiliar. New relations would have to be forged.

Given that Ottoman authority took some time to consolidate its hold on the Holy Land, however, the friars may not have experienced any significant changes at first. To be sure, they would have noticed the presence of soldiers in the region. Moreover, the political center shifted almost immediately from Cairo, the seat of Mamluk power, to Constantinople, where the Ottoman Sultan held court. Local administration, however, seems to have changed much more slowly, and the friars likely found many familiar faces still in charge of the main organs of local governance, including the court of the *kadi* throughout the sixteenth century. However, at the regional level, significant changes were already visible during the first few decades, as the region was incorporated into existing Ottoman structures of authority. The city of Jerusalem and its surrounding area were transformed into a *sanjak* (Ottoman district), one of ten that lay under the authority of the *beylerbei* (provincial governor) of Damascus, an Ottoman appointee.[19] Gradually, at the district level as well, new Ottoman officials were appointed with military and judicial responsibilities: the sanjak-bey who was in charge of the district, calvary officers (*sipahis*), a local garrison of janissaries,[20] *subasis* (police),[21] and judges (*kadis*).[22]

A series of large-scale building projects funded during the rule of Sultan Suleiman I (1520–1566) would have made Ottoman authority even more palpable for the brothers of the Holy Land. These included the well-known soup kitchen built by Hurrem, the consort of Suleiman, and studied by Amy Singer. The soup kitchen was one of many *waqfs* (charitable endowments) constructed in the city as well as in other parts of Palestine to manifest the presence of Ottoman authority in the region.[23] In 1537, Suleiman also ordered the construction of a new, massive wall. The wall, which remains a formidable feature of the Old City to this day, was over forty feet high at the time of completion in 1541 and included thirty-four towers as well as seven gates, all of which were heavily fortified with canons. The wall promised greater protection from Bedouin raids and other external threats, but as Laurent and Reidelmayer also argue, they "symbolically appropriated" Jerusalem for the Ottoman regime much in the way that the other monumental projects marked the region as an Ottoman possession.[24] From the perspective of the friars, the wall must have also promised the unwelcome prospect of closer surveillance by Ottoman authorities. At night, the doors were

---

[19] Amy Singer, *Palestinian Peasants and Ottoman Officials: Rural Administration around sixteenth-century Jerusalem* (Cambridge: Cambridge University Press, 1994).

[20] The *sipahis* and janissaries were assigned to the Citadel, which was under the authority of its own commander, the *duzdar*. K. J. Asali, ed., *Jerusalem in History* (Jerusalem: Scorpion Press, 1989), 203.

[21] Singer, *Palestinian Peasants*, 9, 24. On the administration in Jerusalem, see also Asali, *Jerusalem*, 203. The *sanjaq bey* was almost always an Ottoman Turk, and his responsibilities concerned primarily warfare and the preservation of local order.

[22] The *kadi* (*qadi*) receive more attention in Chapter 2. They were part of the civil administration and their responsibilities were judicial and administrative in nature. See, for example, Rossitsa Gradeva, "On the Judicial Functions of the Kadi Courts: Glimpses from Sofia in the Seventeenth Century," *Islam am Balkan* 2 (2005): 15–43; and Ronald C. Jennings, *Christians and Muslims in Ottoman Cyprus and the Mediterranean World, 1571–1640* (New York: New York University Press, 1993), 74–75.

[23] Amy Singer, *Constructing Ottoman Beneficence: An Imperial Soup Kitchen in Jerusalem* (New York: State University of New York, 2002).

[24] Beatrice St. Laurent and Andràs Reidelmayer, "Restorations of Jerusalem and the Dome of the Rock and Their Political Significance, 1537–1928," *Muqarnas* 10 (1993): 75–84.

locked and monitored by gatekeepers.[25] As we saw with the account of François Savary de Breves discussed earlier, Christian travelers could not move freely through the gates.

Serving both to protect the local urban population and the interests of its new Ottoman overlords, the massive new wall would have been another visible signal to the brothers that they had entered into a new era in the history of the Custody, one that was steeped in uncertainty. The Custody did experience the impact of the Ottoman Empire in other ways as well that more directly impinged upon its operations and, in some cases, even threatened its jurisdiction.

Franciscan sources complained, in particular, about the periodic imprisonment of the *custos* and other friars, raids, the charging of excessive "fees," and most importantly, the loss of privileges in the Holy Places. Because these issues are related to jurisdiction, they will receive more attention in Chapter 2. Broadly speaking, however, it seems fair to say that the transition from Mamluk to Ottoman rule did not fundamentally threaten the traditional spiritual mandate of the Custody. As they did during the many centuries of Mamluk rule, the early modern friars continued to provide pastoral care to local merchant colonies, house pilgrims, lead tours of the Holy Places, perform the liturgical rites, oversee the restoration and ornamentation of Latin chapels, and collect alms in support of the Custody. From 1517 onwards, however, they did so under the watchful gaze of a new Muslim power.

1.3 A SHARED SACRED LANDSCAPE

The Custody oversaw Western pilgrimage in a region that had long lain under the authority of Muslim rulers and which transitioned to Ottoman rule after 1517. To understand the Christian disputes over altars, which are the focus of Chapter 2, we also need to grapple with another reality of the Holy Land, namely, that it was a sacred landscape shared among multiple faiths, and in particular between Muslims, Christians, and Jews. Brian Catlos' description of the late medieval Christian Holy Land as "dizzyingly diverse" could also be said of the region today, even though, sadly, this diversity is retreating from modern view, threatened by religious extremism and nativist models of nationalism among other forces of

---

[25] Dror Ze'evi, *An Ottoman Century: The District of Jerusalem in the 1600s* (New York: State University of New York, 1996), 18; and Asali, *Jerusalem*, 200–201.

change.[26] For early modern European travelers, however, religious diversity would have been an important part of the sensual experience of the region, revealed in the sight of distinctive religious garments, the sounds of chanting in many different languages, the daily calls to prayer emanating from the minarets of local mosques, and shrines remade according to the artistic conventions of the presiding religious culture and which were familiar and meaningful to their devout visitors. By the time this study begins in 1517, the friars lived in a population that recognized several distinctive Muslim, Christian, and Jewish traditions. Sunni Islam was, without question, the dominant Muslim tradition and largest community in a population that also numbered Shiites, Sufis, and myriad other sects. Jewish communities of diverse traditions (karaite, rabbinical) could be found by the time of the Ottoman conquest, in many urban centers, notably Jerusalem and Ascalon, along with at least ten Christian traditions.[27]

During the sixteenth and seventeenth centuries, the demography of the Holy Land shifted in response to forces of religious, political and economic change in the broader Mediterranean, arguably becoming even more diverse in the process. On the one hand, Ottoman expansion into the formerly Mamluk territories encouraged internal migration between Ottoman-held regions. On the other hand, religious changes in Europe saw the Mediterranean awash in forced migrations of diverse religious communities, some of whom found a home in the Ottoman regions of Palestine, Egypt, and Syria. In particular, many Sephardic Jews settled in the Holy Land following their expulsion from Spain in 1492, swelling the local Jewish populations of the cities of Jerusalem, Safed, and Damascus. The Greek Orthodox populations of Jerusalem and Bethlehem also grew in size, many of them drawn from the Arabic-speaking Orthodox communities in the surrounding rural regions but also from other regions of the Ottoman Empire. This local demographic change was one of several factors, we should note, that played into the eruption of conflicts with the Greek Orthodox over the possession of altars by the 1560s that is the focus of Chapter 2.[28] Even with these shifts in local demography, the

---

[26] Brian A. Catlos, *Muslims of Medieval Latin Christendom c. 1050–1614* (Cambridge: Cambridge University Press, 2014), 132.

[27] Catlos, *Muslims of Medieval Latin Christendom*, 132–134; Constantin Panchenko, *Arab Orthodox Christians under the Ottomans 1516–1831* (Jordanville: Holy Trinity Seminary Press, 2016); and Bernard Heyberger, *Les Chrétiens du Proche-Orient au temps de la Réforme catholique* (Rome: École française de Rome, 1994).

[28] On religious migrations and expulsions in the early modern Mediterranean more generally, two important recent interventions are Nicholas Terpstra, *Religious Refugees*

Holy Land was a majority Muslim population throughout the Early Modern Period. The number of Jews and Christians in the region nevertheless remained significant, especially in urban centers, where they were often prominent in local trade as craftsmen and merchants.[29] More generally, the density of Christian populations followed historic demographic patterns. A large Coptic population resided in Egypt, and Syrian Christians could be found in diverse parts of the Holy Land, though they were most numerous in Palestine (particularly the rural areas south of Jerusalem) and Syria. Maronites, who among the many Christian communities enjoyed the friendliest relations with the Latin Church, could be found in significant numbers in the hills of Palestine, notably in and around Mount Lebanon. Both Armenian and Greek Orthodox traditions were well represented across the Custody in urban centers and rural areas. While the majority of the local Greek Orthodox (as well as other local Christians) were Arab-speaking – we should note that they were joined by a growing number of Byzantine Greeks as well in the wake of the Ottoman conquest.

Within this diverse Christian demography, the Latin community was one of the smallest in the Holy Land and it was also widely dispersed. It operated, however, as a vital system of support for the Custody throughout its history, especially as a source of patronage. One could perhaps best describe the Latin community as a loose-knit collection of merchant colonies, convents, and hospices. Prior to the sixteenth century, Latin or "Frankish" mercantile colonies were mostly Venetian, Genoese, or Marseillaise (French), but by the late sixteenth century, this situation began to change in response to the shifting dynamics of Mediterranean trade. Small communities of English and Dutch merchants joined the others, while the French presence swelled as a result of trading alliances forged between the Ottomans and these mercantile states.[30] The early

---

in the Early Modern World: An Alternative History of the Reformation (Cambridge: Cambridge University Press, 2015); and Francesca Trivellato, *The Familiarity of Strangers: The Sephardic Diaspora, Livorno, and Cultural Trade in the Early Modern Period* (New Haven: Yale University Press, 2014).

[29] On the economic roles of Christians, see, for example, Amnon Cohen, *The Guilds of Ottoman Jerusalem* (Leiden: Brill, 2001); and Jacob Norris, "Exporting the Holy Land."

[30] "Frankish" was the old legal designation of Europeans under Islamic law dating back to the time of the Crusades. "Latin" referred to the Roman origins of the Western Christian tradition, distinguishing members of the Western Church (Catholics) from Eastern Christians. On European mercantile communities in the Levant, see, for example, Sylvia Auld, "The Mamluks and the Venetians Commercial Interchange: The Visual Evidence," *Palestine Exploration Quarterly* 123 (1991): 84–102; and Paul Masson,

A Catholic Gateway to the Holy Land 45

modern friars enjoyed close-knit ties with the merchant colonies of France and Venice, in particular, for understandable reasons: they were Catholic. The friars turned to the Venetian consul in Aleppo for aid in 1630, for example, when the Greek Orthodox successfully gained control of their altars in the Holy Sepulcher and the Church of the Nativity.[31] The Catholic mercantile communities in Cairo, Damascus, Tripoli, and Alexandria were also important patrons of the Franciscan mission from the early days of the Custody of the Holy Land, providing not only funds[32] but also acting as important channels of communication and political influence with European and Ottoman authorities. European merchants as well – mostly Venetian – were called upon to act as procurators of the Custody for this reason. This procurator should not be confused with the Franciscan fiscal office. Also known as the "syndic" or "spiritual friend," his role was to provide secular oversight and support for the financial operations of the Franciscan communities. For a religious tradition perpetually concerned about its own worldliness, the procurator was a valued office, and one of its principal tasks was to collect alms from other local Catholic merchants. For this reason among others, procurators were typically chosen from prominent patrons of a given mercantile colony.

The Venetian colony in Aleppo, because it was one of the largest in the Levant, seems to have taken responsibility for gathering from the other Venetian colonies.[33] We obtain a rare glimpse into this community and its

---

Histoire du commerce Français dans le Levant au XVIIe siècle (Paris: 1911; reprint, Burt Franklin, 1967).

[31] ASVe Bailo 109. A series of letters here from 1630 to 1634 between the Bailo and the Venetian consul of Aleppo discuss aiding the friars in the recuperation of the Holy Places. See, for example, one dated September 27, 1632, in which the ambassador refers to the recent arrival of the friars in Aleppo seeking the consul's support: "L'ingresso del Mro R [everen]do Padre Guardiano con suoi li padri in Gierusaleme, che le sue letter mi porta ..." On the role of consul more generally, see, for example, Maria Pia Pedani, "Venetian Consuls in Egypt and Syria in the Ottoman Age," *Mediterranean World* 18 (2006): 7–21; and Viorel Panaite, "French Capitulations and Consular Jurisdiction in Egypt and Aleppo in the Late Sixteenth and Seventeenth Centuries," in *Well-Connected Domains: Towards an Entangled Ottoman History*, ed. Pascal Firges, Tobias Graf, Christian Roth, and Gülay Tulasoglu (Leiden: Brill, 2014), 71–87.

[32] Francesco Suriano, *Treatise of the Holy Land*, trans. Theophilus Bellorini and Eugene Hoad (Jerusalem: Franciscan Printing Press, 1949), 113, n. 1.

[33] We can glean some of the names in surviving sources, though unfortunately they do not often give us much information on the individual. The relation sent by Tomasso Obicini da Novara to the commissioner of the Holy Land in Madrid dated 1621, for example, mentions "our syndic Germano Maria Riztano," who was more than likely a merchant patron based in one of the colonies. AHN OP legajo 1/27/a&b.

relations with the friars in Aquilante Rocchetta's account. In addition to his description of their church discussed earlier, we also learn from Rocchetta that an election was held every year in Aleppo to choose one of the Venetian merchants as the head of the "scuola della santissima Concettione di Nostro Signora," an intriguing detail that points to the existence of an active merchant confraternity (*scuola*) attached to the Venetian church of the Holy Conception. Moreover, every three years the friars in Jerusalem sent three clerics and two laics to Aleppo to provide spiritual services. Of these, two clerics and one laic remained in Aleppo, while one cleric and one lay brother went on to an assignment in Alexandretta (Iskanderon) in Syria. Rocchetta discusses almsgiving as well, stating that every feast day the merchants set aside two funds (*borse*), one intended for Mount Sion, and the other for the poor. It was not unusual, he says, for these to be quite large sums.[34] These financial and spiritual ties were an important facet of relations between the friars and the merchants, but Catholic merchants also served as valuable local connections for visiting pilgrims, providing housing and other kinds of aid on their travels. From the 1620s, the friars would face growing competition for the patronage of French merchants, in particular, as French missionaries (Jesuits, Capuchins, discalced Carmelites) established new missions in the Custody. However, these new communities remained small throughout the Early Modern Period and never fully displaced the Franciscan brothers of the Custody in their pastoral roles.[35] The friars thus had a "local" Latin community that was reliant upon their ministry and supportive of the pilgrimage, one that could also be mobilized in defense of the privileges of the Custody when they were threatened.

1.3.1 Holy Lands

As the discussion thus far has shown, the friars operated in an extraordinarily diverse religious environment, a reality that shaped both the nature and operations of the Custody to a significant degree. This was because the faiths shared a landscape that was sacred to all three Religions of the Book and which was in consequence a revered and vigorous site of international pilgrimage. Indeed, another dimension of local diversity

---

[34] On relations with merchants in Aleppo, see Rocchetta, *Peregrinatione*, 59. "Si mandano attorno per questa Chiesa due borse, l'una assignata per Monte Sion, e llaltra per gli poveri, differente l'una dall'altra, e si san d'ordinario grosse limosne."

[35] See Chapter 4.

was the visibly heterodox nature of worship including the practice of pilgrimage. While Muslims, Christians, and Jews held their own shrines and followed distinctive pilgrimage itineraries, early modern accounts reveal multi-faith caravans traveling the roads of Egypt, Syria, and Palestine, and many shrines and other sacred sites receiving worshippers from more than one faith. This was especially true of sites associated with the biblical patriarchs, but even shrines associated with one tradition could become a locus of heterodox pilgrimage over time. Muslim pilgrims visited the Church of the Nativity, for example, the site of Jesus' birth, because Muhammad purportedly prayed here in reverence of Christ.[36] Marian shrines – of which there were many – drew Muslim, Jewish, and Christian women because of her association with childbirth as well as her relationship with Christ.[37] Indeed, efforts on the part of religious officials to confessionalize the sacred often faced an uphill battle in a region that was historically forged out of vigorous and diverse pilgrimage traffic and which was home to an extraordinarily diverse population as a result.[38]

These signs of religious heterodoxy highlight the Holy Land's significance as a shared sacred landscape. Invoking the language of "sharing" here is quite deliberate, to turn our attention to important commonalities (in addition to critical differences) among the three spiritual traditions that made the Holy Land a meaningful site of spiritual engagement for their devout. It helps us to understand, to begin with, why all three faiths considered the region "holy," and secondly, why Muslims, Christians, and Jews considered it meaningful not only to experience the region first hand but also to maintain an institutional presence near revered sacred sites and sometimes in the same sacred places as other faiths. We need to wrestle, to begin with, the language of "Holy Land" as it was used by

---

[36] Oded Peri, "Islamic Law and Christian Holy Sites: Jerusalem and Its Vicinity in Early Ottoman Times," *Islamic Law and Society* 6 (1999): 97–111. Suriano, for example, mentions the visit of high ranking Mamluk authorities – the governors of Jerusalem and Gaza – to worship during his time in the Custody, which places it before 1514. Francesco Suriano, *Treatise of the Holy Land*, translated by Theophilus Bellorini and Eugene Hoade (Jerusalem: The Franciscan Printing Press, 1949), 136–137.

[37] Suriano also mentions Muslim visitations of the Milk Grotto in Bethlehem. Suriano, Treatise, 106. On the Grotto as a shared shrine, see Lucia Rostagno, "Note su una devozione praticata da cristiani e musulmani a Betlemme: Il culto della Madonna del Latte," *Rivista degli studi orientali* 71 (1997): 159–172; and Alexandra Cuffel, "From Practice to Polemic: Shared Saints and Festivals As 'Women's Religion' in the Medieval Mediterranean," *Bulletin of the School of Oriental and African Studies, University of London* 68 (2005): 401–419.

[38] James Grehan, *Twilight of the Saints: Everyday Religion in Ottoman Syria and Palestine* (Oxford: Oxford University Press, 2014); and Cuffel, "From Practice to Polemic."

the three traditions. Moshe Sharon has argued that Muslims, Christians, and Jews were using similar language to discuss the region of Palestine from early on. In the Jewish tradition, it was "holy" because it was the promised land. It appears in Qur'an as well, when Moses, speaking to the Children of Israel, referred to "the Holy Land which Allah hath written down as yours."[39] While all three faiths shared a conception of the same geographic region (broadly construed) as "holy," the diverse nature of the three faiths and their unique histories suggest that it might be more accurate to speak of multiple holy lands that converged and overlapped at certain geographic points. Still, Sharon argues that a common geographic as well as ideological conception of the Holy Land did emerge by the late medieval period, shaped to a significant degree by medieval Christian writings. For medieval and early modern Catholics, the "Holy Land" (*Terra Sancta, Tierra Santa, terre sainte, terra santa, heigele lande*) referred to the broad expanse of diverse terrain (roughly 24,000 square kilometers) lying between the Mediterranean Sea and modern-day Syria. The same language was also employed in medieval maps dating back several centuries, most famously in the form of T–O maps. T–O maps visually situated the Holy Land at the cosmic, and thus geographic, "center" of the known world, conflating the ideological significance of the region as a site of holiness with its geographic location. They also represented the sacred landscape as a distinct geographic space unto its own, one that, because of its divine state, symbolically and materially transcended the shifting political boundaries that dissected it over the centuries.[40] While Western Catholics shared with the many Eastern Christian traditions a similar conception of the geographic boundaries and ideological centeredness of the Holy Land, Muslims and Jews held their own sacred geographies. For Jews, the "Holy Land" was *Eretz Yisrael*, recognizing Palestine's historic association with the land associated with the biblical Kingdom of Israel (Judah).[41] Islam has a number of "holy lands" within the broader geography discussed here: *balad Mubarak* (a blessed land) in Egypt, *al-Sham* (Northern Syria), and Palestine, known as *al-ard al muqaddasa* (holy land).

---

[39] Moshe Sharon, ed., "Introduction," in *The Holy Land in History and Thought*. Papers Submitted to the International Conference on the Relations between the Holy Land and the World Outside it (Johannesburg 1986) (Brill: Leiden, 1988).

[40] See, for example, Zur Shalev, "Sacred Geography, Antiquarianism and Visual Erudition: Benito Arias Montano and the Maps in the Antwerp Polyglot Bible," *Imago Mundi* 55 (2003): 56–80; and Catherine Delano Smith, "Geography or Christianity? Maps of the Holy Land before AD 1000," *The Journal of Theological Studies* 42 (1991): 143–152.

[41] Sharon, ed., "Introduction."

These sacred geographies reflect the diversity of sacred histories among the three faiths, and they produced unique pilgrimage itineraries. For early modern Christians, the central shrines were the Holy Places, the sites associated with the life of Christ and the apostles. Most clustered in and around the city of Jerusalem, but important ones are also found in Egypt and Syria. For Muslim pilgrims, Egypt, Palestine, and Syria also contained numerous shrines associated with Muhammad, along with others dedicated to Sufi saints and other holy figures. Shi'a as well as Sunni Muslims went to visit the shrine of Husayn ibn Ali (d. 680) in Cairo, for example, and in Damascus the Small Gate cemetery was home to the tombs of household members of the Prophets.[42] However, Palestine, because of its many shrines to Muhammad and the biblical patriarchs Abraham and David, was an especially important pilgrimage destination. Of its many shrines, the Dome of the Rock was unquestionably the most significant, considered the third most important shrine in Islam next to those in Mecca and Medina. Today, as in the early modern past, pilgrims would have seen its golden top glistening from a long distance away, the first of the many shrines to welcome pilgrims to the sacred mysteries awaiting them in the holy city. In mentioning the shrines dedicated to Abraham, David, and other the biblical patriarchs, however, we need to recognize that Muslim, Christian, and Jewish sacred geographies, while they diverged in important ways, also intersected and converged with one another because they were rooted in a shared biblical past. Mount Sinai in Egypt, the shrines of the biblical patriarchs in Hebron and Nablus, the Red Sea parted by Moses – these were among the many sites of multi-faith pilgrimage that contributed to a collective recognition of a common Holy Land. The sharing of sacred sites, along with the clusters of shrines found within certain regions, were one reason why we find caravans filled with pilgrims of diverse faiths traveling together along the main roads of Egypt, Palestine, and Syria long before the Early Modern Period. The Royal Road was a particularly well-known artery, its caravans described in many medieval and early modern pilgrimage accounts.[43] The ancient route stretched from Cairo to Damascus, and passed by Hebron, Jerusalem, and Bethlehem among other sacred destinations (see Figure 1.2).

---

[42] Josef W. Meri, *The Cult of the Saints among Muslims and Jews in Medieval Syria* (2002; reprint, Oxford: Oxford University Press, 2004), 2–4.

[43] It was particularly important for the Hajj. See, for example, Tyler Joseph Kynn, "Encounters of Islam and Empire: The Hajj in the Early Modern World," PhD diss., Princeton University, 2019.

50   *The Holy Land and the Early Modern Reinvention*

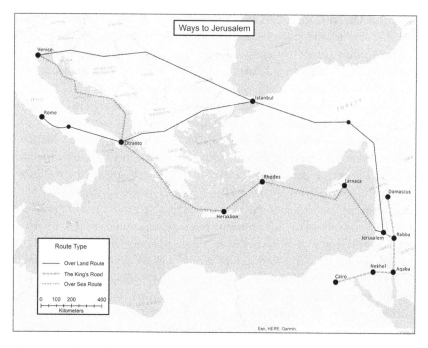

Figure 1.2 Map, pilgrimage routes

A fifteenth-century pilgrimage treatise recently studied by Marianne Ritsema van Eck provides us with an intriguing window into this shared sacred world. Paul Walter von Guglingen, a friar assigned to the Custody, produced what Eck argues was a highly unusual account because of its inclusion of engravings of Islamic shrines and other buildings. What is clear from his text is that Christians also visited some of these places. Guglingen described, for example, traveling with the Franciscan guardian of Mount Sion and other Christians to visit the cave holding the tombs of the Old Testament patriarchs Adam, Abraham, Isaac, and Jacob in Hebron. The enormous Ibrahimi mosque, first established during the seventh century, regulated entrance to the sacred site. Guglingen mentions the party's interest in entering the cave. The *dragoman* (interpreter) negotiated a fee with the Muslim porter to allow them to do so as long as they entered at nighttime and with all lights extinguished. In the end, the group decided not to enter but clearly from their conversation it was not uncommon for non-Muslims to have access to the site. Moreover, Guglingen entered other Muslim sacred spaces, including what he thought was a mosque within the Al Aqsa mosque complex in Jerusalem. In fact, it was a school (*madrasa*).⁴⁴ Still, the friar and his companions received permission to enter the mosque complex, further evidence of a more fluid "local" reality of interfaith engagement between religious leaders across the faiths in the Holy Land in a city that each regarded as "holy."

As one might expect, contemporary accounts portray Jerusalem as an especially intense place of multi-faith engagement, the holy city par excellence because of its containment of multiple sacred pasts: the political and religious center of ancient Israel for Jews, the place of Christ's crucifixion and resurrection for Christians, and home to the Dome of the Rock (*Qubbat Al-Sahkrah*), the site marking Muhammad's ascent to Heaven on his Night Journey (*Isra' and Mi'jra*). The city also occupied a central role in a divine plan for all three faiths – as the site of Creation in the Jewish tradition and of the Last Judgment for Muslims and Jews. In consequence, Jerusalem is typically described as a wondrous place, privileged by God as a site of revelation and a "paradise" on earth. The well-known history of Jerusalem written by Mujir al-Din (d. 1522) serves as a good example. Donald Little argues that this history was significantly influenced by a popular Muslim medieval devotional genre known as the *Fada'il al-Bayt al-Muqaddas* ("In Praise of Jerusalem").⁴⁵ For Mujir al-Din, Muhammad's nighttime flight from Mecca to Jerusalem was part of God's plan, intended to take the Prophet to the place that had long occupied the center of human religious history. Jerusalem was "blessed" with rivers, trees, fruit, and the tombs of the prophets. It was here that "angels and revelation descend and where people will ascend on Judgment day." Jerusalem, in other words, was a continuous site of revelation, the place where God intended to reveal "His miracles and signs."⁴⁶ Al'Din here argues for a privileged role for the sacred city in the unfolding of God's divine plan, but in doing so, his text shows that Muslims as well as Christians considered Jerusalem otherworldly because it transcended the boundary demarcating the material and immaterial

---

⁴⁴ M. Ritsema van Eck, "Encounters with the Levant: The Late Medieval Illustrated Jerusalem Travelogue by Paul Walter von Guglingen," *Mediterranean Review* 32 (2018): 166–168.
⁴⁵ Amikam Elad, *Medieval Jerusalem and Islamic Worship* (Leiden: Brill, 1995), 6–7, 10–11. According to Elad, the *Fada-il* genre flourished during the middle ages. These were essentially guidebooks for pilgrims that also traced an earlier Islamic history. It is considered part of the *hadith* literature.
⁴⁶ Donald P. Little, "Mujir al-Din al'Ulaymi's Vision of Jerusalem in the Ninth/Fifteenth Century," *Journal of the American Oriental Society* 115 (1995): 240–241. Little provides a fine translation of the text that I am using here.

realms of existence. As he also writes, Jerusalem is "the source of all sweet water and wine on earth" because it was closest to Heaven, and it was also the site of Judgment Day when 7,000 angels would descend every night to praise God at Masjid Bayt al-Maqdis (al-Aqsa mosque).

A shared religious character remains a striking feature of the old city of Jerusalem to this day, an urban landscape still crowded with shrines, mosques, temples, and convents. The close proximity of the many sacred sites has also meant that historically worshippers not only cross paths with but also worship near one another, sometimes in the same places and even at the same time, especially when sacred calendars converged. Recent accounts of mounting tension between Muslims and Jews on the Temple Mount only serve to underscore the historically intimate nature of religious life in the holy city, an intimacy that is revealed far too often through interfaith conflict. As one example, on August 11, 2019, violence broke out between Muslim worshippers and Israeli police during the Muslim feast Eid al-Adha. Known to Muslims as the Haram esh-Sharif and to Jews as the Temple Mount, the shared site is a broad plateau at one end of the old city of Jerusalem that is associated with two of the most significant shrines in Islam and Judaism: the Western Wall and the Dome of the Rock. The Western Wall or Wailing Wall is the most holy shrine in Judaism, marking the original location of the Old Temple that was destroyed during Roman occupation of the city in 70 AD. Today it lies opposite one of the main gates of the Al Aqsa mosque complex. This complex was built in 715 AD to mark the ascendance of Umayyad power in the region (661–750 AD), and it remains one of the most commanding religious structures in Jerusalem, its size and Islamic design visually demonstrate Islam as the possessor of the Temple Mount. As mentioned during the earlier discussion of Guglingen, traditionally only Muslims (with some notable exceptions) had permission to enter the mosque complex, a situation that has changed somewhat since the construction of the modern state of Israel. The violent incident in 2019 was sparked by rumours that Jewish visitors would be permitted entrance to honour the day of destruction of the earlier Temples. For a number of the Muslim worshippers, this act was provocative and disrespectful. One of those interviewed in the news account described it as the "storming of the al-Aqsa mosque compound."[47] For our purposes, this episode provides

---

[47] Saphora Smith and Lawahez Jabari, "Muslim Worshippers Clash with Israeli Police at Jerusalem Holy Site," *NBC News*, August 11, 2019. www.nbcnews.com/news/world/muslim-worshippers-clash-israeli-police-jerusalem-holy-site-n1041161.

yet another a vivid reminder that religious violence in the Holy Land has often occurred during festive times because these were occasions of heightened religious sensitivities among the local communities. What can get lost in such disturbing accounts of modern interfaith conflict, however, is that Jerusalem remains a holy city constructed upon centuries of multi-faith devotion; devotion that has carved out places for each tradition within the material fabric of the city because it was spiritually meaningful for each tradition to be present *there*.

This latter point – the importance of being present *in* the Holy Land – reveals another dimension of the Holy Land as a shared religious landscape that is relevant to our broad investigation. Namely, a shared belief in an accessible holiness. As the rich literature on the nature of the sacred makes clear, we need to be careful about over generalizing about the similarities in conceptions of the sacred. One could argue that medieval and early modern Christians held a particularly expansive understanding of the material world as a transformative vehicle, as well as vessel, of divinity. But as Joseph Meri has argued in his study of Jewish and Islamic pilgrimage, both Jews and Muslims believed that holy people and holy places could be "blessed" (*baraka, quadosh*) by divinity that they described as an "innate force." Objects could also be touched by holiness, its divinity accessed by believers to effect change – physiological (i.e., healing), as well as salvific (spiritual transformation).[48] For Jonathan Z. Smith among others, liturgical rites including that of pilgrimage serve as critical, "productive" mechanisms required to obtain these blessings, but the *place* of the ritual defined its meaning and potency. In his response, Ronald L. Grimes criticized Smith's privileging of place, saying that it amounts to little more than "a spatialized theory of ritual." But Smith's observation that liturgical rites are potent because they are "emplaced" would have resonated with early modern pilgrims of all three faiths who accepted that the appropriate rituals must be performed in the appropriate places because the sacred was localized.[49] Because sacrality was localized, moreover, early modern pilgrims shared a belief that the visitation of the shrines was spiritually efficacious. Mujir al-Din, for example, insisted that those who prayed in Jerusalem would be "cleansed

---

[48] Meri, *The Cult of the Saints*, 17–18.
[49] Jonathan Z. Smith, *To Take Place: Toward a Theory of Ritual* (Chicago: University of Chicago Press, 1987). For the response of Grimes, see "Jonathan Z. Smith's Theory of Ritual Space," *Religion* 29 (1999): 261–273.

of sin and restored to primal innocence."[50] Catholic pilgrims were told that the visitation of individual shrines earned them indulgences, spiritual merit that could be used to reduce their time in purgatory after their death. To visit the Holy Land was to make contact with divinity, to be purified and spiritually transformed. Moreover, the experience invested one with spiritual wisdom because the shrines were sites of divine revelation. Jerusalem was particularly revered in this regard, its sacred mountains (Moriah, Zion) living witnesses to millennia of divine communication. For Jews, the Western Wall on Mount Moriah is the "holy of holies," a tangible manifestation of Yahweh's promise to protect the children of Israel (Genesis 17:17), while the Dome of the Rock marked the continuing unfolding of God's divine plan through the visit of the Prophet Muhammad. But many other places in the Holy Land were sites of shared revelation, among them Mount Sinai, where Moses received the Ten Commandments.

As the above suggests, Muslim, Jews, and Christians shared a conception of the Holy Land as a vessel of divine wisdom, wisdom that could be accessed through the visitation of sacred sites, many of which were shared among the three faiths. By privileging contact with the Holy Land, moreover, the three faiths recognized a significant role for the body in the spiritual transformation of the devout traveler. It explains in particular why writers of the various traditions invariably described the experience in sensual terms – the drift of pleasant odours from a tomb, visions, the feel of a sacred object or of the walls of a holy place. According to Meri, light was an especially common attribution in Jewish and Muslim writings. The poet Judah al-Harizi (d. 1235) described light ascending over the tomb of Ezra, while the Muslim writer Ibn al-Hawrani saw lights hover over the tomb of Noah in the town of al-Karak.[51] Similarly, Muji al-Din described Jerusalem as "a marvel renowned for its luminosity."[52] For all three faiths, light symbolized divinity and manifested the otherworldly character of shrines, but it is important to note that it also communicated the living nature of sacrality. Light radiated from the tombs, it was luminous, it moved ("descended"). Touching shrines and leaving mementoes meaningful to the spiritual event marked by it also connected the believer directly to its holiness – for example, a cloth left in the House of Veronica, the saint who wiped Christ's brow during his long

---

[50] Little, "Mujir al-Din al'Ulaymi's Vision of Jerusalem," 241–242, 261–273.
[51] Meri, *The Cult of the Saints*, 22–23.
[52] Little, "Mujir al-Din al'Ulaymi's Vision of Jerusalem," 242.

slow walk with the cross, or written prayers tucked into the crevices of the Western Wall. An anonymous author of a sixteenth-century Muslim pilgrimage account also urged pilgrims to "caress the Tongue with the hand," but not kiss it, insisting that to do so was a "disgraceful innovation."[53] The Tongue of the Rock (*Lisan al-Sakhra*) was one of numerous sacred sites within the al-Aqsa mosque complex in Jerusalem, and his comment suggests that rubbing the shrine had become a routinized part of paying devotion. Similarly, movement *through* a holy space could also mediate contact with divinity, one of the reasons why the rite of pilgrimage itself was so highly valued across the three faiths. For Western and Eastern Christians, the stational liturgy that evolved along the via dolorosa served as the emotional and liturgical focal point of the visitation of the holy city, connecting the devout materially and spiritually with Christ *through* the act of retracing his final footsteps to the Cross.

Recognizing these shared dimensions of the Holy Land – a biblical past, belief in a localized and accessible divinity, and a privileging of the body in processes of spiritual transformation – helps to explain not only the historic religious diversity of the region but also the spiritual importance given by Muslims, Christians, and Jews to being *there*. As Meri argues, Muslims and Jews were urged to seek, experience, and write about "the holy" because it existed on earth and was potentially transformative.[54] Christians like Muslims and Jews also traveled, at times from great distances, for similar reasons. Pregnant women belonging to all three faiths were known, for example, to visit the "Milk Grotto" in Bethlehem, told that her milk flowed from the pillar, and when consumed, ensured a healthy birth. Devotional writings described the experience, moreover, as emotionally as well as physically moving. Mujir al-Din felt "delight and joy as can scarcely be described" at first sight of Masjid al-Aqsa and the "noble" tomb of Abraham," joy that immediately relieved him of "hardship and fatigue."[55] As we may recall, similar feelings of joy and eagerness overtook Savary de Breves and his party when they caught their first glimpse of Jerusalem shimmering in the distance as they made their way to the holy city for the start of the pilgrimage.

---

[53] Elad, *Medieval Jerusalem and Islamic Worship*, 140. Elad includes his translation of the pilgrimage treatise.
[54] Meri, *The Cult of the* Saints, 20–21.
[55] Little, "Mujir al-Din al'Ulaymi's Vision of Jerusalem," 242.

1.3.2 Pilgrimage As an Imperial Project

That the Holy Land was not only deeply meaningful to the three faiths but also forged a tangible material, historical, and ideological link between them helps to explain why the Holy Land saw significant imperial investment in support of the pilgrimage under its new Ottoman rulers. The Ottomans were by no means the first to do so. The Dome of the Rock emerged as one of the most significant pilgrimage destinations in the eighth century with the generous support of Umayyad rulers who built the al-Aqsa mosque in the early eight century, covering its massive dome in gold at enormous expense.[56] The rise of Abbasid influence after 750 saw dynastic interest in promoting the pilgrimage to Jerusalem decline, until the Crusades stoked Muslim interest in the city once again as a sacred place. Investment flowed into Jerusalem under the early Mamluk rulers, who endowed local religious institutions including schools (*madrasas*) as part of a larger initiative to promote Sunni Islam in a city that had by this time become most visibly a Christian pilgrimage destination.[57] Sacred sites received attention as well. Baybars (d. 1277) restored the Qubbat al-Silsila (Dome of the Chain), Qubbat al-Sakhra in Jerusalem, and the Tomb of Abraham in Hebron. Mujir al-Din mentions the rebuilding of the southern wall of al-Aqsa, the resurfacing of the al-Aqsa and al-Sakhra (Dome of the Rock) mosques with marble, and the regilding of their domes during the third reign of the great Mamluk ruler, al-Malik al-Nasir Muhammad ibn Qalawun (709–741/1309–1341).[58] Other sultans contributed as well, including Abu Al-Nasr Sayf ad-Din Al-Ashraf Qaitbay (1468–1496), who ordered the lead roof of al-Aqsa restored, and the building of a number of new monuments in the Haram.

By the time the Ottomans seized control of Jerusalem, however, Mamluk financial investment in Jerusalem and other parts of the Holy Land had waned considerably. Indeed, Mujir al-Din, who lived in Jerusalem at the time, described the era of Qait Bay as full of strife, marked by natural disasters, such as the plague that struck Palestine in 1468–1469, severe droughts, and even a torrential rain in 1472–1473 that destroyed hundreds of places in the city. Uprisings by Bedouin

---

[56] Elad, *Medieval Jerusalem and Islamic Worship*, 53. He mentions, in particular, the patronage of Abd al-Malik (d. 705). For a broad historical overview, see Daniel Pipes, "The Muslim Claim to Jerusalem," *Middle East Quarterly* (2001): 49–66.

[57] Nimrod Luz, "Aspects of Islamicization of Space and Society in Mamluk Jerusalem and Its Hinterland," *Mamluk Studies Review* 6 (2002): 133–154.

[58] Little, "Mujir al-Din al'Ulaymi's Vision of Jerusalem," 244.

Arabs and Kurds and the harsh repression of local inhabitants during the 1490s contributed to the deepening disorder in the kingdom and exacerbated relations between local religious communities.[59] In the midst of these local disturbances, the friars found themselves at times directly affected. In 1489, for example, the Franciscan chronicle known as the *Registro de' fatti memorabili* recorded the abandonment of the Franciscan hospice near the grotto of the Prophet Jeremiah after it was sacked by local Arabs: "Our hospital, which was near the grotto of the Prophet Jeremia, was abandoned because one night the Arabs sacked it and killed all of the friars." Girolamo Golubovich suggests that there is some debate as to whether the hospice in question belonged to the friars or another Christian community.[60] However, the convent of Mount Sion certainly did belong to the friars and it was hard hit later on when the guardian and several friars were arrested and dragged to Cairo for punishment in 1511. It was during this time that Francesco Suriano was brought back from Europe to act as *custos* for a second time, replacing his predecessor who remained in prison for several months.

The political uncertainties of these latter years reflected a weakening Mamluk administration and also explain why the regime found it difficult to invest significantly in the maintenance and promotion of Muslim shrines as it had in earlier times. This situation began to change under Ottoman rule when Suleiman I (d. 1566) assumed power following the death of his father in 1520. Laurent and Riedelmayer argue that Suleiman's motives were political as well as spiritual and economic, since possession of the Holy Land added legitimacy to Ottoman claims of hegemony in the Dar-al-Islam.[61] From the vantage of the brothers of the Holy Land, however, the lavish renovations of the al-Aqsa mosque and other Muslim shrines in Jerusalem were intended to evoke the authority of Suleiman while expressing an altogether more ambitious

---

[59] Little, "Mujir al-Din al'Ulaymi's Vision of Jerusalem," 244–246. The Dome of the Chain is one of the oldest structures on the Temple mount dating back to the Ayyubids. It is a prayer house rather than a mosque or shrine.

[60] Lemmens, ed., *Registro de' fatti memorabili*, 9.

[61] The Ottomans promoted the Hajj pilgrimage for similar reasons. On this, see Tyler Kynn, "Encounters of Islam and Empire." On the religious nature of Suleiman's quest for imperium, see, for example, Cornell Fleischer, "Royal Authority, Dynastic Cyclist and Iban Khaldunishm in Sixteenth Century Ottoman Letters," *Journal of Asia and African Studies* 18 (1983): 198–220; and Caroline Finkel, *Osman's Dream: The Story of the Ottoman Empire 1300–1923* (New York: Basic Books, 2005).

claim to spiritual hegemony over the Three Religions of the Book. It is important to note, however, that the friars and other Christians were also beneficiaries of Suleiman's investment in the pilgrimage, since it involved the repair of fountains, aqueducts, and water pipes as well as the construction of a large pool.[62] Water was essential for the passage of caravans and the performance of daily prayer, and these large structures were also *waqfs*, and thus public demonstrations of imperial piety. Imperial patronage, in other words, was another influential factor in constructing the Holy Land as a shared religious landscape. Christians, Muslims, and Jews not only traveled the same roads together and lived in close proximity to one another but also relied upon the same public works for the practice of pilgrimage as well as other acts of worship – works that they received through the patronage of their Ottoman rulers.

1.3.3 *Christian Relations and the Holy Places*

The Custody operated in a shared sacred landscape that was home to multiple faiths and under the jurisdiction of Turkish rulers. Before moving on to a consideration of the disputes between the Franciscans and the Greek Orthodox, which are the focus of Chapter 2, we need to consider the role of the Holy Places in shaping Christian relations, since these sacred spaces were the loci of the disputes. Local demographic studies show that Christians were drawn to live to near the Holy Places because of their importance to Christian worship. Permanent Christian communities – mostly monastic though also mercantile and artisanal in nature – clustered around the most important shrines and in close proximity to one another. Bethlehem and Jerusalem, the two cities that feature prominently in the early modern disputes, claimed the most revered Holy Places and boasted large and diverse Christian populations as a result. Bethlehem, associated with the birth of Christ, holds one of the most revered Christian shrines – the Grotto of the Nativity. The city was in fact mostly Christian in terms of its religious demography throughout the late medieval and Early Modern Periods. The Armenian and Greek Orthodox comprised the two largest communities and shared jurisdiction with the Latin brothers in the Church of the Nativity. Unusually, Roman Catholics comprised the majority in this city by the late seventeenth century, a fact

---

[62] Amnon Cohen, *Economic Life in Ottoman Jerusalem* (Cambridge: Cambridge University Press, 2002), 3.

that Jacob Norris and Felicita Tramontana attribute to the missionizing work of the resident friars during this period. Over one-third (385) of a population that stood around 1,000 were Catholic according to scholarly estimates. Prior to this time, the Greek Orthodox comprised the single largest religious community.[63] Because of its stature as the sacred center of Christendom, the Christian population of Jerusalem was even more diverse. Surviving tax registers reveal members of at least ten different Christian traditions: Latin, Greek and Armenian Orthodox, Jacobite, Coptic, Nestorian, Abyssinian, Maronite, Syriac, and Georgian Christians.

Tax records for the year 1548–1549 list 1,003 Christian households, roughly one-seventh of the 7,000 households, and one-tenth of "bachelors."[64] Bachelors referred largely to clerics, a segment of the population that was (not surprisingly) quite visible in the holy city. Most were attached to urban monasteries. Today, the four quarters of the old city in Jerusalem are known by the religious identities of their past communities – Armenian, Greek Orthodox, Muslim, and Jewish. During the Early Modern Period, however, these quarters were hardly segregated enclaves but rather home to diverse communities that included the many Christian traditions.[65]

The remarkable Christian diversity found in Jerusalem explains why so many European travelers commented on it, often describing distinctive elements of each tradition, including clothing, liturgical rites, and beliefs. These accounts also depict an early modern Jerusalem bristling with Christian convents, hospices, and other institutions that jostled one another for space in the crowded streets alongside mosques, synagogues, and other religious institutions.

Aquilante Rocchetta, for one, mentioned meeting important officials of a number of the rites including a Greek Orthodox cleric monk (*caloyero*) from the city of Messina and two Greek Orthodox prelates, the bishop of Mount Sinai and the patriarch of Antioch. He was particularly charmed by the patriarch whom, he said, could speak a little Italian. They apparently chatted for about an hour. So many languages were spoken in the

---

[63] Jacob Norris, "Exporting the Holy Land," 16–17; and Felicita Tramontana, *Passages of Faith: Conversion in Palestinian Villages* (Wiesbaden: Harrassowitz, 2014).

[64] Muhammad Adnan Bakhit, "The Christian Population of the Province of Damascus in the Sixteenth Century," in *Christians and Jews in the Ottoman Empire: The Functioning of a Plural Society* (New York and London: Holms and Meier, 1982): 47, and Peri, "Islamic Law and Christian Holy Sites," 13–14.

[65] On neighbourhoods in Ottoman Jerusalem, see Dror Ze'evi, *An Ottoman Century*, 23.

Holy Land, Rocchetta says, that "one could spend many days without speaking with anyone," presumably meaning another Italian.[66]

Rocchetta's observation about language conveys not only the vast cultural distance between Europe and the eastern Mediterranean but also the "smallness" of a European presence in this vast and diverse landscape. Meanwhile, Pierre de la Vergne de Tressan says he was reassured to find so many commonalities between his own Catholic faith and the other Christian traditions. The French pilgrim visited Jerusalem in the 1670s. In his account of the experience, he remarks at one point: "I cannot help but notice, which will demonstrate the confusion of our Calvinists that although all these nations are schismatic or heretical, except the Roman, they faithfully bear the marks of the true Church. They have patriarchs, archbishops, bishops, and priests to whom they confess their sins: they observe their Easter, they perform the sacrifice during the mass with the same belief, and the same intention as us."[67] Tressan's comments reflect upon the divided religious situation of France, a kingdom that at the time of his pilgrimage still recognized two legal faiths, though this situation would change in 1685 following the Revocation of the Edict of Nantes. He was clearly a devout Catholic who considered the existence of the Calvinist tradition unsettling and unnatural. To find similar ecclesiastical structures, beliefs, and practices among the many Eastern rites was comfortably reassuring of the legitimacy of his own Catholic faith and the illegitimacy of French Calvinism.

What also makes Tressan's account of relevance here, however, is its illumination of the Holy Land as an intimate space of Christian encounter. This was an intimacy created through its narrow urban streets and rural roads, caravans and marketplaces, pilgrim hospices, convents, and shared shrines. With an eye to the conflicts between the Latin and Greek Orthodox communities discussed in Chapter 2, we should recognize that the Christian communities of Jerusalem knew one another both on a personal as well as institutional level that is not always conveyed in

---

[66] Rocchetta, *Peregrinatione*, 149.
[67] Pierre de la Vergne de Tressan, *Relation vouvelle et exacte d'un voyage de la Terre sainte ou description* (Paris: Antoine Dezallier, 1688), 131–132. "Je ne sçaurois m'empêcher de remarquer, à la confusion de nos Calvinistes, que quoique toutes ces Nations soient Schismatiques ou Heretiques, exceptés les Romains, ils ont conservé fidelement les marques de la veritable Eglise. Ils ont des Patriarches, Archevesques, Evesques, & Pretres, ausquels ils confessant leurs pechez: ils observant exactement leur Caresme, ils sacrifient toujours à leurs Messes avec la mesme croyance, & la mesme intention que nous."

A Catholic Gateway to the Holy Land 61

surviving sources. Indeed, the Franciscan brothers and the Patriarch of Jerusalem became neighbours of sorts after the friars moved to their new convent of the Holy Saviour in 1558. The palace of the patriarch lay attached to the Church of the Holy Sepulcher, which meant that until the office moved to Constantinople in 1670s, the head of the Greek Orthodox community lived only a short walk down the via dolorosa from the Holy Saviour. Moreover, in Jerusalem many of the Holy Places are located within a few steps of one another, ensuring that pilgrims and clerics of the diverse traditions routinely cross paths with one another (see Figure 1.3). A modern visitor to Jerusalem is immediately struck by the sheer proximity of the many sites, and it would have been the same for the early modern pilgrim. The *via crucis* – the devotional rite that traces Christ's slow, painful march from the palace of Pontius Pilate bearing the cross to the site of his execution on Calvary – is a series of stops (stations) along the same street (the via dolorosa) that ends near the Basilica of the Holy Sepulcher. The Garden of Gethsemane and the many other shrines on the Mount of Olives is only a short hike from the Dung Gate entrance into the Old city. The journey today can be managed by local bus but even on foot

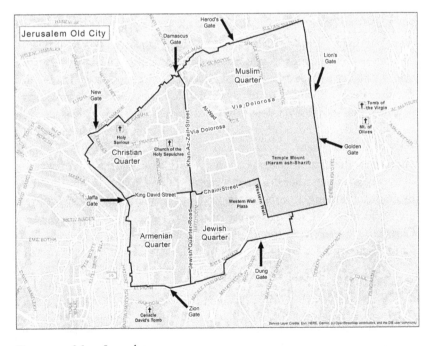

Figure 1.3 Map, Jerusalem

it takes less than an hour at a leisurely pace. From there one can walk down into the Valley of Jehosophat to visit the Tomb of Mary before returning to Jerusalem. Bethlehem lies at a much greater distance (six miles) but is still accessible within a few hours walk of Jerusalem.

The intimacy of the sacred geography of the early modern Holy Land and the fact that Christian sanctuaries were shared among the ten different Christian faiths of the region made them busy sites of worship. This was especially the case in the Holy Places that accommodated altars for multiple Christian faiths, notably the Church of the Nativity and the Basilica of the Holy Sepulcher. Tressan's description of the Holy Sepulcher provides a wonderfully textured and layered image of its complex Christian geography. Indeed, the Basilica is unlike any other Holy Place, its many chapels found on different levels, some seemingly carved haphazardly out of the rocky environment upon which the Basilica was constructed. At Calvary, for example, the site of the crucifixion, Tressan describes a space organized on different levels and requiring pilgrims to alternately climb and descend to visit its many shrines. He begins his description by counting nineteen steps on his climb up to the first chapel on the processional route. From there Tressan walked another ten feet along an arcade that led to the site marking the hole of the cross, which he locates to the left of the entrance in the middle of a large marble stone raised about three feet from the ground. After pausing to describe the sites marked by the crosses of the two thieves, Tressan was on the move again, this time descending to a chapel below the site of Calvary presided over by the Greeks. "The chapel was also covered like the others," he notes, "with small marble stones of diverse colours, and it was about six or seven feet long, and three and a half in length." The Greeks had decorated another altar nearby where they could alone officiate "when it suited them." Tressan was clearly impressed by the enormous number of illuminated lamps, counting thirty alone on the site of the hole of the cross and another dozen at the place of crucifixion.[68] His account is by no means among the most descriptive, but even this one passage conveys quite effectively the sensual nature of the pilgrimage experience for many Christian travelers who found themselves in the revered Basilica, a Holy Place filled with luminous chapels and dark recesses, steps worn from

---

[68] Tressan, *Relation vouvelle et exacte d'un voyage*, 129–131. "Les Grecs y ont dressé un Autel tout auprés, où ils officient seuls, quand bon leur semble. Ils y entretiennent quantité de lampes allumées; je croy qu'il y en a bien trente sur le trou de la Croix, & une douzaine à la place de crucifiement."

centuries of pilgrims' feet, and the mingling sounds of a diverse Christendom engaged in chanting, preaching, and prayer.

1.3.4 Conflict in the Holy Places

The intimate nature of this Christian geography meant that Christians interacted frequently with one another – in city streets, in the marketplaces, and also in the Holy Places. These relations were by no means defined by conflict, a fact attested by both Ottoman and Catholic sources. Christians often shared altars, processed together on feast days, provided one another shelter when traveling, and at times mobilized in political support of one another's privileges.[69] As Chapter 2 will explore at length, however, Christians also often fought with one another in the Holy Land and in particular in the Holy Places. It is fair to say that most of these conflicts concerned access to, and the usage of, these hallowed spaces. The registers of the *kadi* of Jerusalem are particularly revealing about Christian relations. The *kadi* was the local Islamic administrative and judicial official charged with governing religious minorities (*dhimmi*). At his tribunal, with the aid of local legal experts, the *kadi* presided over a wide range of disputes including conflicts over property and ritual transgressions to interpersonal violence. Franciscan records show that the brothers interacted frequently with *kadi* of Jerusalem and Aleppo, in particular, because of their proximity to the main Holy Places and relations with local European merchants. Of the two, the court of the *kadi* in Jerusalem has received significant attention from Ottoman scholars. Its registers show that the friars appeared frequently in the courts both as plaintiffs and as accused in local disputes throughout the medieval and early modern periods. From the 1480s onward, for example, the friars faced multiple challenges to their jurisdiction over the Cenacle from local Christians as well as Muslims and Jews. There was good reason for this because the Cenacle was materially associated with two meaningful sacred places. For Muslims and Jews, it rested upon the Tomb of the biblical King David, while Christians revered it as the site the Last Supper. As Bernard Collins argues, however, the friars seemed to have accepted

---

[69] Multi-faith processions in the Holy Sepulcher were common, especially during the Easter rites. This changed somewhat after the introduction of the Gregorian calendar in the Western Church in 1582. For a discussion, see, for example, Constantin Panchenko, *Arab Orthodox Christians*, 275–277.

the double designation of the site from early on, choosing to recognize David as well in their rites.[70]

Under the Ottomans, Muslim influence ultimately won out, first securing control of the Cenacle in 1530 until 1533, when the friars were reinstated, and definitively in 1551, when the Holy Place was converted into a mosque and the friars ejected from their convent on Mount Sion. Looking more specifically at intra-Christian disputes, the friars faced stiff competition with several local communities throughout the medieval and early modern periods. In 1511, for example, just a few years before the Ottoman conquest, the Georgian Christians challenged Franciscan jurisdiction of the Holy Sepulcher when they briefly gained control of one of their altars. The altar was restored to Franciscan jurisdiction by the *kadi* a year later, though this was not the last time the two communities wrangled over a religious space.[71] During the 1570s, the Georgian community challenged Franciscan possession of the convent of the Holy Saviour.

Though the friars purchased it legally in 1557/1558, the Georgians insisted it had been seized from them illegally and they blamed both the "Franks" (Latins) and Armenians. Almost twenty years later, a petition for the return of the convent to the Georgians was denied on the basis of greater need. The firman upheld Latin possession, noting that while the convent once belonged to the Georgians, at the time of its purchase by the Latins it was rented to three "infidel" women.[72]

That the friars were ultimately successful in retaining this convent may well reflect the waning of Georgian influence in the Holy Places over the course of the sixteenth century. A demographic study of the communities for the period shows that both the Georgian and Coptic communities were shrinking in Jerusalem and likely unable to continue the financial

---

[70] The Dominican friar Felix Fabri mentions conflict between the friars and local Jews over the Cenacle. He made two trips between 1480 and 1483. *The Wanderings of Felix Fabri*, I, pt. 1 (London: Palestine Pilgrim's Text Society, 1896), 303. See also Bernardin Collin, "Les Frères-Mineurs dans le Cenacle," *Studia Orientalia* 2 (1957): 33–34.

[71] As late as 1606, the friars were fending off renewed Georgian efforts to take the altar. A command dated April 14, 1577, to the kadi and sanjak and Jerusalem, for example, ordered these officials to recognize Georgian possession of the disputed chapel. Uriel Heyd, ed., *Ottoman Documents on Palestine, 1552–1615: A Study of The Firman according to the Mühimme Defteri* (Oxford: Clarendon Press, 1960), 181–182.

[72] Agustin Arce, *Documentos y texts para historia de tierra santa y sus santuarios (1600–1700)*, vol. 1 (Jerusalem: Franciscan Printing Press, 1970), 19–22 (doc. 10). The firman (January 22–31, 1596) was issued by Sultan Muhammad III to the *kadi* and *mutawali* of Jerusalem as well as the *beylerbei* of Damascus.

investments involved in maintaining chapels and convents, including the costs of litigation. Even with the declining influence of the Georgian and Coptic communities, however, surviving sources show that the friars were involved in numerous legal conflicts with other Christian communities throughout the seventeenth century, in particular with the Armenian Orthodox and Greek Orthodox. Oded Peri, who has studied these disputes in depth, notes a heightening of competition between these three Christian communities by the late sixteenth century, competition that is the focus of Chapter 2.[73] Indeed, 1604 seems to have been an especially busy year in the courts for the friars who were accused by the Armenians of removing their lamps from altars in the Church of the Nativity. In this matter, the friars were found guilty as charged, but it did not stop them from accusing the Armenians in turn of blocking the burial of Latin brothers and pilgrims in the old cemetery on Mount Sion.[74] The cemetery still belonged to the friars long after they lost their convent at that site. The Franciscan *custos* at the time, Francesco Manerba, mentioned this incident along with other recent disputes in a report to the papal Congregation of the Propaganda Fide. Another of the disputes involved the Syrians and the Greek Orthodox and the removal of some marble from the Holy Sepulcher. In this instance, Manerba accused the Syrian Christians of stealing and then hiding a piece of marble that had fallen from the interior of the great Basilica. Though they later returned it, he complained that the friars were then blocked from replacing the marble by the "maliciousness" of the Greeks ("malignità de' Greci").[75]

More disputes followed. Five years later, a firman issued by the sultan accused the friars of unlawfully forbidding other Christians from hanging lamps in the Grotto of the Nativity.[76] The kadi was ordered to intervene and "not let [the Latins] vex and molest a single person." Seven years later, the friars called upon the French ambassador to the Ottoman Porte – Achilles de Harlay Sancy (d. 1646)– when the Armenians pushed for jurisdiction over the Stone of Unction in the Holy Sepulcher. The Stone of Unction was the place where the three Marys anointed the body of Christ after its removal from the Cross. The shrine has undergone significant transformation since the sixteenth century. Today it is encased

---

[73] Oded Peri, *Christianity under Islam in Jerusalem: The Question of the Holy Sites in Early Ottoman Times* (Leiden: Brill, 2001).
[74] Heyd, ed., *Ottoman Documents on Palestine*, 184.
[75] Leonhard Lemmens, *Acta S. Congregationis de propaganda Fide pro Terra Sancta*, vol. 1 (Rome: Collegio di S. Bonaventura, 1921), 6–9.
[76] Heyd, ed., *Ottoman Documents on Palestine*, 184.

in a larger red stone and raised off the ground. At the time of this conflict, however, the Rock of the Anointing was reportedly a rather unprepossessing slab of either porphyry or marble that lay flat on the ground surrounded with a black and white border. Yamit Rachman-Schrire, who has studied the evolution of this shrine, argues that its location near the entrance of the Basilica was a devotional innovation of the friars which they introduced sometime during to the fourteenth century.[77] By the Early Modern Period, however, the site had clearly become a locus of competition between the Latins and Armenians, and the Armenians emerged victorious from this particular legal struggle. As Charles Frazee notes, the friars "unwisely argued that the Armenians had no rights in Jerusalem and should all be sent off to Cyprus."[78] Tension with the Armenians was clearly still alive and well eight years later in 1622 when friar Ambrosio de la Pola sent off his report to the Spanish commissioner general of the Holy Land. Ambrosio held the office of president, one of the senior positions in the inner council of the convent of the Holy Saviour. Discussing the uncertain state of Latin jurisdiction, De la Pola described the Latin community as "surrounded by schismatics and in particular the Armenians, who," he insisted, were "worse than the Turks." For de Pola, the Armenians posed an ever-present threat to the Custody because they had designs upon Latin altars. As he states quite bluntly in his report, they "strive with all their force to make us waste our funds so that they may seize control of the Holy Places."[79]

1.4 CONCLUSION

The primary objective of this chapter was to introduce the Custody of the Holy Land, a venerable Catholic pilgrimage institution that would become a site of intense Christian contestation by 1517. As discussed,

---

[77] Yamit Rachman-Schrire, "Christ's Unction and the Material Realization of a Stone in Jerusalem," in *Natural Materials of the Holy Land and the Visual Translation of Place, 500–1500*, ed. Renana Bartal, Neta Bodner, and Bianca Kuhnel (London: Routledge, 2017): 216–229. Rachman-Schrire argues that the earliest reports of the stone in its present location date to the late 1320s, and it was recorded regularly in pilgrimage treatises from 1335.

[78] Charles Frazee, *Palestine, Egypt and North Africa* (Cambridge: Cambridge University Press, 1983), 145–150.

[79] AHN OP legajo 1/27/c (July 8, 1622). "... porque estamos rodeados del scismaticos en particular *Armenios peores que los Turcos*, los quales procuran con todas sus fuerças de hazernos gastar los [ojos de la cara] para apoderarse de los santos lugares."

the distinctive character of the Custody was forged at the nexus of Western pilgrimage, sacred space, and Ottoman governance. In other words, the Custody was as much a product of the unique spiritual, political, and material environment of the Holy Land as it was of the Catholic tradition. It may be even more precise to describe it as a Franciscan rather than a Catholic institution given that it has only been governed by members of this order. These myriad contexts set the stage for the following exploration of the Early Modern Custody as a site of intense intra-Christian conflict. The first, and perhaps the most important from the perspective of the brothers of the Custody, was growing competition with the Greek Orthodox over altars in the Holy Places. These legal disputes reveal many of the dimensions of the Custody discussed thus far – the remarkable religious diversity and heterogeneity of the Holy Land, its historic role as a site of multi-faith pilgrimage, the institutionally hybrid character of the Custody, and the local impact of Ottoman governance. More to our broader purpose, they illuminate the Holy Places as historically desirable, and contested, places of Christian engagement because of the Holy Land's status as *the* source of Christian perfection. For two ancient Christian traditions that had long tangled over claims to Christian authenticity, possession of the most important altars served as a powerful and public manifestation of the legitimacy of their claims to Christian primacy.

2

Altars and Christian Precedence in the Holy Places

An Ottoman decree issued in 1692 under Suleiman II (1691–1695) alerts us to brewing conflict between the Franciscan brothers and the Greek Orthodox over chapels in the Holy Places. The decree, which found in favour of the friars, presents us with their description of the most recent events. According to the friars, they were in the midst of performing their rites near the stone of unction in the Basilica of the Holy Sepulcher when they were interrupted by members of "the Greek nation." The Greeks committed many other transgressions as well, including removing Latin lamps from the front of the shrine of the Holy Sepulcher and, "against ancient custom," replacing them with two large stone candlesticks. The Greeks also apparently stole the keys to the doors of the Church of the Nativity in Bethlehem along with three other keys associated with the Grotto of the Nativity, the Holy Place associated with the birth of Christ.

The decree describes several other changes to the use and organization of space by the Greeks including the construction of a door near the "Great Church above its cemetery" and the addition of new seats along the eastern and western sides of the Grotto of the Nativity. The Greeks also walled in two domes that were in front of the door of the Grotto, removed several "ancient" statues, closed two doors leading from the Grotto to two gardens, and made two others.[1]

---

[1] ASVe Bailo 368 (1692). This is the Italian translation of the decree found in the *bailo* records. "Et I religiosi franchi facendo le loro ceremonie nella pietra d'untione la natione greca gli impedi di farle, et [... le sudetti lampade], et insero avanti il santo sepolchro sotto la gran volta dice gran Candeglieri di Pietra contro l'antico costume et due candelle avanti la pietra d'unctione, ricettendo un piccolo banco nella grotta che fù trovasa la Croce, usurpandole chiavi di dire porte della gran chiesa che é nel villaggio chiamata Bethlehem

Altars and Christian Precedence in the Holy Places

As we saw in Chapter 1, it was by no means unusual for the Christian communities of the Holy Land to compete with one another over access to, and the usage of, chapels in the Holy Places. Indeed, one can chart a long history of Christian contestation in these spaces by the time our investigation begins. However, the decree of 1692 emerges from a particularly sustained period of jurisdictional conflict between the Franciscan brothers of the Custody and the Greek Orthodox Patriarchate of Jerusalem. Already visible by the 1560s, this conflict reached particular intensity from the 1630s. Moreover, it played out both in Ottoman courts and in city streets and, as the decree of 1692 also shows, in the chapels of the Holy Places. In these hallowed spaces, Christian rivals "stole" keys, blocked doors, and removed the trappings of the other faith while replacing them with their own.

Our investigation of the early modern Custody as a locus of growing intra-Christian conflict begins with these disputes over altars. While such conflicts were by no means new, the persistent nature of the seventeenth-century disputes and the level of violence is nevertheless striking. Moreover, it was clearly a matter of enormous significance for Catholic leaders in Europe, generating thousands of pages of diplomatic correspondence, financial records, and legal documents. These sources unveil an active international Catholic network operating behind Franciscan initiatives to protect Latin altars. It is because both Catholic leaders and the friars took these legal challenges very seriously that they are the focus of the present chapter. As the following discussion will show, altars in the Holy Places were intensely contested spaces among the many Christians of the early modern Holy Land because they were meaningful material vessels of legal status and spiritual authority. Indeed, as the Ottoman firman of 1692 suggests, these functions were entwined. Its description of stolen keys, locked doors, and interrupted liturgical rites reveals Islamic privileges inflected with Christian meaning because of their role in

---

dove é la grotta che naique Giesù christo, usurpando depuò ingiustamente tre altre chiavi che appartenevano ai Religiosi et i sudetti greci l'impadrovierono di tutti questi luoghi sotto falsi pretesti, et fecero [depuò] a una porta nella gran Chiesa sopra li loro cimiterii, havendone fatta un altra appresso il Presepio di Giesù christo della parte del oriente, é sotto quella una scalla, mettendo sedie appresso la grotta che é tra l'oriente et occidente, et decero murare due cupol[a] ch'erano avanti la porta de Preseppio di Giesu levandone dal detto Preseppio alcune antiche figure cheravo delle parte del Occidente et insero al loro luogo sedie havendo o chiuso le porte di due giardini che dependendevanno dalla grottache nacque Giesù christo facendove due altere."

regulating access to sacred sites that were considered authentic and powerful reservoirs of Christ's authority.

Indeed, the Latin-Greek disputes unveil an even more ambitious struggle over claims to Christian primacy, one in which the greater political status and religious authority of a Christian tradition rested upon its legal and spiritual possession of the most important altars and the Islamic privilege of Christian precedence. This interpretation emerges when we consider, to begin with, the long historic rivalry between the Latin and Greek Orthodox communities over jurisdiction, and secondly, the impact of much more recent political and religious change. It is no coincidence, in particular, that the disputes flared up in the wake of the Ottoman conquest, an event that brought the sacred landscape within the political as well as spiritual reach of the Byzantine Patriarch in Constantinople for the first time in several centuries. Byzantine influence over the Patriarchate of Jerusalem was visible by the middle of the sixteenth century and played a role in catalyzing renewed conflict. The Byzantine Patriarchate had other reasons for targeting Latin jurisdiction by the seventeenth century, including the corrupting impact of religious reforming movements from Europe upon the body of the Greek Orthodox tradition. Calvinist influence and the growing number of Catholic missionaries in Ottoman lands were two pressing concerns for Greek Orthodox leaders by the 1620s. The Catholic missionaries, in particular, posed a serious threat because they arrived in the eastern Mediterranean with the express purpose of converting Eastern Christians.

As should be clear thus far, a complex understanding of the Latin-Greek disputes only emerges when we situate them in the many contexts – political, religious, geographical, historical – that informed them. Doing so, however, illuminates the historic function of the Holy Places as valued sources of spiritual and political legitimacy among the many Christian communities of the Holy Land, especially during a period of profound religious and political change. Section 2.1 sets the stage by providing a brief description of the disputes. Section 2.2 examines the role of Islamic law in shaping Catholic access to the Holy Places, illuminating altars as desirable, and thus contested, vessels of legal and political status and Christian authority. Understanding altars as powerful sources of Christian legitimacy is especially relevant to the discussion in Section 2.3, which considers the disputes in a much longer history of contention between the two communities over claims to Christian primacy in the Holy Places. From this discussion, three themes emerge that are central to the broader investigation of this book: Firstly, that altars were sought after because the Holy Places were revered as authentic, and thus powerful, material reservoirs of Christ's authority. Secondly, that Christian engagement with the Holy Places was mediated, and thus shaped, by Muslim (Mamluk, Ottoman) structures of authority. Thirdly, the Christian communities of the Holy land turned to their sacred pasts to articulate their claims to jurisdiction and thus to Christian authority and leadership.

2.1 THE DISPUTES OVER ALTARS

The disputes discussed here have attracted the attention of other scholars, perhaps as much because of their intensity as the richness of the surviving documentation. Historians, political scientists, and anthropologists have all found the conflicts useful for probing Christian conceptions of sacrality and spiritual purity, the dynamics of religious violence, Ottoman governance, and the nature and possibilities of religious coexistence in a multi-faith city such as Jerusalem.[2] Our objective is somewhat different, namely, to look at them anew as products of the early modern past. More specifically, our objective is to understand their function as rites of spiritual legitimacy for early modern Catholics, members of a religious tradition that was in the throes of profound change by the start of period under investigation. To do so, however, we need to recognize that the legal disputes between Latin and Greek Orthodox were not simple, discreet conflicts but rather multiple, and at times overlapping ones initiated in diverse legal jurisdictions on an array of often interrelated matters. Recognizing that multiple dimensions of meaning also informed each individual legal challenge, this chapter nevertheless treats the various disputes holistically as persistent conflicts in a longer struggle, one that flared up repeatedly over the course of more than a century. That the conflicts were preoccupied in particular with claiming jurisdiction in the two most sacred (and thus most desirable) of the Christian Holy Places – the Church of the Nativity in Bethlehem and the Basilica of the Holy Sepulcher in Jerusalem – is another important element in the following analysis. Finally, while these conflicts continued into the eighteenth century as well, this chapter restricts its analysis to the seventeenth century

---

[2] See, for example, Chad Emmett, "The Status Quo Solution for Jerusalem," *Journal of Palestinian Studies* 26 (1997): 16–28; and Gail Bowman, "In Dubious Battle on the Plains of Heav'n: The Politics of Possession in Jerusalem's Holy Sepulcher," *History and Anthropology* (2011): 371–399.

and devotes most of the attention to two particularly sustained periods of conflict in the 1630s and the 1670s.

As should now be clear, the following brief narrative of the disputes is not intended to be comprehensive. Nor, for that matter, does it claim to present a singular "truthful" account, something that would be hard to do regardless, since it draws from contemporary accounts that do not always agree with one another. Since it relies heavily upon sources pertaining to the Franciscan community, it is also fair to say that the following account is most useful for understanding their perspective as representatives of the Western Church in the region, above all their perception of Christian altars as entwined vessels of legal status and Christian legitimacy. A few observations to note from the start: Firstly, these disputes were simultaneously local and international conflicts. Secondly, they were material as well as legal in nature. Thirdly, they were expensive.

Tension between the Greek Orthodox and Latin communities had been building for several decades by the time of the first of the major seventeenth-century disputes in the 1630s. Since some of the same dynamics were operating in the earlier conflicts, they require a brief discussion here. According to a number of scholars, trouble began brewing following the appointment of the new Patriarch of Jerusalem in 1534. Germanos (1534–1579) was a Byzantine Greek, the first in a succession to occupy this important office. The Patriarchate of Jerusalem was one of four Patriarchs in the Greek Orthodox tradition by the Early Modern Period, the others being those of Antioch, Constantinople, and Alexandria. As the Patriarch of Jerusalem, Germanos oversaw the spiritual life of the Greek Orthodox populations of Palestine and Syria and, importantly, the privileges of the Greek Orthodox Church in the Holy Places. Both Greek and Latin accounts of this period agree that Germanos was eager to expand Greek jurisdiction at the expense of the other Christian traditions, in particular, the Latin and Armenian communities. With this objective in mind, Germanos initiated a number of new measures including the formation of a new clerical community in the 1540s called the Brotherhood of the Holy Sepulcher. From the 1540s onward, the Brotherhood of the Holy Sepulcher (not to be confused with the Catholic confraternity discussed in Chapter 3) became an active arm of the Patriarchate in its many jurisdictional struggles with the friars and other Christian communities. The Greeks and Latins clashed over Latin construction of a bronze altar at the site of the Stone of Unction in the Basilica of the Holy Sepulcher during the 1540s, for example, and over

Latin renovation of the Edicule during the 1550s. The Edicule, also known as the Holy Sepulcher, is the shrine inside the great Basilica built on top of the cave where Christ was believed to have been buried.

A decade later, Germanos apparently sought to assert Greek Orthodox claims to Christian precedence in the Basilica, a move that put him directly at odds with the friars who held this privilege. The Franciscan chronicle known as the *Registro de' fatti memorabili* mentions this petition. It is an admittedly partisan account, written during the seventeenth century by one of the friars attached to the convent in Jerusalem. The chronicle states that Germanos appeared before the "great Turk" in Constantinople and "falsely claimed that the Holy Places had belonged to the Greeks for over thirty years." Germanos lost the case and in response organized a gathering of five hundred Greeks who then "ran through the streets shouting that the Franciscan brothers of Jerusalem were all Spanish and Maltese," that they conspired with the corsairs (likely referring to the Knights of Malta), and "stole sons and sent them to France."[3] The implication of these accusations, of course, was that the friars were conspiring against the Ottoman regime, a damning accusation that the Greeks made repeatedly in later disputes as well. A Greek chronicler of the Brotherhood of the Holy Sepulcher, however, provides a different account of the origins of the Latin-Greek conflicts, instead locating it later in time in 1580. According to Constantin Panchenko, the Greek Orthodox Patriarch Sophronius IV (1579–1608) was upset when the Latin community gave a large sum of money to Ottoman officials in Jerusalem to take control of Golgotha (the site of Calvary) and the chapel of Helen both in the Basilica of the Holy Sepulcher, and the Greek share of the Church of the Nativity in Bethlehem.[4] As Panchenko notes, however, at the time the Latins had held jurisdiction over most of these sites for almost a century. Thus, the two chronicles reveal competing narratives of jurisdiction long before the seventeenth-century disputes, narratives that would be called upon time and again by the two communities in their later struggles over jurisdiction.

---

[3] Leonhard Lemmens, ed., "Registro de' fatti memorabilia di Terra santa," in *Collectanea Terrae Sanctae ex Archivo Hierosolymitano depromta*, vol. XIV, nuova serie, ed. Girolamo Golobovich (Florence: Quaracchi, 1933), 12. "I quali andavano per quella città gridando et escalamando che I Frati franchi di Gerusalemme erano tutti Spagnuoli e Maltesi, nimici del Gran Signore." Lemmens mentions that different versions of this event exist but he found three legal sentences in favour of the friars dated May and June 1566.

[4] Constantin Panchenko, *Arab Orthodox Christians under the Ottomans, 1516–1831* (Jordanville: Holy Trinity Seminary Press, 2016), 273.

While the friars and the Greek Orthodox clashed again a few decades later, first in 1604 and then again in 1611, the legal dispute that erupted in 1630/1631 proved to be a much more serious and long-lasting rupture in relations between the two communities. Rumours circulating at the time suggest that it may have been triggered by recent tension with the friars. In particular, that the friars had caused the arrest of Patriarch Theophanes III (1608–1644) by the Pasha (governor) of Jerusalem.[5] Theophanes managed to escape and fled to Constantinople, where he received a pardon from the Ottoman Porte. It was not long after he returned to Jerusalem to resume his office as Patriarch that he launched a legal suit against Latin jurisdiction in the Church of the Nativity. Initially, it was successful. In 1631, the Patriarch of Jerusalem received a decree (firman) from the *kadi* of Jerusalem forcing the friars to hand over jurisdiction over the Grotto of the Nativity. As discussed in Chapter 1, one of the important responsibilities of the *kadi* was the regulation of relations between local religious communities acting as a court of first instance in a wide array of issues including disputes between Christian communities over privileges in the Holy Places.[6] Like his predecessors in the office of Patriarch, Theophanes bolstered his claim by insisting upon an a priori legal claim to possession of this jurisdiction – in other words, that the friars illegitimately held a jurisdiction that historically and legally belonged to the Greeks. He provided the Ottoman Porte with the requisite supporting documentation, in particular a decree from Sultan Umar (Omar) Ibn al-Khattab, the seventh-century ruler associated with the Pact of Umar, which recognized Greek jurisdiction in the contested chapels.[7] The friars, when confronted by this claim, issued their

---

[5] The Pasha may have been Muhammad ibn Farrukh, a member of the prominent Farrukh dynasty that was powerful in Palestine during the seventeenth century. He followed his father in the office of *sanjak-bey* of Nablus and Jerusalem in 1621 and is referred to as Pasha. He is mentioned, for example, in Dror Ze'evi, *The Ottoman Century: The District of Jerusalem in the 1600s* (New York: State University of New York Press, 1996), 43–45.

[6] On the role of the *kadi* in Jerusalem in local *dhimmi* relations, see, among others, Oded Peri, *Christianity under Islam, in Jerusalem: The Question of the Holy Sites in Early Ottoman Times* (Leiden: Brill, 2001); and Uriel Heyd, *Ottoman Documents on Palestine, 1552–1615: A Study of the Firman according to the Mühimme Defteri* (Oxford: Clarendon Press, 1960).

[7] For example, we find the same accusations made in the 1670s and later on in a petition made by Patriarch Dositheos to the Porte in 1706. See Hasan Çolak, "Between the Ottoman Central Administration and the Patriarchates of Antioch, Jerusalem and Alexandria," PhD thesis, University of Birmingham, 2008, 104.

own petition to the *kadi* in which they accused the Greeks of forging the ancient decree.

For the next five years, the friars, with the vigorous support of the ambassadors of Venice and France, slowly pushed the case through the corridors of power both in Jerusalem and at the Ottoman Porte in Constantinople. Correspondence sent by Giovanni Cappello, the Venetian ambassador (*bailo*) to the Venetian consul of Aleppo between 1630 and 1634, gives us some insight into the active role played by this ambassador in particular.[8] At the height of the conflicts in 1633 and 1634, Cappello was issuing letters every few days and sometimes even more quickly, a rapidity that conveys the urgency of the matter at the time for this Venetian official. Many of these were short, quickly written dispatches, but Cappello did send the Franciscan president in Jerusalem a lengthy one dated October 5, 1633, summarizing recent negotiations with the *visir* and *mufti* in Constantinople regarding the Church of the Nativity. That he sent it to the Franciscan president suggests that the *custos* was traveling outside of Jerusalem at the time, something that he did quite often on matters of business. Five days later, Cappello sent another lengthy letter, this time to the Franciscan *custos*, which captures the breadth of his engagement with Ottoman as well as European officials on behalf of the Custody. He writes, for example, that he had approached the *visir* and *mufti* on several occasions, bearing "the ancient legal writings attesting to our possession" of jurisdiction in the Church of the Nativity. He did so to prove that "we have possessed it for many years" and also informed them of all the other "advantages and considerations that I considered appropriate and useful." Cappello also reminded Ottoman authorities that Latin jurisdiction was meaningful to the Venetian Republic as well as other important powers ("Serenissima reppublica e d'altri patri i grandi"). Cappello nevertheless acknowledged to the Franciscan *custos* that thus far he had been unsuccessful in preventing a judgment favourable to the Greeks. In the end, he said that the *mufti* pronounced against the fathers and ordered that the Greeks be given a key to the Holy Place.[9] On the same day, Cappello also wrote to the consul in Aleppo about the situation regarding the Church of the

---

[8] ASVe Bailo 109 (October 5, 1633). On the *bailo* as a Venetian representative, see, in particular, Eric Dursteler, "The Bailo in Constantinople: Crisis and Career in Venice's Early Modern Diplomatic Corps," *Mediterranean Historical Review* 16 (2001): 1–30.

[9] ASVe Bailo 109 (October 5, 1633). "I fondamenti validi delle scritture, l'antichità del possesso" ("l'uso pratticato per tanti anni")

Nativity, once again stressing that he was "applying all of my will to convince the Visir and the Mufti with the arguments that I considered useful," and that to this end he was working closely with the French ambassador.[10]

As these letters suggest, Cappello felt frustrated by his lack of success in restoring Latin jurisdiction. Although he was able to secure at least a partial restoration that gave the friars access to their former chapels, within a few months the Greeks succeeded once again in forcing the friars out of the Holy Places. It took another two years of intense diplomacy and substantial funds changing hands, but in 1636 the friars were formerly reinstalled in the chapels that they held in 1630. In a dispatch dated July 7, 1636, informing the Venetian Senate of the restoration of Latin jurisdiction, the Venetian ambassador took a moment to convey his "considerable" frustration with the negotiations, likening the experience to a ship faced with a treacherous journey across a sea, "battered by contrary winds" and "dangerous rocks," before finally making it safely to the port. In this case, the safe haven came in the form of a new "catserife" (*hatt-i-serif*) carried by an armed officer (*capigi*) bearing the imperial insignia that ordered the return of the chapels to the "padri zocolanti" (friars). The Greeks, he said, had taken these chapels illegitimately, using trickery ("con male arti") to remove them.[11] Cappello's letter also underscores the unstable nature of Latin possession, reminding the Senate that victory would be fleeting unless funds immediately flowed from Europe to secure the altars. The Greeks, as he explained, had given a great deal of money to acquire the altars two years earlier, and the Latins were expected to do the same.[12] Much later in October, the Venetian ambassador wrote with good news – the brothers reported that the successful

---

[10] ASVe Bailo 109 (October 10, 1633), f. 2. "Nell'affare di Betlem per quei nostri religiosi mi se li adoperato d'ogni efficacia e calor impregondo il talento, e l'applicatgli tutta de miei spiriti in portar le raggioni al Visir et al Mufti con le ponderationi che hò giudicate opportune."

[11] ASVe Dispacci, 117 (July 7, 1636), ff. 45–46. The full passage is here: "Con le ultime mie riverentissime lettere per vostra Serenità, le diedi parta del buon progresso, con che' procedutta la trattatione della recuperatione delli santuarii di Gierusalem, et di Betelem, la quale doppo esser stata combatuta da molte borasche di contrarietà, et doppo haver passato molti scogli di difficoltà, si è finalmente ridotta in porto con haversi ottenuto un novo *catserif* (hatti-serif, catzerifer) e dal Rè informa di segno Imperial e col manuscritto della Maestà sua ... col quale viene annullato il conceduto à Greci già due anni, et commandato di ritornar à Padri zocolanti il possesso di tutti quelli luochi, che le erano stati con male arti levati per l'effettiva essecutione dal quale partiranno questi Padri [Trucimano], et Procuratore, con un Capigi fra due, ò tre giorni."

[12] ASVe Dispacci, 117 (July 7, 1636), 47v–48v.

handover of the chapels in both cities had taken place a few months earlier on July 23 and 24 respectively.[13]

Within a year, however, trouble brewed again. In 1637, the Porte, under pressure from the Greek Orthodox Patriarch of Constantinople, ruled against the friars, reducing their privileges in the Holy Sepulcher and the Church of the Nativity. The friars reclaimed their former jurisdiction more quickly this time but the start of the War of Crete (1645–1669) eight years later prompted yet another legal challenge.[14] A much more serious challenge came twenty years later following the appointment in 1669 of the Byzantine Greek Dositheos to the Patriarchate of Jerusalem.

Dositheos (1669–1707) signaled early on that he was intent upon expanding Greek influence in the Holy Places and in 1672 renewed litigation for control of the previously contested altars in the two most significant of them. The Patriarchate was successful and received the requested jurisdiction that year. However, Dositheos made sure that the moment of Greek triumph was well advertised both in Jerusalem and in the Greek Orthodox tradition more generally when he arranged for the reconsecration of the Church of the Nativity to coincide with the synod of Jerusalem. The synod that met in March saw the most important officials of the Greek Orthodox tradition descend upon the holy city. One can imagine the visual impact of seeing the Greek Orthodox tradition in all its diversity and the richly ornamented robes of its prelates. For the friars, it must have been a bitter reminder of Greek Orthodox triumph in the most recent battle over the Holy Places. It was not long after that they responded with their own petition seeking the restoration of their jurisdiction over the two altars. Surviving sources suggest that tension between the communities only mounted over the next few years.

Reports sent by ecclesiastical officials between 1672 and 1675 described what by now were familiar scenes of liturgical warfare and violence. Juan de Cañizares (Canizares) was a commissioner of the Holy

---

[13] ASVe dispacci 117, f. 374v. This report was sent October 13, 1636, but he refers to a letter sent by the *custos* of the Holy Land to the guardian of the Church of Santa Maria in Constantinople: "... con le quali he avis a il possesso consignato alli padri delli sti luochi già goduti dalla loro Religione per cosi lungo corso di tempo con universal applauso e contentezza di tutte le nato eccettuata quell ache n'è stata spogliata, laudendosi molto, di quell'Agà, che si condusse con loro per il detto effetto che segui x in Gerusalem alli 23 dell'istesso, et in Betlem alli 24."

[14] Charles Frazee, *Catholics and Sultans: The Church and the Ottoman Empire 1453–1923* (Cambridge: Cambridge University Press, 2006), 147. The War of Crete, also known as the War of Candia, was largely between the Ottomans, Venice and her allies and took place around the city of Candia.

Land, one of the officials charged with the collections of alms. He appears in an earlier letter sent to the commissioner general of the Holy Land in Madrid in 1663 as one of three friars sent to Constantinople, including the French friar, Antonio de Bras, and another Spanish friar named Bernardo Soler.[15] By 1675, the time of the latest dispute, the friar had spent almost thirteen years at the seat of Ottoman power. As a prominent official involved in the management of alms collecting, moreover, he became deeply involved in the recuperation of Latin altars. In two letters received by the Propaganda Fide, one dated December 1674 and the other sometime the following year, Cañizares paints a vivid picture of worsening relations characterized by interpersonal conflict and the destruction of sacred objects, art, and architecture. One encounter between clerics of the different faiths left a Greek priest dead. In other related incidents, the Patriarch of Jerusalem purportedly excommunicated the Pope and accused the friars of placing a statue of that "filthy infidel ... pope" on the top of the shrine of the Holy Sepulcher.[16] Perhaps most importantly from the perspective of Cañizares and his Franciscan brothers, the Greeks accused them of illegal possession of their altars. The end of this dispute did not come until 1690, when the Ottoman Porte restored Franciscan jurisdiction to that which they held in 1630. The firman of 1692, however, which is cited at the beginning of this chapter, shows that tensions between the communities over these sacred sites were bubbling again two years later and indeed would continue to define relations between them throughout the eighteenth century as well. Once again at stake for the friars was the loss of keys, doors broken, liturgical rites interrupted, and altars stripped of their Catholic identity.

2.1.1 An International Catholic Network

This narrative of the disputes does little justice to their true complexity, but it does feature key elements that are important for unlocking their meaning for the Catholic community at the center of this discussion as well as its Greek Orthodox rivals. We note to begin with that tension between the Latin and Greek Orthodox communities over altars had been mounting from as early as the 1560s and escalated dramatically after

---

[15] AHN OP legajo 1/12. The letter was sent by Diego de Lardezaval in October 1663.
[16] APF SC I, ff. 447–450. "Che sopra il sepolcro di Christo hanno posto nuovamente li franchi l'immagine di quell'infoedele sporco del loro Papa."

1630. That one dispute quickly followed upon the heels of another is also meaningful, because it points to deep-seated issues that could not easily be resolved by any single legal decision. Mention of the destruction of property and interpersonal violence is yet another striking detail, one that suggests that the disputes were taken very seriously, certainly seriously enough to generate a passionate response from members of both communities. Another important clue lies in the international breadth of Catholic engagement. The seventeenth-century disputes generated thousands of pages of documentation in the form of correspondence, financial registers, legal petitions, and decrees as well as chronicles. Together, this rich source base unveils a powerful international network of Catholic authorities and agents mobilized in defense of the Custody. Since the nature of this support also provides insight into the significance given to the possession of Latin altars, we should briefly consider it here. It took two forms in particular: political and financial.

The correspondence of the Venetian ambassador is especially useful for tracking the international breadth of Catholic political engagement. We note that during the 1630s dispute alone, for example, he was in regular contact with the Franciscan *custos* on the situation in the Holy Places, as well as with the Venetian consuls of Aleppo and Alexandria, two of the cities within the boundaries of the Custody. He wrote frequently to the Venetian Senate as well, providing regular updates on relations between the Christian communities and the progress of the Latin cause. These letters are revealing about the specific negotiations between the Venetian ambassador and Ottoman officials as well as his working relationship with the agents of other Catholic powers including the papacy. In a letter dated August 1631, for example, the ambassador mentions using his influence with the local *mufti* to secure the removal of the *kadi* of Jerusalem, an official that he considered corrupt and responsible for the loss of the Latin chapels. Two letters sent to the Serene Republic in 1633 discussed working closely with the French ambassador and an envoy referred to as "Monsieur la Piccardière," a working relationship that underscores rising French influence at the Ottoman Porte by this time. As shall be discussed further in Chapter 4, the involvement of these officials was consistent with the French monarchy's interest in promoting its status as Protector of the Holy Places.[17] The King of Poland also wrote a supportive letter, though Cappello is not specific about its contents.

---

[17] On the French Protectorship, see Geraud Poumarède, "Les limites de patronage français sur les lieux saints: Autour de l'installation d'un consul à jérusalem dans les années

Such broad political support, needless to say, went hand in hand with substantial financial support because legal cases were costly. A precise accounting of the costs of the individual disputes is unfortunately impossible to determine since they were borne by multiple agencies who provided funds mostly on an a hoc basis. Most letters allude rather generally to payments made. The poor survival rate of financial records also makes tracking the flow of monies in and out of the Custody extremely difficult, especially prior to the 1650s. Franciscan correspondence, along with surviving financial registers belonging to the commissioners general of the Holy Land, show even so that the Custody relied upon the generosity of many princely benefactors as well as parochial donations throughout the Early Modern Period. Princely benefactors provided not only monies in support of the Custody but also devotional objects, supplies for the Franciscan household, and materials for the restoration and decoration of Latin convents and chapels. By the Early Modern Period, almsgiving had become an increasingly organized and centralized practice under Franciscan administration, presided over by commissioners-general based in diverse parts of Europe.[18] Western patronage of the Custody will receive more attention in Chapter 4, but it is important to mention here that the single most generous benefactor of the Custody throughout the late medieval and Early Modern Periods was the Spanish monarchy. Philip II (1556–1598), for example, was largely responsible for funding the restoration of the Dome of the Holy Sepulcher in the 1550s, a massive and expensive undertaking that took several years. More sustained Spanish initiatives included the *cruzada*, a tax placed on the territories of New Spain to support the recovery of the Holy Places[19] and the

---

1620," *Revue de l'histoire de l'Eglise de France* 92 (2006): 73–116. French engagement in the disputes is the focus of Chapter 4.

[18] Patrocinio Garcia Barriuso, *Espana en la Historia de Tierra Santa*, vol. 1 (Madrid: Ministerio de Asuntos Exteriores, 1992–1994), ch. XIII; and Felicita Tramontana, "Per ornamento e servizio di questi santi luoghi: L'arrivée des objets de dévotion dans les sanctuaires de Terre Sainte (xviie siècle)," *Archives de sciences sociales des religions. Façonner l'objet de dévotion chrétien. Fabrication, commerce et circulations (vers XVII–XIX siècles)* 183 (2018): 227–243.

[19] The implementation of the *cruzada* and its contribution to the Holy Land during the Early Modern Period still remains poorly understood despite the magisterial work of Goñi Gatzambide, *Historia de la bula in España* (Vitoria: Editorial del Seminario, 1958). However, an extremely helpful recent discussion of the *cruzada* is Thomas Dandelet's "Praying for the New St Peters," in *Spain in Italy: Politics, Society and Religion 1500–1700*, ed. Thomas Dandelet and J. Marino (Leiden: Brill, 2007), 180–195.

extension of the administration of the commissioners of the Holy Land throughout imperial territories.[20]

The broad nature of financial support for the Custody is a reminder that the Holy Land occupied a singularly important place in Catholic spirituality and had long been a focus of almsgiving throughout the Church. Along with this evidence of more generalized giving, however, we also find more specific indications that the legal cases were regarded as an especially important threat to Latin interests in the Holy Land and merited additional financial investment. Alms placards, for example, mention Greek and Armenian seizure of Latin convents and chapels in their litanies of suffering. These placards, produced by commissioners of the Holy Land and ratified by local secular authorities, were distributed to local parishes across Europe. A number of these survive from the 1650s and 1660s for regions in Italy and France.

One printed in Genoa in 1655, for example, called for alms to cover the extensive costs caused by recent and/or ongoing conflicts with other Christians as well as excessive Ottoman exactions and it mentions specifically the Greek Orthodox and Armenian Christians. Referring to recent challenges to Catholic jurisdiction, for example, the placard noted that the friars "possess other Holy Places, the Grotto, and on Calvary, the site of the crucifixion, and the rock on which Christ our lord was placed by Nicodemus after he removed him from the cross." The Greeks had the money to remove them from these shrines, but the placard assures its Catholic audience that "our friars recovered these places twice for the large sum of 160,000 pezze, 80,000 each time."[21]

In addition to alms placards, the legal disputes with the Greek Orthodox also appear with some frequency in diplomatic requests for aid. A good example is the letter by the *custos* of the Holy Land, friar Joannes dell'Ahaia, sent to the Congregation of the Propaganda Fide in 1637. Ahaia mentions that the recovery of the Holy Places from the

---

[20] Barriuso, *Espana*, vol. I, XIII.
[21] APF Conti Terra Santa, III, SC Miscellanea 1. "Relatione del Misero Stato nel quale si trovano I luoghi santi di Gerusalemme." The broad sheet was published on June 18, 1655 and printed by Gerolamo Marino. "Possedevano frà gli altri Luoghi Santi, il Presepio, e nel Calvario il Luogo della Crocifissione, il bucco dove fù piantata la Croce, e la Pietra sopra della quale fù onto Christo Signor Nostro da Nicodemo, dopò chef ù levato di Croce, li Greci à forza di denari glieli hanno tolti; Li nostri li hanno ricomprati due volte, per cento sessanta milla pezze, ottanta milla per volta."

Greeks was *the* central objective of recent alms collecting[22] and asked the Propaganda Fide to pressure the French monarchy to send along more alms. Ahaia was not the first member of Holy Land community to suggest that the French monarchy was much more ready to intervene politically in the affairs of the Custody than it was to provide it financial support. The brothers made this argument frequently in their communications with the papacy to justify the close administrative and spiritual ties between the Custody and the Spanish monarchy. However, Ahaia's report is relevant here because it also gives us an idea of the costs of the ministry and the organization of alms required to fund it. He warned the Congregation, for example, that the Custody was in grave debt to the sum of 16,000 scuta because of the enormous costs spent on recuperating the Holy Places from the Greeks and that they were having trouble getting rid of it.[23] Debt is a recurring discussion among the friars throughout the Early Modern Period, and borrowing was common to pay for the legal fees involved in the recuperation of altars.

Venetian ambassadorial correspondence during the 1630s mentions a variety of costs that also help us understand a bit better the fiscal demands placed upon the treasury of the Custody because of the legal conflicts. In his report sent to the Senate in 1636 discussed earlier, *bailo* Piero Foscarini (1635–1636) suggested that a combined gift of "centara di migliara de reali" (100,000) would be required "if the Greeks are to be expelled." The funds mentioned here were clearly intended to pay Ottoman officials to shepherd the Latin legal case through to a successful conclusion. He mentions, in particular, that he had told the *Caimecan* (an Ottoman administrative official)[24] that he had amassed 19 m (19,000) reales to give to "diversi ministry" (diverse officials) and another 15,000 for the *kadi* (of Jerusalem). He notes that the Greeks had already given several thousand reales worth of furs and that they would likely provide

---

[22] Leonhard Lemmens, ed., *Acta S. Congregationis de propaganda Fide pro Terra Sancta*, vol. 1 (Rome: Collegio di S. Bonaventura, 1921), 104. "Ut praedictum fratrem Joannem dell'Ahaia moneat, Sancta Loca hoc tempore esse alieno aere gravitissima ob impensas magnas in eorum recuperatione a manibus Graecorum factae, et propterea exactionem praedictorum 16000 scutorum esse sollicitandam, ne usurae gravissimae ad rationem 18–20 pro centenario sortem principalem debitam ita augeant, ut postea majori cum difficultate debitum Sanctorum Locorum extingui possit." Ft. 1 says this was sent to the nuncio in France.

[23] Lemmens, ed., *Acta S. Congregationis de propaganda Fide pro Terra Sancta*.

[24] The spelling is unclear but seems to be referring to the Kiaya, Cahaia, or Cacaia, a steward or lieutenant.

more.[25] Later letters voiced concern that if the payments were not made soon by Christian princes, they risked the loss of the Latin chapels. On July 17, for example, Alvise Contarini (1636–1641), the newly appointed *bailo*, mentions pressure from the Caimecan to pay 1,000 reales for the new mosque in honour of Sultan Ahmed (d. 1617), a payment that the Greek Orthodox had also been asked to pay years earlier when they first received the Latin altars. The Caimecan apparently made it clear to Contarini that if it was not provided soon, the keys would be handed over to the Greeks.[26] Fees were an expected part of legal processes in the Ottoman Empire as well as in European states but the *bailo*'s discussion above seems to point to a form of extortion fueling the wheels of justice at all levels of Ottoman governance. The Greek Orthodox made similar complaints to Ottoman authorities in a number of their own petitions as well.[27] Oded Peri has argued that Ottoman authorities in Constantinople were also worried about local reports of excessive fines and other abuses in these cases, and so it does seem as though certain *kadi* were taking advantage of the Christian conflicts to profit more than permitted by their rulers.[28] For our purposes, however, the discussion of these fees further reinforces the high value given by Western authorities to protecting Latin altars since they were clearly willing to pay a great deal to do so.

The remaining discussion explores Latin altars as desirable vessels of Islamic privilege and Christian authority because they carved a legal, material, and spiritual place for the Catholic tradition in the most sacred of Christian landscapes. Indeed, these functions were entwined, as Christians invested possession of jurisdiction over altars with spiritual meaning as markers of Christian perfection and authority. The brothers of the Holy Land and their powerful Catholic supporters were anxious

---

[25] ASVe dispacci 117 (April 7, 1636), f. 48. "... in quanto sapeva, che Greci havevano fatta provisione di qualche migliaro di reali di molta pelizze di gebellini, di una cinta zogelata di valiente de 4 m tolleri, et che si affattuavano per trovar summe maggiori ...." The currencies given here are all Spanish. The *scuta* or *escudos* was valued at roughly 15–16 *reales* though devaluation significantly changed values during the seventeenth century.

[26] ASVe Bailo 285 (July 17, 1637), ff. 40v–41.

[27] Spero Vryonis, "The History of the Greek Patriarchate of Jerusalem As Reflected in Codex Patriarchicus No. 428, 1517–1805," *Byzantine and Modern Greek Studies* 7 (1981): 29–53. For the *hatt-i-sherif* of Murad IV (1631), see p. 43. A number of the Greek documents in this collection include complaints about excessive fees and other abuses.

[28] Oded Peri, *Christianity under Islam in Jerusalem: The Question of the Holy Sites in Early Ottoman Times* (Leiden: Brill, 2001): 194–195.

about Greek challenges to their altars, in other words, because they threatened the legal and political status of the Custody within the diverse Christendom of the Holy Land and thus its claim to its legitimizing authority. To make this case, we need to return to the descriptions of the disputes and confront the Islamic foundations of custodial authority in the Holy Places. The frequent mention of keys, doors, and lamps takes us into religious spaces carved up and regulated by Islamic law and granted to Christian authorities as privileges. Two questions orient the remaining discussion: Firstly, what did it mean to both Catholics and Greek Orthodox to "possess" altars? Secondly, what did it mean to the Latins and the Greeks to lose their altars to the other?

2.2 ISLAMIC LAW AND CHRISTIAN PRIVILEGES

2.2.1 *Islamic Law and the Custody of the Holy Land*

As an ecclesiastical institution administered by Catholic priests and devoted to Catholic pilgrimage, it is perhaps not surprising that Western scholarship on the Custody of the Holy Land has tended to focus upon its European origins and character. For the friars of our study, however, the Islamic foundations of custodial authority confronted them on a daily basis because the very existence of the Custody was predicated upon its recognition by Muslim rulers. The administration of the Custody, the performance of liturgical rites, and the usage of religious spaces all relied upon a complex web of privileges granted to the Custody over time by a succession of sultans dating back to the fourteenth century (and even earlier). As the Spanish priest Juan Cevero de Vera mused in his sixteenth-century pilgrimage account, in the Holy Land "the religion of Saint Francis exists solely through the grace of the Turks."[29] The most cherished privileges concerned the possession of altars in the Holy Places, for reasons that were political and legal as well as spiritual in nature. Latin altars were ritual sites that oriented Western pilgrimage, providing crucial points of contact between devout believer and the apostolic past. They were at the same time privileges that recognized a place for the Custody in Islamic structures of authority (legal, political) that were essential to the management of its pilgrimage. To understand, to begin

---

[29] Juan Ceverio de Vera, *Viaje de la Tierra Santa, y descripcion de Jerusalem, y del santo monte Libano, con relacion de cosas maravillosas, asi de las provincias de Levante como de las Indias de Occidente* (Madrid: Mathias Mares, 1598), 77.

with, how altars functioned as bearers of legal status we need to first understand them as constructs of Islamic law.

Islamic law is a rather broad term that encompasses a diverse body of juridical learning that evolved over the course of several centuries. For the friars and other Christians living under the rule of Mamluk and Ottoman Turkish rulers, two juridical traditions were especially influential in their affairs: imperial and *shari'a* law.[30] Imperial or dynastic law, as it is also sometimes called, was separate from *shari'a* law and expressed the authority of the sultan.[31]

Under imperial law, all places of worship associated with non-Muslim faiths belonged to the sultan, and it was his prerogative to grant usage of this space. With regard to the Holy Places, this meant that Christians required the permission of the sultan to worship there regardless of whether one was a subject or not. To "possess" a convent, chapel, hospice, or other religious building, in other words, meant to possess the right to use that space and it was codified in the form of an imperial decree. Under both Mamluk and Ottoman governance, imperial decrees took different forms by the sixteenth century. The firman is perhaps the most common one, though Franciscans also received others including the *hatt-i-serif* and *berat*.[32] The decree issued by the Mamluk Sultan al-Nasir, which established Latin jurisdiction in the Cenacle and the Basilica Holy Sepulcher in 1333, for example, was a *hatt-i-serif* (*Catserif, Catzerif*).[33]

---

[30] Important overviews include Wael B. Hallaq, *The Origins and Evolution of Islamic Law* (Cambridge: Cambridge University Press, 2005); and Ovamir Anjum, *Politics, Law, and Community in Islamic Thought: The Taymiyyan Moment* (Cambridge: Cambridge University Press, 2012). On the Ottoman context, see also Leslie Peirce, *Morality Tales: Law and Gender in the Ottoman Court of Aintab* (Berkeley: University of California Press, 2003); and Heyd, *Ottoman Documents*.

[31] Imperial or "dynastic" law issued from the office of sultan. Ottoman sultans ruled both by *shari'a* law and *Kanun* or dynastic (imperial) law. In 1453, following the conquest of Constantinople, Mehmet II issued a *Kanunname*, a codification of customary law. It operated mostly in tandem with Islamic law but could mitigate and even obviate Islamic law. Nuanced discussions on the different arenas of jurisprudence in the Ottoman Empire include Uriel Heyd, Oded Peri, and Leslie Peirce. On discussions of the polylegal nature of Ottoman law, see, for example, Ido Shahar, "Legal Pluralism and the Study of Shari'a Courts," *Islamic Law and Society* 15 (2008): 112–141.

[32] On the different kinds of decrees, see Heyd, *Ottoman Documents*. Heyd argues, however, that by the sixteenth century earlier distinctions had blurred to the point that a number of the decrees served similar functions.

[33] On the decree of 1342, see Felix del Buey and Cristóforo Alvis, "Orígenes de la custodia de Tierra Santa ayuda de los Reinos de Aragón, Nápoles y Castilla," *Archivo Iberoamericano* 65 (2005): 7–96. As suggested here, European orthography of some Ottoman

Imperial decrees were binding because the authority of the Sultan was absolute. Moreover, privileges could be withdrawn at any time, a reality that dogged the ministry of the friars throughout the eras of Mamluk and Ottoman rule. Prior to the seventeenth-century disputes with the Greeks, the friars found themselves shut out of Holy Places on a number of other occasions, most importantly from the Cenacle in 1551.[34] Disputes with other Christians over altars could similarly trigger a realignment of Christian jurisdictions in a given Holy Place as shown in the seventeenth-century disputes. Since decrees were only binding during the regime of the sitting sultan, the succession of a new ruler necessitated petitioning for the recognition of existing privileges. The friars kept a dossier of older decrees and testimonials to their privileges for this very purpose. One is still found in the archives of the Custody of the Holy Land in Jerusalem. From this dossier we can gather that it was more characteristic than not for incoming sultans to recognize existing privileges. Sultan Selim I (d. 1520), for example, abided by a well-established tradition of Islamic rule when he publicly recognized the privileges of the friars and the other Christian communities during his visit to Jerusalem in 1517. Selim's forces had taken control of the city only a few months previously, and his visit cemented the authority of the Ottoman regime over the region including over its religious minorities.

Altars in the Holy Places were privileges granted by Islamic rulers. They could be granted, withdrawn, and reallocated to other Christian communities at any time. Also crucial for interpreting the importance of altars for early modern Catholics is that privileges among the communities varied, in some cases substantially. Jurisdiction over an altar, for example, gave the presiding Christian tradition the right to control its liturgical usage. The friars enjoyed sole jurisdiction in the Cenacle, for example, a privilege that gave them full control of Christian liturgical rites at this shrine. This meant in practice that Christian communities had to seek the permission of the presiding community to worship at any of its altars. But possessing jurisdiction over an altar also did not necessarily guarantee control of the surrounding ritual space. As we have seen, many of the most important Holy Places contained altars belonging to different

administrative and legal terms varies. *Catserif* appears for *hatt-i-serif*, in particular, in many of my Western sources, including Mariano Morone da Maleo's well-known treatise, *Terra Santa nuovamente illustrata* (Piacenza: Giovanni Bazachi, 1669), 368.

[34] The loss of jurisdiction in 1511 is mentioned in several Franciscan accounts including the *Trattato* of Francesco Suriano.

religious communities, most notably the Basilica of the Holy Sepulcher and the Church of the Nativity. This history of multi-faith possession continues today, its Ottoman legal foundations forever enshrined in the Status Quo agreement that received international recognition during the nineteenth century.[35]

An equally complex web of jurisdictions operated around individual altars, which also significantly shaped ritual life within these spaces. Christians could negotiate a menu of privileges, each with a price – the right to officiate on certain feast days, for example, the number of lamps permitted on a given altar, and most valuable of all, the right to control access to that space. For the friars, one of the most cherished privileges took them outside the Holy Places into the streets of Jerusalem on Palm Sunday. The procession, which began outside the city gates at the town of Bethpage, recreated the triumphal arrival of Jesus in the holy city. The Franciscan *custos* played the role of Jesus riding an ass and surrounded by friars and pilgrims bearing palm leaves. Such a public display of Catholic devotion (and entering the city gates on horseback no less!) was not only frowned upon by Islamic authorities but also illegal and required permission from the *kadi* each time to hold the rite.[36] As the treatise of Francesco Suriano also underscores, the right to enclose a space through the building of walls and by possessing keys to doors and gates were also desirable privileges. Among the many achievements during his time in office, Suriano mentioned being especially proud of acquiring the keys to the Grotto of Gethsemane, the cave near the garden of Gethsemane where the disciples slept while Jesus stayed up to pray following the betrayal by Judas Iscariot. More generally, the friar celebrated the many keys acquired by the friars over the centuries to other holy sites – the Cenacle, the Tomb of the Virgin, the Grotto of the Nativity at Bethlehem, the church of Lazarus in Bethany, and the church of the Ascension on the Mount of Olives.[37] Appreciating the importance given by the Christian communities to controlling sacred space helps to explain, more to our purpose here, why keys and doors feature so prominently in Christian petitions to Ottoman authorities and the imperial decrees issued

---

[35] See, for example, Emmett, "The Status Quo Solution for Jerusalem."

[36] The procession receives more attention in Chapter 3. Peri also discusses it as a source of tension with local Muslims, in part because it was noisy. See Peri, *Christianity under Islam*, 86.

[37] Francesco Suriano, *Treatise of the Holy Land*, trans. Theophilus Bellorini and Eugene Hoade (Jerusalem: Franciscan Printing Press, 1949). On the Church of the Ascension, for example, see p. 118. On the Church of the Nativity, see p. 136.

in response. A petition from the Patriarch of Jerusalem to Ottoman authorities in 1630, for example, serves as a good example of this legal mapping of sacred space. The legal document, which has been translated by Speros Vryonis, presents us with a disputed sacred space neatly dissected and catalogued according to its material and liturgical attributes, transformed into a collection of privileges that could be presented in a legal claim for jurisdiction. The list of Greek privileges included the keys to the Grotto of the Nativity that were then held by the friars. The Greeks, as we know, were successful at this time and received, among other privileges, the "keys belonging to the two doors on the right and left which are in it, and the two pieces of garden on both sides of the Church."[38]

As shown thus far, imperial law intruded significantly into the operations of the Custody through its organization of sacred space. In doing so, it also overlapped and engaged with *hanafi* law, the branch of *shari'a* law that regulated state relations with religious minorities (*dhimmi*). This branch of jurisprudence can be traced back to the early years of Islamic conquest, when newly forming Islamic kingdoms wrestled with governing diverse religious populations. The Pact of Umar (738) was an early and important effort at codification. *Hanafi* law was embraced by both Mamluk and Ottoman regimes, both of which had long presided over diverse religious populations.[39] Though the friars were not subjects of the sultan because they remained the subjects of their respective European states, as Christians residing under his rule, they were bound by many of the same strictures on worship among other matters. Under *hanafi* law, for example, the friars were forbidden to evangelize Muslims. It also set clear restrictions upon the usage of religious space, an issue that is especially relevant to our understanding of Christian conflicts over altars. Like other Christians, the friars could not renovate their churches nor build new ones without the permission of Mamluk and Ottoman authorities, nor could they place symbols of their faith (crosses, bells) on the walls of the church. Within designated Christian spaces, however, they were able to perform the liturgical rites for themselves and other

---

[38] Speros Vryonis Jr., "The History of the Greek Patriarchate of Jerusalem As Reflected in Codex Patriarchicus No. 428, 1517–1805," *Byzantine and Modern Greek Studies* 7 (1981): 29–53.

[39] It fell to the *kadi*, for example, to ensure the implementation of both imperial and *hanafi* law.

Christians.[40] In the case of the friars, these designated spaces included not only their chapels in the Holy Places but also ones located in Franciscan convents as well as in the chapels attached to the palaces of European consuls.[41]

Hanafi law, along with imperial law, significantly shaped the nature and function of the Custody as a Catholic institution. It determined where, when, and how Catholics could worship in the Holy Places as well as in other parts of the Holy Land to a degree that deserves much more scholarly attention and which will receive closer attention in Chapter 3. For these reasons, in particular, we should consider the Custody an Islamic institution, since its very existence as a Catholic pilgrimage administration was predicated upon its regulation by Muslim authorities and Islamic law. Perhaps it is more accurate to describe it as a hybrid institution, since it was deeply imbedded in Catholic as well as Ottoman structures of authority and shaped by both cultures.

Some scholars may prefer the term Islamicate as a more accurate description for its hybridity, but I do think it is important to recognize that the institution functioned both *within* as well as *between* diverse governing structures, transgressing imperial boundaries, and as such functioned differently from the many Eastern Christian religious institutions (as well as some Catholic) that were directly governed by the Porte.[42] More to the point for the present inquiry, Catholic authorities from early on accepted the influence of Muslim authorities because it served their political and religious interests in the Holy Land to do so. The papal bull *gratias agimus* that established the Custody in 1342 makes this acceptance clear, since it explicitly reiterated the terms set out by Sultan al-Nasir Muhammad, including the restrictions on evangelization and the privileges allocated to the friars. Moreover, as mentioned with regard to the treatise of Franciscan Suriano, Franciscan chronicles and pilgrimage

---

[40] On these restrictions in the context of Ottoman Palestine, see Heyd, *Ottoman Documents*; and Peri, *Christianity under Islam*.

[41] The consulate chapels are discussed in Chapter 4.

[42] The conquest of the Balkan regions, for example, brought their Catholic populations under Ottoman jurisdiction, investing them with the status of *dhimmi*. These included members of Catholic/monastic communities. See, for example, the extensive work of Anton Molnar on Hungary, including *Le Saint-Siège, Raguse et les missions Catholiques de la Hongrie Ottomane 1572–1647* (Rome-Budapest: Biblioteca Acaemiae Hungariae, 2007) and the dissertation of Ana Sekulic on Ottoman Bosnia, "Conversion of the Landscape: Environment and Religious Politics in an Early Modern Ottoman Town," PhD diss., Princeton University, 2020.

treatises typically included lists of privileges, further indication of broad acceptance of Muslim regulation in the life of the Custody.[43]

2.2.2 *Legal Status and Christian Jurisdiction*

Accepting the influence of Ottoman authority in the life of the Custody was worth any moral quandary Catholic authorities faced about working with a non-Christian regime because it gave the Church legal access to the Holy Places, enabling the reestablishment of Western pilgrimage to the region. But just as importantly, it gave the Catholic Church legal standing in structures of authority necessary to protect and even promote the interests of the Latin community locally. Of particular importance was access to Ottoman courts. As mentioned earlier, the court of the *kadi* was the court of first instance in disputes between religious minorities, responsible for administering both imperial and *hanafi* law. Registers of the *kadi* of Jerusalem show that the friars were experienced users of the court long before the seventeenth century on a wide range of matters. It was at the court of the *kadi*, for example, that the friars sought permission to renovate crumbling chapels, pay the fees of visiting pilgrims, resolve contractual disputes with local workmen, as well as to complain about violations of their spiritual jurisdiction.

Moreover, surviving records of the Custody show that the friars were comfortable appealing to other jurisdictions when they disagreed with the decision of the *kadi*. Indeed, shopping for courts was as typical in Ottoman regions as it was in Europe during the Early Modern Period. Depending upon the issue, the friars could seek redress from the *Beylerbei* (*Beylerbeg*) of Damascus, the provincial official who oversaw the district of Jerusalem, or perhaps the local *mufti* who interpreted *shari'a* law and advised the *kadi*. Other powerful regional authorities appear from time to time as well, their influence reflecting the imperfect consolidation of Ottoman authority in the former Mamluk territories during the seventeenth century. As Amy Singer among others has argued, the Ottoman Porte preferred to work through local authorities in Palestine for most of the sixteenth century and even later rather than exercise direct

---

[43] One finds many examples in early modern pilgrimage treatises, a source explored extensively in this and later chapters. An extensive discussion is also provided in Francesco Quaresmio's *Historica Theologica e Moralis Terra Elucidatio* (Antwerp: Plantiniana Balthasaris Moreti, 1639; reprint, Jerusalem: Franciscan Printing Press, 1989).

control.[44] Doing so was a tried and true strategy of Ottoman conquest that contributed to the existence of a patchwork of overlapping jurisdictions in conquered regions including the Holy Land. The friars, for example, received jurisdiction over the site of the Annunciation in Nazareth in 1620/1621 through negotiations with Emir Fakhr-al-Din, a local Druze prince who was powerful in the region.[45] The site was associated with the birthplace of Mary, and the friars had an earlier convent there.[46] For the friars, however, the Ottoman Porte remained the highest authority and was a frequent resort of the friars because of their close connections with the Venetian and French ambassadors in Constantinople.

As the example of the site of the Annunciation suggests, the friars could use the courts not only to protect their privileges but also to expand the juridical and geographical reach of the Custody within the Holy Land. Indeed, it seems clear that friars were able to develop a working relationship with the Ottoman Turks shortly after the conquest. In 1519, *custos* Gabriele Bruno was given permission by the court of the *kadi* to build a large hospice for pilgrims in Rama (Al-Ram), a village just to the north of Jerusalem that lay on the pilgrimage route. A year later in 1520, *custos* Angelo da Ferraro was given permission to build another church.[47] Several more such projects were approved throughout the next century under Ottoman rule, most importantly the repair of the main dome of the Holy Sepulcher in the 1550s. In addition to the acquisition of the site of the Annunciation and subsequent construction of a small church there, the friars also acquired a convent on Mount Tabor (located in Galilee) in 1631 and the garden of Olives at Gethsemane in 1662.[48] In 1672, the

---

[44] Amy Singer, *Palestinian Peasants and Ottoman Officials: Rural Administration around Sixteenth-Century Jerusalem* (Cambridge: Cambridge University Press, 1994), 278–284. Cyrille Charon notes a similar approach to governance in Syria. Charon, "La Syrie de 1516 à 1855," *Echos d'Orient* 7 (1904): 278–284.

[45] Eugene Roger discusses this acquisition in his pilgrimage treatise. See Chapter 6. Roger was a fascinating figure. A Recollect friar, he was also one of the physicians of the emir, and a member of the Recollect community at Nazareth. Fakhr-al-Din was appointed emir of Arabistan by the Sultan in 1624, a move to bring the powerful local leader more firmly under Ottoman authority.

[46] Chad Emmett, *Beyond the Basilica: Christians and Muslims in Nazareth* (Chicago: University of Chicago Press, 1995), 100–101.

[47] Pietro Verniero di Montepeloso, "Croniche, ovvero Annali di Terra Santa del P. Pietro Verniero di Montepeloso," in *Biblioteca bio-bibliografica della Terra Santa e dell'Oriente Francescana*, vol. 5, ed. Girolamo Golubovich (Florence: Quaracchi Press, 1927), 118.

[48] See, for example, the correspondence in the Archivo General de Simancas (AGS) on the renovations on the Dome sent by friar Bonaficio. AGS sección de Estado, leg. 483, nos. 86, 87, 88 (1556–1557).

friars, once again with French support, were also able to confirm their ownership of Ein Karem, the complex associated with the birth cave of John the Baptist and located in the town of Ein Karem (Ayn Karim), which lies a few miles southwest of Jerusalem. At the time of its acquisition, the site included a Crusader church that was badly in need of restoration. Moshe Sharon argues, however, that even with French aid, local resistance, among other issues, kept the friars from formally renovating and occupying the site until much later in 1693.[49]

By granting permission to the friars and other Christian communities to renovate and/or build structures and acquire new places of worship, Ottoman officials showed that they, like their Mamluk counterparts, were willing to mitigate the strictures of *hanafi* law especially in matters pertaining to religious buildings. It is important to note as well that the friars and other Christians were not necessarily automatically at a disadvantage in legal cases involving Muslim subjects, especially if they could prove their claims to a priori possession. For example, the *kadi* ruled in favour of the friars in a dispute brought against them by a local sheikh named Sayh Daggani in 1614 over their possession of a cemetery on Mount Sion. The sheikh argued that the cemetery had once been the site of a *waqf* (charitable endowment).[50] Under Islamic law, this claim, if proven, would have privileged the sheikh because Muslim religious usage took precedence. As we may recall, the friars lost jurisdiction over the Cenacle in 1551 because the Sultan accepted claims that it was the Tomb of David and that it had once been the site of a mosque. In the case of the sheikh, however, the subsequent investigation found no evidence to verify his claims. To the contrary, it found significant evidence of Franciscan ownership stretching back to pre-Ottoman times.

Perhaps even more striking evidence comes from another dispute, this time concerning the Church of the Nativity. The friars, Greek Orthodox, and Armenian Christians each had altars here during the seventeenth century. But Muslims also visited the site, following in the footsteps of Muhammad who was believed to have visited it to offer prayers to the prophet Jesus during his Night Flight to Jerusalem. In the seventeenth century, Muslim interest in the site seems to have grown, and early

---

[49] Moshe Sharon, ed., *Corpus Inscriptionum Arabicarum Palaestinae*, CIAP 3 (Leiden: Brill, 2004), 155–157.
[50] Agustin Arce, *Documentos y textos para la historia de Tierra Santa y sus santuarios (1600–1700)*, vol. 1 (Jerusalem: Franciscan Printing Press, 1970), 74. The date of the judicial sentence was August 1614.

modern accounts describe imams setting up rest stations within the main choir of the Basilica, while the Greeks, Armenians, and Franciscans continued to lead worship at their own altars in other parts of the Church. In fact, the choir was in bad shape at this time, perhaps one reason why we do not find a concerted effort on the part of the three presiding Christian communities to have Muslim pilgrims legally removed until the last decades. The friars were clearly not happy about sharing space, however, in part because under Islamic law they were obliged to extend hospitality to visiting Muslims, in particular in the form of food and drink. This situation changed in the 1670s, when the Greeks obtained primary jurisdiction in the Church and fixed the roof of the choir. After decades of contention, a firman issued in 1675 forbade Muslim worship there, arguing that it was not "orthodox" to do so.[51] The incident is just one of many examples demonstrating the power of Islamic law to shape Christian experience in the early modern Holy Land through its regulation of sacred space. It also reveals a Latin Custody deeply imbricated in Ottoman political and juridical structures by the end of the sixteenth century through its acceptance of imperial and *hanafi* law.

2.2.3 Altars and the Confessionalization of the Holy Places

As Islamic privileges, altars anchored the Custody in local and imperial structures of authority, structures that could be called upon both to protect and advance its interests in a region that lay well beyond the frontiers of Catholic Europe. For these reasons alone, we can understand why church authorities were willing to invest significant funds and political capital during the seventeenth-century disputes with the Greek Orthodox. But just as importantly, the friars and their supporters had come to see their altars as Catholic in ways that suggest that one impact of Islamic jurisdiction in the Holy Places was the confessionalization of these spaces. To make this claim requires recognizing, to begin with, that it was characteristic of the Catholic tradition throughout its history to fill churches with beautiful ornaments and other works of art as acts of devotion to God and, secondly, that a related intent of this ornamentation of space was to articulate a distinctly "Catholic" identity. Signs of this catholicization of space can be glimpsed in the descriptions of the seventeenth-century disputes, in particular, Greek efforts to strip them

---

[51] Peri, *Christianity under Islam*, 103–106.

of their Catholic identity. To provide just two examples, in a letter sent in 1636, the Venetian ambassador informed the Porte that the friars found their former chapel in a derelict state, the door sealed, and filled with crows and other birds "who had filled it with their filth." According to the account, most of their art and devotional objects had been locked away and left to mold.[52] In the two letters written by Juan de Cañizares discussed earlier, the Franciscan commissioner also complained about material destruction. We should note that the letter dated December 1674 was signed by many of the Catholic leaders in Constantinople, including the heads of the Jesuit and Capuchin communities. Cañizares seems to have been delegated by the Venetian ambassadors and the brothers of the Holy Land to bring their case to Rome, one reason perhaps why we find the long list of ecclesiastical supporters here. The letter includes a healthy list of complaints against the Greek Orthodox in diverse places including Constantinople, the Holy Land, and other Ottoman territories. The Greek clergy, we are told, called the Latins disparaging names ("papisti, Aremyti, cani franchi"), denounced them from pulpits, and in a number of cases treated the friars and their chapels violently. On the island of Scios in 1665, "the Greeks violently usurped these churches, breaking their doors, statues and sacred stones [pietre sacre]." They also "stomped on their crucifixes" and "destroyed their altars."[53] Cañizares may have been referring to the shrine of the Holy Sepulcher in another passage when he wrote that the Greeks "took lamps that were given in the names of the great Christian rulers of Europe that normally burned day and night" and also "impeded with violence the function of our holy church."

The other letter dated 1675 provides a more expansive description of the recent destruction of Latin spaces in the Basilica of the Holy Sepulcher. Together, these letters drive home the material nature of these Christian conflicts, but through them we also glimpse religious spaces brimming with the sights, sounds, textures, and smells of Western Catholicism – for example, a grand lamp placed "in the name of the King of Spain" in the shrine of the Holy Sepulcher, which the Greeks complained left no room for their own, and a Latin chapel despoiled of

---

[52] ASVe dispacci 117 (April 7, 1636), f. 111. "... Cornacchie (crows) et altri animali volatili, che l'hanno riempita d'imonditie."

[53] APF, SC 1 (1675), ff. 447–452. "... usurporono violentemente di quelle chiese, spezzando le porte, Imagini, e Pietre sacre; Calpestrando (stomped on) Crocifissi; destruggendo Altari." Cañizares says that he was sent by the Venetian ambassador and the friars to Rome to ask for help.

not only Latin lamps but also of "ornaments, tapestries and every other thing belonging to the Latins" ("ornamenti tappezzarie è d'ogni altra cosa appartenente à la latini"), including a painting of the resurrection ("un quadro della resurrettione").[54] Unfortunately, modern visitors to the Holy Places will find little evidence of the late medieval and early modern ornamentation that once filled the Latin chapels, lost over the centuries to acts of deliberate destruction, the natural depredations of time, and changing tastes. Contemporary sources, thankfully, allow us to reconstruct, at least partially, what the disputed chapels used to look like for visiting pilgrims. Before the seventeenth century, chronicles and correspondence mention shipments of wood, iron, and precious stone that arrived from Europe for use in renovating several of the Holy Places, including for the repair of the Dome of the Holy Sepulcher during the 1550s. Following its completion, then *custos* Bonifacio Stephano da Stagna purportedly proceeded to fill the space under the completed Dome with white marble and various ornaments.[55] During the seventeenth century, more detail emerges from the financial registers of the commissioners of the Holy Land, many of which can be found in the National Historical Archives in Madrid as well as in the archives of the Congregation of the Propaganda Fide. These registers tend to be rather straightforward lists and not terribly descriptive, but they do allow us to track the movement of art, liturgical paraphernalia, fine textiles, as well as other supplies used for the renovation and ornamentation of chapels.[56] We also cannot overlook the descriptions of the Holy Places provided in early modern pilgrimage treatises. Given the importance of the Custody for members of the Franciscan tradition, it is not surprising to find their accounts among the most detailed. The careful architectural renderings and descriptions of interiors provided by friar Bernardino Amico in his popular treatise *I pianti imagini* evoke a Western Catholic presence in the

---

[54] APF, SC 1 (1675), 450.
[55] Lemmens, ed., *Registro de' fatti memorabili*, 11. Bonificio da Stagna also appears as da Ragusa in some records because he came from this city. See Adam Beaver, "A Holy Land for the Catholic Monarchy: Palestine in the Making of Modern Spain, 1469–1598," PhD diss., Harvard University, 2008, 52–57.
[56] See, for example, the register submitted by Nunez Sanchez to the Propaganda Fide for 1655/1656, APF, *Scripture riferite nei congressi* (SC) Terra Santa, 1. For example, it mentions paintings carried by Friar Ripol intended for the Holy Sepulcher. On the registers, see, for example, Felicita Tramontana, "Per ornamento e servizio di questi santi luoghi: L'arrivée des objets de dévotion dans les sanctuaires de Terre Sainte (xviie siècle)," *Archives de sciences sociales des religions. Façonner l'objet de dévotion chrétien. Fabrication, commerce et circulations (vers XVII–XIX siècles)* 183 (2018): 227–243.

Holy Places that would have been very familiar to its devout readers. He comments, for example, on a painting of the virgin and Joseph that lay over the marble altar in the Grotto of the Nativity. The biblical figures were depicted on their knees "in atto di vedere & adorare il nato Bambino." Praising the artistry of the painter, Amico Amico mentions his skillful rendering of the animals at the birth of Christ and a scene in one corner of the painting of the shepherds visited by the angels in their field.[57] As Amico's description suggests, by the sixteenth century the classically inspired realism of Renaissance art had become another visible representation of the Catholic tradition in the Holy land, one that would have made Latin chapels familiar to visiting pilgrims, while visually distinguishing the Latin community from the other Christian traditions in the same Holy Places.

As we saw from Pierre de la Tressan's description of mosaics and lamps in the Greek Orthodox chapel at the site of Calvary, the friars were by no means the only Christian community to clothe their altars in the art of their own tradition. Indeed, doing so was a long-standing practice among the many different communities that can be traced back much earlier than the seventeenth century. The Basilica of the Holy Sepulcher, in particular, emerges in medieval and early modern accounts as a miniature Christendom unto itself, its many altars and chapels laden with textiles, artwork, and liturgical objects that advertised the religious identity of the presiding Christian community. These visible manifestations of a diverse Christendom suggest that one impact of Islamic jurisdiction was the confessionalization of the Holy Places. To argue that Christian shrines were "confessionalized" perhaps risks using a term that embodies a complex set of meanings more appropriate to discussions of Reformation Europe.[58] However, there, amid the growing religious divide of the Western tradition after 1517, outer forms of worship

---

[57] Bernardino Amico, *Trattato delle piante & immagini de sacri edifizi di Terra Santa: Disegnate in Ierusalemme secondo le regole della Prospettiva & vera misura della lor grandezza Dal R.P. E, Bernardino Amico dal Gallipoli dell' Ord. di S. Francesco de Minori Osservanti* (Rome: Pietro Cecconcelli, 1620), 1–2. "Si vedono anco espressi gl'animali, l'efigie di una notte, che riceve il suo splendore dal Bambino, con mirabilissimo artificio del Pittore, il quale anco ha espresso in una parte più lontana un vago paese, dove si vede l'Angelo ch'apparue alli Pastori, che custodivano il gregge, & una parte di esso gregge tanto naturale, che più non si può desiderare."

[58] For a particularly useful overview of the historiography, see the introduction to Bodo Nischan, John M. Headley, Hans Joachim Hillerbrand, Anthony J. Papalas, eds., *Confessionalization in Europe, 1550–1700: Essays in Honor and Memory of Bodo Nishan* (Aldershot: Ashgate, 2004).

functioned as one of many mechanisms for defining local Protestant and Catholic identities. In this way at least – as visible manifestations of the Catholic tradition – Catholic altars in the Holy land fulfilled a similar purpose as did the altars of the other Christian faiths. Within the diverse Christendom of the Holy Land, Catholic chapels broadcasted the distinctive values and forms of worship of the Catholic faith while staking a claim to a place alongside the other traditions in the Holy Places. Moreover, the stripping of the altars described earlier in the letter of the commissioner Cañizares points to a legitimating function for altars that was no less meaningful to Latin authorities and which would also have been familiar to the friars from their experience of confessional relations in Reformation Europe. This legitimating function hinged upon, on the one hand, a conception of sacred spaces as carriers of divine authority and, on the other, profound Christian disagreement over the nature of the "true" faith.[59] Within this ideological construction of sacred space, erring faiths were a source of pollution that needed to be removed. Consider this view in light of Cañizares description of the events that transpired at the Holy Sepulcher following the arrival of the Patriarch of Jerusalem in 1675.

Patriarch Dositheos came in the company of an armed Ottoman retainer (*capigi*) bearing a firman that handed over Latin altars in the Holy Sepulcher to the Patriarch.[60] The Greeks who accompanied the Patriarch (likely members of the Brotherhood of the Holy Sepulcher among others) then set to work in the Latin chapels. As discussed earlier, Cañizares describes the deliberate destruction of lamps, tapestries, ornaments, and paintings. The Greek clerics also broke (*spezzato*) "many other things" as well that they found in another part of the Church. A particularly powerful and evocative moment in his account, however, concerned the altars themselves. In preparation for the celebration of the

---

[59] See, for example, Eamon Duffy's *Stripping of the Altars* (New Haven: Yale University Press, 1992); Eric P. Nelson, *The Legacy of Iconoclasm: Religious War and the Relic Landscape of Tours, Blois and Vendôme 1550–1750* (St. Andrews: University of Saint Andrew's Center for French History and Culture, 2013); and Alexandra Walsham, *The Reformation of the Landscape: Religion, Identity, and Memory in Early Modern Britain and Ireland* (Oxford: Oxford University Press, 2011).

[60] APF, TS 1 1675, 449–550. "... quale spogliarono dello lampade de Principi Christissimi d'ornamenti tappezzarie è d'ogni altra cosa appartenente à I latini fino ad un [Quadro] della resurrettione. Lo levarono et tutto spezzato si trovò la mattina in un Canton della Chiesa, e per celebrar i Greci la Domenica seguente in domino santo sepolcro lo havorono p.ma [prima] con acqua calda e sapone, tenendo per contaminati, e profanati quell' Altari, dove celebrano I sacerdoti latini."

mass the following Sunday, the Greeks also scrubbed the altars with hot water and soap because, he says, they considered "the places where the Latin priests celebrated to be contaminated and profaned." In these passages, Cagnizares describes religious spaces violently stripped of all the manifestations of Latin worship and then scrubbed of its liturgical presence. Through their stripping and cleansing of the altars, the Greek priests publicly and viscerally communicated their conception of these as profaned spaces because they had been tainted by the presence of the Latin faith. Now cleansed, these altars were restored to their sacred purity and ready for use by their new and more worthy possessors, the Greek Orthodox.

To be sure, the level of violence described in these disputes was not entirely without precedent. Moreover, even smaller, more mundane conflicts, often included acts of removal. We may recall, for example, that in 1604 the Franciscans accused the Syrians of removing marble from a Franciscan chapel in the Holy Sepulcher even as they faced accusations themselves from the Armenians of removing their lamps from the Church of the Nativity. Such acts of removal challenged the legal status of the possessing community, but they could also be read as acts of spiritual erasure because the material objects manifested the identity of the presiding community. Indeed, as a historian of the European Reformations, it is hard not to interpret them as rites of purification since they occurred with seeming regularity and were also aimed at the removal of polluted rivals from revered sacred spaces. After all, similar material conflicts were playing out simultaneously in European churches, cemeteries, and other sacred spaces between Protestant and Catholic communities.[61] Moreover, inasmuch as they were rites of purification, they were also rites of legitimization because the removal of the "other" certified the perfection of the now presiding tradition. This interpretation gains further support when we ponder the special authority of the Holy Land in Christian thought as the *place* of Christ. In Chapter 3, we will delve much more deeply into the spiritual meaning invested by Catholics in maintaining a material presence for their tradition in the Holy Land. For our purposes here, however, it is important to keep in mind that for devout Catholics

---

[61] On intra-faith conflict that seems especially relevant as a point of comparison, see, among others, Walsham, *Reformation of the Landscape*; Barbara Diefendorf, *Beneath the Cross: Catholics and Huguenots in Sixteenth Century Paris* (Oxford: Oxford University Press, 1991); and the wonderful collection of articles edited by Andrew Spicer and Will Coster, *Sacred Space in Early Modern Europe* (Cambridge: Cambridge University Press, 2005).

and other Christians, the Holy Places lay at the apex of all sacred spaces. This was because these marked the original sites associated with the life of Christ and the apostles and a shared a belief in their function as authentic vessels of apostolic authority. To possess an altar was desirable, in other words, because it imbedded that Christian tradition at the very source of Christian perfection, giving direct access to Christ's sacralizing power and in doing so manifesting the spiritual worthiness of its presiding community.

Catholics and the Greek Orthodox alike shared with one another a belief in the sacralizing power of the Holy Places, and they also agreed with one another that there was only one true Christian faith. For this reason, the two traditions cast their rival as the erring one, who contaminated the sacred spaces it occupied. This view underlies friar Henri Castela's sweeping generalization that the Eastern Christians "neither preserved nor revered the churches they stole from the Catholics, and instead pillaged, burned them and committed all sorts of prophanities."[62] Drafted at the height of the disputes with the Greek Orthodox, the alms placard of 1655 discussed earlier also mentions Holy Places "prophaned" by the Greek Orthodox and Armenians. These Christians, according to the placard, were "schismatics" and "slaves of the Turks," denunciations that would have been well understood by Catholics back in Europe. The Greeks and Armenians were "schismatics" because the Eastern traditions broke from the "true" Church of Rome. They were also subjects of the Turks and thus tainted through association with another erring faith. The list of profaned spaces intermingles with ones occupied by Muslims and Greeks, further evidence that the Catholic church considered the Greek and Armenian traditions just as illegitimate as that of Islam: the house of Anna was made into a mosque, the site of the wedding of Cana in Galilee was turned into a "stable" by the Turks, while the house of St. John the Evangelist was a church of the "Greek schismatics." The sight of all this desecration, the placard goes on to say, "brings tears to ones' eyes."[63]

---

[62] Henri Castela, *Le guide et adresse pour ceux qui veulent faire le S. Voiage de Hierusalem par V.P.F. Henry Castela Tolosain religieux observantin et confesseur des Dmes religieuses a Bordeau* (Paris: Chez Laurens Sonnius, 1604), f. 37.
[63] APF Conti Terra Santa, III, SC Miscellanea 1. "Relatione del Misero Stato nel quale si trovano I luoghi santi di Gerusalemme." The original of the two passages is the following: "Vergogna de' Christiani; Li Greci, & armeni, son scismatici, e schiavi de' Turchi," and "... sentasi colle lagrime alli occhi, à qual segno si li rimiriamo del tutto profanati."

That Ottoman privileges could become markers of Christian legitimacy may perhaps seem contradictory in an era when Christians and Muslims regarded the other faith as imperfect and even corrupting. The fact remains that in the specific context of the early modern Holy Land, the intersection of Islamic law, Christian spirituality, and sacred space made Latin jurisdiction over altars immensely significant as markers of Catholic perfection and thus spiritual legitimacy. Pilgrimage accounts produced during the sixteenth and seventeenth centuries make this connection between Islamic privilege and Catholic perfection especially clear. The French Franciscan Jean Thenaud, for one, crowed with no little satisfaction about the greater status of the Catholic tradition in the region because of its possession of beautiful, important religious spaces. Thenaud, who traveled to Jerusalem in 1511/1512, describes the Church in Bethlehem, for example, as "so beautiful that one will hardly find any similar to it in length, size, height and sumptuous decoration."[64] Francesco Suriano similarly measured the length and width of the Latin Chapel of the Apparition in the Holy Sepulcher, the main chapel for Franciscan divine offices in the Basilica, noting that "ours was the largest and airiest of the lot." His account of the Easter processional is especially detailed, describing the usage of vestments of gold brocade and gold vases as well as the prayers and psalms of the liturgy.[65] Forty lamps were burning at all times under the surveillance of two friars. In a similar way, the visit to the Church of the Nativity in Bethlehem became an opportunity to praise the king of England for donating a magnificent leaden roof. According to Suriano, the roof was admired by all: "and therein God was praised both by the Christians and the infidels."[66]

2.3 CHRISTIAN PRECEDENCE, SACRED HISTORY, AND RELIGIOUS AND POLITICAL CHANGE

For pilgrims and the Franciscan brothers of the Holy Land, the location and number of altars, the size of the spaces, and their beauty manifested

---

[64] Jean Thenaud, *Le voyage outremer* (c. 1525; reprint, Geneva: Slatkine Press, 1971), 89–91. The full passage is the following: "qui est si belle que n'en ay veu gueres aultres si singulieres en longueur, largeur, haulteur et sumptuosité de matiere, parce quelle est toute encroustée et pavée de marbe avecques cinquante telles coulompnes que celles qui sont à l'entrée de Nostre Dame la Rotonde à Romme."

[65] Suriano, *Treatise of the Holy Land*, 49–51.

[66] Suriano, *Treatise of the Holy Land*, 134–135. The specific date is not given, but his account ended prior to the Reformation and so the king of England was clearly still very Catholic.

the greater perfection of the Latin tradition among all the Christian traditions in the region. It is clear from the same accounts, moreover, that Eastern Christians countered with their own highly decorated spaces and distinctive acts of devotion, convinced of their own spiritual worthiness. Working within the tight web of legal constraints, the various Christian communities used their artistic skills, liturgical training, and wealth to delineate a place for their own tradition in the homeland of Christ. And as the above examples also suggest, the Catholic tradition did not simply work around Islamic regulations to express Catholic values but *through* them, investing these with meaning as markers of Catholic perfection and leadership. If we turn specifically to the seventeenth-century disputes, we notice that the legal language resonated with this meaning as well. The many accusations of fraud, theft, and forgery that appear in documents from both sides evoke entangled conceptions of spiritual and legal illegitimacy, investing spiritual worthiness in the lawful possession of sacred space. As the legal cases discussed here also made clear, the act of possessing an altar was simultaneously an act of de-possession because it entailed the removal of the legal jurisdiction and the trappings of another faith, at times violently. Oded Peri has argued that Ottoman authorities were shocked at the level of violence between the Christian communities in the Holy Places, considering it something deeply rooted in Christian spirituality and difficult to understand. Indeed, Peri suggests that Mamluk rulers carved up the Holy Places into multiple Christian jurisdictions with peacemaking in mind, hopeful that ensuring the access of multiple communities would temper intra-Christian hostility.[67] Whether this was truly the intent of Mamluk authorities – lucre seems to have been just as important a concern – juridical regulations did little to end conflict over space. Indeed, they may have done a great deal to encourage competition, since jurisdiction was fluid and subject to constant negotiation through resort to the courts and other legal authorities. In fact, one cannot understand the escalation of violence that seems to have accompanied the disputes between the Latin and Greek Orthodox without recognizing the persistent sense of anxiety stimulated by legal systems that facilitated the frequent oscillation of possession from one community to the other over time.

And yet the prolonged nature and intensity of the Latin-Greek conflicts of the seventeenth century is striking. Also striking is the fact that the

---

[67] As a form of peacemaking, for example, see Peri, *Christianity under Islam*, 97–98.

disputes centered upon jurisdiction in the two most revered of the Holy Places. As discussed earlier, location in the Holy Places mattered to Christians. A hierarchy of holiness also governed the Holy Land, investing certain places with special authority because of their proximity to the most important soteriological moments in the life of Christ. Indeed, for most Western pilgrims, the visitations of the Church of the Nativity and the Holy Sepulcher were precisely the point of the pilgrimage.

Taken together, the persistent nature of the conflicts and preoccupation with jurisdiction in these Holy Places argues for another dimension of meaning infusing the disputes. This meaning was one rooted in a long history of spiritual contestation between the two Christian communities, a contestation that seems to have been reinvigorated in the sixteenth century in response to more recent forces of change. In this final section, we will probe each of these dimensions in turn, beginning with the influence of sacred history. The disputes illuminate rival sacred histories animating the disputes over altars, histories that suggest that at stake in the conflicts was a much more ambitious claim to Christian primacy. Particularly revealing in this regard are the many discussions in the sources over the status of Christian precedence, an Ottoman privilege, which, along with the possession of the most important altars, had become a highly valued marker of Christian authority and leadership within the diverse Christian context of the Holy Land. It was because it had become a valued marker of Christian leadership, moreover, that we can understand why the seventeenth-century disputes galvanized international support, in particular that of the papacy and the Byzantine Patriarch of Constantinople.

2.3.1 *Christian Precedence and Sacred Histories*

The issue of Christian precedence echoes throughout the seventeenth-century disputes, asking us to probe its particular significance for both the Latin and Greek communities. That it was another desirable Ottoman privilege is clear. What it meant in practical terms for its holder, however, is more difficult to determine even though it became a highly sought-after marker of Christian status among the many Christian communities of the Holy Land. One problem is that the legal language could be rather vague. Most commonly, it seems to have concerned holding first of place or precedence among Christians in ceremonial rites, including political and/or civic ceremonies and liturgical rites in the Holy Places. Moreover, the privilege varied in its form and nature and was often adapted to local contexts. Under Mamluk rule, for example, the Latin community held liturgical precedence during shared festivals and notably during the Easter rites in the Holy Sepulcher. One notable exception was the procession during the rite of the Holy Fire, which was traditionally led by Greek Orthodox priests. The Holy Fire was the most important ritual in the Greek Orthodox Easter rites and one that typically involved the participation of other Christian communities. Given that one does find other exceptions, it seems fair to say that the privilege of "precedence" at least in terms of liturgical rites was much murkier in practice than initially suggested by the decrees, subject to local, informal interfaith negotiations in the Holy Places.[68] In comparison, precedence in political ceremonials seems to have been more straightforward, granting its holder the privilege of walking in front of the other Christian communities in important public processions. One of the most important of these kinds of events during the Early Modern Period was the visitation of important Ottoman authorities. Even during the era of Mamluk Rule, the Greek Orthodox traditionally held this right as first among the Christian communities. The Greek Patriarch was the first of the local religious leaders to greet Sultan Selim I, for example, when he arrived in Jerusalem in 1517.

While the friars would no doubt have welcomed it in political ceremonials as well, their legal cases with the Greek Orthodox suggest that they were most concerned about precedence in liturgical rites, a privilege that they had come to consider legitimately theirs by the start of the period under consideration in this study. In a letter dated May 1, 1630, for example, written during the first of the major disputes, then Venetian ambassador Giovanni Cappello wrote to the Franciscan *custos* that one of his central objectives was to ensure that the friars and pilgrims would continue "to hold precedence among the Christian nations ... and that no one can celebrate in the Holy Places ... without the permission of the fathers."[69] Precedence featured as a central issue in the disputes of the 1670s as well, at least according to the Franciscan commissioner Cañizares. In his letter dated 1675, he insisted that the Greeks "wish

---

[68] For a discussion of Christian precedence, see, in particular, Peri, *Christianity under Islam*, 100–101; and Panchenko, *Arab Orthodox Christians*, 272–275. Panchenko argues that Greek precedence during the ritual of the Holy Fire was normative even before the change in the Gregorian calendar in 1582, which saw the Latin Easter rites move to a different date.

[69] "... ma che porrino officiar continuar officiar a il loro ... secondo V antico uso senza ... molestie." ASVe Bailo 109 (May 1, 1630), letter 1.

[ed] in everything precedence, that they did not have." In their letters, Cappello and Cañizares were making two important claims. First, that precedence was a central issue for both Christian communities, and second, that it rightfully belonged to the Latins. Unfortunately for the Franciscans and their supporters, the Greek Orthodox were no less convinced in their own claim to precedence, a conviction that is well on display in a remarkable collection of documents produced by the Patriarchate of Jerusalem during the time of the legal disputes studied here.

The collection, known as the Codex Patriarchus no. 428, comprises part of a much larger manuscript collection gathered and published by the nineteenth-century archivist and historian A. Papadopoulos-Kerameus. Spero Vryonis, who has studied it, suggests that the authenticity of some of the legal decrees is difficult to determine. Legal "fictions," however, were not uncommon among the religious communities living under Ottoman governance, and at times these were even accepted on both sides of the disputes.[70] What is important for our purpose here is to understand the objective of its compilers – namely, to create a legal history of Greek Orthodox precedence under Islamic law. Of particular relevance in this regard is a rather lengthy document entitled "Ierousalem katapatoumene" (Downtrodden Jerusalem). The text was the work of Procopius of Nazianus, the official dragoman. As the dragoman, he was learned in Arabic and likely Turkish as well as Greek and represented the institution in the Ottoman courts in its disputes. One of the five parts of the history concerned conflicts with the Latins over the Holy Places and another the similarly long rivalry between the Greeks and the Armenians.[71] Along with this treatise, the codex includes copies of earlier Islamic decrees dating back to the era of Abbasid rule in the eighth century as well as to more recent Ottoman rulers. Of these, one is a copy of the *hatt-i-sherif* issued by Murad IV in 1631 that "restored" the Latin altars to Greek jurisdiction. Addressed to the *kadi* and *emirouran* (local official) of Jerusalem, the decree reiterates a number of accusations made by the Greeks in an earlier petition to the Porte. Referring to the disputed shrines "anciently" belonging to the Greeks, it notes that the Latins were late arrivals in the Holy Places and used trickery and fraud to seize jurisdiction. What is more, it states that the loss of these ancient privileges

---

[70] On the veracity of the documents and the political use of legal "fictions," see Vryonis, "History of the Greek Patriarchate," 36.
[71] On the treatise, see Vryonis, "History of the Greek Patriarchate," 33–34.

had directly led to the decline of the influence of the local Greek Orthodox community: "the people of the Greeks fled afar and grew weak." This statement is particularly intriguing for its implication that the status of precedence went hand in hand with local Christian authority. In other words, the deprivation of precedence prefigured, and perhaps even caused, the decline of Greek influence in the Holy Land.

As should be clear from this discussion, both the Latin and Greek communities asserted claims to Christian precedence throughout the legal conflicts because it had become another valued marker of Christian authority and leadership within the diverse Christian demography of the Holy Land. That they were relying upon an Ottoman privilege to make their claims to Christian primacy further underscores the centrality of Ottoman structures of authority in shaping Christian relations and modes of spiritual engagement. Certainly, it seems clear at the very least, that the Ottoman Porte considered itself the arbiter of Christian authority vis-à-vis the ordering of their religious processions. As the decree states quite bluntly, "we have acknowledged that the patriarch of the Greeks is worthy to command them."[72] What is also clear from the petitions, decrees, and other documents produced during the disputes is that the two Christian communities found support for their claims to Christian primacy in their long histories of spiritual engagement in the Holy Places. These histories articulated competing conceptions of the Christian past, pasts that they traced through periods of Christian as well as Muslim rule to articulate claims to Christian primacy in the Holy Land.

For the Greek Orthodox, the past that most mattered was the era of Byzantine rule. As the Greek petition reminded Ottoman authorities, the Latins were "late comers" to the Holy Places in comparison and had no right to their jurisdiction. Certainly, if we consider the claim of longevity alone, the Greeks had a point. Though the Nestorian, Syriac, and Coptic Christians could claim as a long, or even longer, presence in the Holy Land, the Greek liturgical rites were the most visible of the Christian rites in the Holy Places from the fourth century when Emperor Constantine began promoting Jerusalem as a center of Christian pilgrimage. Egeria described the rites performed at several of the Holy Places during her own travels to the region at the end of the fourth century, which involved visitations of the Holy Sepulcher, the Church of the Nativity, and the

---

[72] Vryonis, "History of the Greek Patriarchate," 43.

Mount of Olives among other shrines.[73] It was during this period as well that Greek Orthodox monasteries began appearing in the Palestinian desert, communities that became instrumental in shaping liturgical traditions in Jerusalem and around the Holy Land over the course of the next centuries. By the time of the first of the medieval crusades in the eleventh century, and really throughout the Early Modern Period as well, the Greek Orthodox tradition was the most prominent and influential of the liturgical traditions in the Holy Land.[74]

While the legal petitions of the Greek Orthodox reminded Ottoman authorities of the community's early arrival in the Holy Land, they devoted even more attention to tracing the numerous privileges that they received during the long periods of Muslin governance. Indeed, Islamic law comprised another thread in the construction of a long sacred past in the Holy Places for both Christian communities. To be sure, the friars may well have been correct when they accused the Greek Orthodox of forging a firman granting them precedence that purportedly dated to the seventh century. The fact remains that the Greeks did manage to retain liturgical privileges in the Holy Places long after the Byzantine Empire lost the Holy Land to the Ummayad dynasty in the seventh century. The brief restoration of Byzantine authority in the Holy Land under Emperor Constantine IX Monomachus (1042–1055) in the eleventh century once again privileged the Greek liturgical rites, though Greek influence diminished once again during the years of Crusader rule in Jerusalem.[75] Throughout these many centuries, however, whether under the rule of Muslim or Christian rulers, the Greek Orthodox community remained a vital liturgical presence in the Holy Places. Moreover, in addition to this long liturgical presence, the Greek Orthodox Patriarch of Jerusalem could brandish an array of privileges acquired over the centuries of Muslim rule that recognized their place as first among the Christian communities.

---

[73] On Egeria and the early pilgrimage, see, among others, Annabel Jane Wharton, "The Baptistery of the Holy Sepulcher in Jerusalem and the Politics of Sacred Space," *Dumbarton Oaks Papers* 46 (1992): 313, 325.

[74] An important recent work on the medieval context and evolution of the Byzantine rites is Daniel Galadza, *Liturgy and Byzantinization in Jerusalem* (Oxford: Oxford University Press, 2018). A very useful overview on the engagement of these traditions is Alexander Rentel, "Byzantine and Slavic Orthodoxy," in *The Oxford History of Christian Worship*, ed. Geoffrey Wainwright and Karen B. Westerfield Tucker (Oxford: Oxford University Press, 2006), 254–306.

[75] See, for example, Robert Ousterhout, "Rebuilding the Temple: Constantine Monomachus and the Holy Sepulcher," *Journal of the Society of Architectural Historians* 48 (2989): 66–78.

Since the Latin tradition made inroads into the Holy Places during the era of Crusader rule in Jerusalem, the Patriarchs of Jerusalem were not wrong when they described the Franciscan brothers as latecomers. To be sure, the Franciscans protested this assertion by insisting that the Catholic tradition was an authentic continuation of the early Christian church. In reality, however, the Latin clergy owed the establishment of the Catholic tradition to the era of Crusader rule in Jerusalem, when Catholic clergy were placed in charge of the liturgical rites in the major Holy Places. To this day, visible markers of this Latin past remain in many of the Holy Places, serving as important witnesses to a living Latin history that also informed their sense of mission in the region. It was a past that the friars took pains to share with visiting pilgrims as well as to incorporate into their chronicles and pilgrimage treatises.[76] More to our immediate purpose here, the early modern rivalry between the two Christian communities may have had its origins in this era of Crusader rule. Bernard Hamilton has argued that while Crusader rulers allowed the Greek Orthodox to worship in Jerusalem, their access was much more strictly regulated. Just as importantly, they refused to allow the Patriarch to oversee Christian rites.[77] Centuries later, memories of this liturgical banishment clearly still rankled Greek Orthodox leaders who described it as a period in which Greek privileges suffered badly.[78]

While the Latin-Greek rivalry in the Holy Places may have begun under Crusader rule, the era of Mamluk rule saw it flourish. This was not immediately the case, however. The friars fled Jerusalem following the Mamluk conquest, retreating to their convents on Cyprus. In their absence, the Eastern Christian communities began to reassert their claims to jurisdiction, and the Greek Orthodox community managed to reclaim its former status as first among Christians in the Holy Land under the

---

[76] Megan C. Armstrong, "Jerusalem in the Reinvention of the Catholic Tradition, 1517–1700," in *Layered Landscapes: Early Modern Religious Space Across Faiths and Cultures*, ed. Eric Nelson and Jonathan Wright (Routledge, 2017), 1–25.

[77] On the Latin rites during the Crusades, see, for example, Bernard Hamilton, "The Impact of Crusader Jerusalem on Western Christendom," *Catholic Historical Review* 80 (1994): 698. Orthodox Eastern Christians were allowed to keep their rites and churches but subject to Western Church hierarchy. See also his book, *The Latin Church in the Crusader States: The Secular Church* (London: 1980), 159–211.

[78] See, for example, Hamilton, "Impace of Crusader Jerusalem," and Richard B. Rose, "Church Union Plans in the Crusader Kingdoms: An Account of a Visit by the Greek Patriarch of Jerusalem Leontius to the Holy Land, AD. 1177–1178," *The Catholic Historical Review* 73 (1987): 377.

leadership of the Patriarch of Jerusalem.[79] By the 1320s, however, the friars had returned to Jerusalem, and the formal establishment of the Custody in 1342 strengthened their foothold in the diverse religious culture of the Holy Land. Whether the Greek codex is correct in suggesting that the Latins held a favoured status vis-à-vis the Greeks and other Christian communities from this time forward is difficult to say given the often challenging relations between the Custody and the Mamluk regime. And yet the era of Mamluk rule did see the jurisdiction of the Custody expand to a degree that would not have engendered friendly relations with the Greek Orthodox. One can well imagine the resentment of succeeding patriarchs as they watched the steady accumulation of new convents, hospices, and altars by their Latin rivals during the course of the fourteenth and fifteenth centuries. Indeed, it seems quite clear that the Latins did enjoy precedence in the liturgical rites in the Basilica of the Holy Sepulcher from the fourteenth century onwards. A firman issued by Sultan al-Nasir Muhammad in 1309, over two decades before the formal establishment of the Custody, gave the friars exclusive right to live in the Basilica. Two decades later in 1332/1333, friar Roger Guerin managed to negotiate Franciscan precedence in the rites. As Yamit Rachman-Schrire has argued, precedence in this case gave the friars liturgical priority at times when space in the multi-faith shrine was limited.[80] In practice, it likely meant that Latin clergy led multi-faith processions and presided over some of the more important, shared rites, in particular at Easter. A number of pilgrimage treatises mention that the friars enjoyed legal precedence at the Church of the Nativity as well by the 1340s. One, produced by a Russian traveler in the late fourteenth century, for example, quoted a Greek Orthodox cleric who said that the Franciscans "owned" the Church of the Nativity.[81]

Why Mamluk rulers would favour the Latin community over the Greek Orthodox is a good question given that the Greeks not only

---

[79] The petition submitted by Patriarch Dositheos in 1706 (see n. 7) reiterated the same charges – recognition by previous caliphs of Greek Orthodox primacy and Latin usurpation of these privileges. Çolak, "Between the Ottoman Central Administration and the Patriarchates of Antioch, Jerusalem and Alexandria," 104–105.

[80] Rachman-Schrire, "Christ's Unction and the Material Realization of a Stone in Jerusalem," in *Natural Materials of the Holy Land the Visual Translation of Place, 500–1500*, ed. Renana Bartal, Neta Bodner, and Bianca Kuhnel (London: Routledge, 2017), 216–229. On the firman, see Golubovich, ed., *Biblioteca bio-bibliografica*, vol. 3, 128–130.

[81] Martiniano Roncaglia, "Sons of St. Francis in the Holy Land," *Franciscan* Studies 10 (1950), 281, ft. 88. "Itineraire Russes."

enjoyed a longer historical presence in the Holy Places but were also much more numerous. One could perhaps point to the increasing integration of the Mamluk Empire in Mediterranean trading networks during the fourteenth and fifteenth centuries and a desire to cultivate powerful European allies to buffer the influence of an expanding Ottoman Empire.[82] Martiniano Roncaglia suggests as well that Mamluk sultans were eager to reward the Latin tradition for its considerable investment in the renovation of the Holy Places during these centuries, investments that helped to promote the pilgrimage trade more generally. He mentions, among other examples, the significant funds gathered from Europe by the *custos* Gerard Chauvet in 1398 to pursue extensive renovations to the roof of the Church of the Nativity in Bethlehem. Wood came from Venice, while England provided the lead. Many more restoration projects followed, continuing on into the Early Modern Period.[83] One cannot overlook the fact, finally, that pilgrimage – whether Muslim, Christian, or Jewish – was a lucrative source of revenue for Mamluk and Ottoman Sultans who promoted it heavily. Attracting Catholic pilgrims, in other words, was of interest to the Muslim rulers of the Holy Land.[84]

Whatever the reason underpinning Mamluk promotion of Latin jurisdiction, Greek documents pertaining to the early modern disputes show that the Patriarchate of Jerusalem viewed the steady expansion of Latin authority during this time as illegitimate and a direct violation of its traditional claims to precedence in the Holy Places. Adding to the intensity of Greek (as well as Latin) concern no doubt was awareness of the stark reality that the Holy Places were finite, delimited spaces under Islamic law. As mentioned earlier, the possession of an altar meant the de-possession of another community. Adding to the sense of injury, as well, was the fact that the Latins had managed to gain control of some of the most significant altars. In addition to the Cenacle, which it held sole authority over for most of its two centuries under Mamluk rule, by the

---

[82] John Wansbrough, "Venice and Florence in the Mamluk Commercial Privileges," *Bulletin of the School of Oriental and African Studies, University of London* 28 (1965): 483–523.

[83] Roncaglia, "The Sons of St. Francis," 282.

[84] Dansette, "Les pèlerinages en terre sainte au XIVè et XVè siècles. Etude sur leurs aspects originaux, et edition d'une relation anonyme," PhD thesis, Université de Paris-Sorbonne, 1977, xxxvii. See also W. Heyd, "Les consulats etablis en terre sainte au moyen age pour la protection des pélerins," in *Archives de l'Orient-Latin*, vol. II (Paris: Ernest Leroux, 1884), 355–364.

sixteenth century, the brothers also tended to three altars in the Basilica of the Holy Sepulcher including two especially important ones marking the sites of the Apparition to Mary and the crucifixion (Calvary). Oded Peri argues, moreover, that until the seventeenth century disputes, the primacy of the Latins in processions in the Holy Sepulcher was recognized under Islamic law[85] and that the Greeks did not challenge Latin claims to it until after the Ottoman conquest. Both the Greeks and the Armenians, however, did frequently challenge the jurisdiction of the Latins over specific altars, especially in the Church of the Nativity and the Holy Sepulcher. It was not until the advent of the Ottomans, however, that the two communities, the Greeks in particular, began to make serious inroads into Latin jurisdiction.[86]

The final section of this chapter (Section 2.3.2) considers the impact of recent change in renewing, or at the very least intensifying, an ongoing rivalry between the two communities over precedence in the Holy Places. A particularly important dimension was its international as well as local character, because the escalation of tension owed a great deal to the active support each community received from powerful allies within their own tradition. The involvement of the papacy and the Patriarch of Constantinople are especially striking indications that the Holy Land had become a renewed site of spiritual competition between these ancient rivals over claims to Christian primacy, an assertion that rested upon not only the acquisition of the most significant altars and the status of Christian precedence but also the souls of local Christians. It was an assertion that was legitimized, just as importantly, by the many centuries of Byzantine rule in Palestine, one that rivaled the claims of the Roman church.

Since Chapter 5 will explore papal engagement at greater length, Section 2.3.2 will focus upon the growing influence of the Patriarchate of Constantinople. Byzantine influence grew in tandem with the expansion of the Ottoman Empire, reaching the Patriarchate of Jerusalem by the 1530s, and it continued to expand over the course of the next two centuries. As the following discussion will suggest, the growing influence of the Patriarchate of Constantinople owed a great deal to its close relations with the Ottoman Porte, but it also reflected an ambitious desire to assert its primacy over the four Patriarchs and a unified Greek Orthodox tradition. Exercising influence over the Patriarch of Jerusalem

---

[85] On Latin primacy under Mamluk rule, see, for example, Peri, *Christianity under Islam*, 100–104.
[86] Peri, *Christianity under Islam*, 100–104.

became a particular concern almost immediately because of the prestige of the Holy Places and the shared importance of the Holy Land for manifesting claims to Christian leadership. What seems to have added some urgency to Byzantine quest for primacy as well were signs of a much more robust Western European campaign for Christian souls in the region by the end of the sixteenth century, both in the form of Calvinism and Catholic missions.

2.3.2 The Ottoman Conquest and Byzantine Influence

That the Ottoman conquest was a catalyst to renewed Christian competition in the Holy Places seems difficult to ignore. Oded Peri and Constantin Panchenko among others have pointed to mounting conflict not only between the Latin and Greek Orthodox communities but also between the Greek and Armenian Orthodox, conflicts that reached periods of particular intensity during the seventeenth century. Indeed, these conflicts were simultaneous. In 1634, for example, at the same time that the Latins were locked in a legal battle over jurisdiction in the Grotto of the Nativity, the Armenians were challenging Greek performance of their rites in the Holy Sepulcher. That the Greek Orthodox Patriarchate of Jerusalem felt emboldened by the Ottoman conquest is not entirely surprising. To begin with, both local Greeks and their Patriarch may have expected to find the new Ottoman regime more receptive than its Mamluk predecessors to its claims to Christian precedence. Oded Peri, in his study of Ottoman jurisdiction in the Holy Places, makes this very point, noting that at the time of the conquest in 1517, the Ottoman Empire already held an enormous Greek Orthodox population within its boundaries. However, the annexation of the Mamluk territories not only significantly increased the Greek Orthodox population of the empire but also brought the four Patriarchs of the Church (Constantinople, Antioch, Jerusalem, Alexandria) together within the same imperial jurisdiction for the first time in over a thousand years. From the perspective of the Patriarchate of Jerusalem, the Ottoman conquest may have augured a potential change for the better, at least in terms of its desire to expand its jurisdiction in the Holy Places, because the conquest brought the community of Jerusalem into a much larger Greek Orthodox context, one that could hopefully be relied upon in its endeavours to reassert its claims to jurisdiction. Moreover, as Halil Inalcik and Hasan Çolak among others have argued, the Porte enjoyed close social and political ties with the Byzantine elite in Constantinople by the early sixteenth century, relations that the Greek

Orthodox community in Palestine may have counted upon when pressing Ottoman authorities for precedence in the Holy Places.[87] The Venetian ambassador Giovanni Cappello voiced precisely this concern when he wrote to the Senate during the 1630s that the Greeks were in greater favour with the Porte than the Latin community.[88]

Further indications of a local Greek community emboldened under Ottoman governance might be the signs of demographic growth discussed earlier, particularly in Palestine and Syria. Following the conquest, Byzantine Greeks began migrating in greater numbers into Syria as well as Palestine over the course of sixteenth and seventeenth centuries. The Greek population in Jerusalem alone doubled between 1562 and 1690.[89] While Amy Singer suggests that most of those who moved to Jerusalem came from the Arabic-speaking populations in the rural areas just outside the doors of the city, the growing size of the local Greek Orthodox population at the epicenter of the jurisdictional conflicts suggests at the very least that the friars had to contend with a larger, and more vocal, local body of Greek supporters. Beyond the question of growing local support, however, significant evidence ties the renewal of the rivalry between the friars and the Patriarch of Jerusalem with the increasing influence of the Patriarchate of Constantinople, the head of the Byzantine Greek Orthodox tradition, over that of Jerusalem. This influence was exerted principally through control over its administration, and it brought with it renewed assertions of Greek Orthodox precedence in the Holy Places.

One of the dangers of talking in broad terms about the Greek Orthodox tradition during this period is oversimplifying the complex nature of its internal relations. It was, and remains, a vast, complex,

---

[87] Halil Inalcik, "The Status of the Greek Orthodox Patriarch under the Ottomans," *Turcica* 23 (1991): 407–435; Hasan Çolak, "Relations between the Ottoman Central Administration and the Greek Orthodox Patriarchates of Antioch, Jerusalem, and Alexandria: 16th–18th Centuries," PhD diss., University of Birmingham, 2013; and Elif Bayraktar-Tellan, "The Pariarch and the Sultan: The Struggle for Authority and the Quest for Order in the Eighteenth-Century Ottoman Empire," PhD diss., Ankara, Bilken University, 2011.

[88] This is a frequent comment on the part of the Venetian ambassadors. See, for example, the reports sent by the *bailo* to the Senate discussing the situation in the Holy Land at this time. ASVe dispacci 112 (1631).

[89] Peri, *Christianity under Islam*, 20–21. We should note that the Armenian community grew even more dramatically during the same period. The Greek Orthodox, however, remained the largest of the Christian communities throughout this period. The Copts, however, reduced dramatically in comparison, numbering 326 in 1562–1563, but only 113 in 1690–1691.

and widely flung tradition that, much like the Catholic Church, has long recognized significant religious diversity within its embrace as well as a multiplicity of authorities. Scholars who work on the tradition have argued, moreover, that it was also changing in significant ways under Ottoman rule. This was not only the case with the Greek Orthodox, because the expansion of the Ottoman Empire from the 1450s onward had profound and indeed transformative consequences for many of the Christian communities that found itself within its embrace, reshaping not only relations with political authorities but also relations *within* each tradition. The Byzantine Church, led by the Patriarch of Constantinople, represents one particularly good and well-researched example of a religious institution and community profoundly altered through its experience of Ottoman rule in ways that had direct implications for Christian relations in the Holy Land, and which are relevant, in particular, for understanding their disputes with the friars over altars.[90] An early and visible manifestation of Byzantine influence in the Patriarchate of Jerusalem was the growing number of Byzantine Greeks who assumed important posts. Many of them were members of the Brotherhood of the Holy Sepulcher, the religious body mentioned earlier, which was formed during the Patriarchate of Germanos (1534–1577) and comprised Byzantine Greek clerics. Though it is difficult to follow the activities of the Brotherhood before the seventeenth century,[91] it appears frequently in the Franciscan accounts as an active clerical body hostile to Latin jurisdiction in the Holy Places. Stronger evidence of Byzantine influence is suggested by the incursion of Byzantine Greeks into the office of Patriarch. Germanos (1534–1579) was the first of several Byzantine Greeks elected in succession during the Early Modern Period, including Theophanes III (1608–1644) and Dositheos (1669–1707), the two Patriarchs at the center of the seventeenth-century disputes.

This succession of Byzantine Greeks in the office of Patriarch likely responded to broader administrative changes at work in the Greek

---

[90] In addition to the work of Tellen and Çolak on administrative change, a growing body of recent scholarship is shedding light on social, religious change among the many Christian traditions during the Early Modern Period. On the Greek Orthodox, see, for example, Febe Armanios, *Coptic Christianity in Ottoman Egypt* (Oxford: Oxford University Press, 2011).

[91] The Brotherhood of the Holy Sepulcher, also sometimes referred to as a confraternity, was established sometime around 1534. Peri discusses it, arguing that it represented essentially a Greek reorganization of the Jerusalem Patriarchate. Peri, *Christianity under Islam*, 99–100.

Orthodox tradition by the Early Modern Period, changes that reveal a Byzantine administration eager to assert its primacy among the patriarchs. As mentioned earlier, the Byzantine elite in Constantinople and the Ottoman Porte enjoyed close ties by the sixteenth century, ties that were used over time to carve out a more prominent administrative and spiritual role for the Byzantine Patriarchate within the broader Greek Orthodox tradition. Hasan Çolak and Elif Tellen both point to a number of changes in administrative and electoral practices by the seventeenth century that privileged Byzantine authority vis-à-vis the four Patriarchates. These changes, they argue, responded in part to Ottoman interest in centralizing and streamlining ecclesiastical administrations among the many *dhimmi* communities.[92] This larger framework of administrative reorganization and centralization helps to explain, in particular, the successive appointment of Byzantine Greeks to the patriarchal office in Jerusalem. Çolak argues that the Patriarch of Jerusalem came under Byzantine influence earlier than the Patriarchs of Antioch and Alexandria in part because of its strategic importance for engaging with other Christian communities as well as its jurisdiction in the Holy Places. Indeed, during the administration of Theophanes III, the Patriarchate purchased a residence in Constantinople. The Patriarch of Jerusalem moved here shortly thereafter and remained until 1867, another tangible manifestation of strengthening relations between these two Greek Orthodox institutions by this time.[93]

Returning to a consideration of the disputes involving the Latin community, however, this larger process of centralization (what some scholars consider a process of "Ottomanization"), while impactful, cannot fully explain the renewal of conflicts over the altars. For that we need to consider, at least briefly, the historic claims of the Byzantine Church to the legitimizing authority of Jerusalem and a historic rivalry that inflected the possession of Christian precedence with added lustre as a marker of Byzantine Christian leadership. In other words, it was important to Byzantine leaders not only to claim possession of altars and the status of precedence but also to do so *at the expense of* the Latin Church.

2.3.3 A Byzantine Sacred History

It is important to recall, to begin with, that a long-running rivalry existed between the Roman and Byzantine Churches over claims to Christian

---

[92] Çolak, *Ottoman Central Administration*, 61–62.
[93] Çolak, *Ottoman Central Administration*, 79.

primacy. This rivalry predated the Schism that ended formal ties between the two institutions in the eleventh century, stretching back to the early centuries of Christian administration in the Roman Empire. It waxed and waned over time, relations between the two Churches were punctuated by periods of tension as well as moderately serious efforts at reunification. Negotiations for reunification were briefly successful at the Council of Florence (1431–1449), for example, an event that has received a fair bit of scholarly attention because of the role of Medici patronage and as an expression of papal hegemonic ambitions.[94] One of the chief objectives of the Council was to unify Eastern Christians under papal leadership. It is fair to say, however, that the Byzantine Church was never receptive to papal assertions of Christian primacy. Indeed, Dimiter Angelov and Judith Herrin have argued that the Patriarch spent the fourteenth and fifteenth centuries promoting itself as the spiritual head of Christendom in myriad ways including the appointment of prelates and negotiations with other Eastern Christian communities.[95]

The conquest of the Byzantine Empire in 1453, less than a decade after the Council of Florence, understandably put a damper on continuing negotiations. The growing conflict between the Latin and Greek Orthodox communities in Jerusalem by the 1540s, however, suggests that the Patriarchate in Constantinople had adapted to Ottoman governance by this time. Moreover, it seems to have found a powerful ally in the Ottoman Porte, one that it turned to repeatedly during the sixteenth and seventeenth centuries to reassert its claims to Christian primacy in the eastern Mediterranean. Asserting Byzantine primacy in the Holy Places served an important legitimizing function in this regard, since Byzantine patriarchs as well as the Roman pontiffs long represented their respective seats of power – Rome and Constantinople – as other "Jerusalems." Like the papacy, Byzantine patriarchs also extracted relics from the Holy Places and imbedded them in the material fabric of the Greek Orthodox

---

[94] The Council of Florence began in Basel in 1431, relocating to Ferrara in 1438 and then Florence in 1439. See, for example, Roger J. Crum, "Roberto Martelli, The Council of Florence, and the Medici Palace Chapel," *Zeitschrift für Kunstgeschichte* 59 (1996): 403–417. An older work but still useful for understanding the question of union is Deno J. Geanakoplos, "The Council of Florence (1438-1439) and The Problem of Union between the Greek and Latin Churches," *Church History* 24 (1955): 324.

[95] See, for example, Dimiter Angelov and Judith Herrin, "The Christian Imperial tradition – Greek and Latin," in *Universal Empire: A Comparative Approach to Imperial Culture and Representation in Eurasian History*, ed. Peter Fibiger Bang and Dariusz Kolodzejczyk (Cambridge: Cambridge University Press, 2012), 149–174. See also Çolak, 40–42.

tradition – in the walls, under altars, and in reliquaries of their many Churches. Alexei Lidov mentions the special importance given in particular to Constantinople's possession of the true cross that was brought by Constantine's mother Helen to the city from Jerusalem in the fourth century. The chapel dedicated to Saint Helen in the Holy Sepulcher paid tribute to her discovery of the fragment while excavating the site of Calvary. The cross became a prized Byzantine relic, paraded through the urban landscape of Constantinople and on the battlefield for important imperial ceremonies. Performance of the liturgical rites associated with the Holy Land, moreover, ensured the continual re-sacralization of the great Christian city.[96] Finally, Byzantine religious leaders, like their counterparts in Rome, also fostered the city as an important pilgrimage destination, promising pilgrims a similar spiritual experience to visiting the real Holy Places. Especially during the long centuries when the two powers were shut out of direct influence over worship at the shrines, these sacralized cities functioned as critical material and ideological conduits of the apostolic past, grounding the claims of its respective leadership both to orthodoxy and leadership. Though the Byzantine emperor was dethroned by the Ottomans in 1453, the Patriarchate of Constantinople remained in charge of the spiritual life of its large body of believers.

Moreover, a conception of a Jerusalem under Byzantine rule persisted throughout the Early Modern Period, encouraged by Byzantine leaders especially in the wake of the Ottoman conquest of the Holy Land. Perhaps the conquest made the possibility much more real to church leaders, but, more immediately, they found it useful for bolstering their assertions of primacy not only vis-à-vis the other patriarchs of the Greek Orthodox tradition but also the many other Christian traditions residing within the Ottoman Empire. An empire, we should emphasize, that had spent the better part of the sixteenth century growing its diverse Christian population. For Constantin Panchenko and Oded Peri, the renewed rivalries between the Greeks, Latins, and Armenian Orthodox reflected a jockeying for status within a new Christian context, that of the Ottoman Empire.[97] More to our purpose here, as Molly Greene has argued recently, the Byzantine Patriarch considered the seizure of Latin

---

[96] Alexei Lidov, "A Byzantine Jerusalem: The Imperial Pharos Chapel as the Holy Sepulcher," in *Jerusalem As Narrative Space Erzählraum Jerusalem*, ed. Annette Hoffman and Gerhard Wolf (Leiden: Brill, 2012), 77.

[97] Panchenko, *Arab Orthodox Christians*, 277–278 and Peri, *Christianity under Islam*, 102–103.

jurisdiction in the Holy Places a restorative act, an interpretation supported by the Greek Codex discussed earlier. As its many documents make clear, resentment over Latin precedence during the eras of Crusader and Mamluk rule lingered into the Early Modern Period, fueled by an equally acute perception that Latin possession was illegitimate because it rightfully belonged to the Greek Orthodox tradition. Thus, as the Byzantine Patriarch moved in the wake of the conquest to assert its authority over an Eastern Christendom, it found in the visible and legal manifestations of Latin jurisdiction a significant ideological as well as political barrier to the assertion of its primacy. But there were other pressing issues that likely convinced the Patriarchs that the removal of Latin jurisdiction was of urgent concern, in particular for containing a corrupting Western influence in its own body.

2.3.4 A Corrupting Christian West: Calvinism, Catholic Missions

Much more work needs to be done on the spiritual engagement between these churches in the Holy Land to test this interpretation, however, it seems much more than a coincidence that the disputes over altars between local Greek and Latin communities intensified at a time when the leadership of the Greek Orthodox tradition was worried about the penetration of Calvinism and Catholicism in its spiritual body. Looking first to the question of Calvinist influence, the disputes of the seventeenth century took place in the midst of a heated controversy over the purported Calvinist writings of Cyril Lucaris. A controversial figure, Lucaris was the Patriarch of Constantinople in 1629 when a book entitled *The Confession of Cyril Lucaris* was printed in Latin in Geneva. Whether Calvinism and other forms of Protestantism were making serious inroads into the Greek Orthodox tradition at this time is unclear, and indeed there is serious debate as to whether the writings of Lucaris were truly Calvinist in nature. Regardless, for many leaders of the Greek authorities, evidence of unorthodoxy in the writings of one of its most influential officials was a serious cause for concern. Indeed, the controversy over Lucaris was clearly important enough to engage the attention of the Venetian and French ambassadors in Constantinople and the Propaganda Fide during the 1620s and 1630s.[98] Lucaris was later murdered while in Ottoman

---

[98] On the Propaganda Fide's interest in Lucaris, see, for example, Lemmens, ed., *Acta*, vol. 1, 32–33.

custody in 1638. Even after his death, however, his writings provoked considerable debate among the leaders of the Byzantine Church, raising concerns about orthodoxy that were later settled at the Synod of Jerusalem in 1672 mentioned earlier.

The synod of Jerusalem is considered historically one of the most important councils in the Greek Orthodox tradition, similar in its impact to the Council of Trent in the Catholic Church. Important matters of doctrine and practice received close attention, including the controversial teachings of Lucaris. Dositheos II, the Patriarch of Jerusalem and a Byzantine Greek, was a leading figure at this reforming synod, articulating a firm Byzantine rejection of core Calvinist doctrines and a reaffirmation of Greek Orthodoxy in the form of a *Confession*.[99] We should note the timing of the synod as well, which followed upon the renewal of disputes with the Latin community, and more importantly, coincided with the re-consecration of the Grotto of the Nativity. The convocation of an important ecumenical council to mark the "restoration" of Greek jurisdiction over the birthplace of Christ was a powerful manifestation of Greek claims both to orthodoxy and Christian leadership. It suggests at the very least that the Byzantine leadership considered this jurisdiction important to the construction of a purified and unified Greek Orthodox body, one that was free of "Latin" unorthodoxy.

In convoking this synod, Dositheos may have also been making a strong statement about growing Catholic influence in the region. Dositheos and the other patriarchs were worried about signs of a reinvigorated and expansionist-minded papacy, one revealed in the growing numbers of missionaries (Jesuit, Capuchin, and Carmelite) arriving in Ottoman lands by the 1620s. Indeed, in an intriguing coincidence, a letter written three years prior to the publication of Lucaris' controversial text points to serious efforts on the part of the French state and the papacy to woo Lucaris, and thus the Byzantine Church, into the Catholic fold. These discussions never amounted to anything serious, but Byzantine leaders would have considered it yet another sign of papal ambitions to expand the reach of the Catholic tradition in the eastern Mediterranean.

Understood in the context of a long history of relations between the two traditions, these signs of Western influence were understandably regarded as a serious threat both to Byzantine leadership and the purity of the Orthodox tradition. Indeed, Molly Greene argues that the

---

[99] On the Lucaris controversy and the synod, see among others, Çolak, 63–65.

Byzantine Church regarded the Latins as a greater threat than the Ottomans to the integrity and authority of the Greek Orthodox for this reason. Just as importantly, the Byzantine Patriarchate came to see the Ottoman Porte as a powerful partner in its quest to reclaim the primacy of the Greek Orthodox tradition in the most sacred of Christian landscapes. As Greene states, "Ottoman power gave the patriarch, and Orthodox clergy across the Greek world, the opportunity to gain back what they had lost to the Latins."[100]

2.4 CONCLUSION

I have argued here that the many legal disputes that erupted between the Latin and Greek Orthodox community reflect the function of altars as valued markers of legal status and spiritual legitimacy. They illuminate at the same time a historic rivalry renewed in the wake of the Ottoman conquest and at a time when both the Catholic and Byzantine traditions were eager to expand their spiritual influence among the Christian communities of the eastern Mediterranean. As this discussion has intended to suggest, the many layers of meaning in the disputes only emerges when studied at the intersection of sacred history, Islamic law, and political and religious change. One critical objective of this chapter has been to assert the important role played by Islamic law in shaping Catholic engagement in the Holy Land through its regulation of Christian access to the Holy Places. Altars were desirable carriers of legal status and spiritual legitimacy for the many Christian traditions in the Holy Land who competed with one another for space to the most significant. On the one hand, altars anchored the Latin Church in Islamic structures of authority, and on the other, they gave the Church access to a sacred landscape that its members considered powerful. It is because the Custody was regulated by Islamic law and subject to the authority of the Sultan that it is treated here as a hybrid institution, one that was equally grounded in Western and Eastern structures of authority, transgressing ideological as well as geographic boundaries to constitute a Western, and Catholic, bastion in an Islamic region. This hybridity informed every facet of custodial authority and also Latin worship, shown most visibly perhaps in the infusion of Islamic privileges with Christian meaning. Lamps, locks, and keys to chapels, as

---

[100] Molly Greene, *The Edinburgh History of the Greeks, 1453–1768* (Edinburgh: Edinburgh University Press, 2015), 94.

well as liturgical rites, were Ottoman privileges, but they were also markers of the distinctive Christian tradition of its holder and of its claims to spiritual purity.

As the remaining chapters will argue, the hybrid character of the Custody made it a crucial gateway to political and spiritual influence for members of the Latin Church, especially once the forces of reform began rattling the very foundations of the Western Church after 1517. It is no coincidence that we find the papacy and the French state deeply involved in the disputes with the Greek Orthodox analyzed here. Each of these powers had a vested interest in protecting a Latin foothold in the Holy Land, a region that promised access both to Ottoman structures of authority as well as to the legitimizing power vested in the Holy Places. For these reasons as well, many Christian powers worked to expand their influence over the administration of the Custody by the end of the sixteenth century, in the process threatening the traditional jurisdiction of the Franciscan brothers. The nature of these Catholic jurisdictional conflicts will receive attention in later chapters. Chapter 3, however, first explores the Reformation as another frontier of conflict facing the Custody by the sixteenth century as Protestant reformers launched a sustained assault upon the spiritual efficacy of the Holy land pilgrimage after 1517. Looking closely at pilgrimage treatises produced by a unique confraternal society known as the Order of the Holy Sepulcher, Chapter 3 argues that the confessional debates worked to elevate the status of the Holy Land as an authentic reservoir of Christ's perfecting power for devout Catholics such as these knights, a power that made it the material equivalent of the Protestant Word. It was an authority that could be called upon by an order of pilgrims to legitimize their claims to spiritual authority and to play a leadership role in a new era of spiritual warfare.

3

The Order of the Holy Sepulcher

It was on the feast day of the Purification February 2, 1617, that the French pilgrim Nicolas Benard became a knight of the Holy Sepulcher. Benard, the son of a well-to-do merchant in Paris, was not much more than twenty years of age at the time. As his pilgrimage account makes clear, the journey leading to this meaningful moment had not been an easy one. Leaving Paris in September 1616, he made his way to the port of Marseilles where he boarded a ship headed for the Levant. This part of the journey lasted several weeks and involved stops at several ports along the way, including in Sicily, Malta, and Cyprus. By the time he set foot on the soil of the Holy Land it was early January, debarking at the port of Saida (Sidon), which today lies within the boundaries of Lebanon. Several days later he arrived at Jerusalem, joining other pilgrims to begin the visitation of the Holy Places in and around the holy city. As his travel account makes clear, however, the personal – and consequently narrative – climax of the entire journey was the knighting ritual that took place during the overnight stay of the pilgrims in the Basilica of the Holy Sepulcher. The overnight stay was a cherished privilege granted by Ottoman authorities, allowing the Latin party to spend several hours locked inside the Basilica to pursue their devotions. After resting for a short time in the dormitory of the Franciscan brothers who lived in a monastery attached to the Basilica, Benard describes being awoken by the Franciscan *custos* at around six in the morning and asked to join a procession. Benard and another French pilgrim named Resteau made their way to the shrine of the Holy Sepulcher, the site of Christ's last resting place. Once inside the small space, the door was closed, and the two men prostrated themselves, bareheaded before the *custos*. Over the course of the subsequent ceremony, the two French pilgrims were interrogated on their worthiness to join the venerable community: What was their state and condition? Were they of noble or base (*routurier*) background? Could they support themselves as knights if called to do so? And would they dedicate themselves to the protection of the Holy Sepulcher? After giving the oath to observe the statutes of "this noble and holy order of knights," the Franciscan *custos* took the sword once held by the Godefroy of Bouillon and tapped the shoulders of first Benard and then Resteau. The ritual continued on from there, as the two newly created *chevaliers* were dressed with the golden chain and golden spurs that marked their new identity, listened to a speech on their responsibilities, exchanged kisses with the friars, and joined in the traditional rites of prayers and hymns before processing back to rejoin the other pilgrims.[1]

Benard's description of the knighting ceremonial is our starting point for the following exploration of the Order of the Holy Sepulcher. Like our young French merchant, many medieval and early modern knights wrote and published accounts of their own journey to the Holy Land that featured their identity as members of the Order. The knighting ritual was an especially popular means of doing so, but these authors also marked their treatises in many other ways that announced their knightly identities. What makes these texts also of interest to our broader investigation is that they were written in a period when the pilgrimage rite that defined the identity of the knights came under intense criticism from Protestant reformers. In other words, their pilgrimage treatises offer critical windows into a distinctive spiritual community, one that found itself on the frontlines of religious controversy by 1520 out of its shared devotion to the Holy Land and desire to protect it. From their texts, and with the consideration of other acts of devotion, a religious ideal emerges that privileged a role for members of the Order as early modern Soldiers of Christ. This was an ideal embodied in the knighting ritual, constructed at the nexus of the Holy Land pilgrimage, a crusading past, and a formative relationship with the Franciscan brothers of the Custody. As we shall discover, it was meaningful to Benard that his transformation into knight took place *at* the foot of Christ's Sepulcher *during* the pilgrimage *with* the sword of Godefroy of Bouillon and *through* the officiation of the Franciscan *custos*.

---

[1] Nicolas Benard, *Le Voyage de Hierusalem et autres lieux de la terre sainct par le Sr Benard Parisien chevalier de l'ordre du St Sepulcre de nostre seigneur Jesus Christ* (Paris: chez Denis Moreau, 1621), 194–201.

Since the purpose of this chapter is to explore the changing character of a unique pilgrimage society through the lens of its pilgrimage treatises, Sections 3.1 and 3.2 will touch upon the history of the Order and evaluate evidence of the devotional life of members to contextualize their texts. Section 3.3 will examine the pilgrimage treatises as modes of religious controversy and expressions of spiritual leadership in the context of the European Reformation. Section 3.4 explores pilgrimage treatises as expressions of a distinctive religious ideal, focusing, in particular, upon their descriptions of the three central elements involved in the creation of the knight: the rite of pilgrimage, crusading past, and relations with the friars. From this discussion, a few observations emerge that speak to our broader interest in exploring the Custody as a gateway to religious and political legitimacy for early modern Catholics. Firstly, the writings of the knights illuminate a changing Catholic tradition, one in which its material cast became much more pronounced in response to the intense ideological battles over the nature of the sacred. Secondly, in this changing context, the Holy Land assumed new importance as an authentic vessel of Christ's authority and thus legitimacy, offering a powerful challenge to Protestant insistence upon the Word as the ultimate source. As a material source of Christ's authority, the Holy Land also invested the knights with spiritual authority that could be used in defense of the Catholic faith because they were creations of the sacred landscape. With this point in mind, one can make a third and final observation: that the pilgrimage treatises of the knights illuminate sacred history as a valued mechanism of spiritual adaptation and reinvention. For the knights of the study, a shared crusading past and personal experience of the pilgrimage invested their writings with authority, allowing them in the process to reimagine a role for themselves as spiritual experts on the frontlines of confessional division in Europe.

3.1 THE ORDER OF THE HOLY SEPULCHER

When Nicolas Benard received his knighthood in Jerusalem in 1617, he joined an international pilgrimage brotherhood with a storied past, one that stretched back at least three centuries. However, whether the origins of the Order of the Holy Sepulcher truly date to the era of the Crusader Kingdom of Jerusalem remains a matter of some debate among its historians. A once widely cited papal charter, for example, recognizing the formation of the fraternity and dated to the year 1100, is now considered to be a sixteenth-century forgery.² A military order of the Holy Sepulcher, akin to that of the Templars and Knights of Saint John, did appear in the Latin kingdom of Jerusalem during the twelfth century, a fact that has been used to support claims to a crusader origin for the society studied here. They were joined around the same time by the Augustinian canons of the Holy Sepulcher, a clerical body that made its way to Cyprus, Perugia, and other parts of Europe at the end of the thirteenth century, following the collapse of the Crusader kingdom. In 1489, Pope Innocent VIII attempted to merge the military Order of the Holy Sepulcher with that of the Knights of Malta, but it failed to take hold. Only a few years later in 1496, Alexander VI restored its independent status but this time claimed the role of grand master, the head of the Order, for the papacy.³ The Order was from this time forward officially a papal institution, but the conferment of knighthood remained the responsibility of the *custos* of the Holy Land in his role as apostolic delegate. While this institutional history is certainly helpful for understanding its early modern counterpart, it does not fully account for its distinctive early modern character, one that was clearly oriented towards the rite of pilgrimage. Indeed, both Jean de Gennes and Antonio Teixidó suggest it represents a later adaptation of the earlier bodies, though they differ somewhat on its source of origin. Teixidó considers it is an ideological conflation of the two earlier orders (the military and canons-regular).⁴ For Jean de Gennes, a member of the present-day Order and its foremost historian, it was more likely a fourteenth-century reinvention of the military Order as a society of pilgrims. This latter interpretation seems likely the case since the earliest description of the knighting ceremonial in the Holy Sepulcher comes from the pilgrimage treatise of German noble Wilhelm von Bodensele written in 1336.⁵

---

² Jean Pierre de Gennes, *Les Chevaliers du Saint-Sépulcre de Jérusalem*, vol. 1 (Paris: Herault, 2004), 33, 42. The charter was attributed to Alexander VI, but there seems to be no surviving trace of the original document. A number of earlier histories of the Order do take its crusading origins seriously, however. See, for example, Prince Xavier de Bourbon, *Les Chevaliers du Saint-Sepulcre* (Paris: Fayard, Prince, 1957).
³ *Cum solerii meditatium* was issued by Innocent VIII on May 28, 1489. De Gennes, *Les Chevaliers du Saint-Sépulcre de Jérusalem*, vol. 1, 130.
⁴ Antonio Martínez Teixidó, "La Orden de Caballería del santo Sepulcro de Jerusalén," *Studia Historica, Historia moderna* 24 (2002): 207–219. The canons regular remained active monastic institutions in Spain and other parts of Europe to the Early Modern Period.
⁵ De Gennes, *Les Chevaliers du Saint-Sépulcre de Jérusalem*, vol. 1, 268–269. See also Colin Morris, *The Sepulcher of Christ in the Medieval West* (Oxford: Oxford University Press, 2005), 337.

Whether the Order of the Holy Sepulcher truly had its roots in an earlier crusading order or emerged later on, reimagined as a pilgrimage society, a wide array of sources, including pilgrimage treatises, notarial accounts, armorials, and paintings, testify to a vigorous society by the fifteenth century, one that was a popular resort of European nobles. Nobility was in fact a stipulation of entry into the Order, a requirement that remained in place throughout the Early Modern Period. However, by the time this study begins, the brotherhood had already evolved into a much more socially diverse institution. A broad survey of its known membership from the fourteenth to the seventeenth centuries undertaken by Jean de Gennes shows that the Order included men from across Western Christendom, reflecting in miniature the significant ethnic and linguistic diversity that characterized the Catholic tradition into the Early Modern Period.

What also seems clear from surviving sources is that the Order continued to attract members at a steady rate throughout the medieval and Early Modern Periods. De Gennes averages the number of knights created annually to between 3.95 during the fourteenth and fifteenth centuries.[6] A comparison of two registers introduced by the Custody in 1561 – one for pilgrims known as the *Navis peregrinorum* and the other for knights (*Registrum Equitum Ssmi Sepulchri*) – suggests that knights continued to be produced at a similar rate throughout the sixteenth and seventeenth centuries.[7] Early modern members included doctors, merchants, diplomatic officials, and nobles as well as a handful of clerics. The Order also included many figures well known to early modern scholars including the cosmographer André Thevet, the famous Dutch engraver Cornelius de Bruyn, and Jean de Thévenot, a French linguist and author of a well-known travel account.

These indications of continuing vigour may perhaps seem surprising when we consider the challenges facing Holy Land pilgrimage by the early sixteenth century, challenges that significantly impacted the flow of European travelers to the region. As discussed in Chapter 2, the number of Western Europeans visiting the region sharply declined after 1519, for a number of reasons that were political as well as religious in nature.

---

[6] De Gennes says that 653 knights were created between 1348 and 1496. De Gennes, *Les Chevaliers du Saint-Sépulcre de Jérusalem*, vol. I, 337.

[7] Arch. Custodia Terra Sancta, Jerusalem. *Registrum Equitum SSmi Sepulchri* (1561–1847). Knights are also mentioned in the pilgrim's register, "Navis peregrinorum, continens nomina, cognomina et nations peregrinorum omnium..."

Given that knights continued to be produced at a steady rate after 1519, it is likely that a higher proportion of pilgrims who did make the pilgrimage during this downturn received the knighthood. But while registers of the knights seem to argue for the continuing allure of the Order for many Catholics throughout the era of the Reformation, they also allude to critical shifts in its demography that may have been caused by the rupturing of the Western Church after 1517. One notes, in particular, a significant drop in the number of German and Dutch members. For example, between 1500 and 1597, the friars created Dutch, French, and German knights at roughly the same rate as those of French origin. French knights numbered 58; the Dutch, 55; and 50 came from German-speaking regions. The numbers shifted dramatically after this time, with 553 French knights created between 1597 and 1739 compared to only 100 German-speakers and 30 from the Netherlands. Such figures suggest that both the Reformation and Counter-Reformation significantly reshaped the demography of the Order by the second half of the sixteenth century. These three regions witnessed the growth of Protestant communities and experienced religious conflict firsthand as a result of mounting tension between the faiths. Of the three, France remained the most staunchly attached to the Catholic faith during the sixteenth century, a fact that likely explains the much larger number of French members by 1597. The emergence of a more militant Catholicism in response to the Reformation may account as well for the dramatic rise in the number of Italian and Iberian members of the Order. Whereas these regions produced 21 and 12 knights respectively between 1500 and 1597, between 1597 and 1739, they produced 161 and 86.[8] But as shall be discussed in Chapter 4, the significant appeal of the Order among the French also likely reflected growing French influence at the Ottoman Porte. Indeed, during the seventeenth century, the Order numbered many important French officials including François Savary de Breves (1560–1628) and Charles Marie François, the Marquis de Nointel (1635–1685), French ambassadors responsible for negotiating the Capitulations treaties of 1604 and 1674 respectively. These were important treatises that laid the foundations for France's emergence during this time as a great Mediterranean economic power.[9]

---

[8] De Gennes, *Les Chevaliers du Saint-Sépulcre de Jérusalem*, vol. 1, 432.
[9] See discussion in Chapter 4.

3.2 A SPIRITUAL BROTHERHOOD

3.2.1 Evidence of a Spiritual Brotherhood?

This brief description of the Order is a prelude to a more in-depth analysis of a unique Catholic institution, one that has received surprisingly little attention from early modern historians even though it remained vigorous throughout the sixteenth and seventeenth centuries. Its absence in scholarship on the Holy Land pilgrimage is especially glaring when we consider the importance of the rite in defining the distinctive identity of this brotherhood as well as the Order's visibility in early modern sources. Indeed, the knights are everywhere in the records – providing alms and other gifts to the Custody of the Holy Land, establishing masses for the dead in local churches, peering from portraits dressed in their distinctive white robes, and discussed in Franciscan writings. The knights also produced pilgrimage treatises, a devotional genre that was enormously popular throughout the medieval and Early Modern Periods and that remains central to scholarly exploration of Western engagement in the Holy Land. Jean de Gennes attributes at least 50 of the over 300 texts produced between 1336 and 1500 to members of the Order.[10] The knights seemed to have been responsible for a much smaller percentage of the treatises produced in the subsequent two centuries. This study found nine texts that can be attributed to knights published between 1520 and 1700. Even with a conservative estimate of 200 treatises published during this time, the contribution of the knights represents roughly 5 percent. Because library and archival catalogues rarely identify authors as members of the Order, however, it is more than likely that several more treatises exist awaiting discovery by an eager historian. More manuscript versions likely exist as well. Of the twelve treatises examined here, three (Affagart, Boisselly, Maggi) were published after the lifetime of the author. In terms of other writings, we should note that a number of knights produced travel accounts that included long descriptions of the pilgrimage. These included three well-known ones penned by Henri de Beauvau, an official attached to the French embassy in Constantinople, the French ambassador François Savary de Breves, and the linguist Jean de Thévenot, but there are more.[11] These accounts will also receive some attention in the following analysis of the Order, though pilgrimage treatises are the

---

[10] De Gennes, *Les Chevaliers du Saint-Sépulcre de Jérusalem*, vol. II, 268.
[11] Henri de Beauvau, *Relation journaliere du voyage du Levant fait et descript par Messire Henry de Beauvau, baron dudit lieu, & de Manonville, seigneur de Fleuville* (Paris: Gilles

primary focus of our investigation. Indeed, a central assertion of this chapter is that the treatises of the knights, much like those produced by the Franciscan brothers of the Holy Land, comprise a sub-genre of Holy Land pilgrimage texts because they were self-conscious products of a distinct community.[12] This view receives further support when we consider their early modern texts alongside the outsized role played by members of the Order in the production of late medieval pilgrimage treatises.

That the knights have yet to be treated as a distinct sub-genre of pilgrimage authors may well reflect a degree of skepticism about the truly devotional nature of the Order by the sixteenth century. Whether one can describe the Order as a confraternity, to begin with, seems a bit of a stretch when we compare it to other confraternities of the period, even though it is officially recognized as such in papal documents from the early sixteenth century. To be sure, the extensive scholarship on confraternities suggests that we should also not generalize about their character. Some were much more demanding than others in terms of collective devotional life. But even on the surface, the Order looked little like the typical confraternities found in cities across Europe by the sixteenth century, lacking as it did a clearly defined administrative structure and intense communal devotional life that was typical of many early modern European confraternities.[13] The Order of the Holy Sepulcher seems to fit somewhere in between this kind of typically urban devotional institution and the quasi-confraternal-chivalric orders Renaissance monarchs were introducing at their courts, for example, the Ordre de Saint-Esprit in France. Indeed, beyond taking an oath to model virtue and to pursue a life of intense personal devotion, the only religious engagement required of members was the pilgrimage to the Holy land and the knighting ceremonial.

Robinot, 1610); and Jean de Thévenot, *Relation d'un voyage fait au Levant* (Paris: Louis Billaine, 1665).

[12] See Chapter 6.

[13] On urban confraternities, a small sampling of the scholarship includes Susan Verdi Webster, *Art and Ritual in Golden-Age Spain: Sevillian Confraternities and the Processional Sculpture of Holy Week* (Princeton: Princeton University Press, 1998); Christopher F. Black, *Italian Confraternities in the Sixteenth Century* (Cambridge: Cambridge University Press, 1989); Nicholas Terpstra, *Lay Confraternities and Civic Religion in Renaissance Bologna* (Cambridge: Cambridge University Press, 2002); Konrad Eisenbichler, *The Boys of the Archangel Raphael: A Youth Confraternity in Florence, 1411–1785* (Toronto: University of Toronto Press, 1998).

That some well-known contemporaries questioned the pious focus of the Order may also have contributed to scholarly skepticism. The German botanist Leonhard Rauwolf and the English traveler George Sandys are both well known to scholars of the pilgrimage because they joined it during their travels and described the experience. Rauwolf, who visited the Holy Land in 1575, specifically mentions the Order in his travel account, dismissing it as more "secular than religious in character."[14] Writing few decades later in 1610, the Englishman George Sandys seems to have agreed with Rauwulf's assessment, observing that the fee of thirty *sultanies* for the knighting ritual was the only real criteria for entrance. Indeed, his description of the society insinuates quite clearly that the noble pious ideal that once inspired the Order had long since dissipated, making it mostly valued as a vessel of noble honorifics. As Sandys states at one point, the Knights wear "five crosses gules, in forme of that which is at this day called the Jerusalem crosse; representing thereby the five wounds that violated the body of our Saviour." The men were to have lived moral lives, be Catholic, and "Gentlemen of the blood," and to possess sufficient means "to maintain a port agreeable to that calling, without the exercise of mechanicall sciences." But now, he says, "they will except against none that bring money, insomuch that at our being there they admitted of a *Romane*, by trade an Apothecary, late dwelling in Aleppo."[15]

Sandys clearly considered the inclusion of a lowly apothecary of Aleppo as a damning indictment of the Order's claims to a noble spiritual brotherhood. Money, more so than status and devotion, he suggests, determined membership. In this regard, Sandys perhaps finds some support from the registries of the knights and pilgrims kept by the friars of the Custody. The *Navis peregrinorum* lists a number of Protestants permitted to joined the pilgrimage. It is possible that a few made it into the Order as well.[16] Since chivalric societies were enormously popular conveyors of noble status and were highly sought after even by the non-elite, it is not unreasonable to accept that many of those who joined the Order during the period of this investigation did so for reasons that had little to do with

---

[14] On Rauwolf, see, for example, Karl H. Dannenfeldt, "Leonhard Rauwolf: A Lutheran Pilgrim in Jerusalem, 1575," *Archiv für Reformationsgeschichte* 55 (1964): 18–36.

[15] George Sandys, *A Relation of a Journey Begun An. Dom. 1610* (London: W. Barrrett, 1615), 159.

[16] Arch. Terra Sancta, Jerusalem. *Navis Peregrinorum*, 28. For example, an entry dated July 21, 1611, lists Pawel Bosepolschy of Pomerania as a "heretic." I wish to thank Justin Vovk for his work identifying central and eastern European pilgrims listed in the *Navis*, including Bosepolschy.

devotion. The Order of the Holy Sepulcher was quite well known and mentioned in a number of early modern treatises on the chivalric orders including those of Andre Favyn and Pierre de Beloy. Favyn, we should note, was also a member of this Order.[17] De Gennes does suggest that many members simply joined it to claim the title. But in addition to pilgrimage treatises, which will receive special attention in this chapter, a rich body of evidence suggests that a shared devotion to the Holy Land profoundly marked the piety of many knights and shaped their religious identities throughout the late medieval and Early Modern Periods. Art historians, in particular, alert us to paintings, engravings, and stained-glass windows commissioned by knights that portray them with recognized symbols of the Order, including images of Jerusalem and the blazon of the Order of the Holy Sepulcher (five red crosses against a white background).[18] A good example is the engraving of Nicolas Benard found in his treatise. Benard's pensive face is featured in an oval, the corners marked with symbols signaling his membership in this pilgrimage society: the palm leaf, Bible, and the cross of Jerusalem. Jean de Thévenot, who included a long description of the pilgrimage in his well-known seventeenth-century travel account, is one of many knights who added the blazon to his family armorial. A particularly stunning example of another armorial can be found in a series of engravings commissioned by the Venetian Carlo Maggi for his own travel account. The manuscript was never published, though it may have been intended for circulation. Maggi, a Venetian citizen, traveled extensively in the Levant between 1568 and 1573 on state business, an itinerary that included a visit to Jerusalem. The narrative of his pilgrimage is a rather straightforward account but includes several striking images including a twelve-part depiction of different scenes of the visitation of the Holy Places. In one scene, Maggi is shown undergoing the knighting ceremonial. Included as well at the beginning of the manuscript is a colourful rendering of the family armorial with the blazon of the Order of the Holy Sepulcher.[19]

---

[17] See, for example, P. de Beloy, *De l'origine et institution des divers orders de chevalerie tant ecclésiastique que profanes* (Montauban: Denis Haultin, 1604); and Andre Favyn, *Le théâtre d'honneur et de chevalerie*, 2 vols. (Paris: Robert Foüet, 1620).

[18] See, in particular, Joanna Woodall, "Painted Immortality: Jerusalem Pilgrims by Antonis Mor and Jan Van Scorel," *Jahrbuch der Berliner Museen* 31 (1989): 149–163; and Bart Holterman, "Pilgrimages in Images: Early Sixteenth-Century Views of the Holy Land with Pilgrim's Portraits As Part of the Commemoration of the Jerusalem Pilgrimage in Germany," PhD diss., Utrecht, 2013.

[19] The "tableau" is no. 11 in the treatise *Le voyage de Charles Magius* (Paris: Editions Anthès, 1992). The original manuscript is found in the Cabinet des Estampes at the Bibliotèque Nationale de France (BNF).

On its own, the blazon was a symbol of devotion to the Holy Land as well as membership in the Order, a devotional intent strengthened when included alongside an account of the pilgrimage. Even more tantalizing evidence of personal devotion to the Holy Land is suggested by membership in local confraternities. Unfortunately, the international reach of the Order means that it is beyond the capacity of the present project to follow every manifestation of local engagement, but the leads uncovered thus far suggest that many more connections existed and merit further investigation. Of local confraternities with demonstrated ties to the Order of the Holy Sepulcher, two existed in Paris, one in Marseilles, and a number in the Low Countries.

From the account of the merchant Jean de Boisselly, we know that a confraternity dedicated to the Holy Sepulcher existed in Marseilles at the time of his pilgrimage in 1643.[20] Regarding the two confraternities in Paris, both are reasonably well documented and emerged in Paris sometime during the fourteenth century. One, simply known as the Confraternity of the Holy Sepulcher, was associated with the church of the Holy Sepulcher on rue Saint-Denis in the area known today as Les Halles. It may have been in existence as early as the 1320s. For at least part of its history, this church also included a hospital for pilgrims. The other confraternity was the Archiconfrérie royale des chevaliers, voyageurs, palmiers et confreres du Saint-Sépulcre de Jérusalem. It was based at the Observant Franciscan community on the rue Saint-Honoré that was also home to a prestigious theology school (*stadium generale*). Both confraternities were still active in the sixteenth and seventeenth centuries, though the archconfraternity affiliated with the Franciscan brothers (Cordeliers) seems to have become quite vigorous from the sixteenth century and was still flourishing on the eve of the French Revolution.[21] A rich depository of notarial contracts exists for this confraternity in particular, and studied together, they provide us insight into the

---

[20] By his own account, Boisselly was knighted along with ten other pilgrims on Holy Friday, April 3, 1643. Jean de Boisselly, *Le pelerinage de Jean de Boisselly en Terre Sainte* (Soc. De Stat. de Mars, XLVII, 67–95). See also De Gennes, *Les Chevaliers du Saint-Sépulcre de Jérusalem*, vol. I, 395.

[21] On the archconfraternity attached to the Paris Grand Couvent, see Béatrice Dansette, "Les pèlerins occidentaux du moyen age tardif au retour de la Terre sainte: confréries et psaumiers parisiens," *in Dei Gesta per Francos, Etudes sur les croisades dédiées à Jean Richard*, ed. Michel Baland, Benjamin Z. Kedar, and Jonathan Riley-Smith (Aldershot: Ashgate, 2001), 301–314; and Megan C. Armstrong, *The Politics of Piety. Franciscan Preachers during the Wars of Religion, 1560–1600* (Rochester: University of Rochester Press, 2004), ch. 4.

distinctive devotional life of this society.[22] We learn, to begin with, that members had funded a chapel dedicated to Jerusalem in the friary church in which they met regularly for communal devotion and as a final resting place for deceased members. A donation made by Pierre Berthault in 1559, for example, requested services every Friday and Sunday in the "chapelle de Jerusalem." His contract also mentions that his wife Jeanne de Sangal was buried there. Another contract dated June 9, 1557, involving the "marchand bourgeois" Jehan le Gros requested a much more elaborate series of rites including a high mass with "diacre soudiacre, acolite," and twelve children "singing and celebrating in the chapel every week of the year at 8:00 am." In addition, the merchant requested a low mass every Friday and a high requiem mass performed every year on the day after Holy Sunday. Le Gros ended his list of bequests with a final touching request that hints at a spiritual brotherhood that he clearly found meaningful, enough so that he hoped its fellowship would continue into the afterlife. Here he dedicated a requiem mass to the "remedy and salvation of the souls of the *voyageurs* of the aforesaid Holy Sepulcher so that their souls remain attached to one another."[23] To aid communal devotion, le Gros made a final request for "lighting and other necessities for the chapel," and perhaps most importantly, to be buried there, sharing the space with his brothers and their wives for eternity.

Le Gros paid a substantial sum for these services, letting us know that he was a member of the wealthy mercantile elite in Paris. The notarial contracts reveal, even so, a confraternity that was socially diverse and which also distinguished between those who made the pilgrimage (*voyageur*) and those who had not (*non voyageur*). For example, a contract dated August 27, 1576, mentions three men as "governors and administrators of the confraternity of the Holy Sepulcher." Gilles Bidault is described as "voyageur de St Sepulcher," Jehan Dol as a master carpenter ("maistre charpentier"), and Felix le Moin, a tombstone maker ("maistre tombier"). All three are described as "bourgeois de Paris," a rather broad

---

[22] The full series of contracts is found in Archives de la Seine D–Q (10), nos. 1299–1317. Knights who left bequests included Pierre Berthault (1559), Philippe de Noyon (1568), and Anthoine Regnault (1568). Regnault produced one of the pilgrimage treatises discussed here.

[23] Both are found in Archives de la Seine D–Q (10) 95=2500, no. 1299–1317. The original passage from Le Gros is the following: "... Que une grande messe de Requiem qui se dira une foys par chacun an le landemain du Dimanche des octaves des pasques pour le remede et salut des ames des voiagers dudict St Sepulcher Que leurs amyes les a liez confederez..."

legal status that marked them as men possessing some property and taxpayers. Another contract involving the bequest of Le Gros includes even more intriguing information on the material and social character of the community. According to the document, which was issued after his death, Le Gros had hung a sign bearing a representation of Jerusalem in front of his house, a wonderfully public statement of personal devotion as well as his membership in the confraternity. We also learn from the contract that the confraternity included prominent members of the Parisian elite. The witnesses, in particular, seem to have come from the ranks of ennobled civil servants associated with the royal courts and other organs of state administration. Baton Gros, seigneur de Bruzol, is described as "valet de chambre ordinaire du roy," and François Georges, sieur de Momay[n], an *avocat* in the Parlement of Paris.

For the confraternity of the Holy Sepulcher located on the rue Saint-Denis, we also have a number of internal records along with a fascinating historical account of the confraternity written by Nicolas Benard. Benard includes this history in his pilgrimage treatise and it is interesting for many reasons including its suggestion of a rather heated local rivalry between the two Parisian confraternities. Clearly, one of Benard's objectives was to assert a longer and more illustrious history for the confraternity on Saint-Denis, a brotherhood that was perhaps worried about competition from a rival that was enjoying a period of renewal. We should not, however, conclude that by including the history of the confraternity in his pilgrimage account Benard was also brandishing his pilgrim-identity to a broader French readership.[24] Outside of France, one finds knights in other pilgrimage societies including a number of Jerusalem confraternities in the Low Countries. These were formed later than those in Paris, the earliest dating to the fifteenth century. Among those that welcomed members of the Order of the Holy Sepulcher, the one in Bruges affiliated with the Adorno chapel is particularly well known. At least two generations of the Adorno family belonged to the Order, a relationship that they advertised in their chapel through their inclusion of the blazon and other symbols of the Order.[25] From confraternal portraits produced by the well-known

---

[24] Benard, *Le Voyage de Hierusalem*, 690ff. The tract is called "De la foundation de l'Eglise du Sainct Sepulcher & Hospital y annexé situez à Paris en la grande ruë S. Deny, & de l'institution de la confrairie du sainct Sepulcher de nostre Seigneur en ladite Eglise ...."

[25] The Adorno (Adornes) family has received a fair bit of scholarly attention from art historians. See, in particular, Kathryn Rudy, "A Pilgrim's Memories of Jerusalem: London, Wallace Collection MS M319," *Journal of the Warburg and Courtauld Institutes* 70 (2007): 311–325.

artist Jan Van Scorel, moreover, one can trace knights to confraternities in the cities of Haarlem, Utrecht, and Antwerp between 1528 and the 1540s. For example, a number of the men included in paintings commissioned by the confraternities are shown wearing the distinctive cross of the Order on the left side of their robes, the designated place for the blazon. Particularly striking is the painting of five members of the Utrecht confraternity studied by Bart Holterman, all of whom are shown wearing the Jerusalem cross.[26]

The visible engagement of these knights in local devotional societies is tantalizing evidence of their Catholic piety, a piety that clearly found special spiritual sustenance through communal devotion to the Holy Land. But more than that, it points suggestively to a claim to local spiritual authority and leadership through their status as knights that may also help to explain the Order's allure for many of its early modern members. That members publicly marked their status as knights while participating in local devotions (displaying the blazon, wearing the robes) should alone be taken as one indication of a claim to spiritual authority, a claim manifested as well through the prominent roles played by knights as patrons and administrators of the confraternities mentioned earlier. These same documents, along with the confraternal paintings analyzed by Holterman, suggest that knights were often favoured as representatives of the local confraternity in its financial and other dealings with the host convent regarding the organization of its devotional life. While it is certainly true that in most cases these men were already prominent members of the local urban elite, a fact that would itself place them in leadership roles, the fact that they also represented themselves as knights in the documents of the confraternities suggests that this status also carried a certain authority within the community.

More dramatic if unusual evidence of claims to spiritual authority is suggested by the involvement of some knights in the production of large-scale replicas of the Holy Places. At least two were created by members of the Order between 1470 and 1520, and both played a prominent role in local urban devotional culture. Don Fadrique Enriquez de Ribera (d. 1539), the Marquis of Tarifa, renovated his palace in Seville upon

---

[26] Holterman, *Pilgrimages in Images*, 35–36. Holterman suggests that the first Jerusalem pilgrimage confraternity was established in Paris but several appeared in the Low Countries after this time. While many of these declined in popularity by the end of the sixteenth century, the seventeenth century saw a noble one introduced in Hoogstraten, and the medieval confraternity in Antwerp restored.

his return from the Holy Land in 1519, transforming it into what quickly became known as the House of Pilate (Casa de Pilatos). The palace, which still stands today, does not truly resemble the original Holy Place but it intentionally evokes its biblical identity through the incorporation of revealing symbols and architectural elements. For example, Ribera named one room the "salon de Pretorio" and placed a reproduction of the pillar of the flagellation inside. Also striking is the portico made of Genoese marble at the front door stamped with three black Jerusalem crosses and the inscription: "I entered Jerusalem on the 4th day of August 1519."[27] These crosses and the inscription, in particular, advertised his identity as a member of the Order of the Holy Sepulcher, placing him in Jerusalem for the ceremony. Quite different from Ribera's House of Pilate is the Jeruzalemkapel in Bruges, which was commissioned by the well-to-do merchant family, the Adorno. The family had already built a church by the time Anselm and his son Jan made their pilgrimage to the Holy Land in 1470–1471. Upon their return to Bruges, they added the Jeruzalemkapel, a unique space that reimagined the topography of the site of Calvary (Station 11). To this day, one can visit the Adorno chapel, which evokes the rocky undulations of Golgotha bearing three crosses for Christ and the two thieves. The stained-glass windows also include a portrait of Jan Adorno with the distinctive blazon of the Order of the Holy Sepulcher.[28]

These two large-scale replicas of the Holy Land visibly articulated the local spiritual authority of their knightly patrons, serving simultaneously as powerful expressions of their piety and as sites of local worship. Fostering local devotion was always one intent of such large-scale replicas according to Robert Ousterhout, and they were enormously popular throughout the medieval and Early Modern Periods. One might ponder, for example, the spiritual impact of encountering the eight Jerusalems nestled in the hilltops of the Piedmont region in Italy. These were all built

[27] On these renovations, see Felipe Pereda, "Measuring Jerusalem: The Marquis of Tarifa's Pilgrimage in 1520 and Its Urban Consequences," *Città et Storia* VII (2012): 77–102. On Enriquez and his journey, see also the extremely useful critical edition of his manuscript account, Pedro García Martín, ed., *Paisajes de la Tierra Prometida: El Viaje a Jerusalén de Don Fadrique Enríquez de Ribera* (Madrid: Miraguano, S. A., Ediciones, 2001); and Adam G. Beaver, "From Jerusalem to Toledo: Replica, Landscape and the Nation in Renaissance Iberia," *Past and Present* 218 (2013), 63–64.

[28] Mitzi Kirkland-Ives, "Capell nuncapato Jherusalem noviter Brugis: The Adornes Family of Bruges and Holy Land Devotion," *The Sixteenth Century Journal* 39 (2008): 1041–1064.

between the sixteenth and eighteenth centuries and transformed the region into a vigorous arena of pilgrimage.[29] Replicas of Jerusalem were constructed in many other parts of Europe as well, and the growing scholarship emerging from their study reveals an extraordinarily exuberant and imaginative local devotional engagement with the Holy Land. Most of these replicas look little like the authentic Holy Places, confident in the belief that to mimic the same dimensions or evoke certain architectural elements of a given Holy Place was more than sufficient to bring its sacrality to full effect locally.[30] In different ways, each replica forged a spiritual and material connection with the Holy Land intended to nourish communal, as well as personal, devotion. Similar objectives would have informed the construction of the Jerusalemkapel in Bruges, a city that was devoutly Catholic and known for its rich devotional culture. Especially at Easter time, Bruges liturgically and visually constructed itself as a "Jerusalem" through art, architecture, and elaborate religious processions.[31] The Jerusalem chapel, containing its unique chapel of Golgotha, was intended to be one focal point of these rites, and it is clear as well that the Spanish knight Ribera had similar ambitions for his Casa de Pilatos in

---

[29] On the *sacri monti*, in particular, there is a growing body of excellent work. See, for example, Bram de Klerck, "Jerusalem in Renaissance Italy: The Holy Sepulcher on the Sacro Monte de Varallo," in *The Imagined and the Real Jerusalem in Art and Architecture*, ed. Jeroen Goudeau, Mariette Verhoeven, and Wouter Weijers (Leiden: Brill, 2014): 215–236; and Pierre Giorgio Longo, *Memorie di Gerusalemme e Sacri Monti in epoca barocca. Vincenzo Fani, devote "misteri" e "magnanime imprese" nella sua Relatione del viaggio in Terrasanta dedicate a Carlo Emanuele I di Savoiva (1615–1616)* (Ponzano Monferrato: Atlas, 2010). As these works show, a number of Franciscans played an important role in fostering these shrines. On this role, see also Alessandro Nova, "'Popular' Art in Renaissance Italy: Early Response to the Holy Mountain at Varallo," in *Reframing the Renaissance. Visual Culture in Europe and Latin America 1450–1650*, ed. Claire Farago (New Haven: Yale University Press, 1995), 113–126, 319–321.

[30] Two recent collections of articles explore this diversity and deserve special attention. These include Goudeau, Verhoeven, and Wijers, eds., *The Imagined and Real Jerusalem*; and Anna Benvenuti and P. Piatti, eds., *Come a Gerusalemme: Evocazioni, riproduzioni, imitazioni dei luoghi santi tra Medioevo ed Età Moderna* (Florence: Sismel Edizioni del Galluzzo, 2013). On medieval examples, see Robert G. Ousterhout, "The Church of Santo Stefano: A 'Jerusalem in Bologna'," *Gesta* 20 (1981): 311–321; and Kathryn Rudy, *Virtual Pilgrimages in the Convent: Imagining Jerusalem in the Late Middle Ages* (Turnhout: Brepols, 2011); and Robin Butlin, "A Sacred and Contested Place: English and French Representations of Palestine in the Seventeenth Century," in *Place, Culture and Identity: Essays in Historical Geography in Honour of Alan R. H. Baker*, ed. Iain S. Black and Robin A. Butlin (Quebec: Laval University Press, 2001), 91–31.

[31] See, for example, Mark Trowbridge, "Jerusalem Transposed: A Fifteenth-Century Panel for the Bruges Market," *Journal of Historians of Netherlandish Art* 1 (2009): 1–22.

Seville. As any modern traveler to Seville knows, the Easter rites remain a central feature of its festive life, and this was certainly the case in the sixteenth century. Ribera's decision to construct a House of Pilate anchored a more ambitious devotional project that involved the introduction of a *via crucis* procession. The new devotional rite, which he formally introduced in 1521, traced a route through the city that led from his palace (Station 1) to the Tempieta, a revered local shrine dedicated to the cross (Station 11). The new route followed the measurements of the via dolorosa, which he had taken personally while in Jerusalem and that he included in a pilgrimage treatise published the same year. Enshrined through these sacred measurements, the new *via crucis* procession symbolically incorporated his palace and the Tempieta as two ends of a new spiritual geography that transformed Seville into another Jerusalem, at least during the Easter rites.[32] We should note that the procession quickly became a popular one, earning it a jubilee indulgence in 1529 from Pope Clement VII.[33]

3.2.2 *The Holy Land Pilgrimage Treatise*

This broader consideration of the devotional life of members of the Order provides a valuable context for the following discussion of their early modern pilgrimage treatises. It is fair to say that pilgrimage treatises devoted to the Holy Land comprised the largest and most important body of Western pilgrimage accounts during the medieval and Early Modern Periods. What makes them a fascinating source for Catholic culture broadly construed is that they were produced in many languages and by authors of diverse social ranks, though most of them were lay authors like the knights of our study. The Order was itself an international society. When we consider as well that knights and authors circulated their texts for public consumption, whether in manuscript or published form, we should read their accounts not only as expressions of personal devotion to the Holy Land but also as assertions of spiritual expertise and leadership.

---

[32] The Tempiete was a small "temple" that covered the cross and was around by the fifteenth century and likely constructed by the Hermandad de negros de Nuestro Señora de los Angeles. The confraternity exists to this day. Enriquez purportedly bought and restored the shrine when he introduced the *via crucis* in 1521.

[33] Amanda Jaye Wunder, "Classical, Christian, and Muslim Remains in the Construction of Imperial Seville (1520–1635)," *Journal of the History of Ideas* 64 (2003): 195–212. The indulgence is mentioned in Pereda, "Measuring Jerusalem," 82.

A central claim of this chapter, however, is that the knights embraced a distinctive Catholic ideal, one that is also visible in their pilgrimage treatises. Indeed, when we consider the significant contribution of the knights to the pilgrimage genre along with the myriad ways in which they marked their texts as products of members of the Order, it seems important to consider their treatises as yet another distinctive act of collective devotion that was meaningful to many members of the Order alongside their participation in the pilgrimage and the knighting ritual. For these reasons, their texts offer valuable insight into the unique religious character of the Order from the perspective of some of its early modern members.

To suggest that Holy Land pilgrimage treatises lent themselves to the exploration of distinct "Catholic" identities may perhaps seem to fly in the face of scholarship that has often emphasized the formulaic nature of this literary genre and even questioned the extent to which we can assume a unique authorial identity in a given text.[34] It is well known, for example, that authors and publishers routinely copied passages and images without attribution. Nicolas Benard, for one, mentions borrowing from other travel accounts to compile his list of distances including the book of an unnamed French friar ("cordelier") who he says made the journey twice.[35] However, a broader consideration of over seventy pilgrimage treatises undertaken during the course of this research suggests that some scholars have failed to take seriously the remarkable facility for self-construction offered by the Holy Land genre precisely because it was predicated upon a well-established narrative of spiritual journeying. To be more precise, the formulaic structure thrusts into relief unique, divergent features of each text that can tell us a great deal about the authors themselves. In the case of members of the Order of the Holy Sepulcher, their treatises illuminate both shared as well as individual features that argue for considering those studied here as cultural products of a unique spiritual society. In order to make this case, however, we need to first

---

[34] For a recent contribution to this debate, see Kathryn Blair Moore, "The Disappearance of an Author, the Appearance of a Genre: Niccolò da Poggibonsi and Pilgrimage Guidebooks between Manuscript and Print," *Renaissance Quarterly* 66 (2013): 357–411. Michael Campopiano also suggests that medieval pilgrimage treatises should be considered "compilations" because of the evident borrowing, see "Islam, Jews and Eastern Christianity in Late Medieval Pilgrim's Guidebooks: Some Examples from the Franciscan Convent of Mount Sion," *Al-Masaq: Journal of the Medieval* Mediterranean 24 (2012): 75–89.

[35] Benard, *Le Voyage de Hierusalem*, 737–738.

confront the distinctive character of the Holy Land pilgrimage treatise as a devotional genre, particularly in terms of its narrative form and devotional function. Most importantly, we need to understand it as a mode of spiritual journeying, because the pilgrimage was a spiritual journey.[36] Typically, they were structured in three parts: the journey to the Holy Land, the visitation of the Holy Places, and the journey home.

This narrative centering of the visitation of the Holy Places was strategic, affirming the spiritual experience of the Holy Land as the entire point of the journey, while underscoring an essential duality of a journey that transcended time as much as it traversed space. The pilgrimage, after all, took the pilgrim-author and their devout readers away from the mundane realities of their own existence in Europe to visit the apostolic past, a past that Catholics were told continued to unfold at the Holy Places because these were sacred sites and thus timeless. The journey was, moreover, an internal one, moving the pilgrim from a state of sin to perfection through his/her first-hand experience of Christ. The objective of the pilgrim was direct contact with Christ, but he/she had to move through physical space (as well as across time) to do so.

Since for most Western Europeans the Holy Places lay in a region that was difficult to access, one that was also culturally unfamiliar and potentially dangerous, pilgrimage treatises served as practical as well as spiritual guidebooks. As a practical resource, the books prepared the reader for the economic and physical realities of the long journey and provided useful observations on local culture. Readers expected to learn about the most common expenses including the costs of travel, food, and clothing. Authors also typically warned about the dangers posed by pirates, Ottoman vessels, and the winds on the Mediterranean Sea. As one example, the French friar Henri Castela includes a list of provisions necessary to survive the rigors of a journey that he says could last between three and six months depending on the vagaries of sea travel. He advised his readers to carry a mattress and listed the fees expected of pilgrims along the journey, for example, the cost of booking passage on a local ship and to pay Turkish officials during their stay. If arriving at Jaffa, for example, the port nearest to Jerusalem, Castela told his readers to go to the nearby city of Rama (Rameh, Ramle, Al-Ram) to purchase the license required to travel through the region from the local Ottoman governor. Castela also advised them on how to avoid irritating Turks while

---

[36] In addition to studies mentioned earlier, see also the seminal work, Alphonse Dupront, *Du sacré: Croisades et pèlerinages-images et langages* (Paris: Editions Gallimard, 2013).

traveling through the region, urging them, for example, not to wear the colour green because it was a sacred colour.[37]

That the journey had to be difficult was of course important to the spiritual narrative of the treatise because pilgrimage was a rite of purification inasmuch as it was an act of devotion. Going to the Holy Land was about being transformed. To signal this purpose, the narrative often shifts gears once the pilgrims arrive at the gates of Jerusalem. The pace slows down, preparing the pilgrim-reader for the profundity of the coming visitation of the Holy Places. That Jerusalem resides on a cluster of hills in a hilly landscape aided the traditional narrative because it allowed for sudden, wondrous encounters with the holy city. More than a few treatises describe climbing up to a peak to find Jerusalem suddenly in view, its shimmering rooftops alerting travelers to the mysteries awaiting them in its ancient streets. Jerusalem still lay a good distance away but for the exhausted travelers it had announced itself and they were encouraged. For the Flemish knight Jean Zuallart, this first glimpse of the holy city became an opportunity to pause and contemplate the city's ancient splendour, recall the momentous biblical past that transformed it into a sacred city, and offer a prayer in thanksgiving.[38] The most meaningful part of Holy Land narratives – the visitation of the Holy Places – began once the pilgrims were safely ensconced in the hospice attached to the Franciscan convent. At each stage of the visitation, the author usually provides some physical description of the sacred site in terms of its architecture and ornamentation along with a brief recounting of its biblical history. Rich descriptions of the performance of Catholic liturgical rites are an especially common feature of early modern treatises, though we do find them in earlier ones as well, because liturgy was important to the devotional function of these texts.

---

[37] Henri Castela, *Le guide et adresse pour ceux qui veulent faire le S. Voiage de Hierusalem par V.P.F. Henry Castela Tolosain religieux observantin et confesseur des Dmes religieuses a Bordeaux* (Paris: chez Laurens Sonnius rue S. Jacques au compas d'or, 1604), ff. 40–47.

[38] Jean Zuallart, *Le tres devot voyage de Jerusalem, avec les figures des lieux saincts, & plusieurs autres, tirées au naturel* (Anvers: Arnould s'Conincx, 1608), Book III, 26. "A l'instant qu'elle fut ainsi apperceuë de nous, suyvant l'ancienne & treslouable coustume des devots Pelerins y arrivans, nous descendismes de noz Asnes & montures: & nous prosternans & baisans la terre, fut chanté le *Te Deum Laudamus*, l'hymne *Urbo beata Jerusalem*... & de telle devotion que plusieurs d'entre nous, à chaudes larmes (glorifiant Dieu de sa bonté immense) le remercierent humblement de ce que par sa divine grace, il nous avoit conduitz iusques là, & faict dignes de voir les lieux Saincts & desirez."

Pilgrim-readers not only wanted to hear about the rites but also participate in them, one of the reasons why pilgrimage guidebooks and the longer treatises provided a list of prayers and psalms performed and the indulgences earned at each place. The third and final section was often the shortest and followed the pilgrim-author home to Europe, now transformed by his/her experience of the most sacred of sacred landscapes.

As the above description is intended to suggest, the sacred geography of the Holy Land grounded Holy Land pilgrimage narratives. In his well-known treatise, the *Historica Theologica e Moralis Terra Elucidatio Elucidation* (1639), friar Francesco Quaresmio outlined several itineraries within Jerusalem alone and surrounding regions alone that took place over the course of many days.[39] These were in addition to itineraries leading to more distant sites – along the river Jordan, for example, which lies just to the east of Jerusalem and flows northward, and which took early modern pilgrims to several other sites – Mount Nebo, the site of Jesus' baptism by John the Baptist at Bethany, the cave where Lot hid during the destruction of Sodom and Gomorrah, and the Dead Sea. From there one could visit the many Holy Places in both lower and upper Galilee, including Mount Tabor, which was associated with the transfiguration of Christ, Bethsaida (where Jesus miraculously fed people fish), and Mary's Well (Ain Maryam), the reputed site of the Annunciation. But the most important visitations were those in and around Jerusalem and, in particular, those familiar through the popular devotional rite known as the Stations of the Cross. The *via crucis* began at the House of Pilate and followed the via dolorosa (road of tears), recreating the Passion of Christ – Jesus' final journey carrying the cross to the site of his execution on Golgotha, also known as Calvary. As Antonio Pereda discusses, the sixteenth century was a formative time in the evolution of this rite, which saw the number of stations gradually increase from seven to fourteen by 1600.[40] These stations continue to direct Western pilgrimage in the city to this day, marking the sites of the condemnation and flagellation of Christ at the palace of Pontius Pilate and the crowning with thorns (Stations 1, 2), the places where Jesus encountered his Mother (Station 4), Simon helped Jesus carry the cross (Station 5), the widow Veronica wiped his brow (Station 6), and Jesus consoled the women of Jerusalem (Station 8).

---

[39] Francesco Quaresmio, *Historica Theologica e Moralis Terra Elucidatio* (Antwerp: Plantiniana Balthasaris Moreti, 1639; reprint, Jerusalem: Franciscan Printing Press, 1989).

[40] Pereda, "Measuring Jerusalem," 91.

Pilgrims along the way also took note of three places where Christ stumbled under the heavy burden of the cross (Stations 3, 7, 9). Stations 10 through 14 concerned the crucifixion and resurrection of Christ and are found inside the Basilica of the Holy Sepulcher. Station 10, which to this day holds one of the chapels belonging to the Franciscans, marks the place where Christ was stripped of his garments and then led to his crucifixion on Calvary (Stations 11, 12). Early modern pilgrimage treatises suggest that Station 13, the site of the anointing, provided one of the most moving moments during the procession of the Basilica, as friars assumed the roles of apostles, removed the body of Christ from the cross, and lay it down on the stone to prepare it for burial. Station 14 marked the final stage of the *via crucis* and the moment when the body of Christ was laid to rest in his tomb only to rise almost shortly thereafter, a spiritual transformation represented through the empty marble Sepulcher.

As suggested here, the sacred itinerary embraced by early modern pilgrimage treatises was intended to be comfortably familiar to its Western Catholic readers. The formulaic structure reassured readers that the most meaningful of pilgrimage destinations was accessible to Catholics whether or not they made the journey in person because they could follow a literary route that remained largely unchanged over time. This function of pilgrimage treatises as "mobile" Holy Lands was certainly an important part of their allure.[41] The vast majority of Catholics simply could not go to the Holy Land in person, whether because of the great expense involved, the difficulties of the journey, or other commitments. While they did promise a familiar journey, pilgrimage treatises were by no means carbon copies because what added authenticity to an early modern account was the assurance that the author had truly gone *there*. It is certainly true that publishers and some authors did borrow from other accounts well into the Early Modern Period – Kathryn Blair Moore's analysis of the many reprintings of Niccolo Poggibonsi's famous treatise provides a particularly good example. A broad survey of seventy treatises undertaken during the course of this study suggests, even so, that most authors by the sixteenth century were writing genuinely first-hand accounts. That the early modern treatises privileged first-hand experience may owe something as well to broader shifts in travel writing during the Early Modern Period. The *relazione* genre, in particular, clearly

---

[41] On pilgrimage treatises as "holy lands," see, for example, Kathryn Rudy, "A Guide to Mental Pilgrimage: Paris, Bibliothèque de l'Arsenal Ms. 212," *Zeitschrift fur Kunstgeschichte* 63 (2000): 494–515.

influenced the Holy Land genre in a number of ways including its association of expertise with personal experience. As shall be argued in the following analysis of the treatises of the knights (see Section 3.3), however, growing conflict between Catholics and Protestants over conceptions of the sacred by 1520 also made "eye-witness" testimony of the pilgrimage much more meaningful.

Whether informed by other travel genres or responding to religious controversy, early modern authors including our knights played with form and content to mark their narratives as *their* journeys. A comparison of the treatises of friar Henri Castela and the Italian knight Aquilante Rocchetta makes this point. Both men traveled within a few years of one another (Rochetta in 1598/1599, Castela in 1600), but their accounts are quite different. To begin with, they took different routes, and secondly, they had different experiences along the journey.

Castela, for example, included a description of a storm to capture the dangers involved in traversing the Mediterranean. In this passage, we learn that fearful passengers retreated to a part of the ship that clearly contained a homely shrine made by the sailors: a place "where sailors kept their bell, and images that they revered of our Lord and the glorious Virgin Mary his mother, and of many other saints." There they "spent every night praying and demonstrating their devotion and zeal for God."[42] These small details ground his account in a material reality that was intended to convey the authenticity of his journey. Once in Jerusalem, Castela describes the practice of Coptic tattooing. Tatoos were one of the more popular mementoes of the journey for many pilgrims and they came in different forms. Castela mentions, in particular, the mark of Jerusalem, no doubt meaning the Jerusalem cross. The Copts used hot needles and some sort of liquid, which he describes as similar to "fiel de boeuf,"[43] a paste often used to treat skin conditions to provide some relief from the pain ("pour en oster la douleur"). The Copts used a distinctive,

---

[42] Castela, *Le Guide*, f. 14v–15. "... leur clochette, & les images qu'ils reverent de nostre Seigneur, de la glorieuses vierge Marie sa mere, & de quelques autres saincts, la ou toutes les nuicts ils vont faire leurs oraisons, presentans devotement leur intention & zele à Dieu ...."

[43] "Fiel de boeuf" was a home remedy in the form of a paste or ointment used for painful skin conditions. See, for example, M. Charles Estienne and Jean Liebault, *Lagriculture, et maison rustique de M. Charles Estienne, et Jean Liebault: Docteurs en Medecine* (Rouen: Charles de la Fontaine, 1601), 227. The book is a later edition and was likely printed in Luneville, Lorraine.

albeit unnamed, "herbe" to blacken the image making it impossible to erase.[44]

These details lent veracity to Castela's account because they are unique to it. In a different way, the Italian Rocchetta authenticated his account by displaying his expert knowledge of recent travel routes. He made the journey in 1598. He begins by noting that Venice was still the best-known port of departure for the Holy Land, but he had been told by a number of Venetians living in Aleppo, Damascus, and Cairo ("certi Venetiani in alcune Città di Turchi") that fewer pilgrims were now passing through it.[45] However, there were in fact many other options. French and Spanish ports were especially useful, he says, because these states had mercantile ties with many of the Levantine ports. Rochetta chose to depart from the port of Messina in Sicily. Malta was another well-traveled port on the way from Europe for merchant ships. We do know that Rocchetta eventually ended up in Alexandria, where he booked passage on a boat named *Le Germe* headed for Cairo. Cairo was a city that fascinated Western travelers, but for pilgrims it also offered access to numerous Christian shrines including several associated with the flight of the Holy Family (Jesus, Mary, and Joseph) from Bethlehem. One of the most significant is the Tree of the Virgin (El Matareya), a sycamore that provided them shelter during their travels.

According to the legend of the shrine, a spring sprang up so that Mary could wash Jesus and the bark was believed to have healing properties. The shrine was a very popular destination for Coptic Christians, in particular, though Catholics also went there to worship. In fact, the Franciscans maintained a small convent nearby that included a chapel. Friar Bernardino Amico visited Cairo not long after Rocchetta and describes it in his *Trattato delle piante* as an "ancient church" belonging to the Catholics in which mass was celebrated every feast day but in particular on the feast of the Madonna.[46]

---

[44] Castela, *Le Guide*, f. 299.
[45] Aquilante Rocchetta, *Peregrinatione di Terra Santa ed'Altre Provincie di Don Aquilante Rocchetta Cavaliere del Santissimo Sepolcro* (Palermo: Alfonso dell'Isola, 1630), 5. "... molt'anni sono si dismise, non vi essendo concorso di Pellegrini, tal che hoggi non vi è piu questo pasaggio."
[46] Bernardino Amico, *Trattato delle piante & immagini de sacri edifizi di Terra Santa: Disegnate in Ierusalemme secondo le regole della Prospettiva & vera misura della lor grandezza Dal R.P. E, Bernardino Amico dal Gallipoli dell' Ord. di S. Francesco de Minori Osservanti* (Rome: Pietro Cecconcelli, 1620), 18.

Rocchetta may have visited the shrine while in Cairo but he seems to have gone there to join the well-known caravan that traveled the Royal Road, the ancient artery that linked Cairo with Damascus and passed close to Jerusalem. This was a popular option for Christians especially at Easter time because it was always accompanied by janissaries whose role was to protect pilgrims, merchants, and other travelers as they traveled the main roads of the region. Rocchetta mentions that the caravan from Cairo typically included "many Christians ... of diverse sects and nations," along with Turkish, Jewish, and Moorish merchants. Unfortunately for Rocchetta, he seems to have arrived at a bad time and instead ended up taking a boat to Jaffa.

Fees receive some discussion as well because they were demanded throughout the journey. Pilgrims, he emphasized, did not want to be caught unprepared or risk being turned away by Ottoman officials. They were required both upon arrival and departure at a Levantine port to cover tolls along the roads and, most importantly, to enter the Holy Places (*kaffara*).[47] All Western travelers must pay them, he emphasized, or risk enslavement. Rocchetta insisted that it was especially bad form to arrive without the fee demanded by the Ottoman porter who monitored entrance into the Basilica of the Holy Sepulcher because it placed the burden upon the friars who themselves "live on very little."[48]

Both Castela and Rocchetta included practical travel information in their treatises, but as these examples make clear, the routes they traveled and the experiences they acquired along the way to Jerusalem differed in ways that advertised the personal nature, and thus authenticity, of their accounts. Featuring themselves as participants in the liturgical rites was important for the same reason. Jean de Boisselly, for example, a Marseillais merchant based in Saida (Sidon), joined the Order of the Holy Sepulcher in 1643 during his pilgrimage to Jerusalem. Along with five companions, he booked passage on a boat that took them first to Acre, the port that is still visually dominated today by the imposing fortress built by the Knights of Saint John Hospitallers. After some time in this city, they boarded another ship to Jaffa and from there traveled overland to the small village of Rama (Al-Ram).[49] Boisselly's account is

---

[47] On fees, see also F. E. Peters, *Jerusalem: The Holy City in the Eyes of Chroniclers, Visitors, Pilgrims, and Prophets from the Days of Abraham to the Beginning of Modern Times* (Princeton: Princeton University Press, 1985), 555.
[48] Rocchetta, *Peregrinatione di Terra Santa*, 6–7.
[49] Boisselly, *Le pelerinage de Jean de Boisselly en Terre Sainte*, 71.

one of those that pays special attention to the liturgical rites, especially ones that were meaningful to him.

Indeed, a wonderful passage on the Palm Sunday procession situates him at the heart of the performance. As Boisselly describes, the procession began just outside the city gates in the small town of Bethpage where the Franciscan *custos*, dressed in a white surplice and stole began chanting the gospel appropriate "for that day" and "at the same place" with one of the other fathers.[50] The guardian then called two of the friars to serve, he says, as "his secretary and companion" for the performance of the office of the apostles, which they did by going down on their knees in front of him. As one began to read out the gospel and reached the words "Ite in castellum," two religious rose and went to get the ass that they said was held nearby at the place of "the Italian Mariano." Boisselly's mention of Mariano similarly locates the author *in* Bethpage *during* the rites since Mariano was clearly a local merchant. While awaiting its arrival, the *custos* gave a beautiful sermon on the biblical event. He then mounted the ass, which was led by the two religious. At this point, Boisselly integrates himself and his fellow pilgrims into the central performance by role-playing the ancient followers of Christ: "we six pilgrims were placed around the ass at the order of the Guardian [*custos*] in this manner: two holding the bridle, of which I was one, and the other was M. Martelly, two on each side and two others at the back of the ass."[51]

We should note that the performance of the procession at the biblical site was central to the spiritual import of the rite for Boisselly, but his description also placed him *in* the Holy Land as a contemporary witness and, just as importantly, as a participant in the rite itself. In other words, he was *there*. The travel narratives of Castela, Rocchetta, and Boisselly may have shared a similar narrative template, but as shown here, each used theirs to highlight the uniqueness of their own journey to, from, and within, the Holy Land. It is in part because authors were eager to establish themselves as real actors in their own pilgrimage dramas that their accounts comprise an important corpus of historical documents on the early modern Holy Land and its pilgrimage. From the three examples provided here, for example, one can see that the early modern pilgrimage

---

[50] Boisselly, *Le pelerinage de Jean de Boisselly en Terre Sainte*, 74. "comme encores ung des autres Pères pour chanter l'évangile de ce jour-là, sur le mesme lieu."

[51] Boisselly, *Le pelerinage de Jean de Boisselly en Terre Sainte*, 74. "Nous estant mis six péllerins à l'entour de l'asne par ordre dudit R.P. vicaire, savoir: deux tenans la bride, don't j'en serois esté ung et le premier avec M. Marielly, deux à costé et deux autres au derrière de l'asne."

was a well-established and regulated travel industry, which was sufficiently flexible to allow pilgrims multiple options along the route to and from Jerusalem including a visit to the Crusader fortress at Acre and its port. They provide intriguing glimpses, moreover, into the materiality of the pilgrimage experience – fees, mattresses, storm-tossed ships, religious diversity, a Palm Sunday procession. For these reasons as well, pilgrimage treatises can be treated as valuable windows into the religious life of the author or, in the case of this study, a pilgrim brotherhood. As the remaining discussion will show, texts produced by members of the Order present us with an important window into the spiritual nature of this brotherhood during a period of profound and destabilizing change for adherents of the Catholic tradition. The Reformation that tore apart the Western Church after 1517 rattled the foundations of the old institution, threatening core Catholic teachings and practices including the rite of pilgrimage. The Holy Land pilgrimage became a particular locus of Reformation controversy early on. Section 3.3 explores the pilgrimage treatises of the knights as modes of controversy with an eye to illuminating the distinctive nature of their shared religious ideal. In preparation for this analysis, we begin by situating the writings of the early modern knights in their Reformation context and, in particular, in debates over the efficacy of the Holy Land pilgrimage.

3.3 REFORMATION POLEMIC AND KNIGHTLY TREATISES

The richness of recent scholarship on the controversy over pilgrimage precludes the need for a full discussion here, allowing us instead to focus upon elements that are most important for interpreting the religious engagement of the knights. It was, to begin with, an enormously destructive controversy. Alexandra Walsham, Andrew Spicer, and Eric Nelson, among others, describe Catholic shrines reduced to rubble in regions penetrated by the new Protestant faiths after 1517, falling victim to local bouts of iconoclastic fury. Other acts of violence left religious statues defaced and chapels denuded of their relics, tapestries, and sacred art that was central to fostering the devotion of Catholic believers.[52] The reasons for this material destruction were multiple and varied but at their heart was a profound

---

[52] See, among others, Alexandra Walsham, *Reformation of the Landscape: Religion, Identity, and Memory in Early Modern Britain and Ireland* (Oxford: Oxford University Press, 2011); and Eric P. Nelson, *The Legacy of Iconoclasm: Religious War and the Relic Landscape of Tours, Blois and Vendôme, 1550–1750* (St. Andrews: St. Andrews Studies in French History and Culture, 2013).

disagreement between Catholics and Protestants over the nature and locus of the sacred. Catholic pilgrimage as an institution rested upon a number of spiritual tenets, in particular, a belief in divine immanence (the capacity of the material to contain divinity), the mediating function of the cult of the saints, and the salvific benefits of the pilgrimage as a penitential and devotional rite. It is also true that the rite had Catholic as well as Protestant critics, among them Desiderius Erasmus and many of his fellow Christian humanists. In his colloquy, "A Pilgrimage for Pilgrim's sake" (1526), for example, Erasmus poked at the credulity of the pilgrim Ogygius when faced with chapels filled with "true" relics of the apostles at the shrine of Saint Mary in Walsingham. Typical of the Christian humanists, Erasmus was concerned about abuse of the rite by the clergy as well as the laity, the former for potential fraudulent promotion and the latter for placing more value upon the outward practice of the rite and not enough upon internal change.[53] Protestant reformers, in comparison, waged a more frontal assault upon the theological legitimacy of pilgrimage than most humanists. In his *Treatise to the Christian Nobility* published in 1520, Luther questioned the scriptural basis of divine immanence, the cult of the saints, and the spiritual benefits of visiting shrines. The German reformer rejected, in particular, Catholic insistence that relics contained the divinity of the saints, challenging in the process the function of shrines as points of intimate contact between devout believer and divinity. He urged that all pilgrimages be stopped because they held no real spiritual benefit and, if anything, were occasions that encouraged sinning. In his *Explanations of the 95 Theses*, which the reformer published in 1518, Luther took pointed aim at Catholic reverence for the Holy Land and other important pilgrimage destinations, arguing that "the Temple in Jerusalem is no more, and now God must be worshipped wherever one happens to be .... For if Christ is sitting at the right hand of his Father, why, then, should we seek Him in Rome, in Campostela, in Aachen, or at the Oak? You will not find god there, you will find the devil."[54]

---

[53] Desiderius Erasmus, "A Pilgrimage for Pilgrim's Sake, *The Colloquies, I. Collected Works of Erasmus*, trans. Craig R. Thompson (Toronto: University of Toronto Press, 1997), 619–675. The rite was a matter of concern, however, within the church hierarchy more generally. See, for example, Charles Zika, "Hosts, Processions and Pilgrimages: Controlling the Sacred in Fifteenth-Century Germany," *Past and Present* 118 (1988): 25–54.

[54] See Graham Tomlin's discussion of Luther on pilgrimage in *Luther's Gospel: Reimagining the World* (London, Oxford: Bloomsbury, 2017), 80. The English translation is taken from Tomlin.

Later reformers including John Calvin and Pierre de Moulin echoed similar challenges to the veracity of the rite. In his *traite des reliques* (1543), Calvin wrote a scathing critique of the veneration of relics, essentially accusing the Church of fraud in its promotion of shrines. Writing several decades later in 1605, the Huguenot minister Pierre Du Moulin sparked controversy in France when he translated the famous *Letter to Kensitor* written by the early church patriarch Gregory of Nyssa (d. 394). Nyssa's text resonated among Protestant reformers, who cited it as evidence of later Catholic misinterpretation of the practice of pilgrimage. One can see the influence of Nyssa in the writings of both Luther and Calvin, particularly Nyssa's insistence that "the changing of one's place does not bring any greater nearness to God." It depended, rather, upon the state of one's soul. If filled with "base thoughts," then even being in the Holy Land, he argued, would not help: "Even if you were present at Golgotha or on the Mount of Olives or by the memorial rock of the Resurrection, you would be as far from receiving Christ in yourself."[55]

Moulin's decision to translate the *Letter to Kensitor* in 1605, and the heated responses it generated from French Catholic leaders, shows that the Holy Land pilgrimage remained a contested issue in a divided French kingdom several decades after the deaths of Luther and Calvin. Richard Coyle suggests in fact that Moulin's treatise directly inspired friar Jean Boucher to write *Le Bouquet sacre compose des plus belles fleurs de la terre sainte*, a popular pilgrimage treatise that receives more attention in Chapter 6.[56] The controversy over the rite of pilgrimage carried on with some intensity in many other European regions as well, in particular, those hit hard by confessional division. To suggest that confessional lines had hardened around the issue of pilgrimage by the seventeenth century, however, would be an overstatement. As recent research on the Protestant traditions makes clear, while most Protestants may have rejected a traditionally Catholic conception of pilgrimage by the seventeenth century, others continued to see them as spiritually meaningful and even

---

[55] Richard Coyle, "Rescuing the Holy Land in Friar Jean Boucher's *bouquet sacre compose des plus belles fleurs de la terre sainte*," in *Through the Eyes of the Beholder: The Holy Land, 1517–1713*, ed. Judy A. Hayden and Nabil Matar (Leiden: Brill, 2013), 97–110. See, in particular, 98–99. For the translations of Nyssa's letters, Coyle relies upon Anna M. Silvas, *Gregory of Nyssa: The Letters – Introduction, Translation and* Commentary (Boston: Brill, 2007): 115–116.

[56] Coyle, "Rescuing the Holy Land."

powerful.[57] The response to pilgrimage among those who stayed with the traditional Church after 1517 was no less fraught. Protestant accusations of fraud among other issues rankled church authorities in particular, playing upon deep-seated concerns about ensuring orthodoxy. To deal with theological among other challenges posed by Protestantism to Catholic practice, the Council of Trent (1545–1563) reasserted the doctrine of divine immanence and the cult of the saints, but it also demonstrated its intent to more closely supervise and regulate the authorization of new cults as well as existing ones.[58]

It is in the context of these debates that we need to situate the pilgrimage treatises of the Order of the Holy Sepulcher because after 1520 Holy Land pilgrimage treatises assumed a new function: that of religious polemic. This is not entirely surprising when we consider the Holy Land's revered status as a pilgrimage destination. Moreover, the genre lent itself to religious controversy. Firstly, it was already a well-established and popular devotional genre in Western Europe by the time of the Reformation, one that was published mostly in vernacular languages and thus accessible to a broad readership. Secondly, as Daniel Vitkus has argued, its distinctive narrative form as a mode of personal journeying and emphasis upon eye-witness testimony lent itself to polemical use by Protestants as well as Catholics. As discussed earlier, by the sixteenth century a central point of the narrative was to emphasize first-hand experience of the Holy Places. In the hands of Protestant authors, these "eye-witness" accounts could be used to instead unmask evidence of Catholic ignorance, gullibility, and clerical fraud through the lens of the visiting Protestant critic.[59] They were, in other words, intentionally

---

[57] See, for example, Walsham, *Reformation of the Landscape*; and Gerrit Verhoeven, "Calvinist Pilgrimages and Popish Encounters: Religious Identity and Sacred Space on the Dutch Grand Tour (1598–1685)," *Journal of Social History* 43 (2010): 615–634.

[58] On this issue, see, William J. Taylor, *Theatre of a Thousand Wonders* (Cambridge: Cambridge University Press, 2016), 55–60; Cécile Vincent-Cassy, "The Search for Evidence: The Relics for Martyred Saints and Their Worship in Cordoba after the Council of Trent," in *After Conversion: Iberia and the Emergence of Modernity*, ed. Mercedes Garcia-Arenal (Leiden: Brill, 2016), 126–152; Claire Copeland, "Saints, Devotion and Canonization in Early Modern Italy," *History Compass* 10 (2012): 260–269; Simon Ditchfield, "Thinking with Saints: Sanctity and Society in the Early Modern World," *Critical Inquiry* 35 (2009): 552–584.

[59] On Protestant accounts of the Holy Land pilgrimage and divine immanence, see Sean E. Clarke, "Protestants in Palestine: Reformation of Holy Land Pilgrimage in the Sixteenth and Seventeenth Centuries," PhD diss., University of Arizona, 2013; Daniel Vitkus, "Trafficking with the Turk: English Travellers in the Ottoman Empire during the Early Seventeenth Century," in *Travel Knowledge: European "Discoveries" in the Early*

subversive modes of controversy, one reason why Vitkus describes Protestant iterations as "anti-pilgrimages." But as the following discussion of the treatises of the knights makes clear, many Catholic authors found the traditional narrative structure just as useful for reaffirming Catholic teachings on the rite.

The twelve treatises examined here were all produced between 1520 and 1700. Collectively, the authors reflect the social and ethnic diversity of the broader membership of the Order. Six were produced by Frenchmen (Greffin Affagart, Nicolas de Hault, Anthoine Regnault, Nicolas Benard, Jacques de Villamont,[60] and Jean de Boisselly), three by Italians (Giovanni Pesenti, Carlo Maggi, and Aquilante Rocchetta), two by Flemish authors (Jean Zuallart and Jean Cotovic, the latter a Catholic priest from Utrecht),[61] and one by the Spaniard Don Fadrique Enriquez de Ribera.[62] That so many knights were drawn historically to this genre is not really surprising when we consider that the Order was first and foremost a society of pilgrims. The Holy Land genre promised European readers first-hand accounts of the experience of the rite, something that our twelve knights could certainly provide since they had all made the journey. It was a genre, moreover, that had long welcomed lay as well as clerical authors, another reason that it would have likely appealed to members of the Order. One notes, for example, that only one of the authors discussed here was a cleric.

Modern Period, ed. Ivo Jamps and Jyotsna G. Singh (Basingstoke: Palgrave, 2001), 35–52; and Paris O'Donnell, "Pilgrimage or Anti-Pilgrimage? Uses of Mementoes and Relics in English and Scottish Narratives of Travel to Jerusalem, 1596–1632," *Studies in Travel Writing* 13 (2009): 125–139.

[60] Jacques de Villamont, The *Voyages du seigneur de Villamont, Chevalier de l'ordre de Hierusalem, Gentilhomme du pays de Bretaigne*, vol. II (Paris: Claude de Montr'oeil et Jean Richer, 1595). Villamont devoted one of his three volumes to the Holy Land and it serves as a pilgrimage narrative. He also published another text in 1597, *Traité ou instruction pour tirer des armes, de l'excellent Scrimeur Hieronyme Calvacabo, Bolognois, avec un discourse pour tirer de l'espec seul, fait par le defunct Patenostre de Rome, traduit de l'italien en François par le seigneur de Villamont, Chevalier de l'Ordre de Hierusalem, & Gentilhomme de la chamber du Roy*.

[61] The Flemish author is Johann van Kootwyck, but De Gennes says that he has become better known by his French name: "Jean Cotovic." De Gennes, *Les Chevaliers du Saint-Sépulcre de Jérusalem*, vol. I, 391. Jean Cotovic [Johann van Kootwyck], *Itinerarium* (Utrecht: Hieryonimus Verdussium, 1619). The preface describes him as "iuris v. doctori equity Hierosolymitano."

[62] Fadrique Enriquez de Ribera (1478–1539) published his pilgrimage treatise in 1521, almost immediately upon returning from his journey in 1520.

Though the Order did include a small number of clerics by the sixteenth century, the majority of members were laymen,[63] and this was especially true of those who decided to write their accounts. The authors, moreover, came from diverse social ranks. The Spaniard Ribera, the Marquis of Tarifa, was the most socially prominent of the knights studied here, though Villamont also came from provincial noble lineage. In the title of his treatise, he is referred to as a "gentilhomme" of the region of Brittany. Yves Berçe provides even more information, telling us that he held the office of a gentleman of the bedchamber.[64] It is harder to place Affagart and de Hault, who respectively held the titles of "seigneur Courteilles du Boise en Maine" and "seigneur de Fromonot & Mortaux." These titles suggest that they owned rural property but they were not automatic carriers of nobility.[65] More likely they were members of the urban (and upwardly mobile) elite, a broad category that also included the French merchants Anthoine Regnault, Jean de Boisselly, and Nicolas Benard, the Italian Pesenti, who came from a prominent mercantile family in Bergamo, and Zuallart, a former mayor of the city of Hainault.

In the following discussion, it is not our intention to confer a special significance upon the literary and intellectual quality of the twelve treatises let alone stake a claim to a broader influence. It is fair to say in fact that most of the texts are unremarkable examples of the pilgrimage genre. For the most part, our authors relied upon narrative and stylistic tropes that were characteristic of early modern pilgrimage texts and were not especially innovative. Moreover, with the notable exceptions of those penned by Jean Zuallart and Aquilante Rocchetta, the treatises of the knights do not display a sophisticated grasp of classical and biblical learning or theology – authorities that were frequently invoked in Reformation controversies and used by many other authors of pilgrimage

---

[63] Jean Cotovic, for example, was a cleric. Jean de Gennes says that the first known cleric in the order was Jean Sorel who joined in 1521. De Gennes, De Gennes, *Les Chevaliers du Saint-Sépulcre de Jérusalem*, vol. I, 412.

[64] Yves Berçe, "Discours de M. Yves Berçe. President de la Société de l'histoire de France en 2005: Les voyages de M. De Villamont (1595), introduction à l'histoire virtuelle," in *Annuaire-bulletin de la société de l'histoire de France* (Paris: Au Siège de la Société, 2006), 3.

[65] Greffin Affagart (d. 1557) traveled to the Holy Land in 1533–1534. His *Relation de la Terre Sainte* was written sometime between 1533 and 1534, close to the time of his pilgrimage, though not published until 1902. *Relation de la Terre Sainte (1522–1534)* (Paris: Librairie V. Lecoffre, 1902); Nicolas de Hault, *Le Voyage de Hieruselam faict l'an mil cinq cens quatre veingts treize* (Paris: Abraham Savorain, 1601).

treatises.[66] Perhaps for this reason only a few of the published treatises received more than one edition during the Early Modern Period. Villamont, for example, seems to have received at least twenty-five editions between 1595 and 1620,[67] a fact that may have owed to the ambitious nature of his *Voyages* and reputation for some learning. Yves Berçe describes him as "a devout Catholic, learned without being erudite, an amateur mathematician and cosmographer." The *Voyages* also included volumes on Italy, Greece, as well as one on the Holy Land and the eastern Mediterranean. Along with that of Villamont, Zuallart's treatise enjoyed several editions including ones in French and Italian.[68]

Since the majority of treatises published by knights received one edition, we can assume that both their readership and impact was likely modest, but then this was characteristic of most pilgrimage treatises published during the Early Modern Period. That they were typical examples of the genre, however, does not undermine their value as unique windows into the spiritual character of the Order. Firstly, their texts reveal important theological fault lines that emerged between Protestant and Catholic believers after 1520, which the knights considered especially threatening to a pilgrimage rite that was deeply meaningful to them. How each author engaged in defense of the pilgrimage, in other words, illuminates shared Catholic beliefs. Secondly, it is in their treatises as well that our authors elucidated their claims to spiritual authority by infusing their texts with the markings of their membership in the Order. For this reason, in particular, we need to consider their pilgrimage treatises as sacred histories of the Order, because they constructed a sacred past that was rooted in the same region once trod by Christ. Looking to begin with at their engagement in spiritual controversy, their treatises show that a particularly thorny issue for the knights was Protestant rejection of the Holy Land as the locus of Christ and the spiritual efficacy of the pilgrimage. As we shall see, how our authors responded to Protestant criticism varied. Collectively, however, their texts unveil a Holy Land that was deeply meaningful to these men as a powerful and tangible vessel of Christian authority and the pilgrimage as a critical and transformative site of encounter between Christ and the devout Christian.

---

[66] See, in particular, Zur Shalev, *Sacred Words, Sacred Worlds: Geography, Religion, and Scholarship, 1550–1700* (Leiden: Brill, 2011).

[67] Berçe, "Discours de M. Yves Berçe," 3. "lettré sans être erudite, amateur d'arithmétique et de cosmographie." These editions were issued in Paris, Lyon, Rouen and Arras.

[68] Rocchetta's was first published in 1630, and there was at least one later edition in 1680.

3.3.1 The Knights and Religious Polemic

Among the twelve treatises, those of Anthoine Regnault and Jean Zuallart are the most pointed and explicit in their engagement in confessional debate. For Regnault, it was Luther's criticism of indulgences that seems to have motivated his own sturdy defense of the practice in his treatise. His willingness to confront Luther head on may also reflect his first-hand experience of religious division in France. One wonders whether it is a coincidence, in particular, that Regnault published his account of the Holy Land pilgrimage in 1573, a year after the infamous Massacre of St. Bartholomews' Day (August 24, 1572). The massacre is one of the most hotly debated episodes of the Wars of Religion because it was a horrific moment of religious violence that saw members of the royal family as well as ordinary Parisians complicit in the slaughter of thousands of Calvinists in the city. Barbara Diefendorf's careful study of the event suggests that the massacre began as a coup against the powerful Calvinist leadership who had arrived in the city days earlier to celebrate the wedding of the King's sister to the Protestant Henry of Navarre. The sounding of a bell to begin the coup triggered widespread panic among the Catholic populace who had heard rumours of a potential Protestant attack for quite some time. Blood poured through the streets of the city over several days as neighbours slaughtered neighbours, violence that quickly spread to other confessionally divided cities across France. The event, which dealt a devastating blow to the morale of the French Huguenots in the short term, was soon heralded by the more militant Catholics as a mark of God's favour and praised from Catholic pulpits.[69] Since Regnault lived in Paris, he may well have witnessed this event firsthand. As a Catholic, he may well have also considered it a sign of God's favour. In the preface of his treatise, for example, Regnault reassures his fellow French Catholics that they were "walking in the faith of the son of God crucified and under the pure doctrine of the holy Catholic Church, and Roman."[70]

While what follows is a mostly traditional recounting of his pilgrimage, Regnault rather unusually includes a short treatise in defense of the practice of the Indulgence. Indulgences were an integral facet of the Holy Land pilgrimage by the Early Modern Period, offering pilgrims

---

[69] On the Massacre of St. Bartholomew's Day, see Barbara Diefendorf, *Beneath the Cross: Catholics and Huguenots in Sixteenth Century Paris* (Oxford: Oxford University Press, 1991).

[70] Anthoine Regnault, "Preface," *Discours du voyage doutre mer* (Lyon: n.p., 1573).

remission from sin after making the arduous journey. Medieval pilgrimage treatises typically recorded these as part of the itinerary, listing the number of indulgences attained at every Holy Place following the performance of the liturgical rites. Naming indulgences remained a characteristic element of early modern treatises as well. In some treatises, the list comprises a separate section, thus encapsulating in one literary space the totality of the remissions obtained through a visitation of the many Christian shrines.[71] Regnault's treatise, however, was clearly intended to undermine Lutheran criticism of the essential sanctity of the practice. After first taking time to describe the theological origins of the indulgence, Regnault then addressed Protestant criticism of corruption head on. He agreed, in particular, that reformers including Luther were not necessarily wrong in finding some instances of abuse by clerics who "pursued money and not the salvation of the people." He nevertheless insisted that the practice was still efficacious even in these cases because it was an expression of God's justice and mercy. A Pope who handed them out "imprudently and with little discretion," he argues, could never squander the "reward" because the treasury of the Church "carried the infinite merit of Christ."[72] Regnault thus draws a distinction between clerical corruption and the practice of the indulgence itself, arguing that it had legitimate theological origins and thus spiritual merit. Indulgences were gifts of God not of the Church, gifts that recognized the active presence of God in this world and the Holy Land as the most important place of encountering that divinity. Luther and other Protestant reformers, he argues, had caused more harm than good through their criticism of a rite that was essentially good and in doing so "greatly increased the present troubles."[73]

---

[71] See, for example, the list of indulgences provided by Rocchetta at the end of his treatise.
[72] Regnault, *Discours du voyage*, 172. The full passage is here: "Comme si par ces indulgences les ministres de l'Eglise pourchassoyent l'argent, & non le salut du people. Si le people soubz l'ombre de ces indulgences delaisse a faire bonnes oeuvres, ou qu'il fust pource plus negligent à fuir peche, ou bien soubz esperance d'en avoir pardon par vertu des indulgences, car ainsi abusant, il s'abuse, & ses pechez ne sont remis, non plus que si le Pape indiscrettement, & imprudemment distribuoit le tresor de l'Eglise, car combine que ce tresor soit infiniment grand, & ne peut ester epuisé, contenant en soy le merite infiny de Jesus Christ."
[73] Regnault, *Discours du voyage*, 172-173. "... je pense l'indult avoir esté saint, & l'intention bonne, mais toutesfoys corrompue par leur meschante avarice, accompagnée d'une plus mauvaise, & insatiable ambition, qui ont donné commencement, & grand accroissement aux presens troubles."

Like Regnault, the Flamand Jean Zuallart came from a region that experienced firsthand the devastating consequences of religious division, a fact that may also explain his direct engagement with Protestant criticism of the pilgrimage.[74] Similar to Regnault as well, he questioned the spiritual integrity of Protestant reformers who criticized the pilgrimage, though, perhaps more typical of his humanist formation, Zuallart attributed their destructive criticism to ignorance of Christian theology. As he argues at one point, "heretics today attack ancient practices and saintly institutions of the Catholic church." They did so by "distracting and misrepresenting devotions and pious conceptions for those eager to do the sacred journey of passed times," suggesting "that these practices were only abusive, diabolical illusions, full of idolatry and without fruit." In this passage, Zuallart argues that Protestant denial of the efficacy of the Holy Land pilgrimage was itself an indication that they were heretics. What clearly bothered him, more to the point for this discussion, was their denial that the pilgrim would truly encounter Christ in the region. Reformers argue, he says, that "pilgrims do nothing but waste time and money, especially those who go to the Holy Land, believing wrongly that they would see the redeemer in Jerusalem, converting, and suffering the death and the passion."[75] They deny this, he notes, even though miracles had been recorded in the Holy Sepulcher. Zuallart's response shows that he was well aware of Luther's indictment of the Holy Land pilgrimage, one that continued to be echoed by Protestant treatises throughout the Early Modern Period. As discussed earlier, Luther had rejected any suggestion that the son of God lived on in the Holy Land, insisting such a belief was folly. He wrote that the "coming of Christ and the holy Spirit" ensured that "God is no longer confined to one place as he was under the old dispensation." God could just as easily be encountered, he said, in one's parish church. Jerusalem was where God chose to live *before* His

---

[74] On the impact of the Reformation in the Netherlands in terms of religious violence and iconoclasm, see, among others, Judith Pollman, "Countering the Reformation in France and the Netherlands: Clerical Leadership and Catholic Violence, 1560–1585," *Past and Present* 190 (2006): 83–120.

[75] Zuallart, *Le tres devot voyage de Jerusalem*, Book I, 12–13. "les heretiques homes mondains, charnelz & contempteurs des anciennes usances & sainctes institutions de l'Eglise Catholique, afin de divertir & faire mepriser les devotions & pieuses conceptions à ceux qui on envie & volonté de faire de S. & salutaire voyage, disans avec les vieux Arriens, Pelagiens, Manicheans & autres heretiques de temps passé, que ce ne sont qu'abusions, illusions diabolicques, pleine d'Idolatrie Y sans fruict."

Advent.[76] One finds similar assertions in the writings of many early modern Protestant travelers to the Holy Land, among them George Sandys and Leonhard Rauwolf.

In challenging Luther directly, Zuallart demonstrated his unshakeable belief in the Holy Land as a tangible and accessible vessel of a living Christ. Though the majority of our authors shied away from direct engagement in controversy, we do find many of them making deliberate stylistic and narrative choices that intentionally amplified a similar conception of the Holy Land. We find this especially characteristic of the longer, more discursive treatises appearing during the early modern period. Several scholars have noted this trend by this time and have attributed it to the influence of new modes of travel writing and scientific thinking as well as changing literary tastes. Several early modern pilgrimage treatises reveal the influence of the popular *Relazione* genre, for example, which privileged greater precision in the representation and analysis of other peoples, animals, landscapes, and institutions, testifying to the expert knowledge and authority of the author.[77] When studied through the lens of religious debate, however, one notices that the more descriptive nature of the early modern treatises was no less useful for evoking a *present* Christ. At least three of our authors – Zuallart, Villamont, and Aquilante Rocchetta – share a similar concern, in particular, with accurately mapping the journey to Jerusalem by providing detailed descriptions of the changing topography and the Holy Places. For example, all three provide specific directions together with descriptions of buildings along the way, sometimes street by street. Villamont's passage on the via dolorosa in Jerusalem serves as a good example. The via dolorosa is the road memorialized in the *via crucis* rite that traces Christ's slow, painful procession through Jerusalem carrying the cross to the site of Calvary. Villamont, playing tour guide, provides clear spatial directions to the reader as they followed in His footsteps:

> ... turning a bit to the left, you see the house of the bad rich man. Going a little further, we come to the place where our Lord turned around, hearing the cries

---

[76] For this translation, see Graham Tomlin, "Protestants and Pilgrimage" in *Exploration in a Christian Theology of Pilgrimage*, ed. Craig Bartholomew and Fred Hughes (Aldershot: Ashgate Publishing, 2004), 114.

[77] Paul Zumthor and Catherine Peebles, "The Medieval Travel Narrative" *New Literary History* 25 (1994): 809–824. On the influence of the *relazione* specifically upon Franciscan Holy Land narratives, see Megan C. Armstrong, "Missionary Reporter," *Renaissance and Reformation/Renaissance et Réforme* 34 (2011): 127–158. However, I argue that the spiritual function remained most important.

made by the women of Jerusalem around him, and where he asked them not to cry for him but for themselves and their children. Twenty to thirty steps past this site, one finds the road that leads to the door of Ephraim, one of the tributes of Israel. Then turning right, near some newly built baths, you will find the place where Simon Cyrene was forced by the Jews to carry the cross of Jesus.[78]

This level of specificity in terms of directions was not necessarily characteristic of medieval accounts, though certainly counting the number of steps between Holy Places as well as providing precise measurements was quite common. As mentioned earlier, Nicolas Benard included a table of distances covering the route to Jerusalem in his own account.[79] Measuring sacred spaces reflected a distinctly Catholic conception of sacrality as wholly consuming of its material environment. Walls, stones, and the earth, as well as any objects contained within, radiated with the divinity of the holy person or event that transformed it, and this included its measurements.[80] This was especially true of the Sepulcher itself, a shrine that marked the *absence* of Christ, at least of his physical body. Christ once lay there but resumed his earthly form when he ascended to Heaven. The measurements were what remained of his former physical existence and were all the more meaningful and potent for that reason.[81] Sacred measurements could be replicated moreover, a fact that made the Holy Places and their sacrality portable, translated to new spaces through the construction of small- and large-scale replicas, engravings, or the medium of print. Bringing the Holy Land home was thus another objective of Don Fadrique Enriquez de Ribera when he incorporated his measurements of the via dolorosa in Jerusalem to mark a direct path from his palace to the Tempieto in Seville. One of his most prized mementoes from the pilgrimage was the band (rope) he used to measure distance. Ribbons used to measure a Holy Place and to touch the shrine were also prized pilgrimage mementoes sent to New Spain during the eighteenth century.[82]

---

[78] Villamont, *Voyages*, vol. II, ff. 154–155.
[79] Benard, *Le Voyage de Hierusalem*, 737–738.
[80] On sacred measurements, see, for example, Zur Shalev, "Christian Pilgrimage and Ritual Measurement in Jerusalem, preprint 384 (Berlin: Max Planck Institute for the History of Science, 2009), 1–20.
[81] See, for example, Caroline Bynum Walker, *Christian Materiality: An Essay on Religion in Late Medieval Europe* (Cambridge, MA: MIT press, 2011).
[82] Pereda, "Measuring Jerusalem," 89. The bull of 1529 apparently recognized the seven main stations of the cross that characterized the devotions at this time. On the New World, see, for example, the discussion of *medidas* (ribbons) used to touch local sacred images in Taylor, *Theatre of a Thousand Wonders*, 59–60.

As mentioned earlier, pilgrimage treatises also functioned as modes of replication that brought the Holy Places into the home and devotional life of the pilgrim through descriptions of their ornamentation, biblical story, rituals, and accurate measurements of each space.[83] But the provision of directions by our early modern authors was no less useful for emphasizing the presence of Christ *in* the Holy Places. Certainly, we need to consider that our authors were responding not only to Protestant rejection of divine immanence but also to scholarly criticism of the accuracy of the traditional itinerary. This is a point made by Zur Shalev and Adam Beaver, in particular. Whether Golgotha truly lay within the walls of the Holy Sepulcher or the real Grotto of the Nativity lay several miles from the site recognized on the traditional itinerary became matters of intense scrutiny, spurred to a significant degree by humanist interest in the Scriptures as well as classical sources.[84] Shalev's close analysis of Zuallart's treatise shows that the Flemish author was directly engaging with this contemporary debate, relying upon his own humanist-informed defense of the accuracy of the itinerary to defend its authenticity. Indeed, his maps and architectural renderings were considered so accurate that they were copied by other authors.[85] But demonstrating the accuracy of the existing itinerary was also important to the spiritual objectives of Villamont, Zuallart, and Rocchetta, since any criticism of the traditional itinerary threatened to undermine Catholic claims of the transformative nature of the pilgrimage. After all, the sacrality of each Holy Place was dependent upon its physical association with the biblical past. It was to disentangle the sacred from the material world that Protestant treatises found scholarly squabbling over the accuracy of the itinerary useful for their own religious objectives. As Sean E. Clarke has argued in his study of Protestant treatises, "a growing sense of the divine as transcendent

---

[83] Kathryn Rudy, "A Guide to Mental Pilgrimage: Paris, Bibliothèque de l'Arsenal ms. 212," *Zeitschrift für Junstgeschichte* 63/64 (2000): 494–515. See also Pnina Arad, "Mapping Divinity: Holy Landscape in Maps of the Holy Land," in *Jerusalem As Narrative Space*, ed. Annette Hoffmann and Gerhard Wolf (Leiden: Brill, 2012), 263–276.

[84] Adam Beaver, "Scholarly Pilgrims: Antiquarian Visions of the Holy Land," in *Sacred History: Visions of Christian Origins in the Renaissance World*, ed. Katherine Van Liere and Simon Ditchfield (Oxford: Oxford University Press, 2012), 267–283; and Shalev, *Sacred Words, Sacred Worlds*. The accuracy of the Christian itinerary continues to be a matter of debate, in particular among archaeologists. See, for example, Joan E. Taylor, *Christians in the Holy Places: The Myth of Jewish-Christian Origins* (Oxford: Clarendon Press, 1993).

[85] Shalev, "Pilgrimage and Measurement," 11–12.

rather than immanent led many Western European Christians ... to view Jerusalem as an historical curiosity." But he notes as well that Jerusalem's "core of religious significance never entirely fell away" for many Protestants. In other words, the sacrality of the Holy Land remained a somewhat contested issue even within the Protestant tradition throughout the Early Modern Period.[86]

In mapping the historic past in modern-day Jerusalem, Zuallart and the other knights were assuring their Catholic readers of the accuracy of the traditional itinerary, but it was a strategy that was no less useful for affirming a Catholic interpretation of the efficacy of the Holy Land pilgrimage because it also confirmed the presence of Christ at these sites. Returning both to Zuallart and Villamont, their detailed descriptions of the passage through streets to each Holy Place were intended to convey a sense of movement, of immediacy, that heightened the reader's sense of journeying to, and through, Jerusalem. Mapping, in other words, served to concretize the historical Christ in the places where he plied his mission, and for Catholics this meant certifying His presence in the places visited by pilgrims. Moreover, evocative descriptions of the interior state of each Holy Place along with the biblical story further rendered Christ a visceral presence in many Catholic treatises including some produced by knights. The passage from Villamont cited earlier, for example, was intended to suggest a biblical story unfolding before the eyes of the visiting pilgrim. The reader watches on as Christ, his face perspiring, stumbles under the weight of the cross and hears the cries of the women of Jerusalem as He passes by them.

That Villamont wished to stir an emotional response in the reader by evoking a living and suffering Christ is clear. It may well reflect the influence of the more affective, "baroque" piety upon his work that scholars find emerging in the wake of the Council of Trent. Marie Christine Gomez-Géraud among others has noted its influence upon pilgrimage treatises by the early seventeenth century including one of the most popular, Jean Boucher's *Le Bouquet sacre compose des belles fleurs de la Terre Sainte*.[87] Gomez-Géraud, who has written an important critical edition of the treatise, argues that Boucher used emotionally charged descriptions of the Holy Places to stimulate inner reflection and

---

[86] Clarke, "Protestants in Palestine," 108–109.
[87] See the excellent introduction in her edition of the Boucher's text. Marie-Christine Gomez-Geraud, ed., *Bouquet Sacre Composé des plus belles fleurs de la Terre Sainte* (Paris: Honoré Champion, 2008).

contemplation.[88] Perhaps Villamont had this objective in mind as well. One could argue even so that an emotive style of description was no less useful for rendering Christ a more palpable presence in pilgrimage narratives for a European readership anxious about Protestant criticism of the efficacy of the rite. Villamont, we should note, was no friend of Calvinism. In fact, he had participated in the religious conflicts in France as a member of the Catholic League in Brittany, the radical association that organized to prevent the succession of the Protestant Henry of Navarre to the throne.[89]

Making Christ palpable seems to have been the objective of Nicolas Benard as well. Of the twelve treatises studied here, that of Benard is the most emotionally charged. Consider, for example, his lengthy description of the visitation of the Basilica of the Holy Sepulcher. For Benard, the great Basilica enclosed the greatest of all mysteries, that of human redemption, and he took his time wandering the Church to contemplate its many "holy objects."[90] These, he argued, were valuable for "engraving and imprinting on the heart and soul a permanent memory of the most holy and salutary of mysteries of our redemption represented by the marks and 'remarques' enclosed in this great Church."[91] In this passage, Benard presents the Holy Sepulcher to the reader as a vessel of a living biblical past, the place where Christ through his crucifixion and resurrection redeemed humankind and from where he continued to reach out to save devout believers. To convey Christ's presence, Benard interweaves descriptions of each space and the biblical scene with that of his own emotional and physical response. Preparing to enter the shrine of the Holy Sepulcher, for example, he mentions being barefoot, on his knees, holding a burning candle. After the group of pilgrims said their devotions "the most devoutly and attentively as possible," Benard describes being

---

[88] Gomez-Geraud, ed., *Bouquet Sacre Composé des plus belles fleurs de la Terre Sainte*.

[89] Yves Berçe mentions that, during his travels, Villamont was in contact with "French habitués" in Naples who were likely "ligueurs." He traveled through France on the way home dressed as a peasant to escape the notice of the troops of Henry of Navarre until he made it safely into the League-controlled territories in Maine and Brittany. Berçe, "Discours de M. Yves Berçe," 3–6. On Villamont's potential connection to the League in Brittany, see also Hervé Le Goff, ed., *La ligue en Bretagne: Guerre civile et conflit international, 1588–1598* (Rennes: Presses Universitaires de Rennes, 2010).

[90] Benard, *Le Voyage de Hierusalem*, 190.

[91] Benard, *Le Voyage de Hierusalem*, 190. "... graver & imprimer au Coeur & en l'ame, pour nous faire avoir tousjours une memoire saincte & salutaire des mysteres de nostre redemption representez par les marques & remarques encloses dans ceste grande Eglise ..."

overcome by joy because he was in the presence of Christ. I was "filled with an inexpressible spirit of joy in the presence of my sweet redeemer Jesus," whom, he noted, "keeps and watches over the place of his Holy Sanctuary" and who worked ceaselessly to raise up the hearts of the most worthless and humble "as well as good and faithful servants through meditating upon his sufferings, humiliations, and hardships. Even the most ignominious and painful death on the cross, suffering through our Lorde Jesus Christ for our redemption."[92] Here Benard expresses feeling overwhelmed by emotions once in the presence of Christ, and he was not alone. Everyone in the great Church, he insisted, felt "ravished" by devotion. Benard captures the eternal nature of the Holy Place when he describes the shrine of the Holy Sepulcher as "His sanctuary, sepulcher, monument." Christ's final resting place was also his present home, a place from which he continued to work for the redemption of souls.

Benard's layering of descriptions of space, biblical story, the performance of the rites, and his emotional response work together to represent the Holy Land as an especially powerful sacred landscape through its hosting of Christ's life. Through Benard's description, we *feel* the presence of Christ consoling the pilgrim and operating upon his hardened heart to bring him to a state of redemption. In rendering Christ palpable, Benard and Villamont were simultaneously demonstrating the truth of Catholic teachings on the sacrality of the Holy Land and the efficacy of the pilgrimage. Perhaps most importantly from the perspective of the Catholic reader, they were also reaffirming the accessibility of Christ to the ordinary believer in the place where he once – and still – lived.

3.4 THE KNIGHT AS SPIRITUAL EXPERT

For Benard and the other knights, *where* Christ lived was significant. Assuring Catholic pilgrims that Christ lived on in the Holy Places and that the pilgrimage was transformative was the primary objective of their texts, a goal that they achieved by illuminating evidence of Christ's presence. In these respects, the treatises of the knights are characteristic

---

[92] Benard, *Le Voyage de Hierusalem*, 192–193. He was filled with an inexpressible spirit of joy in the presence of "mon doux redempteur Jesus, qui sans cesse garde & regarde le lieu de son sainct Sanctuaire, & spirituellement veut ester ensevely dans les coeurs nets & humbles de ses bons & fidelles serviteurs, meditant les douleurs, opprobres, peines & langueurs, mesmes la mort ignominieuse & tres douloureuse de la croix, soufferte par nostre seigneur Jesus-Christ pour nostre redemption."

the Custody.[98] While these texts suggest that the knighting ceremonial was the most common point of connection with other members of the Order in the Holy Land, our authors mention crossing paths with knights at other times – traveling by ship or caravan, eating together at the Franciscan refectory. These more personal moments of engagement exist in many cases alongside other signs of membership in a spiritual family. Particularly intriguing is their penchant for citing the treatises of other knights as reliable authorities. Aquilante Rocchetta, who published his own account in 1599, praises Jean Zuallart's much published account as one that "is most modern and very interesting, truthful."[99] Nicolas de Hault, who traveled to the Holy Land in 1593 and published his treatise in 1601, paid tribute to both Zuallart and Villamont. These authors traveled a few years earlier, he says, and mapped out the same journey in their own treatises "with such acumen (tant bel ordre) that is difficult to do any better."[100] We should regard these inclusions as strategic, intended to establish their expertise on the pilgrimage by reminding readers of their membership in the Order. Authors featured the Order in their narratives in many other ways as well that provide further insight into its meaning as a religious ideal for members. With the exception of those of Affagart and Ribera, for example, all of the treatises examined here include a discussion of the history of the Order of the Holy Sepulcher. In fact, both Villamont and Rocchetta devote entire sections to a description of the Order including its history, regulations, and privileges.[101] More typically, the early modern treatises

---

[98] The practice seems to have been uncommon before the 1620s and rarely more than one a year. From 1630 onwards, it is not uncommon to find clusters of knights produced in absentia. In 1630, at least seven appear in the register, three each in August and October. Arch. Custodia Terra Sancta, *Registrum Equitum S. Sepulchri*, ff. 17v–18.

[99] Rocchetta, "Preface," in *Peregrinatione di Terra Santa*. "Zuallardo, cavaliero del Sanctissimo Sepolcro ... per esser il più modern, e molto curiose, veridico."

[100] De Hault, *Le Voyage de Hierusalem*, 1. "Deux chevaliers de nostre Ordre qui ont faict le voyage bien peu de temps avant moi en mesme vaisseau, soubs mesme Patron, & quasi pendant la mesme famille de Religieux que je trouvai encore in la sainct Cité, l'ont si curieusement, & avec un tant bel ordre descript & ce qui s peult remarquer, qu'il est bien difficile de mieux, l'ung est, Il signor Joani Zuallardo flamand qui fit son voyage lan mil cinq cens quatre vingts quinze & le second le seigneur de Villamont Gentilhomme Breton lan mil cinq cens quatre vingtz& neuf ...."

[101] Rocchetta, *Peregrinatione di Terra Santa*, 391. "militia de' Cavalieri del Santo Sepolcro in memoria della Resurrettione di Christo con l'autorita del Sommo Ponteficem ce cui hebbero 'insegna delle cinque Piaghe di Christo." Villamont mentions that his discussion is in three parts and includes "ordonnances des Grands-maistres & chefs de l'Ordre des Chevaliers du Sainct Sepulcher de Hierusalem."

provide a brief history of the Order alongside a description of the ritual knighting.[102]

The knights thus infused their treatises with the material and manifestations of the Order, calling upon their association with the august society to legitimize their authority as experts on the pilgrimage. By imbedding the Order within the more important narrative of the life of Christ, moreover, they were simultaneously constructing it as a creation of the Holy Land and thus a product of its salvific authority. This conception of the Order as a creation of the Holy Land is most perfectly expressed in the knighting ceremonial, one of the reasons why it is featured in so many of the accounts including that of Benard.[103] If we return to his lengthy description that opened this chapter, one notices that it rested upon three spiritual foundations: pilgrimage, crusade, and Franciscan authority. These elements worked together to shape the distinctive identity and spirituality of the knights, crafting a special role for them as divinely appointed defenders of the Holy Land. It is with the pilgrimage that we begin the final discussion, since it was the first stage in the transformation of the devout Catholic into a knight.

3.4.1 *The Pilgrim-Theologian*

As the early modern readers of the knightly treatises well understood, to be a pilgrim was to possess spiritual wisdom. This was a truism of Catholic thought by the fourteenth century and a central tenet of medieval pilgrimage treatises, which emphasized the transformative nature of the spiritual journey. Such a view recognized, on the one hand, a conception of the Holy Land as a material vessel of a living biblical past and, on the other, a hierarchical conception of sacred space in which the Holy Land operated at the apex of all sacred spaces. As discussed in Chapter 2, early modern Catholics considered the Holy Places, like other sacred places, as irruptions of divinity in the world. But the Holy Places enjoyed a special status within the panoply of sacred spaces because they were vessels of a

---

[102] See, for example, Benard, *Le Voyage de Hierusalem*, 690–716. He includes a history of the Order alongside that of his local confraternity.
[103] Lengthy descriptions can be found in the treatises of de Hault, Benard, Pesenti, Rocchetta, and Villamont. For Pesenti, see, in particular, Giovanni Paolo Pesenti, *Il pellegrinaggio di Gierusalemme di Giovanni Paolo Pesenti: Diario di viaggio di un gentiluomo bergamasco in Terrasanta ed Egitto: 4 settembre 1612–31 agosto 1613*, ed. Ottavio de Carli (Bergamo: Officina dell'Ateneo, 2013), 304–306.

living biblical past. Encountering Christ in the Holy Land, in other words, was to encounter the very source of Christian perfection and thus Christian wisdom. To underscore their acquisition of spiritual knowledge, Benard and his fellow knights described their pilgrimages in detail and emphasized their first-hand experience of each Holy Place. Just as importantly, the knights made it clear to their readers that the ritual knighting took place *during* the pilgrimage *in* the most sacred place. It was especially meaningful that the ritual took place in the Basilica *at the foot of* Christ's sepulcher, the spatial center of the Basilica and focal point of Christian worship.[104] Sacred time similarly invested the knighting ceremonial with special authority. Easter was the most sacred time in the Christian calendar, but in reality, the Custody hosted at least two visitations each year: one at Easter and the other in the fall. Nicolas de Hault, for example, found his way to Venice in late April 1593, only to have to wait several weeks for a ship willing to take a group of pilgrims. It was August before he and his fellow travelers found themselves at the gates of the sacred city. Villamont similarly did not arrive in Jerusalem until the end of September. Meanwhile, Benard visited the Basilica on the Feast of the Purification (February 2), a date that suggests that pilgrimages also occurred outside the two main visitations.[105]

Whether it took place during Easter, the Feast of the Purification, or at another time of the year, Catholic pilgrimage treatises presented accounts of the knighting ceremonial that were quite similar. The experience of being in the same place as Christ and retracing His final days, when performed with a suitably devout mind, simultaneously purified and perfected the pilgrim, investing him with a wisdom that rivaled that of theologians. This was because the Holy Sepulcher, like the other Holy Places, was sacred, and as such, timeless, a view that meant that its biblical past continued to unfold in that place, sanctifying its devout visitors.[106] Thus, in making the Holy Land pilgrimage the central focus of their narratives, the knights, like other authors of pilgrimage treatises, were laying claim to an expertise that was widely recognized in the

---

[104] Colin Morris, *The Holy Sepulcher and the Christian West* (Oxford: Oxford University Press, 2005).

[105] Also known as Candelmas, this feast recognized the presentation of Christ to the Jewish Church forty days after his birth and was marked by a procession to the Basilica of the Holy Sepulcher.

[106] On the special sacrality of the Holy Sepulcher, see Colin Morris, *The Holy Sepulcher and the Christian West* and the discussion in Jonathan Z. Smith, *To Take Place: Toward Theory in Ritual* (Chicago: University of Chicago Press, 1977).

Catholic tradition and which was also very difficult to obtain for most Catholics. To be created a knight in the Holy Sepulcher was to be invested with special authority, moreover, because this place was the site of Christ's resurrection, the pivotal soteriological event that inaugurated a new era defined by the redemption of humankind. It is when we consider the Holy Land's meaning as a source of wisdom and the privileging of personal experience in its acquisition that we can perceive another function of the pilgrimage account, namely, as evidence of the author's spiritual authority.[107] Proof of the journey was expected of all pilgrims, a process that began while they were still in Europe. Would-be pilgrims required the permission of Church officials to make the journey, most often the local bishop, though they had other options including the Latin patriarch in Rome or one of the Franciscan commissioners general of the Holy Land. De Hault, for example, received his from the Latin patriarch in Rome and, like many other authors, he included the text of the certificate in his treatise to endow his account with added authenticity. By the Early Modern Period, the office of Latin patriarch was a titular (honorific) see based at the Basilica of San Lorenzo fuori le Mura in Rome. This was when it was not held ex officio by the Franciscan *custos*. At the time of De Hault's journey in 1593, the patriarch would have been the prominent prelate Fabio Blondus de Montealto (1588–1618).[108] The Frenchman mentions meeting with "Monsieur Legat" as well, though he does not provide any further information on this official except to say that his role was to make sure the pilgrim was "capable" of making the journey. The Church worried about the possibility of spiritual corruption along the way, in particular, about conversion to Islam, hence the emphasis placed upon scrutinizing the character of would-be pilgrims. De Hault insists that one must have the license in hand or risk excommunication. Most important was the certificate provided by the Franciscan *custos* at the end of the pilgrimage, but pilgrims also relied upon other kinds of proof, most commonly in the form of mementoes gathered along the journey. Don Fadrique Enriquez de Ribera reportedly brought back many objects including one hundred candles blessed in Jerusalem and

---

[107] de Hault, *Le Voyage de Hierusalem*, 6–7. "Indultum visitendi S.mum. Sepulchrum."
[108] The office of Latin patriarch seems to have been much more important during the era of the Crusades. The *custos* was granted the status ex-officio in the 1342 bull *gratiam agimus* that established the Custody of the Holy Land. Latin patriarchs were often prominent prelates. For example, Scipione Gonzaga (1585–1588) was a member of the prominent Gonzaga dynasty of Mantua and later became a Cardinal. His brother Francesco became the Minister General of the Franciscan Order.

pebbles from Mount Sinai.[109] Tattoos of the Holy Places were another common pilgrim's "badge" specific to the Holy Land pilgrimage. In a similar way, pilgrimage treatises, with their first-hand narratives and detailed descriptions of sites could also verify the pilgrim status of the author alongside other forms of evidence. As discussed earlier, details mattered in this regard, conveying the unique voice and experience of the author even as it confirmed the essential timelessness of the Holy Land experience. Returning to the treatise of Nicholas de Hault for one such example of proof-making, we note a particular passage in which the Frenchman describes his preparations for the knighting ritual. de Hault describes being awakened early during the overnight stay in the Basilica by one of the friars who then led him to the chapel of Mary Magdalen. Once there he was seated on his own and handed a book describing the ceremonial, which he was asked to read.[110] Even if his description of the ceremony itself seems eerily the same as those provided by other knights, these small, even mundane, details are unique to de Hault's account, situating him *in* the Holy Sepulcher *preparing for* the rite.

3.4.2 A Crusading Past

On its own, the mere act of participating in the pilgrimage invested the knights with expertise because they had experienced firsthand the presence of Christ and been transformed by it, perfected. In making the knighting ceremonial the ritual center of the visitation of the Holy Sepulcher, however, authors were also signaling to their readers that they were no ordinary pilgrims. As we may remember from Benard's account, the would-be knight was separated from the regular group of pilgrims during the course of the visitation to the Basilica and that led to the shrine of the Sepulcher. There he joined a select few others to undergo the knighting ceremony. de Hault shrouds the ritual in danger, describing friars on watch at the door of the shrine lest they were seen by a "Turk" or one of the Eastern Christian worshippers. As several treatises inform their readers, secrecy was crucial, because the Turks did not want new crusaders in their midst. Finally, at the end of the ceremonial, the former pilgrim emerges fully garbed as a knight ready to rejoin the other pilgrims who awaited him in the chapel of the Apparition.

---

[109] Perede, "Measuring Jerusalem," 88.
[110] Le Hault, *Le Voyage de Hierusalem*, 49–50.

Le Hault would not have worn the distinctive robe that members of the Order used today because it became standard dress only at the end of the seventeenth century. He may, however, have pinned the blazon of the Order on his cloak. He does mention being handed the spurs and sword and given a golden chain by the friars in attendance. These affectations of a warlike brotherhood are an important reminder that many medieval Catholics considered crusade another mode of pilgrimage, a conception that clearly continued throughout the Early Modern Period.[111] But our authors were unveiling, just as importantly, their spiritual transformation into knights. The inclusion of a description of the ceremonial conveyed their membership in a special brotherhood, one that had its own unique history in the Holy Land as its defenders. Most meaningful for early modern members was its association with the crusader ruler Godefroy of Bouillon, a history that, as discussed earlier, remains a matter of significant debate among scholars. However, it was by no means the only origin story. The Flemish friar Bernardin (Bernadinus) Surius, for example, was one of many to trace the origins of the fraternity back to the time of Saint Helen's discovery of the true cross in the Holy Sepulcher in the fourth century.[112] According to his account, the knights were the honor guard appointed to protect it. Charlemagne appears in still other accounts as an important patron (and perhaps founder) of the Order following the collapse of Roman rule.[113] For the early modern brethren of this study, however, as well as their modern counterparts, it was a crusading past that exercised a powerful, mythic hold over their corporate identity, one that knights promoted in their pilgrimage treatises and other travel accounts. Anthoine Regnault, Giovani Paolo Pesenti, and Aquilante Rocchetta each insist in their respective accounts that the Order was first formed by Godefroy of Bouillon in 1099,[114] while Nicolas Benard

---

[111] See, for example, Jonathan Riley-Smith, *The First Crusade and the Idea of Crusading* (London: Athlone, 1993).

[112] Bernardin Surius, *Le pieu pelerin ou voyage de Jerusalem divise en trois livres contenans la description topographique de plusieurs Royaumes, pais, villes, nations estrangeres nommement des quatuorze religions orientales, leurs moeurs & humeurs, tant en matiere de Religion que de civile conversation &c.* (Brussels: Francois Foppens, 1663).

[113] Jean Chesneau, *Le voyage de monsieur d'Aramon, ambassadeur pour le roy en levant* ed. Charles Schefer (Paris: Ernst Leroux, 1887), 139. "NOUS SEJOURNASMES AUDICT HIERUSALEM cinq ou six jours où je me fis passer chevalier avec un de mes compagnons, et payasmes chascun ..."

[114] Rocchetta, *Peregrinatione di Terra Santa*, 391; and Pesenti, *Il pellegrinaggio*, 304–305. Pesenti describes the robe as white with the cross, though the portrait in the edition used here has him in a black robe with the cross.

mentions that the sword used in the ceremonial belonged to Godefroy and was blessed by the Crusader ruler.[115] Pesenti adds that, of the four military orders associated with Crusader Jerusalem (Templars, St. John's Hospitallers, Teutonic, Holy Sepulcher), the Order of Holy Sepulcher had specific responsibility for the protection of the Basilica. As another example, Jean Zuallart describes dismounting from his horse at the gates of Jerusalem to walk in imitation of Godefroy when he first arrived at the gates as a Crusader.[116] One should note as well that our knightly authors also made a point of visiting the sepulchers of Godefroy and his son Baldwin. Their tombs were located near the chapel of Saint John in the Basilica and close to the site of Calvary. By the late middle ages, they had become a regular part of the Western pilgrimage itinerary, though they held special meaning for members of the Order. Henri de Beauvau, baron of Manonville, was one of a number of knights who transcribed the inscription on the tomb of Godefroy in his account. Beauvau was in the entourage of the newly appointed ambassador to the Porte, François de Savary de Breves, when he visited Jerusalem in 1605. His travel account is more typical of a relation than a pilgrimage treatise, though it does include a lengthy description of the pilgrimage. In it Beauvau describes the modest room holding the sepulchers including the inscription on that of Bouillon: "Hic iacet inclytus Godefredus de Bouillon, qui totam istam terram acquisivit cultui Christiano, cuius anima regent in Christo."[117]

Godefroy loomed large in the imaginations of the early modern members of the Order, his mythic role as founder evoked in their histories and in their ritual knighting ceremonial. Given the Order's stated mandate to defend the Holy Land, one wonders whether the continuing vigour of the early modern brotherhood was as much a response to Ottoman conquest of the region in 1517 as it was to other forces including the Reformation. There are a number of reasons for thinking that this was the case, especially when we consider the renewed enthusiasm at many European courts for crusade following the conquest of Constantinople in 1453.[118] Enthusiasm rekindled frequently over the course of the sixteenth and seventeenth

---

[115] Benard, *Le Voyage de Hierusalem*, 196–197.
[116] Zuallart, *Le tres devot voyage de Jerusalem*, Book III, 26. They dismounted from their horses and walked "à l'incitation & comme fit le preux Godefroy de Buillon & sa noble compagnie, allans pour tirer ladite saincte Cite des mains des Sarazins infidels."
[117] Beauvau, *Relation journaliere du voyage du Levant*, 223–224.
[118] See, for example, Geraud Poumarède, *Pour en finir avec le Croisade: Mythes et Réalitiés de la lute contre les Turcs au XVIe et XVIIe siècles* (Paris: Presses Universitaires de France, 2009).

centuries whenever fears of Ottoman expansion reemerged. Certainly, several of the knights studied here considered the liberation of Jerusalem from Ottoman hands an important Christian duty. Anthoine Regnault, for one, lamented the sad state of the Holy Land under the control of the Ottomans. "It is not without displeasure," he states, "that I put my hand to writing to begin a description of the Holy Places. When one remembers the rare devotion that one has in these places, and when I realize at the same time that these places are in the hands of Infidels, I am overtaken by such a great melancholy that I lose all desire to write." Regnault implored the rulers of Europe to work together on another crusade: "I beg God that all the Christian princes leave their own ambitions at the door and leave together to come and conquer this Holy Land once again.[119]

We should note that some of the early modern knights went much further. There was a somewhat serious effort to turn the existing Order into a bona fide crusading force during the 1550s under the leadership of Philip II of Spain. An extensive dossier of documents found at the national archives at Simancas points to active negotiations in 1558 during which Philip II agreed to assume leadership of the "archconfraternity of the Holy Sepulcher" and fund a new crusade. This attempt at reorganization, which received the active support of the Pope, seems to have been the brainchild of a Flemish member of the Order named Pierre de Carate (Zarate). A well-publicized general chapter was held in 1558 in Hoogstraten involving thirty knights, most of whom were Dutch. Nothing concrete came of this meeting, however, let alone of a new crusade.[120] A later effort in 1615 involving the Duke de Nevers of France similarly failed to transform the society into a real crusading force. According to Jean de Gennes, Nevers sought the role of Grand Master of the Order but faced intense opposition from the Order of Malta. That Nevers was considered for the role, he argues, reflected a broader

---

[119] "Ce n'est pas sans desplaisir que je mets la main à la plume, pour commencer la description des saincts lieux, tant de la ville de Jerusalem, comme d'alentour. Car me souvennant de la rare devotion qu'on a en ces endroits, & me representant en mesme temps que tous ces lieux sont entre les mains des Infideles: J'entre en une si grand melancolie que je perds quasi toute envie d'en escrire. Et pleust à Dieu que tous les *Princes Chrestiens*, laissans leurs ambitions particulieres derriere la porte sortissent unaniment en campagne pour aller encore de nouveau à la conqueste de ceste Terre saincte."

[120] See, for example, the extensive dossier found in AGS EST leg. 884 discussing the nature and organization of the new militia and the support of Julius III. De Gennes argues that Phillip pursued this endeavour seriously, pressing for papal approval from 1558 to 1563. De Gennes, *Les Chevaliers du Saint-Sépulcre de Jérusalem*, vol. 1, 437.

objective to form an international "milice chrétien" under the leadership of the Bourbon monarch, something that will receive more discussion in Chapter 4.[121]

While the Order failed to mobilize as a true crusading force during the period of this investigation, it is fair to say that members were intentionally promoting its reputation as a bulwark against the forces of Islam as well as Protestantism whenever they wore the blazon in religious processions and other devotions because it evoked a medieval crusading ideal. Returning to the pilgrimage treatises, the descriptions of the knighting ceremonial also incorporated numerous crusading elements – the oath requiring knights to defend the Holy Land from spiritual error, the promise to venture into battle when required with their own horse, and most importantly, dressing the newly created knight in a set of armour, spurs, and with the golden chain bearing the blazon of the Order. But what clearly infused the knighthood with special authority for many members as well was the fact that the knight was created at the foot of Christ's Sepulcher. No longer a simple pilgrim, the newly minted knight was now quite literally a soldier of Christ; one with a responsibility to defend the Holy Land and the true Catholic faith. We find this ideal of the *Christi miles* expressed in a devotional song dedicated to the Order in the account of Anthoine Regnault. In the following passage, for example, Regnault describes the five crosses on the blazon representing the wounds of Christ and urged his readers to meditate upon Christ's suffering in terms that evoked a call to arms:

Contemplate also this sign if it pleases you, which is vermillion, like the red cross. That which was stained during the great conquest of his pure blood which was sorrowfully opened, and within which Christians wish to unite, and with him take over and arm themselves to fight in this lower territory and triumph in eternal glory with the blood of this grand king of Kings, who is Jesus savior, as one believes while showing reverence to the sign of the Cross.[122]

---

[121] De Gennes, *Les Chevaliers du Saint-Sépulcre de Jérusalem*, vol. 1, 42. On Nevers role in the formation of the "milice chretien," see, in particular, Benoist Pierre, "Le père Joseph, l'empire et la Méditerranée au début du XVIIe siècle," *Cahiers de la Mediterranee* 71 (2005): 185–202.

[122] Regnault, *Discours du voyage*, f. 4–4b. "Contemple ausse ce signe s'il te plaist/Qui est vermeil, comme le rouge verre./Las tel fut tainct faisant si grand conquest/De son pur sang en douloureuse serre/Dedans lequel Chrestiens voulut unir/Et annexer avec luy, & munir/Pour milliter en ce bas territoire/ Et triompher en l'eternelle gloire/Avec le sang de ce grand Roy, des Roys/Qui est Jesus Sauveur, comme on doit croire/En reverant le signe de la Croix."

In this passage, Regnault's language intermixes militaristic and devotional elements. By asking readers to meditate on the insignia borne by the confraternity, Regnault is casting his confraternal order in the role of spiritual interpreter and mediator of what he calls the "biens" of the Holy Land. He injects the presence of the Order into his itinerary in other ways as well that ensures that the brotherhood was part of the pilgrim-readers' journey and experience of the region. In other words, Regnault represents the knights as experts on the efficacy of the pilgrimage and militant defenders of the Holy Land from spiritual error including those errors emanating from Europe. Before leaving the knighting ceremonial, however, we need to note yet another element in the formation of the knight that is crucial to understand his claims to spiritual authority in the era of the Reformation. It is represented in the knighting ceremonial by the officiation of the Franciscan *custos*.

3.4.3 *The Franciscans and the Custody*

The officiating role of the Franciscan *custos* (at least in terms of its formal recognition) was an early modern development, a responsibility invested in the office by the papacy sometime between 1495 and 1516, though likely at the request of the friars.[123] Jean de Gennes is of the opinion that the *custos* may have been officiating even earlier, though certainly following the death of Jean of Prussia. John of Prussia was a knight when he joined the Franciscan order as a lay brother and he was responsible for performing the knighting ceremonial from as early as the 1470s. It seems to have been customary for knights to oversee the ceremonial until this time. The death of John of Prussia around 1495 likely saw the role transfer (if unofficially) to the *custos* of the Holy Land. Though Franciscan sources insist that papal recognition came as early as 1496, the earliest document stating so dates much later to the year 1516. Whether reaffirming an existing practice or formally recognizing a new one, however, the timing of this particular document is intriguing. By December 1516, Jerusalem would be overrun by Ottoman forces, stirring new calls for crusade from the Catholic pulpits of Europe. The pope, in

---

[123] De Gennes, *Les Chevaliers du Saint-Sépulcre de Jérusalem*, vol. 1, 107. The Franciscan guardian and *custos* at the time was Friar Nicola da Tossignano. The privilege was formally confirmed in the later bulls of Clement VII (1525) and Pius IV (1561). See *Bullarium Franciscanum Terrae Sanctae*, in *Diarium Terrae Sanctae* V (1912), 14.

The Order of the Holy Sepulcher

recognizing the *custos*, may have been moved by concerns about the spread of Ottoman authority westward even before it penetrated the Holy Land, a concern that led it to declare itself head of the Order of the Holy Sepulcher that same year. The Franciscan *custos*, as apostolic delegate in the Holy Land, was thus the logical local representative to perform the rite. However, it was just as likely that the papacy was simply recognizing the long-standing involvement of the brothers in the ritual formation of the knights. Pilgrimage treatises mention their presence at the knighting ceremonial from as early as the 1330s, long before Jean of Prussia joined the Order.[124]

The administrative role of the Custody further expanded after this time, suggesting that relations between the Order and the venerable pilgrimage institution only strengthened in the era of the Reformation. In addition to the investment of the *custos* with the responsibility of officiating the knighting ceremonial, the oath of knighting was formally codified. The account of Pietro Casola suggests that the formalization of the oath had begun by the 1490s. The cleric visited Jerusalem in 1494 and mentions being present during the creation of knights.[125] In fact, the *custos* asked Casola to write the oaths for the knights according to his instructions. The formalization of privileges continued in 1553 under Bonifacio da Stagna (da Ragusa) who produced a list of eight conceded to the Order up until this time.[126] Further innovations came in 1561 when the Custody introduced the two registries for pilgrims and knights. The privileges of the *custos* regarding the creation of knights received affirmation through instructions issued in 1642 by Pope Urban VIII and a later papal bull in 1655 issued by Alexander VII. A subsequent letter confirming the Order was issued by the papacy in 1683, and in 1708 a decree of

---

[124] De Gennes, *Les Chevaliers du Saint-Sépulcre de Jérusalem*, vol. I, 112. It was issued by Leo X.

[125] "Per carestia de scriptori scripsi paregie littere testimonial, como erano facti cavalieri al Sepulcro, secondo la forma dette el guardian, e lui le sigillava." Pietro Casola, *Viaggio di Pietro Casola a Gerusalemme, tratto dall'autografo esistente nella Biblioteca Trivulzio con note* (Milan: Carpano, 1855), 73. He mentions the creation of knights including D. Zo Symone Fornaro Pavese and a D. Burgho de Anversa de Borgogna. The rest he said were German and Spanish.

[126] De Gennes says that it was printed as "Exemplar litterarum quibus intenditur privilegia equitum dominici Sepulchri, 1553," but he hasn't found an extant copy. De Gennes, *Les Chevaliers du Saint-Sépulcre de Jérusalem*, vol. I, 109–110. It is cited, however, by several sources including Francesco Quaresmio, *Historica theologica et moralies terrae sanctae*, vol. I (1639), 512.

the Congregation of the Propaganda Fide affirmed all earlier papal privileges dating back to 1496.[127]

These early modern innovations point to a relationship between the Order and the brothers that was centuries in the making but also suggest that the Custody was assuming an increasingly important role as the administrative center of the international brotherhood from the turn of the sixteenth century. Other evidence of strengthening administrative ties is suggested by the involvement of knights in the confraternity affiliated with the Grand couvent in Paris, one of the most prestigious and important communities in the Franciscan Order because of its role as a *studium generale*. As discussed earlier, it functioned as another spiritual home for several French knights including Regnault and de Hault. While much more work needs to be done to trace other local connections between Franciscans and members of the Order, the example of Paris suggests that some convents served as proxies of sorts for the Custody. This is not itself surprising given that friaries already played this role, serving as historic transmitters and popularizers of many Holy Land devotional rites including the Stations of the Cross, the Nativity, and the Descent of the Cross.[128] Local friaries also worked with commissioners of the Holy land to gather alms in support of the Custody, while the routine circulation of brothers between Jerusalem and home provinces made friaries important hubs in an increasingly global Franciscan communication network during the Early Modern Period.[129]

Beyond local institutional ties, one also finds evidence of personal ties between knights and friars attached to the Custody, which argue for a mutually beneficial spiritual partnership based upon a shared desire to protect the Holy Land. The meaningful nature of this relationship is most apparent in the writings of the knights and friars and, in particular, their pilgrimage treatises. It is striking, to begin with, to note the visibility of the Order and the friars in one another's treatises. For example, while the friars were the only clerics responsible for the pilgrimage, many medieval and early modern pilgrimage texts do not clearly identify them as Franciscans. It is quite common in fact to find them simply referred to

---

[127] The papal bull of 1655, known as the *Piis Christi fidelium votis* (August 3, 1655), confirmed the privileges and indulgences of the *custos* in general. De Gennes discusses these privileges because they were also mentioned as legitimizing documents of the Order. De Gennes, *Les Chevaliers du Saint-Sépulcre de Jérusalem*, vol. I, 115–116.

[128] On Franciscan promotion of the devotions of the Stations of the Cross and the Nativity in Europe, see, for example, Morris, *The Holy Sepulcher and the West*.

[129] See discussion in Chapter 6.

as "clerics" or "religious." Nicolas de Hault, however, identifies the clerics as friars and also mentions individual brothers throughout his journey. For example, a friar named Leonardo di Bergamo, member of the important convent of San Francesco della Vigna in Venice, helped the French knight arrange his voyage. San Francesco della Vigna appears in many pilgrimage accounts because it had close ties with the Custody of the Holy Land and was a regular feeder of brothers to the region from the Italian peninsula. Another friar named Sebastiano Evangelista organized devotions for the pilgrims on board the merchant ship. Once in the Holy Land, we meet other brothers – greeting the French pilgrims at the gates of Jerusalem, taking them on daily walking tours of the local sites, and leading them throughout the many rites involved in the pilgrimage including the knighting ceremonial.[130] Traveling in 1612, Giovani Paolo Pesenti mentions encountering several friars including the commissioner general of the Holy Land, Reverend Father Grisostomo Capranica.[131] Pesenti is one of several knights, moreover, to discuss the history and privileges of the Franciscan brothers in the Custody. He writes, for example, that the brothers were placed in charge by King Robert of Sicily and that "the fathers established a family in the Custody to edify [the region]." They were sent from many convents "every three years." The Franciscan guardian "held the highest authority" in the Custody.[132] Similarly, in his treatise the French pilgrim Villamont mentions that the *custos* presided over the knighting ceremonial and that he was invested with "episcopal authority." He was, in other words, the highest Latin authority in the region, but he notes as well that the Latin clerics, among all the Christian communities in the region, held the most privileges in the Holy Places.[133]

Franciscan treatises in turn mention individual knights but, in pondering the formative nature of their relationship, it does seem especially significant that Franciscan treatises included descriptions of the Order and promoted it as a spiritual brotherhood. The treatise written by the Flemish friar Bernardin Surius is particularly noteworthy in this regard, providing an extensive description of the history and rituals of the

---

[130] For the two friars encountered early on, see Le Hault, *Le Voyage de Hierusalem*, 3–12.
[131] Pesenti, *Il pellegrinaggio*, 246–247.
[132] Pesenti, *Il pellegrinaggio*, 306.
[133] Villamont, *Voyages*, vol. II, ff. 175–177. For another example, Zuallart mentions early on that the guardian (*custos*) of Mount Sion had the authority to absolve would-be pilgrims who arrived in Jerusalem without first receiving permission to make the journey from church officials in Europe. Zuallart, *Le tres devot voyage de Jerusalem*, Book I, 69.

Order including a particularly lengthy one of the knighting ceremonial. Surius held the office of sacristan in the convent in the Holy Sepulcher, a role that would have had him engaging directly with the knights as part of the organization of the liturgical rites. His account pays significant attention to the officiating role of the *custos* but Surius also makes a point of praising the knights as spiritual exemplars. For Surius, Protestant criticism was clearly very much on his mind when he pondered the many virtues of the Order: "And what do you say my reformed, How can you dare to accuse these zealous knights of any impiety and idolatry, and hold these devout pilgrims as superstitious?"[134] Not all Franciscan texts provide as much attention as Surius to relations with the Order of the Holy Sepulcher. However, collectively they do suggest that they were important. When we consider as well that a number of the treatises produced by the knights also included approbations provided by friars, an even stronger impression of a significant relationship emerges. One of these is found in the treatise of Nicolas Benard which also includes a dedicatory poem by a Franciscan praising his wisdom. A 1607 edition of the treatise of Jean Zuallart similarly includes a poem by friar Petrus Carpin, a lecturer in sacred theology.[135] Through the inclusion of these Franciscan commendations, the knights were touting a relationship with the friars that they believed invested their accounts with spiritual authority because it was coming from religious who were widely regarded as experts on the pilgrimage. The fact that friars provided these accolades is also significant, however, signaling their respect for the Order of the Holy Sepulcher as an effective promoter of Holy Land devotion.

That the friars and knights conceived of their relationship as a spiritual partnership finds further support when we consider the timing of the administrative changes mentioned earlier. It was likely no coincidence that the Franciscans began strengthening their administrative relationship with the Order in the wake of the Ottoman conquest and as Protestant reformers unleased a sustained assault upon the rite of pilgrimage. We should note, to begin with, that a number of the Franciscan treatises including those of Boucher, Bernardino Amico, and Eugene Roger also encouraged the crusading fervour of European readers. Both Boucher and Roger urged the French monarch Louis XIII of France to assume a

---

[134] Surius, *Le pieux pelerin*, 3. "Que dites-vous, mes Reformés? Oseriez-vous accuser ces zeleux Chevaliers de quelque impieté & d'idolatrie, & tenir ces devots Pelerins pour superstitieux?"

[135] Zuallart, *Le tres devot voyage de Jerusalem*, front matter.

leadership role, while the Italian friar Bernardino Amico used his preface to appeal to Cosimo I of Tuscany, asking him to lead the way among Christian princes by "fertilizing devotion and nourishing the land."[136] Amico noted that he had been part of the Observant family in the Holy Land, occupying the important office of president. He also compared himself to Peter the Hermit, the famed medieval preacher who stirred the call to crusade in the twelfth century and insisted that he could testify to the "intolerable treatment faced by Christians" in the region because of their faith.[137] Along with expressed concerns about Islam, Protestant criticism of the pilgrimage visibly informs many the Franciscan treatises as well. Franciscan writings will receive more attention in Chapter 6, which explores the meaning of the Holy Land for members of the Franciscan tradition. It should be mentioned here, however, that their early modern pilgrimage treatises were among the most visceral in terms of their description of the pilgrimage experience. Like those of Zuallart and Regnault discussed earlier, moreover, a number of friars used their treatises to engage directly in religious controversy. In terms similar to that of Zuallart, for example, Bernardin Surius chastised the "heretic" who "in reading his history immediately desired to turn upside down what is founded upon sacred scripture, saying only that the word of God taught them, that pilgrimages are superstitious and impious." But against this novelty and "false" understanding of the word of God, he states, "I take it as my cause to confront them with the pure and well founded."[138]

As these examples suggest, the friars had a great deal in common with the knights through their shared devotion to the Holy Land. When faced by religious controversy after 1520, they also found in these laymen devout champions who would fight alongside with them in defense of the Holy Land pilgrimage. Villamont's description of the exhortation given to the knights by the *custos* during the knighting ceremonial certainly suggests this was the case. Following the completion of the ceremonial, the Franciscan *custos* turned to the newly minted knights and urged them to defend the Holy Land: "I know that you are moved by devotion,

---

[136] Amico, *Trattato delle piante & immagini*, preface.
[137] Amico, *Trattato delle piante & immagini*, preface. "... il quale havendo visitato quei santi luoghi, e vedendo I mali trattamenti, che facevano a' Christiani nemici della nostra Santa fede parendoli cosa intollerabile ...."
[138] Surius, *Le pieux pelerin*, 2. "il luy prendra à l'instant envie de bouleverser tout ce qui est fondé en la sainte Escriture, disant seulement: que leur parole de Dieu leur enseigne, que tous les Pelerinages sont superstitieux, & impies: Mais contre cette nouvelle, & feinte parole de Dieu, j'opposeray la pure, & bien fondée pour ma juste cause, & defense."

or you would not have sought the red, except for the benefit of spreading the faith of Christ, and dying in valiant defense of it."[139]

3.5 CONCLUSION

As discussed here, the traditional role of the knights as defenders of the Holy Places took on renewed meaning for many of its members in the face of profound changes taking place both in the Holy Land and in Western Europe. As of 1517, a new Muslim power lay in charge of the sacred sites that were the locus of their devotional life and the source of their confraternal identity. Perhaps even more disturbingly, the very sacrality of the Holy Places had become a locus of intense debate within the once formerly unified Western Christian body as Protestant reformers challenged the efficacy of the Holy Land pilgrimage. As argued in this chapter, the writings and other devotions of the knights point suggestively to the intensification of the material cast of Catholic spirituality as one important legacy of the Reformation debates. This legacy was demonstrated most vividly through the flourishing of pilgrimages in Europe from the late sixteenth century onwards but also in the presentness of Christ in knightly treatises on the Holy Land and their depictions of the transformative experience of being *there*. Indeed, the pilgrimage treatises of the knights argue for the elevation of the Holy Land as a powerful vessel of Christian wisdom and authority. This makes perfect sense given Catholic belief in divine immanence and acceptance of a hierarchy of the holy even among sacred landscapes. The Holy Land, as the authentic home of Christ and a continuing source of the miraculous, offered a powerful symbol of the truth of Catholic teachings, one capable of countering Protestant insistence upon the Bible as the sole source of Christian wisdom.

The knights rooted their claims to leadership through their firsthand experience of the region, an experience that invested them with wisdom and the responsibility of promoting the efficacy of its pilgrimage. The

---

[139] Villamont, *Voyages*, vol. II, ff. 175–176. "Seigneurs Chevaliers, afin que vous scachiez le grand honneur qui vous a esté maintenant concede par la bonté supresme, je vous diray que c'est celuy mesme que au temps passé recevoient les Chevaliers, Templiers de Hierusalem, lesquels pour un temps furent riches & renommez par tout le monde, mais par leur mauvaise vie & conversation furent privez de leur dignité, & de toutes leurs richesses ... mais je scay que vous autres esmeus de devotion, n'avez procuré la rouge, sinon pour l'augmentation de la foy de Jesus Christ, & mourir en combatant vaillamment pour la defence d'icelle ...."

remaining chapters will show, however, that this legitimizing function made the Holy Places, its altars, and the administration of the Custody a fraught zone of competition within the Catholic tradition as well. By the 1620s, the Bourbon monarchy, the papal Congregation of the Propaganda Fide, and newly reformed Franciscan communities would each begin pressing the Observant administrators with their claims to jurisdiction. Chapter 4 begins with the Bourbon monarchy in its newly acquired Ottoman status as the Protector of the Holy Places. It is through Bourbon intervention in the affairs of the Custody after 1604 that we are confronted with a regime badly shaken by its recent history of civil war and eager to express itself as a great Catholic power in the eastern Mediterranean. The Custody, through its jurisdiction over altars in the Holy Places, gave the monarchy a crucial site of political, religious, and economic engagement in the Ottoman Empire, one that could be harnessed to the construction of its claims to Christian hegemony at the expense, in particular, of its Spanish Habsburg rivals.

4

France, the Protector of the Holy Places

The Order of the Holy Sepulcher also appears in a fascinating dossier of letters received by the Congregation of the Propaganda Fide in May 1661. In this instance, however, the Franciscan *custos* and his fellow friars had little good to say about the two would-be French knights who had traveled to Jerusalem during the recent Easter pilgrimage. Indeed, their letters, which were signed collectively by over forty witnesses, are scathing, accusing the Frenchmen of verbal insults, shouting, and in at least one instance of the physical assault of the presiding cleric. Importantly, this assault occurred on Holy Friday in the Basilica of the Holy Sepulcher during the course of the knighting ceremonial, a ritual discussed at length in Chapter 3.

According to the many reports, one of the two men interrupted the rite to grab the Franciscan *custos* by the chest, seized the sword of Godefroy of Bouillon from his hand, and waved it over him menacingly. Based upon this description alone, one can understand why the Franciscan brothers were offended by the behaviour of the two Frenchmen because they disrupted the solemnity of liturgical rites performed in the most sacred of Christian places and at the most sacred of times of the Catholic festive calendar. In place of an orderly procession of friars and pilgrims winding their way from sacred site to sacred site, peacefully engaged in the performance of the Latin devotions, the Franciscan dossier presents us instead with its inverse: a divided community, rites interrupted, discordant voices, and violence.

We will look more closely at these incidents in the following analysis of an Easter pilgrimage gone terribly wrong because they reveal another jurisdictional controversy brewing in the Custody by the seventeenth century. Whereas Chapters 2 and 3 explored conflicts involving Greek Orthodox and Protestants, the Franciscan dossier points to one that came from within Catholic tradition itself in the form of an expansionist French state. That the friars were intent upon conveying their misbehaviour as acts of French aggression is clear from the dossier, in particular, through their description of the two men as French officials and mention of their anger over a sermon disrespectful to Louis XIV. The ritual inversion of the knighting ceremonial provided the most troubling evidence of all, however, because in snatching the sword that once belonged to the crusader ruler Bouillon from the hands of the *custos*, the French pilgrim symbolically "reclaimed" jurisdiction in the Holy Land for the French kingdom. Bouillon, after all, had been a Frenchman. While it might seem a bit of a stretch to read broader political motives into the misbehaviour of the two French pilgrims, the friars had good reason to be suspicious. Indeed, a closer look at relations between the brothers of the Holy Land and the Bourbon monarchy leading up to this dispute of 1661 illuminates a persistent campaign by the Bourbon regime to use its status as Protector of the Holy Places to expand its authority over the Custody. Of particular concern to the friars were Bourbon efforts to promote a French clerical presence within its jurisdiction, initiatives that began in the 1620s and sparked several conflicts over the course of the seventeenth century including the dispute of 1661. As shall be suggested here, these initiatives point to a desire to transform the Custody into a French institution – one that lay under the authority of the monarchy and in the hands of French clerics.

In seeking to turn the Custody "French," the Bourbon regime likely had many objectives. However, the disputes with the friars suggest that one particularly important one was to evoke France's sacred past as Protector of the Holy Land. This history looked back to Charlemagne, the Crusades, and more recent eras of French involvement in the Holy Places to articulate a bold claim to Christian hegemony for a new dynastic regime plagued by profound challenges to its authority both from within and without France. A number of these challenges are visible in the diplomatic correspondence produced by the disputes informing the engagement of French officials in the affairs of the Custody. One notes, in particular, persistent concerns about religious division in France, growing rivalry with the Spanish Habsburgs, and its enormously valuable but spiritually problematic commercial and political alliance with the Islamic Ottoman regime. While it is certainly true that Bourbon monarchs relied upon an array of strategies to strengthen monarchical authority during the seventeenth century, their interest in turning to a French sacred past in the Holy Land to construct its claims to hegemonic rule provides further evidence of the importance of religion in shaping the imperial structures of the Early Modern Period. The Custody, after all, was a revered Catholic pilgrimage institution that operated visibly in a revered site of global pilgrimage. Moreover, the view from the Custody also raises questions about the changing religious character of the monarchy itself under Bourbon rule. Indeed, the many ways in which the monarchy evoked its authority in the Custody illuminate an institution profoundly transformed through its experience of the Wars of Religion and Catholic reform. The selection of Capuchins and Jesuits for service in the Custody alone alerts us to its changing character, unveiling a governing institution that ventured into the seventeenth century as a self-consciously Catholic, and not simply Christian, institution – one that was confident in its claims to Catholic orthodoxy and perfection and destined for Christian rule.

As in the case of the earlier chapters, this study of the French monarchy develops three themes central to our broader investigation. Firstly, it illuminates the importance placed upon the legitimizing power of the Holy Land by Bourbon rulers as they set upon rebuilding and strengthening the authority of the French Crown. Secondly, it further highlights the formative role played by Ottoman structures of authority in shaping early modern Catholicism not only in terms of Catholic engagement *in* the Holy Land but also relations *within* the Catholic tradition more generally. After all, the French state constructed its claims to Christian hegemony *through* its possession of the Ottoman-granted privilege of Protector of the Holy Places. Thirdly, French pursuit of the status of Protector unveils the continuing potency of a French sacred history in the Holy Land, one that was called upon in this case to legitimize a French monarchy that was in the throes of reinvention, emerging by the end of the seventeenth century as a visibly *French Catholic* institution.

To elucidate these many dimensions, the following chapter begins with a close examination of the dispute of 1661 in Section 4.1, paying attention in particular to its evocation of a Franciscan narrative of Bourbon expansionism vis-à-vis the Custody of the Holy Land. Section 4.2 then situates the dispute in a longer history of jurisdictional conflict dating back to the 1620s. Discussion here centers upon two French policies aimed at transforming the Custody into a French institution: the establishment of French missions and the appointment of French Observants to the central administration. Section 4.3 provides a broader political and religious context within which to elucidate the Custody's utility for evoking French claims to Christian hegemony, in particular, France's alliance with the Ottoman Porte, sacred destiny as protector of the Holy land, rivalry with the Habsburgs, and Catholic reform.

4.1 THE DISPUTE OF 1661

Most of what we know about the dispute of 1661 comes from a dossier of letters sent to the Congregation of the Propaganda Fide from the Franciscan leadership of the Custody. The series of eight letters are dated between April 17 and April 26. Two are especially detailed and provide the foundation of the following analysis. One was written by the Franciscan *custos* at the time, Eusebio Valles (Velles), and the other on behalf of the inner council and the community more generally. Both include the signatures, and in some cases brief statements, of several witnesses, forty-four in all. Of these witnesses, thirty-three were members of the Franciscan community in the Holy Land. The remaining comprised pilgrims who were present at the time of one or more of the conflicts described in the accounts. That the friars took a week to compile the dossier and acquire the signatures of forty-four witnesses is one of many indications that they considered this a serious incident – serious enough to bring it to the attention of the Congregation of the Propaganda Fide. By the 1660s, the Congregation was one of the most powerful organs of papal governance, charged with oversight over Catholic global engagement. Much more will be said about this papal body in Chapter 5, though we should note here that the friars were well aware that it was a very busy institution, one that did not typically concern itself with the misbehaviour of pilgrims.

A notation made by the secretary of the Congregation on the dossier shows that it arrived in late May. This lapse in time between compilation and reception of the dossier in Rome was to be expected given the difficulties of Mediterranean travel. Letters had to first be carried to one of the port cities where they would have to await the departure of a ship heading for Venice, Livorno, or perhaps Marseilles. From there, the dossier required transportation overland to the headquarters of the Congregation in Rome. Today, as in the seventeenth century, the Congregation operated out of a palazzo located near the Spanish steps. Though the trail of documentation after its reception by the secretary is sparse, the matter was clearly considered sufficiently important because it was heard by the officials of the Congregation and they responded.

A series of letters in the months that followed show that the relation of Valles was also circulating more widely, as the friars reached out to powerful allies with their concerns. A letter dated October 2, 1661, mentions that the relation of Valles had reached the ears of the Holy Roman Emperor, who then notified the papal nuncio. The nuncio then conveyed the emperor's concern to the cardinals about the "grave insults used by two French pilgrims against the Guardian of the Holy Land and aforementioned religious." The emperor's officials made it quite clear that these were acts that betrayed the "esteem required of those who go to the Holy Places …"[1] Another letter to the Congregation shows that the relation was being discussed among state officials, with questions raised both about the legitimacy of the account as well as the egregious behaviour of the pilgrims.[2]

Whether the two Frenchmen in question also wrote in their own defense is uncertain based on sources encountered thus far. For this reason, our understanding of the dispute remains largely shaped by the Franciscan administrators of the Custody, men who felt seriously aggrieved by the behaviour of the French pilgrims. Much like a prism, however, when turned and examined in the light from different angles, the dossier reveals other dimensions that are no less integral to unlocking the nature of the dispute. These dimensions give us insight into the motivations of other actors including the Frenchmen at the center of the controversy, European officials, and the officials of the Propaganda Fide who took time in their busy schedules to examine the dossier once it arrived in Rome. That the relation of Valles circulated widely in the months following the Easter pilgrimage serves as a reminder, to begin with, of the Custody's revered status as a Catholic institution as well as its participation in wide-ranging political networks. The Congregation may have been inclined to take the dossier seriously for this reason alone, but a

---

[1] APF SOCG 44 (October 2, 1661), f. 226. The full text is the following: "Essendo stata trasmessa da mons. Nuntio [di Germania] alla santità di NS una distinta relatione di alcune gravi insolenze usate da due Pellegrini Franzesi al Guardiano di Terra Santa, e sudi [tti] Religiosi, che dall'istesso Guardiano è stata inviata al Residente Cesareo di Constantinopoli, e da lui alla Maiesta dell' Imp.re me hà commandato la santità sua di mandarne a VS Illma l'achiusa copia, acciò fatta prima diligenza per haver alcun Riscontio sè sarà possible dell'identità de delinquente, e loro qualità, si contenti di passarne con chi si devi quelli officii[offitii] di doglianza che merita la bene [….] de li successo, e ch'ella stimaria necessarii per tutti quei rispetti, che se non dovuti alla santità del Luogo, et alle sinistere consequenze, che in pregiuditio della Religione christiano possono temersi in quei Paesi da simili attentati …."

[2] Dated October 1661. AVPF SOCG 44, f. 226v.

closer look at the documents suggests that papal officials were likely more concerned about the depiction of a prominent ecclesiastic being publicly humiliated during the performance of the Easter rites by two French officials. The dossier features two incidents, in particular, which would have been of serious concern to the Congregation. Both involved the public disruption of a valued liturgical rite. One concerned the mass on Holy Saturday in the Church of the Holy Saviour and the other the ceremonial knighting for the Order of the Holy Sepulcher on Holy Friday.[3] Since the disruption of the knighting ceremonial opens the two most important letters, it is fair to say that the friars considered it the most controversial of the two.

The following passage taken from the communal letter succinctly lays out the main contours of the incident and serves as a good starting point for our analysis of a pilgrimage gone terribly wrong.

We the undersigned swear under oath say and testify that on Holy Friday at around 4 o'clock in the evening, according to those who were there in the chapel of the angel in the Holy Sepulcher ... in the place where friar Eusebio Valles, the guardian of Mount Sion, came to create the knights of the Holy Sepulcher, and where he came to create two at this time, that is Seigneur Charles du Plessis, a councillor in the Parlement of Paris of his most Christian majesty, and Seigneur Christopher Cadeau, who is the son of a secretary of state of the same king ... [that] when the guardian was in the act of laying the sword as was traditional in the creation of the knights ... Seigneur Charles jumped to his feet and grabbed the guardian by the chest with his left hand, raised up the sword with his right hand, and raised his voice so that it could be heard by the rest of the members of the schismatic nation who were around. He then, exploding violently with the sword, began to threaten the guardian, and tried to injure and abuse him using scolding words and displaying notable contempt ....[4]

---

[3] The document mentions that it took place at four o'clock in the evening, which is possible, though during Easter the knighting ceremonial typically took place early in the morning on Holy Friday following the overnight stay in the Basilica for devotions.

[4] APF SOCG 245 (April 17, 1661), ff. 193–194. "Noi infrascritti con il nostro giuramento diciamo et attestiamo a chiunque perverrà la presente, come Venerdi Santo prossimo passato a 4 hore di notte in circa, stando chi nella cappella dell'angelo, immediata a quella del Santissimo Sepolcro, chi alle finestre di queste, chi vicini alle mura per vedere e sentire, come faceva il M.R.P. frat' Eusebio Valles, guardiano del Sacro Monte Sion, a creare li cavalieri di detto Santissimo Sepolcro, perchè andò da quell'hora per crearne doi, cioè il signore Carlo du Plessis, che dice esser consiglero del parlamento di Parigi di S.M. Christianissima, et il signore Christoforo Cadeau, che dice esser figlio d'un secretario di stato, pure del medesimo re, vedessimo e sentissimo, come gionto detto P. guardiano all'atto di presentare la spada nuda, come si fa in tale fontione fra gl'altri atti, a quelli si creano cavalieri, havendola posta nella mano destra a detto signor Carlo, egli repente saltò in piedi et afferrato il P. guardiano nel petto con la sinistra, alsata la spada con la destra et

From this passage, we can gather some of the most important elements in the Franciscan narrative. Firstly, it took place on Holy Friday (sacred time), in the Holy Sepulcher (sacred place), and during the performance of the knighting ceremonial for the Order of the Holy Sepulcher (sacred ritual). Secondly, the perpetrators were two French pilgrims named Charles du Plessis and Christophe Cadeau, who had ties to the French state. Du Plessis was a royal councillor, while Cadeau was the son of a royal councillor. Thirdly, Du Plessis verbally insulted and laid his hands upon Eusebio Valles during the knighting ceremony. Fourthly, and finally, it was witnessed by members of other Christian communities ("schismatics"). The account of Eusebio Valles, which was dated the same day (April 17) provides further information. It is fair to say his report also provides a much more dramatic reading of the ritual inversion, conveying his personal outrage at the behaviour of Du Plessis, in particular. The report of Valles begins by first suggesting that the pilgrims behaved as though they were "possessed" (si sono portati da doi Demonii). Du Plessis held onto his vestments and yelled at him for over forty-five minutes while brandishing the sword in his direction and even threatened to kill him. It was, Valles insists, an act of "such a great insolence, and wickedness" when one considered the manner, the day, the act and the holy place.[5]

Several witnesses also added personal statements that further elaborated on that of Valles. Don Giorgio, for example, a Maronite priest, noted that he was present during everything that happened in the "holy room" and that "he heard everything" described in the account. The Ragusan pilgrim Tommaso Allapechi described being outside the shrine of the Holy Sepulcher on Holy Friday when he heard the "discourteous words that Du Plessis shouted without respect for the most holy Place." As these and other accounts make clear, the friars and pilgrims who signed the reports in the dossier considered the behaviour of the two pilgrims egregious on multiple fronts. The communal letter succinctly sums up these grievances, stating that Du Plessis spoke "without respect for anyone in the Most sacred place, the time, the person of the guardian who

---

insieme la voce in modo, che non solo da noi, ma da tutte le nattioni seismatiche circonvicine potè esser sentito, fulminante con la spada, si misse a minacciare detto P.M.R., et in atto di ferirlo e di maltrattarlo con dirle parole strapazzatorie, ingiuriose et di notabilissimo disprezzo."

[5] APF SOCG 245 (April 17, 1661), ff. 193–194. Tal insolenza, e sceleratezza, e stata grandissima come l'Eminenze Vostre benissimo concluderò per rispetto del modo, del tempo, del giorno, dell'atto, I dell luogo Smo; in qual si stava, e della persona, Darò per spatio di 3 quarti d'hora."

represented the Pope, despite the dangers of vanity and the greatest scandal that it gave."[6]

4.1.1 Misbehaving Pilgrims and Custodial Authority

It is hardly shocking to find evidence of misbehaving pilgrims in the Holy Land. Enough accounts exist from the earliest days of Western pilgrimage to suggest that some pilgrims behaved badly, whether in the streets of Jerusalem or in its Holy Places.[7] In fact, concern about irreligious behaviour was one reason why church authorities in Europe were wary about authorizing long distant pilgrimages for members of their flock unless certain their intent was truly devotional. The Franciscan brothers also closely scrutinized the pilgrims once they arrived in the region, aware that they could lose privileges and face heavy fines from Ottoman authorities if pilgrims showed any disrespect to Muslim practices or disrupted the local peace.

Ensuring peaceable relations was clearly one objective of the list of regulations read out by the *custos* upon arrival of the pilgrims, a practice mentioned in many pilgrimage accounts. Thankfully, the German Dominican Felix Fabri (Faber) includes a detailed list in his celebrated treatise that he wrote shortly after making two pilgrimages to Jerusalem in the 1480s. Given the nature of these regulations, one can assume that the friars may have been drawing upon past experience when they compiled it. Pilgrims were advised, for example, to avoid laughing at Muslims, giving them wine, and looking at Muslim women. They were urged as well not to travel alone without a Muslim guide or to wear white turbans (only Muslims could). These regulations were clearly intended to steer pilgrims from behaviour that could lead to violent encounters or land them in the court of the local *kadi*, while others reflect serious concerns about ensuring proper reverence for the pilgrimage as a religious rite, above all respectful behaviour towards Franciscan officiants and the Holy Places. For example, pilgrims were ordered to behave peacefully and

---

[6] APF SOCG 245, f. 177 "... e durò per spatio di tre quarti d'hora, senza rispetto alcuno del Luoco Santissimo, del tempo, della persona del P; guardiano, rapresentante il Sommo Pontefice, del pericolo de vanie e del scandolo grandissimo, che dava."
[7] We should note that misbehaving pilgrims comprised a well-known literary trope as well by the time of this study, most famously as depicted in Geoffrey Chaucer's *The Canterbury Tales*.

reverently during worship and warned against desecrating the Holy Places by chipping off fragments or producing graffiti.[8]

Even with these precautions, however, surviving records of the early modern Custody in the form of correspondence and pilgrimage treatises and the registers of the *kadi* in Jerusalem show that some pilgrims behaved badly. Drunkenness, fighting, and noisiness were especially common forms of misbehaviour.[9] Though considered disruptive, the archives of the Congregation suggest that the Franciscan brothers rarely reported such incidents to the papal body. Indeed, the dossier of 1661 is the only detailed account of misbehaving pilgrims in the papal archives encountered during the course of this research, a fact that suggests that the friars typically managed such incidents on their own. The friary did have a prison and the *custos* also possessed the authority to deny badly behaved pilgrims the certificate required by their local bishop to affirm their completion of the rite and even expel them.[10] Since the friars did turn to the Congregation in 1661, we should presume that the nature and/or scale of the disruption was unusual. Indeed, Valles implies as much when he mentions that the two men had been troublesome from early on in the pilgrimage and that initially he hesitated to agree to their request for the knighting ceremonial. In the end, he did so, he said, in the vain hope that it would "pacify" the two men.[11] What may have been even more a concern for the friars, however, was the public nature of their misbehaviour and insolent treatment of the *custos*. As we recall from the Franciscan letter cited earlier, other Christians (*schizmatici*) were present in the Holy Sepulcher at the time of the knighting ceremonial, and several witnesses heard Du Plessis and Cadeau "shouting." Consider, as well, Valles' assertion that Du Plessis "scolded" him, used "injurious" and

---

[8] Felix Fabri, *The Wanderings of Felix Fabri*, vol. 1, pt. 1 (London: Palestine Pilgrim's Society, 1896), 249–255. The regulations mentioned by later pilgrims were likely the same, if not an even longer list.

[9] Felix Fabri (Faber), for one, mentions drunken behaviour. Fabri, *Wanderings*, vol. 1, pt. 1, 34.

[10] See the discussion in Chapter 2. Anthoine Regnault, for example, includes his certificate in his treatise. It was signed by Bonaventure Corsetus, the guardian of Mount Sion on August 23, 1549. Regnault, *Discours du voyage doutre mer* (Lyon: n.p., 1573), 157.

[11] APF SOCG 245 f. 177 (April 17, 1661). "... con occasione di quelle essendo io andato nella Cappella pp.a del Smo sepolcro per farli Cavalieri dell' istesso, cosi da essi supplicate, che con ciò credevo pure, doppo mille alter maniere usati d'aquietarlo."

"contemptuous" language, and publicly declared the friar unworthy of both his office as *custos* and of his Franciscan habit.[12]

Place and time colluded in intensifying the sense of injury on the part of the friars, who found themselves publicly humiliated on important holy days in two places that were deeply meaningful to them: the Basilica of the Holy Sepulcher and the church attached to the convent of the Holy Saviour. Especially during the Easter rites, the Basilica of the Holy Sepulcher was a busy place of worship among the many Christian traditions, and the Holy Sepulcher was an especially visible shrine within it because of its prominent location under the central rotunda.

Pilgrims entering the main door would immediately find themselves under the massive dome, itself an impressive act of engineering that contributed to the majesty of the enormous church. As it does to this day, the rotunda also serves as a central point of access to the many sites of the Basilica as well as a focal point of worship, a centrality reinforced by its containment of the shrine marking the site of Christ's burial and resurrection. Indeed, pilgrims would have immediately seen the shrine as they entered the rotunda, its white marble façade gleaming under the reflected light of hundreds of lamps. Recognizing the spatial centrality and visibility of the Sepulcher within the Basilica, one can well understand the mortification of the Franciscan brothers as they watched the head of their community physically assaulted by a layman, the sounds of his shouting echoing throughout the cavernous spaces of a very public place of worship during the most sacred of Christian rites.

The other significant episode described in the reports reveals a similar preoccupation with the public and insolent behaviour of the two pilgrims. In this case, the setting has changed from the cavernous spaces of the great Basilica to one that was more explicitly Franciscan in character, because it took place in the church attached to the convent of the Holy Saviour. As discussed previously, visiting pilgrims usually stayed with the Franciscan brothers at the hospice attached to the convent and while there joined the Franciscan community for meals and participated in the communal rites held in their church. Bernardin Surius, who was assigned to the Custody during the 1640s, describes it as a small space in the shape of a cross but a deeply meaningful place because it was here that the brothers regularly gathered for worship when not out at one of the shrines. It seems to have

---

[12] APF SOCG 245(April 17, 1661), ff. 275–277. "e detto Carlo mi disse parole di grandissimo disprezzo, con darmi del tù, con dirmi, che Vicario dell'Papa ... indegno soggiongeva dell'officio, e dell'habbito."

been fairly lavish, though Surius is at pains to emphasize the poverty and simplicity of the Franciscan community. The Church held a "great altar" that faced east and that was covered by a dome resting on four pillars. The altar also included seven lamps, and the choir held more than one organ. The church also included two chapels, one dedicated to Saint Francis and the other to Saint Roch. According to Surius, every day after compline the brothers gathered for a "devout procession before the three altars singing the hymns *veni creator, pange lingua* and *exultet caelum laudibus*."

The Flemish friar argues that this procession was their way of "commemorating the mysteries of Mount Sion from which the brothers were chased,"[13] a point of reference that underscores the special spiritual significance attached by the friars to their first convent as a symbol of their community and spiritual purpose. For Valles and his brothers, the disruption of the mass on Holy Saturday represented a direct assault upon the reputation of the Franciscan family because it violated the spiritual peace of an intimate space of Franciscan worship and fellowship. Indeed, Franciscan descriptions of the episode, though concise, hint at a deliberate staging to magnify its message of disrespect. We learn, to begin with, that the mass was attended by other people including the pilgrims. The incident began, moreover, when the two Frenchmen rose to approach Valles just as he was leading the procession down the center aisle. Shouting ensued. A number of the Franciscan witnesses emphasize the solemnity of the ceremony, noting, in particular, that Valles was dressed in his "pontifical" robes of office at the time ("estoit vestry pontificalement").[14] The mention of the robes adds to the intended sense of outrage of the Franciscan account, because it cast the interruption of the rite as an assault upon papal authority as well. Friar Diego della Croce, who also testified as a witness to the misbehaviour of the men, summed it up by saying that they acted "scandalously" (con scandalo grande). As the sacristan, della Croce was one of the friars responsible for ensuring the orderly performance of the liturgical rites, and he must have felt

---

[13] Bernardin Surius, *Le pieux pelerin ou voyage de Jerusalem divise en trois livres contenans la description topographique de plusieurs Royaumes, pais, villes, nations estrangeres nommement des quatuorze religions orientales, leurs moeurs & humeurs, tant en matiere de Religion que de civile conversation &c.* (Brussels: Francois Foppens, 1666), 365–366.

[14] Surius, *Le pieux pelerin ou voyage de Jerusalem*, "... me suis trouvé presente le samedy sant quand le Reverend Pere Guardien estoit vestry Pontificalment, et quil arrive cet bruit que jay neri et entendu."

personally affronted by the disruptive behaviour of these pilgrims. But he was also articulating a sense of grievance that was much more serious. To cause scandal in ecclesiastical parlance was to bring shame upon the community. For della Croce, Valles, and their brothers, the disruption of liturgical rites and disrespect shown to the *custos* were well-recognized signs of spiritual disorder, casting public doubt upon the spiritual worthiness of the brothers in their role as custodians of the Holy Places.

4.1.2 *Papal Authority and the French State*

The Franciscan dossier presented the Congregation with the disturbing image of an important ecclesiastical official berated in public on multiple occasions by two laymen. In one case, the offence took place in the most significant Holy Place. In the other, at the spiritual heart of the Franciscan community in Jerusalem. Such an image was guaranteed to catch the attention of papal officials, especially since the *custos* was a papal office. The head of the Franciscan family in the Holy Land held two simultaneous offices: those of guardian, a Franciscan office recognizing his authority over the brotherhood, and *custos*, which recognized his broader jurisdiction as an apostolic vicar (papal representative). While the Franciscan order elected the *custos* triennially, he was not officially recognized in charge of the Custody until he received approval from the papacy. The Congregation, which assumed responsibility for affirming the office following its establishment in 1622, took this responsibility very seriously, requiring every newly appointed *custos* to go to Rome to receive official recognition of his appointment. This was just one of many new measures introduced by the Congregation during the seventeenth century in an effort to strengthen its influence over the Custody.[15] For our purposes here, it also helps to explain why the friars believed the Congregation would have been concerned about the disrespect shown to Valles in 1661. To insult the *custos*, especially while wearing his "pontifical" robes, was to publicly insult papal authority. As discussed earlier, however, the Franciscans were eager to present the incident as an act of French aggression against their jurisdiction, and it is this intent that preoccupies the remaining analysis. The friars knew firsthand that the papal body was very concerned about the authority of secular powers over religious institutions. Moreover, the Congregation had already

---

[15] The Congregation and its relations with the Custody is the subject of Chapter 5.

presided over several disputes between the friars and the French state beginning in the 1620s. In their reports on the pilgrimage of 1661, the friars deliberately alluded to the involvement of the French state in a number of ways. We learn, to begin with, that the pilgrims had close ties to the Bourbon regime – Du Plessis was a royal official and his friend the son of one. Moreover, the pilgrims insisted their behaviour was justified because they were acting in defense of the honour of Louis XIV. According to multiple accounts, the Frenchmen were outraged over a sermon of a Spanish preacher that seemed to show greater respect to the king of Spain than their own monarch. Bartolomeo Terrench, the Catalan friar at the center of the controversy, recalled giving the sermon. It was likely one of a few given that same day by friars in diverse languages, something that was common given the international composition of the pilgrimage. In his own account of the event, Terrench insists that he offered thanks to both monarchs for their generous patronage of the Custody, but the Frenchmen took umbrage even so because he mentioned Phillip IV (d. 1665) first. Terrench denied having any malicious intent towards the French monarch when he did so (ma ciò fu con ogni semplicità senza ponto di malitia o d'avertenza). To the contrary, he says, the sermons were intended to recognize both rulers as "the principle protectors of these Holy Places."[16] We should note as well that Valles mentions in his account that he only managed to extricate himself from the grasp of Du Plessis by assuring the Frenchman of his "infinite reverence" for the French king as the "Protector of the Holy Places."[17]

---

[16] APF SOCG 245, f. 175 (April 18, 1661). The full passage is here. "Io infrascritto fra BARTOLOMEO TERRENCH, Cattalano, Spagnolo, dico et attesto a ciunque perverirà la presente, anco con il mio giuramento, tacto pectore more sacerdotali, come havendo dovuto fare per obedienza l'ufficio d'hebdomadario la vigilia delle Palme con occasione d'une processione, che si fa ogni sera nel santissimo Sepolcro, nel dire un'oratione, nella quale stavano doi N., credendomi, che queste due lettere fossero per nominare li doi re, Cattolico e Christianissimo, *proferii* prima quello avanti di questo; ma ciò fu con ogni semplicità senza ponto di malitia o d'avertenza, essendo venuto di fresco a questi S. Luoghi, non essendo practico delle buone usanze di T.S., particolarmente di questa, ch'è di dire l'orationi per dette maestà in commune, senza nominarle, atteso, sì come ambe si riconoscono per principalissimi protettori di questi S. Luoghi, cosi si prega incessantemente e indifferentemente per tutti doi."

[17] APF SOCG 245 f. 177 (April 17, 1661). "Poco à poco andai spoglianodomi de paramenti, assicurandolo, che come riconoscevo per singularissimo protettore di quei luoghi S M Xma, cosi lo portava in cima la testa, e tenevo verso la sua gran persona riverenza infinita, che mai havevo fatta cosa in contrario, a gli promessi di tanto osservare in avvenire, e cosi con questi, et altri parole procurai di levar megli dalle mani."

The friars peppered their accounts with other telltale signs of the involvement of the French state, in particular, pointed mentions of the complicity of two French Capuchins and a French Observant preacher in the disruption of the mass on Holy Saturday. Once again, Valles provides us with the most detailed description, writing that "we were in the middle of the traditional procession, engaged in mental prayer and singing the hymn O *Gloriosa Virginum* when the two Capuchins joined the other pilgrims in their devotions." They came, he says, "on the pretext of having received an indulgence" to join in the Easter devotions. Valles' account casts suspicion on their true intentions, noting that at least one of the Capuchins had traveled from Cairo in the company of the two French pilgrims. Rather than pursuing devotions, he states, their true intent was to foment "new tumult." Why Valles believed the presence of the Capuchins signaled the complicity of the French state will become clear when we look more closely at the contested state of relations between these religious leading up to the pilgrimage of 1661. But for our purposes here, we should mention that the two Capuchins were prominent members of missions established through the patronage of the Bourbon monarchy in Cairo and Cyprus. They were also French, the same nationality as the Franciscan preacher whom Valles' implicates as well. This preacher, named Pascal (Pasquale), was a member of the Franciscan family and apparently gave a sermon during the mass on Holy Saturday that left out the mention of the Spanish king entirely. When Valles chastised him for doing so, the French pilgrims rose in support of the French Franciscan preacher, triggering the dramatic confrontation with Valles. As shall be discussed shortly, Pascal was in conflict with Valles on other occasions as well during the 1660s, conflicts that reveal fissures within the Holy Land family along "national" lines that were exacerbated by growing tension with France over jurisdiction.

Were these Frenchmen in fact co-conspirators in a coordinated attack upon the *custos*? It is impossible to say with certainty. Nor is there any concrete evidence that they acted on the wishes of the French monarch or his ambassador at the Ottoman Porte. However, as John Condren shows so effectively (and amusingly) in his study of Bourbon relations with Modena and other Italian states, French officials enjoyed a well-deserved reputation for arrogance and rudeness in diplomatic circles by the reign of Louis XIV.[18] Indeed, these were hallmarks of a French diplomacy that

---

[18] John Condren, "Louis XIV et le repos de l'Italie: French Policies towards the Duchy of Parma, Modena, and Monferrato, 1659–1689," PhD diss., St. Andrews University, 2015.

privileged an aggressive approach to asserting its authority including in public ceremonials and personal diplomatic engagement, especially in regard to states it considered less powerful. That these men displayed some of the same French arrogance, in other words, is not at all unlikely. Whether they were serving as representatives of the state in this matter or not, however, Valles and his fellow friars were intent upon laying the incident at the doorstep of the French state. But the most compelling evidence presented by the friars may have been the ritual inversion of the knighting ceremonial. It would have been impossible for the papal officials of the Congregation to overlook the political implications of Du Plessis' seizure of the sword of Godefroy of Bouillon from the hand of the *custos*. The sword was a symbol of Catholic authority in Jerusalem evoking the years of Crusader rule, but for Frenchmen and -women raised on the accounts of the glorious exploits of Godefroy of Bouillon, Louis IX, and other French crusaders, it was a potent symbol of French governance over Jerusalem.

Du Plessis' actions, the dossier suggested, publicly asserted French governance over the Custody, something that neither the friars nor the Congregation would have accepted lightly. Indeed, a central mandate of the Propaganda Fide was to reclaim papal influence over Catholic missions and other similar Catholic institutions in lands outside of Europe that it had long ceded to various European states. The influence of the Spanish and French states in the Atlantic was a particular sore point for the papacy in the wake of the Council of Trent and explains why the Congregation moved swiftly from its formation in 1622 to organize missions under its own authority in these regions as well as in the Mediterranean.[19] While it is certainly true that the Congregation worked closely with the French and Spanish states to establish new missions as well, it remained ever wary about transgressions against its own authority over Catholic institutions. Indeed, the Congregation may have already been concerned about French influence in the Custody because it had had a front row seat to mounting jurisdictional conflicts between the Observants and the French state dating back to the 1620s. Situating the dispute of 1661 in the context of this longer history of conflict suggests that the suspicions of the friars regarding the ambitions of the French state were not misplaced.

---

[19] On this, see discussion in Chapter 5.

Particularly troubling for the friars was the monarchy's use of its newly acquired Ottoman status of Protector of the Holy Places to promote a larger role for French clerics in the spiritual and administrative life of the Custody. The friars resisted of course, regarding these efforts as a direct assault upon their traditional jurisdiction. In this they were quite correct, but it is the objectives of the Bourbon regime that most concern us here. The documents produced by the disputes, particularly in the form of correspondence involving French officials, the Congregation, and the Observant friars, reveal a French state intent upon rebranding the Custody a French Catholic institution – one that lay under its authority as Protector of the Holy Places and under the management of French clerics. This intent becomes clear when we consider two strategies employed by the state from the 1620s: the expansion of an administrative role for French members of the Holy Land family and the establishment of French missions. These two strategies operated simultaneously from the 1620s, crafting a more visible role for French clerics at the heart of a revered Catholic institution. Section 4.2.1 will consider each of these strategies in turn. As shall soon be clear, both served a similar objective: to promote the visibility and influence of French clerics in the Custody and in consequence the spiritual and political authority of the Bourbon monarchy through its status as Protector of the Holy Places. The conversations that these measures sparked between French officials, the friars, and the Congregation over questions of jurisdiction are also important, revealing a foundational role for the Custody in manifesting Bourbon claim to a French sacred destiny as Christian rulers.

4.2 TURNING THE CUSTODY "FRENCH"

4.2.1 *French Franciscans*

The first indication of French designs upon the administration of the Custody came in the form of a letter sent by Louis Deshayes de Courmenin (c. 1600–1632) to the Congregation in 1621. Deshayes de Courmenin was the French envoy assigned to the Ottoman Porte. He would go on to write a travel account known as the *Voyage de Levant fait par le commandement du Roi en l'année 1621* and even received a few more postings before finding himself at the wrong end of royal authority in 1632. Accused of conspiring against Cardinal Richelieu, Deshayes was arrested and subsequently executed. This unfortunate end lay in the distant future, however, when the French official penned a letter to the

Congregation making a bold request: to increase the number of French Franciscans in the Custody and to hand the office of *custos* to a French friar.[20] We should note that at the time of this request, Deshayes was commissioned by the king to negotiate a consulate in Jerusalem, a move that the Franciscan brothers forcefully resisted. In other words, the envoy may have been reacting to their signs of opposition. His reasoning for the request is nevertheless intriguing because it hints at a strategic importance for the Custody in the imperial ambitions of the Bourbon monarchy. In the letter, Deshayes de Courmenin states quite simply that the Franciscan community in the Holy Land was "full of vassals" of the Spanish state and thus posed a threat to the security of the Custody.[21] The envoy's criticism highlights two features of the administration of the Custody that were of serious concern to French officials from this time forward. Firstly, that its membership mostly comprised Italian and Spanish subjects. In theory, the Custody was open to friars from all provinces of the Order, reflecting a Franciscan conception of the Holy Land as the special missionary ground of their founder, Francis of Assisi.[22] In practice, while still quite diverse, the Franciscan family of the Holy Land drew most heavily from the Italian peninsula and, in particular, from the Veneto, followed by the Spanish and French kingdoms. The remaining membership included a broader array of ethnicities including Flemish, Germanic, and Polish as well as converts from local Christian communities. Moreover, it was customary by the Early Modern Period to place the office of *custos* in the hands of Italian friars, though it did circulate somewhat. Secondly, the letter of Deshayes de Courmenin acknowledged the long-standing importance of the Spanish monarchy as a patron of the Custody. While his assessment of the friars as Spanish "vassals" was an

---

[20] René Pillorget, "Louid Deshayes de Courmenin et L'Orient Musulman (1621–1626)," *Cahiers de l'Association des études françaises* 27 (1975): 65–81. The *Voyage* was published in Paris by Adrian Taupinart.

[21] Leonhard Lemmens, ed., *Acta S. Congregationis de propaganda Fide pro Terra Sancta*, vol. 1 (Rome: Collegio di S. Bonaventura, 1921), 24. Original in APF SA vol 382, f. 36. "Rme Padre! Essendosi novamente verificato, come gli religiosi christiani, quali stanno perstanza nel convento del Smo Sepolchro di gierusalem, et altre persone divote, quale ivi visitano gli Smi Luoghi, sono oltra modo vessati da Turchi, perchè essendo loro vassalli de prencipi christiani loro nemici, non vogliono più detti Turchi soffrire, che habbiano da stare per residenza in Gierusalem et, è anco peggio, che si tiene per cosa certissima, che, se non si rimedia prestamente a questo inconveniente, si corre grandissimo risico, che a fatto tutti gli veri christiani saranno cacciati da quelli Santi Luoghi con pericolo della propria vita et perdita a fatto di questi Sacri Luoghi."

[22] On Franciscan spirituality, see Chapter 6.

exaggeration – most of the brothers of the Holy Land were subjects of other states – he was perfectly correct in highlighting the close ties between the Custody and the Spanish state. As Adam Beaver has argued recently, the Spanish monarchy was the single largest funder of the pilgrimage institution from the fifteenth century onwards.[23] This was certainly still the case in 1661 at the time of the pilgrimage dispute. Sent in November of the same year, for example, a report by friar Paolo da Lodi to the Congregation stated quite bluntly that "with regard to alms, they [the friars] were dependent principally upon those of Spain."[24]

Deshayes de Courmenin's letter reveals significant French discomfort with the leadership of the Franciscan community because of its ties to Spain – ties that the French envoy sought to delegitimize by emphasizing Spain's poor relations with the Ottoman Porte and the much better relations enjoyed between the Turkish Empire and France. In doing so, the French official was also reminding the Congregation of the favoured status of the French monarchy as Protector of the Holy Places. The status of Protector will be discussed in more detail shortly, but we should note here that it was granted to the French king in the Capitulations (*Ahdname*) of 1604 by the Ottoman Sultan Ahmed I (1603–1617). The Capitulations of 1604 was the most recent of several treaties between France and the Ottoman Porte that fostered a valued commercial and political alliance in the Mediterranean between the two great powers. The status of Protector was a recent privilege, one that France would turn to frequently in the following decades to expand its influence in Ottoman Lands, in particular with regard to Catholic institutions. Deshayes de Courmenin's letter is especially interesting, however, because it also points to a changing relationship with the Custody by the 1620s. Until this time, the French state largely interpreted its role as Protector in much the same way as the Venetian Republic – that is, as a defender of the privileges of the Custody, in particular, its jurisdiction over altars. What is intriguing in this particular case is that Deshayes de Courmenin invoked the status of Protector to *challenge* a long-standing privilege belonging to

---

[23] See, in particular, Adam G. Beaver, "A Holy Land for the Catholic Monarchy: Palestine in the Making of Modern Spain, 1469–1598," PhD diss., Harvard University, 2008.

[24] "Circa le lemosine, come da Spagna dependono principalmente: li spagno li sc[uta] le portano le spondono, e cola si mandano li conti dell entrata et uscita. E questo è il nervo di quell governo et intendo che il Rè di spagna senta male che la sac. Conge. voglia ingerirsi della di lui lemosine che manda co là per mezzo de suoi sudeliti fedeli." APF SC Terra Santa I, 297. His letter suggests that Lodi had been sent by the Congregation to report on the state of the Custody, likely in response to the recent troubles.

the Franciscan brothers, one that had been granted by the papacy. The envoy, in other words, was signaling a significant alteration in France's traditional relationship with the pilgrimage institution, one that made the friars uneasy.

The letter thus far highlights three elements important for understanding Bourbon interest in the Custody by the 1620s: Spanish influence, the Custody's importance as a Latin (Catholic) institution in the Holy Land, and French relations with the Ottoman Empire. It also reveals what would become a significant point of tension with the friars from this time forward, namely, the independent nature of custodial jurisdiction. By requesting French control of the office of *custos*, the Bourbon monarchy was trampling upon conventions that had been in place for centuries, because the office lay under the jurisdiction of the central Franciscan administration in Rome. Office-holding and the nomination of friars for service in the Holy Land were decisions made by the Minister General (head of the Order) in consultation with the *diffinitors*, the officials who oversaw the central administration. Major changes to the organization tended to be reserved for the General Chapter meetings that met every few years during the seventeenth century and brought together the administrative heads of the international order to discuss important matters.[25] By requesting French control of this office, Deshayes de Courmenin signaled France's willingness to employ its status as Protector to challenge Franciscan jurisdiction over the Custody. The envoy must have realized it was a provocative gesture. We do know that his letter immediately raised the hackles of the brothers of the Holy Land who responded swiftly through their Cardinal Protector in Rome. The Cardinal Protector, who was charged with representing Franciscan interests with the papacy, defended the existing governance of the Custody, arguing that the Spanish state was a generous benefactor and that the Italian friars had long governed the institution "indifferent" to nation. The Congregation concurred, rejecting the proposed institutional change as a dangerous "novelty" that would cause internal discord.[26]

This was by no means the end of Bourbon efforts to expand the role of the French Franciscans in the central administration of the Custody. The state continued to press for an increase in the number of French brothers

---

[25] On Franciscan organization including the General Chapter, see, for example, John Moorman, *A History of the Franciscan Order* (Oxford: Oxford University Press, 1968).

[26] Lemmens, ed., *Acta*, vol. I, 24–25. The original document is found in APF CG 8, III, f. 5.

throughout the seventeenth century. As late as 1698, for example, then ambassador Pierre Antoine Castagnères, Marquis de Châteauneuf (1689–1692), wrote to the state to ensure that more French friars were sent.[27] More importantly, continuing French pressure resulted in expanding the access of French Franciscans to administrative offices. In 1645, the Order guaranteed one of the two *discreti* to the French nation. The *discrets* served on the inner council, known as the *discretoria*, which oversaw the operations of the Custody including the assignment of friars to various tasks such as alms-gathering, pastoral care and preaching, the maintenance of buildings, the management of funds, and various political matters.[28] In 1658, only three years before the controversial Easter pilgrimage studied here, the General Chapter meeting of the Franciscan order in Toledo issued new regulations for the Custody that further expanded French access to administrative positions. The regulations provided French access in particular to the office of president and one of the two vicars on a rotating basis between the nations.[29] After the *custos*, these were the highest-ranking officials in the Custody, substituting for him during his travels on business.[30] They were, in other words, influential positions and thus desirable.

Internal sources suggest that these administrative changes were controversial and stirred considerable tension between the three main "nations" in the community in the years leading up to the dispute of 1661. A report written by friar Paolo di Migliorico (Miglionico), for example, hints at resistance to the new regulations while also suggesting quite clearly that the French monarchy had played an active role in pushing for the new French offices. His office is unclear from the letter, though he was clearly a senior official in the Custody. Friar Paolo addressed his letter to the Minister General of the Franciscan Order, though its presence in the archives of the Congregation of the Propaganda Fide suggests that it must have been sent along at some point. Dated March 2, 1658, the report

---

[27] ANF B I 380 (April 27, 1698).

[28] On the creation of the *discreti* in 1645, see Bernard Heyberger, *Les Chrétiens du Proche-Orient au temp de la Réforme Catholique* (Paris: Payot, 2012), 288. One was guaranteed to the French nation, one to the Spanish. A third one, granted to the Italian nation, was introduced in 1663.

[29] APF SOCG 245, f. 239. The new regulations issued by the Chapter General of Toledo of 1658 are mentioned, for example, in a letter sent by a French friar named Damien Moran, a Recollect friar from the province of Paris, dated April 20, 1667. On this, see n. 40.

[30] On the function of the discretoria, or inner council, see, for example, Megan C. Armstrong, *The Politics of Piety: Franciscan Preachers during the Wars of Religion, 1560–1600* (Rochester: University of Rochester Press, 2004).

mentions the arrival of a letter in the Custody from "the Emperor our Protector" (The French king), which discussed the recent statutes issued at the Chapter General of Toledo and requested that they be observed. Friar Paolo insisted that he made sure that the statutes were read aloud in the refectory to the brothers during the previous six months as required but they were never implemented.[31] That the new regulations were never implemented is one suggestion that they faced internal resistance in some quarters and likely from those already in charge of the administration. Since the Italian friar moves on to complain about Spanish influence over office-holding in the same letter, we can imagine that some of the resistance to the regulations may have come from these members of the Holy Land family. He complains, in particular, about their influence over financial offices and even accused them of seizing three keys to the "magazei."[32] Friar Paolo seems to be referring to the storerooms in the convent where the friars kept household supplies as well as other goods and funds essential to the orderly operations of the community. His indignation in the letter is palpable, noting that even the guardian did not have direct access but had to go through the procurator. He reported, in fact, that the procurator let it be known that even if the guardian asked for a simple quill ("penna") he would have to seek him out in person.[33] For the Italian friar, the arrogance of this Spanish official was galling, all the more so since he could be vindictive in his use of this authority when aggrieved about some matter. Friar Paolo insisted that it was essential for the "good peace" of the house that the Franciscan guardian also have a key, otherwise he was effectively the "slave" of the Spanish members.

Friar Paolo's report underscores a widely recognized reality in the Custody of the Holy Land, namely. that members of the Spanish nation considered the office of procurator theirs. Indeed, sources on the Custody allow us to trace a consistent Spanish presence in the office during the sixteenth and seventeenth centuries. Friar Martin de Regna, as just one

---

[31] APF SC TS 1 (March 2, 1658), 226.
[32] "Magazei" seems to refer to storerooms for the general community. The sacristy would have had its own separate space where it held devotional objects, liturgical paraphernalia, and other goods necessary for the performance of the rites.
[33] APF SC Terra Santa 1, f. 226. The full passage is here. "Intorno *alle tre chiavi delle Magazei* già che li spagnoli *se l'hanno usurpato* e per la buona pace *è necessario che il superiore si habbia una accioche le robbe* non vaddino per altra strada, come anco il Procuratore ... haverebbe tanta arroganza, *che si ha lasciato intendere*, se il guardiano haveva di bisogno di una penna, e mandasse il suo compagno a chiederla, non ci la darebbe, ma che andasse lui in persona e se l'havessa aggravato di qualche cosa voleva vendicarsi di non dargli niente."

example, appears in several letters regarding the funding of the dome of the Holy Sepulcher during the 1550s. A century later, friar Jacques Goujon wrote in his treatise that the office of procurator "belonged to Spain," showing that little had changed on this front in the intervening century.[34] Miglorico's complaints about the procurator's control of the storerooms hints at the importance of this office within the Custody, one that played an expansive role because it oversaw the flow of funds in and out of the Jerusalem. Indeed, the Spanish monarchy had in fact long insisted upon placing the office with Spanish friars in recognition of its role as the main benefactor of the Custody.

By suggesting that the *custos* was the "slave" of the Spanish members, friar Paolo di Milgiorico may well have been suggesting that there was also tension between Italian and Spanish members over office-holding. But internal resistance to the acceptance of the new statutes – statutes that expanded French access to important offices – points to fraternal hostility involving the French as well. A flurry of letters sent by the French friars to the Congregation after this time show that tension between the French and Spanish was especially acute and may have been aggravated by the election of Eusebio Valles, who followed Migliorico in the office. Like his predecessor, Valles was Italian, but he came from the duchy of Milan and was thus a subject of the Spanish monarchy. His connection to the Spanish monarchy emerges early on in a letter sent by then Franciscan Minister General Angelo di Sambuca to the Congregation dated July 5, 1658. In this letter, Sambuca asked the Congregation to recognize Valles' appointment, mentioning that it was the Spanish king who put forth his name for consideration.[35] Sambuca also mentions that the appointment was urgent because the convent had been without consistent leadership for the last two years. This seems to have been the case, since earlier correspondence discusses the withdrawal of friar Serafico of Milan from the position following his appointment as a *diffinitor* in 1658.[36]

---

[34] Patrocinio Garcia Barriuso, *Espana en la Historia de Tierra santa*, vol. 1 (Madrid: Ministerio de Asuntos Exteriores, 1992), 162. Other Spanish procurators that appear with frequency by the seventeenth century include Antonio Castillo, who wrote a treatise on the Holy Land discussed in Chapter 5. For Goujon, see his *Histoire et voyage de la Terre-Sainte, où tout ce qu'il y a de plus remarquable dns les Saints Lieux, est tres-exactement descript* (Lyon: Pierre Compagnon & Robert Taillandier, 1670), 28–29.

[35] APF SC TS 1, ff. 240–243.

[36] APF SC TS 1, f. 224. The letter is undated but included with other correspondence from 1658. It is from friar Pietro da Quintanilla, a commissioner general of the Holy Land, who mentions the need for the appointment of an interim *custos* until the next Chapter

The matter was urgent as well because of ongoing tension within the Holy Land family, tensions that as we have already discussed, which were disrupting the orderly operations of the Custody. Under Valles, however, the tension clearly not only continued, it intensified. Hints of internal conflict must have reached the Congregation at the end of 1660 because Valles wrote a reassuring letter in response. Dated January 1661, he insisted that he had kept "peace and concord" in the community, adding that he had "removed" those who had tried to disturb it. Though vague on the specifics, the letter does refer to "constitutions," suggesting that office-holding may have been the source of internal division.[37]

When we consider the disruptions to the Easter pilgrimage that took place only three months later, one can safely say that Valles had overstated the pacific state of the community in his letter to the Congregation. Signs of internal dissent remain quite visible in the months that followed as well. In fact, one of the French friars involved in the disruption of the mass on Holy Saturday appears as a plaintiff in a series of letters sent to the Congregation in September. In his letters, Friar Pascal depicts a community riven by tension between the French and Spanish nations and singles out Valles for special criticism. In particular, he accuses the Milanese *custos* of showing favouritism to Spanish friars and of abusive treatment to the French. Consider the following colourful examples: One letter, dated September 6, accuses Valles of nicknaming one of the two prisons in the Custody the "French room" ("Camera de Francesi") in order to mock and shame "members of the nation" as well of imprisoning two French brothers unjustly, the preacher Bernardin de Candal and a lay friar named Stefane. In another incident, a French preacher was beaten in the church by Spanish friars when he rose to take his turn to give a sermon: "And when the French father desired to perform his weekly duty, the Spanish fathers rose up and beat him in the church in the presence of the laity [secolari]."[38] According to Pascal, Valles responded by

---

General, friar Bernardino. As he points out, Mariano Maleo was already in Europe and therefore could not continue in the role.

[37] APF SC TS 1, f. 309. The letter is dated January 27, 1661: "Hò mantenuto semp[e]r questa family *in buona pace*, e s[anta] Concordia, et alcuni soggetti in questi, che me l'hanno volute sturbare doppi fattagli qualche mortification religiosa, in conformità dell'Ordini dattimi da cottesta sac. Congregatione, e delle constitutioni nostre, *gli hò rimandati all loro province.*"

[38] APF SOCG 245 (September 8, 1661), ff. 195. "... e quando Il P[at]re francese volse fare l'ufficio suo per che era hebdomadario, gli Patri spagnuoli si gitarono adesso è l'hanno batuto nella Chiesa in presenza de secolari."

imprisoning the French friar and sentencing him to live only on bread and water "simply because he was French, and even though he was attacked during the legitimate performance of his office as preacher."[39] As a final example, Pascal specifically mentions the violation of the statutes of the community in two other cases involving office-holding, one in which Valles appointed a Spanish friar named Ignatio Murgues to the office of president rather than a French friar and another in which he removed two French *discrets* even though the statutes required an equal number of each nation on the inner council.

Of course, one has to be careful about taking Pascal's complaints of bias and abuse of office at face value. His letters nevertheless offer further evidence of continuing tension within the Holy Land family over office-holding, tension that on many occasions took the form of physical and verbal conflict. Moreover, when one considers these episodes of violence in tandem with the letters discussed earlier, it seems clear that this tension rose alongside, and in response to, persistent efforts on the part of the Bourbon monarchy to expand French office-holding in the Custody. At the very least, the willingness of Pascal and other French friars to voice their complaints to the Congregation suggests that the monarchy's active interest in the Custody emboldened some of these clerics to push for a more prominent role in its administration. But one suspects a degree of collusion between French officials and these brothers as well, suggested not only in their use of a shared language of complaint (Spanish favouritism, violation of regulations) but also in the supportive letters provided by some French officials. More concrete evidence of complicity is found in a letter sent from a French friar named Damien Moran. Sent six years later in 1667, his letter mentions that the French king recently wrote to the Congregation about a disputed office. What is even more intriguing, however, is that he invests significance in the office as a marker of French preeminence. The matter, he emphasizes, was "an affair of importance with regard to the glory of God, the honour of the King, and the reputation of the entire French nation."[40] The French friar thoughtfully attached a copy of the statutes of the Chapter of Toledo of 1658, noting

---

[39] APF SOCG 245 (September 8, 1661), ff. 195. "... e dopo il P[at]re guardian senza haver volute sentire le sue ragioni la fatto state 6 giorni a la camera de francesi cioè la prigione come pane & acqua, per che era francese."

[40] APF SOCG 245, f. 67. "Sa Maiesté tres-Chrestienne escrivant a vostre Eminentissime grandeur comme pareillement a Monseigneur le Duc de Chaumes son Ambassadeur extraordinaire pour une affaire d'importance laquelle regarde la gloire de Dieu, l'honneur et authorité de saditte Maiesté, et la reputation de toute la nation Françoise."

that these were introduced "for the good management of the religious of the Holy Land family of Jerusalem."

If we return to the dispute of 1661, it is important to remember that these conflicts over office-holding were unfolding at the same time and seem to have informed relations between members of the Franciscan family in ways that shed light on the nature of this particular incident. The disputes over office-holding help to explain, in particular, why Valles was quick to consider Pascal's sermon during the mass on Holy Saturday as an attack upon his authority as well as evidence of his complicity with the French pilgrims. As one may recall, his sermon left out any recognition of the generosity of the Spanish king and only acknowledged that of France. But what the dispute of 1661 also makes clear is that, despite the resistance of the Venetian and Spanish friars, the role of the French in the administration was slowly expanding. Certainly, by the end of the seventeenth century, French friars were occupying many of the disputed offices discussed here. Indeed, that Pascal was the guardian of the convent in Bethlehem in 1661 alone points to increased French influence within the Holy Land family by this time. This was an important office in the administration of the Custody, responsible for overseeing the liturgical rites in the second most significant Holy Place, the Church of the Nativity in Bethlehem.

As Section 4.2.2 will also show, French influence in the Custody also expanded through its promotion of French missionaries. Similar to the cases involving office-holding, the actions of the French state threatened Observant jurisdiction and sparked disputes, in particular, with regard to the issues of pastoral care and clerical discipline.

4.2.2 French Missionaries

The growing body of work on the French missions in the Custody means that we can leave aside a detailed description of its history and focus our attention upon jurisdictional conflicts involving the Franciscan brothers, conflicts that reveal a place for these missionaries in the expansionist agenda of the Bourbon monarchy. These disputes began in earnest in 1622, when the Congregation granted permission for the establishment of French Capuchins and Jesuits in five cities that lay within the jurisdiction of the Custody of the Holy Land: Aleppo, Cairo, Beyrouth (Beirut), Saida (Sidon), and Tripoli (in Syria). Since these cities were already home to communities of French merchants, their selection is understandable. The stated reasoning for the new establishments was to provide the cure of souls to subjects of the French nation as well as to aid in the conversion of Eastern Christians.[41] By 1623, a small number of Capuchins arrived to set up their missions, followed in short order by the Jesuits. All came from French provinces of each order: The Capuchins from those of Touronne (Touraine) and Brittany and the Jesuits from Brittany.[42] More French missionaries would follow as the century progressed, in particular, the discalced Carmelites who arrived in the 1630s. Because the most heated disputes involved the Jesuits and Capuchins, however, their relations are the focus of the following discussion.

The Capuchin and Jesuit orders had in fact been seeking entrance into the Holy Land for several decades by this time. Observant chronicles mention two Capuchins causing some havoc during the 1550s, in particular, when they arrived and began preaching in public.[43] Preaching in public was of course forbidden, and they were summarily arrested by Ottoman authorities. A small number of Jesuits also managed to establish a small community in the Custody during the 1590s, twice receiving papal permission to missionize the Copts in Cairo.[44] Both were short-lived efforts, but the arrival of the Jesuits in the Holy Land after 1622 shows that their dream of working in the Levant had not died. This time, moreover, the new missions were fortunate enough to have the generous financial and political support of the French state, support that proved crucial when they found their early missions facing intense opposition from the Franciscan brothers of the Holy Land. To say that the friars were unwelcoming is an understatement, and they quickly mobilized against the missionaries. A letter sent by the brothers of the Holy Land to the Propaganda Fide in 1623, for example, expressed concern that the Capuchins would be a disruptive influence and threaten their ministry.[45] This letter was followed by others, inaugurating a persistent Franciscan

---

[41] On this issue, see the discussion in Chapter 5.
[42] Heyberger, *Les Chrétiens du Proche-Orient*, 291–292. In 1639, the provinces of Touraine and Bretagne assembled twenty-two priests and six laics across eleven residences in the Orient (Egypt, Ethiopia, Chypre, Sattalie, Bagdad, Ispahan). By 1651, the province of Bretagne oversaw fifteen priests in Syria and Touraine three to four.
[43] Pietro Verniero di Montepoloso, "Chroniche ovvero Annali di Terra Santa del P. Pietro Verniero di Montepeloso," in *Biblioteca bio-bibliografica della Terra Santa e dell'Oriente Francescana*, ed. Girolamo Golubovich, nuova serie 6 (Florence: Quaracchi Press, 1936), 120.
[44] See, for example, Robert Clines, *A Jewish Jesuit in the Eastern Mediterranean* (Cambridge: Cambridge University Press, 2019).
[45] APF SA, 196, 117. Also cited in Lemmens, ed., *Acta*, vol. I, 28.

campaign against the French missionaries. The Congregation did not budge, however. Two years later in 1625, and in response to the most recent letters of protest, the Propaganda Fide responded by saying that it had no intention of removing the Capuchins from the Holy Land.[46]

For the Franciscan brothers, papal recognition of the missionary orders represented a shocking innovation to their jurisdiction, a response one can well understand when we consider the many centuries the brothers spent as the visible face of the Catholic tradition in the Holy Land. While it is true that the sacred landscape became home to several Catholic orders during the era of the Crusades, most had to leave following the final collapse of Crusader rule in Jerusalem, including the Carmelites who fled from their base on Mount Carmel to Cyprus.[47] Certainly from the time of the foundation of the Custody in 1342, the Franciscan family comprised the largest Catholic clerical community in the region and was the most politically and spiritually influential through its administration of the Custody. The friars, in other words, were accustomed to a prominent role in the region, one that they were unwilling to share with let alone cede to the new arrivals. No doubt adding to their concern was awareness of the rapid global expansion of these missionary traditions during the course of the sixteenth and seventeenth centuries, but the correspondence of the Franciscan brothers suggests that they were most anxious about their possible designs upon the jurisdiction of the friars. Indeed, with the active support of the French state, the French missionaries began agitating to expand beyond their original geographic and spiritual mandate within a few years of their arrival in the Holy Land, pressing further into the jurisdiction of the friars. Several of the conflicts that erupted from the 1620s onwards reveal a persistent concern about two jurisdictional issues, in particular: the cure of souls and the authority of the *custos* over other religious working in the region.

The cure of souls was a contentious issue from the start, because it was with the promise of serving the pastoral needs of its merchants that the French state first wrangled permission for the establishment of the Jesuit and Capuchin missions in 1622. In their communications with the Congregation of the Propaganda Fide, Bourbon officials argued that

---

[46] Lemmens, ed., *Acta*, vol. I, 29.

[47] On the early history of the Carmelites on Mount Carmel, see among others, E. Friedman OCD, *The Latin Hermits of Mount Carmel* (Rome: Institutum Historicum Teresianum, Studia, I, 1979). A rule for the order was approved by Pope Honorius III in 1226. See also Joanna Cannon, "Pietro Lorenzetti and the History of the Carmelite Order," *Journal of the Warburg and Courtauld Institutes* 50 (1987), 22.

French mercantile colonies in the Levant were growing and required spiritual services in their own language. They were correct in this regard because the French mercantile presence was indeed growing in many of the Levantine port cities as well as Aleppo and Damascus. However, the cure of souls had long been one of the central responsibilities of the Franciscan brothers, a role outlined in some detail in a lengthy *memoriale* produced by the brothers of the Holy Land during a particularly heated dispute with the Capuchins in the 1670s. The Franciscan *memoriale* responded to one recently issued by the Capuchins that challenged their claims to pastoral jurisdiction. Signed by the *custos*, it describes a long history of conflict over the cure of souls in Aleppo dating back to 1626. Aleppo was an immensely important site of Western mercantile engagement. With a population numbering over two hundred thousand at this time, it was the largest city in Syria and one of the three largest in the Ottoman Empire during the Early Modern Period. It was also a bustling, cosmopolitan center of commerce and an important hub in Mediterranean trading networks because it lay close to the port cities of Alexandretta (Iskanderon) and Tripoli and linked caravan routes coming from Mesopotamia through Cairo with the silk road. Until the seventeenth century, the single largest European mercantile colony was the Venetian, though this situation changed as the French colony, comprising mostly merchants from Marseilles, began to grow in size in response to strengthening French commercial and political ties with the Ottoman Porte.[48] The Capuchin *memoriale* was produced in the context of this shift in local European demography and took direct aim at Franciscan claims to pastoral jurisdiction over the French colony. The two Capuchin authors, Henri de Monbazon and Tranquille d'Orleans, criticized the ministry of the friars on multiple fronts including linguistic training and religious zeal. The Franciscan *memoriale* pushed back hard in defense of the training of the friars while underscoring their long history tending to the needs of French merchants. The brothers of the Holy Land had long "held parishes of French merchants in the cities of Aleppo, Alessandretta, Saida, Cairo, Alexandria and Larnaca." Underscoring the universal nature of their ministry, the document reminded the Congregation that friars included not only French, Italian, and Spanish speakers but also Bosnian, Polish, and Portuguese members. However, several of the cures were in the hands of French members including Aleppo, which had both

---

[48] Jan Schmidt, "French-Ottoman Relations in the Early Modern Period and the John Rylands Library MSS Turkish 45 and 46," *Turcica* 31 (1999), 386–387.

French and Venetian friars assigned to parochial duties. The *memoriale* ends with the blunt accusation that the Capuchins were trying to seize their parishes.[49]

The Franciscan *memoriale* testifies to continuing tension over pastoral boundaries five decades after the arrival of the French missionaries. It also reveals Franciscan concern about the erosion of their place in the spiritual life of local Western merchants, concern that informed Franciscan relations with the Jesuits and Capuchins throughout the seventeenth century. Sources on the Custody, however, suggest that the friars were no less anxious about the independence of the French missionaries with regard to the authority of the *custos*. Until 1623, papal and Ottoman legislation recognized the *custos* as having authority over all Latin clerics in the Holy Land regardless of whether they were assigned to work as part of the central administration or traveling for the purposes of pilgrimage or business. The regulations of the Custody required all clerics to present themselves with their patent letters (*obedientia*) before the *custos* and were subject to his discipline while in the region. Visiting clerics were required, moreover, to wear the habit of the family of the Holy Land, essentially that of the Order of Friars Minor but with some distinctive elements. When we consider the profound meaning imbedded in clerical garb as markers of unique spiritual identities, this regulation must have been particularly galling for clerics who were not friars minor. One ponders, for example, what it would have meant to a Jesuit to find his black robe replaced by the distinctive habit and rope belt of the friars. It would have been especially galling for the Capuchins who developed their own unique habit after separating from the Order of Friars Minor.

In reality, there is no evidence to suggest that the French missionaries were ever forced to wear the habit of the Holy Land family. But more threatening to the authority of the *custos* was the administrative independence of the French religious orders. Tied to their provinces of origin, and overseen locally by their own officials, the French missionaries were functionally independent of custodial jurisdiction except in matters pertaining to clerical discipline, a matter over which the *custos*, in theory at least, continued to exercise the highest Latin jurisdiction in the Holy Land. The friars took this authority very seriously as we can see from

---

[49] APF CP 27, ff. 23–30. The specific passage concerning their treat to the Custody is the following: "Da questo decreto si può argomentare ch'I padri Cappuccini in levante ad altro non attendono, che à machinar raggioni a raggioni di stato per ved[er] come possono levare à quelli di Terra Santa le parrochie."

France, the Protector of the Holy Places

the innumerable letters sent to the Congregation detailing the transgressions by missionaries. Their letters show, as well, that they defined this authority broadly, using it to strengthen the juridical, liturgical, and geographic boundaries that confined the French missionaries to their original locations and mandates within the Custody. One persistent concern for the brothers was the illicit movement of French missionaries through the Custody, a concern that saw them seek support from a multiplicity of authorities including the Venetian ambassador, Ottoman officials, and the heads of other local Christian communities.[50] The friars did not hesitate in 1626, for example, to have two Jesuits arrested in Aleppo by the local *kadi*, accusing them of traveling without permission.[51] They reported a rumour that the missionaries were traveling incognito – in other words, not in their own robes – and also that the men failed to present themselves first to the *custos* upon arrival, a privilege that the friars retained through the seventeenth century. The friars knew that such accusations would alarm Ottoman authorities who closely monitored the movement of Western Europeans within their lands.

The friars were as vigilant in surveilling the movements of the French missionaries as they were in defending their rights in matters of pastoral care. What the friars considered a legitimate defense of their privileges, however, was not always regarded as such by the Congregation let alone the other missionaries. A letter dated December 22, 1626, sent from the Congregation to the friars found them culpable of interfering with the ministry of the Capuchins in Aleppo. The particular nature of this dispute is not entirely clear from the surviving sources, only that the Congregation found the Franciscan brothers at fault. The papal body responded that while the friars enjoyed extensive jurisdiction it did not include Aleppo, reasoning that the city was important and diverse and required the work of religious of "other religions to do God's work and procure souls."[52] But struggles over pastoral rites continued. In 1628, the Congregation, fed up with the continuing conflict, tried to impose a

---

[50] This receives more discussion in Chapter 5.
[51] Lemmens, ed., *Acta*, vol. I, 29. In fact, these Jesuits did not have permission from the Porte and would be forced out, though they would return in 1627.
[52] Lemmens, ed., *Acta*, vol. I, 39. Original found in APF *Lettere* 5, f. 265. "L'eccettione nel detto decreto contenua de' luoghi, ove li frati Francescani hanno residenza, non comprende Aleppo, per essere città grande e che per la communicatione, che ha con molte parti del mondo, la medesima Congregatione ha bisogno di mandarvi religiosi d'altre religioni per far il servitio di Dio e procurar la salute dell'animo."

binding settlement, issuing a decree that reaffirmed the privileges for the missionary orders in the original five cities and the authority of the *custos* of the Holy Land to receive new missionaries. Perhaps most importantly from the perspective of the friars, the Congregation also stated firmly that the French missionaries were specifically banned from plying their ministry in Jerusalem, Bethlehem, and Nazareth, sacred cities that comprised the spiritual and administrative heart of the Custody.

No doubt the Congregation hoped that the settlement would appease the Observants who were already complaining that the missionaries were expanding beyond their respective mandates. As the archives of the Congregation make clear, however, disputes over pastoral jurisdiction and the travel of missionaries persisted throughout the seventeenth century. Looking at the disputes leading up to 1661, we find several complaints about the missionaries in diverse parts of the Holy Land, including accusations of illicit preaching by a Capuchin father in 1638. In his letter discussing the incident, then *custos* Andrea d'Arco begins with a sweeping denunciation, accusing a number of Capuchins in Saida (Sidon), Cyprus, and Damascus "of working against our ancient jurisdiction." He singles out two in particular, one who gave a sermon without permission and another who falsely claimed to be able to produce the *patenti*, or licenses, which granted them formal permission. D'Arco states rather dismissively that the Jesuits and Carmelites of Aleppo had tried this before as well. He requested the intervention of the Congregation, insisting that the Capuchins "seem to do nothing but think about usurping our ancient rights under false pretenses."[53]

4.2.3 *Agents of the French State*

The vigilance of the Franciscan brothers in patrolling the frontiers of their jurisdiction shows that they considered every privilege granted to the French missionaries an illegitimate reduction of their own jurisdiction. But just as importantly, it reveals their perpetual worry about any further erosion, worry that is also expressed through voiced suspicions about

---

[53] APF SOCG 118 (August 16, 1638), f. 1. The full passage is the following: "Dall' inclusa lettera ve orà V S Illmas operato *d'alcuni Pri Capucini in Saida,* Cipro, e Damasco *contro le nostre antiche giurisdittioni*: uno de quali ha comunicato la Parola senza licenza, l'altro con ha volute mostrar le Patenti, come anco pretendono fare li Giesuiti, e Carmelitani d'Aleppo, e pare che non pensino *ad altro che usurparci palliatamente il nostro antico ius.*"

missionaries wandering beyond their assigned mandates, whether in terms of their pastoral engagement, geography, or both. Studied in this context of perpetual suspicion, one can understand why Valles and his brothers may have interpreted the involvement of the Capuchins in the disruption of the pilgrimage in 1661 as another assault upon their rightful jurisdiction, a view that would have only been reinforced by their apparent ties with the French pilgrims. Indeed, the correspondence of the friars during their many disputes with the French missionaries make it clear that the brothers considered the missionaries complicit in the expansionist objectives of the Bourbon regime in the Custody, serving as de facto local agents of the state.

Given that the missionary orders enjoyed a great deal of independence in terms of the operations of their missions vis-à-vis the French state, we need to be wary about accepting the Franciscan viewpoint uncritically. It is quite clear from their internal sources that the French missionaries had their own reasons for establishing footholds in the Holy Land, including a strong ideological attachment to the region. Indeed, the Holy Land figures prominently in the origin stories of the three orders that arrived during the 1620s and 1630s. As Chapter 6 will explore in greater depth, both the Capuchins and friars minor considered the Holy Land a legacy of their founder, Francis of Assisi, one that recognized his role as "another Christ" (*alter Christus*), and as the site of his first mission. The origin story for the discalced Carmelites was quite different though no less meaningful to its members. First formed on the slopes of Mount Carmel in the twelfth century, the Order was formally recognized by papal decree in 1238. Carmelite lore, however, charted a much longer past for the contemplative tradition that stretched back to the Old Testament prophets Elijah and Elisha. It was an origin story, in other words, that made them quite literally a product of an ancient biblical past.[54] In comparison to the Carmelite and Franciscan traditions, the Jesuits might seem to have only a tenuous connection to the Holy Land but, as John Olin has argued, "Ignatius' conversion from the very start was ... linked to the idea of a Jerusalem pilgrimage." Ignatius Loyola (1499–1556), founder of the Order, attempted a pilgrimage twice and finally made it to the region in 1523. Unfortunately for the Spanish reformer, the

---

[54] On the place of the Holy Land in the spirituality of these traditions, see, for example, Cannon, "Pietro Lorenzetti and the History of the Carmelite Order"; and John C. Olin, "The Idea of Pilgrimage in the Experience of Ignatius Loyola," *Church History* 48 (1979): 387–398. The quotations of Loyola are taken from Olin's translation.

Franciscan *custos* refused his request to stay permanently and he was forced to leave. But as Olin argues, Loyola, like Francis of Assisi and Dominic (d. 1221), the founder of the Dominican order, invested the pilgrimage to Jerusalem with both penitential and evangelical purpose that shaped his conception of mission. For Loyola, it was a place to seek personal transformation and in which (and from which) to "help souls."

Awareness of these sacred histories adds another dimension to the conflicts between the religious orders studied here. However, one can forgive the Franciscan brothers for viewing the missionaries as agents of the French state because they received substantial material and political support for their endeavours from the Bourbon regime. Other scholars have noted that this material support was significant especially during the first decades of their arrival,[55] providing funds for the purchase of buildings to serve as convents and chapels as well as other necessities required to sustain a mission. Letters in the Congregation give us a good sense of the nature of this support on the ground and point to a close working relationship between the missionaries and French officials. A letter sent to the Congregation in 1626 from the French ambassador to the Porte makes a brief but revealing glimpse into relationship when he mentions that he had just received permission from the sultan to allow the Jesuits a place in Aleppo. The Comte de Césy went on to say that the clerics would have everything they would need to establish themselves because "he had spent everything in his *ufficio*" to support them.[56] French officials and friars discussed the needs of the missions in specific terms as well, including books. Liturgical texts, dictionaries, and catechisms seem to have been especially valued by the French missionaries, something that is not surprising given the demands placed upon them to convert local Christians as well as the cure of souls for French merchants. Housing was another important concern. Letters sent to the Congregation by Pacifique de Province (d. 1648) show that he worked closely with French officials in

---

[55] See, for example, Dominique Dinet, *Vocation et fidelité. Le recrutement des réguliers dans les dioceses d'Auxerre, Langres et Dijon (XVIIe–XVIII siècles)* (Paris: Economica, 1988), 102–117; and Jean Mauzaize, *Le rôle et l'action des Capucins de la Province de Paris dans la France religieuse du XVIIe siècle* I (Lille: Attelier de reproduction des theses, 1978), 60–95.

[56] APF SOCG 112 (October 18, 1626), 16. "dove erano andati senza havene tutto quello che bisognava per il loro stabilimento per il quale spender tutti miei uffici come anco per tutto quello che toccarà al servitio d'iddio et della santa Chiesa Romana secondo le bone intentioni del Rè mio Padrone." A longer letter a year later also discusses providing material support for the Jesuits in Aleppo. See APF SOCG 113 (October 28, 1627), f. 13.

Aleppo to establish a Capuchin mission. Pacifique de Province is better known today more for his mission to Persia, immortalized in his *Relation du voyage de Perse* (1631).[57] As we know from Luca Codignola among others, Pacifique played a central role in the global expansion of Capuchin missions at this time and he undertook several himself including ones to Persia and the Caribbean.[58] However, his first charge was to establish a community in Aleppo that could function as a base of operations for other Capuchin missions in the eastern Mediterranean. Pacifique arrived in Aleppo in August 1626. In one letter written within a few months of his arrival, Pacifique discusses purchasing a house through the agency of the French king that was to serve as a chapel. The French consul of Aleppo may have helped in this regard, since it is clear from the letters that Pacifique relied upon him for array of domestic matters.[59] As a local representative of the French state, the consul was in an important position to support the fledgling missions, enjoying ties with local Ottoman officials and the French ambassador at the Porte, as well as French merchants that were useful for securing financial support, facilitating the flow of new brothers to the region, and providing protection when conflicts arose with the Franciscans and local officials.

The Franciscan brothers of the Holy Land resented Bourbon provision of material and political support because it aided the survival of the new communities but also because it was used in many cases to expand their spiritual footprint in the Custody. A letter sent by friar Jacques de Vendôme to the Congregation in 1631 reveals this latter concern. In the letter, Vendôme discusses brewing tension between the friars and Capuchins over a school recently established by the Franciscans on Mount Lebanon. Vendôme, a French member of the Holy Land family and guardian of the convent of Nazareth, had been sent to Mount Lebanon on other business by then *custos* friar Diego da Sanseverino. According to the French friar, Severino and other Franciscans suspected

---

[57] Pacifique de Provins (d. 1548), also known as da Scala, established another mission in Isphahan in 1627. He is known, in particular, for his travel account, *Relation du voyage de Perse* (1631), which also discusses the Holy Land. APF SOCG 113 (November 25, 1626), f. 351.

[58] Luca Codignola, "Pacifique de Provins and the Capuchin Network in Africa and America," *Proceedings of the Meetings of the French Colonial Historical Society* 15 (1992): 46–60.

[59] APF SOCG 113, ff. 350–360. In one letter, f. 356, Pacifique mentions giving the mass "in una casa la vendita et rendita della quale dependeva di la Me'a [Maiesta] (come e questa casa che ho comprata)."

that the Capuchins were seeking governance over the school. He himself seems to have been skeptical of the rumours, noting that the Capuchins insisted that they were simply seeking a place nearby for "six to seven" members to study local languages. Other friars remained suspicious, however, convinced that the Capuchins were "unjustly" trying to take "whatever they could, not only the chaplaincies but also our Holy Places."[60] Vendome's mention of chaplaincies and the Holy Places here is important, highlighting Franciscan concern about the expansionist ambitions of the French state and its missionaries. In fact, chaplaincies were one of the most visible mechanisms employed by the state to extend its reach within the Custody. This was because the Capitulations permitted consuls their own chapels and clerics for the purpose of personal worship. Letters of appointment sent by French consuls to the Congregation during the seventeenth century are particularly useful for tracking their usage and reveal a distinct preference for appointing French clerics as chaplains from as early as the 1620s. Jesuits were an especially popular choice, one of the reasons why we find them involved in a number of disputes with the friars over the course of the seventeenth century.[61] Jesuit chaplains were at the center of one over the cure of souls in Aleppo, for example, that percolated from 1674 to 1680.[62] The very prospect of Jesuit chaplains in Jerusalem arguably doomed two French efforts to establish a consulate in Jerusalem during the seventeenth century (1624, 1691) arousing vociferous resistance from the resident friars.[63] That the French state was eager to appoint the Jesuits to

---

[60] APF SOCG 149 (December 17, 1631), f. 244. The full passage is here: "il che non ho mai pensato ne anco al hora la perce niente di quella loro pretentione pur non lasciono di prevalersi di questo come d'una persecution publica con detrimento del honor diddio e di questa povera famiglia di terra santa pigliando di cio occasione per coprire le lor ingiusta desegni per togliersi se li fosse possible non solo le capellanie ma anco li nostri Sti Luoghi."

[61] Adina Ruiu, "Missionaries and French Subjects: The Jesuits in the Ottoman Empire," in *A Companion to the Early Modern Catholic Global Missions*, ed. Ronnie Po-Chia Hsia (Leiden: Brill, 2016), chapter 7.

[62] APF CP 27, ff. 122–123. This was part of a dossier produced in 1680 concerning a dispute over cure of souls that had been underway since 1674. "... e nell anno 1674 il signor Marchese di Nointel già Ambasciadore di sua Maestà, ritrovandosi in questa città di ritorno da Jerusalem nel tempo che il signor Dupont essercitava la carica di Console, alle richieste, che li reverendi PP Giesuiti li fecero, di voler fare registrare nella Cancellaria di Aleppo le patenti lettered al Re à loro concedutte per essere loro capellani di sua Maestà delli mercanti suoi sudditi dimoranti nel levante."

[63] Robert Clines, "Fighting Enemies and Finding Friends: The Cosmopolitan Pragmatism of Jesuit Residences in the Ottoman Levant," *Renaissance Studies* 31 (2015): 66–86. The appointment of Jesuits associated with the establishment of a consulate in Jerusalem in

Jerusalem is itself especially intriguing, however, because it reveals a deliberate interest in extending the reach of the missionaries beyond the mandate established for their missions. Indeed, chaplaincies were an effective vehicle for expanding their reach because they lay distributed throughout the many urban centers of the Levant, several in places not served by Capuchin and Jesuit missions.

As these few examples suggest, the French state found the chaplaincies useful for increasing the geographic spread and number of missionaries working within the regions of the Custody. While the friars could not prevent this practice, they were vigilant in restricting the spiritual roles of these men, worried in many cases that they were using the chaplaincies as de facto parish churches. The friars accused the Jesuits of precisely doing just that in Aleppo during the 1670s; a similar charge was made against Capuchin chaplains assigned to Larnaca in Cyprus in an earlier dispute in 1660. For centuries, Cyprus had served as a critical base of operations for Franciscan missions in the Levant, holding important Franciscan convents in the cities of Larnaca and Nicosia. In 1660, the friars accused the Capuchin chaplains in Larnaca of exercising the cure of souls even though this was rightly Franciscan jurisdiction. Arsenio da Milano, the guardian of the Franciscan community, sent a letter to the Congregation that was also signed by several local Italian merchants describing a number of violations. These were mostly concerned with performing liturgical rites for local Catholics and mentioned, in particular, a novena. Arsenio states that the novena involved "all of the French nation" who were rightly "our parishioners."[64] Another two letters, both undated, included with the other ones from Cyprus raised similar concerns about liturgical transgressions. The author was a Spanish friar named Antonio da Pontana, who mentions traveling to Italy specifically to demand restrictions upon the pastoral practices of the French missionaries. He describes several Capuchin transgressions including the performance of parochial rites during Holy Week, singing the masses and vespers every Sunday and

---

1691 is raised, for example, by French ambassador Castagnères de Chasteauneuf in a letter dated September 14, 1691. ANF BI 381.

[64] APF SC TS 1 (undated), 291. "... novenna con espositione del Santissimo, convocanda cola tutti quei della natione loro francese senza farne consapevole noi vere Parochi." The letter is included with other letters regarding the Cyprus dispute beginning with one dated June 28, 1660 (f. 285-289).

feast day, and sprinkling holy water ("solenne aspersione") on Sunday.[65]

The Capuchins responded with indignation, insisting that they always respected the spiritual limitations placed upon their chaplaincies.[66] Either the friars did not believe their denials or they knew that such an accusation might trigger the intervention of the Congregation because their later letters continued to echo with similar suspicions about an expanding liturgical engagement. Moreover, documents generated during disputes over Jesuit chaplaincies suggest that the friars had grounds for suspecting the French state of encouraging French missionaries to expand beyond their permitted spiritual mandate in the Custody. A dossier compiled in 1680 by the friars during the long-running dispute over the Jesuit chaplaincy in Aleppo includes a letter from the French colony that stated that the French merchants were more than content with the ministry of the friars but that the French ambassador, Charles Olier, the Marquis de Nointel, insisted their parish must be attached to the chaplaincy of the consulate.[67] As one often discovers in these disputes, a more complicated history was clearly at work. In this case, we learn that the merchants were already treating the consulate chapel as their de facto parish church by the time of Nointel's announcement. The letter from the merchants mentions that they were forced out of their own church in 1645, when it was turned it into a mosque by the Turks, a move that saw their spiritual services move to the chapel of the consul. In the chapel, the friars continued to "celebrate the mass on all feast days and Sundays," preach, and administer the sacraments as they had before "to the enormous edification and satisfaction of all Christian nations," until they were replaced by the Jesuits in 1674.[68] While it was the prerogative of the consul and

---

[65] APF SC TS 1, f. 289. "se per le fontioni parochiali s'intendono quelle della settimana santa," "annontiar la feste," "lintimar le vigilie," "l'aspersione solemne della domeniche," and the "canto delle messe e vesperi ogni domen e feste."

[66] "Per quello poi, che riguarda a Pri Capuccini, il medisimo segretorio supplica l'CC VV a considerare che per tutto l'oriente I Capuccini si hanno acquistato il posto delle Cappelle de consoli di francia, e con questo pretesto introducono Chiese, et essercitano cure independenti affatto della sede Catholica che non riconoscono in cosa veruna à segno che ne meno si sono degnati di rispondere quando se gli è scritta qualche levera." APF SC, TS 1, f, 285. The date of the report is June 28, 1660.

[67] APF CP 27, ff 122–123. Nointel had apparently made this insistence in 1674, and they were still fighting over it in 1680 according to the dossier.

[68] APF CP 27, ff 122–123. "... ove li Reverendi padri celebrano la messa contata le feste e Domeniche colle prediche, amministrano li sagramenti, e fanno tutte le fontioni coll'istesse cerimonie, che si possono fare in una gran Parocchia nella Chrisitanità, con grande edificatione, e sodisfattione di tutte le nationi Christiani."

ambassador to select the chaplain, one can understand why the Franciscans considered the appointment of the Jesuits a challenge to their parochial jurisdiction since they had fulfilled this role for the French merchants since 1585.

Nor were the friars alone in their conviction that the French missionaries had designs upon their jurisdiction, even the Holy Places. A letter sent by the Venetian ambassador Giorgio Giustinian (1620–1627) to the Venetian Senate in 1622, for example, suggested that French interest in establishing a resident consul in Jerusalem was simply a pretext for introducing the Jesuits into the Holy Places.[69] Three years later, the Congregation responded rather skeptically to a rumour reported by the Venetian ambassador regarding the Jesuits of Aleppo. This rumour was briefly mentioned earlier and involved suspicions about two Jesuits traveling incognito. In the Venetian version, the Jesuits were spotted traveling dressed as Greek monks (*calogeri*), a choice of costume that had a certain narrative logic given that they were also said to be traveling in the company of the Patriarch of Jerusalem with the intent of depriving the Franciscans of their jurisdiction in the Holy Places. Papal officials at the Congregation, however, remained unconvinced and instead suggested that the Franciscan brothers may have played a role in the circulation of this and other rumours.[70] While this was likely the case, Venetian officials such as Giustinian and Nani were doing so as well, a fact that suggests that Venetian authorities also viewed the French missionaries as potential threats to Franciscan administration of the Custody.

Given the recent fraught history between the Venetian state, the papacy, and the Jesuit order, however, Venetian officials may have been ready to be uncritical of suspicions regarding the behaviour of the Jesuits in the Holy Land. In fact, it was less than two decades earlier that the

---

[69] AVSe Dispacci 93 (April 16, 1622): f. 161. "Capito qui li giorni passati con una laetia un Mons. Lempereur spedito dal Re Xsmo a persuasione di questo sa ambasciator, et Gesuiti per resieder consule in Gerusalem, con fine d'introdur poi col suo mezzo essi Gesuiti in quei santi luoghi."
[70] "Calogeri," also written as "Caloyers" in the documents, is the Greek name for the Greek Orthodox monks based on Mount Athos. Lemmens, ed., *Acta*, vol. 1, 29. The relevant part of the letter is the following: "Juvat hoc loco memorare rumores, qui tunc temporis saepius de religiosis Fratres Minores ex Locis Sanctis detruder volentibus circumferebantur. Mense junio 1615 [correct date is 1625] Marcus Nani, bailivus Constantinopoli residens, Venetiam scripsit: Il console di Aleppo scrive, li padri di s. Sepolcro esser ... principalmente afflitti, perchè sono passati in quella parte due Gesuiti travestiti da calogeri accompagnati col patriarca di Gerusalemme con intenzione di privar i Francescani di quei Santi Luoghi."

Venetian Interdict of 1606/1607 saw Jesuits expelled from Venetian territories. The Interdict responded to papal excommunication of the Doge and Senate, a political conflict fueled by competing conceptions of papal jurisdiction. The Senate was displeased, in particular, by the writings of the Robert Bellarmine, the prominent Jesuit theologian who embraced a more expansive view of papal authority than did the Senate.[71] His debate with the Venetian Paolo Sarpi sparked intense controversy at the time, and its impact still resonated in Venetian circles during the 1620s – in other words, at the same time that the Jesuits were establishing missions in the Holy Land. One should recall that the Venetian state regarded the Custody as a de facto Venetian institution in many respects because it provided the majority of its members and administrative leaders and for centuries had played a central role in fielding pilgrimage traffic to Jerusalem. Moreover, even into the Early Modern Period, the Venetian state in the form of its important ambassador at the Porte, the *bailo*, was arguably its most important European protector. Robert Clines suggests that Venetian suspicion of the Jesuits was one important reason why this Order had trouble establishing a home in Jerusalem, a place that Loyola himself had considered an especially meaningful site of mission because of its sacrality and its importance as a diverse site of pilgrimage.[72]

Still, Venetian wariness of the Jesuits in the Holy land had as much, and perhaps even more, to do with their evident ties with the French state. Yet another ambassadorial dispatch to the Senate makes this concern explicit. This one, dated April 5, 1631, raised suspicions about the French envoy sent to negotiate an end to recent conflicts with the Greek Orthodox over altars. The ambassador suggested that "Monsieur de la Piccardière" was more than willing to use any "alterations" in the situation in Jerusalem to discredit the Franciscan brothers of the Holy Land and establish in their place the French Jesuits and Capuchins. He added, quite pointedly, that their numbers in the region were growing.[73]

---

[71] On the Jesuits and the Venetian Interdict, see, in particular, Filippo de Vivo, *Patrizi, Informatori, Barbieri: Politica e comunicazione a Venezia* (Milan: Feltrinelli, 2007); and Francis Oakley, "Complexities of Context: Gerson, Bellarmine, Sarpi, Richer, and the Venetian Interdict of 1606–1607," *The Catholic Historical Review* 82 (1996): 169–396.

[72] Clines, "Fighting Enemies and Finding Friends," 66–86.

[73] ASVe dispacci 112 (April 5, 1631), f. 53. "Per Gierusalem Mons della Picardiera è for[se] gionto fin hora con pensieri di alcuna alteratione se l'occasione l'invitasse ... per discreditar I Padri, *et insinuar I gesuiti, e capuccini*, delli quali sempri quei in queste parti l'accresci il nostro...." La Picardière, the envoy, is also mentioned in the pilgrimage treatise of friar Eugene Roger in Section 4.3.2, who describes him as the "maistre d'hostel" of Louis XIII. Roger, *La Terre Sainte our Description Topographique tres-*

Whether La Piccadière truly was intent upon discrediting the friars is unclear from the surviving records. What is clear is that both Venetian officials and the Franciscans suspected that France had designs upon the administration of the Custody and that they were using the Jesuits and Capuchins to undermine Franciscan jurisdiction. Indeed, evidence of French interest in challenging Franciscan jurisdiction is perhaps nowhere more strongly suggested than its intensive efforts to introduce a consulate in Jerusalem. As mentioned earlier, the French state tried and failed twice to do so during the seventeenth century, first in 1624 and later 1691.[74] In both cases, Franciscan opposition to the appointment of Jesuit chaplains was vigorous and effective, contributing ultimately to their failure. The friars were not about to let the French missionaries gain a foothold in the administrative and sacred sister of the Custody, but this was clearly the objective of the French state according to the correspondence of Bourbon officials. During the second attempt in 1691, for example, the French ambassador to the Porte, Pierre Antoine Castagnères de Chateauneuf, wrote the following to the king of France: "There is no doubt," he says, "that the *Cordeliers* (Franciscans) of the Holy Land detest the establishment of the Jesuits in the city of Jerusalem." However, he insisted that it should not "distance his Majesty from his plan to give the chaplaincy to the Jesuits."[75] He notes that the friars were likely jealous because "the leadership of the [Jesuits] is edifying, and their erudition useful for the spread of the faith." The friars feared that the Jesuits "would be well received by their faithful." Though papal regulations also forbade it, Castagnères for one clearly believed that the French missionaries were legitimate competitors in the spiritual marketplace of the early modern

---

particuliere des saints Lieux & de la Terre de Promission (Paris: Antoine Bertie, 1664), 24.

[74] On the establishment of the consulate, see, for example, Dror Ze'evi, *An Ottoman Century: The District of Jerusalem in the 1600s* (New York: State University of New York Press, 1996), 21; and Charles Frazee, *Catholics and Sultans: The Church and the Ottoman Empire 1453–1923* (Cambridge: Cambridge University Press, 2006).

[75] ANF B I 381 (September 14, 1691). "Il ne faut pas douter que les Cordeliers de la Terre sainte n'ayent beaucoup de repugnance a l'establissment des peres [Jesuites] dans la ville de Jerusalem. La conduitte de ceux cy estant ediffiante et leur erudition [est] utile au progress de la religion il se peut faire que les autres craignent davoir charité des fidelles partagée entr'eux de ce que les suites de ce partage ne ... pas led. interests et la peine que les Cordeliers Italiens et l'Espanols ont eue jusqu'ici d'y souffrir un nombre considerable de Relligieux francois de leur ordre doit faire juger de l'inquietude que leur causera la presence des Jesuittes, mais il nya en tous cela aucune raison qui doive eloigner sa Majesté du dessein quelle a de donner la chappellenie consulaire aux peres Jesuits."

Holy Land for the souls of local believers including in the most holy of holy cities.

4.2.4 A Question of Legitimacy

Chaplaincies were one important mechanism for expanding the reach of the French missionaries, but we should note that the French state also negotiated with the Congregation as well as the Ottoman Porte to establish new communities, and it enjoyed some degree of success. By the time of the dispute of 1661, the Jesuits had managed to establish another mission in Damas in Egypt. The Capuchins of the province of Touronne (Touraine) acquired a hospice in Aleppo, while their brothers from the province of Brittany held convents in the cities of Saida, Beyrouth (Beirut), Tripoli and Abey (Aabey; Mount Lebanon), Damas, and one in Cyprus. The French discalced Carmelites arrived a bit later than the other two Orders, but they quickly established communities on Mount Carmel as well as in Aleppo and Tripoli.[76] Returning again to the dispute of 1661 with this contested spiritual geography in mind, one can better understand friar Eusebio Valles' suspicions of the true motivations of the two Capuchins who traveled to Jerusalem to joined in the Easter rites. Indeed, he would have found it difficult not to read their disruption of the mass as a public, French refutation of his authority in the Custody. This was certainly the message that Valles passed along to the Congregation, counting upon the body's concern about preserving ecclesiastical jurisdiction. That the dispute of 1661 was only the most recent of several involving the friars and the Bourbon monarchy also helps to explain the urgency with which Valles and his brothers treated the matter. However, the dispute also provides tantalizing glimpses into some of the motivations of the Bourbon state, motivations that were commercial and political as well as religious in nature but which were also informed by a powerful, ideological conception of French imperium – a conception predicated upon a sacred past as Protector of the Holy Land. Such an interpretation helps to make sense, in particular, of Du Plessis' symbolic and very public seizure of the sword of Godefroy of Bouillon from the hand of the Franciscan *custos* but also French complaints about the influence of the Spanish king in the Custody and their insistent brandishing of France's hard-won status as Protector of the Holy Places.

---

[76] Heyberger, *Les Chrétiens du Proche-Orient*, 284–285.

In the remaining discussion, we will probe more deeply the legitimizing function of the Custody for the Bourbon state. Along with consideration of the correspondence produced by Bourbon officials, the dispute of 1661 illuminates a new dynastic regime with hegemonic ambitions but one faced with serious challenges to the establishment of its authority after 1589. At home in France, the Bourbon monarchy confronted the daunting task of restoring the authority of a French Crown badly weakened by decades of religious civil war. Beyond its own borders, the Bourbon regime faced serious challenges to its imperial ambitions in the Atlantic and Mediterranean from another great Catholic power, the Habsburg monarchy of Spain. It was the inheritor, at the same time, of a valuable but controversial alliance with the powerful Ottoman Empire, which was crucial to the expansion of its spiritual, political, and economic influence in the eastern Mediterranean. Studied within this broader context, Bourbon interest in turning the Custody "French" illuminates its importance for asserting a claim to Christian hegemony. A Custody cloaked with the visible markings of French Catholicism and under the protection of the French monarchy was useful for pacifying Catholics at home, reassuring them of the essential Catholicity of the throne. It was no less useful for challenging Spanish claims to universal Christian dominion, and it could even be used to legitimize a controversial but valuable alliance with an "infidel" regime. In Section 4.3.1, we will consider each of these contexts in turn. We begin with the Ottoman alliance, since it was through this alliance that the monarchy could stake a legal, as well as ideological, claim to the role of Protector of the Holy Places.

4.3 THE PURSUIT OF CHRISTIAN HEGEMONY

4.3.1 *Protector of the Holy Places and the Ottoman Alliance*

That the Bourbon regime staked its claims to Christian orthodoxy and leadership upon its possession of Ottoman privileges may seem surprising given Western Christian perceptions of Islam. The fact of the matter is that it was nothing new. French potentates negotiated with Mamluk sultans to secure access to the Holy Places for their pilgrims throughout the fourteenth and fifteenth centuries, privileges that they subsequently used to magnify their pious reputations at home. They relied upon a wide array of other Mamluk privileges as well because these were essential for the pursuit of trade in the Muslim kingdoms that ranged around the southern and eastern perimeters of the Mediterranean. With specific regard to the Ottomans, France entered into commercial relations with the Porte as early as 1528, and many of the privileges granted in in the Capitulations were already enjoyed by France as of this time. Christine Isom-Verhaaren argues that these early relations were by no means unusual but rather reflective of the integration of the Ottoman Empire in Mediterranean trade networks by this time, networks that included France.[77] For King Francis I (1515–1547), an Ottoman alliance opened up Ottoman-controlled port cities to French ships, but he was no less concerned about growing Habsburg power in the Mediterranean, a concern that the Ottomans also shared. While the most recent scholarship is skeptical about the existence of a formal treaty that year, negotiations in 1535 significantly strengthened relations that enhanced the status of Marseilles as a commercial hub in the Mediterranean and gave the French monarchy a permanent ambassador in Constantinople and thus proximity to the seat of Ottoman power.[78] It wasn't until the early seventeenth century that one can truly talk about a standing French ambassador in Constantinople, but a steady stream of officials were appointed after this time, gradually laying the foundations for a strong French political presence in the city. Certainly by the 1620s, the French ambassador, ensconced in his palace among the foreign communities in the neighbourhood of Pera, had emerged as an influential local representative of the French state in matters of commerce and military affairs as well as religion.

Relations with the Ottoman Empire would wax and wane in intensity throughout the remaining years of the sixteenth century, though Nathan Michalewicz argues that they remained more central to French political and economic interests than usually understood.[79] Indeed, French

---

[77] Christine Isom-Verhaaren, *Allies with the Infidel: The Ottoman and French Alliance in the Sixteenth Century* (London: I. B. Tauris, 2011). See also Viorel Panaite, "French Capitulations and Consular Jurisdiction in Egypt and Aleppo in the Late Sixteenth and Seventeenth Centuries," in *Well-Connected Domains: Towards an Entangled Ottoman History*, ed. Pascal Firges, Tobias Graf, Christian Roth, and Gülay Tulasoglu (Leiden: Brill, 2014), 71–87.

[78] On the debate over the "Capitulations" of 1525, see, in particular, Gilles Veinstein, "Les Capitulations Franco-Ottomanes de 1536 sont-elles encore controversables?," in *Living in the Ottoman Ecumenical Community*, ed. Vera Constantini and Markus Koller (Leiden: Brill, 2008), 71–88. On the role of Marseilles, see, for example, Junko Takeda, *Between Crown and Commerce: Marseilles and the Early Modern Mediterranean* (Baltimore: John Hopkins University Press, 2011).

[79] Nathan Michalewicz, "Franco-Ottoman Diplomacy during the French Wars of Religion, 1559–1610," PhD diss., George Mason University, 2020.

influence in the Mediterranean grew because of the alliance, as the French state received permission to establish new consulates across the Levant including ones in Tripoli (1548) and Algiers (1565). Since consuls played a central role in regulating Western trade in the Levant, these officials extended the diplomatic reach of the French state within Ottoman lands as well as other states under Ottoman influence. They strengthened commercial ties with Marseilles, in particular, a French city that was already imbricated in Mediterranean trading works and which became an increasingly important hub of French engagement from this time forward. Many of the new consuls came from the ranks of its mercantile elite.[80] The first formal treaty with the Ottomans, known as Capitulations (*Adhname*), came in 1569 and was followed by several more over the course of the sixteenth and seventeenth centuries (1581, 1597, 1604, and 1673). These further expanded French influence eastward while strengthening French status at the Ottoman Porte. The designation of the French king as "friend" in the Capitulations of 1569, for example, is often pointed to as a particularly significant sign of strengthening ties, though Ottoman scholars challenge any suggestion that it recognized the French king as an equal to the Ottoman sultan. As Gunes Isikel has argued recently, this was never the intent of the Ottoman Porte. Rather, it signaled France's integration into a larger system of Ottoman political relations, one that included other European and Islamic states but in which "the Ottoman state was the most powerful and its primary support."[81] Given that French officials touted it as a sign of equality, one might think they simply misunderstood its political meaning. It seems more likely, however, that they had their eye on Europe, and the rhetoric of friendship was politically useful for bolstering French status both at home and abroad.

At the very least, the status of "friend" served as a meaningful indication of strengthening relations, and it was one in a growing array of privileges that Bourbon officials would rely upon to assert French precedence at the Porte in its dealings with other Western ambassadors. The same treaty, for example, also granted *pavillon* to French ships – the right to bear the goods of non-allies of the sultan under the French flag. This privilege in particular provided a crucial impetus to the growth of

---

[80] The first ambassador was Jean le Fôret, and he brokered the treatise.
[81] He describes it as "un ordre interétatique." Gunes Işikel, "Les méandres d'une pratique peu institutionalisée: La diplomatie ottomane, XVe–XVIIIe siècle," *Monde* 5 (2014): 43–55.

France's importance as a great Mediterranean power after this time.[82] For François Savary de Breves, who negotiated the Capitulations of 1604, the right of *pavillon* was one of the most significant of French privileges because it manifested France's special status at the Porte. In his treatise discussing the most recent Capitulations, Savary de Breves emphasized this point, stating that many nations including the Spanish, Portuguese, Catalans, Ragusans, and even the Venetians and English "and generally all other nations, whoever they are, may freely trade through our country, under the security of the banner [flag] of France, which they display as their safeguard."[83]

This history of strengthening ties provides us with a crucial context for understanding the political and spiritual importance given by the French state to the status of Protector of the Holy Places, a privilege that it obtained in the Capitulations in 1604 and that became its primary mechanism for expanding French influence over the Custody of the Holy Land after this time.

On the surface, the new status seems to have been mostly a composite of existing privileges. Friar Alessio, who sent a report to the Propaganda Fide in 1606, copied the twelve clauses of the Capitulations he considered especially relevant to the operations of the Custody. These included permission for Catholic pilgrims to visit the Holy Places without impediment, the protection of the "religiosi" living in the Holy Land from violence, access to the Basilica of the Holy Sepulcher and other Holy Places for Catholic worship, permission to restore buildings that lay under the jurisdiction of the Latin brothers, and the right of the friars to turn to the French ambassador and consuls to represent their interests before Ottoman authorities.[84] Protection for pilgrims was not new,

---

[82] On the various Capitulations, see, for example, Schmidt, "French-Ottoman Relations."
[83] The text of the Capitulations is included with his travel account. See François Savary de Breves, *Relation des voyages de Monsieur de Brèves, tan ten Grèce, Terre Saincte et Aegypte qu'aux royaume de Tunis et Arger, ensemble un traicte faict l'an 1604 entre le roy Henry le Grand et l'empereur des Turcs* (Paris: Nicolas Gasse, 1628), 6. Number IV, and v. Number IV states: "Que des Venitiens & Anglois en là, les espagnols, portugais, Catelans, Ragusois, Genevois, Anconitains, Florentins & generalement toutes autres nations, quelles qu'elles soyent, puissant librement venire trafiquer par nos pays, sous l'aveu & seureté de la banniere de France, laquelle ils porteront, comme leur sauvegarde."
[84] Relation of friar Alessio de Bagnolo, in Lemmens, ed., *Acta*, vol. I, 14–17. Alessio copied the chapters in his report on the Custody given to Paul V upon his return to Rome in 1606. The treaty is dated and signed at Constantinople, "the year of the prophet, 1013" (February 1605). "Commandiamo espressamente per questo nostro alto et sublime segno, che per l'innanzi tutti li religiosi et peregrini, che sotto il nome et protettione dell'imperador di Francia verranno a visitare i Santi Luoghi di Gierusalemme, et quelli

though until the sixteenth century it typically referred to the protection of French pilgrims and not all Catholics. However, during the sixteenth century, the various Capitulations expanded the French mandate to include pilgrims of French allies as well as the Latin clerics assigned to work in the Holy Places.[85] Two important changes in the Capitulations of 1604 were the formal recognition of the status of "Protector of the Holy Places" and the attachment of the protection of the Latin clergy assigned to the Holy Places as a specific privilege of the Protector.[86] These new elements proved useful for representatives of the Bourbon monarchy who insisted that these privileges gave precedence to the French state and his ambassador in matters pertaining to the business of the Custody. Just as importantly, French ambassadors from this time forward employed the status to promote, more generally, French claims to leadership of the entirety of the Latin (Catholic) tradition in Ottoman lands.

The sources on the Custody reveal two ways in which the Bourbon monarchy employed its status as Protector to articulate a more broadly construed leadership role: firstly, through representing the interests of the Custody at the Porte and secondly, through acquiring privileges that expanded the influence of the French state over custodial administration. With regard to its representative role, one can argue that the Bourbon monarchy began playing a more assertive role as a defender of the interests of the Custody from 1599 onwards, when it intervened in the disputes with the Greek Orthodox over chapels in the Holy Places. We do have earlier instances of the French state moving to the aid of the friars including in 1549 when the friars were threatened with expulsion from their main convent.[87] François Savary de Breves' successful conclusion of the dispute in 1599, however, seems to have marked a much more interventionist role, publicly celebrated at the time by the administration of King Henry IV as a great success and reflection of true spiritual

---

vi verranno a starvi per servirli, vi possino venire, stare et andare sicuramente et liberamente senza alcuno impedimento o disturbo, et che sotto pena di castigo alcuno ardisca inquietare i detti santi Luoghi, et questo tanto che l'imperator di Francia haverà amicitia con la nostra eccelsa Porta."

[85] W. Heyd, "Les consulats établis en terre sainte au Moyen Age pour la protection des pélerins," in *Archives de l'Orient-Latin*, vol. II (Paris: Ernest Leroux, 1884), 355–363.

[86] See, for example, Giles Ferragu, *Eglise et diplomatie au Levant au temps des Capitulations*, Rives Méditerranéennes 6 (2000): 69–78.

[87] The envoy Gabriel D'Aramon was involved in the mediation of this dispute. See Jean Chesneau, *le voyage de Mr. D'Aramon*, ed. Charles Schefer (Geneva: Slatkine Reprints, 1970), 38–46. Chesneau says that the friars greeted Aramon like a messiah: "comes les Juifs attendant leur Messias ...."

leadership. Savary de Breves subsequently used France's engagement in this matter to negotiate the status of Protector of the Holy Places for the French monarch in the Capitulations of 1604.[88] Only a year later, a serious legal conflict over Franciscan jurisdiction in the Basilica of the Holy Sepulcher offered Savary de Breves another opportunity to capitalize on France's status as Protector. In 1605, the Georgian Christians legally challenged Latin control of its prestigious altar at the site of Calvary. In his report discussed earlier, friar Alessio wrote of the ambassador's successful negotiations with the Ottoman governors of Judea and of Gazza, praising his work on behalf of the Custody. Alessio was privy to the affair because he had accompanied Savary de Breves from Constantinople. Given his own intimate knowledge of the Custody as a former *custos*, he may have played an active role as well.[89] While not all French ambassadors who followed him in the post were as attentive to the affairs of the Custody as Savary de Breves, a broad consideration of their relations during the seventeenth century suggest that most considered the defense of its privileges an important responsibility, especially with regard to privileges in the Holy Places. In fact, French ambassadors played a critical role during the many disputes with the Greek Orthodox discussed in Chapter 2, a relationship that is particularly well documented in the correspondence of the Venetian ambassadors. As one final example, French ambassadors played a vital role in the successful negotiations with the Druze leader Fakhr-al-Din and the Ottoman sultan in 1620 for possession of two important shrines: the Annunciation in Nazareth and on Mount Tabor and the shrine of St. John the Baptist in the village of Ein Karem. These acquisitions were cherished by the early modern friars and celebrated in their histories and pilgrimage treatises.

As these examples suggest, the French ambassador used his precedence at the Porte to protect the privileges of the Custody. By doing so, it is fair to say that he was assuming a representative role that had long been played by Catholic ambassadors at the Porte, most importantly the Venetian ambassador.[90] However, the Bourbon regime was also signaling its rising influence at the Porte vis-à-vis other European powers, influence

---

[88] Frazee, *Catholics and Sultans*, 79.
[89] The letter was signed in Constantinople (March 12, 1605). Lemmens, ed., *Acta*, vol. I, 17–18.
[90] On the history of Venice's relations with the Custody, see, for example, Giovanni Bissoli, "La Republica di Venezia e la custodia di Terra Santa," in *La custodia di Terra Santa e l'Europa: I rapport politici e l'attività culturale dei Francescani in Medio Oriente*, ed. Michele Piccirillo (Roma: Il veltro, 1983), 83–94.

that was not only economic and political in nature but also religious. The same objective helps to explain its vigorous promotion of French missions and office-holding in the Custody, since these measures aimed to imprint a French face upon the most visible and influential of Latin institutions within the vast reach of the Ottoman Empire, one that was also revered throughout Europe because of its association with Western pilgrimage to the Holy Land. The status of Protector, in other words, was far from an empty honorific. The French state used it in tandem with other privileges to strengthen its standing at the Ottoman Porte, standing that enhanced its political clout across the Mediterranean more generally. It certainly gave France some leverage among some European powers, notably the papacy, in their dealings with Ottoman authorities. France's status as Protector was an important reason why it received permission to establish French missions, which were no less useful to papal interests in the eastern Mediterranean.

By pressing for the appointment of French religious to the Custody, however, the French state was playing a much more interventionist role in its affairs than had been the case before. In fact, it is quite clear that it was intent upon extending its authority more directly over this Latin institution as part of a broader agenda regarding the Latin tradition in Ottoman lands. Other scholars working on different parts of the Ottoman Empire have noted its more interventionist approach, in particular regarding the older, well-established mendicant communities found in Constantinople, the island of Scios, and elsewhere.[91] Ambassadorial dispatches show that this engagement was quite deliberate and strategic, focused upon elevating the local influence of French missionaries. To be sure, not every ambassador was as enthusiastic as Philippe de Harlay, the Comte de Césy (1621–1630), an official who seems to have been quite comfortable in wielding the power of the French state to expand its interests in Ottoman lands. The correspondence of other ambassadors suggest that he was not well liked in their circles for his rather heavy-handed wielding of French influence including his strident insistence upon French precedence during state occasions.[92] As his

---

[91] See, among others, Adina Ruiu, "Conflicting Visions of Jesuit Missions to the Ottoman Empire, 1609–1628," *Journal of Jesuit Studies* 1 (2014): 260–280.

[92] See, for example, G. R. Berridge, "Notes on the Origins of the Diplomatic Corps: Constantinople in the 1620s," *Discussion Papers in Diplomacy* 92 (2004): 1–20. Berridge is discussing mostly the response of the English ambassador, but the dispatches sent to the Senate by the Venetian ambassador reflect a similar dislike of Césy as essentially pushy and arrogant.

own correspondence makes clear, Césy enjoyed testy relations with the Franciscan and Dominican mendicant communities of Constantinople. In a series of letters sent to the Congregation in 1628, for example, the ambassador accused various Dominican and Franciscan friars of preaching without permission and immoral behaviour, as well as conspiring against the French Jesuits. Needless to say, his energetic promotion of French missionaries was a particular sore point for the mendicant communities based in Constantinople just as it was for the friars of the Custody.[93] With specific regard to expanding French influence in the Custody, Césy's support for the Capuchin community in Aleppo has already received some discussion, but he was no less active on behalf of the Jesuits. What deserves a bit more discussion here, however, is his enthusiastic efforts to introduce a consulate in Jerusalem. At the time the Bourbon state first proposed a consulate in 1621, there were no European consulates in Jerusalem, though this had not always been the case. A number of European consulates were established in the fifteenth century, mostly to facilitate Western pilgrimage.[94] These officials, however, had disappeared before the seventeenth century. The French proposal, which was being discussed as early as 1620/1621,[95] was briefly realized in 1624 with the appointment of Jean Lempereur. That the negotiations were initially successful owed a great deal to Césy who pushed hard for the consulate with the Ottoman Porte. Lempereur only lasted a few months in the office, however, before being summarily removed. It seems as though his abrasive personality, as well the vociferous opposition from the friars and other Christian communities, played a role in the consulate's failure. In fact, Lempereur found himself arrested and thrust into prison by the Pasha of Damascus, forced to pay a hefty fine for his release.[96] Serious efforts to establish a consulate were made once again in 1691, but these negotiations collapsed. Though they failed, French

---

[93] See, for example, the series of letters regarding the Franciscans and Dominicans in Pera in 1628. APF SC *Lettere di Levante* Vol 111, ff. 9–13.

[94] On consulates in Jerusalem in the fifteenth century, see Heyd, "Les consulats établis en terre sainte au Moyen Age." As he points out, these were Italian consuls and their main purpose was to support Western pilgrimage. They seem to have been appointed only between 1413 and 1476.

[95] On the discussions surrounding the establishment of the French consulate, see Géraud Poumarède, "Les limites du Patronage Français sur les Lieux Saints: Autour de l'Installation d'un Consul à Jerusalem dans les Années 1620," *Revue d'Histoire de l'Eglise de France* 92 (2006): 147–163.

[96] Ze'evi, *An Ottoman Century*, 21–22. He cites a letter to the king of France dated November 20, 1624.

efforts to establish a consulate in Jerusalem provide further evidence of its intention to strengthen its influence at the heart of the Custody. Viewed from the perspective of the friars, the consulate would have placed a senior French official not only at the sacred heart of the Christian Holy Land but also in close proximity to the main administration of the Custody at the very same time that it was seeking to place its administration in the hands of French clerics. That in both instances French officials also intended to appoint French Jesuits as chaplains would have only further confirmed the fears of the friars as well as Venetian officials that these French religious had designs upon the Custody itself.

4.3.2 A French Sacred History

As just discussed, the status of Protector gave the French state a legal and political foothold from which to present itself as a defender of the interests of the Custody as well as the Latin tradition more generally. In doing so, the Bourbon state was crafting its image as a great Catholic power, one who could wield its influence on behalf of Europe more generally within Ottoman lands because of its privileged standing at the court and thereby better represent, and expand, its own interests. The promotion of French clerics similarly manifested Bourbon influence, demonstrating its privileged status by imprinting a French face upon a revered Catholic pilgrimage institution. In doing so, one could argue that the state was intent upon transforming the Custody into a French Catholic institution, an interpretation that makes even more sense when we consider the continuing potency at the French court of a French sacred past as "protector" of the Holy Places. This past informed French negotiations for the Ottoman status of Protector from the start. One finds it elucidated, for example, in the published memoir of François Savary de Breves, the *Discours sur l'alliance qu'a le Roy, avec le Grand Seigneur, & de l'utilité qu'elle apporte à la Chrestienté*. The *Discours* was based upon memoirs kept by Savary de Breves while ambassador to the Ottoman Porte, subsequently published posthumously by Jacques du Castel, one of his secretaries. Savary de Breves' description of the pilgrimage to Jerusalem was discussed in Chapter 1, but our interest here lies in his justification of the Ottoman alliance as a critical manifestation of France's historic claims to Christian leadership. In the *Discours*, Savary de Breves argues that France first formed an alliance with the Ottomans because it was for "the universal good of Christianity" and not simply for the benefit of France. It gave Christians access to markets throughout the Mediterranean as well as the "Indes Orientales" but, in addition to these considerations, it was also important for "the preservation of the Christian name, and of the Catholic religion ...." Savary de Breves goes even further, however, insisting that Christian subjects of the sultan were looking to the French monarchy for protection precisely because of France's historic role as a defender of Christendom. French protection was crucial, he explains, to ensure that Christianity continued to flourish in these regions, including in the Holy Land. Indeed, the king of France "was the sole protector of the sacred place where the Saviour of the world wished to be born and die."[97]

In casting the treaty with the Ottomans as a Christian act and marker of spiritual leadership, Savary de Breves was clearly anxious to quell lingering concerns in France about a French alliance with an Islamic power, an association that, as Gillian Weiss among others have argued, dogged Bourbon efforts to cast itself as an orthodox Catholic power throughout the seventeenth century.[98] The status of Protector was useful in this regard because it recognized a divine mandate for the Bourbon regime as a Christian leader, and one of its most important responsibilities was the protection of the Holy Land from the corruption of erring faiths including that of Islam. The organization of French missions similarly honed this image of Bourbon Christian leadership by placing the French state on the frontlines of confessional relations in defense of a broadly construed Christendom. This is certainly the argument made by le Sieur de La Croix in a treatise published in 1695. Nicholas Dew, who has worked extensively on La Croix, notes that he remains a rather shadowy figure in history even though he was a respected orientalist and wrote extensively on the Ottoman East. Indeed, adding to the confusion over his identity is that there were two French diplomats named La Croix in service to the French ambassador at much the same time.[99] We do know that he had a long career in service, spending over twenty years assigned

---

[97] François Savary de Breves, "Discours sur l'alliance qu'a le Roy, avec le Grand Seigneur," in *Relations des voyages de Monsieur de Brèves tant en Grèce Terre Saincte et egypte qu'aux royaumes de Tunis et Arger* (Paris: Nicolas Gasse, 1628), 8.

[98] Gillian Weiss, *Captains and Corsairs: France and Slavery in the Early Modern Mediterranean* (Stanford: Stanford University Press, 2011).

[99] The other was named Petit le Croix and was also an orientalist. I want to thank Nicholas Drew for sharing his paper on La Croix. Nicholas Dew, "Jerusalem and the Sun King: The Memory of the Crusades in the Cult of Louis XIV," Cambridge: Paper for the Comparative Social and Cultural History Seminar, November 1998. See also Paul Sebag, "Sur deux Orientalistes français du XVIIe siècle: F. Petis de la Croix, et le Sieur de la Croix," *Revue des mondes musulmans et de la Méditerranée* 25 (1978): 89–117.

to the embassy in Constantinople, including a stint as secretary to Charles Marie François Olier, Marquis de Nointel. Nointel was the French ambassador from 1670 to 1679 who presided over the negotiations of the Capitulations of 1674. Since le Sieur de La Croix published a printed edition of the treaty the same year, we can safely say he was well-versed in its provisions regarding the status of Protector. However, we find a particularly strong expression of Bourbon Christian leadership in a treatise he wrote twenty years later, *La Turquie chrétienne sous la puissante protection de louis le Grand, Protecteur unique cu Christianisme en Orient*. La Croix dedicated the treatise to Louis XIV and used it to encourage the king to establish a seminary for French missionaries in the Ottoman Empire, arguing that it would assist the French ambassador in his representation of all Christians in the region. The "pauvres Orientaux" he said, were persecuted under Ottoman rule, and required the protection of the French king: "You are the only Protector of Christianity in the Ottoman Empire."[100] Insisting that the Eastern Christians were asking to be "freed" from the Ottoman yoke, La Croix included a "tableau naturel" of "your piety, and that of the emperors of France, your predecessors," as well as "the missions that your majesty maintains in the Ottoman empire, established under Henry the Great [Henry IV]."[101]

Similar to the *Discours* of Savary de Breves, La Croix argues here for an expansive role for French engagement in Ottoman lands, casting the French monarch in the role of designated protector of a broadly construed, diverse Christendom that was under threat from Islam. Some Franciscans seemed to have shared a similar view of the French monarchy, no doubt in part because of personal allegiance as well as the Order's ties to the Custody of the Holy Land. In a funeral sermon given by the prominent Portuguese preacher Jacques Marie de Suarez upon the death of Henry IV in 1610, for example, the friar praised the monarch for

---

[100] Sieur de La Croix, *La Turquie chrétienne sous la puissante protection de louis le Grand, Protecteur unique cu Christianisme en Orient, contenant l'état present des Nations et des Eglises Grecques, Arménienne et Maronite dans l'Empire Ottoman* (Paris: P. Håérissant, 1695), epistle. "Vous estes le Protecteur unique du Christianisme dans l'Empire Ottoman, & l'azile des Peuples & des Princes persecutez, d'ecouter les voeux de ces pauvres Orientaux, qui representent leur necessité spirituelle . . . ."

[101] La Croix, *La Turquie chrétienne sous la puissante protection de louis le Grand*, epistle. "... tableau naturel de votre pieté, & de celle des Empereurs de France, vos predecesseurs, et des Missions que V.M. entretient dans l'Empire Ottoman, établis par Henri le Grand."

fulfilling the traditional role of French kings by offering his protection to the Custody and the Franciscan brothers: "We say in our order of Saint Francis that we always felt content under his protection, and in consequence all Christians of the Catholic Church." In particular, the preacher mentions Franciscan convents in the Holy Land, which, he states, are "the only place for Latin Christians" in the region. Referring to the most recent disputes between the friars and the Greek Orthodox over altars in the Holy Places, Suarez insisted that the removal of the friars was only prevented "by the sole authority of the deceased King who intervened through is ambassador" with the sultan.[102] As a royal preacher, Suarez held a patronage position, a fact alone that might explain his praise of Henry IV. However, we also find similar sentiments in the writings of a number of French friars who were assigned to the Custody. A treatise published in 1644 by friar Eugene Roger offers a particularly strident, and evocative, example. Roger was assigned to the Custody during the late 1630s not long after the first of the major seventeenth century disputes. He includes a lengthy passage describing the successful negotiations of the French envoy La Piccardière for the protection of Latin altars but then went on to insist that the role of Protector "was not the least of the favours our kings of France received from heaven [Ciel]." French monarchs were chosen by God from among all the kings of the world to "ensure that Holy Places, under their favour, would remain inhabited and served by Catholic Christians and visited by pilgrims under the banner and standard of the Fleurs de Lys."[103] Roger says, moreover, that the French monarchs manifested their divinely allotted role by providing military protection, alms, and beautiful ornaments for devotion in the chapels but also through entering into treaties with Islamic rulers. The

---

[102] Jacques Suarez de Sainte-Marie, *Sermon funebre fait aux obseques de Henry IIII, roy de France et de Navarre, le 22 Juin dans l'eglise de St Jacques de la Boucherie* (Paris: Nicolas du Fosse, 1610), 56. The full passage is the following: "Nous pouvons dire en nostre religion de S François que nous nous sommes ressentis bien avant de sa protection, & par consequent tous les Chrestiens de l'Eglise Catholique, Apostolique & Romaine: Car nous avons en la terre saincte six convents de nostre Ordre, lesquels seuls sont la retraitre des Chrestiens latins, lors ue leur devotion les transporte par delà pour visiter les lieux saincts & ausquels seuls se celebre le divin mystere selon l'usage Romain: desquels le grand Turc a voulu chasser les religieux pour le dommage que celà apportoit à sa secte, tant pour la vie exemplaire de nos peres, que pour les instructions qu'ils donnent aux habitans du pays: lequel coup a esté empesché par la seule authorité di defunct Roy, qui intervint par le moyen de son Ambassadeur envers le grand Seigneur."
[103] Roger, *La Terre Sainte our Description Topographique*, 23–24.

Capitulations with the Turks, in other words, were legitimate and expected manifestations of France's sacred responsibilities as a Christian leader.

In this passage, Roger has inflected the status of Protector with a sacred history that claimed a destiny for the French throne as *the* Christian protector of the Holy Places. He also imbeds it in a longer narrative of French protection that included Saint Louis, the great Crusader king, stating: "Wasn't it out of love, devotion and respect that Saint Louis went to the Holy Land leaving his own kingdom ... using all his power, even his life, to deliver this glorious country from the possession of tyrannical barbarous nations that prophaned it?"[104] Roger's invocation of Louis IX (1214–1270) was clearly intended to remind readers that France had its own past in the Holy Land, one that also legitimized its assumption of the Ottoman status of Protector. Indeed, as Sean Heath and Eric Nelson have argued recently, the cult of Saint Louis found new life under the Bourbon rulers, invoked in diverse contexts from the reign of Henry IV onwards to reaffirm the dynasty's claims to orthodoxy and divine right.[105] In doing so, the Bourbon rulers were recognizing the cult's historic place in the construction of royal authority in France, featured most notably in the ceremonies known as the *religion royale* that took place during the coronation of the French king. The cult had in fact declined somewhat in royal favour before this time. Nelson argues that it had been hit hard by the religious wars, devalued as a marker of divine rule both by the Calvinists, who questioned the divine basis of royal authority, and the radical Catholics, members of the Catholic League, who emphasized divine immanence.[106] Heath shows, moreover, that the cult faced some controversy even in the seventeenth century including from Catholic historians who were critical of the medieval king's management of the kingdom. For these early modern commentators, the Crusades were ultimately a failure, while Louis' long absences from France led to the

---

[104] Roger, *La Terre Sainte our Description Topographique*, 24.
[105] Sean Heath, "The Bourbon Monarchy and the Cult of Saint Louis, 1589–1792," PhD diss., St. Andrews, 2017, 55–58.
[106] Eric Nelson, "Religion Royale in the Sacred Landscape of Paris: The Jesuit Church of Saint Louis and the Re-Sacralization of Kingship in Early Bourbon France (1590–1650)," in *Layered Landscapes: Early Modern Religious Space across Faiths and Cultures*, ed. Eric Nelson and Jonathan Wright (Abingdon: Routledge, 2017), 171–184.

neglect of other important duties.[107] The saintly monarch was nevertheless useful to the ambitions of the Bourbon rulers because he provided a direct genetic link to the throne as well as an image of religious orthodoxy and devotion useful for affirming Bourbon orthodoxy in a religiously divided kingdom. Nelson goes even further, situating the cult as one foundation of a "royal political theology" that reified the French monarchy as a channel of transcendent divine authority on earth.[108] But as friar Eugene Roger's description also makes clear, Louis' prominent role in the Crusades also served the hegemonic ambitions of the Bourbon rulers because it invested them with an important precedence as international leaders of the Christian faith. This was precisely Roger's intent, to legitimize Bourbon claims to Christian leadership more broadly. Indeed, Roger went so far as to suggest that the Ottoman sultan recognized the monarchy's sacred destiny when it gave Henry IV the status of Protector: "Even the Grand Seigneur, although Muslim, and an enemy of the Christian faith," called him "protecteur & conservateur de la sainte Jerusalem."

The cult of Louis was thus useful for elevating the political and spiritual authority of the Crown over a divided populace, and it was just as useful for asserting Bourbon claims to hegemony. Returning to the texts cited above, one can see that French officials and clerics were giving the status of Protector a historic French significance that was integral to its construction from the start. In fact, Jean-Philippe Mochon argues that the name of Protector was specifically requested by the Bourbon regime to evoke its sacred history with the Holy Land. The title "Protector of the Holy Places" was first bestowed upon Charlemagne by the pope in 798, when he intervened successfully to protect Latin interests in the Custody during a particularly serious dispute.[109] Later monarchs, including Louis IX, assumed the title, notably during the era of the Crusades. The century of French rule in Jerusalem under Godefroy of Bouillon and his son Baldwin (d. 1197) and the celebrated Crusade led by Saint Louis each added new threads to a sacred history that continued to evolve as it entered the Early Modern Period, informing the renewed crusading esprit of the French nobility and court discussed by Benoist Pierre and Géraud

---

[107] Heath, "The Bourbon Monarchy and the Cult of Saint Louis."
[108] Nelson, "Religion Royale," 172.
[109] Jean Philippe Mochon, "Le Consul Général de France à Jérusalem: Aspects historiques, juridiques et politiques de ses fonctions," Annuaire français de droit international 42 (1996): 929–945.

Poumarède among others.[110] For Jean-Philippe Mochon and Charles Frazee, the expanded religious role of the king granted in the sixteenth century Capitulations reflected the continuing potency of this living sacred past among the Valois rulers of the sixteenth century. Poumarède has noted, moreover, that the accession of a new monarch was invariably followed by the recycling and adaptation of prophecies foretelling the "consecration" of the King in the Levant. This sacred destiny followed a certain mythic pattern, beginning with France's triumphant conquest of the West, organization of a great expedition to the Holy Land, defeat of the "infidels," construction of a new monarchical regime ("royauté"), and the end of history.[111]

As Poumarède argues, Bourbon interest in the Custody of the Holy Land was one important indication that these rulers, just like their Valois predecessors, found this notion of a mythic past appealing because it presaged both divine election and hegemonic rule for French rulers.[112] It may have been especially useful for Henry IV, in particular, the monarch who negotiated the status of Protector in 1604. Henry IV was dogged by suspicions of unorthodoxy throughout his reign because of his Protestant past. He was raised as a Calvinist by his mother, the Queen of the Kingdom of Navarre, who was among the many French nobles to convert to the faith during the late 1550s. Jean Calvin had sent teams of preachers into the kingdom of his birth with the specific objective of conversion, and his efforts proved successful. The spread of the new faith, however, sparked internal dissent that erupted into outright conflict between leaders of the two faiths and their followers from the 1560s onwards. Religion was by no means the only cause of tension during the Wars of Religion, the cluster of civil wars that pestered the unity of France throughout the last four decades of the sixteenth century and into

---

[110] On resurgent crusading fervour more generally, see, for example, Phil McCluskey, "Les ennemis du nom Chrestien": Echoes of the Crusade in Louis XIV's France," *French History* 29 (2015): 46–61; and Géraud Poumarède, *Pour en finir avec le Croisade: Mythes et Réalitiés de la lute contre les Turcs au XVIe et XVIIe siècles* (Paris: Presses Universitaires de France, 2009).

[111] "... prophéties perpétuellement recyclés et adaptés qui prévoient pour le souverain une consécration en Levant." Geraud Pomarède, "La France et Jérusalem (XVIe–XIX e siècle)," *Annuaire-Bulletin de la Société de l'histoire de France* (2008): 39–42.

[112] Pomarède, "La France et Jérusalem." "Jerusalem est d'abord la *Jerusalem desirée des projets de reconquête*, des attentes et des prophéties qui dessinent pour les rois de France comme une destinée manifeste dans les Lieux saints."

the early seventeenth century.[113] However, it was an important one, posing a particular challenge for Henry IV who found himself, a Calvinist, the legal heir of Henry III following his assassination in 1589. Faced with the challenge of pacifying a majority Catholic population, Henry converted to Catholicism in 1593. Suspicions of heresy nevertheless lingered throughout his reign complicating his efforts at pacification. As Eric Nelson and Bernard Dompnier among others have shown, the government sought to assuage popular concern through an intense campaign involving public acts of Catholic devotion including processions, the patronage of religious institutions, and the sponsorship of missions in Protestant regions of France. Nelson describes this as a program to re-sacralize the throne, a program that was initiated under Henri IV and continued actively under his successors, Louis XIII and XIV. It included, for example, the construction of the chapel of Saint Louis under the direction of Louis XIII.[114] The status of Protector should be viewed as another strategy in this public relations campaign, employed to highlight the orthodoxy of Henry IV by having him follow in the footsteps of earlier French rulers who protected the Holy Places and, in particular, Louis IX. It was likely no coincidence, for example, that the French state chose to intervene in the disputes involving the Greek Orthodox only a few months after the promulgation of the Edict of Nantes by the Parlement of Paris (February 1599).[115] The treaty, which ushered in nine decades of legal and political recognition for the Protestant faith in

---

[113] In addition to works cited earlier in this section, a sampling of the vast scholarship on the religious and political dimensions of the Wars of Religion includes Mack P. Holt, *The Politics of Wine in Early Modern France* (Cambridge: Cambridge University Press, 2018); Penny Roberts, *Peace and Authority during the French Religious Wars c. 1560–1600* (Cambridge: Cambridge University Press, 2013); and Denis Crouzet, *Les guerriers de Dieu. Le violence au temps des troubles de religion, vers 1525–1610* (Seyssel: Champ Vallon, 1994).

[114] In addition to Sean Heath and Nelson (nn. 105–106), see also Michael Wolfe, *The Conversion of Henri IV: Politics, Power and Religious Belief in Early Modern France* (Boston: Harvard University Press, 1993). For Louis XIV and his promotion of the cult of Louis, see also Bruno Neveu, "Du culte de Saint Louis à la glorification de louis XIV: La maison royale de Saint-Cyr," *Journal des savants* Jul–Dec (1988): 277–290.

[115] The edict was controversial and widely criticized at the time. See, for example, Megan C. Armstrong, "La réaction des frères mineurs Capucins à la publication de l'Edit de Nantes en 1599," in *Paix des armes, paix des âmes*, actes du colloque international tenu (sous l'égide de la Société Henri IV), ed. Paul Mironneau et Isabelle Pedbay-Clottes (Pau: Société Henri IV, 2000), 261–268; and Frederic Baumgartner, "The Catholic Opposition to the Edict of Nantes, 1598–1599," *Bibliothèque d'humanisme et Renaissance* 40 (1978): 525–536.

France, did little to assuage the fears of some Catholics that their monarch was still a crypto-Protestant.

A well-publicized role defending the most revered Catholic pilgrimage and sacred landscape provided a useful counter-narrative to any suspicions of royal unorthodoxy that were reignited in the wake of the Edict. Negotiations for the Capitulations of 1604, in other words, took place in this hotbed environment of suspicion regarding the orthodoxy of the monarchy in France.

While it is true that Louis XIII and Louis XIV were not dogged to the same degree by suspicions of unorthodoxy, memory of the civil wars still haunted France throughout the century in ways that continued to pose challenges to Bourbon rule. For Louis III and Louis XIV, the legal recognition of two faiths represented a particularly persistent and troubling manifestation of their divisive impact.[116] Protestant revolts erupted in southern France in 1621–1622, leading to the first significant reduction of Huguenot privileges granted under the Edict. The Frondes (1648–1653), along with divisive debates over Jansenism, rocked the peace of the state during the 1640s and 1650s. During 1670s and 1680s, Louis XIV also found himself at odds with the papacy over the right of the *régale*, a serious controversy that seemed to renew old debates about the relationship between the papacy, the king, and royal authority over a "Gallican" (French) Church. Unfortunately in this case, for Louis XIV, the papacy had some support within certain parts of the French episcopacy, especially over concerns about the intrusion of the royal courts into ecclesiastical affairs. Joseph Bergin suggests that the revocation of the Edict of Nantes in 1685 may have been intended by Louis XIV to "soften" the papacy's position on the *régale*, advertising as it did the "purified" and Catholic state of the French kingdom under his rule.[117] Innocent XI, however, was not easily persuaded and the conflict

---

[116] Recent work on memory and the Wars has underscored its shaping impact upon seventeenth century France. See, for example, David Van der Linden, "Memorializing the Wars of Religion in Early Seventeenth-Century French Picture Galleries: Protestants and Catholics Painting the Contested Past," *Renaissance Quarterly* 70 (2017): 132–178. On local and state relations under the Edict of Nantes, see, for example, Keith P. Luria, *Sacred Boundaries: Religious Coexistence and Conflict in Early-Modern France* (Washington, DC: The Catholic University Press of America, 2005).

[117] Joseph Bergin, *The Politics of Religion in Early Modern France* (New Haven: Yale University Press, 2014), 3. Bergin says, however, that Innocent XI was "unimpressed" by the gesture.

continued to trouble Louis' efforts to govern French religious institutions after this time.

Faced as they were with these and other manifestations of religious conflict throughout the seventeenth century, Bourbon rulers employed the status of Protector as one of several strategies to highlight the orthodoxy of the Bourbon dynasty but also its place on the frontlines in the battle against religious error. Discussions of organizing a *milice chrétien* took place in this context, for example. The idea may have already been taking shape under Henry IV, who asked Pope Paul V to recognize the establishment of a new chivalric order, the Ordre de Notre-dame de Mont Carmel. Père Joseph, the Capuchin advisor to Richelieu, seems to have been an early and active promoter of a new Crusade, one that would comprise an international nobility under the direction of the French monarchy. The objectives included not only the "rescue" of the Holy Land from the Turks but also its many Christian subjects, who were eager (so officials argued) to be brought within the embrace of the French Catholic state. We find similar calls for a French-led crusade echo in the writings of a number of French friars attached to the Custody, a fact that is hardly surprising when we consider not only that they were French but also that the brothers of the Holy Land promoted the Order of the Holy Sepulcher. In one rather poetic passage taken from his well-known pilgrimage treatise, the *Bouquet sacre*, friar Jean Boucher bemoans the pitiful state of Jerusalem, saying that its children were ready to restore it to its "ancient luster and antique splendour." A second Mars was coming, one that was "generous, courageous, valiant and powerful ... my Prince and my King Louis XIII."[118] Roger, in turn, praised Louis XIII for ensuring the survival of the Catholic cult, "protecting it from the extortions and tyrannies that the infidels inflict upon the servants of the God who are based there to praise God and demand blessings for all of Christianity." For Roger, Louis XIII was fulfilling a royal duty by doing so, since it was "nos Roys Tres-Chrestiens" who established it.[119]

Both authors wrote during the reign of Louis XIII, but notions of a *milice chretien* clearly continued to percolate under Louis XIV as well, suggested, for example, by the treatise of le Sieur de La Croix discussed earlier. Together these texts, written by French diplomats and friars, suggest that the role of Protector remained important to Bourbon rulers

---

[118] Jean Boucher, *Bouquet sacre composé des plus belles fleurs de la Terre Sainte* (Paris: Denis Moreau on the rue St Jacques Salamanderie, 1620), 156.
[119] Roger, *La Terre Sainte our Description Topographique*, 24.

for manifesting their claims both to orthodoxy and Christian leadership throughout the seventeenth century. One could argue that the efforts of French officials to promote French clerics in the Custody from the 1620s onwards should be understood in similar terms, manifesting its custodial role through the visible presence of French religious performing the liturgical rites in the Holy Places and tending to the material care of its sacred spaces. The timing of these measures, however, also draw our attention to two other forces shaping French interest in the Custody: a resurgent Bourbon-Habsburg rivalry and the forces of Catholic reform in France. These forces further imbued French control of the administration with importance as a manifestation of its Catholic perfection and designated role as protector of the true faith.

4.3.3 The Custody and Habsburg-Bourbon Rivalry

That the Custody had become another site of Bourbon-Habsburg rivalry by the 1620s is also clear from the correspondence of the Franciscan disputes. It is suggested in a number of ways but most notably through the persistent concerns voiced by French officials about Spanish influence and the evident competition over office-holding between members of the two nations. Similarly, usage of the traditional medieval titles of the two monarchs in diplomatic correspondence – "The Most Christian King" (French) and "The Most Catholic King" (Spanish) – highlighted rival claims to Christian leadership.[120] The rivalry was certainly on display during the dispute of 1661, notably in the public signs of outrage expressed by the French pilgrims over the Spanish sermon. By this time, the two major powers had been embroiled in a power struggle that was close to two centuries old and had achieved global dimensions. John C. Rule argues that the rivalry ebbed and flowed in intensity over time, while Nathan Michalewicz suggests that it was a central factor shaping Valois interest in an Ottoman alliance by 1535 and remained so throughout the sixteenth century.[121] In fact, François de Noailles, who had served as French ambassador to the Porte from 1571 to 1575, specifically mentions concern about the "House of Austria" and its ambitions in the Mediterranean in a *discours* addressed to King Henry III on the

---

[120] See, for example, their usage in letter responding to the relation from the French nuncio. AVPF SOCG 44, f. 226v.
[121] Michalewicz, "Franco-Ottoman Diplomacy."

Ottoman alliance. Written in 1578, the document deserves a brief discussion here because it reveals the entwining of French concerns of imperium with growing Habsburg power and the Holy Land prior to the seventeenth century. Noailles begins by stating that the King and his royal predecessors were engaged in the Levant for three principal reasons. The first was religious, because France was responsible for protecting the Holy Sepulcher and ensuring safe passage for all pilgrims "who wished to visit the region out of devotion." Popes, moreover, had "always" turned to French kings for help in stopping "infidel" armies from "molesting the lands of the church" that were in their path. The second reason was to establish and protect the commerce of French subjects living in the regions of Provence and Languedoc, commerce that was increasing during the sixteenth century. The third principal reason was to restrain the "excessive grandeur of the House of Austria," which was growing through their "usurpation of the best kingdoms [couronnes] and states of Europe outside of France."[122]

Noailles letter suggests that Habsburg power was very much on the minds of the later Valois rulers of France, even though the Wars of Religion proved to be a persistent distraction. The timing of the jurisdictional disputes between France and the Franciscan brothers of the Holy Land in the seventeenth century seem to fit with signs of a reenergized rivalry during the reigns of Louis XIII and LXIV. Rule notes that the 1620s–1640s and the 1660s–1700 were periods of particular intensity marked by economic competition and warfare.[123] Viewed within this frame, for example, the dispute of 1661 could be read as an early and deliberately public warning to the friars and the Spanish monarchy of the emergence of a more bellicose Louis XIV following the death of his closest advisor, Cardinal Mazarin. Mazarin died in March 1661, only a few weeks before the infamous Easter pilgrimage that opens this chapter. His death ushered in the era of Personal Rule, which was marked as much by sustained warfare with the Habsburgs as it was by the transformation of the French administration and military and the construction

---

[122] Gallica, BNF Français 7161, 7a–15b. *Discours de Monsieur de Noailles Evesque d'Acs Ambassadeur pour le Roy a la porte du grand Seigneur Touchant l'alliance avec le Turc.* I want to thank Nathan Michalewicz for sharing this fascinating document with me, as well as his expertise on sixteenth-century French diplomacy.

[123] John C. Rule, "The Enduring Rivalry of France and Spain," in *Great Power Rivalries*, ed. William R. Thompson (Columbia: University of South Carolina Press, 1999): 31–59. See, in particular, 33–34.

of Versailles.[124] The rivalry continued during the last decades of the seventeenth century, only ending when the Spanish throne passed to a Bourbon heir in 1700.

This broad overview serves as an important reminder that the jurisdictional conflicts between France and the brothers of the Holy Land must be interpreted within a geopolitical frame of relations between the two great Catholic empires. But it also asks us to ponder the particular utility of the Custody for these powers given its location in a sacred region that had long been important for constructing claims to imperium among adherents of the three Religions of the Book. Modern struggles for dominion over the dusty landscape serve as a potent and bitter reminder of this long-standing function. The friars of this study trod roads and plied their ministries within the walls of structures left behind by a succession of imperial states – Rome, Byzantine, Abbasid, Crusader, Mamluk, Ottoman – each of which had been eager to claim jurisdiction over the sacred landscape to manifest its spiritual and political leadership. That the Custody itself became a fraught zone of competition between the two Catholic powers in the seventeenth century also testifies to the success of Muslim rulers in tightening their control over the region by the thirteenth century, shutting out Christian rulers from direct rule from this time forward. The establishment of the Custody in 1342 gave Western rulers rare access to a region that they considered the very source of Christian authority, an access that made the Custody a revered pilgrimage institution and as such a site of intra-Catholic competition. This competition took mostly the form of patronage and was visible from the earliest days of the institution. One considers, to begin with, that the Custody emerged as a result of a struggle between the Crowns of Aragon and Naples to reestablish a Catholic pilgrimage institution in Jerusalem following the collapse of the Crusader Kingdom in 1291.[125] Naples proved more

---

[124] On French military, political, and economic engagement in the Mediterranean during the period of Personal Rule, some of the more recent work includes Gillian Weiss, *Captivity and Corsairs: France and Slavery in the Early Modern Mediterranean* (Stanford: Stanford University Press, 2011); Jeff Horn, "Lessons of the Levant: Early Modern French Economic Development in the Mediterranean," *Journal of French History* 29 (2015): 76–92; and Junko Takeda, *Between Crown and Commerce: Marseilles and the Early Modern Mediterranean* (Baltimore: John Hopkins University Press, 2011). See also the special collection of articles in Megan C. Armstrong and Gillian Weiss, eds., "France and the Early Modern Mediterranean." *French History* 43 (March 2015).

[125] See, for example, discussions on the first century of the Custody in Felix del Buey and Cristoforo Alvis, "Origenes de la custodia de Tierra Santa," *Archivo ibero-americano* 65

successful its negotiations with the Mamluk Turks, and its monarchs became the most important patrons of the Custody until the kingdom was absorbed by the Crown of Aragon in 1504. Even before this time, Isabella of Castille had begun developing ties between the Crown of Castille and the Custody, providing a sizeable annual sum to support its operations from as early as the 1480s. Throughout the sixteenth and seventeenth centuries, Spain remained the single most generous funder of the mission, a relationship that both the friars and the Spanish monarchy publicized.[126] The *Patrimonio Seraphico de Tierra Santa*, for example, a text that receives a closer look in Chapter 6, was produced by a Spanish press established at the convent of San Francisco in Madrid. One of its central objectives was to advertise Spanish patronage of the Custody.[127] Its author, Francisco Jesus Maria de San Juan del Puerto, was a commissioner general of the Holy Land for the kingdom of Spain and he dedicated his work to its newly crowned monarch, King Louis I (d. 1724). In his dedication, he thanked the monarch for supporting the religious who "serve the cult of the Holy Places" but also all Christian Catholics "of these countries" who benefit from "the increase in alms that come from Spain."[128]

To appreciate French desire to uproot Spanish influence in the administration of the Custody, we need to consider two related facets of Spanish patronage used to construct Habsburg claims to Christian hegemony: the ornamentation of chapels, and the traffic in alms and pilgrimage mementoes.

4.3.4 Chapels and Imperial Rivalry

Surviving sources including registers of expenses and pilgrimage treatises suggest that Spanish authority would have been a palpable presence in the Latin chapels of the Holy Places. It was on display in the expensive gilt

---

(2005): 7–96; and Sabino de Sandoli, *The Peaceful Liberation of the Holy Place in the Fourteenth Century* (Jerusalem: Franciscan Center, 1991), 36.

[126] Victor de Lama, "Un breve de Inocencio VIII dirigido a los Reyes Católicos, que nunca recibieron, y la financiación de los Santos Lugares," *España Medieval* 38 (2015): 231–240.

[127] See Karen Melvin, "The Travels of *El devoto peregrino*: A Franciscan Holy Land Comes to New Spain," in *Five Hundred Years of Franciscans in New Spain*, ed. Thomas Cohen, Jay Harrison and David Rex Galindo (forthcoming).

[128] "... las crecidas Limosnas, que vàn de España." Francisco Jesús Del Puerto and Maria de San Juan, *Patrimonio Seraphico de Tierra Santa, fundado por Christo nuestro redentor con su preciosa Sangre, prometido por su Magestad à N.P.S. Francisco para sì, y para sus Hijos, adquirido por el mismo santo, heredado, y posseìdo por sus Hijos de la Regular Observancia, y conservado hasta el tiempo presente* (Madrid: Imprenta de la V.M. Maria de Jesus de Agreda, 1724), 3a.

ornaments used to decorate the chapels, works of art including royal portraits, and in the vestments worn on the bodies of the officiating Franciscan priests. Just as importantly, it was carved into the walls of the Holy Places since Spanish wealth paid for most of the renovations during the Early Modern Period. Some of the more striking discussions in the sources include Spanish funding of the renovation of the Dome of the Holy Sepulcher during the 1550s, a massive engineering achievement mentioned earlier that was extremely expensive and involved the work of Spanish craftsmen and materials. The Spanish king also provided lavish gifts to fill the renovated spaces and to help modernize the convent of the Holy Saviour.[129] Spanish patronage was sufficiently visible to merit mention in many pilgrimage accounts, whose authors typically paid close attention to the ornamentation of chapels, providing physical descriptions and attributions. Unfortunately, these descriptions often stop short of describing stylistic elements that allow us to recreate "Spanish" spaces in terms of design, but they do refer to gifts from the Spanish monarchy. Several seventeenth century accounts mention, for example, a large "lampadario" on the main Franciscan altar in the Holy Sepulcher. The French linguist Jean de Thévenot, who traveled to the Holy Land in the 1670s, remembered being impressed by the beautiful lamps given by various monarchs for the Latin altars in the Basilica but, in particular, an enormous silver one given by the Spanish monarchy.

He notes that it was covered in eight places with the coat of arms of Spain and was a magnificent object, one that he insists was highly coveted by the Muslims themselves.[130] This was likely the "lampada argentea" donated by the Philip IV in 1626 mentioned in the records of the Propaganda Fide, which cost the vast sum of "16,000 aureorum." Francisco Jesús de San Juan del Puerto may have been describing this lamp as well in his *Patrimonio* when he mentions one made of silver that was located at the door of the shrine of the Holy Sepulcher. It was donated by Philip IV in memory of his father Philip III who died in 1621 to burn eternally in his "reverent memory," testifying to his Catholic piety.[131]

---

[129] On these renovations, see Chapter 1.
[130] Jean de Thévenot, *The Travels of M. Thévenot* (London: H. Clark, 1687), 187–188. Francisco Jesús Maria de San Juan del Puerto's *Patrimonio Seraphico de Tierra Santa* (1724), which was written by a former commissioner of the Holy Land, mentions the historic generosity of the monarchs including a "Lampara de plata de docientas libras Españolas, en que hasta oy, à la puerta de el Santo Sepulcro de nuestro Salvador, arde siempre viva su Catholica, y reverente memoria."
[131] Lemmens, ed., *Acta*, vol. 1, 39. The original document was APF CG 20 (April 1626), NR. 16, f. 46v.

Early modern Christians were skilled interpreters of signs. They would have read the Spanish gifts as markers of Catholic devotion and their status as rulers. They would have also interpreted them, because of their specific location and visual prominence in the sacred geography of the Holy Places, as claims to possession of these spaces and thus of its sanctifying power. Asserting Spanish claims to Christian hegemony was precisely the point of royal patronage of the Custody according to Adam Beaver, an objective that also led Philip II to commission histories that traced Habsburg rule to the biblical monarchs.[132] As Fabien Montcher has argued recently, the Habsburg rulers of Spain, like the Bourbon monarchs of France, turned to the medieval French King Louis IX to construct their claims to Christian hegemony. Both dynasties could trace their lineage to the medieval ruler, a connection that Philip III of Spain in particular cultivated, finding the medieval monarch useful both as a symbol of royal piety and as grounds for justifying Spanish "protection" of the Holy Places.[133] Spain of course was by no means the only European power to see the sanctifying value of a visible presence in the Latin chapels. Venice, along with the Holy Roman Empire and the king of Poland, were generous benefactors throughout the medieval and Early Modern Periods but there were many others. A report submitted by the outgoing *custos* Franciscus Manerba in 1604, for example, crowed about the generous gifts recently provided by the kings of Poland and Portugal, the Grand Duke of Tuscany, and the Duke of Olica.[134] The gifts of these rulers competed with those of Spain for the eye of the pilgrim, articulating a relationship with the Holy Land that was devotional as well as political in nature. Some of these other powers clearly had hegemonic ambitions as well, notably the Medici dukes of Florence. In 1601, Fernando I de' Medici, the Grand Duke of Tuscany (1589–1609), gave an elaborate marble slab to the Custody for the Latin altar in the chapel at the foot of Calvary known as the site of the Nailing of the Cross (Station 11). The gift was part of negotiations that sought to move the Holy Sepulcher from

---

[132] Adam G. Beaver, "Scholarly Pilgrims: Antiquarian Visions of the Holy Land," in *Sacred History: Visitations of the Christian Past in the Renaissance World*, ed. Simon Ditchfield and Kate Van de Liere (Oxford: Oxford University Press, 2012), 267–283.

[133] Fabien Montcher, "L'image et le culte de saint Louis dans la Monarchie hispanique. Le role des 'reines de paix' (du milieu du XVIe siècle au milieu du XVIIe siècle)," in *"La dame de Coeur." Patronage et mécénat religieux des femmes de pouvoir dans l'Europe des XIVe–XVIIe siècles*, ed. Murielle Gaude-Ferragu et Cecile Vincent-Cassy (Rennes: Presses Universitaires de Rennes), 167–192.

[134] Manerba's report is included in Lemmens, ed., *Acta*, vol. I, 10.

Jerusalem to the Medici chapel in Florence. One could hardly imagine a more visible symbol of Florentine and Medici power than its possession of Christ's resting place. These negotiations failed in that regard, though the altarpiece remains in its original location in the Basilica of the Holy Sepulcher to this day, announcing the wealth and power of an early modern ruler who was then in the midst of transforming Florence into an important commercial power. Fernando I was responsible, we should remember, for turning Livorno into a vibrant free port during the seventeenth century to compete with Marseilles, Venice, and other European port cities.[135]

In comparison to these rulers, French monarchs stand out as rather parsimonious patrons of the Custody until the seventeenth century, and even then, their financial support never matched that of Spanish rulers – a point made repeatedly by the Franciscan brothers when challenged about Spanish influence. While the Bourbon regime could not (or would not) match Spanish financial generosity, it could use its political influence at the Porte and with the papacy as Protector to push its own claims to Christian leadership by seeking to minimize if not uproot Spanish influence in the Custody. This objective underlay, for example, French arguments with the Congregation that the ties with Spain endangered the security of the Custody, but it also helps to explain Bourbon interest in giving French clerics a more influential role in its administration. To begin with, the larger number of French clerics rendered French Catholicism a more visible presence throughout the Custody. Secondly, the greater access of French friars to the inner council of its administration could buffer the influence of Spanish as well as Venetian clerics over the performance of the liturgical rites and preaching, both important public roles that were managed by the council. But in seeking to control the council, French officials may have been just as concerned about Spanish influence over a bustling global traffic in alms and pilgrimage mementoes. This was another important facet of custodial business that has yet to receive attention here but which was especially important for amplifying Spanish claims to Christian hegemony well beyond the confined spaces of the Holy Places.

---

[135] On Florence as a Mediterranean empire, see, in particular, Francesca Trivellato, *The Familiarity of Strangers: The Sephardic Diaspora, Livorno, and Cultural Trade in the Early Modern Period* (New Haven: Yale University Press, 2014).

4.3.5 Alms and Mementoes

The incomplete nature of financial records for the sixteenth and seventeenth centuries make it challenging to discuss with any specificity the size and nature of this commerce. A fascinating picture is slowly emerging, however, thanks to Ottoman and New World scholars working on diverse ends of this global trade. Their studies reveal a network that by the seventeenth century carried pilgrimage mementoes (miniature replicas of the Holy Places, vials of the River Jordan) produced by Christian craftsmen in Bethlehem (and perhaps other cities in the Holy Land) to distributors in Europe and from there to the colonial regions of the Atlantic world.[136] The central administration of this trade lay with the commissariat of the Holy Land, a fiscal structure that was tied to the Custody and was managed by teams of friars who gathered and carried alms and other "gifts" to Jerusalem. That this commerce was growing throughout the sixteenth and seventeenth centuries also seems important for understanding Bourbon interest in the Custody because it testified to a productive partnership between the Spanish monarchy and the Franciscan brothers that would have been concerning. Patrocinio Barriuso, who has written on Spanish fiscal relations with the Custody, shows that the commissariat expanded significantly during the sixteenth and seventeenth centuries as resident commissioners-general were established in diverse parts of Europe. The Chapter of Valladolid of 1593 recognized the establishment of thirteen commissariats,[137] with one in France established later in 1615. The commissioners-general, who oversaw the circulation of alms and mementoes to and from Jerusalem, served as important lynchpins in the growing global trade, especially once Spain opened its colonial territories to Franciscan commissioners for alms collection in 1606. By the end of the seventeenth century, the Spanish New

---

[136] On the Bethlehem workshops, see Jacob Norris, "Exporting the Holy Land: Artisans and Merchant Migrants in Ottoman-Era Bethlehem," *Journal of Middle East Migration Studies* 2 (2013): 14–40; and Felicità Tramontana, "Per ornamento e servizio di questi santi luoghi: L'arrivée des objets de dévotion dans les sanctuaires de Terre Sainte (xviie siècle)," *Archives de sciences sociales des religions. Façonner l'objet de dévotion chrétien. Fabrication, commerce et circulations (vers XVII–XIX siècles)* 183 (2018): 227–243.

[137] By 1698, they were established in Vienna, Paris, Madrid, Lisbon, Naples, Messina, Malta, Venice, Milan, Florence, Turin, Marseilles, and Genoa. Heyberger, *Les Chrétiens du Proche-Orient*, 215.

World was the single largest contributor to alms.[138] These Franciscan officials, we should note, were mostly Spanish throughout the early modern period, much like the procurator attached to the Custody who received the alms.

French officials were well aware that the traffic in alms and mementoes emmeshed the Custody in the imperial networks of France's rival because it was heavily dependent upon the support of Spanish officials, merchants and ships, and political access to Spanish markets in the New World and elsewhere. This trade also simultaneously gave Spain a local foothold in the Levant, a region to which it lacked direct political and economic access for most of the seventeenth century because of its frayed relations with the Ottoman Porte. But looking beyond its evident commercial value, both monarchies would have considered the trade another effective means of broadcasting their claims to Christian hegemony on a global scale. One can imagine what Louis XIII and Louis XIV thought about the sight of the powerful Spanish Empire presiding over an ever-flowing circulation of alms and religious mementoes carried in the hands of Spanish friars by Spanish ships to the distant regions of the known world.[139]

4.3.6 France and Catholic Reform

The imperial rivalry so visible in disputes of the friars is another important reminder of the centrality of the Catholic tradition inshaping the expansionist ambitions of early modern states. It was because the Custody gave Catholic powers such as France and Spain a spiritual foothold in the most sacred of Christian landscapes, a region pulsing with the spiritual authority of Christ, that both were eager to bring it within their sphere of influence and lay claim to its sanctifying power. Imprinting the Custody with the markings of Bourbon jurisdiction was thus intended

---

[138] The expansion of alms collection can also be traced in the archives of the Propaganda Fide, which issued permission for the organization of alms in the New World. For example, a decree dated December 20, 1690, authorized alms collected in Brazil. Heyberger, *Les Chrétiens du Proche-Orient*, 215. On alms collection in the New World, see, in particular, Melvin, "The Travels of *El devoto peregrino*." I want to thank Dr. Melvin for sharing her article, providing critical new information on the organization of alms in the New World including the role of the Franciscan Custody.

[139] In addition to Karen Melvin, "The Travels The Travels of *El devoto peregrino*." See also Agostino Arce, OFM, *Expeditiones de España a Jerusalen 1693–1842* (Madrid: Relaciones culturales imprenta del ministerio de asuntos exteriors, 1958).

to legitimize the French claims to Christian hegemony above those of its Habsburg rivals, a claim for which the Bourbon regime could point to its destiny as ruler of the Holy Land. As a final observation, the disputes reveal another factor motivating Bourbon interest in transforming the Custody into a French institution. This was an emergent and increasingly self-confident French Catholicism. The dispute of 1661 hints at this dimension when it depicts two lay Frenchman inverting the knighting ceremonial of the Order of the Holy Sepulcher to humiliate the Milanese Franciscan *custos*, Valles. As we may recall from our discussion of the Order of the Holy Sepulcher in Chapter 3, the ritual created new members of a religious brotherhood that historically enjoyed close ties to the Custody. But by 1661, the Order of the Holy Sepulcher had become a predominantly French brotherhood, a demographic shift that is explicable when we consider not only the Ottoman Empire's absorption of the Holy Land in 1517 and its tightening political and commercial relations with France but also an early modern France engulfed by the forces of religious reform.

On its own, Du Plessis' seizure of the sword from a papal official was a striking claim to spiritual authority by a layman. When studied in the context of broader French engagement in the Custody, his actions could also be read as a particular assertion of French spiritual worthiness. A broad consideration of the correspondence exchanged by Bourbon officials during the many disputes involving the Custody finds a number of Bourbon officials making precisely this claim to justify Bourbon efforts to expand its religious influence in the Levant. It is suggested, for example, in the disdain frequently expressed by Bourbon officials as well as French missionaries for the friars and other established mendicant orders. A letter sent by the French ambassador Césy to the Propaganda Fide in 1628 serves as a particularly colourful example. As context, we should note that the ambassador was writing in response to the recent expulsion of Jesuits from Constantinople by the Porte, an expulsion that he insisted had been orchestrated by the local mendicant communities and the Venetian ambassador among others. The communities in question were old ones, tracing their foundations back to the thirteenth century. Similar to the Franciscan brothers of the Custody, they were also less than warm in their reception of the French missionaries that began arriving in their city after 1604. Césy's suspicion of their complicity in the expulsion, in other words, was not necessarily misplaced.[140] More relevant here is his

---

[140] On the Jesuits in Constantinople, see, among others, Ruiu, "Conflicting Visions."

language, which is, to say the least, scathing in its assessment of the moral and spiritual character of the mendicant communities. A furious Césy writes, for example, that "considering the religious who usually come here ... it seems that superiors seek out those to send here whom the galleys reject ... in place of individuals, [moral] examples that would impress all nations."[141] He followed by praising the French clerics, stating that "I can no longer delay in [louer] praising the Jesuit and Capuchin fathers, who are admired here."[142]

Césy's letter suggests that the older orders had fallen to the corrupting influences of the Islamic East.[143] They were morally and spiritually compromised. French missionaries were uncorrupted, and as a result, more worthy of representing the Latin tradition in Ottoman regions. We may recall that another ambassador, Pierre Antoine de Châteauneuf, marquis de Castagnères (d. 1728), attributed Spanish and Italian Franciscan resistance to the establishment of Jesuits in Jerusalem in 1691 to their recognition that the ministry of the Jesuit chaplains would be more "edifying." That Castagnères in the same letter referred to the Jesuits as "our religious" is another intriguing element, underscoring the close ties between the Jesuits and the French state, but it also articulates a shared sense of French Catholic identity. We should note that some of the Capuchin and Jesuit missionaries also criticized the spiritual worthiness of the Franciscan brothers. Often these criticisms centered around issues of linguistic training and pastoral care. One also finds more pointed suggestions of spiritual corruption, however, such as a letter sent by a French Capuchin named Vincent, which accused the Franciscan *custos* of consorting with heretics. The letter, dated July 22, 1636, was sent to the Congregation of the Propaganda Fide. The Franciscan *custos* in question was Paolo da Lodi. According to Vincent, Lodi "frequented the churches of heretics and schismatics," a clear reference to local Eastern Christian communities. As we shall see in Chapter 5, the papacy was preoccupied with the conversion of Eastern Christians, but it went hand in hand with concerns about preserving Catholic orthodoxy. Vincent was implying

---

[141] APF Lettere di Levante 111 (January 25, 1628), ff. 9–11. "En fin Rme Sgr, considerant les religieux quy viennent icy ordinayrement il semble que les superieurs cherchent ceulx dont les Galeres ne veulent point pour les envoyer icy, au lieu de choysir des personnes, exemplayres pour satisfayre toutes les nations."

[142] APF Lettere di Levante 111 (January 25, 1628), ff. 9–11. "Et sur ce propos je ne puys m'empescher de louer les peres Jesuytes et les peres Capuchins lesquels se sont icy admirer d'un chascun."

[143] APF SOCG 195, f. 133.

here that Lodi, by mingling with the other Christian communities, was flirting with spiritual contagion if he had not already been fully consumed by it.

Accusations of corruption were a popular strategy for delegitimizing the arguments of an ecclesiastical opponent during the early modern period, whether a rival community or a senior official. When one considers, moreover, that similar assertions of spiritual worthiness were emerging from other "nations" at the same time, however, perhaps most notably that of Spain, it does not seem to be going too far to suggest that the French officials of this study may have genuinely believed in French worthiness as well. It is important to note, to begin with, that the two letters of Castagnères and Césy discussed here were directed at fellow French officials, suggesting a shared esteem for the Jesuits and disdain for the established mendicant traditions. Secondly, by the 1620s, France was in the throes of powerful forces of Catholic reform. Indeed, one might well argue that the rhetoric of worthiness invoked by these officials reflected the religious sensibilities of members of a monarchical institution that had been transformed in the "purifying" fires of the Wars of Religion and by the distinctive forces of religious change that followed, emerging from it a more self-consciously French Catholic institution that was confident in its claims to spiritual perfection and thus global leadership.

Much more work must be done on the religious attitudes of Bourbon officials to make this case, but a growing body of scholarship on the changing religious character of France and its monarchy under the Bourbons provides some support. One must consider, to begin with, the powerful forces of Catholic reform unleashed in France in the wake of the Wars of Religion that fundamentally altered the nature of the Catholic tradition in France and its institutions by the middle of the seventeenth century.[144] As Barbara Diefendorf, in particular, has argued in a series of works including most recently a comparative study of monastic institutions, Catholic reform in France was distinctive and diverse in nature, shaped by local forces in addition to those emanating from outside the kingdom. For Diefendorf, a shared preoccupation with

---

[144] A small but important sampling on this vast scholarship must include Joseph Bergin, *The Politics of Religion in Early Modern France*; Barbara Diefendorf, *From Penitence to Piety: Pius Women and the Catholic Reformation in Paris* (Oxford: Oxford University Press, 2005); Denis Crouzet, *Les guerriers de Dieu. Le violence au temps des troubles de religion, vers 1525–1610* (Seyssel: Champ Vallon, 1994); and Alison Forrestal, *Vincent de Paul, the Lazarist Mission, and French Catholic Reform* (Oxford: Oxford University Press, 2017).

purity was one important feature of French monastic reform marked in particular by a certain militancy and thirst for rigorous asceticism.[145] The monarchy played an active role fueling these and other reforming movements, moreover, first under Henry IV and continuing under Louis XIII and Louis XIV. These monarchs promoted internal missions and patronized new charitable endowments and monastic institutions with the shared objective of re-Catholicizing the kingdom. Purifying France thus meant removing a faith considered heretical by French Catholics, "restoring" the kingdom to its natural state as one governed by one king, one God and one faith. Joseph Bergin argues, moreover, that the Bourbon monarchs shared this objective with the French episcopacy even if some serious differences over governance plagued their relations during the seventeenth century.[146]

Recent scholarship on French engagement in the Mediterranean is similarly suggestive of an emergent, self-confident French Catholicism among French officials by the seventeenth century. Benoist Pierre's study of the Capuchin advisor to Richelieu, Père Josef, locates this reformed piety as a central pillar of an ambitious plan for global hegemony under Louis XIII. Under the direction of Père Joseph, the French state sponsored numerous missions across the Ottoman Empire from the 1620s.[147] The French missionaries who arrived in the Custody, we should note, were members of the same reformed religious orders that the French state charged with the missionization of France in the decades after the Wars of Religion, suggesting an important relationship between the religious policies and objectives of the Bourbons both at home and abroad. With a specific eye to the Mediterranean context of French engagement as well, Gillian Weiss has argued that the public redemption of slaves under Louis XIV articulated a conception of French identity that was intentionally, and inherently, Catholic, casting Calvinism as a polluted faith and Calvinists as *de natura* non-French subjects.[148] Taken together, these various studies suggest that the Wars of Religion and its legacy of religious division haunted the Bourbon regime throughout the seventeenth century and fostered the emergence of a more self-consciously French

---

[145] Barbara Diefendorf, *Planting the Cross: Catholic Reform and Renewal in Sixteenth and Seventeenth Century France* (Oxford: Oxford University Press, 2019).
[146] Bergin, *The Politics of Religion*.
[147] See, in particular, Benoist Pierre, *Le Père Joseph: L'Eminence grise de Richelieu* (Paris: Perrin, 2007).
[148] Weiss, *Captives and Corsairs*.

Catholic institution – one that came to read its experience of religious warfare and subsequent reform as perfecting.

The Bourbon officials of this study were products of this reformed culture. Whether or not they believed in a form of French spiritual exceptionalism is impossible to say with certainty. It would be more accurate, rather, to suggest that by the seventeenth century they were devout Catholics who considered the Crown as *de natura* a Catholic institution, one that had a responsibility to play a role in strengthening the Catholic faith both at home and abroad. There is tantalizing evidence, moreover, that they may have shared a belief in the French monarchy's destiny as a Christian leader, one that privileged a role for French jurisdiction in the Holy Land. The growing number of French officials who undertook the pilgrimage is particularly striking. In addition to the two French pilgrims, Du Plessis and Cadeau, who disrupted the Easter rites in 1661, the register of pilgrims kept in the Custody reveals a steady flow of officials arriving in Jerusalem throughout the seventeenth century, either en route to their new postings or on the way back to France at the end of their tenures.[149] Many of them also wrote accounts of their pilgrimage, including François Savary de Breves (d. 1628) and le Sieur La Croix (d. 1704). Just as intriguingly, quite a few joined the Order of the Holy Sepulcher, including several ambassadors to the Porte and officials attached to their household.[150] As discussed in Chapter 3, the Order became a predominantly French society over the course of the sixteenth and seventeenth centuries, a demographic shift that asks one to ponder the Order's emergence at this time as another valued manifestation of French Catholic identity under Bourbon rule. This was an Order, as we should recall, whose spiritual identity was closely associated with Godefroy of Bouillon, the first Crusader ruler of Jerusalem. Anthoine Regnault, for example, described the king of France as the first "grand master "of the Order in his pilgrimage treatise. Regnault was referring to Godefroy of Bouillon, but Jean de Gennes suggests, that he may have also been anxious to claim the Order for the Bourbon monarchy and at the expense of the Spanish monarchy. After all, it was only a few years after his pilgrimage that Philip II entered into serious negotiations with the papacy to assume the role of grand master.[151] Regnault, however, uses

---

[149] Arch. Custodia Terra Sancta, *Registrum Equitum SSmi Sepulchri* (1561–1847).
[150] See the discussion in Chapter 2.
[151] Jean De Gennes, *Les Chevaliers du Saint-Sépulcre de Jérusalem*, vol. 1 (Paris: Herault, 2004), 44.

Bouillon to trace a much longer royal lineage linking the French monarchy to the Holy Land, one that began before Charlemagne and ends with Charles IX (d. 1574). He mentions that Charles IX "pacified the entire kingdom, frustrating all rebellions and "the enemies of the holy Catholic faith and the Roman Church."[152]

It is interesting that Regnault, a member of the Order of the Holy Sepulcher, ends his pilgrimage treatise at this very point with the recent triumph of Charles IX over "rebellions" in France. As we may recall, the Massacre of St. Bartholomew's day took place during his reign in August 1572, and Regnault published his treatise only a year later. He may well have been reflecting on this bloody episode, one that was celebrated by many Catholics and horrified the Huguenots. Echoing with the sounds of religious crusade, this passage further suggests that the Order if the Holy Sepulcher offered an ordinary Parisian merchant as well as many French officials another French sacred past in the Holy Land. At the very least, it served as another strand in an existing French mythic past that rooted their kingdom in the legitimizing soil of the most sacred of Christian landscapes. Returning to the disputes that started this chapter, a similar legitimizing function was served by turning the Custody French, because it placed the Holy Land and its pilgrimage under the visible control and protection of the French state. A wonderfully evocative painting recently discovered in a Parisian hotel expresses these very hegemonic ambitions. Unearthed during renovations and dating to 1674, the painting by the artist Arnaud de Vuez places the French ambassador Charles Olier de Nointel at the center of the canvass in front of the gates of Jerusalem (see Figure 4.1). Nointel made the journey a year earlier in 1673. Seated on a rearing horse and accompanied by an aristocratic retinue, the ambassador's noble and official status is also immediately apparent from his luxurious clothing. But Vuez also chose to illuminate the figure of Nointel by dressing him in white and gold, colours that evoked divinity. At the back of the frame one notices the glimmering of the coming dawn heralding the arrival of Nointel and his party at the gates of the holy city. Nointel commissioned the work to commemorate the signing of the Capitulations in 1674, and it is a powerful scene that was clearly intended to evoke a French *milice Chretien* at the doors of Jerusalem, a Christian army led by his most important official – the French ambassador – in Ottoman lands. Given that Nointel was also member of the Order of the

---

[152] Regnault, *Discours du voyage doutre mer*, 202.

256   The Holy Land and the Early Modern Reinvention

Figure 4.1 *Marquis de Nointel at Jerusalem* (1672). Artist: Arnould de Vuez. Location: Oscar de la Renta Boutique, Paris, France. Julien Mignot/The New York Times/Redux.

Holy Sepulcher, this militant depiction seems more than appropriate, investing his role as the highest French representative in Ottoman lands with spiritual purpose as a divinely designated defender of the Holy Places on behalf of a Christendom united under French leadership.

4.4 CONCLUSION

As this chapter has argued, from the 1620s onward, Bourbon administrators filled the Custody with French missionaries and pushed for the appointment of French Observants to its central administration in an effort to bring the venerable pilgrimage institution under its jurisdiction. They did so by flaunting its status of Protector of the Holy Places, one obtained through negotiations with Ottoman rulers. The many disputes that erupted over jurisdiction with the Observants illuminate a Catholic institution that was immensely valuable to the new Bourbon dynasty France for legitimizing its rule, an importance tied to its intimate connection with the Holy Land. Henry IV inherited a throne that was reeling from powerful forces of change, in particular religious division and a resurgent and increasingly global rivalry with the powerful Spanish Habsburgs. Faced by these serious challenges amongst others, the Bourbon monarchy turned to its alliance with Ottoman rulers and France's sacred past in the Holy Land to construct its claims to Christian hegemony. Chapter 5 places the spotlight on another Catholic power with hegemonic ambitions, which also involved the Custody of the Holy land. By the 1620s, the Observant brothers found their jurisdiction under threat from a post-Tridentine papacy eager to expand its spiritual influence in Ottoman lands. The Custody, because of its responsibilities at a diverse site of global pilgrimage assumed special importance both as an agent of conversion and as a manifestation of papal primacy.

5

The Congregation of the Propaganda Fide

In Chapter 4, the archives of the Congregation of the Propaganda Fide served as a crucial window into the many disputes between the Bourbon monarchy and the brothers of the Holy Land. These same documents, however, reveal a papal institution that had its own ambitions regarding the Custody. Indeed, the Congregation became deeply emmeshed in the affairs of the pilgrimage institution within a few years of its establishment in 1622, an engagement that was not always welcomed by the Franciscan brothers, who viewed a number of its measures as intrusions into their traditional jurisdiction. Long accustomed to managing the affairs of the Custody with little interference from external Catholic authorities including the papacy, the friars were more than a little perturbed to find their operations under greater scrutiny. At the same time, they recognized that the Congregation, as a new embodiment of papal authority, could not be easily ignored. The task of the present chapter is to look more closely at relations between the Congregation and the Custody during the seventeenth century. Doing so reveals a papacy with hegemonic ambitions, ambitions that privileged an important role for the Holy Land and the Custody in the construction of its claims to universal Christian governance.

For the Congregation of the Propaganda Fide, an institution forged in the fires of Tridentine reform and charged with expanding the global reach of Catholic tradition, the Holy Land represented an especially important site of engagement because of its spiritual significance as a shared religious landscape and strategic location in the diverse religious realities of the Ottoman Empire. The Holy Land, in other words, was of central concern because it served as both a *frontier* and spiritual *center* of an expanding Catholic tradition. These two conceptions of the Holy

Land – spiritual *center* and Catholic *frontier* – operated in tandem to shape papal policies regarding the Custody throughout the seventeenth century, revealed, in particular, through the Congregation's preoccupation with moulding the Observant brothers into a pliant and obedient missionary body. The Congregation understood the unique capacity of the Custody to expand its authority both locally and globally through its responsibilities with the Catholic pilgrimage and its locus within a diverse religious landscape.

Indeed, relations between the Congregation and the Custody from the 1620s onward point to interest in reshaping the Observant ministry to involve the evangelization of local Christians. As shall soon be clear, the growing influence of the Congregation illuminates the continuing potency of an older conception of Christendom shaping papal engagement in the Holy Land, one that recognized Jerusalem as the spiritual heart of a unified Christendom under the authority of the bishop of Rome. To possess altars in the Holy Places, fill the Holy Land with the bodies of Latin clerics, and convert local Christians rendered the Latin tradition visible and palpable at the place where Christianity began, thus ratifying its historic claims to Christian leadership. Doing so simultaneously evoked Jerusalem's historic significance as a site of continuing revelation, signaling the start of a new era of Christian renewal under papal direction.

However, in seeking to transform the Franciscan brothers into missionaries in the service of a restored Christendom, the Congregation had to overcome the traditional independence of the Franciscan brothers of the Holy Land. The papal body found a number of strategies useful in this regard, all aimed at expanding its influence in the Custody at the expense of the jurisdiction of the friars. It is with its efforts to transform the brothers into a pliant and obedient ministry that this chapter begins. Section 5.1 traces the emergence of a more interventionist papacy in the Custody in the form of the Congregation of the Propaganda Fide. Given particular attention are four strategies employed by the Congregation to expand its authority at the expense of the traditional jurisdiction of the friars: the approval of incoming *custos*, regular reporting, the introduction of the French missionaries, and mediation. Sections 5.2 and 5.3 explore the Custody's importance in papal objectives through a consideration of the Holy Land's twin functions as a *Catholic frontier* (site of evangelization) and a *spiritual center* (place of Christ). Studied in tandem, these functions illuminate the Custody as a critical gateway to spiritual and political legitimacy for another important early modern Catholic institution, in this case a papacy hit hard by the forces of reform and struggling to reconstruct its status as a great Christian authority in an increasingly diverse global religious landscape. As in the case of earlier chapters, this investigation locates the spiritual significance of the Holy Land for a changing early modern papacy at the nexus of Catholic spirituality, Ottoman governance, and sacred history. Three themes, in particular, emerge as especially important for understanding papal objectives: Firstly, the reification of the Holy Land as a material vessel of Christian authority grounded in the global ambitions of the early modern papacy. Secondly, the Custody's strategic importance as a *local* institution in Ottoman lands, which allowed the papacy to spread its influence *there*. Thirdly, the Congregation's focus upon conversion intentionally recalled the papacy's mythic Roman past as the leader of a unified Christendom. Reconciling Christians to the "true" faith manifested early modern papal claims to global Christian leadership, and for this reason one should interpret the many endeavours of the friars and Congregation to secure local conversions as modes of sacred history-telling.

5.1 THE EXPANSION OF PAPAL INFLUENCE

5.1.1 *The Congregation of the Propaganda Fide*

For an institution that would emerge as a powerful arm of the papacy during the course of the seventeenth century, the Congregation of the Propaganda Fide remains surprisingly understudied, especially for the Early Modern Period. More and more scholars, however, are discovering the richness of its vast, byzantine holdings for exploring the global engagement of the Catholic Church. The present study contributes to a growing body of scholarship examining the Congregation's engagement on the ground in diverse regions, in this particular case involving a revered Catholic institution in the Levant.[1] Interpreting these "local" relations, however, still necessitates a solid grasp of the organization and operations of a unique and complex papal body. The foundational work of Giovanni Pizzorusso and Josef Metzler, in particular, has been enormously important for understanding its internal operations and

---

[1] Bernard Heyberger, *Les Chrétiens du Proche-Orient au temps de la Réforme Catholique.* (Rome: Ecole Française de Rome, 1994); Robert Clines, *A Jewish Jesuit in the Eastern Mediterranean* (Cambridge: Cambridge University Press, 2019); Felicita Tramontana, *Passages of Faith: Conversion in Palestinian Villages (17th Century)* (Wiesbaden: Otto Harrassowitz, 2004); and Adina Ruiu, "Conflicting Visions of Jesuit Missions to the Ottoman Empire, 1609–1628," *Journal of Jesuit Studies* 1 (2014): 260–280.

processes of decision-making during its formative first century as well as its place within broader papal objectives.[2] From their work we know that the new Congregation took shape relatively quickly following the appointment of thirteen cardinals in 1621. Its administrative form and mandate were hammered out in a series of regular meetings over the subsequent months leading to the formal recognition of the new organ of papal governance in January 1622 in the form of the papal bull *Inscrutabili Divinae*. During the intervening months, the Congregation received a palazzo on the Piazza della Spagna in Rome to serve as its headquarters. The palazzo, which was designed by Gian Lorenzo Bernini and completed by Francesco Borromini, remains an imposing expression of baroque Rome and its powerful papal ruler. From this site, the members of the Congregation undertook an ambitious mandate to expand the global reach of the Church, one that charged them with responsibility for reconciling Protestant "heretics" as well as bringing the faithful of other religions into the Catholic fold. As Pizzorusso has argued recently, the Congregation's focus upon evangelization should be understood within a much broader program of religious outreach developed by a post-Tridentine Church, one that was as concerned about preserving orthodoxy and determining error within the Catholic body as it was about expanding its membership.[3] The conversion of the many Eastern Christian communities in the Levant became a particular priority early on, one of the reasons that the Custody was of interest to the Congregation from the start.

Initially, the Congregation met only a few times a month and it functioned with a remarkably rudimentary administrative structure that relied almost entirely upon the office of the secretary. As it happened, the choice of Monsignor Francesco Ingoli (1622–1649) as the first secretary proved formative in the development of the institution. Metzler and Pizzorusso, among others, credit Ingoli with playing a singularly

---

[2] See, in particular, the many works of Giovanni Pizzorusso, including *Governare le missioni, conoscere il mondo nel XVII secolo. La Congregazione Pontificia De Propaganda Fide* (Rome: Sette Città, 2018); the multi-volume collection of articles in Joseph Metzler, ed., *Sacrae Congregationis de Propaganda Fide Memoria Rerum*, 3 vols. (Rome, Freiburg, Vienna: Herder, 1971–1976). With regard to Metzler on the early organization, see "Foundation of the Congregation de Propaganda Fide by Gregory XV," 79–111; and "Orientation, programme et premières décisions (1622–1649)," 146–196. Also useful as a legal view of its establishment is Raphael H. Song, *The Sacred Congregation for the Propagation of the Faith* (Washington, DC: The Catholic University of America Press, 1961).

[3] Pizzorusso, *Governare le missioni*, 1.3.2.

important role in ensuring the new papal body's rapid rise in influence. Under his long watch, the secretary became the fulcrum of internal operations and the most important point of contact between the Congregation and the many Catholic institutions and communities found throughout the known world. For the Franciscan brothers of the Custody, Ingoli was the face of the Congregation during its early years, his signature visible in the extensive correspondence exchanged with the *custos* and other Franciscan officials from the 1620s to the 1640s. Indeed, Ingoli's influence went well beyond establishing institutional procedures because he was very much involved in shaping the decisions of the body regarding local ministries as well. In the case of the Custody, for example, he is credited with securing the appointment of friar Diego da Sanseverino as *custos* of the Holy Land in 1628, a controversial move that opened the Custody to the influence of a reformed Franciscan tradition, known as the *Riformati*, for the first time.[4] As Chapter 6 will show, this appointment was not well received by the Franciscan brothers who were traditionally in charge, and it had lasting consequences for the internal administration of the Custody. Other early initiatives by Ingoli that would prove consequential to the ministry of the brothers of the Holy Land included the establishment of a printing press in 1626 dedicated to the production of missionary texts (dictionaries, alphabets, catechisms, preaching aids) and the Collegio Urbano in Rome. The College continues to operate today as a central training ground for indigenous missionaries.[5] Other developments that would have long-term consequences for the Custody included the introduction of new officials to represent the authority of the Congregation in the field, notably the apostolic vicar (1650). All of these initiatives reflected the Congregation's preoccupation with conversion as a critical mechanism for the expansion of the Catholic tradition and as a central function of its far-flung clerical body.

With this broad description of its organization and mandate in mind, we turn to examine the Congregation's relationship with the Custody after 1622. The voluminous holdings on the Custody in the archives show that the venerable pilgrimage institution was a concern of the papal body

---

[4] Paolo Pieraccini discusses this intervention in *The Franciscan Custody of the Holy Land in Cyprus: Its Educational, Pastoral and Charitable Work and Support for the Maronite Community* (Jerusalem: Terra Santa, 2013). See, in particular, the discussion in ft. 64.

[5] On Ingoli's influence, see the excellent entry of Giovanni Pizzorusso in *Dizionario biografico degli Italiani* 62 (2004), www.treccani.it/enciclopedia/francesco-ingoli_%28Dizionario-Biografico%29/. On the general organization of the College and the press, see, for example, Metzler, "Foundation under Gregory XV."

from the earliest days of its establishment. Particularly important for charting the growth of papal influence in the Custody is the *scritture*, the multivolume collection of reports, letters, financial documents sent from the Custody to the Congregation, and the *Acta*, which contain the decisions of the papal body along with an array of other communications. These documents reveal a fledgling institution that was making its authority felt in the affairs of the Custody from early on. Since many of the documents useful for tracing papal authority have already received close attention in other chapters, this chapter will not delve into the same detail in order to avoid unnecessary repetition. Rather, our objective here is to strike a balance between highlighting some of the more revealing evidence of papal influence in its relations with the friars and providing a broader historical context within which to interpret their meaning. At the same time, it is beyond the capacity of this investigation to probe the many dimensions of the Congregation's involvement in the affairs of the Custody for a simple reason: its engagement was broad, complex, flexible, and mutable. Given the visibility of the Congregation in the records of the Custody, however, and its evident influence, it is important that it be included in our broader investigation. Thankfully, the excellent quality and growing body of scholarship exploring many dimensions of the Congregation's relations with the Custody give us some leeway to focus upon evidence that speaks more specifically to its interest in reducing the independence of the Franciscan brothers. The Congregation's steady erosion of the jurisdiction of the friars after 1622 is one of our first indications that it had grand ambitions for the Holy Land. Some of the strategies it employed included asserting papal right of approval of the *custos*, regularized reporting procedures, the promotion of other missionary orders, and mediation. Each of these strategies will be discussed in turn.

5.1.2 The *Custos* and Papal Scrutiny

For the brothers of the Holy land, one early indication of a more interventionist – and scrutinizing – papacy was a decree issued on June 23, 1622. The decree, which was issued almost immediately upon the establishment of the new body, put the many religious missionary orders on notice. Responding to a petition sent by the Franciscan Minister General regarding the appointment of religious officials, the cardinals decreed that newly appointed religious officials headed for work on a mission must first visit the Congregation for examination and receive its approval, risking deprivation of office if they failed to do so.[6] One should not be surprised to find that the Minister General of the Franciscan Order was the stated recipient of this directive. Much like the other mendicant traditions, the Franciscans had enjoyed significant independence in the management of their many missions since the Order's foundation in the thirteenth century. This independence was essentially a pragmatic one. For all that the medieval papacy held universalist ambitions, it fully recognized the logistical challenges inherent in managing Catholic institutions that operated in regions outside its direct jurisdiction.[7] The mendicant orders including the Franciscans were especially useful in this regard because they embraced an evangelical model of spirituality that privileged a mobile ministry. Moreover, they developed reputations early on for producing highly trained and effective preachers and confessors. For these and other reasons they were well situated to assume the burden of mission in the Church, a role that they were still actively fulfilling in the eastern regions of the Mediterranean during the Early Modern Period.[8]

The decree of 1622, however, was one of many new directives signaling a shift in papal views on mission by this time. In particular, the papacy had come to view the independence of the older missionary traditions as a significant barrier to the consolidation of its authority over an increasingly global Catholic institution. The Custody experienced the impact of this directive early on when a new *custos* was appointed in 1623 and was forced to travel to Rome. The election of the *custos* was a cherished privilege of the Franciscan order, and since 1430, so was the specific responsibility of the General Chapter meetings of the Order, which took place every few years.[9] A broad survey of the clerics chosen as *custos*

---

[6] *Collectanae S. Congregationis de Propaganda Fide seu Decreta Instructiones Rescripta pro apostolicis Missionibus* (Rome: ex typographia polyglotta s.c. propaganda fide, 1907), 5. "Quod Generales et alii Superiores Regularium religiosos sibi subditos quos ad propagandandam fidem in quascumque mundi partes mittere contingent, Sacrae Congni prius nominent, ad hoc ut priusquam mittantur ab eadem examinentur et approbentur."

[7] See, for example, Jean Richard, *La papauté et les missions d'Orient au Moyen-Age (XIII–IVème siècle)* (Rome: Ecole Française de Rome, 1977); and more recently, Amanda Powers, "Going among the Infidels: The Mendicant Orders and Louis IX's First Mediterranean Campaign," *Mediterranean Historical Review* 25 (2011): 187–202.

[8] See, for example, Anton Molnar, *Le Saint-Siège, Raguse et les missions Catholiques de la Ongrie ottoman (1572–1647)* (Budapest: METEM, 2007); and Ana Sekulic, "Conversion of the Landscape: Environment and Religious Politics in an Early Modern Ottoman Town," PhD diss., Princeton University, 2020.

[9] In the eighteenth century, the election became the responsibility of the Minister General and the council of *diffinitors*.

during the sixteenth and seventeenth centuries suggests that the central administration of the Order took this responsibility seriously, selecting men who were already highly experienced administrators in their own communities and trained in theology and preaching. However, other skills were required as well.[10] We can gain some insight into the ponderings of Franciscan officials from the treatise written by Mariano Morone da Maleo and published in 1669.[11] A former *custos* of the Holy Land, Morone devoted one section on the selection of friars for service. That he presided during a particularly turbulent time in the Holy Land family may help to explain some of his more pointed observations, but it also highlights the wealth of administrative experience among the leaders of the community, experience that informed their oversight of the Custody. Morone begins by insisting that only the "best friars," whether lay or clerical, should go to work in "Christianità" because they would be working with "all nations" of the world. They needed to be of good character, have some language training, and also be in good health because the living conditions were arduous.

Morone emphasizes that some places were "fatal to those who arrive with bad eyes, limbs" or other health issues.[12] Friars also required a strong digestive system ("buon stomaco") to adapt to the local diet. In addition to concerns about moral worthiness and physical health, Morone tasked administrators with sourcing skills that were essential for the good operations of the Custody. It was particularly important, he writes, to ensure that the community could provide preaching in multiple languages. Clerics who were highly educated and experienced administrators were especially valued since these men would be recruited to serve on the inner council, as guardians of convents, and in other important administrative offices. These officials would work closely with the *custos* on an array of important matters. Other highly valued offices included those of confessor and chaplain since these had to do with the pastoral ministry of the friars as well as the performance of the liturgical rites for the pilgrimage.

---

[10] Several also rose to high Franciscan office, including Francesco Maria Rhini, who followed his term as *custos* (1664–1669) with that of Minister General of the Order (1670–1674).

[11] Mariano Morone da Maleo, *Terra Santa Nuovamente Illustrata dal P. Fr. Mariano Morone da Maleo* (Piacenza: Stampa Ducale di Giovanni Barachi, 1669).

[12] Morone, *Terra Santa*, 51. "... anzi fatali à chi patisce mal d'occhi, di gambe, di crepatura."

The most important role was that of *custos*, and for this reason Morone insisted that it should only be handed to well-experienced administrators. The demands upon this office were enormous, requiring the management of a diverse Franciscan body in a region that posed significant challenges to the daily operations of the mission, politically as well as financially. Good judgment was essential since the *custos* played a critical role in securing worthy friars and assigning them to appropriate offices. The weight of choosing well applied to the consideration of lay friars as well as clerics, reflecting the practical challenges involved in supporting a Catholic institution that lay at a significant distance from Europe and that needed to support a busy local ministry. Morone advised the future *custos*, for example, to seek out not only "good theologians and preachers" but also a good organist, woodworkers, doctors, bakers, cooks, tailors, and shoemakers among others.[13]

As the above suggests, the selection of the *custos* was of particular concern. Perhaps for this reason the central administration of the Franciscan order took this responsibility seriously. In fact, the Congregation does not seem to have rejected any of their nominations for the office during the period of this investigation, though it is certainly true that it was less than pleased with the performance of some while in office. The Congregation did, however, begin to rigorously enforce their right of approval as of 1622, and we know of at least one *custos* who fell afoul of the Congregation by testing their resolve. Curiously, the friar in question was none other than Eusebio Valles (1658–1661), the Milanese *custos* who found his authority challenged by badly behaved French pilgrims in Chapter 4. Following his appointment in 1658, Valles made the mistake of traveling directly to the Holy land in clear violation of the directives of the Congregation.[14] A flurry of letters between Valles and the Congregation after this time reveals a papal body that was not about to be ignored and a new *custos* who was doing his best to avoid returning to Rome to face it. In one letter, the Congregation threatened him with removal if he did not return immediately. Valles responded with apologies but also insisted that his actions were guided by the best interests of the Custody, an institution that was in a desperate fiscal situation and required an immediate delivery of alms from the king of Spain. That it took several months before Valles finally acquiesced and returned to Rome is perhaps less surprising than the fact that the Congregation did

---

[13] Morone, *Terra Santa*, 54.
[14] See Chapter 2.

not move to replace him earlier. However, it may have found his excuses reasonable. The Custody was truly in difficult shape at this time, wracked by internal conflicts and financial scandal. Without a *custos* in place as well, the institution was struggling. Valles also claimed a lengthy illness that prevented him from responding immediately to the letters of the Congregation and which also delayed his journey back to Europe. In a letter dated October 18, 1658, for example, Valles mentions that he had been "sick in bed for over forty-five days, weak with a fever and unable to move."[15] Perhaps more important to the Congregation, however, was the fact that Valles clearly had powerful supporters who vouched for the urgency of delivering alms. His letter included testimonials from the Grand Master of the Order of Malta, friar Antonio del Castillo, who was the commissioner general of the Holy Land, and Francesco della Madre di Dios, the general procurator of the Holy Land. These officials all played a role in the traffic of alms in and out of Jerusalem.

5.1.3 *Instructions and Reports*

The importance of having an obedient and effective cleric in charge of the Custody explains the implementation of other measures as well after 1622 that were clearly aimed at ensuring closer direction over the operations of the administration. These included the provision of instructions and the requirement of outgoing reports. The first mention of instructions involving the Custody appear in the *acta*, which include a request for instructions from the newly appointed *custos* in 1623. Instructions (*istrucciones*) were by no means a new mechanism of papal authority when adopted by the Congregation. However, the fledging body embraced it with alacrity and it quickly became a distinguishing feature of its engagement with the far-flung institutions under its jurisdiction. Instructions were essentially directives given by the Congregation and intended for implementation by the local administration. Some were quite general in nature, while others were quite specific, detailing policies and practices tailored to address particular local situations. The instructions issued to the new Franciscan *custos* in 1628, for example, included directives for pacifying ongoing jurisdictional conflicts with the

---

[15] For the correspondence, see APF SC TS 1, ff. 248–265. "... 45 giorni fa in questa infermaria, sopra un letto, infermo di febre, et almente privo di forze, e destrutto, che non posso muovere altro."

Capuchins. It also requested that the friars organize festivities in the Custody to go in tandem with those organized in Rome for the upcoming Jubiliee.[16]

As this example suggests, instructions communicated the interests of the Congregation, a function that also makes them useful as historical windows into the particular concerns of the institution vis-à-vis the Custody. But along with the final report, they were also a means of controlling the office of *custos*, in particular, since it was this official's responsibility to ensure that the directives were followed. Adding another important layer of scrutiny over the office of *custos* was the triennial report. Reports, like instructions, were not new instruments. A few survive from the first decade of the seventeenth century, a fact that suggests they were required during the Clementine Congregation, the predecessor to the Congregation of the Propaganda Fide.[17] The Congregation of the Propaganda Fide, however, made the report a routinized part of the responsibilities of the *custos*, who was expected to submit it sometime before the end of his tenure in office. Reports were often more detailed than the typical letters exchanged with the Congregation since their purpose was to provide an overview of the state of the Custody. Gathering information was of critical importance to members of the Congregation, who relied upon the local expertise of missionary institutions to develop its policies and strategies.[18] In some cases, we find reports issued in the midst of an administration, often responding to especially challenging problems facing the Custody.

Whether issued at the end of a term or earlier on, reports tended to follow a similar format, a fact that suggests the officials of the Congregation were expecting certain kinds of information. We should note, to begin with, that they were quite pragmatic documents, concerned with analyzing the present circumstances of the Custody (political,

---

[16] Leonhard Lemmens, ed., *Acta S. Congregationis de propaganda Fide pro Terra Sancta*, vol. 1 (Rome: Collegio di S. Bonaventura, 1921), 49–50.

[17] See the report of Francesco Manerba to Clement VIII (1604) in Lemmens, ed., *Acta*, vol. 1, 3.

[18] On the importance of local reports, see, for example, Metzler, "Origines." An important point for comparison would be the Venetian *relazione*, diplomatic reports that may have informed the nature of these reports as well. On the *relazione*, see, in particular, the work of Filippo de Vivo, including "How to Read Venetian relazioni," *Renaissance and Reformation/Renaissance et Réforme*, Special Issue, "Things Not Easily Believed: Introducing the Early Modern Relation," ed. Thomas Cohen and Germaine Warkentin (2011): 25–59; and *Information and Communication in Venice: Rethinking Early Modern Politics* (Oxford: Oxford University Press, 2007).

religious, economic) and its operations. Recent political events and disputes with other Christian communities, for example, were common elements, especially when these issues impacted the orderly operations of the Custody. The Congregation also expected to hear about the diverse facets of the Franciscan ministry, in particular, maintenance of chapels and shrines and, increasingly, efforts at conversion. A report sent by Eusebio Valles in January 1661 serves as a typical example. Valles wrote the report eighteen months into his term – roughly halfway. He begins with recent events including the death of the Greek Orthodox Patriarch of Jerusalem and complaints about the excessive fiscal demands (*avania*) made by the new Bassa and *kadi* of the city upon the Custody. Valles also assured the Congregation that the Franciscan family was much more peaceful now that it was under his direction, before moving on to discuss evidence of their spiritual progress among local Christians. He was especially proud of the establishment of a school in the convent in Bethlehem, where they taught the "sons of our Catholics to speak, read and write French." Valles then addressed the problem of alms, or rather the lack of alms, noting that they had been delayed. As the Congregation knows, he says, the Holy Places are maintained "with these two things, with good religious and with alms, without which they cannot be preserved."[19]

In this report, Valles touched upon local politics, the economy of the mission, internal order, and evangelization. Other surviving ones show that the outgoing *custos* understood full well that his success was defined in part through the achievement of directives that were important to the Congregation. The instructions and the report, in other words, set the frame for the administrative tenure of the *custos*, providing a greater degree of direction from and accountability to the papacy than was the case prior to the establishment of the Congregation. That the friars do not seem to have been particularly resistant to these formal mechanisms may suggest that they found them useful for legitimizing their jurisdiction in the Custody. Indeed, the friars were facing serious challenges to their jurisdiction from new missionary orders throughout much of the seventeenth century, and so these signs of papal recognition must have seemed all the more valuable. But just as importantly, the report offered the friars a designated space in which to craft their own narratives of their tenure – whether to promote their endeavours as efficacious or, when necessary, to justify decisions that were likely to meet with papal criticism. Finally, the

---

[19] APF SC Terra Santa, I (January 27, 1661), ff. 309–311.

report enabled friars to highlight their local expertise by mentioning, for example, their relations with local officials and the heads of other religious communities and knowledge of local structures of authority.

Another report, this time from the outgoing *custos* Francesco di S. Floro in 1697, reveals these three functions at work simultaneously.[20] S. Floro uses his to celebrate signs of success as well as some of the more serious challenges. Successes included the establishment of a school for Maronites on Mount Lebanon. Challenges numbered the recent sacking of a Franciscan convent in Nazareth as well as tension with Maronite leaders over pastoral rights. Suffering was a regular motif in Franciscan reports, useful for highlighting the demands of the work and the selflessness of the brothers. The issue involving Maronite leaders, however, seems to have been a particularly delicate one because S. Floro was clearly on the defense and concerned that it would reflect badly on the ministry of the friars. His report responded directly, in particular, to recent accusations that they had abused their jurisdiction. He may have been responding to a letter sent to the Congregation by the Maronite Catholic Patriarch of Antioch months earlier, though several letters in the archives testify to tension between the communities at this time over spiritual jurisdiction. In the letter, which is dated November 20, 1695, the Patriarch accused the friars of deliberately interfering in the pastoral ministry of the Maronite priests. The friars wished to "deprive [the priests] of their jurisdiction" by forbidding the observance of their rites, and in doing so they were sowing "dissension and discord" in the Maronite community. He accused them in particular of trying to persuade women to disavow their husbands, of "renaming" women, blocking marriages, and even threatening to excommunicate Maronites living in Jerusalem "who do not observe their rites."[21] After listing these various transgressions, the Patriarch asked the Congregation to intervene on their behalf and inform the friars that they could not "interfere in the matters

---

[20] Lemmens, ed., *Acta*, vol. 1, 291–294. It is dated 1697. The original is in APF CG 18. XII.1696 nr. 15, f. 260v.

[21] Lemmens, ed., *Acta*, vol. 1, 289. The full passage is the following: "che i medesimi pretendono di privare i parochi marroniti dei loro dritti, di prohibere l'osservanza dei riti loro e che seminano dissensioni e discordie tra li medesimi e i loro sudditi; inoltre che fanno maritare zitelle di nove e dieci anni, che persuadono le donne a repudiare i loro mariti, che ribatezzano, che impediscono i matrimonii, servendosi del braccio turchesco; che in Gierusalemme scommunicano chi non segue il rito loro; che non vogliono, che si nominino più Marroniti, che hanno fatto dichiarare dai Turchi, che i *Marroniti di Gierusalemme non sono sudditi del loro patriarca, ma del guardiano di Terra Santa.*

of the Maronite nation with regards to their rites or the authority of their priests," and, in particular, in their marriages.[22] Though S. Floro does not engage in a point by point response, he clearly took the accusations of the Patriarch seriously and insisted that they were false. To bolster his defense, he went even further by attaching a letter signed by other leaders of the Maronite community in support of the ministry friars.

By attaching this letter, S. Floro strengthened the Franciscan case in two important ways. Firstly, it offered eyewitness testimony refuting the earlier complaints from the Maronite Patriarch. Secondly, it demonstrated the local expertise of the brothers by highlighting their imbrication in local networks of authority, in this case their ties with members of the Maronite community. One finds other Franciscan *custos* tailoring their responses to protect as well as promote the orderly nature and productivity of their own administrations and highlight their local expertise and connections. In other words, reports and instructions were also useful for protecting Franciscan jurisdiction. Still, these mechanisms also demonstrate the Congregation's intent to play a more active role in the affairs of the Custody by scrutinizing the office of *custos* and directing the ministry of the friars on the ground. The Congregation relied upon two other mechanisms as well for expanding its jurisdiction locally: the admission of new missionary orders and the mediation of disputes. These mechanisms also intentionally trampled upon the traditional jurisdiction of the friars but in ways that were even more concerning. Both served the objectives of a papal body intent upon creating a more dependent and pliant Franciscan brotherhood in the Holy Land.

5.1.4 *The New Missionary Orders*

As Rafael Moya has argued, introducing new missions was a tried and true strategy of the Congregation for expanding its reach locally at the expense of well-established spiritual communities. Indeed, it was a general directive of the Congregation to reduce the monopolies of established Catholic jurisdictions, whether it took the form of the Patronato Real of the Iberian monarchs in the New World or a locally influential mendicant

---

[22] Lemmens, ed., *Acta*, vol. 1, 289. "Supplica pertanto questa S.C., a dar ordine, che i sudetti padri non s'ingeriscono nelle cose della natione marronita nè quanto ai riti, nè quanto ai diritti degl'ecclesiastici come nè anco nei matrimonii."

institution.[23] From the perspective of the Congregation, the Custody was one such spiritual monopoly because it operated largely independently of papal administration throughout the first three centuries of its history. This tradition of independent governance posed a significant barrier to papal influence in the Holy Land in a number of ways, but in particular because the Franciscan family was quite comfortable exercising its autonomy and was well-connected and knowledgeable about local structures of authority. For centuries, it had used this expertise to expand the spiritual, liturgical, and material reach of the Catholic Church in the region. And as earlier chapters have also demonstrated, the brothers were formidable advocates of the Custody in European political circles, having cultivated close ties with a broad array of European powers over time. For these reasons among others, the friars represented a valuable local proxy for papal interests in the region by the seventeenth century. For these reasons as well, the brothers also represented a potential barrier to the expansion of papal influence because they were the only permanent local representatives of the Catholic Church until 1622.

French interest in planting French missionaries in the Custody thus offered the papacy an opportunity to break the long-standing spiritual monopoly of the Order of the Friars Minor and, in doing so, to extend its influence across the Holy Land. The new orders expanded papal influence in three important ways: Firstly, by limiting the legal and spiritual jurisdiction of the Franciscans, secondly, by introducing men who were dependent upon the authority of the Congregation for their missions, and thirdly, by giving the papacy broader access on the ground in the Holy Land through the profusion of new clerics. As discussed in Chapter 4, the introduction of the new orders disrupted the spiritual monopoly of the friars in a number of ways, in particular with regard to the provision of pastoral care to the merchant colonies and clerical discipline. What also made the missionaries useful was their greater dependence upon papal authority. It is important to note, to begin with, that the new orders required papal permission as well as that of the Ottoman sultan to establish within the boundaries of the Custody. The Congregation also defined the nature of their engagement. As we saw in the letter issued in 1622, for example, which announced the introduction of the new orders, the Congregation determined *where* they could establish (the five cities) and *what* spiritual role they could play (pastoral care,

---

[23] Rafael Moya, "Hacia una participación fructuosa de los religiosos en las misiones de Propaganda," *Sacrae Congregationis* I, 439–464.

evangelization). From the correspondence of the many disputes that erupted between the Observants and the missionaries after this time, it is also clear that the Congregation was in the regular business of renegotiating the privileges of the missionaries. The Capuchins, Jesuits, and Carmelites all benefited, in particular, from papal permission to establish new convents and hospices outside the original five-city mandate. As a final example, we may recall from a rather heated dispute in the 1670s that it was the Congregation that ultimately allowed the Jesuit chaplains attached to the consul of Aleppo to provide pastoral services to local French merchants despite Franciscan opposition.[24]

The French missionaries were well aware that the nature and success of their enterprises in the Holy Land depended significantly upon good relations with the Congregation, and this is one of the reasons why one finds them in close contact with the papal body throughout the seventeenth century. From the perspective of the Congregation, their dependence made them a pliable clerical body or at least one that was much more receptive to its directives. But just as importantly, the new missions also offered the Congregation a larger, more diverse, and dispersed clerical footprint in the Custody after 1622. To be sure, the friars remained a much larger presence throughout the seventeenth century, but the number of French missionaries did increase over time. According to Bernard Heyberger, the Capuchins were by far the largest of the two new orders, at their peak numbering in the range of twenty members. The Jesuits and Carmelites were smaller missions. By the 1670s, the Jesuit presence included eight priests and four *coadjuteurs* and the discalced Carmelites six priests and two lay brothers.[25] Though smaller in number, however, these communities operated independently of Franciscan authority in diverse contexts within the Holy Land. The French missionaries thus collectively broadened and diversified the base of papal engagement on the ground in the Holy Land, offering the Congregation alternative conduits of information and local networks useful for expanding its spiritual influence locally.

---

[24] See Chapter 4.
[25] Heyberger, *Les Chrétiens*, 290–292. He also cites Eugene Roger, who claims that there were no more than 110 Catholic religious in the Custody during his time in the Custody (1640s) across all institutions. Eugene Roger, *La Terre Sainte our Description Topographique tres-particuliere des saints Lieux & de la Terre de Promission* (Paris: Antoine Bertie, 1664), 378–380.

5.1.5 Mediation

Thus far we have touched upon the greater scrutiny being paid to the *custos* and the appointment of new missionaries as mechanisms for expanding the reach of the papacy in the Custody. While these mechanisms fulfilled multiple functions, one shared intent was to make the Franciscan brothers more responsive to, and dependent upon, papal jurisdiction while expanding the local influence of the Congregation. No less important for understanding the steady expansion of papal authority in the Custody was its assertion of its role as mediator of ecclesiastical disputes. As discussed earlier, the Congregation mediated numerous disputes involving the friars, the French monarchy, and the French missionaries between 1622 and 1700.

However, these were by no means the only ones because the friars worked within a complex and shifting matrix of relations in the Holy Land and these also at times produced conflicts that involved the Congregation. It is possible that the loss of much of the central archives of the Custody has artificially obscured an active mediating role by the papacy in the affairs of the Custody prior to the seventeenth century. However, when considered alongside relevant sources that survive for the earlier period, including the sixteenth century correspondence of the Venetian ambassadors to the Ottoman Porte and the Spanish monarchy, it does seem quite clear that the foundation of the Congregation marked a much more interventionist role for the papacy in the affairs of the Custody, including many of its disputes.

Indeed, it is difficult to overstate the rapidity with which the Propaganda Fide constructed a central mediating role for itself after 1622, assuming a responsibility that until this time had been most commonly fulfilled by the central administration of the Franciscan order in Rome. Given that the early modern friars had conflicts with a wide array of institutions, officials, and communities throughout the seventeenth century, the Congregation was a very busy mediator indeed. During the first decade of its existence alone (1622–1632), for example, the Propaganda Fide was directly engaged in mediating disputes involving the friars with a diverse array of authorities as well as local communities. The nature of these conflicts varied, though most concerned disputes over pastoral duties, spiritual jurisdiction, and office-holding.

Looking specifically at the correspondence for the year 1624, for example, we find the friars protesting the recent (and controversial) appointment of the French consul Jean Lempereur to Jerusalem,[26] along with numerous complaints about Capuchin and Jesuit missionaries. These disputes were by no means the extent of their relations with the Congregation at this time. In the same year, the friars also consulted regularly with the Congregation about the delegation led by friar Jacques de Vendôme, the Franciscan guardian of Nazareth, to discuss the possibility of union with the patriarchs of the Armenian and Greek Orthodox.[27] Disputes nevertheless comprised a significant portion of the business involving the friars with the papal body in 1624 just as they did throughout the seventeenth century.

That the friars voluntarily sought out the intervention of the Congregation in many of these cases suggests that they were willing to recognize its jurisdiction, especially when they perceived a threat to their own. Nor were the friars alone as we can see from the parade of European ambassadors, prelates, heads of religious orders, leaders of local Christian communities as well as Ottoman officials seeking the attention of the papal body in matters pertaining to the Custody and its Franciscan administrators. One could argue that willingness of the brothers to accept its role as a mediator reflected a typical early modern sensibility regarding authority since these men operated in a political and religious world that was already crowded with competing jurisdictions. As administrators of an institution imbricated in Ottoman and European structures of authority, they could (and usually did) call upon a multiplicity of authorities depending upon the issue at hand, including not only the local *kadi* and the *mufti* but also the *Pascha* (governor) of Damascus or officials attached to the *divan* (imperial council) at the Ottoman Porte. Close by and useful as well were the European consuls in the port cities and ambassadors at the Porte. And in Europe as well, the friars comfortably turned to their Minister General, European powers, and ecclesiastical officials, all depending upon the nature of the issue. That the friars embraced the Congregation as another in a multitude of useful jurisdictions is thus in itself typically early modern behaviour. But in doing so, they were also setting precedents that facilitated the expansion of papal influence in the Custody, one case at a time.

We can see this creeping influence through the Congregation's management of the many fraternal disputes that wracked the Franciscan

---

[26] Lemmens, ed., *Acta*, vol. I, 30. The original is found in APF CG 22 1624, nr. 4, f. 84v.
[27] Lemmens, ed., *Acta*, vol. I, 30. The original document is found in APF CG 3 XII. 1624, nr. 12.

family during the course of the seventeenth century. Indeed, the alacrity with which disgruntled friars turned to the Congregation to air their fraternal grievances is striking. Whether secular or other ecclesiastical, the leadership of the regular orders never looked kindly on members who went outside their own Order for the resolution of internal conflicts because they considered them family matters and ignoble signs of disorder. During the seventeenth century, however, several brothers did just that.[28] Some of these conflicts were fueled by divisions between nations (French, Spanish, Italian) and received attention in Chapter 4. Others, which are the focus of Chapter 6, responded to differences over Franciscan reform (*Riformati*, Recollect, regular Observance). In each case, certain friars called upon the Congregation to mediate an internal conflict with the hopes of righting a perceived wrong and restoring order. In doing so, however, they opened the door to greater papal influence in the administration of the Custody. A good example concerns an intense dispute that rocked the Franciscan family between 1654 and 1656. The slippery and contested nature of the early modern sources suggests that there were several layers to the conflict, a number of which receive more attention in Chapter 6. On the surface, the dispute involved charges of maladministration against then *custos* Mariano Morone da Maleo, the author of the treatise discussed earlier. The accusations were numerous and varied, though among the most serious was that of fiscal malfeasance. In particular, he was accused of failing to keep good records of alms donations as well as expenses, accusations that he vociferously denied. Though Morone would go on to complete his second term in office, finally leaving Jerusalem for Europe in 1657, the Congregation used the dispute to initiate a broad ranging and thorough investigation of the finances of the Custody, first demanding the production of a full inventory of the possessions of the Custody in 1654 and then later mandating the regular submission of alms registers by the commissioners of the Holy Land to the Congregation. One finds these registers in the *scritture*, the earliest dating to the year 1654/1655, the time of the dispute.[29]

The Minister General also wrote letters about the controversy, one indication that the head of the Franciscan order remained an important and influential arbiter in the affairs of the Custody. In this case, however,

---

[28] See, for example, Megan C. Armstrong, "Spiritual Reform, Mendicant Autonomy, and State Formation: French Franciscan Disputes before the Parlement of Paris, 1500–1600," *French Historical Studies* 25 (2002): 505–530.

[29] On this dispute, see Chapter 5.

the Congregation emerged as the central mediator, a role that ultimately saw its influence increase over the internal administration of the Custody especially with regard to financial matters. In a similar way, the papacy's mediation of their disputes with the French missionaries after 1622 served to expand papal influence in the administration on a case by case basis because each intervention increasingly defined the nature and extent of their jurisdiction while asserting the Congregation as the determining authority. We should note that the influence of the Congregation as a mediator rested upon its foundation as an arm of papal authority, which it wielded principally through the medium of correspondence and that came to serve as an ever-building body of missionary jurisprudence. Pizzorusso argues that the *scritture* should be regarded as a central mechanism of an emergent papal "imperial" bureaucracy, providing a critical legal as well as political connective tissue between Rome and the innumerable Catholic institutions that lay well outside the immediate sphere of influence of the See. Important to understanding this function is that these letters were *de natura* expressions of papal authority because the papal bull *Inscrutabili* recognized the Congregation as its vehicle. Whether this authority was expressed in the form of letters, or instructions, or formal decrees, *every* communication of the Congregation carried the weight of papal authority. The Congregation was, in other words, not only an administrative but also a juridical body, one that used its decision-making in the Franciscan disputes to expand the scope of its jurisdiction. And as mentioned already, it did so on a case by case basis, setting precedents that then came to shape the operations of the Custody over time as well as relations between the two institutions.

The importance of the *scritture* for expanding papal influence lay also in its promise of a legal history of relations with the missionary orders. As Pizzorusso suggests, the *scritture* from the start was envisioned as central to the construction of a "missionary jurisprudence," one developed over time through the routine bureaucratic interactions of the Congregation and the missionaries in the field. These interactions, contained in reports, letters, and other forms, could be used to develop policies and protocols that could be applied more universally within the Catholic tradition as well as to address more regionally and culturally specific practices and concerns. The mediation of disputes in the Custody served these objectives, providing an evolving body of decisions that could be used as precedents in later decision-making to sharpen and/or alter existing jurisdictions and authorities. During the disputes involving the Capuchins and the friars between 1623 and 1628, for example, we notice that, letter by letter, the Congregation and friars worked to articulate their respective spheres of authority in the Custody as well as those of the missionaries. The Instructions issued in 1628 point to a growing clarity about the geographic organization of the missions and their mandates by this time, clarity that was clearly being demanded by the religious orders as well as the Congregation. Just as importantly, the friars as well as the missionaries would return to previous decisions made by the Congregation when they felt their jurisdiction was threatened. In fact, it was for this purpose among others that the friars kept an extensive register of these decisions at their friary beginning in the 1670s. The *Registro de lettere scritte al nostro Sommo Pontefice alla sacra congregatione de propaganda fide co'ad altri Prelati, cosi occidentati, come Orientali per si bisogni di Terra Santa e per l'aumento della nostra santa fede* is a remarkable collection of documents, providing copies of letters as well as summaries of decisions made by a range of officials but in particular the Propaganda Fide. It was compiled in 1673 under the direction of then *custos* Teofilo Testa de Nola. The earliest document is a *memoriale* issued by Clement X on August 28, 1670, which granted them permission to perform the following rites: "the office of Pentecost in S. Salvatore, the office of the Resurrection in the Holy Sepulcher, the office of the Nativity in Bethlehem, and the office of the Annunciation in the holy house of Nazareth."[30] This particular decree concerned liturgical rites, but the register as a whole reveals the broad reach of the Congregation's influence in the Custody by this time, touching on matters ranging from pastoral care to the renovation of religious buildings and the conversion of Eastern Christians.

As the *Registro* makes clear, many if not all of the decisions of the Congregation regarding the Custody were responses to specific points of contention between the friars and other parties. However, the cumulative impact of individual decisions led to a significant rethinking and reshaping of the nature of the Franciscan ministry and jurisdiction in the Custody. But as the *Registro* also suggests, this was a negotiated process, one that hinged upon Franciscan willingness to recognize the jurisdiction of the Congregation. This is not to say that the friars always welcomed the mediation of the Congregation let alone its routine intervention in their affairs. Indeed, as we saw in the disputes involving the French

---

[30] Arch. Custodia terrae sanctae. *Registro de lettere scritte al nostro Sommo Pontefice alla sacra congregatione de propaganda fide co'ad altri Prelati, cosi occidentati, come Orientali per si bisogni di Terra Santa e per l'aumento della nostra santa fede.* (September 12, 1673), 3.

missionaries discussed in Chapter 4, the friars protested any "innovations" repeatedly and vigorously, brandishing their traditional privileges in defense of the status quo. And, in many instances, they were successful. While the friars found ways to negotiate with the Congregation and mitigate some of its more painful decisions, however, they could not have easily ignored its authority because of the expansive nature of papal jurisdiction. As devout Catholics, the brothers recognized the pope as the supreme head of their tradition. Moreover, the Custody, inasmuch as it was regulated by Islamic law, was no less subject to canon law. Finally, the friars also benefited from having good relations with the Congregation. While the friars found their former monopoly of pastoral rites irreparably broken after 1622, the Congregation consistently protected Franciscan jurisdiction over the Custody and its spiritual monopoly in the most important spiritual centers, the holy cities of Jerusalem, Bethlehem, and Nazareth. Indeed, it is worth repeating that the Franciscans remained the single most influential religious order in the Custody throughout the Early Modern Period and the most important representative of the Catholic Church in its dealings with Ottoman authority. Still, little by little, the friars, through recognizing the mediating role of the Congregation, became complicit in expanding and shaping its authority within the Custody on a case by case basis, often at the expense of its own autonomy.

As of 1622, the Franciscan brothers of the Custody thus faced a persistent and ultimately successful effort on the part of the Congregation to expand its influence over their administration. It came in the form of new procedures, new missionaries, and also the mediation of disputes. The question remains now to ask about the Custody's significance in the objectives of the papal body, since it is clear from its frequent interventions that the Congregation considered the pilgrimage institution very important indeed. With a specific eye to our interest in the Holy Land as a source of spiritual legitimacy, the remaining discussion situations their relations in the contemporary religious and political context that shaped the emergence of the Congregation as a new arm of papal administration. This era of change, as we shall see, added new importance to papal engagement in the Holy Land because of its global significance as a shared sacred landscape and site of pilgrimage, and a papal sacred history in which the possession of the Holy Places and conversion of Eastern Christians were important elements in a broader plan of spiritual restoration and renewal. These intersecting contexts invested the early modern Holy land with heightened importance as a source of legitimacy, one that was useful for an ancient institution struggling to reassert itself as a powerful Christian leader by the middle of the sixteenth century. It proved especially useful for casting the papacy as the legitimate head of a "restored" Christendom.

To help make sense of the ways in which these contexts privileged a role for the Custody in the construction of papal claims to Christian leadership, Sections 5.2 and 5.3 will consider the Holy Land from two vantage points – as a Catholic *frontier* and as a spiritual *center*. For the papacy, the Holy Land offered a critical and fruitful zone of encounter with its diverse local Christian populations as well as a Roman Christian past that grounded its claims to global Christian leadership. Indeed, it is when studied as both a Catholic *frontier* and a spiritual *center* as well that we can better understand the Congregation's efforts to create a more pliant and obedient Observant family in the Custody. The Congregation had little interest in removing the Franciscans from their custodial responsibilities because they were well established and well connected locally and had acquired privileges in the Holy Places that provided the Church with crucial sites of contact with the other faiths. The friars, in particular, offered the Church a well-established and influential mechanism for pursuing the conversion of other Christians, an objective that, alongside the protection of altars and the promotion of Latin devotion in the Holy Places, the papacy had long considered important for articulating its claims to Christian primacy.

5.2 A CATHOLIC *FRONTIER*

The Congregation's active role in promoting the Holy Land as a site of evangelization has already received significant attention from scholars, in particular, Bernard Heyberger and Felicita Tramontana.[31] These scholars have explored the organization of the new missions, modes of evangelization, as well as relations with the Congregation, particularly with regard to the conversion of the Eastern Christian traditions of the Holy Land. The intent of this section is not to reiterate the findings of this rich scholarship but rather to elucidate the Custody's importance within the global mandate of the Congregation for constructing its claims to Christian hegemony. With this objective in mind, the Holy Land offered the Church an immensely significant place of contact with the many

---

[31] Heyberger, *Les Chrétiens*; and Tramontana, *Passages of Faith*.

Eastern Christian traditions of the eastern Mediterranean because it was itself an extraordinarily diverse Christian landscape. The Holy Land was a Catholic frontier in this sense, serving as an important place to engage with other faiths in a region that lay outside the reach of the Western Church because it was under the jurisdiction of a Muslim regime.[32]

It was at the service of this mandate of global evangelization that we find the Congregation working to transform the friars into a missionary body from shortly after its establishment, an objective that the Congregation clearly believed required a more interventionist role in the affairs of the Custody. One of the most important indications of this intent emerges in the triennial reports of the *custos*, which devoted significant discussion to local evangelization. By the 1650s, a standard format for the report emerged that included a list of recent conversions. Individual names were rarely given but the *custos* included the religion of origin and location in the Holy Land. these documents also usually listed the establishment of schools, the number of students, and other signs of spiritual progress. In the report that he sent to the Congregation in 1697, for example, S. Floro informs the papal secretary that the Custody supported one hundred students between its three schools, a number that he says represented a significant increase over the previous five years. Five years earlier, there were only twelve students. S. Floro mentions, moreover, that the brothers converted five "renegade" Christian slaves and freed two Christian slaves.[33]

The introduction of schools is one of many indications of the growing influence of the Propaganda Fide in the Custody, reflecting its origins in Tridentine reform. It reveals, among other things, the Congregation's interest in conversion. For Tridentine reformers, education was a critical mechanism for ensuring orthodoxy but it was no less critical for the conversion of other believers. A preoccupation with education was one of the reasons why the Congregation worked closely with the Jesuits, a religious Order that enjoyed a reputation for the excellence of its schools in Europe and incorporated them in its missions.[34] The Congregation

---

[32] On the usage of "frontier" for thinking of early modern missions, see the introduction by Alison Forrestal and Seán Alexander Smith eds., *Frontiers of Mission: Perspectives on Early Modern Missionary Catholicism* (Leiden: Brill, 2016). On the Holy Land, see the following article in this collection, Megan C. Armstrong, "Spiritual Legitimization? Franciscan Competition over the Holy Land, 1517–1700," 159–180.

[33] Lemmens, *Acta* I, 289, and APF CG 18.XII.1696, n. 15, f. 260v.

[34] The scholarship on education in the context of Tridentine reform is vast. With more specific regard to its place in Jesuit conceptions of "mission," see for example, John O'Malley, "How the First Jesuits became involved in Education," *Saints or Devils*

began establishing its own colleges in many missionary zones by the end of the seventeenth century as well. In most cases, these were managed by members of diverse missionary orders including the Franciscans.

As David Rex Galindo shows, the friars played an important role overseeing a number of these institutions in New Spain during the eighteenth century.[35] Looking more specifically at the Custody, Jesuit and Capuchin missionaries established schools within a few years of their arrival, and the Franciscan brothers of the Holy Land were clearly under pressure from the Congregation to do the same. In addition to schools, the friars could point to other initiatives as well that demonstrated their diligence at evangelization. In particular, they were developing local Christian flocks. Bernard Heyberger argues that the establishment of an "Arab cure" in the Custody in 1630 was a particularly important (and early) initiative to reach out to local Christians. These cures were initially attached to Franciscan convents in Jerusalem and Bethlehem as well as other Franciscan residences. This responsibility was considered parallel to the pastoral care provided to European merchants, hence the name "Arab" cure, since most local Christians spoke Arabic. By 1692, the flock attached to the Custody had grown large enough to warrant the establishment of a coadjutor (teacher) to assist with the communities in Bethlehem and Jerusalem. A central intent of the Arab cure was to train the youth of local Eastern Christian communities in Christian doctrine and provide spiritual services for local converts.

Through the establishment of schools and the Arab cure, the friars were showing their willingness to take evangelization more seriously as one of their custodial responsibilities. In doing so, they were pushing back at the accusations of the French missionaries who had questioned their mastery of local languages and thus their ability to be effective missionaries. The French missionaries were not entirely wrong. Since pilgrimage was the central mandate of the Custody from the start, Franciscan administrators were much more concerned about ensuring the Custody had sufficient diversity in European languages. Like other Europeans based in the Levant, the friars relied upon the linguistic and diplomatic services of local dragoman to negotiate the complexities of local and imperial

---

Incarnate? Studies in Jesuit History (Leiden: Brill, 2013), 199–215, and Jennifer D. Selwyn, *A Paradise Inhabited by Devils: The Jesuits Civilizing Mission in Early Modern Naples* (Aldershot: Ashgate Publishing and the Jesuit Historical Institute, 2005).

[35] David Rex Galindo, *To Sin No More: Franciscans and Conversion in the Hispanic World, 1683–1830* (Stanford: Stanford University Press, 2017).

governance as well as on other business in the region.[36] However, the Custody always included some brothers who could work in local languages, above all Arabic. By the middle of the seventeenth century, moreover, the numbers of friars who could do so was clearly growing. The Franciscan *memoriale* (1680) mentioned in Chapter 4 is one of many documents that discuss linguistic training. Written by the Franciscan *custos* during the height of a dispute with the Capuchins of Aleppo, the tone of the *memoriale* is understandably defensive. After first asking (rather sarcastically) whether the Capuchins "possessed this gift of the holy spirit of knowing all the oriental languages," the *custos* ventured into a rather lengthy discussion of Franciscan knowledge of local languages. He notes that Arabic was the most important because it was the most common language in Syria and Egypt and then gave the names of eighteen friars trained in Arabic, a number that represented roughly 20 percent of the Franciscan family at the time. Moreover, some of these friars, like Paolo Bertonii, were versed in other languages, in his case Chaldean and Greek.[37] With regard to acquiring local languages, the friars could study them at schools established in Rama, Aleppo, and Bethlehem as well as at San Pietro Montorio in Rome. As a final point, the *custos* mentions that the Maltese brothers came to the Custody as Arab speakers.

Though evangelization would never supersede their duties with the pilgrimage, the brothers began playing a more active role in local conversion during the seventeenth century. Moreover, they enjoyed some success, though hardly the "thousands" reported converting in the New World by Spanish friars during the sixteenth century. Felicita Tramontana, who has looked closely at surviving baptismal records as well as the correspondence of the friars and local Ottoman records, suggests that the friars were particularly successful in Bethlehem.[38] Bethlehem was unusual in the context of the Holy Land because it was a mostly Christian city throughout the medieval and Early Modern Periods. Even more unusually, by the seventeenth century, the single largest of the Christian communities was the Latin (Catholic) because of recent conversions. Both Tramontana and Jacob Norris suggest that the

---

[36] See in particular the extensive body of work on the dragoman by Nathalie Rothman, most recently *The Dragoman Renaissance: Diplomatic Interpreters and the Routes of Orientalism* (Cornell University Press, 2021).
[37] APF CP 27, ff. 23–26.
[38] Felicita Tramontana, *Passages of Faith*, 92–94.

visible wealth and power of the Western Church may have been a central reason for its allure among local Christians. Many if not the majority of converts were relatively poor and may have hoped the Custody would provide an influential local protector as well as a source of economic patronage and charity.[39] In fact, many of the new Catholics had business ties with the Bethlehem community. Local Christians were involved in the production of Holy Land mementoes, served as interpreters, and provided domestic help among other tasks. But Tramontana suggests that these conversions may have also been triggered by the growing size of the local Greek Orthodox community in the wake of the Ottoman conquest. The Catholic tradition, in other words, in the form of the Bethlehem convent, may have offered a more appealing choice between the two faiths for at least some local Christians.

Outside of Bethlehem, the brothers of the Holy Land had some success in conversion as well, though on a much smaller scale. Most important to recognize here, however, is the fact that the focus upon conversion represented a significant shift in the traditional nature of the Franciscan ministry, one that had until the 1620s been largely preoccupied with the management of the pilgrimage. This shift, moreover, came at the direction of the Congregation. That the Congregation was pushing for a more aggressive program of evangelization in the Custody is not surprising given its global evangelizing mandate and the ideological significance attached by Church authorities to the conversion of Eastern Christians. As mentioned earlier, the Congregation was a product of Tridentine reform, the name given to the ambitious reform program formulated at the Council of Trent (1545–1563). The Council undertook the unenviable task of reshaping the sprawling institution of the Church to address the many issues nibbling at the foundations of its authority by the sixteenth century. As in the case of the French state, the early modern papacy faced threats both from within the Catholic body and from without. Most damaging of all, for many reasons, was the schism in 1517, but church authorities were also anxious about the Ottoman Empire's steady absorption of states in central and eastern Europe during its progress westward around the Mediterranean, states that had once been Catholic. The

---

[39] Jacob Norris argues that some of these local Christians were hoping to break into the global trade linking the Custody with Spain and the New World, at least by the eighteenth century. Norris, "Dragomans, Tattooists, Artisans: Palestinian Christians and Their Encounters with Catholic Europe in the Seventeenth and Eighteenth Centuries," *Journal of Global History* 14 (2019): 68–86.

emergence of new European empires (Spain, Portugal, France) and their indigenous populations posed other challenges to the leadership of the Church, in particular with regard to evangelization and pastoral care.

The formation of the Congregation in 1622 reflects some of the central tenets to emerge from the Council, above all its contention that the route to a reformed, stable, and powerful Catholic Church required not only a more powerful and centralized papal government but also an ambitious program of evangelization to "reclaim" members lost to other faiths and the conversion of indigenous peoples.[40] Pizzorusso considers the Congregation the last "fruit" of the reorganization of the roman curia first undertaken under Sixtus V.[41] It was, more directly, an outgrowth of the pontificate of Pius V (1566–1572), the reforming pope who made the first serious attempt to establish a central administration for Catholic missions based in Rome. As a Dominican, Pius V was a product of an influential missionary tradition, and he was also a prominent supporter of the reform initiatives promulgated at Trent. In 1568, a commission dedicated to the conversion of "infidels" was formed but did not last long.[42] Other regional commissions for Germany and Greece were introduced after this time and similarly disappeared after a brief period of activity. It was during the papacy of Gregory XIII that the idea for a central organ overseeing all missions circulated, and an early attempt was implemented under Clement XIII (1592–1615). The Clementine congregation seems to have ceased to exist by 1603/1604,[43] and the paucity of records make it difficult to assess the level and nature of its activity. It does seem clear, however, that this early body provided an important template for the Congregation that was finally established through the papal bull *Inscrutabili* in 1622. As the bull states, the mission of the Congregation was twofold: to reclaim direction of all Catholic missions for the papacy and to propagate the Catholic faith. In the service of this mandate, the

---

[40] Among the important studies of the Council, see John O'Malley, *Trent and All That: Renaming Catholicism in the Early Modern Era* (Cambridge, MA: Harvard University Press, 2000); Alain Tallon, *La France et le Concile de Trente (1518–1563)* (Paris: Cerf, 2000); and the older but still seminal work of Hubert Jedin, *A History of the Council of Trent*, 4 vols. (Edinburgh: Thomas Nelson and Sons, 1957–1976).

[41] Giovanni Pizzorusso, "Le Monde et/ou l'Europe: La Congrégation de Propaganda Fide et le politique missionaire du Saint-Siège (XVII siècle)," *Bulletin de l'institut de Réformation* (2014): 1–20; and Song, "The Sacred Congregation."

[42] This first endeavour seems to have emerged in discussion with Francis Borgia, the Master General of the Jesuit Order and the Portuguese ambassador Alvaro Castro.

[43] Song finds no evidence of meetings after 1601, but they may have continued until the end of the 1603. "The Sacred Congregation," 11–13.

Congregation was invested with an expansive jurisdiction that made it a powerful representative of papal authority in the regions that lay under its jurisdiction. Pizzorusso describes a circular letter issued simultaneously to papal nuncios as "a veritable program of action," requiring nuncios to work closely with the new Congregation in service of the global expansion of the Catholic Church. Two months later, on March 22, 1622, the body established a geographic template for its organization. The globe was divided into thirteen zones each under the responsibility of one of the cardinals, with the Custody falling under the responsibility of the Cardinal in charge of the province of Syria and Egypt.

This broad mandate makes it easier to understand the Congregation's interest in the Custody, because one objective of the papal body from the start was the conversion of Eastern Christians. The conversion of Eastern Christians was in fact an old concern by this time, dating back to the time of the Great Schism of the eleventh century that left the Western and Byzantine Churches irreparably divided. As discussed in Chapter 2, the Schism resonated just as strongly in Byzantine circles, giving birth to a rivalry over claims to Christian primacy that lasted for centuries and that was well on display in the heated disputes over altars in the Holy Places. For papal officials, the conversion of Eastern Christians represented another important manifestation of papal primacy, one that gained new urgency in the wake of the Council of Trent. Decades before the Congregation received formal recognition, the papacy had already established colleges in Rome to train missionaries for work among the Eastern Christian traditions. In Rome, colleges for the Greek Orthodox and Maronites were established in 1576 and 1584 and the Illyrian college in Loretto in 1584.[44] The papacy's interest in the conversion of Eastern Christians reflected an old understanding of relations, namely, that Eastern Christians were schismatics. They had left the "true" (Roman) Church and were corrupted versions of the Christian faith. The conversion of Eastern Christians, in other words, was a process of reconciliation, returning them to their authentic spiritual home, thus restoring the unity of Christendom.[45]

---

[44] Heyberger, *Les Chrétiens*, 231–233.
[45] With regard to the issue of reconciliation and the medieval Church, see, for example, Andrew Jotischky, "Penance and Reconciliation in the Crusader States: Matthew Paris, Jacques de Vitry and the Eastern Christians," *Studies in Church History* 40 (2004): 74–83; and J. Muldoon, "The Avignon Papacy and the Frontiers of Christendom: The Evidence of Vatican Register 62," *Archivum Historiae Pontificiae* 17 (1979): 125–195.

Given this understanding of Christian relations, the Congregation's implementation of a more active program of evangelization in the Holy Land after 1622 makes perfect sense because few regions held as many Eastern Christian communities as the Holy Land. Moreover, while Mamluk and later Ottoman authorities forbade the conversion of Muslims upon pain of death, the conversion of other Christians was another matter entirely. The Holy Land, with its many Eastern Christian communities was thus a valuable frontier of spiritual engagement, one that the Church already had access to through the Custody, and after 1622, in the form of the French missionary orders. The more interventionist role of the Congregation in the administration of the Custody, even so, is one indication that the Congregation also viewed the Franciscan brothers as a potential obstacle to its objectives. One can understand why when we consider, to begin with, that it was an institution that was defined legally, politically, and historically by its pilgrimage mandate. Secondly, centuries of self-governance made the Holy Land family comfortable in their claims to expertise. Thirdly, as demonstrated in their many disputes with other Christians, the brothers enjoyed broadreaching support both within the Holy Land as well as in Europe more generally. Since the Congregation made no move to remove them from their administration and instead affirmed their jurisdiction over the Custody throughout the seventeenth century, one can suggest that the papal body valued Franciscan expertise. But to redefine their ministry to incorporate evangelization posed significant challenges both to the existing organization of the ministry of the Custody as well as the formation of its members, challenges that the Congregation also clearly believed required greater papal oversight of the administration of the Custody.

Thus, it was with an eye to molding the brothers as agents of conversion that we can understand the Congregation's interest in bringing the Custody and its Franciscan administrators firmly under its direction after 1622. While the friars had played an evangelizing role during the first centuries of the history of the Custody, it is fair to say that they found both the scope and nature of their role significantly reshaped under the direction of the Congregation. During the fourteenth and fifteenth centuries, for example, one finds a number of Franciscans delegated to treat with spiritual leaders in pursuit of union with the Roman Church. These legations were usually at the behest of the papacy and reflected an assumption that wooing patriarchs would open the door to the conversion of the communities under their care. One of the better-known delegations was that of the fifteenth century Belgian friar Griffon

(Gryfon), no doubt because it was also one of the more successful. Griffon was sent to work among the Maronites. Francesco Suriano writes that Griffon had studied Arabic and preached in this language among the community and produced a translation of the Bible.[46] Perhaps most importantly, he was credited by Franciscan chroniclers with facilitating a formal union between this Christian community and the Roman church in 1469.[47] The Maronites were most heavily concentrated in and around Mount Lebanon, and by the time of the formation of the Congregation, they were considered the closest allies of the Latin tradition in the Holy Land. While it is clear from the report of S. Floro discussed earlier that tension percolated between these communities at the end of the seventeenth century over questions of spiritual jurisdiction, Franciscan records show that the friars were accustomed to sharing their altars with Maronite priests and joining them in worship on the major feast days as well as providing spiritual services such as preaching.[48]

Union with the Maronites represented an early success story of sorts for the medieval Church, but it was a rare one. With perhaps the notable exception of the Chaldeans in the sixteenth century,[49] negotiations with Eastern Christian leaders rarely progressed very far. The papacy continued to send delegations throughout the Early Modern Period even so, though a noticeable change during the late sixteenth century was its increasing reliance upon members of the Jesuit order. Under Gregory XIII (1572–1585), Jesuit delegations were sent to the Maronites on Mount Lebanon and to the Melkite Greeks and Syrians in Aleppo. In 1592, Clement VIII sent a new delegation to the Coptic Christians. After 1622, negotiations with patriarchs continued, perhaps most famously with the controversial Greek Orthodox patriarch Cyril Lucaris.[50] Along with the Jesuits, we also find a number of friars sent as delegates including

---

[46] Francesco Suriano, *Treatise on the Holy Land*, trans. Theophilus Bellorini and Eugene Hoade (Jerusalem: Franciscan Press, 1949), 82.

[47] Augustin Arce, "Maronitas y Franciscanos en el Libano 1450–1516," *Miscelánea de Tierra Santa 2, Estudios críticos y documentos*, Jerusalem (1973): 184.

[48] Arce, "Maronitas y Franciscanos," 184; and Pierre Moukarzel, "Les Franciscains dans le sultanat Mamelouk des années 1330–1516," *Le Moyen Age* CXX (2014): 135–149.

[49] The Chaldean Patriarchate emerged from a schism in the Nestorian tradition, established in 1552, and was formally recognized by the Holy See as part of the Catholic Church in 1553. The first Patriarch was Mar Shimun VIII who led the negotiations. Relations with Rome fluctuated throughout the Early Modern Period, leading to a rupture in 1692 with the formation of the Assyrian Church of the East in 1692. Full communion with Rome was reestablished in 1830.

[50] Lucaris is discussed in Chapter 2.

Jacques de Vendôme, who was sent to treat with the Armenian and Greek Orthodox in 1624,[51] and Tommaso Obicino da Novara and Francesco Quaresmio, who were assigned to the Chaldeans during the 1620s.[52]

That the Congregation embraced delegations in the pursuit of ecclesiastical union shows that the early modern papacy continued to see local spiritual leaders as important pathways to conversion. One reason may have been pragmatic, recognizing the very real financial and political challenges of manning a significant effort to convert on the ground given the restrictions placed upon both the size and spiritual mandate of Custody. Bernard Heyberger argues, however, that both for theological as well as practical reasons, the papacy regarded Eastern recognition of the papacy as the "father" of a diverse Christendom was itself considered a worthy spiritual goal. The underlying assumption, of course, was that long-term relations would lead to the inculcation of Catholic values and practices. He argues that the post-Tridentine mind was less troubled by differences among the Christian traditions in terms of liturgical rites because the traditions agreed in matters of faith if not wholly in form. For this reason, the discussion of union tended to pivot upon recognition of Roman authority and not the adoption of the Catholic rites. As he states, the "idea that a different ritual could express a different theological conception was foreign to post-Tridentine thinking."[53] Heyberger may well be correct, but when we consider the vigour with which the Greek Orthodox set about cleansing the altars seized from the Latin community during their many disputes in the seventeenth century and the equal vigour with which the friars "restored" their chapels to good Catholic order after they had been occupied by the Greek Orthodox, one has to wonder whether papal authorities as well as the Franciscan religious made such a neat distinction between doctrine and rite. Indeed, as Heyberger also states, the Congregation frowned upon Catholic participation in the liturgical rites of the Eastern Christians, a concern that suggests that the Congregation viewed such rites as potentially corrupting, or at the very least, illegitimate.

---

[51] See, for example, the discussion of a delegation by friar Jacques de Vendôme to the Armenian and Greek Orthodox patriarch in 1624. Lemmens, ed., *Acta*, vol. I, 30.

[52] Heberger suggests that Francesco Quaresmio was particularly unsuited to the task because of his authoritarian manner and ignorance of the Eastern traditions. Bernard Heyberger, "Le Terre Sainte et mission au XVIIe siècle," *Dimensioni et problemi della ricerca storica* (1994): 1–33, see, in particular, ft. 12.

[53] Heyberger, *Les Chrétiens*, 235. "Car l'idée qu'un rituel different puisse exprimer une conception théologique differente est étrangère au mode de pensée post-tridentin."

While the Congregation continued to embrace delegations as a necessary path to the reconciliation of Eastern Christians, the sources on the Custody discussed thus far show that it was also initiating a more ambitious program of evangelization in the form of local missions. That one finds this shift to a more active role on the ground by the 1620s may well reflect a heightened sense of urgency on the part of the papacy to manifest the authority of the Western Church in the sacred landscape. One reason to consider was the growing influence of the French monarchy at the Ottoman Porte, influence that opened up the Ottoman regions to Catholic missions during the early decades of the seventeenth century. Another that seems to have been just as important was growing local competition for the bodies and souls of local Christians.

While more research needs to be done, intriguing new studies suggest that the Holy Land was becoming a particularly active and fertile zone of religious reform among many other religious traditions in the region.[54] This was certainly true of the Greek Orthodox tradition. The papacy would have had difficulty ignoring the signs of Byzantine influence in particular, especially as the local Greek Orthodox population began to swell with new arrivals from other parts of the Ottoman Empire and Greek clerics assumed control of the Patriarchate of Jerusalem.[55] As discussed in Chapter 2, the Byzantine Church was no less worried about the growing missionary engagement of the Western Church in Ottoman regions. Indeed, the fierce competition for altars in the Holy Places that we find in the seventeenth century was one important indication that the Holy Land had emerged as an especially fraught zone of spiritual competition between the two Christian traditions. But in addition to rising Byzantine influence, the Congregation of the Propaganda Fide may have been concerned as well about a rise in Christian conversions to Islam. Whether one can talk about the sixteenth and seventeenth centuries as a period of intensive Islamicization remains a matter of vigorous debate among Ottoman historians. However, they do agree that the Muslim population in the Holy Land was growing during the course of the

---

[54] See, for example, James Grehan, *Twilight of the Saints: Everyday Religion in Ottoman Syria and Palestine* (Oxford: Oxford University Press, 2014); and Constantin Panchenko, *Arab Orthodox Christians under Ottoman Rule, 1516–1831* (Jordanville: Trinity Seminary Press, 2016).

[55] Oded Peri, "The Christian Population of Jerusalem in the Late 17th Century," *Journal of the Economic and Social History of the Orient* 39 (1996): 398–421.

sixteenth and seventeenth centuries.[56] In fact, we find some evidence of the fluidity of local conversions in the records of the Custody that was clearly a matter of serious concern to the friars. The former *custos* Antonio da' Gaeta, for example, was accused by at least one friar of losing several recent converts to Islam. This was a damaging accusation and its veracity questionable given the state of the sources, but it was by no means the only time we find the friars bemoaning the loss of losing recent converts to the majority faith.[57]

The Congregation recognized that the conversion of Eastern Christians – indeed, members of any faith in the Holy Land – was no easy task, especially in a revered, and shared, sacred landscape. Living in the Holy Land was to see and experience every day the manifestations of an ancient past that was deeply meaningful to members of each tradition. Being *there*, in other words, was affirming for Eastern Christians just as it was for Catholic pilgrims and the Franciscan brothers. Effecting conversions at the sacred *center* of Christendom was thus bound to be an uphill battle, one that required a more aggressive approach on the ground that involved education and pastoral care. It was for this reason that the Congregation eagerly sponsored the French missions in the 1620s even though doing so ruffled the feathers of the Franciscans. We should note that these missionaries belonged to orders (Jesuit, Capuchin, discalced Carmelite) that the Church had already relied upon in other missionary contexts, and which, as a number of scholars have argued, shared with the Congregation a similar evangelizing *esprit*. Benoist Pierre insists, for example, that Père Joseph, the Capuchin advisor of Cardinal Richelieu, was inflamed with a millenial vision of a "a new world dominated by the Catholic Church" when he devised his global plan of French missions.[58] Père Joseph naturally considered his own tradition, the Capuchin, the

---

[56] On Palestine, see, for example, Amy Singer, *Palestinian Peasants and Ottoman Officials: Rural Administration around Sixteenth-Century Jerusalem* (Cambridge: Cambridge University Press, 1994). Important recent interjections into the discussion of Islamicization more generally include Tijana Krstic, *Contested Conversions to Islam: Narratives of Religious Change in the Early Modern Ottoman Empire* (Stanford: Stanford University Press, 2011); and Marc Baer, *Honored by the Glory of Islam: Conversion and Conquest in Ottoman Europe* (Oxford: Oxford University Press, 2011).

[57] On Gaeta, see also the discussion in Chapter 6. The relevant document is APF SC TS 1, ff. 118–123.

[58] Benoist Pierre, *Le Père Joseph: L'Eminence grise de Richelieu* (Paris: Perrin, 2007), 123–124, and 130–135. Pierre shows that Joseph was also involved in mobilizing an international crusade of princes (a *milice chrétien*) around 1615.

finest expression of a militant Church ("la fine fleur de l'Eglise militante"), and he used his influence to situate it on the vanguard of French global engagement. Robert Cline and Adina Ruiu find a similar globalizing evangelical zeal among the Jesuits assigned to Ottoman lands.[59] Relations with the Congregation show that papal officials believed that the Franciscan brothers of the Custody could similarly be harnessed to the cause of conversion. But to do so their ministry needed to be reshaped to engage effectively in local evangelization, an observation that explains why many of the discussions between the Congregation and the Custody by the 1630s centered upon the pastoral formation of the friars (linguistic training, liturgical rites) as well as their spiritual jurisdiction vis-à-vis other communities including the Maronites. To be effective missionaries, the brothers were expected to preach in local languages, invite other Christians into their churches and chapels, and teach them the principles of the Catholic faith. Establishing schools, the Arab cure, learning local languages – these were important mechanisms for expanding the local reach of the Catholic tradition and ensuring that it had continuing institutional support locally. The Congregation in turn facilitated their work in the field through its production of catechisms, dictionaries, grammars, and devotional texts in local languages, as well as ongoing guidance from Rome.

Reshaping the ministry of the Observant friars to include evangelization, however, clearly posed a serious challenge to an already overstretched ministry according to the sources of the Custody. This was because it required a more direct engagement in the religious lives of local Christians. Indeed, the correspondence of the friars suggests that evangelization raised a host of new concerns for the brothers as they became more emmeshed in the lives of their flock and as they had to negotiate the new strictures placed upon their ministry by the Congregation. The issue of marriage, in particular, emerges as a frequent point of tension between the friars and their flock, other priests, and even with the Congregation. In addition to the report of S. Floro discussed earlier, two letters written by friars assigned to the Chaldeans during the 1630s point to marriage as

[59] Robert Cline, "Fighting Enemies and Finding Friends: The Cosmopolitan Pragmatism of Jesuit Residences in the Ottoman Levant," *Renaissance Studies* 31 (2015): 66–86; and Adina Ruiu, "Missionaries and French Subjects: The Jesuits in the Ottoman Empire," in *A Companion to the Early Modern Catholic Global Missions*, ed. Ronnie Po-Chia Hsia (Leiden: Brill, 2016), 181–204. For a broader approach, see Luke Clossey, *Salvation and Globalization in the Early Jesuit Missions* (Cambridge: Cambridge University Press, 2008).

a persistent challenge for their ministries. They reveal, moreover, friars struggling to interpret their Catholic ministry in an urban context shaped by competing social, economic, and cultural priorities, in this case the bustling commercial center of Aleppo. In a letter dated February 23, 1635, for example, the French friar Vincenzo da Gallicano (Vincent) is clearly frustrated with the Patriarch of the Maronites because he officiated the marriages of two female converts with Christian "schismatics." What clearly bothered Vincenzo was that the Patriarch allowed them to continue to observe their own rites ("le lascoranno viver nel rito loro"). As we know from Keith Luria and Giovanni Pizzorusso among others, church authorities wrestled with the legitimacy of such unions.[60] From the perspective of the Congregation, converts should steer clear of marrying non-Catholics, but local realities in many missions made such enforcement virtually impossible. In the eastern Mediterranean, Islamic law permitted intermarriage between the faiths with certain restrictions, in particular, it forbade non-Muslim men from marrying Muslim women. Intermarriage was in fact quite common in the Holy Land as well as elsewhere, and it would have been hard as well for the small number of Catholic converts to remain truly endogamous. Marriage was simply too important as a vehicle of social and economic stability, too essential to the generational transference of wealth and power, to be easily restricted to a community of a few hundred people, especially when a much larger population of Christians – as well as the devout of other faiths – resided nearby.

Poverty appears as another issue challenging the pastoral work of the friars, visible, for example, in Vincenzo's mention of four Catholic converts who wished to marry but couldn't afford to do so.[61] As Tramontana argues, many of the converts were quite poor. Bernard Heyberger says that the friars resorted at times to paying small sums and offering gifts to lure local Christians to worship, an enticement that in many cases did not lead to the desired conversion. In fact, it seems to have been quite common for potential converts to disappear as soon as they received the promised offering. A letter sent by Antonio da Veglia, a *Riformati* friar and guardian of the Aleppo community, similarly alludes to the challenges of maintaining orthodoxy in such a religiously diverse

---

[60] Keith Luria, "Catholic Marriage and the Customs of the Country: New Religious Community in Seventeenth-Century Vietnam," *French Historical Studies* 40 (2017): 457–473; and Giovanni Pizzorusso, "I dubbi sui sacramenti dalle missioni "ad infideles": Percorsi nelle burocrazie di Curia," *Mélanges de l'école française de Rome* 121 (2009): 39–61.

[61] APF SOCG, 59, f. 102–104.

environment. Writing in October 1634, Veglia describes a porous religious reality, noting that many of those "who live in conformity with the Roman rites, were European by birth [Franchi]." Because they married Christians of the region, however, many were following "the rites of these parts." Veglia is arguing, in other words, that the spiritual life of local Catholics was being shaped through its exposure to other Christian rites and, in particular, through the practice of intermarriage.[62] He was seeking the advice of the Congregation, clearly unsure how to determine his role as a pastoral advisor in a Christian population that showed significant signs of liturgical as well as cultural intermingling.

Once the Franciscan brothers became entangled in a pastoral ministry, they had to wrestle with the daily demands of administering the sacraments and the formation of converts in a religiously diverse region. Intermarriage was a reality of religious relations in the eastern Mediterranean, and it was a one that posed serious challenges to a Catholic ministry that not only recognized marriage both as a potential road to conversion but also as a boundary demarcating membership in the Catholic community. But there were many other threats limiting the influence of the Catholic tradition, including the very real issue of access to the services of the friars. As Veglia also mentions in his letter, Chaldeans were going to Nestorian churches for their services because they were, quite simply, located nearby. Given the sacrality of the Holy Land, the diverse population of the region, and the influence of competing social, economic, and other values among other challenges, converting the local populace of the Holy Land was never easy. One can appreciate the frustration of Francesco Quaresmio, who, after his work with the Chaldeans, apparently stated that it "would take a miracle" to convert local Christians. As these examples suggest, the transformation of the Custody of the Holy Land into an early modern mission was a work in progress throughout the seventeenth century. It is also fair to say that it never assumed the forms one finds in the New World because the demands of the pilgrimage continued to supercede its other duties. Still, the ministry of the friars was changing in the seventeenth century as conversion became a more important duty under the direction of the Congregation.

---

[62] APF SOCG (October 19, 1634), f. 109. "Ho trovato qui che molte creature, che vive conforme i riti della Chiesa Romana, *essendo nate da Franchi*, congiungodosi in matrimonio con I christiani di questi [paesi], essendo *con il costume antico, sequetano i riti di queste parti.*"

5.3 A SPIRITUAL *CENTER*

As Section 5.2 has argued, the Holy Land was an important frontier of Catholic engagement because it linked the Church with a diverse Christian landscape in the Levant through its possession of altars in the Holy Places and its ties with other local communities. The Franciscan brothers thus remained crucial to the achievement of the grander ambition of the Congregation to construct a truly global Catholic Church. In emphasizing the Holy Land's importance as a frontier of Catholic engagement, however, we need to recognize that it was a valued Catholic frontier because it was also a shared sacred landscape and a global site of pilgrimage. The conversion of Eastern Christians, in other words, also responded to the Congregation's interest in capitalizing upon the Holy Land's status as a sacred *center* of Christendom. This objective emerges into view when we study it with an eye to an evolving papal sacred history, one that envisioned the "restoration" of a Christendom unified under the Church of Rome. In this history, Jerusalem served as a critical place in which to manifest these hegemonic ambitions because it once lay under Roman rule and it was a globally recognized vessel of Christ's authority. Indeed, the very act of Catholic evangelization should be understood as a mode of sacred history-telling intended to recall Rome's mythic past as leader of a unified Christendom.

It is beyond the capacity of this discussion to wade deeply into the complexities of this papal sacred history, though thankfully it has received significant attention from medieval and early modern scholars.[63] A few strands that are immediately relevant here include the Roman origins of the papacy, the "loss" of the Holy Places to the forces of Islam, its long history of schism, and Jerusalem's soteriological importance as the place of Christ's sacrifice and resurrection. With a specific eye to this theme of restoration, we should note that the medieval papacy promoted the Crusades as restorative acts. These were rescue missions because the Holy land had been "seized" illegitimately from its "Roman" rulers and soiled by the presence of the erring Muslim faith. In rescuing

---

[63] See, for example, James Hankins, "Renaissance Crusaders: Humanist Crusade Literature in the Age of Mehmed II," *Dumbarton Oaks Papers* 49 (1995): 111–207; Nikalaos G. Chrissis, "The City and the Cross: The Image of Constantinople and the Latin Empire in Thirteenth-Century Papal Crusading Rhetoric," *Byzantine and Modern Greek Studies* 36 (2012): 20–37; and Nicholas Muldoon, *Popes, Lawyers, and Infidels: The Church and the Non-Christian World* (Philadelphia: University of Pennsylvania Press, 2015).

the Holy Land, the papacy was simply reclaiming its traditional jurisdiction over the sacred landscape for the Roman Church. Moreover, as the bishop of Rome, the pope was the "papa" of all Christians, the legitimate head of Christendom. While this sacred history evolved over time, its central assertion of papal primacy and the Holy Land as a sacred *center* of Christendom shaped papal narratives into the Early Modern Period. Indeed, as several scholars have argued, this sacred history found new purchase during the fifteenth and sixteenth centuries in response to the growing might of the Ottoman Empire. Some of the more important new strands threading the mythic crusading narrative by the early sixteenth century featured the Ottoman conquests of Constantinople in 1453 and the Holy land in 1517 and the battle of Lepanto in 1571.[64] In response to these and other events, Rome issued new calls for Crusade. Selim I's conquest of Egypt in 1517 and seemingly inexorable advancement into central Europe especially worried Pope Leo X, who turned to Francis I of France to lead a new Crusade. Negotiations continued throughout the fall of 1517, and Leo X eventually granted Francis a crusading tithe to impose in his kingdom in support of the venture, though in the end nothing came of it.[65] As we may recall, the papacy also entered into negotiations with Philip II of Spain in 1558 and in 1615 with Louis XIII of France to lead another.[66]

Buoying these calls to Crusade was a narrative that was already well familiar to early modern Catholics, that of a Christendom under attack by a powerful and expanding Muslim empire. Rescuing the Holy Places from the clutches of a rapacious and repressive Ottoman Empire emerges as a persistent cry, along with the rescue of the many Eastern Christians living under Ottoman rule; Christians who eagerly awaited "union" with their true spiritual home, the Catholic Church. The conversion of Eastern Christians mandated by the Congregation after 1622 similarly participated in the construction of papal claims to Christian hegemony through its restoration of the spiritual integrity of the Christian body. Eastern Christians were doubly victims because they lived under Islamic rule and were members of corrupted Christian traditions. In this context, conversion was a restorative act because it healed the fractured Christian body

---

[64] See, among others, Hankins, "Renaissance Crusaders." On the council, see, for example, Deno J. Geanakoplos, "The Council of Florence (1438–9) and the Problem of Union between the Greek and Latin Churches," *Church History* 24 (1955): 324–346.

[65] Kenneth M. Setton, *The Papacy and the Levant*, vol. III (Philadelphia: The American Philosphical Society, 1975): 175.

[66] See discussion in Chapter 3.

inasmuch as it returned these erring Christians to a state of spiritual perfection. But to convert Eastern Christians living in a sacred region that was also considered a site of continuing revelation had added significance for the hegemonic objectives of the early modern papacy because it testified to the Christian legitimacy of the Catholic tradition.

That conversion could assume this function – as visible testimony of Christian perfection and authority – was by no means something new to the Early Modern Period though it was embraced with gusto as missions expanded the frontiers of Catholic engagement. The Franciscan missionaries who claimed the rapid conversion of thousands of indigenous peoples during the early years of the missions in New Spain, for example, were confident in these as signs of a new era of Christian renewal under Catholic and, more precisely, Franciscan leadership.[67] To convert Eastern Christians at the spiritual *center* was an especially potent sign of Catholic legitimacy and authority because it recognized the place of Christ as an ever-flowing source of his perfection.

Moreover, it was a site of global pilgrimage among the three faiths and thus a visible platform for articulating papal claims to primacy. One only has to consider, to begin with, that conversions made the Latin tradition more visible within the diverse Christian demography of the region, both by increasing the number of Catholic bodies *there* and by offering tangible local evidence of Catholic perfection. Such conversions were, at the same time, recognized signs of spiritual renewal, a message that must have seemed especially meaningful as well as useful for church leaders who were engaged in a massive reformation of their own religious institution.

Thus, even if few in number, Catholic converts in the Holy Land offered papal authorities a powerful symbol of a rejuvenated and galvanized Catholic Church, one that had global resonance because the Holy Land belonged to so many different faiths. Conversion and Crusade, in other words, worked in tandem to manifest papal authority both *over* and *within* the Holy Land, and in doing so legitimized its historic claims to Christian primacy. While no Crusades materialized during the time of this study, papal authorities could point at least to conversions as evidence of

---

[67] On Franciscan missions and spiritual renewal, see, for example, William J. Taylor, *Theatre of a Thousand Wonders: A History of the Miraculous* (Cambridge: Cambridge University Press, 2016); Osvaldo Pardo, *The Origins of Mexican Catholicism: Nahua Rituals and Christian Sacramentals in Sixteenth-Century* Mexico (Ann Arbor: University of Michigan Press, 2006); and the still seminal work, John Leddy Phelan, *The Milennial Kingdom of the Franciscans in the New World* (Berkeley: University of California Press, 1956).

Catholic renewal and authority. And they had other ways as well of manifesting a Latin presence in the Holy Land. The arrival of the new missionaries increased the number of clerical bodies in the region and expanded the geographic distribution of the Church. Moreover, the Congregation recognized the enormous ideological value of the Custody itself as a Latin institution because it was revered and operated at the heart of the most sacred of Christian landscapes. Indeed, it is quite clear from the sources discussed thus far that the Congregation's interest in bringing the Custody more closely under its direction reflected its recognition of its importance for rendering the Latin tradition visible in the region and, in particular, in the Holy Places. As we should recall, the papacy worked tirelessly alongside the friars to protect, preserve, and when possible, expand Latin jurisdiction in the Holy Places throughout the sixteenth and seventeenth centuries. It was also through the advocacy of the papacy that we find the alms-gathering network of commissioners of the Holy Land penetrating new European regions, eventually reaching the colonies of New Spain and Brazil by the end of the seventeenth century. That the Congregation used its authority to expand papal scrutiny over its financial administration, demanding inventories of the Custody and the submission of expense reports from the alms commissioners is further evidence that it considered the custodial responsibilities of the friars extremely important to the maintenance and orderly operations of the pilgrimage. Papal support was no less important for ensuring that Catholic chapels in the Holy Places were perpetually impressive sites of spiritual encounter with the other faiths through the regular performance of the liturgical rites, renovation, and lavish decoration of these spaces.

Given the revered status of the Holy land among the Religions of the Book, papal preoccupation with the provisioning of the Custody and its administration thus makes a great deal of sense. Through its material, liturgical, and political engagement in the Holy Land, the Custody was the most visible face of the Latin Church in the region and a central mechanism for expanding its influence locally as well as globally. As the face of Western pilgrimage, moreover, the Custody connected the outer Catholic world to Jerusalem and the many Holy Places of the Holy Land. Indeed, as recent work on missions has made quite clear, the expansion of the Catholic tradition during the sixteenth and seventeenth centuries did little to challenge Catholic conception of the Holy Land as the *center* of Christendom, serving rather to reify its significance as the source of a shared faith and focus of devotional engagement. One is struck in particular by the popularization and indigenization of *via crucis* processions and the Virgin Mary in so many diverse regional contexts.[68] Holy Land replicas as well not only mushroomed across Europe but also in the New World, the migrating house of the House of Loreto being a particularly intriguing example. In her recent monograph, Karin Velez traces Mary's "home" as it flew from the Holy Land to Italy and from there to myriad sites in New Spain. But alms-gathering and the trade in pilgrim's mementoes also did brisk traffic in these regions, integrating the friars from their base in Jerusalem in a broader, global Catholic community. Thus, ideologically and materially, the Holy Land provided the papacy with a sacred landscape that was useful for defining a shared Catholic identity as well as a claim to Christian primacy, one that could embrace indigenous converts as well as schismatics reconciled to the Church. Moreover, as Karen Melvin has argued, what made mementoes such as the *medidas* meaningful to early modern Catholics in New Spain was the fact that they had come *from* the Holy Land. They were made from local materials, blessed there, and in many cases had "touched" a Holy Place.[69] The papacy understood the power of the Holy Land to express its claims to Christian primacy for this reason, because it contained *the* source of Christianity: Christ.

The spiritual significance given to having a Catholic presence *there* also helps to explain why medieval and early modern pontiffs worked to promote Rome as another Jerusalem. Beginning with the papacy of Sixtus V, Roman authorities worked with architects, historians, artists, and liturgists to illuminate Rome's ancient Christian past. They did so by situating it both materially and ideologically within a sacred landscape that included Jerusalem, creating a unity of sacred space defined through a shared ancient Roman administrative past, and the wanderings of Christ and the apostles. As Simon Ditchfield has argued, this past was carefully choreographed in particular to highlight Rome as a place of

---

[68] Karin Vélez, *The Miraculous Flying House of Loreto: Spreading Catholicism in the Early Modern World* (Princeton, Princeton University Press, 2019); and Olivier Christin, Fabrice Flückiger, and Naïma Ghermani, eds., *Marie mondialisée: L'Atlas Marianus de Wilhelm Gumppenberg et les topographies sacrées de l'époque* (Neuchâtel: Presses universitaires suisses, 2014).

[69] Karen Melvin, "The Travels of El Devoto Peregrino: A Franciscan Holy Land Comes to New Spain," in *Five Hundred Years of Franciscans in New Spain*, ed. Thomas Cohen, Jay Harrison, and David Rex Galindo (forthcoming); and Brian Larkin, *The Very Nature of God: Baroque Catholicism and Religious Reform in Bourbon Mexico City* (New Mexico: University of New Mexico, 2010).

martyrdom and the papacy as a spiritual legacy of St. Peter.[70] There were many layers of meaning operating in this reconfiguration of Rome as a sacred city, but certainly one that is immediately relevant to our study was its assertion of the legitimizing power of the relics brought from the Holy Places, in particular, through its possession of the bodies of the apostles. Holding pride of place in the reconfigured sacred geography of Church of Saint John's Lateran was the head of Saint Peter, the first bishop of Rome. Promoting its material connection to the Holy Land through local devotions and possession of the bones of martyrs and other relics grounded the papacy in the sacralizing power of Christ through a shared Christian past.

It was because it recognized the ideological as well as spiritual significance of "possessing" the Holy Land that the early modern papacy worked vigorously to protect a place for the Catholic tradition in the true Holy Places in the form of the liturgical rites, Catholic structures, and Catholic bodies (clerics and pilgrims). These too were material conduits linking the sacrality of the Holy Places with Rome and the outer Catholic world, reaffirming the Western Church as the "true" Church and the papacy as its legitimate leader. A particularly intriguing indication of this intent is the discussion of Jubilee celebrations briefly mentioned earlier. The instructions of 1628 touched upon a number of matters involving the ministry of the friars, including an order to organize local Jubilee festivities in coordination with those in Rome. Contemporary reports of the Jubilee years in Rome describe elaborate festive rites attracting hundreds of thousands of devout Catholics. In Jerusalem, they would have been much more modest affairs, but in organizing the festivities, the Congregation was showing its intent to make papal authority much more visible in the Holy Land. If it could not do so by exercising direct jurisdiction over the many Holy Places, it could still make itself visible through liturgical rites performed in shared sacred places at the *center* of Christendom.

5.4 CONCLUSION

As this chapter has argued, the papacy was another Catholic power testing the jurisdiction of the early modern Franciscan brothers. As in

---

[70] Simon Ditchfield, "Reading Rome as a Sacred Landscape, c. 1586–1635," in *Sacred Space in Early Modern Europe*, ed. Will Coster and Andrew Spicer (Cambridge: Cambridge University Press, 2005), 167–192. Important to his discussion is Gregory Martin's *Roma Sancta (1581)*, ed. G. B. Parks (Rome: Edizioni di Storia E Letteratura, 1969).

the case of the Bourbon regime, the early modern papacy was a Catholic power facing serious challenges to its authority by the sixteenth century both from within the structure of the Church as well as from without. These challenges were multiple and serious, and one consequence was its embrace of transformative change in the form of Tridentine reform. The Congregation of the Propaganda Fide was a product of this reform, charged with an ambitious evangelizing mandate, one aimed at "restoring" papal authority over a unified Christendom. As discussed here, the Holy Land occupied a special role in this ambitious mandate because of its importance as a site of contact with the many faiths of the Levant and as a revered sacred landscape. Because it was important both as a Catholic *frontier* and a spiritual *center*, the Congregation moved quickly to expand its authority over the Franciscan family in charge of the Custody. One objective was to transform them into a missionary body to convert Eastern Christians. The other was to capitalize upon the Custody's importance as a pilgrimage institution, a role that made it a privileged global as well as local platform from which to articulate the hegemonic ambitions of the early modern papacy.

As I have tried to argue here, Jerusalem remained a revered spiritual center within the expanding boundaries of the early modern Catholic tradition. The Custody, through the work of the friars, also served as a crucial transmitter of the sacralizing authority of the region to the distant expanses of the Catholic tradition, and for this reason it was a powerful vehicle of papal authority as well. In Chapter 6, we turn our attention to the Franciscan brothers themselves, to understand the significance of the sacred landscape for the men charged with the management of Western pilgrimage. By the seventeenth century, the Observant friars, who had been in charge since 1431, faced serious challenges to their jurisdiction from reformed members of the Franciscan family. These conflicts illuminate a special place for the Holy Land in the Franciscan tradition as a source of legitimacy through its intimate association with the life of Francis of Assisi. These disputes and the writings of the friars illuminate a Franciscan Holy Land, one in which the Custody exercised enormous meaning as a legacy of Francis to his most faithful followers.

6

A Franciscan Holy Land

Christ confided this land, this land of blessings, of His life and death, to the legitimate inheritors of his suffering and humility on the cross: because among all the religious, those in abidance with the will of our holy patriarch [Francis] renounced in particular and in general every sort of possession. Christ wished to reward their trust, by giving them guardianship ... of the most precious place on earth. This Holy land is so fully the possession of the religious of the Observance of saint Francis ... that other religious have not been able to establish ... under threat of "major" excommunication and when they come they must only wear the habit of the religious of the Observance.[1]

        Jacques-Florent Goujon, *Histoire et voyage de la Terre Sainte*

In our earlier chapters, the Holy Land emerges as an ebullient, inventive source of sacred history for early modern Catholics – an ever-flowing reservoir of Christian authority that could be called upon to legitimize claims to spiritual authenticity and authority for a diverse body of Catholic communities and institutions threatened by forces of religious

---

[1] "Il leur a confié cette terre de benediction de sa naissance, de sa vie & de sa mort, comme aux legitimes heritiers de des souffrances & de l'humilité de la Croix: comme entre tous les Religieux, conformément à la volonté de nostre saint Patriarche ils ont renoncé en particulier, & en general à toute sorte de possession Jesus-Christ a bien voulu recompenser leur confiance, leur donnant en garde & en depost ce qu'il avoit de plus precieux en terre. Cette Terre Sainte est si bien dans la possession des Religieux de l'Observance de saint François, appellez Cordeliers en France, qu'aucuns autres Religieux ne peuvent s'y establir, ny fonder sous peine d'excommunication maieure, & ne viennent la visiter qu'apres avoir pris l'habit desdits Religieux de l'Observance." Jacques-Florent Goujon, *Histoire et voyage de la Terre-Sainte, où tout ce qu'il y a de plus remarquable dans les Saints Lieux, est tres-exactement descript* (Lyon: Pierre Compagnon & Robert Taillandier, 1670), 12.

reform and political change. The histories of the Order of the Holy Sepulcher, the Bourbon regime, and the papacy served two simultaneous purposes, affirming the perfection of Catholicism as the true Christian message and manifesting their own claims to authority within the Catholic tradition. These claims to a sacred past were predicated, however, on being *there*. The Catholics of this study staked a claim to the spiritual authority of the Holy Land by incorporating themselves into the landscape. Negotiating legal privileges, the construction and renovation of Catholic buildings, and the presence of Catholic bodies (pilgrims, clerics) literally grounded their claims to Christian leadership, connecting them with their earlier Christian pasts in the region.

This observation – about the spiritual and political authority obtained by being *there* in the Holy Land – is also critical to unlocking the meaning of Jacques-Florent Goujon's bold claim to Franciscan "possession" of the Holy Land. The passage comes from his pilgrimage treatise, which was first published in 1670. Goujon was a fur merchant from the French city of Lyon who later in life adopted the Franciscan habit. The community he joined belonged to the Order of Friars Minor (OFM), one of three branches comprising the Franciscan tradition by the seventeenth century and the one charged with jurisdiction over the Custody. He made at least two trips to the Holy Land, the first in 1636 and another in 1666, the second time as a member of the Franciscan family in the Holy Land. In his address to the reader, Goujon mentions that he worked across the extent of the Custody, spending time in Jerusalem, Bethlehem, and Nazareth as well as parts of Egypt and Syria. As guardian of the Franciscan convent in the Basilica of the Holy Sepulcher in 1668, Goujon also held the highest office in a community responsible for performing the Latin rites in the great Basilica. He mentions leaving the Holy Land unhappily, however, having run out of time to finish "his work and prayers." For this friar, the mysteries of the region were simply too vast to be comprehended in the span of three years. Indeed, with tongue firmly planted in cheek, Goujon "marveled" at the long volumes written by pilgrims who had only "spent a month there."[2] The French friar clearly believed that the five years he spent in the Holy Land and his personal experience of its mysteries invested his text with much greater authority. But even more significant, he suggests, was the long spiritual engagement of the friars that began with the visit of Francis of Assisi in 1219 and that continued on in the

---

[2] Goujon, *Histoire et voyage de la Terre-Sainte*.

ministry of the Custody.³ Thus, from the very start of his treatise, Goujon anchors his claims to authority on the pilgrimage in a long Franciscan past in the Holy Land, a past that continued to unfold for his early modern readers in his descriptions of Franciscans busy with their spiritual ministry in the same places once occupied by Christ and the apostles.

As this brief description suggests, Goujon included a Franciscan sacred history in his pilgrimage treatise, one that existed alongside the traditional narrative of the life of Christ and that privileged a special role for the friars as custodians of the Holy Land. His is one of several such Franciscan texts produced during the period of our investigation, and together they unveil a veritable industry of sacred history writing emanating from the early modern Custody. It is with these texts that we finally turn our attention to the friars at the center of our investigation, members of a religious tradition with deep ties to the Holy Land who were proud of the Order's long tenure in charge of the Custody. When we consider as well that the brothers wrote their histories at a time when their jurisdiction over the Custody was being threatened on multiple fronts, one can appreciate the allure of a Franciscan sacred past that ratified their authority. But in addition to the visible intrusions of the French state and the papacy upon their jurisdiction, the growing local influence of the Greek Orthodox in the Holy Places, and the more existential threat posed to the pilgrimage by Protestant theology, their texts point to yet another serious threat, one that may have seemed especially troubling because it came from within the Franciscan family itself. By the seventeenth century, new reformed traditions in the form of the Capuchins, Recollect, and *Riformati* friars began pressing for access to the Custody and waged a multifrontal assault upon the traditional spiritual monopoly of the mainstream (regular Observant) members of the Franciscan Order. This fraternal competition provides another crucial context for interpreting their sacred histories, unveiling a Holy Land inflected with meaning as a privileged source of Franciscan authority through its hosting of the life of Francis of Assisi as well as Christ. As shall soon be clear from the following discussion, it was meaningful to friars like Goujon that Francis went *there*. His visit to the Holy Land demonstrated his perfect modeling of the life of Christ and thus legitimized Franciscan claims to apostolic succession. Moreover, in the context of brewing debates over the true nature of the Franciscan ideal, the historic presence of Francis of Assisi

---

[3] Goujon, *Histoire et voyage de la Terre-Sainte*, 3.

also invested custodial jurisdiction with special purpose as a marker of Franciscan perfection.

Thus, the primary objective of this chapter is to explore the Holy Land as a source of Franciscan legitimacy for members of a religious tradition divided by disagreements over the true nature of the Franciscan ideal. With this in mind, our first task (Section 6.1) is to look more closely at the nature of the fraternal disputes in the Custody, highlighting dimensions that speak to a shared interest in possessing jurisdiction. Sections 6.2 and 6.3 explore the ideological and historical context shaping these fraternal struggles through an examination of Franciscan sacred histories of the Custody. Two narrative strategies receive particular attention, each serving to construct the Holy Land as the spiritual home of the Franciscan tradition and the Custody as a spiritual legacy of Francis. The first involved locating Francis of Assisi historically and spiritually *in* the Holy Land. The second illuminated a Franciscan ministry in the same places and same roles as the apostles. These narrative were often entwined. Together, they show that the friars, much like the other early modern Catholics studied here, turned to a sacred past in the Holy Land to legitimize their claims to spiritual authority. That their possession of custodial jurisdiction became a valued marker of Franciscan perfection, moreover, further underscores the importance of Ottoman structures of authority in shaping not only Catholic access to and experience of the Holy Land but also its formative influence upon Catholic spirituality. The fraternal squabbles over jurisdiction allow us to make one final observation as well, this time regarding the Holy Land's infinite capacity for spiritual reinvention. They illuminate an influential religious tradition in the throes of profound change, which, as in times past, sent reformed brethren to the Custody fueled with zeal to prove their worthiness. For the brothers of this study, in other words, the Holy Land was a place of perpetual Franciscan reinvention because it was a revered vessel of an authentic Franciscan past. It was a Franciscan Holy Land.

6.1 FRATERNAL CONFLICTS, 1517–1700

6.1.1 *Strands of Reform*

One of the challenges of working on the Franciscan tradition during the Early Modern Period is wrestling with its extraordinary diversity, diversity that was the product of centuries of internal reform. Sixteenth century Europe was a busy patchwork of Franciscan traditions, their distinctive characteristics shaped locally inasmuch as they were formed through intellectual and administrative engagement in an international religious community. Because of this extraordinary diversity, designations of "friar," "Franciscan," or "sister," can obscure differing Franciscan conceptions and modes of life even within the same community, and this is the case we find with the Franciscan brothers of the Holy Land. In this investigation, the brothers of the Holy Land have also been referred to as friars or Franciscans, names that drew from their collective membership in the largest of the Franciscan branches of the Order at the time, the Order of Friars Minor (OFM Obs.). This is in addition to "the Holy Land family" (famiglia della terra santa), language that the brothers often used to describe themselves and that seems appropriate for distinguishing this unique, international community. However, by the seventeenth century, stark differences existed within the community over conceptions of the Franciscan ideal, reflecting the existence of a multiplicity of Franciscan identities. Since these differences were a source of serious tension within the brotherhood during the period of our investigation, we need to come to terms with the Franciscan character of the Custody in all its complexity. Doing so means using the language of the brothers of the Holy Land themselves, who, as we shall see, were much more comfortable describing themselves as Observants, Recollects, and *Riformati* than they were in using the common designation of "friar." Why this was so becomes clear when we examine the transformation of the Holy Land family during the seventeenth century, a community whose Franciscan diversity became difficult to ignore for its administrators by the 1620s as reformed brethren began making their way to the region.

   It was only a matter of time before the reforming movements that wracked the Order of the Friars Minor reached the Custody. The Capuchins, who arrived in 1622, were followed in short order by members of the Recollect and *Riformati*. By 1625, the brothers of the Holy Land, who were traditionally drawn from the more mainstream (regular Observant) communities thus faced a multifronted challenge from fellow Franciscans, fraternal struggles that are the focus of the present discussion. As is often typical of familial disputes in the Church – and certainly those that plagued the Franciscan tradition throughout its history – the fraternal conflicts in the Custody were at times quite heated affairs that disrupted internal peace and the orderly operations of the administration. One important reason for this is that they were animated by deep-seated differences in their conceptions of the Franciscan ideal. Indeed, as we know from the rich scholarship on the

Order, internal reform was a perpetual and powerful engine of Franciscan diversification from the thirteenth century onwards.

The Observant movement that gained momentum over the course of the fifteenth century proved to be especially popular and transformative, stimulating the foundation of new communities across Europe as well as the reformation of many existing ones. The result of this was the formal division of the Franciscan Order in 1517 into two distinct families each possessing its own administration: the Conventual (OFM. Conv.) and Observant, the latter known conventionally from this time forward as the Order of Friars Minor (OFM Obs.) because it was the largest.[4] This formal division did little to resolve internal differences, however, and the Order of Friars Minor in particular remained wracked by internal debate throughout the Early Modern Period.[5] One would be hard pressed to easily categorize the reform movements that flourished within its body during this time except to say that there were many of them and that they differed from one another in ways that were meaningful to their adherents. Moreover, while some remained quite local in impact others spread widely. The three traditions that managed to penetrate the boundaries of the Custody by the seventeenth century – the Capuchin, Recollect, and *Riformati* – were among the more influential, and each represented a distinct interpretation of Franciscan spirituality. From the 1620s onwards, the Custody was thus a diverse Franciscan landscape, a change that the brothers of the Holy Land resisted from the start. One can understand why they did so when we consider the deep-seated nature of disagreements among the traditions over the Franciscan ideal. Until the 1620s, the community drew its members from the more mainstream Franciscan communities in Europe, known as the "regular" Observants because they continued to adhere to an Observant Franciscan tradition that the reformed movements rejected as corrupted. The sources of the early modern Custody make it clear that these fraternal disagreements impacted the Holy Land family by the early seventeenth century. They show, moreover, that the regular Observant members worried that criticism of their spiritual worthiness by the reformed brethren would

---

[4] On the reform movements in the early years of the Order, see, for example, David Burr, *Olivi and Franciscan Poverty: The Origins of the Usus Pauper Controversy* (Philadelphia: the University of Pennsylvania Press, 1989); Bert Roest, *Order and Disorder: The Poor Clares between Foundation and Reform* (Leiden: Brill, 2013); and John Moorman, *History of the Franciscan Order* (Oxford: Oxford University Press, 1968).

[5] Moorman, *History*; and Duncan Nimmo, *Reform and Division in the Medieval Franciscan Order* (Rome: The Capuchin Historical Institute, 1987).

jeopardize their control of the central administration. Indeed, concerns about spiritual worthiness comprised a persistent source of tension within the Holy Land family throughout the seventeenth century, emerging into view in the form of legal conflicts, episodes of physical and verbal violence, and even the production of sacred histories. These signs of fraternal tension make one thing perfectly clear: possession of jurisdiction in the Custody had become a valued marker of Franciscan authenticity within the fractured body of the Order of Friars Minor by the seventeenth century.

Relations between the Capuchins and brothers of the Holy Land have already received significant attention in Chapters 4 and 5. However, the question of Franciscan identity and reform also animated their many disputes. For this reason, the nature of Capuchin reform requires a brief discussion here as well. Of the three reform movements, the Capuchin was the only one to formally separate from the Order of Friars Minor during the time of this investigation. In 1525, only a few years after the division of the Order into two branches, the papacy recognized the Capuchins as a third one (OFM Cap.). To say that animosity characterized relations between the Capuchins and the Friars Minor throughout the Early Modern Period is not an exaggeration, as it was rooted in starkly different interpretations of Franciscan spirituality. The Capuchins became known in particular for their mystical piety and embrace of extreme austerity, celebrated in Europe for walking barefoot even in the harshest conditions, and engaging in visceral public reenactments of the *via crucis*.[6] More to our immediate purpose here, they were vocal critics of the spirituality of the regular Observants. Some of the more typical Capuchin criticisms levied at these friars concerned perceived laxity in convent life as well as their pastoral ministry – they ate too well, slept on mattresses and not straw, wore sandals, owned property, and lacked the evangelizing zeal embodied by Francis.

Needless to say, these kinds of criticisms alone help to explain why the brothers of the Holy Land were less than welcoming to the Capuchins when they began arriving in the Custody. No doubt adding to their frostiness was an awareness of the rapid growth of the rival Order. Indeed, by the 1620s, the Capuchin order had become a serious global rival to that of the Friars Minor, its communities were found in many

---

[6] See, for example, Bernard Dompnier, *Enquête au pays des frères des anges: Les Capucins de la province de Lyon au XVIIe et XVIIe siècles* (Lyon: Publications de l'Université de Saint-Etienne, 1993).

parts of the Atlantic World, Europe, and the eastern Mediterranean.[7] The repeated insistence of friars such as Eusebio Valles that the Capuchins had designs upon their administration makes sense in the context of this historic rivalry, a fear that was also not unreasonable when we consider the history of Franciscan reform in the Custody. A similar Franciscan rivalry saw the Custody pass from the hands of Conventual friars to the Observant tradition in 1431, a change in regime that was perhaps on the mind of Valles when he accused the two Capuchins of plotting to undermine his authority during the Easter pilgrimage in 1661. As we may recall from the discussion in Chapter 4, Valles was suspicious of their intentions for a number of reasons, including the fact that they were French. As members of a rival Franciscan Order, however, they were doubly suspect.

While the brothers of the regular Observance clearly worried about Capuchin designs upon their own administration, sources on the Custody suggest that they had much more reason to be concerned about the Recollect and *Riformati*. Unlike the Capuchins, these reformed brethren remained firmly attached to the Order of Friars Minor throughout the Early Modern Period, an administrative relationship that ultimately made it possible for them to penetrate the Holy Land family itself. Both were offshoots of the "the strict observance," a reform movement within the Observant tradition that was already making itself known by the end of the fifteenth century.

Generally speaking, this movement called for a more rigorous observance of the Franciscan Rule, showing particular concern for a more demanding penitential life, simpler diet and living conditions, focus upon prayer, as well as an active evangelical ministry. The *Riformati* was formally recognized as a distinct community of the strict reform in 1532 and it became influential in Italy, Austria, and Poland. In contrast, the Recollect movement took root in France and the Netherlands.[8] According to Frédéric Meyer, the French tradition was heavily influenced

---

[7] See, for example, Dompnier, *Enquête*; and Megan C. Armstrong, "La réaction des frères mineurs Capucins à la publication de l'Edit de Nantes en 1599," in *Paix des armes, paix des âmes*, actes du colloque international tenu (sous l'égide de la Société Henri IV) au Musée national du château de Pau et à l'Université de Pau et des Pays de l'Adour les 8, 9, et 10 octobre 1999, réunis par Paul Mironneau et Isabelle Pedbay-Clottes (Pau: Société Henri IV, 2000), 261–268.

[8] Frédéric Meyer suggests that anti-Italian sentiment in France made it difficult to establish the *Riformati*, hence the greater appeal of French Recollects. Frédéric Meyer, *Pauvreté et assistance spirituelle: Les franciscains récollets de la province de Lyon aux XVIIe et XVIIIe siècles* (Lyon: Université de Saint-Etienne, 1997), 20.

by the Spanish movement of strict observance associated with the reforming friar Peter of Alcantara (d. 1562). The origins of the name "recollect" is a matter of scholarly debate, though it may owe to the emphasis given by this particular tradition to spiritual reflection as a regular facet of conventual devotional life. The first Recollect communities began appearing in France at the end of the sixteenth century, including ones in Nevers (1592), Limoges (1596), and Paris (1603).[9] Like the Capuchins, the Recollects would also eventually make their way into the Atlantic and Mediterranean regions with the support of the French monarchy.[10]

Certainly by the 1620s, the Recollect and *Riformati* traditions had made inroads into the Holy Land family, securing places for members at the heart of the administration of the Custody alongside the Observants. The many lacunae in the sixteenth and seventeenth century sources make it difficult to track the membership on a year to year basis. However, the regulations of the Custody issued in 1633 and published in pamphlet form in 1636 confirm that the Custody included both regular Observant and reformed members by this time. In its discussions about the travel of friars from their home communities, for example, the regulations specifically mention those coming from regular or reformed provinces ("proprie provincie, ò Riforme").[11] The French Recollects achieved an important recognition when they were given their own convent in Nazareth in 1627/1628,[12] but we also find these brothers assigned to other convents. Bernardin Surius, for example, fulfilled the role of president of the convent in the Basilica of the Holy Sepulcher from 1644 to 1647. Eugene Roger, who also wrote one of the pilgrimage treatises analyzed here, spent twenty months in the convent at Nazareth as well as a year assigned to the convent in Bethlehem. He emerges as one of the more intriguing characters among the Holy Land family in sources on the Custody. A loyal French subject and ardent Recollect, Roger was also

---

[9] Meyer, *Pauvreté et assistance spirituelle*, 22–28.

[10] See, for example, Caroline Galland, *Pour la gloire de Dieu et du roi: Les récollets en Nouvelle-France au XVIIe et XVIIIe siecles* (Paris: Editions du Cerf, 2012).

[11] APF CP 27, ff. 150–153. The pamphlet is entitled *ordinationi intorno all buon governo delli luoghi santi di Gierusalemme I Religiosi che van, e vengono fatted al reverendissimo P fra Pietro Iouer, vicario generale di tutto l'ordine del nostro padre S. Francesco* (Rome: Ludovico Grignani, 1636). The regulations were originally approved at General Chapter in Toledo, 1633.

[12] Benard Heyberger, *Les Chrétiens du Proche-Orient au Temps de la Réforme Catholique* (Rome: École Française de Rome, 1994).

apparently a physician who served in this capacity to the Druze prince Emir Fakhr al-Din. Al-Din played a critical role in Franciscan acquisition of the convent of Nazareth in 1620.[13] Of the reformed traditions, the *Riformati* assumed an even larger presence in the Holy Land family over the course of the seventeenth century. An inventory of the Custody from 1654 to 1655, for example, includes a list of twenty-seven priests assigned to the Custody. Of these, six are listed as Recollects, seven *Riformati*, and the remaining fourteen were likely regular Observants.[14] Twenty-two years later, in 1677, a report sent by the *custos* on the state of the Custody included a list of friars who had preached during a recent plague epidemic. Two came from *Riformati* provinces of Corsica and Milan, three are described as Observant, and another two friars receive no provincial origin.[15] A list of friars sent to the Propaganda Fide in 1704 suggests that the *Riformati* came to rival the friars minor in numbers by this time. Organized by region and Franciscan identity, the list notes that of the forty-seven friars from Italy, nineteen were *Riformati*, the regular Observants numbered twenty, and two were Recollects. Among the twenty Spanish friars, nineteen were Observants, one Recollect. Of the eleven remaining, most of which came from France (though one is described as Irish), we find two *Riformati*, two Observants, and two Recollects in addition to four members of the Third Order.[16]

6.1.2 *Fraternal Tension in the Holy Land Family*

As the above suggests, the two reformed traditions were well established in the Custody by the 1650s, creating a Holy Land family that was not only diverse linguistically and ethnically but also in terms of its Franciscan identity. That the regular Observants were no more welcoming to these friars than they were to the Capuchins is also not surprising. Signs of

---

[13] Eugene Roger, *La Terre sainte, ou description topographique tres-particuliere des saints Lieux* (Paris: Antoine Bertier, 1664). The first edition came out in 1646. On Roger, see Hafez Chehab, "Reconstructing the Medici Portrait of Fakhr Al-Din Al-Ma'Ani," in *Muquarnas: An Annual on Islamic Art and Architecture*, vol. XI (Leiden: Brill, 1994), 118; and Frédéric Gabriel, *Christian-Muslim Relations: A Bibliographical History*, ed. David Thomas and John Chesworth, vol. 9 (Leiden: Brill, 2017), 447–452.
[14] APF SC TS I, ff. 46–47. We should note that of the lay brothers, only three are identified as *Riformati* and one as Recollect.
[15] APF CP 27, f. 120. The report was signed by *custos* Fra Teofilo de Nola (April 24, 1677).
[16] APF SOCG (January 14, 1704), f. 29rv–30r. See also Heyberger, *Les Chrétiens*, 287.

tension between the traditions emerge in the sources almost immediately, in particular, over office-holding and internal reform.

These issues were among the more persistent ones to trouble internal relations throughout the seventeenth century, introducing yet another layer of tension into a community already divided over regional differences. The Observants seemed to have had especially fraught relations with the *Riformati*, a situation that may have owed something to their shared Italian origins. As discussed in Chapter 4, the Italian states, and in particular the Venetian Republic, traditionally filled the most important offices in the administration of the Custody. It may have been because they were also Italian that we find *Riformati* entering administrative positions in greater numbers than the Recollects, a fact that made them a more immediate threat to the jurisdiction of the friars minor. In fact, the records show that the *Riformati* began holding important offices from early on, including the important ones of vicar and president. During his time in the convent of the Holy Saviour in Jerusalem, for example, Michele da Filettino occupied the offices of vicar and president, while friar Antonio di Fagnano was president of the community in Cairo.[17] More egregiously (at least from the perspective of the regular Observants), quite a few *Riformati* were appointed as *custos*. Indeed, it was likely no coincidence that several heated disputes erupted between the 1620s to the 1660s, decades that saw a succession of *Riformati* elected to the lofty office. Diego da Sanseverino was the first, appointed *custos* in 1628 by then Minister General Bernardino da Senna (1625–1631). One may recall from Chapter 5 that his appointment was initially encouraged by none other than the secretary of the Propaganda Fide, Monsignor Francesco Ingoli. Ingoli had pushed for his appointment because the regular Observant administrators of the Custody were resisting the Congregation's efforts to establish the French missionaries. In daring to appoint a *Riformati* to the highest office in the Custody, Ingoli knew that he was challenging a cherished privilege of the Friars Minor, one that had become the special purview of the regular Observants. Perhaps it was for this reason that the secretary advised Sanseverino and the reformed brothers who accompanied him to travel to Jerusalem without fanfare and arrive at nighttime so as to take the Observant brothers unawares. The surprise tactic seemed to have worked, because Sanseverino was able to establish his authority from the start. His election also laid the path for

---

[17] APF SC TS 1, ff. 46–47. Filettino was elected vicar in 1637 and *custos* in 1658. He died in Jerusalem on March 22, 1660.

a succession of *Riformati* in the office, a streak that continued without interruption until the election of Mariano Morone da Maleo in 1651/1652.[18]

The appointment of Morone ended twenty-three consecutive years of *Riformati* governance, placing the office back in the hands of the Observant friars. It remained there until 1658, when two *Riformati* were chosen as *custos* in succession: Eusebio Valles (1659–1662) and Isidore da Oggione (1662–1664). Francesco Maria Rhini da Polizzo, a regular Observant, was appointed thereafter and held the office until 1669.[19] Girolamo Golubovich, an Observant himself, has argued that the appointment of the *Riformati* represented a serious rupturing of the traditional jurisdiction of the regular Observants and was never intended to be permanent. Morone's appointment in 1651, in other words, represented a return to normative Observant authority. It was a view clearly shared by the Observant administrators of the seventeenth century. Indeed, one of the first initiatives of Rhini following his election to the office of Minister General of the Order in 1670 was the reaffirmation of Observant jurisdiction over the Custody. Rhini held the office of *custos* just prior to his election to the highest office in the Franciscan Order, and he used his elevated position to secure it *ad futuram* for his tradition, the regular Observant.[20] And with a few exceptions, the friars minor did retain control of the office of *custos* from this time forward. What is more to our purpose here is that the oscillation of the office from one to the other tradition between the 1620s and 1650s responded to internal competition between the *Riformati* and regular Observants over spiritual and political direction of the community.

A particularly evocative example of this competition comes from a series of letters sent to the Congregation of the Propaganda Fide between 1635 and 1636 from a *Riformati* brother named Giacinto. He was most likely Giacinto da Verona, a *Riformati* friar who came from the province

---

[18] Heyberger, *Les Chrétiens*, 88.
[19] On this oscillation in office-holding, see Paolo Pieraccini, *The Franciscan Custody of the Holy Land in Cyprus: Its Educational, Pastoral and Charitable Work and Support for the Maronite Community* (Jerusalem: Terra Santa, 2013), 41, ft. 64.
[20] On Rhini, see Girolamo Golubovich, *Serie cronologica dei reverendissimi superiori di Terra Santa, ossia, dei provinciali custodi e presidenti della medesima: Già commissari apostolici dell' Oriente e sino al 1847 in officio di gran maestri del S. Militare Ordine dal SS. Sepolcro: attuali prelati mitrati, provinciali e custodi di T.S., guardiani del Monte Sion e del SS. Sepolcro di N.S.G.C. ecc* (Gerusalemme: Con. di San Salvatore, 1898), 80. Rhini, a Sicilian, served as *custos* from 1664 to 1667 and as the Minister General of the Order of Friars Minor from 1670 to 1674.

of San Antonio in the Venetian state. Between 1635 and 1637, he served as president in the convent of the Holy Saviour in Jerusalem, an office preoccupied with internal discipline among other responsibilities.[21] In a series of letters sent to the Congregation, the first written within a matter of weeks of his arrival, Giacinto touched upon a number of important issues facing the Custody including internal dissent. On July 24, for example, he mentions "certain lay brothers of the [Observant] family who had been in charge here for years" and insist that only they provided good governance in the Custody. These brothers argued that it was the *Riformati* "who always disturb the good order of the house."[22] But for Giacinto, blame for any unrest fell squarely upon the Observant members of the community. Another letter sent to the Congregation in April 1636 mentions one troublesome Observant friar in particular, a lay brother named Giulio da Venetia whom Giacinto had threatened with excommunication. Excommunication of course was a very serious threat because it would have removed Giulio not only from participation in the liturgical rites but also from the community itself. The seriousness of this threat helps to explain why Giulio appealed the matter to "a higher authority" ("al superior Maggiore"). In doing so, however, the lay brother only infuriated Giacinto further, leading the president to remark that he did not see how the Observants and the *Riformati* could live together because "the Observants refused to be governed by them."[23]

Friar Giacinto does not provide us with a description of Giulio's misbehaviour, except to say that he was excommunicated for disobedience ("il quale non havendomi voluto obedire"). The lay brother may have simply preferred the governance of members of his own tradition, or perhaps he was involved in some sort of illicit act – perhaps drinking excessively, traveling without permission, or even sexual misconduct. Some friars got into serious trouble for these reasons among others. It does seem more likely, however, that Giulio was one of a number of Observant brothers who resisted the reforming endeavours of *Riformati* officials. As Giacinto readily admits in one of his letters, reform was his objective. He notes at one point, for example, that the Custody was an Observant and not a *Riformati* institution but that he had no choice but

---

[21] Golubovich, *Serie cronologica*, 131.
[22] ASVP SOCG 135 (July 24, 1635), f. 385. "Sono qui *certi frati laici della familia*, è gia molti anni regnano qui; pare à essi, è a chi non conosc. la verita, che terra santa non starebe senza loro; ma in vero sono di molto dano al buon governo, che hano tanto in e cose il nome, è viver di Reformati, che sempre met[t]ono male in casa."
[23] APF SOCG 135, f. 417.

to govern all Franciscans the same. He lamented that it was "difficult if not impossible to reduce the brothers of the Observance to live the *Riformati* way." Indeed, he insisted that they had little interest in being "restrained" because they were used to living "broadly," a clear insinuation that the regular Observant tradition was much less rigorous than his own. Reform, in other words, was an upward struggle in the Custody. Clearly feeling sorry over his own situation, Giacinto ends his letter stating that the "poor superior of the Holy Land" must have enormous patience because the Observant brothers were sure to complain whenever he tried "to remove ... their abuses." And yet, to let them continue to "live so irreligiously" was unadvisable, because it would "give rise to many disturbances."[24]

Giacinto returned to the Veneto in 1637, and there is little evidence in the archives to suggest that he had pacified, let alone reformed, the community before doing so. Indeed, a serious scandal that rocked the community in the 1650s suggests that the *Riformati* and Observants continued to hold deep-seated grievances regarding jurisdiction. The scandal in question, which concerned the financial accounts of the Observant *custos* Mariano Morone da Maleo, received a brief discussion in Chapter 5. It first emerges into view in the archives of the Congregation in 1654 and remained a matter of intense debate over the course of the next two years. There is no question that the controversy was a deeply disruptive event in the life of the Custody, raising profound questions about its fiscal operations, the authority of the *custos*, as well as the nature of the Franciscan ideal itself. The brisk exchange of accusations over the following two years also make it virtually impossible to assess the legitimacy of the many grievances. Indeed, the many differing accounts speak to a polarized Franciscan body. What does seem clear at the very least is that intense disagreement erupted between the *Riformati* and Observant members over Morone's tenure. Morone, an Observant, had

[24] APF, SOCG 135 (April 30, 1636), f. 417. The full passage is the following: "Ho voluto il tutto significar di nuovo à cotesta sac. cong.ne acciò voglino l'EEVV la difficoltà per non dire impossibilità che vi è di poter ridurre li frati dell'osservanza al vivere de frati Riformati; posciache essendo quelli avvezzi à vivere largamente non vogliono restringersi; et al povero superiore di Terra Santa tocca haver patienza se esso superiore vuol levare qualche loro abuso *contra la purità della nostra Regola si lamentano*; se egli dichiara levo la regola, ò fa alcuni ragionamenti spirituali, gli pigliano in mala parte, è volendo essi vivere à modo loro non viene tenuto, ne obedito il superiore quando gli vuol rimovere per rimediare à qualche inconveniente, mormorando di quello con dire che gli perseguita; è non essendo conveniente che si lascino vivere cosi irreligionamente; percio ne nascono molte volte disturbi."

fulfilled the posts of lecturer and preacher in his province of Milan before being elected to the office of *custos* in March 1652, following the unexpected death of his predecessor, friar Ambrogio da Pola. Morone arrived in Jerusalem shortly after his election to find himself in charge of a deeply divided community. He was elected for a second term in 1654 and stayed in office until September 27, 1657, and it was during this second term that Morone found himself under fierce attack from some members of the community.

An extensive dossier of documents loosely titled *Causa de Maleo* outlines the main charges and includes the testimony of accusers as well as supporters. Among the many accusations against Morone, one concerned his long absence from Jerusalem, an absence that began in July 1654 and lasted until September. According to the documents, Morone traveled first to Constantinople before making his way to Rome for the General Chapter meeting of the Franciscan Order. It was common for the *custos* to leave the Custody on business, but such a lengthy absence was unusual. In his response, Morone defended his absence, arguing that his return from Rome took longer than usual because it was a difficult time of the year to travel for someone "at an already failing age," and also because he had been advised to take advantage of the water in Testaccio by a doctor "as the only remedy for my illness." Morone vigorously defended himself from other more serious accusations as well, in particular, suggestions of fiscal incompetence and possible malfeasance. Among his accusers, the *Riformati* Michael da Filettino was one of the most vocal, summing up his governance as "very poor" ("poco buono"). Friar Giovanni Battista da Veneti described him as "capricious and imprudent," mentioning that he spent the large sum of 100,000 pezze d'a otto on fees to Ottoman officials among other expenses. Poor expense reporting was apparently another accusation because Morone also took time to address this concern. Morone mentions, for example, that he wasn't specific in noting the dates of purchase or the quantity of the silk, clothes (*panni*), wax, and sugar that they purchased to give to the Turks, and nor did he include those for the initial donation of alms because he thought that it was only important to note when these items were received.

Morone went even further, insisting that he had accomplished a great deal as *custos*. He mentions several projects, including the reacquisition of the Venetian chapel in Cairo and restoration projects involving the chapel of the Calvary in the Holy Sepulchre, the Tomb of Mary, the Garden of Gethsemane, and the holy house of Nazareth. From Morone's perspective, these were important legacies of his turn in office and demonstrated the kind of diligence that was expected of administrators of the Custody.[25]

On the surface, the dispute presents itself as a concern about good governance, but a closer look suggests that it was another manifestation of ongoing disagreements between the *Riformati* and Observants. We note, to begin with, that a number of his most vocal critics, including Michele Filettino, were *Riformati*. Secondly, accusations of poor governance were invoked in early disputes as well. A fascinating document included in the *Causa de Maleo* dossier offers a lengthy account of *Riformati* governance of the Custody, that is, to say the least, scathing. Unfortunately, parts of the document are missing, including the date and the name of the friar who wrote it, though it is clearly an account written by one of the Observants. Internal dating suggests it was likely written sometime between 1655 and 1656. The document begins by noting that the *Riformati* were guardians for twenty-five years and had governed badly. Under their watch expenses rose sharply, while the jurisdiction of the Custody vis-à-vis the Holy Places suffered because of the poor relations between *Riformati* administrators and the Greek Orthodox community. The document also accused the reformed brothers of incompetence vis-à-vis their liturgical duties, stating that they failed to perform the traditional Palm Sunday procession and even questioned the viability of some of the conversions that took place under their watch. It mentions, in particular, a *Riformati* friar named Alessandro di Palermo, who apparently converted to Catholicism and then later back to Islam ("à farsi Turco"). The report also singled out individual *Riformati* for special criticism including the former *custos* Antonio da Gaeta (1648–1651). Gaeta stood accused of presiding over several such failed conversions as well as of being a very poor administrator. The document sums up his administration rather pithily when it describes it as "so terrible, the expenses so exorbitant, and there were so many disorders."[26] One particular statement, however, is especially suggestive of fraternal conflict. It comes near the end of the document and seems to directly challenge *Riformati* criticism of the Observants when it states that the *Riformati* were no more obedient than Observant administrators. As evidence, it mentions the *Riformati* brothers Giuseppe d'Ottaieno and P. Diego di

---

[25] APF SC TS 1, ff. 34–38.
[26] APF SC TS 1, ff. 118–123. "... fù tanto tanto malo il governo, cosi essorbitanti le spese, e sue essere tanti dissordini."

Sorrento who refused to perform their duties as chaplains on the Feast day of Saint Francis in 1654. The document is blunt, stating that they "publicly rebelled by not going to their assigned chaplaincies." Friar Giuseppe seems to have been especially obdurate to the point of insisting that he would "reveal the secrets of the Holy Sepulcher" to the Turks if forced to attend to his duties. Apparently these were "secrets" that he knew through his former role as sacristan, though what they concerned is unclear.[27]

This account, along with the many other documents included in the *Causa da Maleo*, illuminate deep-seated differences between the *Riformati* and the regular Observants thirty years after the first admittance of the reformed brethren into the Holy Land family, differences that circled around questions of governance, Franciscan identity, and spiritual reform. Looking back to our earlier discussion in Chapter 4 of the disrupted Easter pilgrimage in 1661, it seems reasonable to wonder whether the subsequent election of a member of the *Riformati* (Eusebio Valles) as *custos* was another animating force stirring internal conflict. Valles followed the Observant friar Morone in the office in 1658.[28] As a final example, letters involving the commissioners general of the Holy Land show that tensions with the *Riformati* faced the Observants on their travels to and from the Holy Land as well, at least while passing through the kingdom of Naples. A wonderfully colourful letter dated November 29, 1636, concerns the fraught visitation of the convent of Santa Trinità in Naples by an Observant commissioner general, Antonio di' Cerigliano. Franciscan convents, particularly those located near important hubs of the alms trade, were required to provide hospitality to traveling commissioners. Naples was the earliest and still one of the most important hubs dating back to the fourteenth century. The convent of Santa Trinità, however, was in the hands of the *Riformati* at the time of the Cerigliano's visit in 1636. In his letter, Cerigliano describes a hostile environment, complaining that during his two months stay he was "treated as if he was a prisoner." The living conditions were extremely uncomfortable – he was forced to sleep on a table, and the cell was

---

[27] APF SC TS 1, f. 119. "... et il sudetto fr. Giuseppe protestò, che se lo mandava per forza, sarabbe andato à revelare à Turchi tutti secreti del Santo Sepulchro, e lei li sapeva per che era statto sagrestano ...."
[28] On this conflict, see Chapter 3. Valles was elected at the General Chapter held at Toledo on June 8, 1658, and was reconfirmed June 25, 1661, at Valladolid. Golubovich, *Serie cronologica*, 80.

extremely cold. The commissioner general was eventually moved to a cell provided for a "forastiero" (stranger).[29]

The linguistic choice of *forastiero* its itself revealing. Cerigliano was likely referring to cells set aside for nonmembers who were visiting the community or passing by on their travels. However, the implication would have been clear to the officials of the Propaganda Fide – that he was being treated as an outsider of this Franciscan community. Perhaps not surprisingly, the *Riformati* guardian disputed Cerigliano's account, insisting in his own letter that they had provided him with good accommodations, noting that five to six cells were assigned near the stairs close to the choir for the use of the commissioner general and his companions. The suggestion barely hidden in his response was that the commissioner was overly demanding and perhaps "unreformed."[30]

****

As this brief exploration of internal conflict is intended to suggest, other concerns in addition to regional identity fissured the Holy Land family during the Early Modern Period. Lurking barely beneath the surface were deep-seated differences over conceptions of spiritual purity and Franciscan identity, differences that tugged at the threads of communal unity in the Custody and tested the mediating capacities of its governors. For scholars who work on the Franciscan order in other regional contexts, these signs of conflict must seem uncomfortably familiar. No other religious order enjoyed as fractious a reputation as the Franciscan, especially when it came to issues involving internal reform. That these internal debates were playing out in the context of the Custody of the Holy Land, however, argues for the local context of the conflicts as another factor shaping their meaning. As Barbara Diefendorf argues so persuasively in her recent study of monastic reform in seventeenth-century France, the impetus to reform played out in local contexts that significantly determined their nature and impact.[31] This was very much the case in the Custody, a Catholic institution that was unique in terms of its

---

[29] APF SOCG 195, f. 295. "... Di modo che da due mesi in circa mi tratenuto come carcerato; E fatto dormire sopra tavola; *et havesse incon[vinc]iato à far freddo mi volsi ritornare in una cella dal forastiero*." Santa Trinità was an Observant community that was given to the *Riformati* in 1594.

[30] APF SOCG 195, f. 327. Undated.

[31] Barbara Diefendorf, *Planting the Cross: Catholic Reform and Renewal in Sixteenth and Seventeenth-Century France* (Oxford: Oxford University Press, 2019).

membership, administrative character, and spiritual mandate because of its location in the Holy Land. Indeed, when studied in conjunction with Franciscan writings on the Holy Land, the fraternal conflicts illuminate a sacred landscape potent with spiritual meaning because of its intimate association with the life of Francis of Assisi as well as Christ.

The writings represent the Holy Land as another place of Francis, one in which his followers could prove their fidelity to his spiritual vision by exercising jurisdiction over the Custody. Since these texts were produced in the midst of the fraternal conflicts, it is not unreasonable to suggest that they can serve as useful windows into the Holy Land community. In fact, a holistic study of their writings suggest that Francis and his spiritual ideal were very much on the minds of our authors as they grappled with the divisions within their community. What is also clear from their texts is that they were eager to incorporate their traditions in the Holy Land, materially, spiritually, and administratively. Pietro Verniero di Montepeloso, for example, diligently traces the ascendance of his tradition, the *Riformati*, in office-holding during the seventeenth century, in particular, those who held the office of *custos*.[32] Similarly, Eugene Roger and Bernardin Surius introduced their readers to Recollect brothers and institutions under their care. Both take time to describe, for example, the Recollect convent in Nazareth. As the Home of the Virgin Mary and site of the Annunciation, Nazareth was one of the most sacred cities in the Holy Land. A Franciscan convent once existed here but it was abandoned in 1548 because of local violence.[33] In 1620, however, French negotiations to establish a chapel near the site of the Annunciation of Mary led to the reestablishment of a community in the city, this time under the administration of a Recollect guardian and several brothers. Both authors celebrated this achievement by providing brief histories and a description of the community. Of the two, Surius' is the most detailed, mentioning, for example, that five to six friars lived there at the time under the direction of friar Jacques de Vendôme and that the chapel was built attached to the mountain where the Angel Gabriel announced the coming

---

[32] Pietro Verniero di Montepoloso, "Chroniche ovverro Annali di Terra Santa del P. Pietro Verniero di Montepeloso," in *Biblioteca bio-bibliografica della Terra Santa e dell'Oriente Francescana*, ed. Girolamo Golubovich, vol. 10 (Florence: Quaracchi, 1936), 132.

[33] Girolamo Golubovich, ed., "Registro de' fatti memorabili per gli anni 1429–1699," in *Collectanea Terrae Sanctae ex Archivo Hierosolymitano depromta*, Biblioteca bio-bibliografica della Terra Santa e dell'Oriente Francescano, vol. XIV, nuova serie (Florence: Quaracchi, 1933), 10.

birth of Christ to Mary.[34] Most of the sacred histories discussed here, however, were produced by Observant friars. This is not surprising since these were the brothers who had governed the Custody since 1431 and who comprised the largest segment of the Franciscan family during the time of this study. As one might expect as well, their histories provided strident defenses of Observant jurisdiction in the Custody in particular. Whether regular Observant, Recollect, or *Riformati*, however, they were all connected ideologically through their Franciscan heritage and their membership in the Order of Friars Minor. Lurking in the myriad writings of the brothers, in other words, is a shared Franciscan sacred history, one that celebrated the followers of Francis as the rightful possessors of custodial jurisdiction because of the perfect apostolic piety of their founder, Francis of Assisi. For reformed friars as well as the regular Observants, moreover, to be *in* the Holy Land and part of the administration of the Custody carried special meaning as a marker of Franciscan fidelity and authenticity.

Sections 6.2 and 6.3 probe the construction of a Franciscan sacred history of the Custody by looking at two narrative strategies that proved particularly useful: firstly, placing Francis of Assisi in the Holy Land and secondly, constructing Observant administration of the Custody as a continuation of the apostolic ministries of both Christ and Francis. In preparation for this discussion, Section 6.2 begins with a brief introduction to the writings of the early modern friars.

6.2 AN OBSERVANT SACRED HISTORY

6.2.1 *The Sources*

Among the many Catholic orders, the Franciscan had long been active producers of sacred histories. It is not surprising, in other words, to find several penned by members of the Custody, especially since these were being used to celebrate their long tenure in charge of its administration. Other scholars have remarked on this as well, most recently Andrew Jotischky and Mirianne Ritsema van Eck. Ritsema argues that the

---

[34] Roger, *La Terre sainte*, 433; and Bernardin Surius, *Le pieu pelerin ou voyage de Jerusalem divise en trois livres contenans la description topographique de plusieurs Royaumes, pais, villes, nations estrangeres nommement des quatuorze religions orientales, leurs moeurs & humeurs, tant en matiere de Religion que de civile conversation &c.* (Brussels: Francois Foppens, 1666), 305–306.

writings produced by Observant friars expressed a certain "territoriality" about the Holy Land, constructing the sacred landscape as a spiritual and material possession of the Franciscan tradition.[35] A similar observation shapes this exploration of their texts as well, though particular attention is given to elucidating those material, legal, and spiritual dimensions intended to evoke custodial jurisdiction as a marker of Franciscan legitimacy. Their sacred histories took other forms as well including material representations, and so the decision to focus upon texts may seem somewhat limiting.[36] I would suggest, however, that their texts provide us with the most layered and complex sacred history narratives. Indeed, many of their texts also incorporate other media including engravings that contribute to the richness of their histories. Detailed descriptions of the performance of liturgical rites similarly provide a sense of materiality that engages with the more typical scholarly observations about past events (biblical, Franciscan, imperial), geography, and local culture to construct a Franciscan sacred history. Moreover, Franciscan texts also played with different literary genres.

This project has identified sixteen texts that incorporated some form of sacred history that were published between 1500 and 1725. This is in addition to two chronicles that were written at the time but published later. The eighteen texts represent a mix of genres – pilgrimage treatises, chronicles, juridical and liturgical compendia, theological tracts, grammars. More such writings likely exist, especially in manuscript form.[37] We should note that the diversity of genres employed by these friars was not in itself unusual, reflecting both the missionary mandate of the order as well as the particular demands of fulfilling a spiritual ministry in a diverse site of global pilgrimage. Grammars were important for engaging with the many local Christian and Muslim communities; liturgical handbooks described the distinctive rites held in the Holy Places for pastoral as well as devotional

---

[35] Marianne P. Ritsema, *The Holy Land in Observant Texts (c. 1480–1650): Theology, Travel, and Territoriality* (Leiden: Brill, 2019);Andrew Jotischky, "The Franciscan Return to the Holy Land (1333) and Mt Sion: Pilgrimage and the Apostolic Mission," in *The Crusader World*, ed. Adrian Boas (London: Routledge, 2016), 241–258.

[36] See, for example, Kathryn Blair Moore, *The Architecture of the Christian Holy Land: Reception from Late Antiquity through the Renaissance* (Cambridge: Cambridge University Press, 2017).

[37] The fourteenth-century treatise of Niccolo Poggibonsi, for example, was still being reprinted in the Early Modern Period. Kathryn Blair Moore, "Disappearance of an Author and the Emergence of a Genre: Niccolò da Poggibonsi and Pilgrimage Guidebooks between Manuscript and Print," *Renaissance Quarterly* 66 (2013): 357–411.

usage. Learned compendia were needed to engage with an international scholarly community on the biblical past, while chronicles of the Custody traced a continuing Western Christian, and mostly Franciscan, ministry in the Holy Land. Pilgrimage treatises, finally, which were produced in multiple languages, served as handy guides and devotional aids for an international Catholic community eager to participate in the spiritual journey.

The writings of the friars thus served many purposes beyond that of sacred history, though it is this function that concerns our investigation here. Of the genres, chronicles and pilgrimage treatises provide the richest sacred histories. The four chronicles were compiled between 1600 and 1724. Two were published during this time, including those of Calahorra and del Puerto. Juan de Calahorra's *Chronica de la provincia de Syria y Tierra Santa de Gerusalen* traces a Franciscan history in the Holy Land from 1219 to 1632. He was a former member of the inner council in the Custody and thus familiar with the inner workings of the Custody.[38] Pietro da Verniero di Montepoloso completed the *chroniche overro annali di Terra Santa* in the 1630s during his tenure as *custos*. An anonymous chronicle is known as the *Registro de' fatti memoriali*. It may be the "annal" mentioned in a statute issued during the tenure of Minister General Sambuca that required the guardian and the *discrets* (*discreti*) of the Custody to choose one doctor from the family to produce a historical record of the most important matters.[39] Both chronicles seem to have relied upon internal documents once housed in the convent of the Holy Saviour, many of which were destroyed in the nineteenth century. The last of the four chronicles is Francisco Jesus Maria de San Juan del Puerto's *Patrimonio Seraphico de Tierra Santa, fundado por Christo nuestro redentor con su preciosa*. Del Puerto's account is the most expansive but clearly relied significantly upon the earlier chronicles for its history of the Custody. In addition to these chronicles, two scholastic treatises are also important to this investigation: Francesco Quaresmio's *Eluctio Terra Sanctae* (1639)[40] and Mariano Morone da Maleo's *Terra Santa Nuovamente Illustrata* (1669).[41] Both authors occupied

---

[38] Juan de Calahorra, *Chronica de la provincia de Syria y Tierra Santa de Gerusalen contiene los progressos que en ella ha hecho la religion serafica, desde el año 1219 hasta el de 1632* (Madrid: Juan Garcia Infançon, 1684).

[39] Golubovich, ed., "Registro de' fatti memorabili per gli anni 1429–1699," 1–55.

[40] Francisco Quaresmio, *Historica Theologica e Moralis Terra Elucidatio* (Antwerp: Plantiniana Balthasaris Moreti, 1639; reprint, Jerusalem: Franciscan Printing Press, 1989), 417, 423.

[41] Mariano Morone da Maleo, *Terra Santa Nuovamente Illustrata dal P. Fr. Mariano Morone da Maleo* (Piacenza: Stampa Ducale di Giovanni Barachi, 1669).

prominent positions in the Custody – Francesco Quaresmio as a commissioner general of the Holy Land and Morone as *custos*. The *Elucidatio* is a fascinating scholastic study of the Holy Land that combines history, geography, and theology, but it also includes substantive discussion about the Custody and Franciscan administration. Harder to categorize is the *Liber de perenni cultu Terrae Sanctae et de fructuosa ejus peregrinatione* by Bonifacio Stephano. Published in Latin in 1573, Stephano intersperses a discussion of the central liturgical rites in the Holy Places with some discussion of history.[42]

The majority of Franciscan writings took the form of pilgrimage treatises, a fact that is not surprising given the pilgrimage mandate of the Custody. Though older treatises were still being published in the Early Modern Period as well, most notably that of the fourteenth-century friar Niccolò Poggibonsi, the twelve studied here were first published between 1500 and 1700 and thus products of the early modern Custody. Four were written by friars who traveled for the purposes of pilgrimage or business and the remainder were the work of brothers who had spent significant time on the mission, usually between three and six years. The authors, moreover, came from diverse linguistic and ethnic backgrounds, with five French friars (Jean Thenaud, Henri Castela,[43] Jean Boucher, Goujon, Eugene Roger), one Flemish friar (Bernardin Surius), four Spaniards (Antonio de Aranda, Pantaleo Daveiro, Antonio Castillo, Medina), and three Italians (Bianchi, Suriano, Amico).[44] Of course, categorizing the authors by region let alone by Franciscan identity does little to tell us about the authors themselves. This is a shame because their writings hint at a diverse and interesting cluster of personalities worthy of further exploration. As a historian immersed in their work, I have wondered what it would be like, for example, to sit in on a conversation between the elegant, humanist-trained Venetian Francesco Suriano, the fiery Recollect Eugene Roger, and the very serious if (reportedly) truculent Francesco Quaresmio. Unfortunately, as well, it is also beyond the capacity of this discussion to explore their texts as unique products of their authors, though it bears stating that they stand on their own as literary creations. Instead, our focus lies upon their participation in a collective

---

[42] Bonifacio Stephano, *Liber de Perenni Cultu Terrae Sanctae et de Fructuosa eius Peregrinatione* (Venice, 1573; reprint, Venice: L. Merlo Ioh. Bapti. Filii, 1875).

[43] Henri Castela, *Le guide et adresse pour ceux qui veulent faire le S. Voiage de Hierusalem par VPF Henry Castela Tolosain religieux observantin et confesseur des Dmes religieuses a Boreaux* (Paris: chez Laurens Sonnius, 1604).

[44] The full citations for their texts will be provided in the course of this analysis.

sacred history that invested jurisdiction in the Custody with significance as a marker of both Franciscan authenticity and apostolic authority. Sections 6.2 and 6.3 explore two related strands of this narrative, each of which traces a long Franciscan history in the Holy Land. Section 6.2 begins at the beginning with the historic journey of Francis of Assisi.

6.3 A FRANCISCAN HOLY LAND: FRANCIS OF ASSISI

In 1219, Francis and a contingent of brothers traveled to Syria to join the Fifth Crusade (1217–1222), an expedition that set out to restore Jerusalem to Crusader authority after having lost it to the forces of Sultan Saladin in 1187. Within the Franciscan tradition, this trip is considered a defining time in the life of Francis as well as the development of the order as a missionary body, though we learn little about it from surviving historical sources. It is unclear, in particular, whether Francis preached before the sultan of Egypt, an event still celebrated in Franciscan sources on the life of their founder. There is also little evidence to suggest that Francis ever traveled to Jerusalem. It is not mentioned, for example, in his early biographies.[45] Most likely, he returned home to Italy after spending several months in Syria in the service of the Crusade. Whether Francis did make a visit to the Holy Land or not, his followers in the Custody insisted that he did. Moreover, they insisted that his visit marked a crucial moment of spiritual transmission between Christ, Francis, and his later followers because it placed the Holy Land in the spiritual care of the Franciscan Order. Goujon is making precisely this connection when he argues that Christ gave the Holy Land to Francis and his faithful followers. Similarly, Francesco Suriano insists that the friars received the guardianship of the Holy Land "from Francis and the Holy Ghost."[46] To be sure, both Goujon and Suriano were careful to highlight Observant jurisdiction in the Custody as the natural spiritual outgrowth of this transmission of authority within the Franciscan tradition. Suriano remarks in another passage of his *Trattato*, for example, that the Observants replaced the Conventuals in the Custody in 1431 because they were the most perfect followers of Francis. The Venetian friar was a proud Observant who lived to see it assume formal shape as the Order of

---

[45] John Tolan makes this point in *Saint Francis and the Sultan: The Curious History of a Christian-Muslim Encounter* (Oxford: Oxford University Press, 2009).

[46] Francesco Suriano, *Treatise of the Holy Land*, trans. Theophilius Bellorini and Eugene Hoade (Jerusalem: Franciscan Printing Press, 1949), 78.

Friars Minor in 1517. But more generally, these and other Franciscan authors were concerned first and foremost with representing Francis as the divinely designated mediator of apostolic authority, a role that continued to be fulfilled by his sons through their possession of jurisdiction over the Custody.

In Section 6.3.1, we will look more closely at Franciscan narratives of the visit of Francis to understand its construction as a marker of apostolic succession. Three strategies receive particular tradition: firstly, a model of *imitatio Christi*; secondly, as the origins of the first Franciscan ministry; and thirdly, as a site of mystical encounter with Francis. Each of these elements drew upon different facets of the life and spirituality of the saint, together recognizing a special role for the Holy Land as a powerful and transformative vessel of the authority of their founder for his faithful followers.

6.3.1 Alter Christus

Though the visit of Francis is mentioned by most of our early modern authors, the level of description varies as do their points of view. One widely shared objective, however, was to underscore Francis' reputation as "another Christ" by placing him in the same region as Christ and in the service of his preaching ministry. An important historical lynchpin for this narrative was the famed audience of Francis with the sultan, celebrated in many of the early Franciscan biographies of the saint. Two of the most influential biographies are those of Thomas of Celano (d. 1260) and Bonaventure of Nursia (d. 1274). Both recount the audience of Francis with the sultan with enormous pride, highlighting it as a moment of spiritual bravery but also as evidence of his early ministry in the region. Thomas of Celano, a contemporary of Francis, emphasized his suffering, dedication, and righteousness. Along the route, Francis was captured and beaten by soldiers, though the future saint was undaunted and eventually made his way into the presence of the sultan of Egypt. Here he was treated graciously and offered many gifts, though he resisted all such overtures. Celano insists that Francis' refusal to be corrupted impressed the Muslim ruler who "was overflowing with admiration and recognized him as a man unlike any other." The ruler, according to Celano, saw the spiritual truth in Francis' preaching, though he refused to convert out of fear of alienating his people. Bonaventure of Nursia sets a similar scene in his own biography, though the gift giving assumes a more spiritual purpose when he suggests that the sultan gave the gifts for "for his own salvation." Francis refused to accept them, even when the sultan suggested giving them to the Christian poor and churches.[47]

While these early accounts differ somewhat in their interpretation of the journey of Francis to Syria and his audience with the sultan, they drew a material connection between Francis and the sacred region that shaped the early modern narratives studied here, in particular, those of Goujon and Quaresmio. In their accounts, Francis expressed a desire to go to the Holy Land from early on, noting that he failed twice before finally succeeding in 1219. That he joined the Crusade and met the sultan similarly highlighted continuity with the mission of Francis in the region, providing another link between a Franciscan presence in a longer history of Christian engagement. Goujon is suggesting as much when he states that the children of Francis "learned from the mouth of their father" that they must carry the world of God to "the Orient." The "orient" in this case referred to the Levant, the primary missionary ground of Christ and the early apostles who traveled the roads of Egypt, Syria, and Palestine to spread the Word of God. In Goujon's account, Francis of Assisi felt compelled to introduce his own preaching ministry in the same region and in doing so, the French friar was reminding readers of Francis' reputation as *alter Christus*. The spiritual tradition developed by Francis and formally approved in 1210 embraced an interpretation of the life of Christ that privileged a wandering preaching ministry and the shunning of wealth and other forms of worldliness. His reception of the stigmata on Mount La Verna in 1226 became a powerful symbol of his faithful rendering of the life of Christ and was memorialized by innumerable artists, including Giotto, in paintings and sculptures.[48] The ubiquity of representations of Francis in parochial churches across the global expanse of the Catholic tradition testifies to his popularity as *alter Christus* throughout the medieval and early modern periods, and the shrine on Mount La Verna remains a popular pilgrimage destination to this day.[49]

---

[47] Thomas of Celano, "The Life of Francis of Assisi," in *Francis of Assisi-The Saint: Early Documents*, vol. 1, ed. Regis J. Armstrong, J. A. Wayne Hellmann, and William J. Short (New York: New City Press, 2005), 231–232; and Bonaventure of Nursia, *Life of Saint Francis* (London: J. M. Dent, 1914), 101–103.

[48] See, for example, H. W. van Os, "St. Francis of Assisi as a Second Christ in Early Italian Painting," *Simiolus: Netherlands Quarterly for the History of Art* 7 (1974): 115–132.

[49] See, in particular, Anne Derbes, *Picturing the Passion in Late Medieval Italy: Narrative Painting, Franciscan Ideologies, and the Levant* (Cambridge: Cambridge University Press, 1996).

For the followers of Francis, including the early modern friars studied here, the reception of the stigmata marked Francis as the perfect interpreter of Christ's message. Through it he had become "one" with the Son of God and embodied His perfection. Along with the stigmata, the journey of Francis to Syria in 1219 served as another authentic demonstration of the *imitatio Christi* because Francis quite literally followed in the footsteps of Christ, fulfilling his role as a latter-day apostle.

That our Franciscan authors placed the founder of their tradition in the Holy Land, however, meant that they had embraced a reinterpretation of his early journey that better supported their construction of custodial jurisdiction as a spiritual legacy. While there is little evidence to suggest that Francis did make it to Jerusalem let alone visit the Holy Places, the majority of Franciscan treatises discussed here insisted that he did so. Goujon, for example, mentioned that Francis visited "every place," while Quaresmio insisted that a divine revelation sent Francis directly from the audience with the sultan to Palestine. Because we find similar statements made in diverse Franciscan sources, including the chronicles of Calahorra and del Puerto that will be discussed shortly, it does seem as though the visit to the Holy Land had become part of Franciscan lore long before the time of this study.[50] For the brothers of the Custody, it was a lore that was especially useful for grounding their claims to custodial jurisdiction because it placed Francis in the same places that witnessed the life and death of Christ, further elucidating a spiritual connection between the apostolic past and a Franciscan present that affirmed their status as latter-day apostles. The friars were thus divinely chosen as mediators of Christ's message, a role that legitimized their jurisdiction in the Holy Places. That Francis was the most perfect guide to the mysteries of Christ was also the message communicated to readers in the accounts of Henri Castela and Bernardin Surius when they included a tour of shrines associated with Francis as part of their journeys to the Holy Land. While passing through Italy on the route to Venice in 1600, for example, Castela stopped to visit the burial places of Francis and Clare in Assisi before going on to the site of the first church built by Francis, known as Santa Maria of Portiuncula. He noted that it was at this church that Francis established his Order. Even more important to his account was the visit to the shrine on Mount La Verna marking the site of the stigmata. Here Castela states proudly that this mountain belonged "entirely to our religious." After describing a

---

[50] Jotischky makes this point as well. Jotischky, "The Franciscan Return to the Holy Land (1333)," 241–258.

miracle in which Francis was saved by an angel from falling down a crevice, the friar playfully redrew the sacred geography of the Holy Land to include La Verna. Its rocky terrain, he insists, brought to mind the "four rocks which experienced the death and passion of our Lord, that is to say Mount Calvary, Mount Sinai, the Mount of Olives and finally that of Averna."[51]

As Kathryn Blair Moore has argued, medieval Franciscan art featured La Verna as one of the four holy mountains, most notably in the cycles of the life of Saint Francis that could be found at Assisi and the shrine at La Verna, indeed throughout the surrounding region.[52] Castela thus drew upon a well-established conception of Francis, but by making the mountain shrine an early stop on his journey to Jerusalem he was also making the site of his transfiguration the gateway to the Holy Land pilgrimage experience. La Verna also features prominently in the account of Bernardin Surius. In comparison, his description is much more sensual, evocative of the spiritual experience of being in that holy place. His account also reinforces popular identification of Francis with Christ, the founder's mission with that of his early modern followers, and the Franciscan path as the correct path to fully comprehend the meaning of the Holy Places.[53] In fact, Surius devotes an entire section to the mountain. He begins by situating it spatially along his journey from Rome and describing its visual impact upon the viewer. We discover, to begin with, that Mount La Verna is located in Tuscany in the Appenines, the mountain chain that runs through the center of Italy. Its summit "bristled with green trees" that formed a "pennache" (plume) of sorts because the mountain was scored on three sides with "deep and terrifying" crevices. The fourth side was "protected" by a wall made of rugged stones ("pierres rudes"). Thus far Surius has prepared his reader for a holy place that was challenging to access but whose ruggedness also embraced it in a protective hug. Moreover, the mountain was verdurous, filled with "all kinds of trees and medicinal herbs," while two rivers, the Arno and the Tiber, flowed at its feet. The mountain was also "extremely high," and its "admirable" rocks and steep precipices "raise the hair" of those who look on it. Surius' description conveys the hardship, suffering, beauty, and

---

[51] Castela, *Le guide*, 18–19. "... et me feust dict que ces grosses masses de pietre estoient mises au reng des quatre rochers, qui se sendirent à la moret & passion de nostre Seigneur, à scavoir celuy du mont de calvaire, du Mont Sinay, du mont des olives, & finalment cestuy de l'Averne."

[52] Moore, *The Architecture of the Christian Holy Land*, 124–125.

[53] Surius, *Le pieux pelerin*, 43–44.

renewal that awaited the pilgrim who braved the climb, elements that worked in tandem to secure the salvation of his/her soul. The mountain emerges at the same time as an animate force, transformed and energized by the sacrality that coursed through its landscape and that was complicit in the spiritual transformation of the devout visitor. As Surius writes: "This place, I don't know by what grace and blessing of God moves hearts to stop, and to hate sin, and even to despise the world [mespriser le monde]." It is as if whoever climbs the mountain hears a voice stating: "This place is sacred, stop sinning." The mountain was sacred, he says, because it had been visited by Christ, his mother, infinite Angels, and also the "humble Francis" among a host of other saints.

Like Castela, Surius presents the mountain as a Franciscan sacred landscape because it was a site of divine revelation. At the time of his visit, seventeen churches and chapels marked the sacred presence of Francis on the mountain. These included the oldest chapel that covered the site of the stigmata, a large church built beside it in the fifteenth century to handle the "grand multitude" who flocked on pilgrimage, and a beautiful chapel on the site of his cell that he had made in a simple fashion from straw and tree branches. Surius uses the description of this chapel to underscore the Franciscan path as the most authentic because of Francis' true humility. Indeed, along with the site of the stigmata, the cell was another crucial site of spiritual transmission on the mountain because it was here that Francis communicated directly with Christ. Directing the reader to look at the center of the chapel, Surius describes a four-sided stone covered by iron lattice marking the spot where Francis used to meditate. It was while in meditation that Jesus communicated with Francis, granting him and his followers four privileges: firstly, that "his order would last until the end of the world; secondly, that "all those who loved his Order, no matter how great sinners they were, God would so move their hearts that they would repent"; thirdly, that all those who persecuted his Order, if they never were truly penitent, would not live long; fourthly, that no religious of the Order would live a sinful life for long, thus they must abandon sin or leave the order."[54] Surius' message to the reader is clear: Christ recognized the friars as His apostolic successors, promising as well a rather nasty threat of divine retribution for any who

---

[54] Surius, *Le pieux pelerin*, 44. "Troisièment que tous ceux qui persecuteroient son Ordre, si ce n'est qu'ils en fissent penitence, ne vivroient gueres; quatriesmement, que nul Religieux de son Ordre ne fera long-temps mauvaise vie, ains quiter a le peché our abandonnera l'Ordre."

tried to harm or undermine the Order. Having established the Order's apostolic credentials, Surius then leads readers to the chapel of the five wounds for what becomes an extended meditation on the meaning of the momentous spiritual event. However, along the way, Surius turns their attention to other physical signs of a spiritual connection between La Verna and the Holy Land. These included a large rock where an angel appeared to Francis to say that this particular rock, along with other ones, had been created on Holy Friday "during the death of our Lord." Once in the chapel, Surius describes the moment when Francis received the five wounds from the angel, writing that the future saint was deep in meditation at the time, pondering an image of Christ on the cross in a small oratory that he had built in his honour. All of a sudden, Francis felt Christ and was overwhelmed with both "sadness and joy." His experience of Christ was mystical and visceral and in this regard typically Franciscan. For Surius and his brothers, the path to salvation was sensual in nature because it worked upon the soul through the body. The love of Christ burned, pierced, engulfed. As he describes the experience: "O what loving inflictions! O what a painful love this perfect lover experienced from this time on, see that he died pierced, sick, languishing of a love for two years after" he received this "loving impression."[55]

6.3.2 *The Origins of a Franciscan Ministry in the Holy Land*

In featuring Francis as a spiritual mediator, the early modern friars were also forging a place for his followers as divinely chosen custodians of the Holy Places. When we consider the many challenges they were facing to their jurisdiction by the sixteenth century, one can certainly understand why they felt doing so was important. As their histories, pilgrimage treatises, and other writings argued, who were better suited to tend to the care of the places associated with the ministry of Christ and interpret their message of redemption than the followers of His most faithful servant, Francis? The presentness of Francis of Assisi in their narratives, however, is one of many indications that the early modern brothers were wrestling with the profound spiritual divisions that were tearing apart the Franciscan body during this time. When understood as a legacy of

---

[55] Surius, *Le pieux pelerin*, 48. "Pourtant cét ardent Seraphin marqua exterieurement imprimé dans son ame l'amour. O quelles amoureuses peines! Ô quel penible amour sentoit ce parfait Amant doresnavant, veu qu'il mourut transpercé, malade, & languissant d'amour deux ans aprés cette impression amoureuse."

Francis, the Custody held understandable allure for the fledgling reforming traditions as well as the regular Observants. To begin with, as a revered pilgrimage institution, the Custody offered a highly visible platform from which to tout their authenticity as faithful followers of Francis. Secondly, it demonstrated a continuing Franciscan presence in the region that stretched back to the life of the founder of the Order. One could argue for this reason as well that custodial jurisdiction manifested the *imitatio Francisci* for the followers of Francis because it recalled the apostolic ministry of Christ. By going to the Holy Land, the friars were walking in the footsteps of their founder and pursuing his ministry.

Such a view of custodial jurisdiction also explains why the visit of Francis appears in the Franciscan treatises as the starting point of a Franciscan administration in the region. Two of the better-known chronicles associated with the Custody serve as good examples. Both were written by regular Observants. Published in 1724, the *Patrimonio Tierra Santa* of Francisco Jesus Maria de San Juan del Puerto lies just outside the period of this study. However, it shows continuity with the other treatises discussed here and for this reason will receive a brief discussion. The full title makes this objective clear from the start when it describes the Holy Land as "a seraphic Patrimony" created by Christ and promised to Saint Francis and his sons of the regular Observance...."[56] Once again, we find here a specific plea for the special authority of the regular Observants, but more pertinent is the emphasis upon the chain of transmission from Christ to Francis to his followers. A much more broadly construed Franciscan sacred history emerges throughout the chronicle, though it is the preface that is of immediate relevance here for its elucidation of an unbroken Franciscan ministry in the Holy Land from the thirteenth to the early eighteenth century. Written by a friar named Domingo Lossada, the preface insisted that Francis not only visited the Holy Land but also preached there: "Francis traveled throughout all of the Holy Land, and his zeal resulted innumerable conversions which he sowed with tears in this ungrateful Land." As this description suggests, Francis established the first framework for the

---

[56] Francisco Jesus Maria de San Juan del Puerto, *Patrimonio Seraphico de Tierra Santa, fundado por Christo nuestro redentor con su preciosa Sangre, prometido por su Magestad à N.P.S. Francisco para sì, y para sus Hijos, adquirido por el mismo santo, heredado, y posseido por sus Hijos de la Regular Observancia, y conservado hasta el tiempo presente* (Madrid: Imprenta de la V.M. Maria de Jesus de Agreda, 1724), b. The title of the preface is "Censura del muy R.P.Fr. Domingo Lossada, lector Jubilado Complutense, examinador synodal del arçobiscopado de Toledo."

modern-day mission and in doing so made the region a historic spiritual responsibility of his Order. The "sons of Saint Francis," he states, "have held possession of the Holy Places for over five centuries." Lossada argues that it was always Francis' intention to hold the Holy Land as a Franciscan mission, noting that the saint took "possession" of Jerusalem but then left, leaving it in the hands of his followers "to oversee and protect it." Indeed, they had never left "the bed of the divine Solomon," maintaining a continual ministry in the Holy Land to the present day.[57] As another example, the chronicler Calahorra wrote that the Friars Minor were the legitimate inheritors "of the Holy city and land of Jerusalem." They inherited it from Francis, whom, he says, lay claim to its jurisdiction through his own travels in the region: "With each step of his holy feet [Francis] inscribed the land with the authentic legitimacy for the inheritance of his sons and their possession thereafter."[58]

As should be clear from this discussion, the chronicles of Calahorra and Del Puerto represented the visit of Francis to the Holy Land as mission in its own right, one that the founder of the Order used to stake a claim to spiritual possession of a region that was deeply meaningful to him because of its intimate association with Christ. Goujon and Quaresmio make similar arguments in their pilgrimage treatises. After insisting that Francis was given possession of the Holy land by Christ, Goujon insisted that Francis had the satisfaction of experiencing the "promised land" first hand, and in doing so, "he took it in his possession, and all the places he visited belonged to him."[59] And it was God's intent that his "children" assumed responsibility for its care: "There are no other religious except those of the Observants of Saint Francis intended to be the guardian angels of the glorious sepulcher of his son Jesus Christ." The friars had preserved it for 356 years, he went on to say, "in its original purity with more care than for their own lives which they

---

[57] Del Puerto, *Patrimonio Seraphico de Tierra Santa*, b. "... y tomò possession non una vez sola, dexando sobre Jerusalèn por centinelas, y guardias constituidos sus hijos, que hasta oy dia no se han apartado de aquel lecho del Divino Salomòn."

[58] Calahorra, "Pues aviendo la peregrinado con sus santissimos pies, y adorado con devocion cordialissima el Apostolico Abrahan, y Caleb Evangelico N. Serafico Padre San Francisco, cada passo, que por aquella Tierra daba, era un [renglon], con que escrivia entonces la legitimidad autentica, para que sus hijos la heredassen, y posseyessen despues."

[59] Goujon, *Histoire et voyage de la Terre-Sainte*, 14. "... il entrera dans sa possession, & tous les lieux qu'il visitera, luy appartiendront."

abandoned at all times for His honour and glory."[60] Of the accounts discussed here, Quaresmio's is the most suggestive of the establishment of an early Franciscan administration in the Holy Land. He notes, to begin with, that the saint traveled to Syria with twelve companions. After arriving at Acre, he distributed his companions to different regions, traveling in twos. According to Quaresmio, once Francis arrived in Palestine, he stayed for a year to establish a Franciscan administration.

In attributing an early Franciscan administration to Francis of Assisi, Quaresmio was not necessarily wrong. Regardless of the truth of his visit to the Holy Places, Francis did make the Holy Land a privileged space of Franciscan mission from early on. In fact, two years before he joined the Crusades in Syria, Francis established the Province of the Holy land in the Franciscan administration. Within a few years of his return to Europe, friars were working in diverse parts of the Levant under the oversight of the Province. Cyprus served as a critical local base of operations for the Province from this time forward, and it was through its provision of an ongoing local Franciscan ministry that the friars were able to negotiate altars in Jerusalem as well as the renowned convent of Mount Sion by the 1330s. Thus, though it is difficult to draw a direct line between Francis and the formation of the Custody, the early establishment of the province of the Holy land and subsequent organization of missions were powerful indications that the Holy Land was an important site of spiritual engagement for the founder of the Franciscan Order, a fact alone that would have made jurisdiction in the Custody meaningful to his followers.

6.3.3 Encountering Francis

As discussed thus far, the visit of Francis to the Holy Land provided another important thread in the Observant narratives anchoring Franciscan claims to custodial jurisdiction. Placing Francis in the Holy Land reminded readers of his reputation as *alter Christus* while staking a claim to the Holy land as a Franciscan mission. Both facets of the visit articulated a role for Francis as the perfect interpreter of his Christian message. But another facet of his visit is also important for understanding

---

[60] Goujon, *Histoire et voyage de la Terre-Sainte*, 14. "ne veut point d'autres Religieux que ceux de l'Observance de saint François, pour ester les Anges tutelaires du Glorieux Sepulchre de Jesus-Christ son Fils, qui depuis 356 ans le conservent dans sa premiere pureté plus soigneusement que leurs vies qu'ils abandonment à tous momens pour son honneur & pour sa gloire."

its meaning for the early modern followers of Francis, namely, its function as a Franciscan sacred space. Calahorra alludes to this when he insists that Francis left behind vestiges of his journey – vestiges that only served "to increase the devotion of his sons to the Holy Places." Following in the footsteps of Francis is a common refrain in many of the Franciscan texts discussed here, but one also finds it in some of their surviving correspondence, including those of the Capuchin missionaries. Pacifique de Provins, for example, who established the first Capuchin community in Aleppo, wrote to the Propaganda Fide in 1627 saying that he still felt the fervor and zeal that first led him to Rome to aid in the salvation of others and compared it to the zeal felt by Francis.[61] In another letter, this one sent just a few months earlier, he reiterated a traditional conception of the Holy Land as the "inheritance" of "our father Saint Francis," mentioning as well that it had been entrusted to the Saint by Pope Benedict with the objective of converting the "orient."[62] When one considers the historic allure of the founder for his followers, these examples suggest that many of the early modern friars who went to the Holy Land, whether as members of the Holy Land family or on one of the Capuchin missions, were also intent upon encountering Francis in the place that inspired his distinctive ministry. That the Saint's charisma has been proven to be a vigorous stimulus to internal renewal in the tradition is also difficult to deny. Scholars have offered it as an important explanatory framework in particular for understanding the spiritualists of the thirteenth century and the Observant reform movements of the fourteenth and fifteenth centuries, as well as the later formation of the Capuchin, *Riformati*, and Recollect traditions discussed here.[63] For Franciscans, returning *ad fontem* meant returning to the source of their own spiritual tradition and that

---

[61] APF SOCG 113 (June 12, 1627), f. 363. "... subito mi vienne una allegrezza al cuora, al ricordo che ho dal fervore et del zelo col quale mi andava animado in Roma alla prochura della salute delle Anima, sia Ste la nostra *come quella del nostro et nostro gloriossissime Padre St Francesco.*"

[62] APF SOCG 113 (Nov 24, 1626), f. 252v. "È ardisco de dire che le VV SS Ill hanno magior obligo di servirse di questa povera, ma seraphica Congre di Capucini, che di qual si voglia altra, non solamente perche pare che Xpto Benedetto habia fatto il suo servitor S Francesco nostro Padre, herede di tutta questa terra per il spiritual è che habbia destinato di convertire tutto l'oriente per li Religiosi gli questo Ordine ...."

[63] On the charisma of Francis as a facet of internal reform, see, in particular, David Burr, *The Spiritual Franciscans: From Protest to Persecution in the Century after Saint Francis* (University Park: Penn State University Press, 2003); and Nimmo, *Reform and Division in the Medieval Franciscan Order*. On charisma in other religious orders, see, for example, Sean Smith, *Fealty and Fidelity: The Lazarists of Bourbon France 1660–1756* (Aldershot: Ashgate Publishing, 2015).

was the life of their founder. The importance of Francis for his followers was something noted outside the tradition as well and even used to undermine their influence. In the popular Protestant polemic, *The Alcoran of the Franciscans* (1542), the German reformer Erasmus Alber insisted that the appeal of Francis for his followers transcended that of Christ as a model of perfection.[64] This was of course a blasphemous assertion, since it suggested that Francis rather than God was the real focal point of Franciscan devotion. It would be more accurate to say that Francis was the gateway to Christian perfection, and it was to his life that the brothers turned repeatedly to understand the path to righteousness. The allure of the Holy Land for brothers at times of spiritual reform is thus understandable, because to go to the region was to encounter Francis in the sacred place that had inspired his distinctive spiritual ministry. That participation in its administration offered a recognized path to Franciscan legitimacy is also why the regular Observants were extremely concerned about the arrival of the reformed traditions in the Custody, all the more so because they were not shy about accusing the Observants of laxity. As the Observants knew full well, charges of corruption had been used quite successfully in the past to unseat Franciscan rivals in the Custody. They themselves had managed to wrestle control of the Custody from the Conventual friars on grounds of spiritual laxity in 1431.[65] In Francesco Suriano's description of this event, European rulers clamoured for the removal of the Conventuals from the Holy Places because they comported themselves "sinfully and dishonestly" and were thus unworthy of tending to the Latin altars.[66] The Observants were chosen instead, a role that Suriano proudly noted they continued to hold to his day. Every three years the central administration of the Order selected worthy Observants to send to the region, friars who were sufficiently "learned, lived a holy life, and zealous on behalf of the Christian faith."[67]

6.4 APOSTOLIC SUCCESSION

Placing Francis in the Holy Land grounded Franciscan claims to custodial authority by constructing this jurisdiction as a legacy of their founder, a religious reformer who made the journey *there* to the homeland of Christ.

---

[64] I want to thank Ian MacCormack for urging me to look at the *Alcoran of the Franciscans*.
[65] *Registro da fatti memorabili*, 7–8, n. 1; and Moorman, *History*, 447–448.
[66] Suriano, *Treatise of the Holy Land*, 112.
[67] Suriano, *Treatise of the Holy Land*, 124.

The early modern narratives crafted ideological and material ties between the Custody and their founder in other ways as well that further legitimized their jurisdiction, in particular by representing the early modern ministry as a continuation of the apostolic one that inspired the spiritual ideal developed by Francis of Assisi. They did so in particular by situating the early modern ministry in the same places once occupied by the apostles and elucidating their custodial responsibilities as adaptations of the early ideal. Four strategies receive special attention here: tracing a Franciscan presence, the Cenacle and Mount Sion, martyrdom, and the veneration and the renovation of the Holy Places.

6.4.1 Tracing a Franciscan Presence

In seeking to collapse the distance between the early modern ministry and the apostolic past, Franciscan authors found multiple ways to evoke spiritual continuity, but one of the most effective was to make their presence in the region palpable in the same places as the apostles. The authors did so in myriad ways. Goujon, for example, provided readers with a spatial and administrative mapping of the ministry in a section dedicated to the Custody entitled "des convents, hospices & cures qu'ont les religieux de l'Observance en la Custodie de Terre Sainte." Goujon begins by first underscoring the Custody's role as *the* home for European travelers regardless of region or status: "Every sort of person, pilgrim or other is well received by us wherever we have a convent in the Holy Land." Also welcome were "all sortes of religious," though it is curious that he specifically mentions the Benedictines, Dominicans, Augustinians, and Carmelites, Capuchins and Recollects. Left out are the Jesuits, who were certainly present in the Custody at the time. While it is less surprising to find the Capuchins included in his list since they were a separate Franciscan order, the Recollects were certainly legitimate members of its administration by the 1660s. However, Goujon is clearly eager to emphasize "Observant" possession of jurisdiction, an objective that also explains his rather pointed comment that many traveling religious "set aside their *capuces*" once in the Custody to adopt the habit of the Holy Land family in order to "to avoid the *avanies* imposed by Turkish officials upon religious in new habits."[68] In mentioning *capuces*, Goujon was likely referencing the Capuchins whose distinctive hoods became visible

---

[68] Goujon, *Histoire et voyage de la Terre-Sainte*, 22.

markers of their reformed Franciscan spirituality. Goujon's implication here was clear, that the Order of Friars Minor was the highest Catholic authority in the Holy Land.

As the administrative center of the Custody, the convent of the Holy Saviour in Jerusalem provided Goujon with another opportunity to highlight the extensive reach of Franciscan jurisdiction. He informs us that this was the home of the *custos* who held the dual authority of apostolic commissioner. His local authority in this role was expansive because it came from the papacy and extended "over all Roman Catholic Christians, habitants, travelers, pilgrims, consuls, merchants, captains of vessels, sailors and seamen" as well as "all religious who arrive as missionaries in the Levant." Goujon then proceeds from here to map a Franciscan presence in the Holy Land using his own time in the Custody to provide a spatial and temporal point of reference. In fact, he wrote his treatise while assigned to the convent of the Holy Sepulcher in Jerusalem, stating that he "had the honour of leading the convent of the Holy Sepulchre in the year 1668, during which time I wrote this book." We learn, moreover, that there were ten to twelve members in this convent at all times, while Bethlehem had as many as fifteen to sixteen priests, Nazareth twelve, and so forth. Here and there we glimpse a certain self-conscious Frenchness about this friar as well, for example, when Goujon makes a point of mentioning that the president of the hospice in the city of Alexandretta (Iskenderun) was almost always a French friar and responsible for the "cure" of the French nation in the city. Other details unique to his account include his discussion of the Franciscan hospice in Saida, describing it as the most beautiful and commodious of the Latin houses and an active hub of the Franciscan pastoral ministry. Four to five religious resided there, he says, though as many as eighteen to twenty used it as a base while traveling.[69]

The size of the communities in the Holy Land may perhaps seem quite small when compared to some of the better-known ones in Europe. Convents such as that attached to the Basilica di Santa Maria in Aracoeli in Rome or the famous *studium generale* in Paris were home to hundreds of friars. However, those in the Custody were more typical of Franciscan communities, especially those found outside of the major urban centers. Much more importantly, Goujon's description highlights their local administrative role and authority while placing them in close

---

[69] Goujon, *Histoire et voyage de la Terre-Sainte*, 23–24.

proximity to the most important Holy Places and in the major cities, sites routinely visited by pilgrims during their travels. For all intents and purposes, the friars were the face of the Latin tradition in the Holy Land, a perception that Goujon reinforces by featuring personal encounters with other friars busy about their duties. Friars populate other Franciscan pilgrimage treatises for similar reasons, encountered along the journey from Europe but most meaningfully in the streets and sacred spaces of the Holy Land. The French friar Jean Thenaud, who made the journey in 1512, for example, describes meeting Francesco Suriano while the latter was guardian of Mount Sion.[70] It was another *custos* who impressed Jean Boucher during his pilgrimage in 1609. Boucher records first meeting Gaudenzio Saibante di Verona (Gaudant Saybant) on the day of his arrival at the convent. Saibante was a Venetian friar from the province of San Antonio, elected to the office of *custos* in 1608.[71] Boucher describes being overwhelmed with tears of joy at the warm greeting of the Franciscan official who came and kissed him on the cheek. Saibante then led the pilgrims to the church attached to the Holy Saviour for prayers and the expected ritual washing of their feet. He features later on in Boucher's account as a knowledgeable conversationalist who engaged frequently with the French preacher during their meals together on a wide array of matters.[72] Boucher was clearly both flattered and impressed by these exchanges, describing Saibante as "a noble Venetian, a very pious and learned and prudent man who is no less versed in affairs of the world as he is in those of religion."

That the *custos* is often the most visible Franciscan in early modern pilgrimage treatises is not surprising given the importance and visibility of this official. But early modern readers encountered many other friars as well. The Flemish friar Bernardin Surius, for example, mentions several friars from the start of his journey, beginning with the commissioner general of the Observants for the Low Countries, friar Pierre (Petrus) Marchant. It was Marchant who gave Surius and his traveling companion, the lay brother Philippe Sinceliers, the necessary permission to travel

---

[70] Jean Thenaud, *Le voyage Outremer et itineraire de oultre mer faict par frere Jehan Thenaud, maistre és ars, docteur en theologie et gardien des freres mineurs d'Angousleme* (1512: reprint, Geneva: Slatkine Reprints, 1971), 3–4, 93.

[71] On Saibante, see P. Guido Zanelli, OFM, "I missionari veneti in Terra santa nel scoli XVII–XVIII e XIX," *Le Venezie Francescane* 15 (1948): 148.

[72] "Un homme fort experimenté [en] les saints Lieux, & verse en toutes les sciences." Jean Boucher, *Le Bouquet sacre compose des plus belles fleurs de la Terre Saincte* (Paris: Denis Moreau on the rue St Jacques Salamanderie, 1620), 189–191.

to the Holy Land. Once in Jerusalem, we meet many more members of the order including the *custos*, Andrea de Luca, one of our chroniclers, Pietro Verniero di Montepeloso,[73] and Hilaire Tounon. That Tounon was a fellow Flamand may explain why Surius provides a bit more biographical information about him than many others. Apparently, he was the longtime companion of Tommaso Obicino da Novara who served as *custos* during the 1620s and was later appointed as papal legate to treat with the Patriarch of the Chaldeans. If Surius is correct, Tounon must also have been one of the longest serving of the brothers at the time because he claims he spent over thirty years there. At the very least, Surius was impressed by their encounter, describing Tounon as "a man extremely knowledgeable about the Holy Places and versed in all the sciences."[74]

However, as the texts of Boucher and Surius demonstrate quite clearly, the most visible manifestation of the Franciscan order was the author himself, the spiritual guide of the journey. Of the two authors, Boucher comes across as especially present in his recounting of the events if at times a bit self-satisfied, at least with regard to his learning and talents as a preacher. At one point, for example, Boucher informs us that the Franciscan *custos* was so impressed by their conversation that he asked him to stay longer and preach during the Easter services in Jerusalem. The French friar understood that this request was unusual because preachers were typically chosen for the Custody by Franciscan authorities in Europe. However, the *custos* could appoint friars as needed. Boucher was certainly flattered, but the fact that he mentions it suggests that he found the invitation useful as well for affirming his credentials as a spiritual guide to the Holy Land. To this end, he mentions that he preached in another language (Italian) in "many places" and that those who listened "were pleased by it."[75] To be sure, not all of the Franciscan authors inserted themselves into the narrative to the extent of Boucher. But every author made it perfectly clear to readers that he was a member of the Franciscan family, noting it on their title page or in the introductory material of their texts, and in some cases providing biographical information. Typically, these mini biographies mentioned the friar's Franciscan province of origin, offices held (e.g., president, lecturer of

---

[73] Surius, *Le pieux pelerin*, 9–10, 271.
[74] Surius, *Le pieux pelerin*, 284. On Novara's role as papal prelate, see Chapter 5.
[75] Boucher, *Le Bouquet sacre*, 193–197. "... de quoy je m'acquitte par la grace de Dieu, au contentement de mon auditoire preschant en langue Italienne, d'autant que tous mes auditeurs estoient Italiens de nation ou de langage."

theology), and just as importantly, the length of time spent in the Holy land.

6.4.2 *The Cenacle and Mount Sion*

Franciscan treatises populated the Holy Land with Franciscan bodies, an effective technique for manifesting spiritual as well as juridical possession of the Holy Land. They also ensured that the reader was accompanied throughout the journey by a Franciscan guide in the form of the narrator. In doing so, they made the Franciscan tradition their gateway to experiencing the Holy Land. Placing the friars spatially in the apostolic past was no less useful for evoking claims to apostolic succession; and for this reason, Franciscan authors featured the ministry of the friars in the same places associated with the ministry of Christ and the apostles. Of special meaning for the friars was the Cenacle and the convent that they built adjacent to it in 1333.[76] The brothers would have been keenly aware of the spiritual significance of this location within the sacred geography of Jerusalem as well as within the Christian tradition more generally. The Cenacle lies on Mount Zion (Sion), the highest of the sacred mountains that embrace Jerusalem and one that has long been revered as a continuous divine revelation among Muslims, Christians, and Jews. As discussed earlier, the Cenacle was itself a site of multifaith pilgrimage through its association both with the Last Supper and the Tomb of King David. Within the sacred geography of Jerusalem, in other words, the friars occupied a privileged place that must have been useful for visibly manifesting their claims to divine authority among the diverse population of the holy city. Indeed, from their perch on the Mountain, the friars overlooked the Western Wall and the Dome of the Rock, the two shrines most sacred to Jews and Muslims. As their writings make clear, however, the convent most importantly connected them materially and spiritually to the apostolic ministry of Christ.

A wonderfully rich description of the Cenacle and its apostolic meaning for the brothers can be found in the pilgrimage treatise of the Spanish friar Antonio de Aranda. Aranda visited the region in 1530 and his account was published just a few years later. It was clearly important to Aranda to feature the friars engaged in their ministry in the Cenacle, and

---

[76] On the significance of Mount Sion, see also Jotischky, "The Franciscan Return to the Holy Land (1333)."

so we learn that thirty friars lived on Mount Sion at any given time and that they came from all nations, including France, Spain, Germany, Hungary and Slavonia (Croatia).[77] He also gives us some sense of the material character of the complex, mentioning that it was a "large and sumptuous church with three naves whose foundations declare earlier greatness." It was also surrounded by a village cemetery. Once inside the Holy Place, the reader follows Aranda on a tour of its chapels – the one holding the heart of Saint Stephen "the protomartyr," another on the site of the Assumption,[78] the place where the apostles elected a bishop of Jerusalem, and, most importantly, the site of the Last Supper.[79] The sanctity of the Holy Place was palpable, and Aranda mentions one particular cell (*celda*) below the Cenacle that exuded "such a great gentleness" and "a smell that [the brothers] insisted it must be celestial and a divine fragrance." This, he insists, "is a true and proven thing."[80] The convent of Mount Sion also appears during the course of the tour and Aranda locates it for the reader by describing it as lying along the meridional wall of the Cenacle. He notes that it had cost the friars a great deal to build it because they required permission from Ottoman authorities. In other words, the convent was a significant Franciscan privilege, one that Aranda was proud to flaunt to their readers. Connecting the convent of Mount Sion to the Cenacle was the chapel associated with the apparition of Christ to his apostles. In other words, the friars had free access to its hallowed spaces because they were materially a part of the Holy Place. This was also meaningful, that it was physically (and thus spiritually) connected; and indeed, Aranda's description of the convent itself is rather cursory in comparison to the Cenacle. It does seem to have been on the small side since he mentions that it held only enough cells for twenty brothers even though the community had thirty. He insisted, however, that the friars never complained because of the special holiness

---

[77] Antonio de Aranda, *Veradera informacion de la tierra sancta segun la disposicion en que en año de mil y quinientos y treynta. El muy reverend padre F. Antonio de Aranda de la orden de sant Francisco Provincial de la Provincia de Castilla sa vio y paseo Agora nuevamente en esta ultima impression muy corregida y enmendada* (Madrid: Francisco de Cormellas y Antonio de Robles, 1563), f. 61.

[78] Aranda must be referring to the site where Mary "fell asleep" and ascended to heaven, today marked by the Church of the Dormition.

[79] Aranda, *Veradera informacion*, f. 59.

[80] "Os hago saber por cosa muy cierta y averiguada, que debaxo del santo Cenaculo, ay una celda delas que moran los frayles donde los moradores della sienten en algunos tiempos tan gran suavidad y olorque juzgan ser celestial y divinal fragancia." Aranda, *Veradera informacion*, f. 61.

and renown of the convent. To their mind, even the smallest room was larger and more beautiful than any found in the rich and grand palaces of Galiana.

Aranda had not yet finished with his discussion of the Cenacle and Mount Sion at this point because he wanted to provide a more detailed physical description of the interior of the Cenacle and its significant biblical past. It is after this that he returns to ponder the long relationship between the friars and the Cenacle itself, a history that clearly was on his mind because of recent events. At the time of Aranda's journey to the region, the friars were briefly shut out of the Cenacle by Ottoman authorities, though they were still living in part of the convent of Mount Sion. The reason given for their expulsion was sacrilege. Specifically, they were accused of walking over the grave of King David whenever they were in the lower area of the Cenacle. Aranda writes that they were forced to leave the Holy Place, only to watch it rededicated to the "rite of Muhammad." Though officially banned, the friars found an ally of sorts in the *santon*, the Muslim religious official placed in charge of the entrance. Plied with gifts, the *santon* let the brothers enter freely at nighttime for worship. However, they could not do was perform the divine offices, a situation that clearly distressed Aranda, who noted that it was something that they traditionally did "for their own great consolation, that of all Christians of this land, and for our pilgrims."[81]

Reflecting upon their recent troubles, Aranda asked his readers to sing for the consolation of the brothers who "continually suffered" at the hands of their Muslim overlords. He reminded them that the Cenacle was the first altar received for the Latin faith from the Mamluk Sultan in 1333 and that it had long been the specific responsibility of the friars. In fact, he insisted that the friars were divinely appointed to care for this Holy Place because it was the start of the apostolic ministry. As he states, the Cenacle was the "first church [established] in the world ... and it is here that will once again see Christ reign."[82] In this passage, Aranda is arguing that he and his Franciscan brothers were true inheritors of the apostolic mantle, a claim that was problematic given that friars had lost access to the site that defined their role as missionaries. For this reason, he

---

[81] Aranda, *Veradera informacion*. "Carescen empero de no poder celebrar el officio divino enellos, segun solian que era gran Consuelo a ellos y a todos los christianos desta tierra, y a nostros peregrinos."
[82] Aranda, *Veradera informacion*, ff. 61–62.

insisted that the friars must one day regain possession of the Cenacle so that Christ could once again reign at "Syon."[83]

Unfortunately, this was not to be. While the friars were briefly reinstalled shortly after the publication of Aranda's treatise, in 1551/1552, the Cenacle was once again seized and this time turned into a mosque. The friars were also expelled from their convent, never to return to live there again. Later accounts depict this event as a devastating loss for the community. Writing in the 1650s, the Flemish friar Bernardin Surius reflected on the earlier expulsion, expressing considerable anger at Ottoman authorities. How arrogant of the Ottoman Sultan (Suleiman), he said, to refuse to restore the Cenacle and the friary to the friars. This place "was sanctified by Jesus Christ by so many beautiful and divine mysteries." Like Aranda, Surius represents Mount Sion as a place of continuing suffering in the name of an apostolic ministry. The "children of Saint Francis," he says, "have fought victoriously for so many years over this place under His glorious standard, and it has often been bathed in, and tainted with, their blood."[84]

As a final example, the Cenacle is also evoked as a site of Franciscan apostolic succession in the treatise of the Italian Bernardino Amico. First published in 1609, D'Amico's *Trattato dell piante et imagine dei sacri edificii di Terra Santa* became popular because of its detailed renderings of the Holy Places. In form it was more a visual journey than a straightforward pilgrimage narrative, though it does take the reader on a tour of the Holy Places. In his preface, Amico recounts the early mission of friar Roger Guerin who was sent in 1332 to conduct Latin worship at the Cenacle. The friar pays tribute to the King and Queen of Naples for providing financial and political support, but he credits Guerin with laying the foundation of a Franciscan ministry at the Cenacle, in particular for obtaining permission for the right to worship and to build a convent. He adds, moreover, that the Franciscan mission was modeled on the apostolic one. In fact, the first brothers numbered twelve at the

---

[83] Aranda, *Veradera informacion*, ff. 61–62. "Estos es el lugar donde mis pies estaviero yo glorificare consuelasse estos nostros religiosos y dando buenas nuevas a todos los lugares sanctos ca. tan diziendo."

[84] Surius, *Le pieux pelerin*, 385. "... quand on considere que ce lieu que Jesus-Christ a sanctifié par tant de beaux & divines mysteres, & où les Enfans de sant François ont guerroyé victorieusement tant d'années sous son glorieux estandart, & souventesfois baigné, & teint de leur sang, soit maintenant prophané de ces chiens circoncis."

A Franciscan Holy Land 345

insistence of their patron, Queen Sancia.[85] Amico presents Guerin and the early community of friars on Mount Sion as a critical continuation of the early apostolic ministry, a ministry that continued on through Franciscan administration of the Custody.[86]

6.4.3 Martyrologies

As Aranda and many other Franciscan authors hastened to inform their readers, the friars also suffered in the Holy Land. Virtually every treatise mentioned brothers who had died, or at the very least suffered, in the pursuit of their mission. Indeed, by the seventeenth century, tracing a long history of suffering had become a more common and formalized element of Franciscan chronicles and pilgrimage texts. Several incorporated martyrologies. In reality, disease was the cause of most of the Franciscan deaths. Bouts of plague, fever, and other infections carried off friars and pilgrims each year, some before ever setting foot on the soil of the Holy Land. Suffering caused by persecution resonated more powerfully as a mark of apostolic succession, however, since, like the early apostles, the friars were operating their mission under a regime that they considered hostile to their faith. For this reason, the most common references to suffering and martyrdom were examples of persecution by the ruling Muslim regime. Francesco Suriano provides quite a few of these in his account, including the arrest of two predecessors as *custos*, Bartholomew of Piacenza and Bernardino da Vecchio. Piacenza was twice *custos* (1489–1493, 1496–1499), while Vecchio was *custos* at the time Suriano arrived in 1512. Both officials had been publicly beaten by Mamluk authorities. Vecchio and several other friars were imprisoned as retribution for recent conflict between the Mamluk Turks and the Knights of Saint John. Suriano arrived in Jerusalem in the midst of European negotiations for their release and noted with some sadness that relations with Mamluk authorities had deteriorated since his first time as *custos* between

---

[85] Bernardino Amico, *Trattato delle piante & immagini de sacri edifizi di Terra Santa: disegnate in Ierusalemme secondo le regole della Prospettiva & vera misura della lor grandezza Dal R.P. E, Bernardino Amico dal Gallipoli dell' Ord. di S. Francesco de Minori Osservanti* (Rome: Pietro Cecconcelli, 1620), preface.

[86] On the early history of the friars before the formation of the Custody, see, for example, Félix del Buey and Cristóforo Alvis, "Orígenes de la custodia de Tierra Santa ayuda de los Reinos de Aragón, Nápoles y Castilla," *Archivo Ibero-americano* 65 (2005): 7–96; and Sabino da Sandoli, *The Peaceful Liberation of the Holy Places in the Fourteenth Century* (Jerusalem: Franciscan Center of Christian Oriental Studies, 1990).

1481 and 1484. By 1512, a new sultan (Al-Gawri) was in power, one less friendly to the friars. Relations with local authorities seemed no easier. Giving voice to these difficulties, Suriano said that "I find it extremely tiring and difficult, remembering the protection provided during my first time as custos, to see the return of the old swindles and extortions...."[87]

Since Suriano also spoke of good relations with the previous Mamluk ruler, the arrest of Vecchio is one important reminder that relations between the Custody and Muslim authorities were complex and fluid throughout the medieval and Early Modern Periods. The Custody would not have existed had the friars not found a way to work well with Mamluk and Ottoman authorities much of the time, but relations could change and quickly for a variety of reasons. However, for the friars, these and other challenging moments became part of a long narrative of suffering that was no less useful for asserting their apostolic credentials. To be sure, disease posed the most persistent danger to the Franciscan ministry. We may recall the lengthy relation of Tommaso Obicino da Novara from 1621, which described a Franciscan community ravaged by plague. Plague epidemics were not new to the Levant during the sixteenth and seventeenth century, and as discussed earlier, a particularly large one swept through between 1620 and 1621 in North Africa and the regions of the Holy Land. The Franciscans of the Custody were hit hard, losing fourteen brothers including the vicar and procurator. The contagion was so severe that the previous guardian, named Francesco Dulcedo, and the remaining brothers were forced to retreat to Bethlehem.[88] Because it was in the service of their ministry, these deaths were also treated as martyrdoms in Franciscan accounts, but death through persecution seems to have received special attention for evoking claims to apostolic authority. Perhaps the most extensive martyrology among the Franciscan texts studied here is that provided by Eugene Roger. Roger included an entire chapter dedicated to Franciscan martyrs, which begins in the thirteenth century and continues through to the time of his own mission to the region in the 1640s. Perhaps because they were closer to his time, or more likely because they ably demonstrated continuing suffering, the more recent martyrdoms are the most detailed. As his account makes

---

[87] Suriano, *Tratatto*, 117. "... me parse molto fatichoso e duro, recordandome de la immunità del primo mio Guardianato, che havevamo, per essere ritornati in quelli primi affanni e manzarie et extorsione e graveze insopportabili."
[88] AHN OP Legajo 1/27/d, 3.

clear, the 1620s and 1630s witnessed several killed and virtually all at the hand of Turkish authorities or armies.[89]

In the Franciscan texts, it mattered *where* as well as *how* Franciscan martyrs died. Suffering was an expected feature in early modern missionary accounts, a recognized mark of true devotion, fidelity to Christ, and zeal. However, Franciscan suffering was intended to evoke that of the apostles, the original Christian martyrs.[90] While the early modern brothers could not claim to be roasted on spits, flayed or crucified like the early martyrs, they could trace a long history of suffering in the very same landscape. Franciscan authors pointed to specific places where the blood of the friars mingled with that of the apostles, thus tracing material as well as spiritual connections between the past and present missions. This objective helps to explain why the most detailed of the examples of martyrdom given by Roger was one of recent memory and he says it took place in the convent of "Mount Sion."[91] It is also the only one for which he provides a specific date – 1637. According to Roger, in 1637, the Order lost the largest number of friars to Ottoman aggression. The details are worth noting: twelve brothers were killed on Mount Sion, while the rest were imprisoned. Twelve represented the number of the original apostles, further signifying the apostolic origins of the Observant mission. But it was also meaningful that these friars died at their convent on Mount Sion. Roger was likely referring to the convent of the Holy Saviour, the convent that they moved to in 1558. The seventeenth-century brothers often still referred to as "Mount Sion."[92] That they continued to

---

[89] AHN OP Legajo 1/27/d, 430–436.
[90] The scholarship on Christian martyrdom is vast. On martyrdom in the early Christian tradition, see, for example, the many seminal works of Peter Brown including *The Body and Society: Men, Women and Sexual Renunciation in Early Christianity* (New York: Columbia University Press, 2008); and Elisabeth Anne Castelli, *Martyrdom and Memory: Early Christian Culture Making* (New York: Columbia University Press, 2004). Several scholars consider the Early Modern Period a new age of martyrdom. See, among others, Hitomi Omata Rappo, "Memories of a 'Christian Past' in Japan: The Museum of the Twenty-Six Martyrs in Nagasaki," *Anais de história de além-mar* 18 (2017): 249–282; Anne Dillon, *The Construction of Martyrdom in the English Catholic Community, 1535–1603* (Ashgate Publishing, 2002); and Brad Gregory, *Salvation at Stake: Christian Martyrdom in Early Modern Europe* (Boston: Harvard University Press, 2001). Concerning its place in the Franciscan tradition, see, for example, Christopher MacEvitt, "Martyrdom and the Muslim World through Franciscan Eyes," *The Catholic Historical Review* 97 (2011):1–23; and Isabelle Heuillant-Donat, "Martyrdom and Identity in the Franciscan Order (Thirteenth and Fourteenth Centuries)," *Franciscan Studies* 70 (2012): 429–453.
[91] Roger, *La Terre sainte*, 438–439.
[92] For example, the *custos* often signed letters *custos* or guardian of Mt. Sion.

use this name further underscores the spiritual significance invested by the friars to their earlier jurisdiction in the Cenacle and location on Mount Zion. As a final observation, the date of this martyrdom was also significant because it was recent. Roger joined the Custody only a few years after this event. Rogers was illuminating a Franciscan family that continued to suffer in the service of the same spiritual ministry and in the very same places as the apostles.

6.4.4 Liturgical Performance

Martyrdom and the Cenacle/Mount Sion were two of the most widely used tropes of apostolic succession in the Franciscan treatises, employed to evoke shared apostolic virtues and evangelical practices. The Cenacle witnessed the birth of the early church in the form of the apostles and its later reform in the hands of their successors, the friars. And like the early Apostles, the friars demonstrated their fidelity to Christ by suffering in his service. But also effective for collapsing the distance between the earlier and later missions were descriptions of liturgical performances.

Experiencing the performance of the rites in the Holy Places was, after all, the objective of the Holy Land pilgrimage because it was through the rites that the mysteries of the site were unveiled, its biblical past brought to life, and the pilgrim transformed. For these reasons, the rites also offered the friars an ideal theatrical space within which they could delineate an intimate association with an apostolic past. An in-depth look at how the friars used liturgical performances in their treatises to construct their sacred histories is far beyond the scope of this investigation. However, it is precisely because they were central to the pilgrimage experience that their use of role-playing and reenactment merits at least a brief discussion here. An early and particularly dramatic example can be found in the treatise of Francesco Suriano when he invites his readers to join the friars and the three Marys on a procession through the Basilica of the Holy Sepulcher wrote the treatise for his sister who belonged to a community of Poor Clares in Venice. His virtual pilgrimage likely features a female apostolic past for this reason. In this passage, Suriano first called upon the sisters to join the traditional procession and asked them to assume the roles played by the friars. This procession, however, was to be led by the Virgin Mary and the abbess assigned the role of the standard bearer. Other sisters formed the choir. Once assembled, the nuns began their virtual visitation: "And as the friars begin in our chapel, in like manner let the chantresses begin, inviting all to weep and lament in the participation of the pains of your spouse Christ, the only Son of the Virgin Mary, Master of Magdalen and the other Marys, underwent at the time of his passion, crucifixion and burial."[93] As this brief excerpt alone suggests, Suriano's gendered reimagining of one of the central rites of Christendom deserves a much more serious exploration than it receives here. Why, for example, did Suriano have the nuns play the roles of the friars rather than just accompany them as pilgrims? What seems more immediately pertinent to our discussion here, however, is that he used the procession to evoke Franciscan claims to apostolic succession. Firstly, the Clares were members of the Franciscan tradition. Secondly, by including them in the procession, Suriano effectively collapsed the historical distance between the apostolic past and Franciscan present. The Clares walked in the footsteps of Christ in the company of the Marys, holy figures who were often described as apostles in their own right.

More typically, Franciscan treatises featured the friars in important male apostolic roles but with the same intent of evoking apostolic succession. Bernardin Surius, for example, provides a detailed description of the performance of the Descent of the Cross in which friars assumed the roles of Joseph of Arimathea and Nicodemus. By the seventeenth century, the *depositio* was a well-established and popular rite during the Easter devotions in many parts of Europe. The rite also had a long history in the Custody, and it seems likely that it was exported from the Holy Land. Surius' description suggests that the friars made sure it was an especially dramatic and emotional moment during the rites in Jerusalem. Indeed, his account of it is touching, presenting the reader with a scene that was suitably solemn because it marked the moment of Christ's great sacrifice but also imbued it with a loving intimacy as the friars and pilgrims slowly, mournfully conveyed a lifelike wooden Christ to the site of Calvary. The *custos* was dressed in a black robe and led a procession of forty friars. At the center of the procession was the figure of Christ, carried in the arms of a prominent member of the community who wore a white stole. Surius describes the wooden figure as almost lifelike. It was "made with such artifice to the last detail that one can bend and turn all of its members in accordance with the devotions."[94] Along the path to the crucifixion, the procession stopped at "the prison of our savior" as well as "other holy

---

[93] Suriano, *Treatise of the Holy Land*, 52–76.
[94] Surius, *Le pieux pelerin*, 496. "Au milieu de la Procession marche une des plus honorables Peres revestu seulement d'un estole, qui porte un Christ entre ses bras, si

places." At each stop they sang the psalm *miserere mei deus* in what Surius describes as a sombre register ("accent lugubre"). Once at the site of Calvary, the friars reenacted the crucifixion, bringing everyone to tears "as they listened to the sound of the blows by the hammer on the nails attaching Christ to the cross." The pilgrims and the friars cried, lamented, and "beat their stomachs." After a period of meditation, the religious playing the role of Joseph of Arimathea took Christ down from the cross and covered him in linen, while another four religious wrapped a black cloth over the cross. From there the figure of Christ was carried to the stone of unction where his body was prepared for burial by Joseph and Nicodemus who filled the church with the smells of their "poudres odoriferantes." At last, the figure of Christ was raised again, covered in a "beautiful shroud" ("beau suaire"), and carried into the shrine of the Holy Sepulcher where devotions continued until the following morning.[95]

Surius' emotional description of the *depositio* is a reminder that this ritual, while popular, held special importance for members of the Franciscan tradition. This was in part because of its celebration of the human, suffering Christ, a conception that the Order had long fostered. Another reason was its evocation of spiritual fidelity, a central tenet of Franciscan spirituality.[96] Francis called on his followers to faithfully imitate Christ, a path that he insisted required humility and selflessness. For the friars as well as the other mendicant orders, worthy exemplars of humility and fidelity could be found among the apostles, in particular, those that stayed by his side throughout the final days and tended to his body by performing the final rites. The Marys and Joseph were rewarded for their selfless devotion by becoming the first to witness His resurrection.[97] Liturgical rites that had the *custos* play the role of Christ were also effective for visually communicating Franciscan apostolic succession. Because it took place in public, the Palm Sunday procession offered a particularly prominent opportunity for doing so. The *custos* played Christ on other occasions as well, however, in particular, the ceremonial washing of the feet of pilgrims upon their arrival at the Jerusalem convent for

---

artificiellement fait à petits resorts, qu'on peut plier & tourner tous les members à sa devotion."

[95] Surius, *Le pieux pelerin*, 496–497.

[96] See, for example, Solange Corbin, *Le Déposition liturgique du Christ au vendredi saint: Sa place dans l'histoire des rites et du theater religieux (Analyse de documents portugais)* (Lisbon: Libraria Bertrand, 1960; Paris: Société d'Editions "Les Belles Lettres," 1960).

[97] Katherine Ludwig Jansen, *The Making of the Magdalen: Preaching and Popular Devotion in the Later Middle Ages* (Princeton: Princeton University Press, 2001).

the pilgrimage. Later, on the eve of Holy Thursday, he washed the feet of twelve religious at the door of the Holy Sepulcher. This ritual recalled Christ's washing of the feet of the poor in the Gospel of John (13:1–17), a moment celebrated as a demonstration of His humility. Since humility was also a central tenet of the Franciscan tradition, the ritual was intended to evoke not only Christ but also Francis. Jean Boucher was clearly at pains to make this connection explicit in his description of the ritual when he describes a prominent ecclesiastical official (the *custos*) dressed in a simple white robe of fine linen decorated with a white star ("une estolle blanche") bending over the feet of pilgrims. "He washed our feet," he says, "with such devotion and humility, and with such a sweet majesty, that there was no one in the group, in my opinion, whose face was not bathed in burning tears [larmes bouillantes]"[98] In this moment, the *custos* was playing both the role of Christ and Francis, manifesting the latter's embodiment of the true message of Christ, a message that lived on in the ministry of the early modern brothers.

6.4.5 Renovation and Veneration

As Section 6.4.4 suggests, role-playing the apostles in the liturgical rites was useful for conflating the early modern ministry of the Observants with that of the apostolic past. Occupying the same spaces, liturgical role-playing, and suffering in the name of Christ cast the early modern ministry of the Observants as a faithful rendering of the *imitatio Christi* that was also modeled by their founder, Francis of Assisi. Even at the most literal level, the visual impact of Franciscan nuns and friars walking alongside the apostles or playing their roles conveyed the notion of apostolic succession quite effectively both to onlookers and readers alike, all the more so since these rites were reenacting the biblical moments at the very sites where they first occurred. At the same time, however, the narrative weight given to liturgical performances is just one of many reminders in the texts of the brothers that the early modern ministry was quite different in nature from that which first traveled the roads of the Holy Land. Centuries of Muslim rule over the sacred landscape had moved Christian ministries from the roads of Palestine to enclosed spaces,

---

[98] Boucher, *Le Bouquet sacre*, 191. "... le Reverend Pere Gardien revestu d'une Aube de fin lin, & orné d'une estolle blanche, nous lava les pieds avec tant de devotion & d'humilité, & avec une si douce majesté, qu'il n'y avoit aucun de la troupe, à mon advis, qui ne baignast sa face de larmes boüillantes ...."

spaces that were closely regulated by Islamic law. Moreover, the primary purpose of the ministry had also changed in response to the region's subjugation to Muslim powers, transformed from one defined primarily by evangelization and aimed at conversion to a ministry dedicated to fostering devotion through the rite of pilgrimage. The pilgrimage remained their first and most important duty into the seventeenth century even as evangelization became a more important custodial responsibility. Thus, representing the early modern ministry as a continuation of the early apostolic one posed a thorny problem for Franciscan authors, who solved it by promoting their role as preservers of a Latin material and liturgical presence in the Holy Land. Since the liturgical rites have already received a fair bit of discussion, we will devote more attention in Section 6.4.6 to descriptions of the material care of the Holy Places. Franciscan texts devoted significant space to describing the material renovations of the Holy Places. Moreover, they often imbed these descriptions in a longer history of Western Christian engagement in the Holy Land, one that highlighted in particular the eras of Byzantine and Crusader rule. These were eras, we should note, that were associated with massive building campaigns in the Holy Places.

Francesco Suriano and the chronicler Pietro Verniero di Montepeloso were among the many Franciscan authors who recorded important contributions to the mission in the form of new buildings as well as renovations to existing ones. In his *Trattato*, Suriano celebrates numerous material contributions made not only by himself but a number of his predecessors. These included several renovation projects, among them the rebuilding of the chapel attached to the convent of Mount Sion during the 1450s and the repair of the apse of the Holy Sepulcher. The latter project was an especially expensive one, costing 11,000 Venetian ducats. John of Tomicello, who preceded Suriano's first term as *custos*, repaired the wooden roof of the church of the Nativity in Bethlehem in 1480 at the cost of 7,000 ducats. Not surprisingly, Suriano provides the most detailed description of his own contribution to the material care of a Latin presence. He seems to have been particularly proud of the beautiful marble altar commissioned for the Church of the Nativity, the renovation of the main convent of Mount Sion (including the dormitory for pilgrims), and the acquisition of a Latin altar in the Holy Sepulchre at the site of Calvary.[99] Each of these accomplishments were expensive projects that

---

[99] Suriano, *Treatise of the Holy Land*, 123–128.

demonstrated the administrative skill as well as the devotion of Suriano, but just as importantly, the preservation and promotion of the Latin tradition in the Holy Land. For similar reasons, Pietro Verniero di Montelpeloso included renovations and the acquisition of religious privileges alongside other spiritual accomplishments in his *chroniche ovvero annali di terra santa*. He praised the *custos* Gabriele Bruno, for example, who built a large hospice for pilgrims in the city of Rama in 1519. His successor Angelo da Ferrara also earned praise for negotiating the construction of a new religious structure in Jerusalem from the *kadi* of Jerusalem. It seems to have been another massive project, requiring shipments of iron, lead, and wood from Europe along with the labour of European master masons, ironworkers, and carpenters.[100] Perhaps the most significant project that engaged the early modern mission was the rebuilding of the dome in the Holy Sepulcher during the 1550s.

The dome was a legacy of the Crusades, and a massive structure in its own right that required frequent renovations by the early modern period. As discussed in Chapter 4, the renovation in the 1550s depended significantly upon the generosity of Philip II, the King of Spain, but it was overseen by the brothers of the Holy Land under the direction of Bonifacio Stephano. It is clear that it was an enormously expensive and demanding project, and a highly visible one, because it covered the most prominent of the Christian Holy Places. Several Franciscan accounts celebrate this project including Stephano himself in his work *de perenni cultu*.[101]

It is not surprising to find Franciscan accounts paying tribute, in particular, to the acquisition of new religious buildings, whether in the form of a hospice, church, or most importantly of all, a chapel in one of the Holy Places. The footprint of the *dhimmi* traditions was strictly delimited under Islamic law, and the friars faced serious competition from other Christian communities when it came to the Holy Places in particular. This meant in practice that such acquisitions were rare and were regarded by the friars as well as other Catholic authorities as significant expansions to the geographic and spiritual reach of the

---

[100] Verniero, *Croniche* 115–118.
[101] Bonifacio Stephano, *Liber de Perenni Cultu Terrae Sanctae et de Fructuosa eius Peregrinatione* (Venice, 1573; reprint, Venice: L. Merlo Ioh. Bapti. Filii, 1875), 275–278. On his close relationship with Philip II, see Adam G. Beaver, "Scholarly Pilgrims: Antiquarian Visions of the Holy Land," in *Sacred History: Visions of the Christian Past in the Renaissance World*, ed. Kate van Liere, Simon Ditchfield, and Howard Louthan (Oxford: Oxford University Press, 2012), 267–84.

Custody.[102] However, Franciscan authors also celebrated the renovation of Latin structures because these were challenging tasks that demonstrated their attention to the promotion of a Latin presence at the spiritual center of Christendom. They required significant funding, the organization of labour, and just as importantly, the support of local political authorities. For this reason among others, the friars represented these responsibilities as other markers of their spiritual worthiness.

Such was the case for liturgical rites as well. Eugene Roger notes, for example, that the friars in the three main convents of Bethlehem and Jerusalem had special privileges to celebrate "the feasts and the divine offices of Abraham, of Job, of Joseph the Just, of Moses, prophet David, and all the prophets, of Anne the prophetess, the good thief, of Longis, of Joseph of Arimathea and Nicodemus." This is just the first part of a more extensive listing of the liturgical rites permitted to convents across the Custody.[103] That Roger and other friars acknowledged these spiritual privileges as Ottoman privileges in their texts is further evidence of the Custody's imbrication in Islamic and Christian structures of authority but also a vivid reminder that the Christian rites were shaped to a significant degree by the nature and degree of access granted through these privileges. More to our purpose in Section 6.4.6, the possession of legal access to the Holy Places and permission to perform the rites placed the spotlight on the continuous usage of the same spaces by the "true" faith and its ministry. To a similar end, authors incorporated the Custody in a longer history of Christian veneration in the Holy Places that celebrated the massive building programs undertaken during the eras of Byzantine and Crusader rule.

Given their central role in transforming Jerusalem into a center of pilgrimage, it is not surprising that Franciscan accounts feature the contributions of the Roman Emperor Constantine and his mother Helen. Constantine and Helen invested substantial sums into the construction of impressive religious buildings to mark sites believed to have witnessed important biblical moments from the life of Christ. Collectively, these came to comprise the sacred itinerary of Christian Jerusalem that was still being followed by the early modern pilgrims. Francisco Quaresmio, for example, devotes extensive discussion in the *Historica Theologica* to the

---

[102] See, for example, the importance given to the acquisition of the Church of the Annunciation in Nazareth in 1620. Roger, *La Terre sainte*, 434; and Golubovich, ed., "Registro de' fatti memorabili," 16.
[103] Roger, *La Terre sainte*, 433.

contributions of Constantine and Helen, insisting that Constantine had grand plans for transforming Jerusalem into a sacred imperial city, and more precisely, a sacred Christian imperial city. Among other Roman sources, Quaresmio cites Eusebio's *vita* of Constantine, a text that dated the promotion of the cult to 325, the same year as the council of Nicaea. It was after this council, he argues, that Constantine decided that the place of Christ's resurrection deserved veneration, and so he undertook the construction of a church that took ten years to complete. He also built two other churches, one on Mount Calvary and one at the place where the "true cross" was found.[104] Quaresmio informs us that this church was dedicated to Helen, Constantine's "most pious" mother "who went herself to Jerusalem, the place of the sepulcher, to help her son purify it and take care of it."[105]

In the above passage, Quaresmio is discussing the first chapels that would come to comprise the Basilica of the Holy Sepulcher, the most important and lasting legacy of Constantinian rule in the Holy Land. The Basilica was constructed to house multiple shrines dedicated to the final days of Christ and, most importantly, the sites of Christ's crucifixion and resurrection.[106] By the time of the mission of Quaresmio and his brothers in the seventeenth century, few remnants of the Constantinian era remained visible in the fabric of the Basilica. It was nevertheless important for the friars to pay tribute to the contributions of son and mother where possible. This is why, for example, Franciscan pilgrimage treatises often used the visitation of the chapel dedicated to Saint Helen to praise her material contributions as well as those of her son. As it is to this day, this chapel is located on the lower level of the Basilica at a short distance from the site of Calvary. The chapel lay under the jurisdiction of the Greek Orthodox at this time and was likely built during the time of the Crusades.[107] By the sixteenth century, pilgrimage treatises make it clear that it was a regular part of the procession through the Basilica. It contained a white marble chair and pilgrims were told that the empress

---

[104] Quaresmio, *Historica Theologica e Moralis Terra Elucidatio*, 223.

[105] Quaresmio, *Historica Theologica e Moralis Terra Elucidatio*, 223–234.

[106] John Baldovin, *The Urban Character of Christian Worship: The Origins, Development, and Meaning of Stational Liturgy* (Rome: Orientalia Christiana Analecta, 1987), 47; Edward D. Hunt, "Constantine and Jerusalem," *The Journal of Ecclesiastical History* 48 (1997): 405–424; Annabel Wharton, "The Baptistery of the Holy Sepulchre in Jerusalem and the Politics of Sacred Landscape," *Dumbarton Oak Papers* 46 (1992), 313–325.

[107] Robert Ousterhout, "Rebuilding the Temple: Constantine Monomachus and the Holy Sepulchre," *Journal of the Society of Architectural Historians* 48 (1989), 71.

sat in it while overseeing the search for the true cross. Friar Henri Castela provides one of the more detailed descriptions of the room, writing that it was richly ornamented and included a bronze sculpture that looked like a crown as well as mosaics depicting the emperor and empress under the dome of the grand altar. As many as two hundred lamps strung from iron chains hung from the ceiling, an enormous number whose illumination would have widely announced the sacrality of this space to pilgrims walking through the dark, cavernous hold of the Basilica. Castela includes a poem as well, a rather unusual, even whimsical, element in the narrative that celebrated Helen's role in promoting the cult in Jerusalem. One line in particular is especially relevant: "Helen came to Jerusalem in person to help her son cleanse the Holy Land and rebuild it."[108] In one sentence, Castela conveys a central connection between the renovation of the Holy Places and spiritual renewal, a task that was a central responsibility of the ministry of the Custody.

Castela's tribute to Helen imbeds the Franciscan ministry in a longer history of Christian renewal defined by the restoration and veneration of religious spaces, a history that stretched back to Byzantine rule. It was a history that included the era of Crusader rule as well. The Christian landscape of Jerusalem was transformed during this time through a vast building campaign that brought workers and artists from Europe as well as building materials and devotional objects.[109] Francesco Suriano mentions several Crusader structures still visible in the city during his time in the Custody including the House of Saint Ann that he says had once been home to the sister of King Baldwin of Jerusalem.[110] As was the case during the time of Constantine and Helen, the Basilica of the Holy Sepulcher was the focus of the building campaign in Jerusalem following the seizure of the city in 1099. Mariette Verhoeven argues that the Basilica was radically transformed to create unity between its many shrines, most importantly those marking the sites of Calvary and the resurrection. Enormous pillars were constructed on either side of the main entrance. The internal space was reorganized as well through the addition of new chapels, a cloister to house the resident Benedictine canons, and a bell

---

[108] Castela, *Le guide*, 219–221.
[109] Adrian Boas, *Jerusalem in the Time of the Crusades: Society, Landscape and Art in the Holy City under Frankish Rule* (London and New York: Routledge, 2001); and Jaroslav Folda, *Crusader Art in the Holy Land from the Third Crusade to the Fall of Acre, 1187–1291* (Cambridge: Cambridge University Press, 2005).
[110] Suriano, *Treatise of the Holy Land*, 105–106.

tower.[111] A church that was also European in design was added along one side of the existing Basilica as part of this reconfiguration of space.

Crusader rule set out to free the Holy land from the "taint" of another erring faith, Islam. In doing, so Crusader rulers, with the active support of the papacy, remade the Holy Places as Latin Christian spaces, an act of transformation that the Franciscan brothers represented in their treatises as an earlier manifestation of Catholic devotion and spiritual renewal. By the end of the fifteenth century, much of the medieval ornamentation of these interior spaces had disappeared. The bell tower attached to the Holy Sepulcher collapsed in 1549, and in 1555, the friars completely rebuilt the Edicule that contained the sepulcher of Christ. Still, traces remained and these formed part of the Franciscan itinerary for visiting early modern pilgrims – the imposing columns at the front entrance already mentioned, for example, and the distinctive vaulted arches so familiar from medieval European church architecture. For many pilgrims, however, and in particular the Knights of the Holy Sepulcher, the most tangible indication of Crusader devotion must have been the sepulchers of the Latin rulers of Jerusalem. As discussed in Chapter 3, Godefroy and his son Baldwin represented a sacred past that was meaningful to members of the Order of the Holy Sepulcher. Along with their many building projects, the bodies of these rulers also anchored the Custody in a long history of Latin engagement in the Holy Land. For this reason, the friars also included their burial places in their literary pilgrimages. In his account published in 1601, friar Henri Castela describes the room in which they lay, noting that that the sepulchers were elevated on four pillars and inscribed with an inscription in Latin, one that many other pilgrim-authors also felt bound to include in their texts.[112]

6.4.6 Francis of Assisi: Renovation, Renewal and Reinvention

As this chapter has argued, Observant authors constructed a long sacred history of the Custody in their treatises, one that cast the early modern ministry as a continuation of that of Christ and the apostles. Marking a long material and spiritual presence in the region was important to

---

[111] Mariette Verhoeven, "Jerusalem As Palimpsest: The Architectural Footprint of the Crusaders in the Contemporary City," in *The Imagined and Real Jerusalem in Art and Architecture*, ed. Jeroen Goudeau, Mariëtte Verhoeven, and Wouter Weijers (Leiden: Brill, 2014), 114–135.

[112] Castela, *Le guide*, 245.

legitimize their claims to custodial jurisdiction. In situating the friars in the same places as the apostles and role-playing them in liturgical performances, Observant authors were recalling the spiritual ideal of their founder, a saint who enjoyed a reputation in his own lifetime as the Other Christ. Indeed, especially important for grounding their claims to jurisdiction was his historic visit, a visit that assumed mythic importance for the brothers of the Holy Land as the spiritual and legal foundations of their jurisdiction over the Custody. For the friars of this study, the visit of Francis was a form of *imitatio Christi*, testifying to the authenticity of Francis' model of ministry through the faithful imitation of the life of Christ. The brothers of the Holy Land presented custodial administration in similar terms to underscore the apostolic origins of their authority. Read in the context of the early modern disputes between the diverse Franciscan traditions in the Custody, the sacred histories of the brothers studied here also show that the Custody had assumed importance by the seventeenth century as a marker of Franciscan authenticity within a Franciscan tradition that was increasingly diverse. The presentness of Francis of Assisi in the early modern narratives studied here suggests that, for many of his followers, going to the Holy Land was about making contact with Francis as well as Christ, contact that was material as well as mystical in nature because the Holy Land was another place touched by his life and infused with his sacrality. To go to the Holy Land as part of the ministry of the Custody thus was to follow in the footsteps of Francis, a mode of *imitatio Francisci*.

With this in mind, one can understand Goujon's assertion at the start of this chapter that custodial jurisdiction manifested the perfection of the spirituality of the regular Observants. To his mind, the Observants were the most perfect followers of Francis, and the reason why they were given guardianship of a region that was deeply meaningful to their founder was because it had inspired his spiritual ideal. That they demonstrated this fidelity through acts of veneration and renovation did not challenge the authenticity of their rendering of the apostolic ideal because these acts, along with evangelization, traced a material and spiritual presence for the "true" Christian faith in the place where it all began. Indeed, these more material and liturgical facets of custodial business also had antecedents in the life of Francis, ones that evinced an ambitious plan of spiritual renewal through the restoration of the true faith. Restoring the Church was Christ's reason for recognizing Francis as his apostolic successor, a role that his early biographers suggested already defined his ministry when he began rebuilding local churches near Arezzo.[113] In one of the most celebrated episodes of his life, Francis personally repaired the dilapidated chapel of San Damiano in Italy as well as other chapels. Among the better known was the church of the Portiunicula, which is mentioned in the account of Henri Castela.[114] These restorative acts suggest that Francis interpreted God's injunction to "rebuild his Church" rather literally, but his biographers insisted that it manifested his role as a restorer of the universal Church, a role that his later followers also celebrated. As Goujon insisted, "Saint Francis was chosen to repair" a church mired in "filth and idolatry."[115]

The restoration of San Damiano is just one of many reminders that the mystical cast of Franciscan spirituality coexisted with an acceptance of the material in the fostering of devotion to God. Rebuilding places of worship promoted veneration, facilitating the much more important spiritual transformation of individual believers. Indeed, building projects played an important role in the Franciscan tradition from the very start, and so it is not surprising that the Franciscan brothers of the Holy Land also cast their renovation and ornamentation of the Holy Places as restorative acts. For the followers of Francis who shared his reformist ambitions, the Holy Land was the natural starting point for the restoration of the true Church because it was a powerful vessel of the authority of Christ. As his followers repeatedly insisted, Francis was a reformer with universalist ambitions. Suriano describes him as the "standard-bearer of Christ" who went everywhere in the service of the true faith.[116] Jacques Goujon writes that Francis was driven by a desire to save the world and argued that his journey to the "orient" was always his principle concern because it was "the land of redemption." That it was home to a multitude of erring faiths as well as the Catholic one made this place all the more in need of a Franciscan ministry. Moreover, God gave Francis responsibility for the Holy Land because he "always saw [Francis] as the restorer of Holy Calvary." The Holy Land was polluted through its subjugation to Muslim rule and the corruption of "new" Christians and "reduced to agony by the perfidy of the Jews who abused the glorious blood [sang

---

[113] On the visit of Francis and spiritual renewal, see for example, Tolan, *Saint Francis and the Sultan.*

[114] Castela, *Le guide*, 11–19.

[115] Goujon, *Histoire et voyage de la Terre-Sainte*, 19–20. "... ordure, de saleté & d'idolatrie, pour en estouffer la memoire, iusqu'à y eriger la statuë d'un Jupiter furieux, & d'une Venus impudique: & Saint François est choisi pour reparer ces desordres."

[116] Suriano, *Treatise of the Holy Land*, 19.

adorable] which continues to flow and that God gives freely to all men." In this passage, Goujon elevates the Holy Land as a singularly powerful vessel of Christian authority, one that was the natural starting point for a new era of spiritual renewal. It reminds us of Suriano's description of the Holy Land as ever-flowing fountain of sacrality in the world, an active, pulsating vessel of the crucified Christ. The region was drenched in His blood and tears, blood and tears that flowed perpetually in the service of the redemption of humankind.

These two facets of Franciscan ideology – the role of Francis as a restorer of the Church and the Holy Land as an ever-flowing vessel of Christ's sacrality – infused the Custody with special meaning for the followers of Francis as a manifestation of their claims to apostolic succession. Franciscan jurisdiction only certified the perfection of the Franciscan tradition but also their mandate as spiritual reformers. And it was no less useful for legitimizing a distinctive Franciscan interpretation within the Franciscan body. One can understand the allure of custodial administration for members of a Franciscan tradition disrupted, but also reinvigorated, by the forces of internal reform at a time when the Catholic Church more generally was wracked by accusations of corruption and disorder. As Surius insisted, "[the Custody] was truly a great favour bestowed upon these religious, who through their poverty possessed the greatest riches and treasures of the world, and for that reason they protect those places which salvation of humankind takes place."[117] In flocking to the Holy Land, however, the reformed brothers were acknowledging another well-recognized function of the sacred landscape in the Franciscan tradition: as a site of Franciscan reinvention. Like the regular Observants before them, the Capuchins, *Riformati*, and Recollects went to the Holy Land to legitimize their claims to Franciscan perfection. In doing so, they were seeking legitimacy for a Franciscan tradition that was changing.

---

[117] Surius, *Le pieux pelerin*, 119.

Conclusion

The Holy Land: Renewal, Revelation, and Reinvention

The year 1700, which marks the end of this investigation, did usher in some notable changes in the life of the Custody. The death of the last Spanish Habsburg monarch in November saw the throne transfer to the Bourbon line, signaling the coming end to an imperial rivalry that had raged in the Custody as well as other global arenas for over a century. While France would remain an important ally of the Custody at the Ottoman Porte for several decades more, its influence in the Mediterranean was declining by the end of the century, especially once the forces of Revolution began tearing at the foundations of the monarchy. The Franciscan brothers arguably faced a more serious challenge to their administration of the pilgrimage from the new enlightenment culture emerging in Europe at this time, which embraced among other things a certain skepticism about the Catholic Church and its doctrine including belief in divine immanence. Still, while perhaps much more muted in tone than in the previous century, pilgrimage treatises produced after 1700 make it clear that Reformation debates over the efficacy of the pilgrimage continued to haunt the Custody. And there were other signs as well that many of the conflicts that beset the venerable pilgrimage institution by 1517 were still testing the administration of the friars. Internal sources show, in particular, that differences over nation and reformed identity remained sources of tension within the Holy Land family. The competition with the Greek Orthodox over altars also reignited in 1701, leading to several more decades of episodic conflict. Indeed, by the end of the eighteenth century, the Greek Orthodox would succeed in asserting their claims to precedence in the Holy Places. And yet, for the brothers of the Holy Land, there were some welcome signs of continuity as well. As in times past, Catholic pilgrims arrived each year in the Holy Land to visit its many sacred sites. Alms continued to flow into Jerusalem from all corners of an increasingly global Catholic tradition in support of the ministry of the Custody and Franciscan jurisdiction persisted. Despite the many challenges the friars faced to their jurisdiction after 1517 from other Christians – including other Catholics and even fellow Franciscans –they continued to exercise control over the Custody after 1700, and the Order of Friars Minor remains in charge to this day.

As argued throughout this book, these manifestations of an early modern Custody engulfed by intra-Christian conflict provide an intriguing glimpse into a venerable pilgrimage institution during a period of profound religious and political change for early modern Catholics. A central assertion here is that the Custody emerged as site of intense intra-Christian contestation by 1517 because of its intimate association with a revered sacred landscape, an association that assumed added significance for early modern Catholics because of the profound changes reshaping their world. Some of the more disruptive (and formative) ones discussed over the course of the six chapters of this investigation include the Ottoman conquest of the Holy Land, the division of the Western Church, Catholic reform, and growing imperial competition in the Mediterranean. These changes intersected with one another and together heightened Catholic belief in the material sacrality of the Holy Land as a vessel of a still living, and powerful, Christ.

Chapters 1 and 2 discussed the formative impact of the Ottoman conquest of the Holy Land in 1517, an event that brought the Holy Land within the embrace of the Ottoman Empire, forever severing its ties with its former Mamluk rulers. In the short term the change in governance revived Western calls for Crusade and forced the Franciscan brothers of the Custody to adapt to a new institutional framework. What proved perhaps the most troubling legacy of the conquest from the perspective of the friars and Catholic authorities, however, was its renewal of competition with the Greek Orthodox community over altars. The division of the Western Church by 1517 also had important consequences for the Custody, in particular through its stirring of debate over the nature and locus of the sacred. As we saw in the pilgrimage treatises written by members of the Order of the Holy Sepulcher, Protestant rejection of a present and accessible Christ and the efficacy of the Holy Land pilgrimage troubled the devout knights, transforming them into ardent defenders of a traditional Catholic understanding of the Holy Land. Both the experience of religious division and internal reform profoundly reshaped the Church in myriad other ways that would also heighten Catholic interest in the Holy Land and its venerable Catholic pilgrimage institution, accounting in particular for the growing influence of the French state and the papacy, the introduction of the Jesuit and Capuchin orders, and internal competition within the Order of Friars Minor for access to the administration in the Custody.

As these cases suggest, it was in response to the profound religious and political changes of their era that many Catholics reinvested in the Holy Land as a material and thus tangible and accessible source of Christian authority and legitimacy. The material nature of its sacrality also made the jurisdiction of the Custody immensely valuable because the pilgrimage institution was the gatekeeper to its legitimizing authority. But as this book has also argued, the Custody was valuable because it was a product of the Holy Land, a region that was extraordinarily diverse in terms of its religious culture and governed for many centuries by Muslim rulers. This study of the Custody, in other words, privileges a formative interaction between Catholic spirituality, Ottoman governance, and political and religious change to explain the religious and political significance of the early modern Custody and in consequence the legitimizing function of the Holy Land for early modern Catholics.

To elucidate this argument, three broad assertions thread the six chapters: Firstly, that the intra-Christian conflicts reveal the reification of the Holy Land as a material and thus tangible and accessible vessel of Christ's authority. Secondly, the Catholics of this study turned to sacred pasts in the Holy Land to justify their claims to jurisdiction. Thirdly, Catholic engagement with the Holy Land operated *through* Ottoman structures of authority and, in doing so, shaped the nature of Catholic engagement.

Firstly, with regard to its reification, Catholics and Catholic powers spent enormous sums to visit the region in person, acquire and build Catholic convents and chapels, and support a permanent Franciscan ministry. That they did so reflected the meaning attached to experiencing the region firsthand, in other words, to being *there*. Because the Holy Land was a vessel of a living Christ, having access to His authority was important because it was transformative. As pilgrimage treatises insisted, to visit the region was to be perfected, because the ministry of Christ and the apostles continued on in the same places where they once lived and worked. In a period of profound and disruptive change such as the Reformation, the Holy Land, through its possession of the most revered of Christian pasts, could also serve as a powerful riposte to a Protestant emphasis upon the Bible as the central vehicle of Christ's authority. For many of the early Catholics discussed here, the Holy Land was another *biblia sacra*, the Word writ material.

Understanding the Holy Land as sacred history is critical to the second assertion, namely, that it was through a sacred past in the Holy Land that the early modern Catholics of this study articulated a claim not only to Catholic legitimacy but also to Christian leadership. Catholics shared a conception of their tradition as the most perfect, one of the reasons why in diverse ways they sought to imbed the manifestations of their tradition in a region that they considered a sacred center of Christendom but also an ever-flowing source of perfection. Doing so sanctified their tradition while advertising its claim to spiritual orthodoxy and legitimacy by rendering it visible, in particular, in the Holy Places and other shared shrines. But it also comprised a critical strand in the construction of a Catholic sacred history, or more accurately, sacred histories. As this study has also shown, the Holy Land was an endlessly inventive source of sacred history for Catholics. Each of the ones discussed here traced a material presence in the region to frame their narratives. This is true whether one is discussing the Roman past that anchored a papal sacred history, a French past that stretched back as far as Charlemagne, the crusading origins of the Knights of the Holy Sepulcher, or a Franciscan history rooted in the visit of Francis of Assisi.

These long pasts were invoked to assert claims to Christian authority and leadership as much as they were used to defend existing privileges in the Holy Land, brandished, for example, to fend off Greek Orthodox claims to Latin altars, refute Protestant criticisms of the Holy Land pilgrimage, or in the case of the papacy, assert its claims to spiritual leadership over the many Eastern Christian traditions of the eastern Mediterranean. In each of these cases sacred history was used to trace a long historical and material connection between early modern Catholics and the region, to protect their own tradition from accusations of spiritual corruption, and to justify their claims to leadership. These sacred histories were no less useful for asserting claims to leadership within the Catholic tradition as well, one of the reasons why we find various Catholic powers and religious communities eager to bring the Custody within the embrace of their own authority. Together, this multiplicity of Catholic sacred histories thrusts into relief the much-valued legitimizing function of the Holy Land because it was not simply a vessel of an authentic biblical past but *the* vessel.

This leads to another related argument, namely, that sacred history was called upon in many cases to legitimize a Catholic tradition that was changing. For many early modern Catholics, the biblical past offered a site of reinvention precisely because it was an eternal source of Christian perfection. It offered not only legitimacy but also an imaginative space within which to rethink a tradition – in this case the Catholic – thus enabling it to adapt to a world that was changing. That the Holy Land would play this function makes perfect sense because it was a site of continuing revelation for Christians as well as Muslims and Jews. The mountains of Jerusalem were witnesses to the successive revelations of Isaiah, Jesus, and Muhammad among other prophets, and each led to a new era marked by spiritual renewal but also spiritual change as the revelations charged new directions for members of these traditions. The Franciscans were making such a claim about their founder Francis, who went to the Holy Land eager to usher in a broad ranging spiritual transformation of the Christian tradition. The early modern friars similarly insisted that they were latter-day apostles, charged with the responsibility of "restoring" the Church. But their vision of the "true" church was hardly that of Francis let alone Christ, rather one that had evolved over time in response to external change as well as internal rethinking of the nature of the Franciscan ideal. Such a view helps to explain the allure of the Holy Land for the Capuchin, Carmelite, and Jesuit missionaries as well who envisioned themselves as leaders ushering in a new age of spiritual renewal, or a Bourbon monarchy presiding over a French kingdom engulfed by the forces of religious reform. Going to the Holy Land offered these Catholic powers and communities a place to re-root their conception of the Catholic tradition, and in the process, reinvent it. The past, in other words, at least in the case of the biblical past of the Holy Land, offered the path forward to a new Catholic future.

Thirdly, and just as importantly, to understand the Custody's emergence as a site of contestation, we need to recognize the formative influence of Ottoman structures of authority in mediating Catholic engagement *in* the Holy Land. Critical to understanding this role was the fact that the Custody was both a Catholic and Ottoman institution shaped by canon and Islamic law. Imbedded in Ottoman as well as Western structures of authority, the Custody gave the Catholic tradition a home in a region that otherwise lay well outside the jurisdiction of Western powers, including the papacy. This point leads to a number of observations made during the course of this investigation. Firstly, that because the Custody had a material and liturgical presence in the Holy Places and in the regions of the Holy Land more generally, its jurisdiction became a sought-after marker of Christian orthodoxy and leadership. This makes sense when we consider that every privilege acquired from Ottoman authorities either reaffirmed or enhanced the place of the Catholic tradition *in* the Holy Land. The most meaningful privileges were those associated with the Holy Places, in particular, the possession of altars. Because these were meaningful markers of Christian orthodoxy and legitimacy, the control of these spaces was especially valued, notably as it concerned doors, keys, and gates. But lamps were also cherished privileges, as were the many and diverse forms of liturgical rites that could be performed on the feast days as well as on more ordinary occasions, because each delineated a place for the Catholic tradition at the source of Christian perfection. Viewed from this standpoint, the jurisdiction of the Custody was contested because it manifested Catholic authority locally and, in consequence, globally, because the Holy Land was the center of Christendom.

This leads to a second observation: that Ottoman governance, through its regulation of Christian access to the Holy Land and its sacred places, also shaped its religious culture to a greater extent than is often understood. It is an observation that deserves much more attention than it receives in this investigation. The Holy Land pilgrimage, however, was deeply meaningful to medieval and early modern Catholics, and it had operated for centuries in a decidedly Muslim context. For this reason, it seems important to ponder the influence of Islam, or perhaps more accurately, the Muslim cultures of the eastern Mediterranean, upon the organization and practice of the Catholic rite. As discussed at several points, Islamic law shaped where, when, and how Christians could worship. Islamic Law and Ottoman authorities also regulated the organization of spaces of worship and ornamentation. So much more work needs to be done to tease out the main dimensions of interfaith engagement, but one has to think it had broader influence in Catholic culture in Europe because the liturgical rites developed in the Holy Land were exported home and promoted through Franciscan friaries. It seems a fitting end to this investigation to offer, as a final observation, that this study argues for the formative impact of the Franciscan tradition upon early modern Catholicism. I am by no means the first scholar to make this argument. The influence of Franciscan spirituality upon the work of Renaissance artists and the lasting legacy (good and bad) of Franciscan missions are just two particularly well-known examples.[1] Franciscan administration of the Custody strengthens the case for its influence because it places the

---

[1] The work on Franciscan missions, in particular, is robust and discussed in Chapters 5 and 6. On the influence of Franciscan piety in the Renaissance, see, for example, Louise Bourdua, *The Franciscans and Art Patronage in Late Medieval Italy* (Cambridge: Cambridge University Press, 2004); Rona Goffen, *Piety, Patronage and Venice: Bellini, Titian, and the Franciscans* (New Haven: Yale University Press, 1986); and more recently, Kathryn Blair Moore, *The Architecture of the Christian Holy Land: Reception from Late Antiquity through the Renaissance* (Cambridge: Cambridge University Press, 2017).

distinctive religious community at the spiritual center of an increasingly global Catholic tradition. As should be clear from this investigation, the brothers of the Holy Land presided over an institution that was global as well as local in nature. Their convents were homes to traveling diplomats, merchants, and pilgrims, and they traveled the world in pursuit of alms as well as political support for their ministry. The friars developed, promoted, and disseminated pilgrimage treatises and liturgical rites, all of which brought the Holy Land to the outer reaches of the early modern Catholic world. But it was a Holy Land seen through the eyes of the Franciscans, packaged in the recognizable garb of Franciscan piety. There is so much more to explore to understand the nature of its global influence through its jurisdiction over the Custody, but William Taylor's observation about Franciscan involvement in the promotion of image shrines in New Spain offers a great deal of food for thought, particularly for thinking about shrines as mechanisms of spiritual renewal and the Holy Land as a place of continual revelation. As he argues, the Franciscans (along with the Augustinians) contributed to what he describes as "the air of the marvelous in New Spain." Shrines, he suggests, had a special place in Franciscan spirituality because "they traditionally looked to miracles and revelation as the greatest source of God's truths."[2]

---

[2] William J. Taylor, *Theatre of a Thousand Wonders: A History of the Miraculous* (Cambridge: Cambridge University Press, 2016).

Bibliography

ARCHIVES

Israel

Arch. Custodia Terrae Sanctae

Index Rerum et decretum S. Congr. De Propaganda Fide
Navis peregrinorum: Ein Pilgerverzeichnis aus Jerusalem von 1561 bis 1695. Bachem: 1938.
Questioni giurdici
Registro de lettere scritte al nostro Sommo Pontefice alla sacra congregatione de propaganda fide co'ad altri Prelati, cosi occidentati, come Orientali per si bisogni di Terra Santa e per l'aumento della nostra santa fede.
Registrum Equitum SSmi Sepulchri (1561–1847).

Italy

Archivio Storico de Propaganda Fide (APF)

Acta Sacrae Congregationis (Acta) I Congregazioni Particolari (CP) 27
Scritture riferite nei congressi (SC) Terra Santa I, II, III Lettere 5, 111
Miscellanea I (Conti Terra Santa III)
Scritture originali riferite nelle congregazioni generali (SOCG) 3, 8, 18, 22, 44, 59, 95, 104, 112, 113, 118, 135, 149, 245

Archivio di Stato Venezia (AVSe)

Bailo 109, 285, 368
Dispacci 93, 112, 113, 117

France

Archives Nationales de France (ANF) BI 380, 381
Archives de la Seine D–Q (10), nos. 1299–1317

Spain

Archivo Histórico Nacional, Madrid (AHN) OP legajo 1/ 12, 27
Archivo Général de Simancas (AGS) legs 483, 1319

PRIMARY SOURCES

Amico, Bernardino. *Trattato delle piante & immagini de sacri edifizi di Terra Santa: Disegnate in Ierusalemme secondo le regole della Prospettiva & vera misura della lor grandezza Dal R.P. E, Bernardino Amico dal Gallipoli dell' Ord. di S. Francesco de Minori Osservanti.* Rome: Pietro Cecconcelli, 1620.

Affagart, Greffin. *Relation de la Terre Sainte (1522–1534).* Reprint, Paris: Librairie V. Lecoffre, 1902.

Aranda, Antonio de. *Veradera informacion de la tierra sancta segun la disposicion en que en año de mil y quinientos y treynta. El muy reverend padre F. Antonio de Aranda de la orden de sant Francisco Provincial de la Provincia de Castilla sa vio y paseo Agora nuevamente en esta ultima impression muy corregida y enmendada.* Madrid: Francisco de Cormellas y Pedro de Robles, 1563.

Arce, Agustin. *Documentos y textos para la historia de Tierra Santa y sus santuarios (1600–1700).* Vol. 1. Jerusalem: Franciscan Printing Press, 1970.

——— . *Expediciones de España a Jerusalén 1693–1842.* Madrid: Relaciones culturales imprenta del ministerio de asuntos exteriors, 1958.

——— . "Maronitas y Franciscanos en el Libano 1450–1516." In *Miscelánea de Tierra Santa 2, Estudios críticos y documentos*, 149–269. Jerusalem: Imprenta de Tierra Santa, 1973.

Beauvau, Henri. *Relation journalière du voyage du Levant fait et descript par Messire Henry de Beauvau, baron dudit lieu, & de Manonville, seigneur de Fleuville.* Paris: Gilles Robinot, 1610.

Beloy, P de. *De l'origine et institution de divers ordres de chevalerie tant ecclésiastique que profanes.* Montauban: Denis Haultin, 1604.

Benard, Nicole. *Le Voyage de Hierusalem et autres lieux de la terre sainct faict par le Sr Benard Parisien chevalier de l'ordre du St Sepulchre de NRE seigneur Jesus Christ.* Paris: chez Denis Moreau, 1621.

Boisselly, Jean de. "Le pelerinage de Jean de Boisselly en Terre Sainte en 1643–1645." In *Société de Statistique de Marseilles* 47 Valence: Imprimerie Valentinoise, 1908: 67–95.

Bonaventure of Nursia, *The Life of Saint Francis of Assisi.* London: J. M. Dent, 1914.

Boucher, Jean. *Bouquet Sacre Composé des plus belles fleurs de la Terre Saincte. Par le P. Boucher Mineur observantin, revue, corrigé, augmenté, et enrichi par l'Autheur d'un excellent discours de la noblesse sur la creation des chevaliers du Saint-Sépulchre.* Paris: Denis Moreau, 1620.

Bouquet Sacre composé des plus belles fleurs de la Terre Sainte. Edited by Marie-Christine Gomez-Geraud. Paris: Editions Anthès, 2008.

"Bullarium Franciscanum Terrae Sanctae."*Diarium Terrae Sanctae* (1912).

Calahorra, Juan de. *Chronica de la provincia de Syria y Tierra Santa de Gerusalen contiene los progressos, que en ella ha hecho la religion serafica, desde el año 1219 hasta el de 1632.* Madrid: Juan Garcia Infançon, 1684.

Casola, Pietro. *Viaggio di Pietro Casola a Gerusalemme, tratto dall'autografo esistente nella biblioteca Trivulzio con note.* Milan: P. Ripamonti-Carpano, 1855.

Castela, Henri. *Le guide et adresse pour ceux qui veulent faire le S. Voiage de Hierusalem par VPF Henry Castela Tolosain religieux observantin et confesseur des Dmes religieuses a Boreaux.* Paris: chez Laurens Sonnius, 1604.

Castelli, Elisabeth Anne. *Martyrdom and Memory: Early Christian Culture Making.* New York: Columbia University Press, 2004.

Ceverio de Vera, Juan. *Viaje de la Tierra Santa, y descripcion de Jerusalem, y del santo monte Libano, con relacion de cosas maravillosas, asi de las provincias de Levante como de las Indias de Occidente.* Madrid: Mathias Mares, 1598.

Chesneau, Jean. *Le voyage de monsieur d'Aramon, ambassadeur pour le roy en levant,* edited by Charles Schefer. Paris: Ernest Leroux, 1887.

Collectanea S. Congregationis de Propaganda Fid e seu Decreta Instructiones Rescripta pro apostolicis Missionibus Rome: ex typographia polyglotta s.c. propaganda fide, 1907.

Cotovic, Jean [Johann van Kootwyck]. *Itinerarium.* Utrecht: Hieryonimus Verdussium, 1619.

De Breves, François Savary. *Relation des voyages de Monsieur de Brèves, tant en Grèce Terre Saincte et egypte qu'aux royaumes de Tunis et Arger.* Paris: Nicolas Gasse, 1628.

Del Puerto, Francisco Jesús María, San Juan. *Patrimonio Seraphico de Tierra Santa, fundado por Christo nuestro redentor con su preciosa Sangre, prometido por su Magestad à N.P.S. Francisco para sì, y para sus Hijos, adquirido por el mismo santo, heredado, y posseìdo por sus Hijos de la Regular Observancia, y conservado hasta el tiempo presente.* Madrid: Imprenta de la V.M. Maria de Jesus de Agreda, 1724.

Erasmus, Desiderius. "A Pilgrimage for Pilgrim's Sake." In *The Colloquies, I. Collected Works of Erasmus.* Vol. 39/40, translated by Craig R. Thompson, 624–655. Toronto: University of Toronto Press, 1997.

Favyn, Andre. *Le theatre d'honneur et de chevalerie ou L'histoire des Ordres Militaires des Roys, & Princes de la Chestienté, & leur Genealogie: De l'Institution des Armes, & Blasons; Roys, Heraulds, & Poursuivants d'Armes; Duels, Ioustes, & Tournois; & de tout ce qui concerne le faict du Chevalier de l'Ordre.* 2 vols. Paris: Robert Foüet, 1620.

Fabri [Faber], Felix. *The Wanderings of Felix Fabri.* 2 vols., translated by Aubrey Stewart. London: Palestine Pilgrim's Society, 1896.

Bibliography

Golobovich, Girolamo, ed. *Biblioteca bio-bibliografica della Terra Santa e dell'Oriente Francescano.* 5 vols. Annales Minorum in quibus res omnes trium ordinum a S. Francisco institutum. Florence: Quaracchi, 1906–1927.

Goujon, Jacques-Florent. *Histoire et voyage de la Terre-Sainte, où tout ce qu'il y a de plus remarquable dans les Saints Lieux, est tres-exactement descript.* Lyon: Pierre Compagnon & Robert Taillandier, 1670.

Hault, Nicolas de. *Le Voyage de Hierusalem faict l'an mil cinq cens quatre vingts treize.* Paris: Abraham Savorain, 1601.

Heyd, Uriel, ed. *Ottoman Documents on Palestine, 1552–1615: A Study of the Firman according to the Mühimme Defteri.* Oxford: Clarendon Press, 1960.

La Croix, Sieur de. *La Turquie chrétienne sous la puissante protection de louis le Grand, Protecteur unique cu Christianisme en Orient, contenant l'état present des Nations et des Eglises Grecque, Arménienne et Maronite dans l'Empire Ottoman.* Paris: P. Hérissant, 1695.

Lemmens, Leonhard, ed. *Acta S. Congregationis de propaganda Fide pro Terra Sancta.* 2 vols. Rome: Collegio di S. Bonaventura, 1921.

"Conspectus Missionum Familiae Cismontanae Ordinis Fratr. Minorum an. 1627–1628 conscriptus." *AFH* 22 (1929): 379–390.

"Registro de' fatti memorabilia di Terra santa." In *Collectanea Terrae Sanctae*, in *Bilbiografica della Terra Santa e dell'Oriente Francescano*, vol. XIV, nuova serie, edited by Girolamo Golobovich, 1–64. Florence: Quaracchi, 1933.

Isler-de Jongh, Ariane and François Fossier, eds. *Le voyage de Charles Magius, 1568–73.* Paris: Editions Anthèse, 1992.

Martín, Pedro García, ed. *Paisajes de la Tierra Prometida: El Viaje a Jerusalén de Don Fadrique Enríquez de Ribera.* Madrid: Miraguano, S. A., Ediciones, 2001.

Medina, Antonio. *Viaggio di Terra Santa con sue stationi e misterii del M.R.P. Antonio Medina Spagnuola dell'Ordine di S. Francesco di gli Scalz.* Italian translation by Pietro Buonfanti. Florence: Giorgio Marescotti, 1590.

Morone da Maleo, Mariano. *Terra Santa Nuovamente Illustrata.* Piacenza: Stampa Ducale di Giovanni Barachi, 1669.

Nau, Michel. *Voyage nouveau de la Terre-Sainte, enrichi de plusieurs remarques particulieres qui serve à l'intelligence de la Sainte Ecriture.* Paris: J. Barbou, 1679.

Pesenti, Giovanni Paolo. *Il pellegrinaggio di Gierusalemme di Giovanni Paolo Pesenti: Diario di viaggio di un gentiluomo bergamasco in Terrasanta ed Egitto : 4 settembre 1612–31 agosto 1613*, edited by Ottavio de Carli. Bergamo: Officina dell'Ateneo, 2013.

Quaresmio, Francesco. *Historica Theologica e Morales Terra Elucidatio.* Antwerp: Plantiniana Balthasaris Moreti, 1639.

Regnault, Anthoine. *Discours du voyage doutre mer au Sainct Sepulcre de Jerusalem, et autres lieux de la terre saincte.* Lyon: n.p., 1573.

Rocchetta, Aquilante. *Peregrinatione di Terra Santa ed'altre Provincie di Don Aquilante Rocchetta Cavaliere del Santissimo Sepolcro*. Palermo: Alfonso dell'Isola, 1630.

Roger, Eugene. *La Terre Sainte our Description Topographique tres-particuliere des saints Lieux & de la Terre de Promission*. Paris: Antoine Bertie, 1664.

Sandys, George. *A Relation of a Journey Begun An. Dom. 1610*. London: W. Barrrett, 1615.

Schmidt, Jan. "French-Ottoman Relations in the Early Modern Period and the John Rylands Library MSS Turkish 45 and 46." *Turcica* 31 (1999): 375–364.

Smith, Saphora, and Lawahez Jabari. "Muslim Worshippers Clash with Israeli Police at Jerusalem Holy Site." *NBC News*. August 11, 2019. www.nbcnews.com/news/world/muslim-worshippers-clash-israeli-police- jerusalem-holy-site-n1041161.

Stephano, Bonifacio. *Liber de Perenni Cultu Terrae Sanctae et de Fructuosa eius Peregrinatione*. Venice, 1573. Reprint, Venice: L. Merlo Ioh. Bapti. Filii, 1875.

Suarez de Sainte-Marie, Jacques. *Sermon funebre fait aux obsequies de Henry IIII, roy de France et de Navarre, le 22 Juin dans l'eglise de St Jacques de la Boucherie*. Paris: Nicolas du Fosse, 1610.

Suriano, Francesco. *Trattato di Terra Santa e dell'Oriente*, edited by Girolamo Golobovich. Assisi: Artigianelli, 1900.

  Treatise of the Holy Land, translated by Theophilus Bellorini and Eugene Hoade. Jerusalem: The Franciscan Printing Press, 1949.

Surius, Bernardin [Bernardinus]. *Le pieu pelerin ou voyage de Jerusalem divise en trois livres contenans la description topographique de plusieurs Royaumes, pais, villes, nations estrangeres nommement des quatuorze religions orientales, leurs moeurs & humeurs, tant en matiere de Religion que de civile conversation &c*. Brussels: Francois Foppens, 1666.

Thenaud, Jean. *Le voyage Outremer. c. 1525*. Reprint, Geneva: Slatkine Press, 1971.

Thevenot, Jean de. *Relation d'un voyage fait au Levant*. Paris: Louis Billaine, 1665.

Thomas of Celano. "The Life of Francis of Assisi." In *Francis of Assisi – The Saint: Early Documents*, edited by Regis J. Armstrong, J. A. Wayne Hellmann, and William J. Short, 275–308. New York: New City Press, 2005.

Tressan, Pierre de La Vergne de. *Relation vouvelle et exacte d'un voyage de la Terre sainte ou description*. Paris: Antoine Dezallier, 1688.

Van Os, H. W. "St. Francis of Assisi as a Second Christ in Early Italian Painting." *Simiolus: N Netherlands Quarterly for the History of Art* 7 (1974): 115–132.

Verniero di Montepoloso, Pietro. *Chroniche ovvero Annali di Terra Santa del P. Pietro Verniero di Montepeloso*. In *Biblioteca bio-bibliografica della Terra Santa e dell'Oriente Francescana*. Vol. 5, edited by Girolamo Golubovich. Florence: Collegio di Bonaventura, 1936.

Villamont, Jacques de. *The Voyages du seigneur de Villamont, Chevalier de l'ordre de Hierusalem, Gentilhomme du pays de Bretaigne*. Paris: Claude de Montr'oeil et Jean Richer, 1595.

Traité ou instruction pour tirer des armes, de l'excellent Scrimeur Hieronyme Calvacabo, Bolognois, avec un discourse pour tirer de l'espec seul, fait par le defunct Patenostre de Rome, traduit de l'italien en François par le seigneur de Villamont, Chevalier de l'Ordre de Hierusalem, & Gentilhomme de la chamber du Roy. Paris: Claude Montr'oeil & Jean Richer, 1595.

Wadding, Lucas. *Annales Minorum in quibus res omnes trium ordinum a S. Francisco institutum, XV*. Rome: Typis Rochi Bernabò, 1836.

Zanelli, P. Guido, OFM. "I missionary veneti in Terra santa nel scoli XVII–XVIII e XIX." *Le Venezie Francescane* 15 (1) (1948): 147–155.

Zuallart, Jean. *Le tres devot voyage de Jerusalem, avec les figures des lieux saincts, & plusieurs autres, tirées au naturel*. Anvers: Arnould s'Conincx, 1608.

SECONDARY SOURCES

Angelov, Dimiter, and Judith Herrin, "The Christian Imperial Tradition – Greek and Latin." In *Universal Empire: A Comparative Approach to Imperial Culture and Representation in Eurasian History*, edited by Peter Fibiger Bang and Dariusz Kolodzejczyk, 149–174. Cambridge: Cambridge University Press, 2012.

Anjum, Ovamir. *Politics, Law, and Community in Islamic Thought: The Taymiyyan Moment*. Cambridge: Cambridge University Press, 2012.

Arad, Pnina. "Mapping Divinity: Holy Landscape in Maps of the Holy Land." In *Jerusalem As Narrative Space*, edited by Annette Hoffmann and Gerhard Wolf, 263–276. Leiden: Brill, 2012.

Armstrong, Megan C. "Jerusalem in the Reinvention of the Catholic Tradition, 1517–1700." In *Layered Landscapes: Early Modern Religious Space Across Faiths and Cultures*, edited by Eric Nelson and Jonathan Wright, 1–25. London: Routledge, 2017.

"Journeying to an Antique Christian Past." In *Reading the Ancient Near East in Early Modern Europe*, edited by Jan Grogan, 35–52. Oxford: Oxford University Press, 2020.

"La réaction des frères mineurs Capucins à la publication de l'Edit de Nantes en 1599." In *Paix des armes, paix des âmes*, actes du colloque international tenu (sous l'égide de la Société Henri IV) au Musée national du château de Pau et à l'Université de Pau et des Pays de l'Adour les 8, 9, et 10 octobre 1999, réunis par Paul Mironneau et Isabelle Pedbay-Clottes, 261–268. Pau: Société Henri IV, 2000.

"The Missionary Reporter." *Renaissance and Reformation/Renaissance et Réforme* 34 (2011): 127–158.

The Politics of Piety: Franciscan Preachers during the French Wars of Religion, 1560–1600. Rochester: University of Rochester Press, 2004.

"Spiritual Reform, Mendicant Autonomy, and State Formation: French Franciscan Disputes before the Parlement of Paris, 1500–1600." *French Historical Studies* 25 (2002): 505–530.

"Spiritual Legitimation? Franciscan Competition over the Holy Land, 1517–1700." In *The Frontiers of Mission*, edited by Alison Forrestal and Sean Smith, 159–180. Leiden: Brill, 2016.

Armstrong, Megan C., and Gillian Weiss, eds. "France and the Early Modern Mediterranean." *Special Edition of the Journal French History* 43 (March 2015).
Auld, Sylvia. "The Mamluks and the Venetians Commercial Interchange: The Visual Evidence." *Palestine Exploration Quarterly* 123 (1991): 84–102.
Arad, Pnina. "Mapping Divinity: Holy Landscape in Maps of the Holy Land." In *Jerusalem As Narrative Space*, edited by Annette Hoffmann and Gerhard Wolf, 263–276. Leiden: Brill, 2012.
Arce, Agostino, OFM. "De origine custodiae Terrae Sanctae." *Miscelánea de Tierra Santa* III (1975): 75–139.
 Expediciones de España a Jerusalen, 1673–1842, y la real cedula de Carlos III sobre los Santos Lugares en su abiente internacional. Documentos y contribuciones a la historia internacional de Tierra Santa. Madrid: Direccion general de relaciones culturales, 1958.
 "Los Franciscanos en Tierra Santa." *Miscelánea de Tierra Santa* III (1975): 156–164.
 "Maronitas y Franciscanos en el Libano 1450–1516." In *Miscelánea de Tierra Santa I, Estudios críticos y documentos*, 149–269. Jerusalem: n.p., 1973.
Armanios, Febe. *Coptic Christianity in Ottoman Egypt*. Oxford: Oxford University Press, 2011.
Asali, K. J., ed. *Jerusalem in History*. Jerusalem: Scorpion Press, 1989.
Baer, Marc. *Honored by the Glory of Islam: Conversion and Conquest in Ottoman Europe*. Oxford: Oxford University Press, 2011.
Bakhit, Muhammad Adnan. "The Christian Population of the Province of Damascus in the Sixteenth Century." In *Christians and Jews in the Ottoman Empire: The Functioning of a Plural Society*, edited by Bernard Lewis, 19–66. New York and London: Holms and Meier, 1982.
Baldovin, John. *The Urban Character of Christian Worship: The Origins, Development, and Meaning of Stational Liturgy*. Rome: Pont. Institutum Studiorum Orientalium, 1987.
Barriuso, Patrocinio Garcia. *Espana en la Historia de Tierra Santa*. 2 vols. Madrid: Ministerio de Asuntos Exteriores, 1992–1994.
Bayraktar-Tellan, Elif. "The Pariarch and the Sultan: The Struggle for Authority and the Quest for Order in the Eighteenth-Century Ottoman Empire." PhD diss., Ankara, Bilken University, 2011.
Beaver, Adam G. "From Jerusalem to Toledo: Replica, Landscape and the Nation in Renaissance Iberia." *Past and Present* 218 (2013): 55–90.
 "A Holy Land for the Catholic Monarchy: Palestine in the Making of Modern Spain, 1469–1598." PhD diss., Harvard University, 2008.
 "Scholarly Pilgrims: Antiquarian Visions of the Holy Land." In *Sacred History: Visions of Christian Origins in the Renaissance World*, edited by Katherine Van Liere and Simon Ditchfield, 267–283. Oxford: Oxford University Press, 2012.
Benoist, Pierre. *Le Père Joseph: L'Eminence Grise de Richelieu*. Paris: Editions Perrin, 2007.
Benvenuti, Anna, and P. Piatti eds., *Come a Gerusalemme: Evocazioni, riproduzioni, imitazioni dei luoghi santi tra Medioevo ed Età Moderna*. Florence: Sismel Edizioni del Galluzzo, 2013.

Berçe, Yves. "Discours de M. Yves Berçe. President de la Société de l'histoire de France en 2005: Les voyages de M. De Villamont (1595), introduction à l'histoire virtuelle." In *Annuaire-bulletin de la société de l'histoire de France*, 3–12. Paris: Au Siège de la Société, 2006.

Bergin, Joseph. *The Politics of Religion in Early Modern France*. New Haven: Yale University Press, 2014.

Bernstein, Hilary. *Historical Communities: Cities, Erudition, Knowledge and National Identity in Early Modern France*. Leiden: Brill, 2020.

Berridge G. R., "Notes on the Origins of the Diplomatic Corps: Constantinople in the 1620s." *Discussion Papers in Diplomacy* 92 (2004): 1–20.

Bissoli, Giovanni. "La Republica di Venezia e la custodia di Terra Santa." In *La custodia di Terra Santa e l'Europa: I rapport politici e l'attività culturale dei Francescani in Medio Oriente*, edited by Michele Piccirillo, 83–94. Rome: Il veltro, 1983.

Black, Christopher F. *Italian Confraternities in the Sixteenth Century*. Cambridge: Cambridge University Press, 1989.

Boas, Adrian. *Jerusalem in the Time of the Crusades: Society, Landscape and Art in the Holy City under Frankish Rule*. London and New York: Routledge, 2001.

Bourbon, Prince Xavier de. *Les Chevaliers du Saint-Sepulcre*. Paris: Fayard, Prince, 1957.

Bourdua, Louise. *The Franciscans and Art Patronage in Late Medieval Italy*. Cambridge: Cambridge University Press, 2004.

Bowman, Gail. "In Dubious Battle on the Plains of Heav'n: The Politics of Possession in Jerusalem's Holy Sepulchre." *History and Anthropology* (2011): 371–399.

Brown, Peter. *The Body and Society: Men, Women and Sexual Renunciation in Early Christianity*. New York: Columbia University Press, 1988.

Buey, Félix del, and Cristóforo Alvis. "Origenes de la custodia de Tierra Santa ayuda de los Reinos de Aragón, Nápoles y Castilla." *Archivo Ibero-americano* 65 (2005): 7–96.

Burkhart, Louise M. *Holy Wednesday: A Nahua Drama from Early Colonial Mexico*. Philadelphia: University of Pennsylvania Press, 1996.

Burr, David. *Olivi and Franciscan Poverty: The Origins of the Usus Pauper Controversy*. Philadelphia: The University of Pennsylvania Press, 1989.

Butlin, Robin. "A Sacred and Contested Place: English and French Representations of Palestine in the Seventeenth Century." In *Place, Culture and Identity: Essays in Historical Geography in Honour of Alan R. H. Baker*, edited by Iain S. Black and Robin A. Butlin, 91–131. Quebec: Laval University Press, 2001.

Bynum Walker, Carolyn. *Christian Materiality: An Essay on Religion in Late Medieval Europe*. Cambridge, MA: MIT Press, 2011.

Campopiano, Michele. "Islam, Jews and Eastern Christianity in Late Medieval Pilgrims' Guidebooks: Some Examples from the Franciscan Convent of Mount Sion." *Al-Masaq* 24 (2012): 75–89.

Cannon, Joanna. "Pietro Lorenzetti and the History of the Carmelite Order." *Journal of the Warburg and Courtauld Institutes* 50 (1987): 18–28.

Catlos, Brian A. *Muslims of the Medieval Latin Christendom, c. 1050–1614*. Cambridge: Cambridge University Press, 2014.
Charon, Cyril. "La Syrie de 1516 à 1855." *Echos d'Orient* 7 (1904): 278–284.
Chehab, Hafez. "Reconstructing the Medici Portrait of Fakhr Al-Din Al-Ma'Ani." In *Muquarnas: An Annual on Islamic Art and Architecture*. Vol. XI, edited by Gülru Necipoglu, 117–124. Leiden: Brill, 1994.
Chrissis, Nikalaos G. "The City and the Cross: The Image of Constantinople and the Latin Empire in Thirteenth-Century Papal Crusading Rhetoric." *Byzantine and Modern Greek Studies* 36 (2012): 20–37.
Christin, Olivier, Fabrice Flückiger, and Naïma Ghermani, eds. *Marie mondialisée: L'Atlas Marianus de Wilhelm Gumppenberg et les topographies sacrées de l'époque*. Neuchâtel: Presses universitaires suisses, 2015.
Clarke, Sean E. "Protestants in Palestine: Reformation of Holy Land Pilgrimage in the Sixteenth and Seventeenth Centuries." PhD diss., University of Arizona, 2013.
Clines, Robert. "Fighting Enemies and Finding Friends: The Cosmopolitan Pragmatism of Jesuit Residences in the Ottoman Levant." *Renaissance Studies* 31 (2015): 66–86.
A Jewish Jesuit in the Eastern Mediterranean. Cambridge: Cambridge University Press, 2019.
Clossey, Luke. *Salvation and Globalization in the Early Jesuit Missions*. Cambridge: Cambridge University Press, 2008.
Codignola, Luca. "Pacifique de Provins and the Capuchin Network in Africa and America." *Proceedings of the French Colonial Historical Society* 15 (1992): 46–60.
Cohen, Amnon. *Economic Life in Jerusalem*. Cambridge: Cambridge University Press, 2002.
The Guilds of Ottoman Jerusalem. Leiden: Brill, 2001.
Çolak, Hasan. *Between the Ottoman Central Administration and the Patriarchates of Antioch, Jerusalem and Alexandria*. PhD thesis, University of Birmingham, 2008.
"Relations between Ottoman Central Administration and the Greek Orthodox Patriachates of Antioch, Jerusalem, and Alexandria: 16th–18th Centuries." PhD diss., University of Birmingham, 2013.
Collin, Bernardin. "Les Frères-Mineurs dans le Cenacle." *Studia Orientalia* 2 (1957): 19–34.
Condren, John. Louis XIV et le repos de l'Italie: French Policies Towards the Duchy of Parma, Modena, and Monferrato, 1659–1689," PhD Diss., St Andrews University, 2015.
Copeland, Claire. "Saints, Devotion and Canonization in Early Modern Italy." *History Compass* 10 (2012): 260–269.
Corbin, Solange. *Le Déposition liturgique du Christ au vendredi saint: Sa place dans l'histoire des rites et du theater religieux (Analyse de documents portugais)*. Paris: Société d'Editions "Les Belles Lettres", 1960.
Coster, Will, and Andrew Spicer, eds., *Sacred Space in Early Modern Europe*. Cambridge: Cambridge University Press, 2005.
Coyle, Richard. "Rescuing the Holy Land in Friar Jean Boucher's *bouquet sacre compose des plus belles fleurs de la terre sainte*." In *Through the Eyes of the*

Beholder: The Holy Land, 1517–1713, edited by Judy A. Hayden and Nabil Matar, 97–110. Leiden: Brill, 2013.

Covaci, Valentina. "Contested Orthodoxy: Latins and Greeks in Late Medieval Jerusalem." *New Europe College Yearbook* (2020): 53–78.

"Praying for the Liberation of the Holy Sepulchre: Franciscan Liturgy in Fifteenth Century Jerusalem." *Acta ad archaeologiam et Artium Historiam Pertinentia.* 31 (2019): 177–195.

Crouzet, Denis. *Les guerriers de Dieu. Le violence au temps des troubles de religion, vers 1525–1610.* Seyssel: Champ Vallon, 1994.

Crum, R. J. "Roberto Martelli, The Council of Florence, and the Medici Palace Chapel." *Zeitschrift für Kunstgeschichte* 59 (1996): 403–417.

Cuffel, Alexandra. "From Practice to Polemic: Shared Saints and Festivals As 'Women's Religion' in the Medieval Mediterranean." *Bulletin of the School of Oriental and African Studies, University of London* 68 (2005): 401–419.

Dandelet Thomas. "Praying for the New St Peters." In *Spain in Italy: Politics, Society and Religion 1500–1700,* edited by Thomas Dandelet and J. Marino, 180–195. Brill: Leiden, 2007.

Dannenfeldt Karl H. "Leonhard Rauwolf: A Lutheran Pilgrim in Jerusalem, 1575." *Archiv für Reformationsgeschichte* 55(1964): 18–36.

Dansette, Bermadette. "Les pèlerins occidentaux du moyen age tardif au retour de la Terre sainte: confréries et psaumiers parisiens." In *Dei Gesta per Francos, Etudes sur les croisades dédiées à Jean Richard,* edited by Michel Baland, Benjamin Z. Kedar, and Jonathan Riley-Smith, 301–314. Aldershot: Ashgate, 2001.

"Les pèlerinages en terre sainte au XIVè et XVè siècles. Etude sur leurs aspects originaux, et edition d'une relation anonyme." PhD. thesis, Université de Paris-Sorbonne, 1977.

De Gennes, Jean. *Les Chevaliers du Saint-Sépulcre de Jérusalem.* 2 vols. Paris: Herault, 2004.

De Klerck, Bram. "Jerusalem in Renaissance Italy: The Holy Sepulchre on the Sacro Monte de Varallo." In *The Imagined and the Real Jerusalem in Art and Architecture,* edited by Jeroen Goudeau, Mariette Verhoeven, and Wouter Weijers. Leiden: Brill, 2014.

De Lama, Victor. "Un breve de Inocencio VIII dirigido a los Reyes Católicos, que nunca recibieron, y la financiación de los Santos Lugares." *España Medieval* 38 (2015): 231–240.

Derbes, Anne. *Picturing the Passion in Late Medieval Italy: Narrative Painting, Franciscan Ideologies, and the Levant.* Cambridge: Cambridge University Press, 1996.

De Vivo, Filippo. "How to Read Venetian relazioni." *Renaissance and Reformation/Renaissance et Réforme.* Special Issue, "Things Not Easily Believed: Introducing the Early Modern Relation," edited by Thomas Cohen and Germaine Warkentin (2011): 25–59

Information and Communication in Venice: Rethinking Early Modern Politics. Oxford: Oxford University Press, 2007.

Patrizi, Informatori, Barbieri: Politica e comunicazione a Venezia. Milan: Feltrinelli, 2012.

Dew, Nicholas. "Jerusalem and the Sun King: The Memory of the Crusades in the Cult of Louis XIV." Cambridge: Paper for the Comparative Social and Cultural History Seminar, November 1998.

Diefendorf, Barbara. *Beneath the Cross: Catholics and Huguenots in Sixteenth Century Paris*. Oxford: Oxford University Press, 1991.
— *Planting the Cross. Catholic Reform and Renewal in Sixteenth and Seventeenth-Century France*. Oxford: Oxford University Press, 2019.
Dillon, Anne. *The Construction of Martyrdom in the English Catholic Community, 1535–1603*. Aldershot: Ashgate Publishing, 2002.
Dinet, Dominique. *Vocation et fidelité. Le recrutement des réguliers dans les dioceses d'Auxerre, Langres et Dijon (XVIIe–XVIII siècles)*. Paris: Economica, 1988.
Ditchfield, Simon. *Liturgy, Sanctity and History in Tridentine Italy: Pietro Maria Campi and the Preservation of the Particular*. New York: Cambridge University Press, 1995.
— "Reading Rome as a Sacred Landscape, c. 1585–1635." In *Sacred Space in Early Modern Europe*, edited by Will Coster and Andrew Spicer, 167–192. Cambridge: Cambridge University Press, 2005.
— "Thinking with Saints: Sanctity and Society in the Early Modern World." *Critical Inquiry* 35 (2009): 552–584.
Dompnier, Bernard. *Enquête au pays des frères des anges: les Capucins de la province de Lyon au XVIIe et XVIIe siècles*. Lyon: Publications de l'Université de Saint-Etienne, 1993.
Duffy, Eamon. *Stripping of the Altars*. New Haven: Yale University Press, 1992.
Dupront, Alphonse. *Du sacré: Croisades et pèlerinages-images et langages*. Paris: Editions Gallimard, 2013.
Dursteler, Eric. "The Bailo in Constantinople: Crisis and Career in Venice's Early Modern Diplomatic Corps." *Mediterranean Historical Review* 16 (2001): 1–30.
Eisenbichler, Konrad. *The Boys of the Archangel Raphael: A Youth Confraternity in Florence, 1411–1785*. Toronto: University of Toronto Press, 1998.
Elad, Amikam. *Medieval Jerusalem and Islamic Worship*. Leiden: Brill, 1995.
El-Mudarris, Hussein I., and Olivier Salmon, eds. *Le Consulat de France a alep au XVIIe: Journal de Louis Gedoyn, vie de François Picquet, Mémoires de Laurent d'Arvieux*. Aleppo: Diplomatic and Consular Service, 2009.
Emmett, Chad. *Beyond the Basilica: Christians and Muslims in Nazareth*. Chicago: University of Chicago Press, 1995.
— "The Status Quo Solution for Jerusalem." *Journal of Palestinian Studies* 26 (1997): 16–28.
Ferragu, Giles. "Eglise et diplomatie au Levant au temps des Capitulations." *Rives Méditerranéennes* 6 (2000): 69–78.
Finkel, Caroline. *Osman's Dream: The Story of the Ottoman Empire 1300–1923*. New York: Basic Books, 2005.
Fleischer, Cornell. "Royal Authority, Dynastic Cyclist and Iban Khaldunishm in Sixteenth Century Ottoman Letters." *Journal of Asia and African Studies* 18 (1983): 198–220.
Folda, Jaroslav. *Crusader Art in the Holy Land from the Third Crusade to the Fall of Acre, 1187–1291*. Cambridge: Cambridge University Press, 2005.
Forrestal, Alison. *Vincent de Paul, the Lazarist Mission, and French Catholic Reform*. Oxford: Oxford University Press, 2017.

Frazee, Charles. *Catholics and Sultans: The Church and the Ottoman Empire 1453–1923*. Cambridge: Cambridge University Press, 2006.
Palestine, Egypt and North Africa. Cambridge: Cambridge University Press, 1983.
Friedman, E., OCD. *The Latin Hermits of Mount Carmel*. Rome: Institutum Historicum Teresianum, Studia, I, 1979.
Gabriel, Frédéric. "Eugene Roger." In *Christian-Muslim Relations: A Bibliographical History*, edited by David Thomas and John Chesworth, 9: 447–452. Leiden: Brill, 2017.
Galadza, Daniel. *Liturgy and Byzantinization in Jerusalem*. Oxford: Oxford University Press, 2018.
Galland, Caroline. *Pour la gloire de Dieu et du roi: les récollets en Nouvelle-France au XVIIe et XVIIIe siecles*. Paris, Editions du Cerf, 2012.
Galindo, David Rex. *To Sin No More: Franciscans and Conversion in the Hispanic World, 1683–1830*. Stanford: Stanford University Press, 2017.
Gatzambide, Goñi. *Historia de la bula in España*. Vitoria: Editorial del Seminario, 1958.
Geanakoplos, Deno J. "The Council of Florence (1438–9) and the Problem of Union between the Greek and Latin Churches." *Church History* 24 (1955): 324–346.
Goffen, Rona. *Piety and Patronage in Renaissance Venice: Bellini, Titian, and the Franciscans*. New Haven: Yale University Press, 1986.
Golubovich, Girolamo. *La questione de' Luoghi Santi nel Periodo degli Anni 1620–1638. Nuovi documenti dall'incarto dell'ambasciatore Filippo de Harlay, conte di Césy*. Florence: Quaracchi, 1921.
Serie cronologica dei reverendissimi superiori di Terra Santa, ossia, dei provinciali custodi e presidenti della medesima: Già commissari apostolici dell' Oriente e sino al 1847 in officio di gran maestri del S. Militare Ordine dal SS. Sepolcro: Attuali prelati mitrati, provinciali e custodi di T.S., guardiani del Monte Sion e del SS. Sepolcro di N.S.G.C. ecc. Gerusalemme: Con. di San Salvatore, 1898.
Gomez-Geraud, Marie Christine. *Le Crépuscule du Grand Voyage. Les récits de pèlerins à Jérusalem (1458–1612)*: Paris: Honoré Champion, 1999.
Goudeau, Jeroen, Mariette Verhoeven, and Wouter Weijers, eds. *The Imagined and the Real Jerusalem in Art and Architecture*. Leiden: Brill, 2014.
Gradeva, Rossitsa. "On the Judicial Functions of the Kadi Courts: Glimpses from Sofia in the Seventeenth Century." *Islam am Balkan* 2 (2005): 15–43.
Gregory, Brad. *Salvation at Stake: Christian Martyrdom in Early Modern Europe*. Boston: Harvard University Press, 2001.
Greene, Molly. *The Edinburgh History of the Greeks, 1453–1768*. Edinburgh: Edinburgh University Press, 2015.
A Shared World: Christians and Muslims in the Early Modern Mediterranean. Princeton: Princeton University Press, 2000.
Grehan, James. *Twilight of the Saints: Everyday Religion in Ottoman Syria and Palestine*. Oxford: Oxford University Press, 2014.
Hallaq, Wael B. *The Origins and Evolution of Islamic Law*. Cambridge: Cambridge University Press, 2005.

Hamilton, Bernard. "The Impact of Crusader Jerusalem on Western Christendom." *Catholic Historical Review* 80 (1994): 695–713.
  The Latin Church in the Crusader States: The Secular Church. London: Variorum Publications, 1980.
Hamilton, Bernard, and Richard B. Rose, "Church Union Plans in the Crusader Kingdoms: An Account of a Visit by the Greek Patriarch of Jerusalem Leontius to the Holy land, AD. 1177–1178." *The Catholic Historical Review* 73 (1987): 377.
Hamilton, Tom, and David Van der Lindon. "Introduction: Remembering the French Wars of Religion." *French History* 35 (2020): 1–6.
Hankins, James. "Renaissance Crusaders: Humanist Crusade Literature in the Age of Mehmed II." *Dumbarton Oaks Papers* 49 (1995): 111–207.
Harline, Craig. *Miracles at the Jesus Oak: Histories of the Supernatural in Reformation Europe.* New Haven: Yale University Press, 2003.
Heath, Sean. "The Bourbon Monarchy and the Cult of Saint Louis, 1589–1792." PhD diss., St. Andrews University, 2017.
Hendrix, Scott. "Re-Rooting the Faith: The Reformation As Re-Christianization." *Church History* 69 (2000): 558–577.
Heyberger, Bernard. *Les Chrétiens du Proche-Orient au temps de la Réforme Catholique.* Rome: Ecole Française de Rome, 1994.
  "Le Terre Sainte et mission au XVIIe siècle." *Dimensioni et problemi della ricerca storica* (1994): 1–33.
Heyd, Uriel. *Ottoman Documents on Palestine, 1552–1615: A Study of the Firman according to the Mühimme Defteri.* Oxford: Clarendon Press, 1960.
Heyd, W. "Les consulats etablis en terre sainte au Moyen Age our le protection des pèlerins." In *Archives de l'Orient-Latin*, vol. II., 355–363. Paris: Ernest Leoux, 1884.
Holt, Mack P. *The Politics of Wine in Early Modern France.* Cambridge: Cambridge University Press, 2018.
Holterman, Bart. "Pilgrimages in Images: Early Sixteenth-Century Views of the Holy Land with Pilgrim's Portraits As Part of the Commemoration of the Jerusalem Pilgrimage in Germany." PhD diss., Utrecht, 2013.
Horn, Jeff. "Lessons of the Levant: Early Modern French Economic Development in the Mediterranean." *Journal of French History* 29 (2015): 76–92.
Inalcik, Halil. "The Status of the Greek Orthodox Patriarch under the Ottomans." *Turcica* 23 (1991): 407–436.
Işikel, Gunes. "Les méandres d'une pratique peu institutionalisée: la diplomatie ottomane, XVe–XVIIIe siècle." *Monde* 5 (2014): 43–55.
Isom-Verhaaren, Christine. *Allies with the Infidel: The Ottoman and French Alliance in the Sixteenth Century.* London: I. B. Tauris, 2011.
Jansen, Katherine Ludwig. *The Making of the Magdalen: Preaching and Popular Devotion in the Later Middle Ages.* Princeton: Princeton University Press, 2001.
Heuillant-Donat, Isabelle. "Martyrdom and Identity in the Franciscan Order (Thirteenth and Fourteenth Centuries)." *Franciscan Studies* 70 (2012): 429–453.

Jedin, Hubert. *A History of the Council of Trent*. Vols. 1–2. Edinburgh: Thomas Nelson and Sons, 1957–1961.
Jennings, Ronald C. *Christians and Muslims in Ottoman Cyprus and the Mediterranean World, 1571–1640*. New York: New York University Press, 1993.
Jotischky, Andrew. "The Franciscan Return to the Holy Land (1333) and Mt Sion: Pilgrimage and the Apostolic Mission." In *The Crusader World*, edited by Adrian Boas, 241–258. London: Routledge, 2016.
"Penance and Reconciliation in the Crusader States: Matthew Paris, Jacques de Vitry and the Eastern Christians." *Studies in Church History* 40 (2004): 74–83.
Kynn, Tyler Joseph. "Encounters of Islam and Empire: The Hajj in the Early Modern World." PhD diss., Princeton University, 2020.
Kirkland-Ives, Mitzi. "'Capell nuncapato Jherusalem noviter Brugis': The Adornes Family of Bruges and Holy Land Devotion." *The Sixteenth Century Journal* 39 (2008): 1041–1064.
Klimas, Narcy. "I danni subiti nei secoli dall'Archivio gerosolimatano: Principale cause è fattori." *Antonianum* 3 (2009): 531–564.
Krstic, Tijana. *Contested Conversions to Islam: Narratives of Religious Change in the Early Modern Ottoman Empire*. Stanford: Stanford University Press, 2011.
Larkin, Brian. *The Very Nature of God: Baroque Catholicism and Religious Reform in Bourbon Mexico City*. New Mexico: University of New Mexico, 2010.
Le Goff, Hervé, ed. *La ligue en Bretagne: Guerre civile et conflit international, 1588–1598*. Rennes: Presses Universitaires de Rennes, 2010.
Lidov, Alexei. "A Byzantine Jerusalem: The Imperial Pharos Chapel as the Holy Sepulchre." In *Jerusalem As Narrative Space Erzählraum Jerusalem*, edited by Annette Hoffman and Gerhard Wolf. Leiden: Brill, 2012.
Little, Donald P. "Mujir al-Din al'Ulaymi's Vision of Jerusalem in the Ninth/Fifteenth Century." *Journal of the American Oriental Society* 115 (1995): 237–247.
Longo, Pierre Giorgio. *Memorie di Gerusalemme e Sacri Monti in epoca barocca. Vincenzo Fani, devote "misteri" e "magnanime imprese" nella sua Relatione del viaggio in Terrasanta dedicate a Carlo Emanuele I di Savoiva (1615–1616)*. Ponzano Monferrato: Atlas, 2010.
Luria, Keith. "Catholic Marriage and the Customs of the Country: Building a New Religious Community in Seventeenth-Century Vietnam." *French Historical Studies* 40 (2017): 457–473.
Sacred Boundaries: Religious Coexistence and Conflict in Early-Modern France. Washington, DC: The Catholic University Press of America, 2005.
Luz, Nimrod. "Aspects of Islamicization of Space and Society in Mamluk Jerusalem and Its Hinterland." *Mamluk Studies Review* 6 (2002): 133–154.
Martin, Pedro García. *Paisajes de la Tierra Prometida: El Viaje a Jerusalén de Don Fadrique Enríquez de Ribera*. Madrid: Miraguano, S. A., Ediciones, 2001.
MacEvitt, Christopher. "Martyrdom and the Muslim World through Franciscan Eyes." *The Catholic Historical Review* 97 (2011): 1–23.

Martin, Gregory. *Roma Sancta (1581)*, edited by G. B. Parks. Rome: Edizioni di Storia E Letteratura, 1969.
Masson, Paul. *Histoire du commerce Français dans le Levant au XVIIe siècle*. Paris: 1911. Reprint, New York: Burt Franklin, 1967.
Mauzaize, Jean. *Le rôle et l'action des Capucins de la Province de Paris dans la France religieuse du XVIIe siècle*. Vol. 1. Lille: Attelier de reproduction des theses, 1978.
Mazumdar, Shampa, and Sanjoy Mazumdar, "Religion and Place Attachment: A Study of Sacred Places." *Journal of Environmental Psychology* 24 (2004): 385–397.
McCluskey, Phil. "'Les ennemis du nom Chrestien': Echoes of the Crusade in Louis XIV's France." *French History* 29 (2015): 46–61.
Melvin, Karen. "The Travels of El Devoto Peregrino: A Franciscan Holy Land Comes to New Spain." In *Five Hundred Years of Franciscans in New Spain*, edited by Thomas Cohen, Jay Harrison, and David Rex Galindo. Forthcoming.
Meri, Josef W. *The Cult of the Saints among Muslims and Jews in Medieval Syria*. Oxford: Oxford University Press, 2002. Reprinted 2004.
Metzler, Joseph. "Foundation of the Congregation de' Propaganda Fide by Gregory XV." In *Sacrae Congregationis de Propaganda Fide Memoria Rerum: 350 anni servizio delle missioni=350 jahre im Dienste der Weltmission=350 years in the Service of the Missions*. Vol. 1, edited by Joseph Metzler, 79–111. Rome: Herder, 1971.
"Orientation, programme et premières decisions (1622–1649)." *Sacrae Congregationis* 1 (1971): 146–196.
ed. *Sacrae Congregationis de Propaganda Fide Memoria Rerum: 350 anni servizio delle missioni=350 jahre im Dienste der Weltmission=350 years in the Service of the Missions*. Vol. 1. Rome, Freiberg, Vienna: Herder, 1971.
Meyer, Frédéric. *Pauvreté et assistance spirituelle: Les franciscains récollets de la province de Lyon aux XVIIe et XVIIIe siècles*. Lyon: Université de Saint-Etienne, 1997.
Michalewicz, Nathan. "Franco-Ottoman Diplomacy during the French Wars of Religion, 1559–1610." PhD diss., George Mason University, 2020.
Mochon, Jean Philippe. "Le Consul Général de France à Jérusalem: Aspects historiques, juridiques et politiques de ses fonctions." *Annuaire français de droit international* 42 (1996): 929–945.
Molnar, A. *Le Saint-Siège, Raguse et les missions Catholiques de la Ongrie ottoman (1572–1647)*. Budapest: METEM, 2007.
Montcher, Fabien. "L'image et le culte de saint Louis dans la Monarchie hispanique. Le rôle des "reines de paix" (du milieu du XVIe siècle au milieu du XVIIe siècle)." In *"La dame de coeur." Patronage et mécénat religieux des femmes de pouvoir dans l'Europe des XIVe–XVIIe siècles*, edited by Murielle Gaude-Ferragu and Cecile Vincent-Cassy, 167–192. Rennes: Presses Universitaires de Rennes, 2018.
Moore, Kathryn Blair. *The Architecture of the Christian Holy Land: Reception from Late Antiquity through the Renaissance: The Undiscovered Country*. Cambridge: Cambridge University Press, 2017.

"The Disappearance of an Author, the Appearance of a Genre: Niccolò da Poggibonsi and Pilgrimage Guidebooks between Manuscript and Print." *Renaissance Quarterly* 66 (2013): 357–411.
Moorman, John. *A History of the Franciscan Order*. Oxford: Oxford University Press, 1968.
Morris, Colin. *The Sepulchre of Christ and the Medieval West: From the Beginning to 1600*. Oxford: Oxford University Press, 2005.
Moya, Rafael. "Hacia una participación fructuosa de los religiosos en las misiones de Propaganda." *Sacrae Congregationis de Propaganda Fide Memoria Rerum* I, (1971): 439–464.
Moukarzel, Pierre. "Les Franciscains dans le sultanat Mamelouk des années 1330–1516." *Le Moyen Age* cxx (2014): 135–149.
Muldoon, J. "The Avignon Papacy and the Frontiers of Christendom: The Evidence of Vatican Register 62." *Archivum Historiae Pontificiae* 17 (1979): 125–195.
Muldoon, Nicholas. *Popes, Lawyers, and Infidels: The Church and the Non-Christian World*. Philadelphia: University of Pennsylvania Press, 2015.
Nelson, Eric. *The Jesuits and the Monarchy: Catholic Reform and Political Authority in France (1590–1615)*. Rome: Institutum Historicum Societatis, 2005.
The Legacy of Iconoclasm: Religious War and the Relic Landscape of Tours, Blois and Vendôme, 1550–1750. St. Andrews: St. Andrews Studies, 2013.
"*Religion royale* in the Sacred Landscape of Paris: The Jesuit Church of Saint Louis and the Resacralization of Kingship in Early Bourbon France (1590–1650)." In *Layered Landscapes: Early Modern Religious Space across Faiths and Cultures*, edited by Eric Nelson and Jonathan Wright, 171–184. Abingdon: Routledge, 2017.
Neveu, Bruno. "Du culte de Saint Louis à la glorification de louis XIV: La maison royale de Saint-Cyr." *Journal des savants* Jul–Dec (1988): 277–290.
Nimmo, Duncan. *Reform and Division in the Medieval Franciscan Order*. Rome: The Capuchin Historical Institute, 1987.
Nischan, Bodo, John M. Headley, Hans Joachim Hillerbrand, and Anthony J. Papalas, eds. *Confessionalization in Europe, 1550–1700: Essays in Honor and Memory of Bodo Nishan*. Aldershot: Ashgate, 2004.
Norman, Corrie. "The Franciscan Preaching Tradition and Its Sixteenth-Century Legacy: The Case of Cornelio Musso." *The Catholic Historical Review* 85 (1999): 208–232.
Norris, Jacob. "Dragomans, Tattooists, Artisans: Palestinian Christians and Their Encounters with Catholic Europe in the Seventeenth and Eighteenth Centuries." *Journal of Global History* 14 (2019): 68–86.
"Exporting the Holy Land: Artisans and Merchant Migrants in Ottoman-Era Bethlehem." *Journal of Middle East Migration Studies* 2 (2013): 14–40.
Nova, Alessandro. "'Popular' Art in Renaissance Italy: Early Response to the Holy Mountain at Varallo." In *Reframing the Renaissance: Visual Culture in Europe and Latin America 1450–1650*, edited by Claire Farago, 113–126, 319–321. New Haven: Yale University Press, 1995.
Oakley, Francis. "Complexities of Context: Gerson, Bellarmine, Sarpi, Richer, and the Venetian Interdict of 1606–1607." *The Catholic Historical Review* 82 (1996): 169–396.

O'Donnell, Paris. "Pilgrimage or Anti-Pilgrimage? Uses of Mementoes and Relics in English and Scottish Narratives of Travel to Jerusalem, 1596–1632." *Studies in Travel Writing* 13 (2009): 125–139.

Olin, John C. "The Idea of Pilgrimage in the Experience of Ignatius Loyola." *Church History* 48 (1979): 387–398.

O'Malley, John. "How the First Jesuits Became Involved in Education." In *Saints or Devils Incarnate? Studies in Jesuit History*, 199–215. Leiden: Brill, 2013.

Trent and All That: Renaming Catholicism in the Early Modern Era. Cambridge, MA: Harvard University Press, 2000.

Ousterhout, Robert. "Architecture As Relic and the Construction of Sanctity: The Stones of the Holy Sepulchre." *Journal of the Society of Architectural Historians* 62 (2003): 4–23.

"The Church of Santo Stefano: A 'Jerusalem in Bologna'." *Gesta* 20 (1981): 311–321.

"Rebuilding the Temple: Constantine Monomachus and the Holy Sepulchre." *Journal of the Society of Architectural Historians* 48 (2989): 66–78.

Panaite, Viorel. "French Capitulations and Consular Jurisdiction in Egypt and Aleppo in the Late Sixteenth and Seventeenth Centuries." In *Well-Connected Domains: Towards an Entangled Ottoman History*, edited by Pascal Firges, Tobias Graf, Christian Roth, and Gülay Tulasoglu, 71–87. Leiden: Brill, 2014.

Panchenko, Constantin. *Arab Orthodox Christians under the Ottomans 1516–1831*. Jordanville: Holy Trinity Seminary Press, 2016.

Pedani, Maria Pia. "Venetian Consuls in Egypt and Syria in the Ottoman Age." *Mediterranean World* 18 (2006): 7–21.

Peirce, Leslie. *Morality Tales: Law and Gender in the Ottoman Court of Aintab.* Berkeley: University of California Press, 2003.

Pereda, Felipe. "Measuring Jerusalem: The Marquis of Tarifa's pilgrimage in 1520 and Its Urban Consequences." *Città et Storia* VII (2012): 77–102.

Peri, Oded. *Christianity under Islam in Jerusalem: The Question of the Holy Sites in Early Ottoman Times.* Leiden: Brill, 2001.

"Islamic Law and Christian Holy Sites: Jerusalem and Its Vicinity in Early Ottoman Times." *Islamic Law and Society* 6 (1999): 97–111.

Peters, F. E. *Jerusalem: The Holy City in the Eyes of Chroniclers, Visitors, Pilgrims, and Prophets from the Days of Abraham to the Beginning of Modern Times.* Princeton: Princeton University Press, 1985.

Phelan, John Leddy. *The Millennial Kingdom of the Franciscans in the New World.* Berkeley: University of California Press, 1956.

Pierre, Benoist. *Le Père Joseph. L'Éminence grise de Richelieu.* Paris: Perrin, 2007.

"Le père Joseph, l'empire et la Méditerranée au début du XVIIe siècle." *Cahiers de la Mediterranee* 71 (2005): 185–202.

Pieraccini, Paolo. *The Franciscan Custody of the Holy Land in Cyprus: Its Educational, Pastoral and Charitable Work and Support for the Maronite Community.* Jerusalem: Terra Santa, 2013.

Pillorget, René. "Louid Deshayes de Courmenin et L'Orient Musulman (1621–1626)." *Cahiers de l'Association des études françaises* 27 (1975): 65–81.

Pipes, Daniel. "The Muslim Claim to Jerusalem." *Middle East Quarterly* (2001): 49–66.

Pizzorusso, Giovanni. "I dubbi sui sacramenti dalle missioni 'ad infideles': Percorsi nelle burocrazie di Curia." *Mélanges de l'école française de Rome* 121 (2009): 39–61.

Governare le missioni. Conoscere il mondo nel XVII secolo la Congregazione Pontificia de Propaganda Fide. Rome: Sette Città, 2018.

"Le Monde et/ou l'Europe: la Congrégation de Propaganda Fide et le politique missionaire du Saint-Siege (XVII siècle)." *Bulletin de l'institut de Réformation* (2014): 1–20.

"Monsignor Francesco Ingoli." *Dizionario biografico degli Italiani* 62 (2004). www.treccani.it/enciclopedia/francesco-ingoli_%28Dizionario-Biografico%29/.

Pollman, Judith. "Countering the Reformation in France and the Netherlands: Clerical Leadership and Catholic Violence, 1560–1585." *Past and Present* 190 (2006): 83–120.

Poumarède, Geraud. "Les limites de patronage français sur les lieux saints: Autour de l'installation d'un consul à jérusalem dans les années 1620." *Revue de l'histoire de l'Eglise de France* 92 (2006): 73–116.

Pour en finir avec le Croisade: Mythes et Réalitiés de la lute contre les Turcs au XVIe et XVIIe siècles. Paris: Presses Universitaires de France, 2009.

"La France et Jérusalem (XVIe–XIX e siècle)." *Annuaire-Bulletin de la Société de l'histoire de France* (2008): 39–62.

Powers, Amanda. "Going among the Infidels: The Mendicant Orders and Louis IX's First Mediterranean Campaign." *Mediterranean Historical Review* 25 (2011): 187–202.

Rachman-Schrire, Yamit. "Christ's Unction and the Material Realization of a Stone in Jerusalem." In *Natural Materials of the Holy Land and the Visual Translation of Place, 500–1500*, edited by Renana Bartal, Neta Bodner, and Bianca Kuhnel, 216–229. London: Routledge, 2017.

"Christ's Side-Wound and Francis' Stigmatization at La Verna: Reflections on the Rock of Golgotha." In *Steinformen.Materialität, Qualität, Imitation*, edited by Isabella Augart, Maurice Sass, and Iris Wenderholm, 45–58. Berlin: De Gruyter, 2019.

Rappo, Hitomi Omata. "Memories of a 'Christian Past' in Japan: The Museum of the Twenty-Six Martyrs in Nagasaki." *Anais de história de além-mar* 18 (2017): 249–282.

Rentel, Alexander. "Byzantine and Slavic Orthodoxy." In *The Oxford History of Christian Worship*, edited by Geoffrey Wainwright and Karen B. Westerfield Tucker, 254–306. Oxford: Oxford University Press, 2006.

Reinburg, Virginia. *Storied Places: Pilgrims Shrines, Nature, and History in Early Modern France.* Cambridge: Cambridge University Press, 2019.

Riley-Smith, Jonathan. *The First Crusade and the Idea of Crusading.* London: Athlone, 1993.

Richard, Jean. *La papauté et les missions d'Orient au Moyen-Age (XIII–IVème siècle)*. Rome: Ecole Française de Rome, 1977.
Ritchey, Sara. *Holy Matter: Changing Perceptions of the Material World in Late Medieval Christianity*. Ithaca: Cornell University Press, 2014.
Ritsema, Marianne P. *The Holy Land in Observant Texts (c. 1480–1650): Theology, Travel, and Territoriality*. Leiden: Brill, 2019.
Roberts, Penny. *Peace and Authority during the French Religious Wars c. 1560–1600*. Cambridge: Cambridge University Press, 2013.
Roest, Bert. *Order and Disorder: The Poor Clares between Foundation and Reform*. Leiden: Brill, 2013.
Roncaglia, Martiniano. "The Sons of St. Francis in the Holy Land." *Franciscan Studies* 10 (1950): 282.
Ronen, Avraham. "Portigiani's Bronze 'Ornamento' in Jerusalem." *Mitteilungen des Junsthistorischen Institutes in Florenz* 14 (197): 415–442.
Rose, Richard B. "Church Union Plans in the Crusader Kingdoms: An Account of a Visit by the Greek Patriarch of Jerusalem Leontios to the Holy land, AD. 1177–1178." *The Catholic Historical Review* 73 (1987): 371–390.
Rostagno, Lucia. "Note su una devozione praticata da cristiani e musulmani a Betlemme: Il culto della Madonna del Latte." *Rivista degli studi orientali* 71 (1997): 159–172.
"Pellegrini Italiani a Gerusalemme in Età Ottomana: Percorsi, Esperienze, Momenti d'incontro." *Oriente Moderno* 17 (1998): 63–157.
Rothman, Natalie. *Brokering Empire: Trans-Imperial Subjects between Venice and Istanbul*. Ithaca: Cornell University Press, 2012.
The Dragoman Renaissance: Diplomatic Interpreters and the Routes of Orientalism. Ithaca: Cornell University Press, 2020.
Rudy, Kathryn. "A Guide to Mental Pilgrimage: Paris, Bibliothèque de l'Arsenal Ms. 212)." *Zeitschrift fur Kunstgeschichte* 63 (2000): 494–515.
"A Pilgrim's Memories of Jerusalem: London, Wallace Collection MS M319." *Journal of the Arbur and Courtauld Institutes* 70 (2007): 311–325.
Virtual Pilgrimages in the Convent: Imagining Jerusalem in the Late Middle Ages. Turnhout: Brepols, 2011.
Ruiu, Adina. "Conflicting Visions of Jesuit Missions to the Ottoman Empire, 1609–1628." *Journal of Jesuit Studies* 1 (2014): 260–280.
"Missionaries and French Subjects: The Jesuits in the Ottoman empire." In *A Companion to the Early Modern Catholic Global Missions*, edited by Ronnie Po-Chia Hsia, 181–204. Leiden: Brill, 2016.
Rule, John C. "The Enduring Rivalry of France and Spain." In *Great Power Rivalries*, edited by William R. Thompson, 31–59. Columbia: University of South Carolina Press, 1999.
Sandoli, Sabino de. *The Peaceful Liberation of the Holy Place in the Fourteenth Century*. Jerusalem: Franciscan Center, 1991.
Scribner, Robert. "The Reformation, Popular Magic, and the 'Disenchantment of the World'." *The Journal of Interdisciplinary History* 23 (1993): 475–494.

Sebag, Paul. "Sur deux Orientalistes français du XVIIe siècle: F. Petis de la Croix, et le Sieur de la Croix." *Revue des mondes musulmans et de la Méditerranée* 25 (1978): 89–117.

Sekulic, Ana. "Conversion of the Landscape: Environment and Religious Politics in an Early Modern Ottoman Town." PhD. diss., Princeton University, 2020.

Selwyn, Jennifer D. *A Paradise Inhabited by Devils: The Jesuits Civilizing Mission in Early Modern Naples.* Aldershot: Ashgate Publishing and the Jesuit Historical Institute, 2005.

Sessevalle, François de. *Histoire Generale de l'Ordre de St. François.* 2 vols. Paris: Editions de la Revue d'histoire Franciscaine, 1935.

Setton, Kenneth M. *The Papacy and the Levant.* 4 vols. Philadelphia: The American Philosophical Society, 1976.

Shahar, Ido. "Legal Pluralism and the Study of Shari'a Courts." *Islamic Law and Society* 15 (2008): 112–141.

Shalev, Zur. *Christian Pilgrimage and Ritual Measurement in Jerusalem.* Preprint 384. Berlin: Max Planck Institute for the History of Science, 2009.

Sacred Words, Sacred Worlds: Geography, Religion, and Scholarship, 1550–1700. Leiden: Brill, 2011.

Sharon, Moshe, ed. *Corpus Inscriptionum Arabicarum Palaestinae.* CIAP 3. Leiden: Brill, 2004.

ed. *The Holy Land in History and Thought.* Papers Submitted to the International Conference on the Relations between the Holy Land and the World Outside it (Johannesburg 1986). Leiden: Brill, 1988.

Singer, Amy. *Constructing Ottoman Beneficence: An Imperial Soup Kitchen in Jerusalem.* New York: State University of New York Press, 2002.

Palestinian Peasants and Ottoman Officials: Rural Administration around Sixteenth-Century Jerusalem. Cambridge: Cambridge University Press, 1994.

Silvas, Anna M. *Gregory of Nyssa: The Letters – Introduction, Translation and Commentary.* Boston: Brill, 2007.

Smith, Catherine Delano. "Geography or Christianity? Maps of the Holy Land before AD 1000." *The Journal of Theological Studies* 42 (1991): 143–152.

Smith, Jonathan Z. *To Take Place: Toward a Theory of Ritual.* Chicago: Chicago University Press, 1987.

Smith, Sean. *Fealty and Fidelity: The Lazarists of Bourbon France 1660–1756.* Aldershot: Ashgate Publishing, 2015.

Soergel, Philip. *Wondrous in His Saints: Counter-Reformation Propaganda in Bavaria.* Berkeley: University of California Press, 1993.

St. Laurent, Beatrice, and Andràs Reidelmayer. "Restorations of Jerusalem and the Dome of the Rock and Their Political Significance, 1537–1928." *Muqarnas* 10 Essays in Honor of Oleg Grabar (1993): 75–84.

Takeda, Junko. *Between Crown and Commerce: Marseilles and the Early Modern Mediterranean.* Baltimore: John Hopkins University Press, 2011.

Tallon, Alain. *La France et le Concile de Trente (1518–1563).* Paris: Cerf, 2000.

Taylor, William J. *Theatre of a Thousand Wonders: A History of the Miraculous.* Cambridge: Cambridge University Press, 2016.

Teixidó, Antonio Martínez. "La Orden de Caballería del santo Sepulcro de Jerusalén." *Studia Historica, Historia moderna* 24 (2002): 207–219.

Terpstra, Nicholas. *Lay Confraternities and Civic Religion in Renaissance Bologna*. Cambridge: Cambridge University Press, 1995.

Religious Refugees in the Early Modern World: An Alternative History of the Reformation. Cambridge: Cambridge University Press, 2015.

Tolan, John. *Saint Francis and the Sultan: The Curious History of a Christian-Muslim Encounter*. Oxford: Oxford University Press, 2009.

Tomlin, Graham. *Luther's Gospel: Reimagining the World*. Oxford: Bloomsbury, 2017.

"Protestants and Pilgrimage." In *Exploration in a Christian Theology of Pilgrimage*, edited by Craig Bartholomew and Fred Hughes, 110–125. Aldershot: Ashgate Publishing, 2004.

Tingle, Elizabeth. "Long-Distance Pilgrimage and the Counter Reformation in France: Sacred journeys to the Mont Saint-Michel 1520–1750." *The Journal of Religious History* 41 (2016): 158–180.

Tramontana, Felicita. *Passages of Faith: Conversion in Palestinian Villages*. Wiesbaden: Otto Harrassowitz, 2014.

"Per ornamento e servizio di questi santi luoghi: L'arrivée des objets de dévotion dans les sanctuaires de Terre Sainte (xviie siècle). *Archives de sciences sociales des religions. Façonner l'objet de dévotion chrétien. Fabrication, commerce et circulations (vers XVII–XIX siècles)* 183 (2018): 227–243.

Trivellato, Francesca. *The Familiarity of Strangers: The Sephardic Diaspora, Livorno, and Cultural Trade in the Early Modern Period*. New Haven: Yale University Press, 2014.

Trowbridge, Mark. "Jerusalem Transposed: A Fifteenth-Century Panel for the Bruges Market." *Journal of Historians of Netherlandish Art* 1 (2009): 1–22.

Van der Linden, David. "Memorializing the Wars of religion in Early Seventeenth-Century French Picture Galleries: Protestants and Catholics Painting the Contested Past." *Renaissance Quarterly* 70 (2017): 132–178.

Van Eck, M. Ritsema. "Encounters with the Levant: The Late Medieval Illustrated Jerusalem Travelogue by Paul Walter Von Guglingen." *Mediterranean Review* 32(2018): 153–188.

The Holy Land in Observant Franciscan Texts (c. 1480–1650). Brill: Leiden, 2019).

Van Liere, Katherine, Simon Ditchfield, and Howard Louthan, eds. *Sacred History: Uses of the Christian Past and the Renaissance World*. Oxford: Oxford University Press, 2012.

Varlik, Nuket. *Plague and Empire in the Early Modern Mediterranean World: The Ottoman Experience, 1347–1600*. Cambridge: Cambridge University Press, 2015.

Veinstein, Gilles. "Les Capitulations Franco-Ottomanes de 1536 sont-elles encore controversables?" In *Living in the Ottoman Ecumenical Community*, edited by Vera Constantini and Mark Koller, 71–88. Leiden: Brill, 2008.

Vélez, Karin. *The Miraculous Flying House of Loreto: Spreading Catholicism in the Early Modern World*. Princeton: Princeton University Press, 2019.

Verhoeven, Gerrit. "Calvinist Pilgrimages and Popish Encounters: Religious Identity and Sacred Space on the Dutch Grand Tour (1598–1685)." *Journal of Social History* 43 (2010): 615–634.

Verhoeven, Mariette. "Jerusalem As Palimpsest: The Architectural Footprint of the Crusaders in the Contemporary City." In *The Imagined and Real Jerusalem in Art and Architecture*, edited by Jeroen Goudeau, Mariëtte Verhoeven, and Wouter Weijers, 114–135. Leiden: Brill, 2014.

Vincent-Cassy, Cécile. "The Search for Evidence: The Relics for Martyred Saints and Their Worship in Cordoba after the Council of Trent." In *After Conversion: Iberia and the Emergence of Modernity*, edited by Mercedes Garcia-Arenal, 126–152. Leiden: Brill, 2016.

Vitkus, Daniel. "Trafficking with the Turk: English Travellers in the Ottoman Empire during the Early Seventeenth Century." In *Travel Knowledge: European "Discoveries" in the Early Modern Period*, edited by Ivo Jamps and Jyotsna G. Singh, 35–52. Basingstoke: Palgrave, 2001.

Vryonis, Spero. "The History of the Greek Patriarchate of Jerusalem As Reflected in Codex Patriarchicus No. 428, 1517–1805." *Byzantine and Modern Greek Studies* 7 (1981): 29–53.

Walsham, Alexander. "The Reformation and 'The Disenchantment of the World' Reassessed." *The Historical Journal* 51 (2008): 497–528.

———. *The Reformation of the Landscape: Religion, Identity, and Memory in Early Modern Britain and Ireland*. Oxford: Oxford University Press, 2011.

Wansbrough, John. "Venice and Florence in the Mamluk Commercial Privileges." *Bulletin of the School of Oriental and African Studies, University of London* 28 (1965): 483–523.

Webster, Susan Verdi. *Art and Ritual in Golden-Age Spain: Sevillian Confraternities and the Processional Sculpture of Holy Week*. Princeton: Princeton University Press, 1998.

Weiss, Gillian. *Captivity and Corsairs: France and Slavery in the Early Modern Mediterranean*. Stanford: Stanford University Press, 2011.

Welle, Jason. "The Status of Monks in Egypt under early Mamluk Rule: The case of Ibn Taymiyya." *LOGOS: Journal of Eastern Christian Studies* (2014): 41–67.

Wharton, Annabel Jane. "The Baptistery of the Holy Sepulchre in Jerusalem and the Politics of Sacred Space." *Dumbarton Oaks Papers* 46 (1992): 313–325.

Wunder, Amanda Jaye."Classical, Christian, and Muslim Remains in the Construction of Imperial Seville (1520–1635)." *Journal of the History of Ideas* 64 (2003): 195–212.

Williams, Wes. *Pilgrimage and Narrative in the French Renaissance: The Undiscovered Country*. Oxford: Oxford University Press, 1999.

Whyte, William. "Buildings, Landscapes and Regimes of Materiality." *Transactions of the Royal Historical Society* 28 (2018): 135–148.

Wolfe, Michael. *The Conversion of Henri IV: Politics, Power and Religious Belief in Early Modern France*. Boston: Harvard University Press, 1993.

Woodall, Joanna. "Painted Immortality: Jerusalem Pilgrims by Antonis Mor and Jan Van Scorel." *Jahrbuch der Berliner Museen* 31 (1989): 149–163.
Ze'evi, Dror. *An Ottoman Century: The District of Jerusalem in the 1600s.* New York: State University of New York Press, 1996.
Zumthor, Paul and Catherine Peebles. "The Medieval Travel Narrative." *New Literary History* 25 (1994): 809–824.

Index

Abu Al-Nasr Sayf ad-Din Al-Ashraf Qaitbay, 56
Acre, 145
Adorno family, *See* Order of the Holy Sepulcher
Affagart, Greffin, author, 164
Ahaia, Joannes dell', *custos*, 81
Al-Aqsa Mosque, 50, 52, 55
    Ottoman renovations, 57
Al-Din, Mujir, 53, 55
    on Jerusalem, 51, 56
Aleppo, 206
    description, 209–212
Alessio, *custos*, 226
Alexandretta, 35, 209, 338
Alexandria, 35
Al-Malik-al-Nasir Muhammad, Mamluk Sultan, 29, 56
alms-giving, 46, 78, 80, 248
    Custody of the Holy Land, 81
    and imperial rivalry, 249
Altars
    and Islamic law, 85
    jurisdiction, 71
    Latin, 81–82
    sites of intra-Christian conflict, 63–66, 69
Ambassadors
    French, 65, 201, 214, 218, 220, 230
    role in Christian disputes, 75
    Venetian, 76, 79, 219
Amico, Bernardino, friar, 95, 144, 344, *See also* Franciscan authors
Angelo da Ferraro, *custos*, 91

Annunciation, shrine, Nazareth, 91, 191, 228, 278
Antonio de Aranda, friar, 341, 343
Antonio di Fagnano, friar, 312
Antonio di' Cerigliano, friar, 318
Arco, Andrea d', *custos*, 212
Armenian Christians, 66, 81, *See* Holy Places: material destruction
    population, 44
Arsenio da Milano, friar, 217

Baroque piety, 160
Baybars, Mamluk Sultan, 56
Beauvau, Henri de, author, 127, 171
Benard, Nicolas, author, 121, 130, 133, 158
    on the Holy Sepulcher, 161
Bethlehem
    Christian artisans, 248
    Christian communities, 58
    Greek Orthodox community, 59
    Latin community, 58
Bethpage, 87
Beyrouth (Beirut), 206, 222
Boisselly, Jean de, author, 145, 151, 164
Bonaventure of Nursia, Franciscan biographer, 326
Boucher, Jean, friar, 160, 178, 339, 351
    on French crusade, 240
    on the ritual Washing of the feet, 351
Bourbon-Habsburg rivalry, 223, 241–242
    Custody of the Holy Land, 194
Brotherhood of the Holy Sepulcher, 72, 113
Byzantine influence
    upon Patriarchate of Jerusalem, 113

Byzantine-Roman rivalry
  Council of Florence, 115
Byzantine-Roman rivalry, history, 70, 114

Cadeau, Christophe, seigneur, French pilgrim, 187
Cairo, 35
Calahorra, Juan de, friar, 333
Calvary, Holy Sepulcher, 62, 73, 246, 316, 349
Calvinism, 161, 237, 253
Cañizares, Juan de, friar, 77, 94, 103
Capello, Giovanni, *bailo*, 79
Capitulations, 126, 224–225
Capitulations of 1604. *See* Protector of the Holy Places
Cappello, Giovanni, *bailo*, 75, 103
Capuchins, 206, 212, 217, 307
  Dispute of 1661, 195
  disputes with friars, 209
  distinctive piety, 308
  missionary rivalry with Observant friars, 308
Caravans and pilgrimage, 47–58, 60, 145
Carmelites, discalced, 207, 212, 213
Casola, Pietro, author, 175
Castela, Henri, friar, 99, 143
  on Francis of Assisi, 328
  on St. Helen and spiritual restoration, 356
Cave of the Patriarchs, 50, 56
Cenacle, the, 29
  and apostolic succession, 341, 343
  description of, 342
  expulsion of friars, 86
  expulsion of friars, 1530s, 343
  Franciscan jurisdiction, 86
  a shared shrine, 341
  site of intra-competition, 63
Césy, Comte de, French ambassador, 214, 250
Chapel of St. Helen, Holy Sepulcher, 73, 355
Chaplaincies, 35
  conflicts over, 217–218
  Jerusalem, 221
Charlemagne, 236
Charles IX, King of France, 255
Châteauneuf, Pierre-Anthoine, Marquis de Castagnères, French ambassador, 201, 221, 251
Christian precedence, 102
  Greek Orthodox, 104
  Latin, 108

Church of the Annunciation, Nazareth, 320
Church of the Holy Conception, Aleppo, 35, 37
Church of the Nativity, 33, 47, 73
  description of, 35
  Grotto of, 36, 68, 96
  legal disputes, 1670s, 93
  Muslim-Christian disputes, 92
  renovations, 352
  site of Muslim worship, 92
Commissioners of the Holy Land, 66, 78, 95, 244, 318
  global traffic, alms, 248
  registers, 80
Confessionalization
  and religious conflict, 94
  Holy Sepulcher, 96
  material destruction, ornamentation, 94
  on material destruction, renovation, 94
  theory of, 21
Confraternities
  scuola della santissima Concettione di Nostra Signora, Aleppo, 46
Confraternities of the Holy Sepulcher, Paris, 131, 176
Congregation of the Propaganda Fide
  disputes between friars and France, 185, 190, 211
  Latin-Orthodox disputes, 78
  legal disputes, 82
  relations with France, 196
Constantine IX Monomachus, Emperor, 106
Constantine, Emperor, 17, 29, 354
Constantinople
  as Jerusalem, 115–116
Consuls
  Aleppo, 37, 45, 79
  Alexandria, 79
  French, 215
  Venetian, 75
Contarini, Alvise, *bailo*. *See also* Ambassadors: Venetian
Convents
  Bethlehem, 338
  Cyprus, 217
Custody, 30
  Holy Sepulcher, 121, 338
  Mount Tabor, 91
  Nazareth, 215, 320
  San Francesco de la Vigna, Venice, 177

Conventuals, 31, 325
  loss of Custody, 336
Conversion
  as spiritual restoration, 297
Coptic Christians, 44, 64
Cotovic, Jean, author, 151
Council of Trent, 150
  on divine immanence, 163
Courmenin, Louis Deshayes de, French envoy, 197, 199
Crusade
  resurgent interest after 1500, 171, 173
Crusader architecture, 92, 353–357
Custodial jurisdiction
  and Franciscan legitimacy, 305
  as *imitatio Christi*, 354
  as *imitatio Francisci*, 358
  reinterpretation of apostolic ideal, 354
Custody of the Holy Land
  administration, 4
  convents, 1517, 34
  convents, 1627, 35
  fees for Ottoman officials, 316
  finances, 82
  a Franciscan institution, 200
  Franciscan martyrologies, 345
  geography, 38
  as a global Catholic institution, 298
  history, 28
  and Islamic law, 84
  languages, 33
  legacy of Francis of Assisi, 331
  material character, 34
  merchant colonies, cure of souls, 209
  relations with Mamluk rulers, 346
  renovations, 109, 311
custos
  authority, 31, 193, 210
  Palm Sunday procession, 87
  a papal office, 193
  role-playing Christ, 350

Damas, Egypt, 222
De Breves, François Savary, French ambassador, 26, 55, 126, 226
  on Protector of the Holy Places, 231
  relations with Custody, 227
Descent of the Cross, 176, 349 *See also* Processions
Dhimmi and Islamic law, 63
Diego da Sanseverino, *custos*, 215, 312

disease, 38, 345–346
Dispute of 1661, 190, 192, 206, 213, 222
  witness testimony, 188
Dome of the Chain, 56
Dome of the Rock, 49, 341
Dositheos II, Patriarch of Jerusalem, 77, 97, 118
Du Plessis, Charles, seigneur de, French pilgrim, 187

Easter rites. *See* Descent of the Cross; Holy Fire; Palm Sunday Procession; Pilgrimage
Edicule. *See* Holy Sepulcher, shrine
Ein Karem, 92
Enriquez de Ribera, Fadrique, author, 134, 137, 151, 158, 168

Faber (Fabri), Felix, friar, author, 189
Fakhr-al-Din, Emir, 91, 228, 311
Favyn, André, author, 130
Ferdinand I, Grand Duke of Tuscany, 246
France
  Catholic renewal, seventeenth century, 250, 252
  chaplaincies, 216, 218, 251
  consulate in Jerusalem, 198, 216, 221, 230
  Dispute of 1661, 185
  Jurisdiction. *See also* Protector of the Holy Places
  jurisdiction, Holy Land, 183, 196
  missionaries, 214, 253
  missionaries as agents of the French state, 206
  monarch as Christian leader, 233
  promotion of French friars, Custody, 201, 205
  Protector of the Holy Places, 183
  relations with Ottoman Empire, 223, 225
  religious context, 154, 223
  religious divisions, seventeenth century, 239
  sacred destiny, 232, 237
  Wars of Religion, 237–238
Francesco Ingoli, secretary, Congregation of the Propaganda Fide, 312
Francis I, King of France, 224
Francis of Assisi, 303
  as *alter Christus*, 326, 330
  audience with the Sultan, 326

Francis of Assisi (cont.)
　charisma and internal reform, 335
　involvement in the Crusades, 325
　as latter-day apostle, 332, 359
　Province of the Holy Land, 334
　renovation and restoration, 358
　as spiritual restorer, 360
　visit to the Holy Land, 321
Franciscan administration
　guardian, 31, 50, 193
　history, 34
　mobility, 32, 38
Franciscan authors, Custody, 324
Franciscan family, Holy Land, 198
　arrival of reformed brothers, 304, 310
　conflict with reformed brethren, 312
　disputes between nations, 201, 203–204
　on its diverse Franciscan nature, 306
　fraternal conflicts, office-holding, 312
　fraternal conflicts, reform, 314
　international membership, 198
　numbers, 35
Franciscan Order, 303
　General Chapter, 201, 205, 248
　global influence, 367
　internal reform, 4, 306, 335
　Minister General, 323
　Observant reform, 307–308, *See also* Recollects, *Riformati*
Franciscan spirituality, 351, *See* Francis of Assisi; Franciscan Order
　apostolic succession, 330
　influence in Catholic culture, 366
　on material and mystical character, 359
　mystical character. *See also* Francis of Assisi
　sensuality, 330
Franciscan writings, 304
　on diversity of genres, 322
　martyrologies, 345
　sacred history, 320–322, 338
Francisco Jesus Maria de San Juan del Puerto, friar, 244, 323
Fraternal competition. *See also* Capuchins; Franciscan family, Holy Land; Recollects; *Riformati*
French missionaries
　disputes with friars, 217
Friars, mistreatment of, 57

Gabriele Bruno, *custos*, 91
Garden of Gethsemane, 91, 316
Garden of Gethsemane, Grotto of, 34
Georgian Christians, 64, 228
Germanos, Patriarch of Jerusalem, 72, 113
Giacinto, friar, 314
Giovanni Battista da Veneti, friar, 316
Giustinian, Giorgio, *bailo*, 219
Godfroy of Bouillon, 122, 236
　and Baldwin, sepulchers, 357
　founder of the Order of the Holy Sepulcher, 170, 182
Goujon, Jacques, friar, 32, 203, 303, 325, 337
　Holy Land as legacy of Christ to Francis, 360
　on legitimacy of Observant jurisdiction, 333
Goujons, Jacques
　on Francis of Assisi, 327
Greek Orthodox
　Holy Land, 112
　influence of Calvinism, 117
　Patriarch of Jerusalem, 61
　population, 43
　relations with Ottoman empire, 111–112, 115
　rituals, 105
Greek Orthodox tradition
　organization, 112
Gregory of Nyssa, *Letter to Kensitor*, 149
Guerin, Roger, friar, 31
Guglingen, Paul walter von, friar, 50

Hault, Nicolas de, author, 151
　knighting ceremonial, 169
Helen, St., true cross, 116, 170, 355
Henry IV, King of France, 227
　concerns about unorthodoxy, 238
Holy Fire, 103
Holy Land, the
　as *Biblia Sacra*, 364
　as a Catholic *frontier*, 298
　Christian communities, 59
　demography, 43
　early Franciscan missions, 334
　as a Franciscan "possession", 333
　as a Franciscan sacred place, 304, 321
　as the *home* of Christ, 157
　imperial building projects, 56

as an inventive source of Catholic sacred
    histories, 364
Jewish sacred geography, 48
location, 28
as many Holy Lands, 48
as a material vessel of Christian authority,
    303, 363
Muslim sacred geography, 48
Ottoman conquest of, 28
as a *place* of Francis, 334
Protestant views, 159
and Reformation controversy 159
reinvention of Catholic tradition, 364
religious diversity, 42
and the restoration of papal authority, 301
sacrality, 53–54
and sacred history, 302
as a shared sacred space, 47
as site of Franciscan reinvention, 360
as site of imperial competition, 243
as a site of revelation, 297
as spiritual *center*, 298
and spiritual reinvention, 3
spiritual significance of, Catholicism, 48
spiritual significance of, Islam, 48
spiritual significance of, Judaism, 47
Suleiman I, patronage, 57
Holy Land replicas, 135–136, 142, 299
    Casa de Pilatos, Seville, 136
    Jeruzalemkapel, Bruges, 135
Holy Places, the
    Christian conflict, 58
    Christian violence, 78
    Greek privileges, 88
    Latin privileges, 87
    legal disputes, 43, 63
    material destruction of, 97–98
    materiality, 84
Holy Roman Emperor, 186
Holy Saviour, convent, 3, 27, 187
    church, 187–191
    description, 36
    library, 36
Holy Sepulcher, Basilica, 29, 40, 100, 182
    description of, 62, 191
    intra-Christian conflict, 68
    renovations, 95
Holy Sepulcher, shrine, 73
    as a material vessel of Christ, 161
House of Loreto, shrine, 299
House of Pilate, shrine, 135

House of Saint Ann, shrine, 356
Humanism
    on the legitimacy of pilgrimage, 159
Hurrem, consort of Suleiman
    soup kitchen, 41

Imperial patronage
    Custody of the Holy Land, 246
Indulgences
    Catholic, 54
    Reformation controversy, 154
Islamic law, 365
    Custody, 108
    description, 85
    and *dhimmi* worship, 353
    Hanafi, 88
    influence upon Christian religious
        practice, 89
    renovation of *dhimmi* religious buildings,
        88

Jerusalem
    religious diversity, 51
    as site of Revelation, 51
    Umayyad period, 52
Jesuits, 206, 211–212, 216
Jesus Maria de San Juan del Puerto, friar,
    332
Jews, Sephardic, 43
Joseph of Arimathea, 350, 354
Juan de Calahorra, friar, 323

kadi, 90
    Christian conflict, the Holy Places, 63
    court of, 40
    Jerusalem, 74, 79
    Muslim-Christian disputes, 92
    regulation of Christian communities, 90
    renovations of Christian buildings, 92
    renovations, Custody, 353
keys, 87
King of Poland, 79
knighting ceremonial, Holy Sepulcher, 121,
    130, 167, 182
    crusading elements, 173
    Dispute of 1661, 187–188, 222
    French pilgrims, 196

La Piccardiere, French envoy, 234
La Vergne de Tressan, Pierre de, 60
    description of Holy Sepulcher, 62

La Verna, Mount
  site of pilgrimage, 330
Lamps, 100, 192, 366,
  See Confessionalization:
  ornamentation of space
Latin Christians
  population, 44
Latin history
  Crusader rule of Jerusalem, 107
  era of Mamluk rule, 107
Latin-Greek Orthodox legal disputes
  1630s, 74, 76
  1670s, 77
  sixteenth century, 72
Lempereur, Jean, consul, 230
Liturgical rites. See also ; Custody of the
  Holy Land; Islamic law; Processions
Liturgical rites and Islamic law
  privileges, 69
Lodi, Paolo di, custos, 199, 251
Louis IX, King of France, 235–236, 246
  cult of, 236
Louis XIII, King of France, 240
Louis XIV, King of France
  tensions in France, 239
Lucaris, Cyril, Patriarch of Constantinople,
  117

Maggi, Carlo, author, 130, 151
Mamluk Empire, 4, 29
  Holy Land, 40, 107
Manerba, Francesco, custos, 65, 246
Marian shrines. See also ; Church of the
  Annunciation; Milk Grotto; Tomb of
  the Virgin Mary
  El Matareya, Egypt, 144
Maronites
  population, 44
Marseilles, 30, 131, 225
Massacre of St. Bartholomew's Day,
  154, 255
Mazarin, Cardinal, 242
Medici Patronage, 246
Merchant colonies, 44
  Aleppo, 218
  Alexandretta, 46
  French, 207, 209
  procurator, 45
  Venetian, 45
Michael da Filettino, friar, 316
milice chrétien, 240, 255

Milk Grotto, Bethlehem, 55
Missionaries, French, 46, 70, 118, 195
  disputes over cure of souls, 208
  disputes with friars, 207–208, 210
  established in Custody, 206
  expansion in Custody, 222
Moran, Damien, French friar, 205
Morone da Maleo, Mariano, custos
  on financial scandal, 315–316
  renovation projects, 316
Mount La Verna, 327, 329
Mount Moriah, 54
Mount Sion, convent, 29, 31, 57,
  334, 347
  and apostolic succession, 342
  cemetery, 92
  description, 342
  expulsion from, 64
  memories of, 192
  renovations, 352
Mount Zion, 54, 341
  as site of revelation, 341
Mufti, 75
Muhammad
  Muslim shrines, 49, 55
  Night Flight to Jerusalem, 51, 92
  Naples, 318
  patronage of rulers, Robert and Sancia,
  30

Noailles, François de, French ambassador,
  241

Obicino da Novara, Tommaso, custos,
  38, 340
Observants, 31, 306, See also Franciscan
  Order
Olier, Charles Marie, Marquis de Nointel,
  French ambassador, 126, 218, 233
  painting, 255
Order of the Holy Sepulcher, 122, 357
  blazon, 130
  a chivalric society, 129
  confraternities, 133
  a crusading society, 172, 179, 240
  Franciscan governance, 174–175
  a French institution, 126, 182, 254
  history of, 123
  impact of the Reformation, 126
  membership, 125–126, 129, 132, 151
  papal recognition, 176

pilgrimage treatises, 127–128, 151
pilgrimage treatises as polemic, 153
sacred histories, 165
on the spiritual authority of the knight, 168
a spiritual brotherhood, 128, 165
Ottoman administration
　decrees, 85, 104
　Holy Land, 40
　Holy Places, 74
　influence upon Christian worship, 365
Ottoman conquest, 40
　Jerusalem, 86
Ottoman officials
　Beylerbei, 90
　the Caimecan, 82
　Holy Land, 40
　sangiac, 27
Ottoman Porte, 90
　Constantinople, 40
　costs of litigation, fees, 83

Pacifique de Provins, Capuchin, 215, 335
Pact of Umar, 88
Papal bulls
　gratias agimus, 89
　Inscrutabili Divinae, 261, 277
Pascal, French friar, 195, 204
Pascha, Damascus, 230
Patriarch of the Chaldeans, 340
Patriarchate of Constantinople, 70, 77, 110
　influence in Holy Land, 113
Patriarchate of Jerusalem, 104
Père Joseph, Capuchin, 240, 253
Pesenti, Giovanni, author, 151, 171, 177
Philip II, King of Spain,
　80, 246, 254, 353
Philip III, King of Spain, 246
Philip IV, King of Spain, 194, 245
Piero Foscarini, *bailo*, 82
Pilgrimage
　Catholic liturgical rite, 148
　decline after 1519, 125
　guidebooks, 37
　and French Catholicism, 254
　impact of Reformation in Europe, 147
　as a liturgical rite, 53
　misbehaving pilgrims, 182, 189, 192
　proof of journey, 168
　sacred itineraries, 141
　sensual experience, 161
　travel routes, 144, 146

Pilgrimage, Catholic
　debates over accuracy of Holy Land itinerary, 159
Pilgrimage mementoes, 35, 169, 248, 299
Pilgrimage and Reformation controversy,
　147, 149, 156
　Council of Trent, 150
　Desiderius Erasmus, 148
　Martin Luther, 148
Pilgrimage treatises. *See also* Order of the Holy Sepulcher
　as authentic journeys, 143
　as a distinctive genre, 138–139
　as a mode of spiritual journeying,
　　140–141
　as religious polemic, 150, 153
　as sacred histories, 153
Poggibonsi, Niccolò, friar, 324
Pola, Ambrosio de la, friar, 66
Pope Alexander VI, 124
Pope Innocent VIII, 124
Pope Sixtus V, 299
Pope Urban VIII, 175
Processions
　Descent of the Cross, 349
　Holy Saviour, church, 192
　Holy Sepulcher, 348
　Palm Sunday, 87, 146, 317
　via crucis, 61, 141
　via crucis, Seville, 137
Protector of the Holy Places
　and Christian leadership, 235
　French influence, 228
　jurisdiction, 227
　and legitimacy of French state, 240
　Ottoman privilege, 197, 199, 226

Quaresmio, Francesco, friar, 141, 324, 354

Rauwolf, Leonhard, author, 129
Recollects, 33, 215, 306, *See also* Franciscan Order
　Convent in Nazareth, 320
Reformation, the, 154
régale controversy, 239
Regnault, Anthoine, author, 151, 164, 254
　on crusade, 172
　crusading rhetoric, 173
　religious polemic, 154
Renovation as spiritual restoration, 351, 358

Renovation of the Holy Places
   under Byzantine rule, 356
   under Crusader rule, 352, 357
   Dome, Holy Sepulcher, 353
   under Mamluks and Ottomans, 352
Richelieu, Cardinal, 240
Riformati, 306
   conflict with Observants, 314, 317–318
Rocchetta, Aquilante, author, 37, 46, 143, 151
   on Christian diversity in Holy Land, 59
Rock of the Anointing (Stone of Unction), Holy Sepulcher, 66, 68
Roger, Eugene, friar, 234, 310, 320, 354
   on French crusade, 240
   martyrology, 346
Rome
   as another Jerusalem, 299
Rosetta, Egypt, 35
Royal Road, the, 49, 145

Sacrality
   sensual experience, 54
Sacred histories
   Carmelites, 213
   France, 236
   Franciscan, 304
   Greek Orthodox, 104, 106
   papal, 296
Sacred history, Greek Orthodox, 105
Sacred measurements, 158–159
Saibante di Verona, Gaudenzio, *custos*, 339
Saida (Sidon), 35, 206, 338
Sandys, George, author, 129
Scios, 94
Selim I, Ottoman Sultan, 86
Shrines and religious violence, 52
Shrines, shared, 47, 63
   biblical patriarchs, 49
   Hebron and Nablus, 49
Sieur de La Croix, 233
Small Gate Cemetery, 49
Soler, Bernardo, friar, 78
Sophronius IV, Patriarch of Jerusalem, 73
Spanish patronage
   Custody of the Holy Land, 80, 198, 202–203, 243–244
   global traffic in alms, 248
Stations of the Cross, 141, 176, *See also* Processions: *via crucis*
Stephano da Stagna, Bonifacio, *custos*, 175, 324, 353

Suarez, Jacques Marie de, friar, 233
Suleiman I, Ottoman Sultan, 344
   building projects, 41
Suriano, Francesco, *custos*, 1, 3, 32, 57, 324, 345, 348, 352
   description of Franciscan privileges, 87
   on legitimacy of Observant jurisdiction, 336
   on renovations during era of Crusader rule, 356
   renovation as spiritual restoration, 359
Surius, Bernardin, friar, 177, 192, 310, 320, 329, 339, 350, 360
   on shrine at La Verna, 329
Synod of Jerusalem, 77, 118
Syrian Christians, 65, 98

tatoos, 143, 169
Temple Mount, Jerusalem, 52
Terrench, Bartolomeo, Spanish friar, 194
The Alcoran of the Franciscans, 336
The Marys, 350
Thenaud, Jean, friar, 100, 339
Theophanes III, Patriarch of Jerusalem, 74, 114
Thévenot, Jean de, author, 130, 245
   Order of the Holy Sepulcher, 125
Thevet, André
   Order of the Holy Sepulcher, 125
Thomas of Celano, Franciscan biographer, 326
Tomb of David, 63
Tomb of the Virgin Mary, 33, 62, 316
Tounon, Hilaire, friar, 340
Tripoli, 206, 209

Valles, Eusebio, *custos*, 185, 222, 309, 318
   conflict with French friars, 203
   Dispute of 1661, 188, 192
Vendôme, Jacques de, friar, 215
   guardian, Recollect convent, Nazareth, 320
Veneration of the Holy Places
   and apostolic succession, 354
   under Byzantine rule, 355
Venetian Chapel, Cairo, 316
Venetian Interdict, 220
Venice
   on relations with Custody, 220
   suspicion of Jesuit missionaries, 219

Index

Verniero de' Montepeloso, friar, 353
Verniero di Montepeloso, Pietro, friar, 320, 323, 353
via dolorosa, Jerusalem, 157
Villamont, Jacques de, author, 151–152, 161, 177
   description of via dolorosa, 157
Vincent, Capuchin, 251
Visir, 75

War of Crete, 77
Washing of the feet, ritual, 27, 348
Western Wall, Jerusalem, 52, 341

Zuallart, Jean, author, 140, 151, 178
   on the presence of Christ in the Holy Land, 156
   religious polemic, 156

CPSIA information can be obtained
at www.ICGtesting.com
Printed in the USA
LVHW111916030821
694401LV00001B/73